D0915631

THE GROWTH OF LITERATURE

VOLUME I

THE GROWTH OF LITERATURE

BY

H. MUNRO CHADWICK

AND

N. KERSHAW CHADWICK

VOLUME I

THE ANCIENT LITERATURES OF EUROPE

CAMBRIDGE
AT THE UNIVERSITY PRESS
1932
REPRINTED
1968

Published by the Syndics of the Cambridge University Press
Bentley House, 200 Euston Road, London, N.W. 1
American Branch: 32 East 57th Street, New York, N.Y. 10022

PUBLISHER'S NOTE

Cambridge University Press Library Editions are re-issues of out-of-print standard works from the Cambridge catalogue. The texts are unrevised and, apart from minor corrections, reproduce the latest published edition.

Standard Book Number: 521 07422 3
Library of Congress Catalogue Card Number: 33–6470

First published 1932
Reprinted 1968

First printed in Great Britain at the University Press, Cambridge
Reprinted in Great Britain by John Dickens & Co. Ltd, Northampton

SOCIETATI
AULAE DE CLARE

CONTENTS

PREFACE

IS it possible to trace the operation of any general principles in the growth of literature? We shall endeavour to answer this question by a comparative study of the literary genres found in various countries and languages and in different periods of history.

For such comparative study the modern literatures of the West offer only a very limited amount of material. Owing to the constant interaction of these literatures upon one another for several centuries past, and before that to the common influence of Latin upon all of them, they have had little chance of independent development. The most valuable material for our purpose comes from ancient records unaffected, or only partially affected, by the influence of Latin or other languages of wide circulation, and from isolated or backward communities of the present day which are still unaffected by cosmopolitan literature.

The plan which we have set before ourselves is, in the first place, to examine a number of literatures, some ancient and some modern. In making our selection, the guiding consideration has been to find such literatures as would seem to be at least partly independent. And here we may remark that the possibility of external influence is a factor which can never be wholly ignored; wherever evidence pointing to connections occurs it must be noted. But other considerations also have had to be taken into account—the accessibility of the material and the limitations of our own knowledge. For instance, we have no doubt that a study of early Chinese records would prove very instructive; but such a study would be entirely beyond our powers. In general, we have had to limit the scope of our enquiry to literatures of which we have some personal knowledge, or which are intelligible to us through translations and other sources of information.

An initial obstacle to studies of this kind is presented by the fact that the literatures which one would expect to be most independent are generally those for which information is most difficult to obtain. We refer to the literatures of isolated and remote peoples. These are as a rule 'unwritten' literatures; and they are now fast perishing before the incoming tide of cosmopolitan literature. A similar course of history may be traced in our own part of the world. Our ancestors once had unwritten literatures of their own, which in time had to give way before the tide of cosmopolitan late Roman or medieval literature. Fortunately something of the old order has been preserved in both cases—in the former partly by the European travellers, missionaries and officials of last century, and partly by natives who had received a foreign education; in the latter perhaps almost entirely by educated natives. In both cases alike the records committed to writing and preserved by these persons supply the material upon which we have to draw.

But it is not only in remote lands, such as Central Africa and the islands of the Pacific, that we now find unwritten literature independent—more or less—of cosmopolitan literature. Even in Christian and Mohammedan countries such literatures often flourish, side by side with a written literature which is cultivated by the religious and educated. In these cases the former is probably never wholly unaffected by the latter; but it sometimes retains a remarkable amount of vitality and independence. 'Backward' literatures of this type, like the literatures of more remote lands, were little known to the outside world before last century. Intrinsically they are less valuable than the latter for our purpose; for they are usually limited to certain genres, and even these often show traces of learned or foreign influence. But they have been more systematically studied, and consequently have yielded a much larger amount of material.

In the course of our enquiry we shall take examples from the literatures of both remote and backward communities of the present day, as well as from ancient literatures. In each literature we shall attempt a descriptive analysis of the available records with a view to ascertaining how far the genres and the general features of the various literatures correspond, and wherein the chief differences lie. Not until this is done will it be possible to formulate any general principles governing the growth of literature.

We are not concerned with the origins of literature. That is a subject which must be left to those who have made a special study of the most primitive peoples. None of the literatures which have come under our notice gives an impression of recent origin. There can be little doubt that in the civilised world literature has had a history of several thousand years.

On the other hand we shall not, in general, pursue our examination beyond the stage at which writing comes into regular use for literary purposes. On this point a word of explanation is perhaps necessary. We are accustomed to think of literature as inseparably bound up with writing. But in reality the connection between the two is accidental, and belongs only to a secondary phase in the history of literature. There are peoples with highly developed literatures who until recently seem to have made little use of writing for literary purposes, though they have been acquainted with the art of writing for thousands of years. Somewhat similar conditions are said to have prevailed among the ancient Gauls. Our own ancestors were acquainted with writing for centuries—perhaps many centuries—before they applied it to the preservation of literature. Again, most of the literary genres familiar to us are found among peoples to whom writing is—or was until yesterday—wholly unknown. And there is no reason for doubting that among our ancestors, if not throughout the whole civilised world, these genres had taken form before writing was employed. In this formative period, as among remote and backward communities of the present day, 'literature' must have consisted of records of intellectual activities preserved in speech, not in writing. A man's memory was his library.

The remains of ancient literatures, however, are usually—in Europe without exception—preserved only in the form of written records; and many of these records were doubtless written from the beginning. Indeed in the ancient[1] (pre-medieval) literatures of Europe, with which we are concerned in this volume, it is only seldom that a work now surviving is definitely known to have been in existence before the time of written literature. On the other hand there is usually sufficient evidence that literature of some kind—on lines similar, apparently, to existing types—was cultivated before this time. And in all these literatures there are a number of records which may have been composed, not necessarily in their present form, long before they were committed to writing, though decisive evidence to this effect is not often to be found.

In regard to the origin of these records much difference of opinion prevails. Those whose interest lies in comparative studies generally tend to lay weight upon the resemblances between the early records of

[1] Some readers may perhaps demur to our use of the word 'ancient', which is commonly applied only to the literatures and history of Rome, Greece and the East. We use it also for the earliest literatures of the British Isles. It is true that the latter do not begin—as written literatures—until much later than those of Rome and Greece, though they come next among the literatures of Europe. But there is no other suitable word. The term 'medieval', sometimes applied to them, is misleading, since it is also, and more commonly, applied to the more or less 'cosmopolitan' literature of the succeeding period, which was essentially different. The transition took place to a large extent during the times with which we have to deal; but the medieval element was of foreign origin, and had nothing in common with the native elements, which concern us. The latter had literary traditions of their own, which in our belief had had a long history—certainly reaching back to 'ancient' times—before anything was written down.

different literatures; and where definite evidence, literary or historical, for connection is wanting they are inclined to attribute such resemblances to parallel development in the growth of literature during its earlier ('spoken') phase. On the other hand those whose interest is concentrated upon the history of one special literature tend to stress the fact that such records have usually much in common—sometimes only in diction and metre, sometimes also in subject-matter—with records which certainly belong to the 'written' phase. They see no adequate reason for distinguishing between the two series of records, and are inclined to ascribe everything to the written phase, except in cases where there is definite evidence to the contrary. These scholars usually attribute resemblances between the early records of different literatures to the influence of written texts, just as in later times. In all the ancient European literatures, except Greek, their tendency is to reduce the native element to a minimum and to trace foreign (Latin) influence in the presentation of subjects, even when the subjects themselves are derived from native tradition. It may be observed here, parenthetically, that a similar tendency is to be found in recent works dealing with the modern backward literatures of Europe.

A generation ago, when the study of Comparative Philology was flourishing, the former school of thought was in the ascendant. But in recent years the decline in the study of Comparative Philology has led to the neglect of other comparative studies; and now it is often declared with confidence by those who adhere to the opposite school that in this literature or that the case has been finally settled in their favour. Yet little new evidence of a convincing character appears to have been produced. The case of the 'comparative' school would seem rather to have been allowed to go by default owing to the general neglect of comparative studies, as against the increasing tendency to specialise in one literature only, or perhaps in two literatures which are not independent of one another. The change of attitude has also been affected no doubt by a growing distrust in the speculative theorising which was popular with the last generation, especially in regard to the composite authorship of various ancient works, and which is not always easy to avoid in comparative study. On the other hand very little account seems to have been taken of the new material for comparative study which has been made accessible during the last half century. We think therefore that the time has come for a restatement of the 'comparative' case by a wider collection of material and in the light of new evidence derived from it.

Twenty years ago in *The Heroic Age* one of the authors called attention to many striking analogies between ancient Teutonic and Greek heroic poetry, and endeavoured to show that these were due to parallel development, arising from similar social and political conditions. Subsequent study convinced him that this parallel development between the two literatures was by no means limited to the category or genre in question. But owing to the pressure of teaching duties it was impossible for many years to make any further systematic study of the subject.

About nine or ten years ago both authors began to take the work seriously in hand. By this time we had realised that in order to obtain a sound basis for such comparative study it was necessary to make a detailed examination of other literatures, both ancient and backward. But in the course of the next two or three years we became more interested in the general aspect of the problem than in its special application to ancient Teutonic and Greek literature. Hence the work has changed its character and grown to much larger dimensions than was at first intended.

The plan of the book is explained in the introductory chapter. The greater part of it consists necessarily of a descriptive analysis of the material. In the present volume the ancient literatures of Europe—those which we believe to be wholly or partly independent—are treated concurrently. In the following volumes other literatures will be examined according to the same scheme; but a separate section will be devoted to each literature. The work will conclude with a general survey of the results to which the evidence leads.

It would be out of place here to anticipate these results. In the present volume, which is merely preliminary, we have practically confined our attention to the literatures concerned. References have not often been given to the evidence of other literatures, though our judgment has doubtless been influenced by it. It will be seen that we believe (unwritten) literary tradition to have been a more developed and potent force and to have had a longer life than many scholars are willing to allow. We cannot admit that the MS. was quite so formidable a foe to this tradition as the printing press now is among remote and backward peoples, or that it won its way so quickly. The evidence seems to us to point to a long period of transition, during which in the northern literatures the native tradition became restricted in scope—somewhat as in the modern backward literatures noticed above—before it was finally submerged. But this restriction was due to the religious influences which accompanied the introduction of the MS., rather than to the influence of the MS. itself.

General considerations such as these must wait for discussion later. But in the meantime there is one aspect of the subjects treated in this volume which we would take the opportunity of pointing out to British readers, though it lies apart from our main theme. It will be seen that of the five 'ancient literatures of Europe' discussed here, four belong to languages which were formerly current in this country, while three of them are spoken here still. And this is not due to any arbitrary selection. The five literatures in question are the only ancient European literatures of native growth which have left any substantial records.

This country is in all probability unique in the opportunities which its early records afford for the comparative study of literature. It may be of some interest therefore to see how far these opportunities are recognised.

Curiously enough Greek, the only literature of the five which is essentially foreign, is the only one which has been long and widely studied.

The Celtic literatures are practically unknown, except to persons who have spoken the languages from childhood. A few adaptations of early Irish sagas have recently had a certain vogue; but it may safely be said that very few people in this country have any conception of the extent and value of early Irish literature.

Half a century ago early Norse literature also was practically unknown in this country, except to a small number of private scholars. In recent years its study has made a good deal of progress. But it is still neglected in a number of our Universities; and, so far as we know, no permanent endowments have been provided anywhere for its study or teaching. This literature, owing to its varied character, is perhaps the most valuable of all for comparative purposes.

Anglo-Saxon is now far more widely known than any other of the northern languages. But its position in the educational system of the country seems to be somewhat anomalous, and indeed pathetic. In most of our Universities it is hardly recognised, at least in principle, as possessing a literature, but rather as an accessory to the study of the English language. One must admit that the amount of literature which is of independent native origin is much smaller in Anglo-Saxon than in Irish and Norse; but it is of singular value and interest and by no means deserves the sad fate which has befallen it. We claim that more provision should be made for its study, not as ancillary to a later literature which, owing to the break in continuity, can contribute nothing to its elucidation, but for its own sake, and with the aid of other literatures, e.g. early Norse and Celtic, in a similar stage of growth. Not until this is done shall we be able to get rid of certain widely prevalent fantasies, such as e.g. that every element of thought and culture which the literature contains must be derived from Roman sources, and that the English themselves down to the time of their conversion were thoughtless and uncultured boors.

It is not only in the domain of literature that the unintelligent use of Anglo-Saxon is to be deplored. Who would think of making any serious study of Classical Latin without a knowledge of Roman history or of Roman history without a knowledge of Latin? But in our enlightened educational system the student of Anglo-Saxon is not required to know the history of the period, nor is the student of early English history required to know Anglo-Saxon—the two subjects belong to different 'schools'. Yet Anglo-Saxon is far more valuable to the student of English history than to the student of English literature. It is the language of our early laws and of important historical records, the knowledge of which is essential to any true understanding of early English history and institutions.

Again, the student of Latin is expected to have some knowledge of Roman antiquities, and the student of Roman archaeology to have some knowledge of Latin. In recent years great progress has been made in archaeology—more perhaps than in any other branch of knowledge—and much light has been thrown upon the early Anglo-Saxon period, as well as upon the periods which preceded it. But here again there is in general no co-ordination with literary and linguistic studies. The literary schools, owing to their one-sided and narrowly linguistic tradition, contribute little or nothing to the knowledge of Anglo-Saxon civilisation, while the British archaeologist, unlike the Roman or Greek archaeologist, regards the study of literary and linguistic evidence as lying outside his sphere and unnecessary. It is true that much can be done in the study of material culture without such evidence. But the more enterprising archaeologist will not rest content with the study of museum objects. He is attracted by problems relating to the settlement and early history of the country—problems which usually cannot be settled by archaeological evidence alone—and here unfortunately, owing to the lack of co-ordination, the results of important work are too often vitiated by an uncritical use of literary records.

It is to be hoped that before long the study of Anglo-Saxon may be freed from its present anomalous position and allowed to develop on its own lines, in connection with studies which can both benefit it and be benefited by it. We refer to the study of the early history and civilisation of our country and to that of literatures which are related or in a similar phase of growth.

Of these literatures the early Norse is the most important; indeed it is essential to the progress of Anglo-Saxon studies. This literature cannot be regarded as wholly foreign. Much of it relates to this country; the language was once widely spoken and some of the existing poetry composed here. But apart from this historical connection, Anglo-Saxon and early Norse literature have common elements reaching back to a high antiquity; and our defective knowledge of Anglo-Saxon civilisation and thought can be supplemented very largely from the richer stores of Norse literature.

The early Celtic literatures should not be ignored, as they are at present. It is a question how far they can be utilised, owing to the serious linguistic difficulties which they present. But much can be done by translations, just as in Greek and other literatures which will be noticed in this book. And we would take this opportunity of impressing upon Celtic scholars the need of good and accessible translations, provided with commentaries. Early Celtic records are perhaps even more important for the history of institutions than for that of literature.

For the full development of such studies as we have indicated further endowments are required; and it may be urged that conditions at present are unfavourable and that there are needs of a practical character more pressing than the study of the past. All very true. But in our country, as in all civilised countries, there are still many people who are interested in the study of the past. Even in recent years many generous endowments have been provided for Classical studies, with the result that these studies are still able to draw upon a large proportion of the best intellects in the country.

Why is the same generosity not shown to the study of our own past? The chief reason is simple enough. Because it is not believed to be worthy of it.

Our ancestors had a language, which may be studied with advantage by those who are interested in the later history of our language. They had institutions and laws of some kind, which may be studied to a limited extent, but only in translations, by a different set of people, those who are interested in the later history of English institutions.

They had also certain distinctive elements of material culture, e.g. in weapons, utensils and ornaments, which may be studied by a third set of people. But they are hardly recognised as possessing an intellectual culture before they came under Roman influence. And the idea that their civilisation should be worthy of study as a whole, like those of Rome and Greece, seems so unfamiliar and fantastic as not to deserve serious consideration.

Hence, naturally, endowments are not forthcoming. Who would endow Latin studies if such studies were only to be utilised here for illustrating the history of the French language, there for first lessons in Roman Law? The house must first be put in order, and the study of British antiquity established on the same footing as that of Roman or Greek antiquity[1].

It may be long before this is accomplished. Apart from the widespread ignorance of British antiquity and the lack of interest in it, which prevails throughout our educational system, our studies are under the great disadvantage that they are usually controlled by authorities who have little or no personal knowledge of them. They are attached—something here and something there—to other studies, to which they are made subservient. We do not deny of course that in this function they may serve a useful purpose, just as a knowledge of Roman history is helpful to the study of later history, and a knowledge of Latin to various other studies. But this should be only a secondary object. The primary object of a school of British antiquity, like that of a school of Classical studies, should be to devote its energies to the promotion of its own subjects as a whole; and for this object it is essential that such schools should be made independent as soon as possible.

As University teachers we have entered upon the academic side of these questions perhaps at greater length than we ought to have done—for which we must crave the reader's pardon. We are aware that in the study of British antiquity the Universities have not always—perhaps not even usually—led the way. The great progress in our knowledge made last century was due in the main to private students. And in

[1] The mistake of narrowing down the scope of Anglo-Saxon studies was made in the closing decades of last century, and arose out of the establishment of examination courses in English. The earlier scholars, like Kemble, realised clearly enough the many-sided importance of these studies. The chair which I have the honour to hold was founded for the promotion of the study of 'the antiquities and history of the Anglo-Saxons', as well as 'the Anglo-Saxon language and the languages cognate therewith'. H. M. C.

archaeology, which is now the most progressive branch of our studies, the work is at present being done more in connection with museums than with Universities. But it is to be regretted that on the literary and linguistic sides there is less activity outside the Universities than there was formerly. Yet the private student of today is better off in many respects—e.g. in linguistic handbooks, translations, and works of reference—than his predecessor of last century.

The contents of this volume will, it is hoped, give some idea, incidentally, of the field which is to be explored in literature and of the attractions which it offers. To those who are interested in the study of antiquity it may perhaps help to expose the groundlessness of the prevalent notion that the Greeks and Romans were the only 'ancients' whose history and literature are worth study, and to make clear that our own ancestors had literary traditions and intellectual activities of their own, less familiar to us but of equal interest. Aesthetic considerations are not our concern; but we think that if anyone will be at the pains to examine for himself the records in the northern literatures to which we refer, he will find that in general they will bear comparison with the Greek records. In narrative poetry we have nothing equal to the Homeric poems; but on the other hand the northern literatures are frequently rich in genres which are barely represented in early Greek. With Latin literature and Attic and later Greek literature comparison is of course impossible; for these belong to a more advanced stage of growth. But we venture to doubt whether those who have devoted an equal amount of time to the study of Classical Latin and early Norse would as a rule prefer the former to the latter. At all events the northern literatures are all, in greater or less degree, products of independent native growth, which is not the case with Latin literature.

A few words more must be said here with regard to the treatment of our proper theme—the comparative study of literary genres. The best that can be hoped for by one who embarks upon an unfamiliar line of work is that he may stimulate others to follow it up to better effect. It is needless to say that we ourselves are quite aware of many defects; and many more will doubtless come to light in course of time. A new departure cannot hope to be more than tentative at the best.

We have not often entered upon the discussion of views opposed to our own[1]. Had we done so the task would have been endless; for we do

[1] For a learned and able treatment of the Teutonic material, from a point of view opposed to ours (cf. p. xi f.), the reader may be referred to Heusler, *Altger-*

not suppose that there are many pages in the book to which one scholar or another would not object. Many scholars also, who regard literature as a kind of *lusus naturae*, will consider the whole work to be mistaken in principle.

One criticism we may as well anticipate. It may very justly be brought against us that we "do not know the (modern) literature of the subject"—or rather of the various subjects included in this volume. In order to save critics the trouble of looking for references we may state at once that we do not know the literature of any of the subjects treated in this book. We have read some books which happen to have come in our way; and to some of these we refer occasionally. But we do not for a moment claim to have made any exhaustive examination of the modern literature bearing on these subjects. We have doubtless missed many important works, and thereby failed to obtain much valuable information. If we had read more widely we should not have completed the book—which perhaps might have been the better course. The amount of time at our disposal is limited; and we have preferred to give as much of it as possible to the primary authorities.

In the spelling of Greek, Anglo-Saxon and Norse names we have followed the same system as in *The Heroic Age*. In Irish names we have generally followed Thurneysen, *Die irische Helden- und Königsage*—a work to which we are indebted more than to any other in this volume —but the quantity of the vowels has not been marked, except (by accents) in italics. It will be found that there is a good deal of inconsistency in the writing of certain names (e.g. *Coirpre*, *Cairpre*, *Cairbre*); but this is hardly to be avoided, unless one normalises, as many scholars do, according to the later forms. In Welsh names we have used modern orthography in the writing of the consonants. Its consistency is a great advantage, and it seems to represent the pronunciation of early times more clearly than does that of the MSS.—though we do not deny that objection may be taken to such forms as *Gwallawg*. The medieval vowels have commonly been written, though not according to the earliest MSS.; but sometimes we have used modern forms, as in *Cadwallon*. In the same way we write such names as *Edwin* and *Alfred* in their modern form.

We are indebted to Professor A. D. Nock of Harvard University, formerly Fellow of Clare College, for many valuable references and for

manische Dichtung in the *Handbuch der Literaturwissenschaft*. Similar views will be found expressed in many important recent works, among which we may mention Thurneysen's *Irische Heldensage* and Chambers' *Beowulf*.

the kind encouragement which he gave us in the earlier stages of the work; to Mr J. M. de Navarro, formerly Fellow of Trinity College, for valuable help in the final stages[1]; and to Mr N. G. L. Hammond, Fellow of Clare College, for kindly letting us consult him about certain Greek passages. More especially we have to thank Mr C. E. Wright, B.A., of Clare College, and Mr K. H. Jackson, B.A., of St John's College, for reading the proofs and for much helpful criticism. The great care which Mr Wright has bestowed upon the work is responsible for the removal of many oversights and obscurities.

As in the past, we have to thank the staff of the Cambridge University Library for the kind attention which we have constantly received from them. For special favours we are under obligations to the Librarians of the National Library of Wales and of Trinity College, Cambridge.

Lastly, we have to thank the Syndics of the Cambridge University Press for undertaking the publication of the book and the staff for the efficiency with which it has been printed. Among the latter we may mention Mr H. A. Parsons, who has prepared the Index.

H. M. C.
N. K. C.

The work for this volume has been done by the two authors in collaboration. Nearly all the material for the Irish sections has been supplied by my wife; and she has also contributed largely to the other sections. But I am responsible for its form.

And, in accordance with the wishes of us both, I ask the Master and Fellows of my College, which has sheltered and supported me for over forty years, to accept it, as a tribute, small but sincere, of gratitude.

H. M. C.

[1] We had hoped to receive much valuable help also from another friend and colleague, the late Dame Bertha Newall. To our great sorrow it was too late.

CHAPTER I

INTRODUCTION

IN the Middle Ages Latin was in general use as the language of serious literature throughout western and central Europe. In the literature of entertainment the same uniformity did not prevail. French was in use in England, as well as in France; but this was due to political causes. Elsewhere the vernaculars of the various countries were commonly employed. Yet there was an underlying uniformity; from the twelfth century onwards literature was dominated everywhere to a great extent, in both form and substance, by French and Provençal models. Since that time various changes have taken place; movements in literature and thought have arisen in different countries. But contact and interaction have never ceased.

From times earlier than the latter part of the eleventh century hardly any literature of entertainment has been preserved in the vernaculars of the Continent. A certain amount of vernacular literature has been preserved in Germany and a little in France; but in both cases this consists almost wholly of translations and adaptations from Latin. For literature of this period which is independent of Latin, whether it be literature of entertainment, thought, celebration, or any other kind of literature, we have to turn to the islands—the British Isles and Iceland.

It will be seen, therefore, that in western and central Europe, from the Arctic to the Mediterranean, the materials available for a comparative study of literature—we mean of course independent literature—are very limited. Practically we have to take into account only Latin and the languages of the islands. The latter, of course, had a very different history from the former. They did not find their way into writing for literary purposes before the seventh century—in Iceland not until much later.[1] Latin, on the other hand, was essentially a written language and had possessed a written literature for many centuries before this time.

In the east of Europe written literature in the Middle Ages was limited in the main to the two ecclesiastical languages, Greek and Church Slavonic. The history of the latter goes back to the ninth

[1] Not until the twelfth century (cf. p. 9); but many of the poems are known to date from the ninth and tenth centuries.

century; but it was almost wholly inspired and dominated by the former. In Russia a modified form of this language, which seems not to have differed greatly from the vernacular, was written as early as the eleventh century. But literature independent of foreign inspiration does not make its appearance before the twelfth at the earliest, though in modern times it is richly represented.

Hence it may be said that in Europe as a whole, before the eleventh century, independent literature is preserved only in Greek, Latin, and the languages of the islands—before the seventh century only in Greek and Latin. Both the latter had a written literature of great antiquity. Yet for the purpose of comparative study Latin literature is practically useless, since it was almost wholly modelled upon Greek from the time of its earliest records.

Greek literature itself contains certain foreign elements, especially the ecclesiastical element, which was derived chiefly from Hebrew and Aramaic. But in the main it appears to be a product of independent native development. Its history is all-important; for it can be traced back to—and even beyond—the time when writing came into use for literary purposes. We believe the same to be true in the case of the island languages—more than twelve hundred years later.

From what has been said it will be seen that for the comparative study of literature—independent literature—in Europe the following materials are available:

(i) Greek literature, which has been preserved in writing from the seventh century B.C.—earlier according to some authorities.

(ii) The island literatures, which have been preserved in writing from the seventh century A.D., or later—in so far as these are independent of Latin (ultimately Greek) influence.

To these we may add (iii) the vernacular literatures of the Continent, which are preserved in writing from the eleventh century, or later—in so far as these also are independent of Latin influence. It is to be observed that in general these literatures were essentially literatures of entertainment or celebration. Any literature of thought which they have to show is translated or derived, directly or indirectly, from the ecclesiastical book-languages, Latin or Greek.

There can be no doubt that in all these three groups written literature was preceded by a time when poetry or saga (i.e. prose story) of some kind was cultivated. Indeed we may say that, in so far as it was independent, the written literature was derived in some form from this 'unwritten literature', though opinions may often differ as to the precise nature of the relationship between the two. In eastern Europe 'unwritten literature' has been preserved and cultivated down to our own times.

At this point it will be well to define what we mean by the word 'independent' when we are speaking of the island literatures. Hitherto we have used the word in the sense of 'independent of Latin'. By this we do not mean that any one of these literatures as a whole was free from Latin influence, even in the times when it was first written, but that each of them contained elements, by no means inconsiderable, which were not of Latin origin. But further, it is certain that the island literatures themselves were not wholly independent of one another. In this case, however, we may distinguish between influence through written texts and influence conveyed through oral channels, especially before the days of writing. We are under the impression that influence of the former kind is limited in general—we will not say wholly—to those elements which are ultimately of Latin origin. But influence through oral channels seems to be much more widespread. The earliest English poetry has much in common with early Norse poetry, preserved in Iceland; and these common elements clearly date from before the time of written literature. As traces of the same elements are to be found in Germany, we should in this case perhaps speak of a common Teutonic poetry, rather than of influence. Again, early Welsh and early Irish poetry have elements in common, which clearly show the influence of one upon the other. It is not likely that in general this influence was conveyed through written texts. Or, to take an instance from our third group, it is clear that much of the matter contained in French romances of the twelfth century is ultimately of British origin; but there is little or no satisfactory evidence for written sources.

A word may be said here as to the fate of the three groups of literature. (i) Greek literature became, indirectly, the main source of European literature. (ii) The island literatures, or rather the native elements contained in them, withered away gradually. English disappeared quickly after the Norman Conquest, to some extent probably even before. Only Irish maintained its vitality down to modern times. Certain elements of British heroic story, however, obtained a new lease of life in French literature, by which they were carried over the greater part of Europe. (iii) The Continental literatures of entertainment, which appear first in the eleventh century or later, maintained themselves throughout the Middle Ages—Spanish even down to the present time in remote places. In Germany native elements reappeared by the end of the twelfth century, though the form of the poetry was borrowed from Romance. In the North also native elements reappeared, somewhat later, in the heterogeneous literature of ballads. In the east of Europe, with probably one important exception, native elements, independent of the Greek-Slavonic book-literature, hardly make their appearance until towards the close of the sixteenth century, though we believe they had long existed in oral tradition. For the most part indeed they did not find their way into writing before the nineteenth century. Both poetry and saga are still current orally in many districts.

This brief survey will be enough to show that the native literatures, in so far as they retained their independent character, have not been able to maintain themselves against the current of modern civilisation and the cosmopolitan literature (of Greek ancestry) which accompanies it. For the survival of oral literature in the south-east of Europe—whether Yugoslav, Greek, Spanish or Albanian—we have to thank the unprogressive conditions arising from Turkish government.

The scheme of comparative study which we have adopted is as follows. In this volume we have attempted to treat the early history of Greek literature and the island literatures parallel. Since ancient Greek literature was the source from which the main current of European literature is derived, we have usually taken this first; but in cases where the Greek evidence is less full or clear we have begun with one or more of the island literatures.

We have not attempted in this volume to treat any of the medieval and modern literatures included in our third group. To treat them all according to our scheme would of course be impracticable—the material is far too great. Moreover their evidence for the history of literature as a whole is much less valuable than that of the island literatures. In certain branches or categories of literature some of them supply very full and important evidence. But other categories are represented feebly or not at all—owing to the fact that in every case there existed beside the vernacular language a learned language which more or less monopolised the literature of thought. The influence of the latter makes itself felt also in various other ways.

It has been necessary therefore to make a selection; and in the next volume we propose to examine two of these literatures—Russian and Yugoslav—in so far as they appear to be of purely native origin. We have chosen these two partly because they are the fullest and most varied, and partly because they supply abundant evidence as to the way in which an unwritten literature is preserved and cultivated. Our plan is next to examine a selected number of representative non-European literatures, some of which in general resemble the first and second groups noted above, while others, which belong to Christian or Mohammedan peoples, resemble the third group. When this has been done, we hope it may be possible to formulate some general principles in regard to the history of literature. The present volume, however, is concerned only with the history of literature in Europe before the Middle Ages, and must be regarded as merely preliminary.

We believe that in Europe the only parallels to our first two groups are to be found among the Finns and related peoples; and we are under the impression that these peoples possess a good deal of material which would be of importance for the comparative study of literature in its earlier stages. But unfortunately only a small portion of this material is easily accessible; beyond that one is faced with linguistic and other difficulties, which are prohibitive.

In this volume we shall see that the early literatures of Greece and of the islands have very many features in common. Indeed we may say that in general their history seems to have followed very similar lines, though separated by an interval of a thousand to fifteen hundred years. Yet the parallelism extends only to a certain point. Greek literature appears to have had an unbroken history. But the independent development of the island literatures was cut short by the introduction of Christianity and of the Latin literature which accompanied it. Nowhere does it seem to have been extinguished all at once. Literature of thought usually succumbed—or underwent a complete transformation—long before literature of entertainment. The former was incompatible with Christianity. The latter gave way, gradually except in England, before the introduction of new fashions from the Continent. Our task is to trace the history of literature down to the point where parallelism ceases.

As mentioned above, there is no doubt that the island literatures were originally oral. Writing was used occasionally even before the Roman alphabet became known. But the intimate connection between literature[1] and writing, which is familiar to us from childhood, was

[1] Purists may perhaps object to this use of the word on the ground that etymologically it implies writing. But there is no other term available, apart from cumbrous circumlocutions. Commonly we use the expression 'poetry and saga'; but this is not entirely comprehensive. The reader will doubtless understand what we mean, and that is enough.

wholly foreign to our ancestors before the introduction of Roman writing. Indeed the evidence clearly indicates that a long period elapsed even after this event before writing was generally employed for vernacular literature. We are under the impression, for reasons which will be considered later, that similar conditions prevailed in Greece until about the close of the seventh century—or, to take the country as a whole, between 650 and 550 B.C. It is about this time that the parallelism between Greek literature and the island literatures ceases, just before the great advance in Greek thought, to which the island literatures never attained.

We may now take the material in the various languages seriatim.

In Greek we have the *Iliad* and *Odyssey*, the Homeric *Hymns*, the poems and fragments attributed to Hesiod, and a large number of short poems and fragments in hexameter, elegiac, iambic, and various lyric metres, including a number of epitaphs and a few oracles. No written prose, beyond a few short inscriptions, has survived from this period. It is believed that apart from laws and legal documents, which have perished, prose literature had hardly begun. But some of the stories recorded by Herodotos, Plutarch and other writers may date substantially from these times.

In English a very considerable amount of literature has survived from the period between the seventh and the twelfth centuries. But we have to distinguish between literature of native origin and literature derived or inspired from foreign (Latin) sources. To the latter—apart from works written in Latin—must be assigned all translations, adaptations, religious poems, sermons, legal documents due to ecclesiastical (Roman) law, and various other works of similar origin. Even the *Saxon Chronicle* cannot properly be regarded as a native product, though only the first part of it—down to the ninth century—is translated from Latin sources. What remains is only a small proportion of the whole. The poetry amounts to perhaps between 5000 and 6000 lines and includes poetry of thought, as well as poetry of entertainment and celebration. In prose, apart from the Laws, which are largely native, only a few short pieces of narrative and description are preserved.

It would seem that for some time after the introduction of Christianity, which began at the end of the sixth century, native and foreign literature ran largely in separate channels. There can be little doubt that heroic poetry was the most highly cultivated form of native literature. Yet it is never noticed by Bede, who wrote c. 700–735. The first ecclesiastic who refers to it is Alcuin, who wrote towards the end of the eighth century, and who condemns it in unsparing terms for its heathen associations. Yet all the poetry of native types which has come down to us contains passages of a Christian character, while references to heathen beliefs have disappeared, with rare exceptions, though in other respects native characteristics seem to have been well preserved. Religious (Christian) poetry, which began in the latter part of the seventh century and was soon widely cultivated, took over the diction and metre of the native types. In the ninth century English was much written and became the language of education, owing to the decay of the knowledge of Latin. But by this time Latin learning had been assimilated to a considerable extent.

Welsh poetry earlier than the twelfth century is by no means so well preserved as English. With one exception the poems are known only from medieval or later MSS., of which the four most important date from c. 1150 to 1350. Three of these MSS. contain religious poetry of Latin ancestry; but the majority of the poems belong to the native tradition. In these latter also passages of a Christian character occur frequently; but references to heathen beliefs and ideas are more in evidence than in the English poems—a curious fact, since Britain had been nominally a Christian country since the Roman period. On the other hand, in contrast with English poetry which, with rare exceptions, is purely native in form, Welsh poetry regularly shows rhyme, which is presumably of Latin origin. The use of stanzas, of three, four or more lines, is also extremely frequent. Native features are, however, preserved in the frequent prevalence of alliteration and in the occurrence of much irregularity in the length of the lines. In other respects Latin influence seems to be slight. The poetry is of very varied character; but narrative is practically wanting. Very little prose survives from before the twelfth century, and this is of Latin derivation. But from the twelfth and following centuries there are a small number of stories, especially the four *Mabinogion*, which belong to the native (saga) tradition, in form as well as in substance. A few others are under French influence. A large amount of native tradition is summarised in the form of *Triads*, some of which will be quoted later. The Laws, though late, appear to be of native origin, in form and substance.

A large proportion of the poems and *Triads* relate to persons of the sixth century, the majority of whom belonged to Scotland and the north of England. We use the term 'British' when speaking of this period. Difficulties of every kind—textual, linguistic and historical—abound both in these and many other poems. Some of them appear to be veritable palimpsests; in others the train of thought is extremely obscure. The chief MSS. have been published in a way which leaves nothing to be desired. But numerous variants require consideration; and there is everywhere the most urgent need of new translations and commentaries.

Ireland and Iceland are the chief homes of saga literature. Both countries have preserved a large amount of literature from native tradition.

In Ireland Latin literature begins in the fifth century with the writings of St Patrick. Irish, apart from inscriptions, seems to have been first written in the seventh century, both in Laws and in religious literature of Latin derivation. The writing of literature from native tradition can be traced back to the early part of the eighth century, though none of the existing MSS. of it are earlier than the twelfth century. Many forms of native literature are represented; but saga is perhaps the most extensive and important. Much of it relates to very early times. Latin influence is often visible, but usually it is more or less superficial. Heathen beliefs are of common occurrence; and even gods are frequently introduced, though they are not described as gods. The poetry is not so well preserved as the prose. Apart from what is contained in sagas, it consists very largely of fragments. In form two strata can be distinguished. The later type, which is clearly of Latin origin, shows rhyme (assonance), a fixed number of syllables in the line, and stanzas with a fixed number of lines, usually four. The earlier type has none of these features, but shows alliteration. In sagas a poem of this type is called 'rhetoric' (*retoric*). Many intermediate types are found. Lastly, we may mention that there is a very large amount of antiquarian literature, both prose and poetry, in which Latin learning and native tradition are commonly combined.

Iceland also possesses an extensive and varied literature. This is in part of native origin, especially the saga literature. But much of the poetry and of the tradition contained in the sagas was brought from Norway during the period of colonisation (c. 870–930) or later. As a rule therefore we use the term 'Norse' for this literature, although the sagas were doubtless composed in Iceland. In Norway itself literature of native tradition seems to have gone out of favour in the course of the twelfth century. The literature which survives in that country is partly of religious character, derived from Latin, partly romance literature from the Continent. A certain amount of Latin literature too has been preserved. All these are found also in Iceland. But Iceland has become the sole repository of literature of native tradition, whether from the homeland or the colonies. Both in Norway and in Iceland the writing of the vernacular seems to have begun with the Laws, which were written early in the twelfth century. In Iceland the writing of the sagas began not much later. Of these the most important are the 'Sagas of Icelanders' (*Íslendinga Sögur*)—stories from oral tradition of men and families belonging to the period c. 870–1030. Next come the 'Sagas of the Kings' of Norway (*Konunga Sögur*), which were compiled by literary men from similar stories. On the other hand the 'Sagas of Ancient Times' (*Fornaldar Sögur*), relating to times anterior to c. 870, are largely works of imagination, composed in the twelfth century or not much earlier, though some of them are based on early poems or traditions. As records of ancient times this last series is of much less value than the Irish heroic sagas. Much poetry has been preserved from heathen times, i.e. before A.D. 1000. In addition to works by known poets, we may mention especially the collection of anonymous poems commonly called *Edda*, some of which deal with stories of the gods, others with heroic stories. Hardly a trace of Latin influence is to be found in all this literature, except a few of the 'Stories of Ancient Times'. Even in antiquarian works it is extremely rare.

It has been mentioned above (p. 3) that the earliest English poetry has much in common with early Norse poetry, and that traces of the same elements are to be found in Germany. These common elements certainly date from early times—hardly later than the sixth century. They apply to both the diction and the metre of the poems, as well as the subject-matter; and they may be taken as reflecting characteristics of a poetry which was once common to the various Teutonic peoples. Much additional information relating to Teutonic poetry and tradition is supplied by Latin and Greek writers of the sixth century and earlier. We may therefore speak of the characteristics of this poetry with some confidence, though nothing of it has been preserved in its original form.

There are also elements common to early Welsh and Irish poetry. The relationship here is by no means so close as between English and Norse. Thus the heroic stories of the two peoples are totally distinct.[1] But there are certainly common elements in metre and diction which point to communication between the two countries. These may be due

[1] One Welsh poem is concerned with an Irish heroic story; and there is other evidence that Irish heroic stories were not unknown in Wales. But the two series of stories are entirely independent.

in part to the ecclesiastical connection which began in the fifth century and would seem to have been especially close in the sixth. Instances occur as late as the ninth. But there are other parallels, especially in 'mantic' poetry, which must point to a connection by no means confined to the Church. The problems arising from these parallels will be discussed in Ch. XV. But evidence is not wanting for a much earlier connection than this—a connection which seems to be shared by the Gauls of the first century B.C. This subject will require notice in Ch. XIX. The evidence points to the existence of what we may call a common Celtic element. But this common element is of much earlier date, and the traces it has left in our records are much slighter than is the case with the common Teutonic element in English and Norse.

In the present volume, as already indicated, we shall attempt a parallel treatment of these five literatures. The enquiry will be limited to the purely native elements in each literature. Reference to the elements of Latin derivation will be merely incidental, in so far as they contribute evidence of value for the history or interpretation of the native elements.

The material will be arranged according to subjects, not according to form. Poetry and prose will be treated together in each section.

First we have to distinguish between literature relating to individuals and literature of general reference. The former of these is then to be divided according as it relates to specified or unspecified individuals, and again according as it relates to human beings or to deities and other supernatural beings.

By far the largest of these classes is that which comprises literature relating to specified human beings; and this it will be convenient to subdivide. Now every one of the peoples with whom we are concerned in this volume possesses what is generally called a 'Heroic Age', which has come to an end long before the close of the period of literature comprised within the scope of our study. Many stories, though not all, which relate to this Heroic Age are commonly known as 'heroic' stories. We may therefore perhaps speak of 'heroic literature' and also of 'non-heroic literature' relating to the Heroic Age, without reference to the times when such literature was composed, whether during the Heroic Age itself or later. For literature relating to times later than the Heroic Age we may conveniently use the term 'post-heroic'.

We shall not at this point attempt to define the term 'heroic'. The word 'hero' and its derivatives are of great antiquity, as we shall see in the next chapter. So far as Greece is concerned, no ambiguity as to the meaning of the expression 'Heroic Age' is possible; and we believe that similar 'Ages' are to be traced in the past history of the other peoples now under discussion. Some scholars, however, in relation to Anglo-Saxon and Norse literature use the expression in a wider sense—without analogy to the Greek 'Heroic Age'. In order to avoid any misunderstanding therefore we must state that what we mean[1] by the expression—in this volume—is 'an age famous in literature or tradition, in which heroic conditions are predominant'. What we mean by 'heroic conditions' will, we think, be made clear for all practical purposes in the next few chapters. But the underlying principles or causes cannot profitably be discussed until we have considered the evidence available from other peoples. In the meantime it will be seen that 'heroic' conditions are still predominant in certain parts of the world. Consequently we ought perhaps to regard the first part of our definition of 'Heroic Age' as not essential, though it is valid for this volume. On the other hand we must emphasise the word 'predominant'. Heroic conditions occur, for example, sometimes in the sagas of Icelanders; but they were not the predominant conditions of Iceland in that period.

We shall not attempt to take the various divisions of our subject, as noted above, in what may be called their logical order. In this volume, which is merely preliminary, it is convenient to use the history of one literature, as far as possible, as a standard of comparison, and for obvious reasons we have chosen Greek literature. We begin with heroic literature (poetry and saga), because Greek literature, as known to us, begins with heroic poetry. Literature relating to unspecified individuals does not make its appearance as such in the earliest times of Greece; consequently it will be left until late in the volume (Ch. xiv).

Heroic literature is all-important in the earliest times; and we shall therefore devote several chapters to special aspects of it. But antiquarian literature, though it is in part based upon heroic stories, is also concerned with traditions and speculations relating to many other subjects. We shall therefore treat this in a special chapter, independently of the divisions noted above. Mantic literature requires similar treatment. The 'descriptive' literature which comes within the scope of this volume is usually of general, not particular, reference; and it is often

[1] It is the same meaning in which the expression is used in *The Heroic Age* (Cambridge, 1912).

very closely connected with gnomic literature. We shall therefore treat these two subjects in consecutive chapters.

After this chapter we shall generally use the expression 'poetry and saga' instead of 'literature'. As a description of the material this expression is less liable to misconception; and in general it applies to all the subjects treated except the four last mentioned. Of these two—mantic literature and 'descriptive' literature—consist almost wholly of poetry, so far as they come within our province, while we doubt whether the term 'literature' is properly applicable to all the antiquarian traditions and speculations which require to be noticed—some of them may never have assumed any definite literary form.

The next fourteen chapters are occupied with the discussion of the various categories of literature—heroic, non-heroic, antiquarian, etc.—noted above. The last five chapters are concerned, not with separate categories, but with questions relating to the growth and preservation of literature in general.

CHAPTER II

THE HEROIC AGE[1]

THE story of mankind, as told by the poet Hesiod, is divided into five stages, each of which is represented by a separate race. The first stage is that of the Golden Race, who were blessed with every joy and knew nothing of sorrow, and who, when they died 'as overcome by sleep', became good spirits upon the earth. Next came the Silver Race, far inferior to their predecessors. Then, thirdly, came the Race of Bronze, who had all their implements and weapons of bronze, since iron did not yet exist. This was a fierce and insolent race, wholly given up to warfare. They died by each other's hands, and their names perished with them.

A further and final stage of deterioration is marked by the Race of Iron; but before this is reached the poet introduces another race, juster and better than the last—"a godlike race of Hero men who are called Demigods, who of old peopled the boundless earth. These too were destroyed by war and the roar of battle, some at Thebes of the seven gates, the land of Cadmos, striving for the flocks of the son of Oidipus, and others at Troy, whither they had been led by war in ships, over a great expanse of sea, for the sake of fair-haired Helen. There indeed did some of them meet their end in the embrace of death, while others were granted life and abodes apart from men by the Father, Zeus the son of Cronos, and planted at the ends of the earth".

In Teutonic legend also references to a Golden Age are not unknown; but the people of this are represented as divine. Nothing is said of a Silver Age; and all memory of the Age of Bronze had faded away before the time of our earliest records. On the other hand all Teutonic peoples long preserved vivid memories of an Age of Heroes, who are celebrated alike in English, German and Norse poetry. Among the earliest references to this age is a passage in Jordanes' *History of the Goths*

[1] This and the following chapters (III–V, VII, VIII) are concerned to a large extent with the subjects treated in *The Heroic Age*, by H. M. Chadwick (Cambridge, 1912), to which—in order to save unnecessary repetition—the reader is referred for a more detailed study of the material. In general the Greek and Teutonic evidence is treated more briefly in the following chapters. We adhere to the views expressed in the former work, except that we now recognise the existence of non-heroic stories relating to the Heroic Age.

(cap. 5), which states that the Goths "used to sing to the strains of the harp, in ancient poetry, the deeds of their ancestors...Fridigernus, Vidigoia and others, who have a great reputation in that nation. The marvellous ancient world[1] can hardly claim that its Heroes were their equals". We may also refer here to another passage in the same work (cap. 13). The context contains a historical error; but this hardly affects the passage itself, which offers a rather interesting parallel to the one quoted above from Hesiod. The Goths "now called their chiefs, to whose good fortune it would seem that they owed their victory, not mere men but Demigods, that is Ansis".[2]

In both the Greek and the Teutonic worlds the Heroic Age was the earliest period of which memory survived. In both cases it forms the subject of the oldest literature which has come down to us. And later, as new literary forms grew up, it continued to supply them with themes. Thus the Athenian drama of the fifth century drew almost all its subjects from this source. In the North the heroic stories were treated first in poetry of the native traditional type, then in prose narratives, and later again in rhyming verse and popular ballads—some of which may still be heard in remote islands even in our own day.

The Heroic Age of the Teutonic peoples has no direct connection with this country, although it is in English poetry that its earliest records are preserved. There is, however, another Heroic Age, which belongs wholly to Britain. Its earliest records are to be found in Welsh poetry; but the persons and events celebrated in these poems appear to be distributed over various parts of the country, from the Channel to the Forth.

In later times many of the British heroes were forgotten. Those who were remembered were mostly drawn into connection with King Arthur—who figures in very few of the early poems—and the scene came to be laid usually in Wales and on the Welsh borders. In Wales itself the heroic stories were preserved probably in the form of saga or traditional prose narrative. But from the twelfth century onwards, if not somewhat earlier, they gained a much wider circulation—apparently through Breton channels—in France and among the Normans settled in England; and before long they became famous as themes of poetry throughout the greater part of Europe.

[1] The world of ancient Greece is meant.

[2] *Non puros homines sed semideos, id est Ansis, uocauerunt. Ansis* is doubtless identical with the Norse *Aesir*, 'gods', though there is a difference in the use of the name.

The Britons possessed also a learned literature, mainly religious, which began probably before the time of any of the heroes of whom record has survived. In early times, however, this literature seems to have been wholly in Latin, and consequently, from the fifth century onwards, confined to ecclesiastical circles. So far as the secular world is concerned the Heroic Age may be said to occupy the same position in Welsh literature as it does in Greek and Teutonic.

The British heroes, being Christians, did not become 'demigods'; but they seem to have been regarded as superior, at least in size, to people of later times. In the *Dream of Rhonabwy*, King Arthur deplores that the country should now be in the keeping of men like Rhonabwy and his companions, so puny in comparison with the men of old. The same idea recurs elsewhere both in medieval and modern stories.

Ireland also had a Heroic Age of its own. The records of this Age are more abundant than those of any of the preceding, if we exclude the late foreign outgrowths of the British. They are mostly in the form of saga, though a large amount of poetry also is preserved, chiefly in the sagas themselves. Many of the heroic stories relate to times apparently anterior to either the Teutonic or the British Heroic Ages, and among these are to be found the longest and most famous. But there are other stories, which can only be regarded as heroic, dealing with times when the Teutonic and the British Heroic Ages had come to an end. The Irish Heroic Age therefore covers an exceptionally long period.

Until recently the heroic stories were widely known among uneducated people both in Ireland and in the Gaelic-speaking parts of Scotland, whither they had been carried in the course of time. Indeed there are persons still living, at least in Ireland, who can recite some of the stories. But nearly everything seems to have been committed to writing long ago—for the most part between the eighth and the eleventh centuries.

The more famous stories and their heroes were regarded with a kind of veneration, as may be seen, e.g., from the way in which they are introduced at times into legends of saints. According to one (late) story St Ciaran wrote the *Táin Bó Cuailnge* at the dictation of the hero Fergus mac Roich, who had been raised from the dead for the purpose. In another, much earlier, story St Patrick at King Loegaire's request brings CuChulainn in his chariot before him. In a third story Cailte, the comrade of Finn, is represented as entertaining St Patrick with accounts of his adventures. Here, as elsewhere, the heroes are described as men of much greater size than people of later times—though Cu-Chulainn is always said to be small.

Next, we may consider briefly the question of date. It will be seen at once that the Greek Heroic Age is separated from the others by a long interval of time.

There is no difficulty in fixing approximately the date of the Teutonic Age; for many of the persons and events mentioned in the poems are well known from the writings of contemporary Roman and Greek historians. The period to which these belonged extends from the fourth to the sixth century; but it is probable that a few of the earliest heroes lived in the third century. The latest reference which can be fixed is to the presence of Aelfwine (Alboin), king of the Lombards, in Italy, i.e. about the year 570. The Heroic Age therefore coincides with the period of upheaval which preceded and followed the fall of the Roman Empire in the west—the period generally known as the Age of National Migrations.

The British Heroic Age was in part contemporary with the Teutonic, though it began and ended later. Most of the heroes belong to the sixth century. Arthur, however, may have lived before the end of the fifth century; and there is one—doubtful—case of still earlier date. On the other hand, if Cadwallon be included, the Heroic Age extends down into the seventh century. Cadwaladr, the son of Cadwallon, figures in a number of poems; but these are of a totally different character, and will require discussion in a later chapter.

The limits of the Irish Heroic Age are more difficult to determine. There are a number of heroic stories relating to events of the seventh century, but after this they are rare. The evidence of two early lists of sagas, which are believed to come from a common original, probably of the tenth century, seems to point to the same date. Many of the stories mentioned are unknown; but very few of them appear to fall after 700, although there is one well-known story—found in both the lists and therefore presumably derived from the original—which is concerned with events as late as the early part of the tenth century. In truth, any date which may be fixed for the end of the Irish Heroic Age must be more or less arbitrary; but for practical purposes we prefer to date it early in the eighth century. We may perhaps include the story of the Battle of Allen (*Cath Almaine*), A.D. 718.

As to the beginning of the Irish Heroic Age all that can be said with certainty is that it goes back to prehistoric times. Genealogies and the chronological schemes of the early chroniclers refer a number of stories to times even anterior to the Christian era. Until some corroborative evidence is forthcoming little trust can be put in such dating, although we suspect that the value of the genealogies has been underrated by many modern writers. Our view is that Irish heroic tradition may well reach back, in some form or other, to the early centuries of the Christian era, and possibly still further. No external evidence is available before the fifth century—the time of St Patrick—and very little before the seventh; but we see no reason for doubting that St Patrick's times were separated by a long interval from those of Cormac mac Airt, who is assigned by the chronologists to the third century, and the latter again by another long interval from the period to which the Ulster stories relate. The question as to the historicity of these early periods will have to be noticed later.

The Greek Heroic Age is wholly prehistoric. The persons and events recorded in the poems are known to us only from native tradition. No certain reference to any of them has yet been found in Egyptian or other foreign contemporary records;[1] and there are still scholars—though by no means so many as formerly—who regard them all as mythical. The ancients, however, believed them to be historical, and in the Alexandrian period, at least from the third century onwards, the leading events of the Heroic Age were included in various chronological schemes. These schemes themselves were based on calculations made by writers of the fifth century (and earlier) from genealogies; but unfortunately the mistake was made, usually it would seem, of reckoning forty years to a generation. Consequently, in order to obtain the dates really indicated by the genealogies it is necessary to deduct about twenty-five per cent. from the figures actually given.[2] The trustworthiness of the genealogies is, of course, a different question. But their evidence, such as it is, points to c. 1000 B.C., or perhaps even rather later, for the end of the Greek Heroic Age.

It is of importance to note the difference which exists between the records of the Heroic Age and those of later times in Greece. Stories relating to the Heroic Age are numerous and the persons mentioned in them amount to many hundreds—perhaps thousands—while the

[1] The recently discovered Hittite records will be noticed in Ch. VII. The most probable identifications derived from them relate to times long anterior to those of the heroes celebrated in the Homeric poems.

[2] This has been disputed. The question will be discussed briefly in Ch. VII (*ad fin.*).

centuries which intervene between it and the beginning of the historical period are practically blank, except for the bare lists of names which occur in a handful of genealogies. Yet the stories which can properly be called heroic—as distinguished from aetiological myths—are represented as extending over only a small number of generations, such as might amount to two, or possibly three, centuries.

Several questions relating to all the Heroic Ages discussed above must be reserved for consideration in later chapters. (1) What is it that constitutes a Heroic Age? Is the Heroic Age—or can it be—a purely 'literary' phenomenon, or does it necessarily involve the existence of certain social and political conditions? (2) Is the presence of historical elements essential to a heroic story? As said above, opinion on this subject has changed somewhat; but many scholars still hold to the old position, especially in regard to the Irish stories. (3) Is it justifiable to speak of the 'beginning' of a Heroic Age, as we have done? Does the fact that there are no heroic stories before a certain date mean anything more than that all the earlier heroic stories are lost and forgotten? It will be seen that these questions are all connected with one another, more or less closely.

CHAPTER III

HEROIC POETRY AND SAGA

GREEK literature begins with the two great heroic epics, the *Iliad* and the *Odyssey*. Of other such works we have only 'tables of contents', together with a few brief quotations. The only exception is the *Shield of Heracles*, a short heroic poem traditionally ascribed to Hesiod, but now generally assigned to a later date, though not later than the seventh century. Not long afterwards heroic subjects began to be treated in lyric poetry, but of such poems also we have only short fragments before the end of the sixth century. By this time a new field for the treatment of heroic subjects was supplied by the Athenian drama. In still later times the same subjects were treated in various kinds of poetry and in prose works, but with these we are not concerned.

The earliest phase of Teutonic poetry is represented by the English heroic epic *Beowulf*, with the fragments of *Finn* and *Waldhere*. The elegy of *Deor* and the catalogue poem *Widsith* date from approximately the same period. They deal with heroic subjects, though they are not primarily narrative poems like the other three. The German *Hildebrandeslied*, a fragment of a heroic narrative poem, closely resembles the English pieces and belongs no doubt to the same phase. But the great mass of German heroic poetry dates from a much later time—not earlier than the twelfth century—and shows a totally different style and metrical form. From the tenth century, however, there is a Latin heroic poem *Waltharius Manu Fortis*, dealing with the same story as the Anglo-Saxon *Waldhere*.

Of extant Norse poems none are believed to be earlier than the ninth century, at least in their present form. Among the oldest are those contained in the large collection commonly known as *Edda*, which range in date probably from the ninth to the eleventh century, and of which more than half deal with heroic subjects. A few other heroic poems, such as the *Battle of the Goths and Huns* and a fragment of the *Bjarkamál*, seem to belong to the same period. From the thirteenth century we have prose narratives—largely paraphrases of poems—on heroic subjects.

In the present chapter we shall deal first with the *Iliad* and *Odyssey* and with the earliest Teutonic narrative poems, *Beowulf*, *Finn*, *Waldhere* and *Hildebrand*; next with the other Greek poems, and with *Deor* and *Widsith*; and then with the Norse poems.

Now if the Homeric poems be compared with the earliest Teutonic narrative poems, it will be seen that there are many striking resemblances between the two groups. It will be convenient to give a list of these and at the same time to call attention to the chief points in which they differ.

Four characteristics common to the two groups may be noted at once:

(1) They are primarily narrative poems; the main object in each case is to relate a story.

(2) The stories are essentially stories of adventure.

(3) They were clearly composed for the purpose of providing entertainment rather than instruction.

(4) The stories, as we have already seen (p. 13 ff.), relate in each case to a definite period—the Heroic Age.

These characteristics seem to be constant in the poems which we are now considering. It is true that *Beowulf* contains a number of didactic passages, partly of a religious (Christian) character; but these are not sufficient to affect the general character of the poem.

As a further characteristic common to the two groups of poems we may add (5) that they may for all practical purposes be regarded as anonymous. This is strictly true of the Teutonic poems, though it is to be remembered that three of them are mere fragments. The *Iliad* and *Odyssey* were ascribed by Greek tradition to 'Homer'; but it is extremely doubtful if anything was really known of this person. At all events the personality of the author is never disclosed. Such expressions as "Tell me, O Muse" (e.g. at the opening of the *Odyssey*), or "to my knowledge" or "I have heard" (in *Beowulf*) doubtless represent conventional diction; and though sententious passages occur not unfrequently in *Beowulf*, there is no reason for supposing that they do more than voice the generally recognised opinions of the day.

Further, in regard to form, the two groups of poems have the following features in common:

(6) A uniform type of verse in either case.

The Greek and Teutonic types differ from one another considerably. The Greek poems with which we are dealing are in one metre (hexameter), which, like all ancient Greek metres, is governed by quantity, without regard to accent. The number of syllables is fixed, and so also is the quantity in each case, except the last syllable of the line. The metre of the Teutonic poems is also uniform.[1] But Teutonic metre is governed by accent as well as by quantity, the latter being regarded only in accented syllables. In certain unaccented positions the number of syllables may vary considerably. The Teutonic poems are governed also by alliteration, which is unknown in Greek.

Anglo-Saxon and early German poems have the same metrical form, each half-line containing two accented units[2] and two or (less frequently) three unaccented units or units with secondary accent. The chief difference between Anglo-Saxon and German metre is that half-lines containing five units are comparatively rare in the former and practically confined to the first half of a line, whereas in German they are more frequent and may occur in either half.

(7) An unbroken flow of verse.

Neither the Greek nor the Teutonic poems have strophe or stanza. In the Greek poems sentences usually end with the end of the line, but stops in the interior of the line are quite frequent. In the Anglo-Saxon poems interior stops are almost as frequent as those at the end of the line.

(8) The introduction of speeches.

Speeches are of frequent occurrence in the Homeric poems and are often of considerable length. The space devoted to them varies a good deal in different books—generally from one-third to four-fifths—but in both poems the total amount of the speeches exceeds that of the narrative. In *Beowulf* they are nearly as prominent and occupy in all more than two-fifths of the whole poem. They occur also in the fragments of *Finn*, *Waldhere* and *Hildebrand*.

(9) Fullness of description, even of familiar occurrences.

This is a marked feature both of the Homeric poems and of *Beowulf*. Typical examples may be found in descriptions of the arrival and reception of visitors, e.g. the reception of Telemachos and Peisistratos at the court of Menelaos (*Od.* IV. 20 ff.) and that of Beowulf at the court of Hrothgar (*B.* 325 ff.). Other instances of the same leisurely type of narrative occur in the accounts of the movements of royal personages in their palaces (e.g. *Od.* I. 328 ff., IV. 121 ff.; *B.* 920 ff.,

[1] Apart from a few examples of an extended type of line, which occurs in pairs or short groups. The *Hildebrandeslied*, however, is less regular.

[2] An accented unit consists either of one long syllable or of two syllables, of which the first is short. Unaccented units may in certain positions contain more than one syllable—sometimes up to four or five.

1162 ff.) and in the descriptions of funerals (e.g. *Il.* XXIII. 110 ff.; *B.* 3134 ff.) and of quite uneventful voyages (e.g. *Od.* II. 413 ff.; *B.* 205 ff., 1903 ff.). Even the undressing of heroes, when they go to bed, is described in the same leisurely style (e.g. *Od.* I. 436 ff.; *B.* 671 ff.).

(10) The abundance of static epithets.

This is the feature which most clearly distinguishes the language of the earlier heroic poems, both Greek and Teutonic, from that of later poetry and of prose. Examples are extremely numerous in the Homeric poems and plentiful enough in *Beowulf*. The epithets sometimes consist of simple or compound descriptive adjectives or adjectival expressions, sometimes of nouns in apposition. Thus, where we should say 'the sea', the Homeric poems and *Beowulf* commonly add an epithet, e.g. 'grey' (πολιός, *fealu*). Similarly, a ship is often described as 'hollow' (κοῖλος) or 'broad-bosomed' (*sidfæðmed*); or, again, as 'curved' (κορωνίς), which is also possibly the meaning of *wundenstefna*, etc. Headlands or cliffs have the epithet 'breezy' (ἠνεμόεις, *windig*). Buildings are called 'lofty' (ὑψηλός, *heah*). Heroes have various epithets, denoting prowess, etc., applied to them, while their squires or personal followers are often described as 'dear' or 'own dear' (φίλος, *swæs*). Not unfrequently also we meet with more picturesque expressions, such as 'the dawn clad in saffron' (ἠὼς κροκόπεπλος) or 'the sun clad in radiance' (*sunne sweglwered*).

In addition to these adjectival descriptions there are others which contain nouns, often in apposition with personal names, e.g. 'lord of men' (ἄναξ ἀνδρῶν) or 'lord of knights' (*eorla dryhten*). One of the most noticeable of these is the description of a king as 'shepherd' or 'keeper' of troops (ποιμὴν λαῶν, *folces hyrde*). Other expressions, of a more metaphorical character, are 'rampart' of a nation (ἕρκος Ἀχαιῶν, *eodor Scyldinga*) and even 'helmet', in the same sense (*helm Scyldinga*). Periphrases like 'sons of the Achaioi' or 'sons of the Geatas' are also of common occurrence.

It may be added that repetitions and recurrent lines are extremely frequent both in Greek and in English. We may note especially the formulae with which speeches are introduced.

Perhaps the most distinctive feature in the diction of Teutonic—as against Greek—heroic poetry is the love of 'kennings' or periphrastic expressions. There are indeed many expressions in the Homeric poems which would be regarded as kennings in Teutonic poetry. They occur especially as descriptions of heroes and deities, e.g. when 'husband of

Hera' is used for Zeus. But it is less easy to find analogies for the use of such expressions as 'road of the whale' or 'bath of the gannet', which occur so frequently for the sea in Anglo-Saxon poetry.

The chief distinctive feature of Greek—as against Teutonic—heroic poetry is the love of similes. These are, of course, by no means unknown in the early Teutonic poems; but they are much less numerous, and seldom run to more than a few words. It is only very rarely, as in *B.* 2444 ff., that one meets with a simile of the lengthy and detailed character which is so striking a feature of the *Iliad.*

The characteristics common to Teutonic and Greek heroic poetry which we have discussed above are for the most part such as are often known as 'epic'. It will be seen later that they are likewise characteristic of the extempore narrative poetry of modern barbaric peoples; and there can be little doubt that their origin is, in part at least, to be traced to a desire to make the entertainment last over as long a time as possible.

Next we may notice certain common features of a different character:

(11) Length of time covered by the action.

The events narrated in the *Odyssey* are represented as extending over a period of not more than six weeks, while the action of the *Iliad* is limited to a still shorter period. In both cases a considerable proportion of this time is passed over in the course of a few lines. *Beowulf* really consists of two stories, connected merely by the person of the hero, and separated from one another by an interval of more than half a century. The action of the first part (1–2199), apart from the introduction, is limited to four or five days; that of the second may be said to extend over two or three weeks, though nearly the whole takes place in one day. As regards the fragments, it is impossible to speak with certainty; but the action of *Waldhere* and *Hildebrand* probably covered only a few days.

This concentration of the action upon a brief period is doubtless to be connected with the tendency to fullness of detail noted above.

(12) Time of the action relatively to the poet.

The Homeric poems sometimes[1] use the phrase 'such men as there now are', contrasting the men of the poet's own day with the heroes of the stories. But this phrase does not necessarily mean that the heroes were regarded as belonging to a very remote past, for similar expressions are put into the mouths of the heroes themselves,[2] when they are speaking

[1] E.g. *Il.* v. 304 (οἷοι νῦν βροτοί εἰσι).

[2] Cf. *Il.* I. 272.

of the generation next before their own. Indeed there is no indication in the poems that the times of the heroes were believed to be very remote. The same remark is true of *Beowulf.* It is plain that the events related are regarded as belonging to the past; but there is nothing to show that they happened very long ago.

The above list of characteristics common to the two groups of poems is by no means exhaustive. Thus in both we frequently meet with episodes in the form of stories relating to the past, usually but not always contained in speeches. Stories of the past which are not contained in speeches seem to be proportionately more frequent in *Beowulf* than in the Homeric poems. In both also we find changes of scene, where the narrative passes from one character or set of characters to another; but in this case the examples found in *Beowulf* (e.g. 1591, 1605) are much less striking than those in the *Iliad*, while *Beowulf* has no parallels to the transitions from one strand of narrative to another, which form one of the chief features of the *Odyssey*. In addition to these there are certain other common characteristics—the concentration of interest upon individuals, the aristocratic milieu, the presence of both historical and unhistorical elements—which we shall have to consider in the following chapters. For the moment, however, the list given above will be sufficient.

Up to now our discussion has been confined to the *Iliad* and *Odyssey* on the one hand and to *Beowulf*, *Finn*, *Waldhere* and *Hildebrand* on the other. The *Shield of Heracles*, apart from the long description of the shield itself (139–320), conforms to the same type, though the narrative is more condensed—a feature which is perhaps observable in *Finn* as compared with the other Teutonic poems. The lost Cyclic poems also seem in general to have been of this type, if we may judge from the few fragments and references which have been preserved. There are, however, certain indications of the presence in these poems of elements of a different character, as we shall see in a later chapter.

It is difficult to form an opinion as to the character of Greek lyric heroic poetry from the minute fragments which have come down to us. The evidence, however, such as it is, would seem to indicate that these poems differed considerably from the type discussed above. The object appears to have been to depict a scene rather than to tell a story; and they were occupied apparently more with situations and emotions than with adventures. Their metrical character was of course entirely different.

Greek tragedies, the great majority of which derive their themes from heroic stories, follow and develop the line set by the earlier lyric poets. Apart from the fact that the stories are drawn from the Heroic Age and that the action is limited to a brief period—much briefer indeed than in the epics—the characteristic features discussed above are almost wholly wanting in these works.

The Anglo-Saxon poems *Deor* and *Widsith* are concerned with heroic themes; but they do not conform to the type which we have been considering. They cannot properly be described as narrative poems, although they contain narrative elements. The references to adventure which occur in them are merely incidental, and it can hardly be said that their primary object is to entertain. *Widsith* indeed has much in common with didactic poetry, for it consists largely of catalogues—which will be discussed in a later chapter. *Deor* also is a short catalogue of scenes from heroic story. Both poems, however, contain passages describing what purport to be personal experiences of the authors, and which—at least in the case of *Deor*—approximate to 'occasional' poetry.

Both poems are in the ordinary Teutonic alliterative metre mentioned above. *Deor*, however, is divided into short sections of unequal length, which are separated from one another by a refrain. *Widsith* has no refrain; but, except from the brief prologue, the close of the sentence almost invariably comes at the end of a line. Both poems, apart from the prologue in *Widsith*, are in the form of speeches by the authors. They contain no internal speeches. In language and metre they show no remarkable differences from the poems discussed above.

Both poems profess to be the work of court minstrels of the Heroic Age. Deor states (35 ff.) that he had been the minstrel of the Heodeningas—an expression which seems to mean Heoden and his family or perhaps Heoden himself—and that he had been displaced from his position by an accomplished poet named Heorrenda. The first of these persons is without doubt the famous hero Heðinn of Norse tradition, called Hetele in the medieval German poem *Kudrun*, while the second is clearly Horant, the minstrel of Hetele. Widsith describes his visit as a minstrel to the courts of Eormenric, king of the Goths, and other famous kings. His permanent abode was at the court of Eadgils, prince of the Myrgingas, who were neighbours of the English in their Continental home.

It is a disputed question whether the statements given in the poems are to be accepted at their face value, i.e. whether we are to believe that the poems are really the work of the persons who are represented as their authors. Against this it is urged that Widsith claims to have visited kings who lived in different periods, e.g. Eormenric who died c. 370 and Aelfwine, king of the Lombards, who died c. 570. If the poem was originally composed in Eormenric's time, considerable additions must have been made to it subsequently. As a matter of fact it contains a certain amount of material derived from Latin sources, which can hardly have formed an original part of it, unless it was composed at a late date.

There is no reason for doubting that poetry of the 'occasional' type was composed in the Heroic Age. Historical evidence for this is to be found in Procopios' *History of the War against the Vandals* (II. 6). When Gelimer, the last king of the Vandals, was besieged by the Romans on Mt Papua in 534, he wrote to the commander of the besieging army, begging him to send him a harp. The explanation given by the messenger was that the king had composed a song upon his misfortunes, and as he was a good minstrel he was anxious to accompany it with a mournful tune on the harp, as he bewailed his fate.

The case of poems which bear the names of ancient authors is one which we shall encounter again, and discussion of this question must therefore be deferred for the present. It may, however, be observed here that we have no knowledge of the poets Deor and Widsith from other sources. The name *Widsith* ('Far-travelled') is indeed clearly fictitious. It occurs only in the prologue, which is perhaps a subsequent addition to the poem.

Several of the heroic poems of the *Edda* conform in general to the type discussed on p. 20 ff. Such are *Völundarkviða*, *Helgakviða Hundingsbana I*, *Sigurðarkviða hin skamma*, *Atlakviða*, *Atlamál*, *Hamðismál*, and probably the fragmentary *Sigurðarkviða hin meiri*. To these may be added the *Battle of the Goths and Huns*, which is preserved in *Hervarar Saga*. All these may fairly be described as narrative heroic poems, dealing with stories of adventure and composed for the purpose of entertainment.

There are, however, other heroic poems in the *Edda* which can hardly be described as narrative, and which deal with situations and emotions rather than with adventure. Such are *Guðrúnarkviða I*, *Helreið Brynhildar*, *Oddrúnargrátr*, and *Guðrúnarhvöt*.[1] In all these cases the object

[1] Intermediate between the two classes stands the short poem *Guðrúnarkviða III*, in which the narrative is outweighed by the speeches.

of the poem seems to be rather to depict a scene than to tell a story.

Thus *Guðrúnarkviða I* consists chiefly of a dialogue, depicting the grief of Guðrún after Sigurðr's death and the efforts made by her relatives and others to comfort her. This poem may be compared with the final scene in the *Iliad* (XXIV. 719 ff.)—the lamentation over Hector. Both cases are examples of a widespread custom, which we shall meet with in several other regions—the lamentation over a dead man by his wife and relatives. Irish parallels will be noticed below.

A different kind of situation is depicted in the *Helreið Brynhildar*. The heroine on her way to Hell encounters an ogress, who upbraids her for the calamities she has brought about. The greater part of the poem is occupied with Brynhildr's apologia.

The other two poems, *Oddrúnargrátr* and *Guðrúnarhvöt*, consist largely of dialogue, leading up in each case to a longer speech by the heroine, in which she gives a retrospect of her experiences. With these we may compare *Guðrúnarkviða II*, which is wholly in the form of a retrospective monologue.

All these poems, except *Guðrúnarkviða I*, contain a story—the story of the speaker's life—told in the first person; but in all cases[1] it is not so much the story as the situation or feelings of the speaker at the moment to which our attention is chiefly called.

Here also we may refer to two other poems, *Helgakviða Hjörvarðssonar* and *Helgakviða Hundingsbana II*, which consist almost wholly of dialogue. Each of these is divided into a number of scenes, the connecting narrative being supplied in prose. It would seem that the *Bjarkamál* also was a dialogue poem, if we may judge from the Latin version given by Saxo.

Mention may also be made of the *Grottasöngr*, a poem preserved in the *Prose Edda*, if this can properly be regarded as a heroic piece. The subject is the plight of two giant maidens, who are forced to grind gold on the quern Grotti for Fróði, the legendary peace king of the Danes. The greater part of the poem is occupied with a grinding spell, by means of which they eventually bring a raid upon Fróði; and the quern breaks.

Lastly, there remain three *Edda* poems, *Reginsmál*, *Fáfnismál*, and *Sigrdrífumál*, which form a connected Trilogy, relating to the early adventures of Sigurðr, and ought perhaps to be treated as parts of a single work. They consist wholly of speeches, with connecting narratives

[1] Except perhaps *Guðrúnarkviða II*; but the end of this poem is lost.

in prose. But in these poems the predominant element is didactic. In the *Sigrdrífumál* indeed the story furnishes little more than an opening for a discourse by the Valkyrie Sigrdrífa on magical and gnomic lore, similar to the second half of the didactic poem *Hávamál*.

Among the 'speech' poems themselves therefore we have to distinguish between two different types—a type dealing with situation or emotion, and a type of predominantly didactic interest. It will be convenient now to describe the three types of heroic poems in the *Edda* as follows:

Type A: Narrative poems.

Type B: Poems dealing with situation or emotion, and consisting wholly or mainly of speeches.

Type C: Poems of didactic interest. The examples in the *Edda* are speech poems; but in the following pages we shall meet with didactic heroic poems which are not of this character.[1]

The English narrative poems, discussed on p. 19 ff. above, correspond, as we have seen, in their primary characteristics to the poems of Type A, and may be classed under the same heading. But it is not clear that there are any English poems corresponding to the other two types. The personal elements in *Deor* and *Widsith* may be referred to Type B if we are to regard these poems as speeches in character, like *Guðrúnarkviða II*; but this is uncertain. And in any case the personal elements form only a minor part of either poem. *Widsith* might be referred rather to Type C, if the author is not speaking *in propria persona*; for in that case the catalogues, of which the poem is largely made up, will be of a quasi-didactic character—comparable, of course, not with the magical and gnomic didacticism of the *Sigrdrífumál*, but with the slight antiquarian element found in the *Fáfnismál*. The first catalogue indeed can hardly be regarded otherwise than as antiquarian, whatever view be taken of the poem as a whole; and the same remark applies to certain elements in the other catalogues in their present form.[2] But even *Beowulf* contains an appreciable amount of didactic matter—of the gnomic variety—though it is merely incidental.

There is, however, one English poem—the short piece which stands at the beginning of the Riddles in the *Exeter Book*—which may perhaps be taken as an example of Type B. It consists of a speech by a woman addressed to a man called Eadwacer. The piece is full of diffi-

[1] Where necessary we shall distinguish between CA, CB, etc.

[2] To the catalogues in *Widsith* we shall have to refer again in the chapter on antiquarian poetry. It may be mentioned here that similar catalogues seem to have been cultivated by the Goths and other Teutonic peoples.

culties and has been variously interpreted—by some as a riddle, by others as a scene from some heroic story. The latter would seem to be the more probable explanation, although the story cannot be identified with certainty. It is hardly possible to regard this piece as a genuine case of personal poetry.

In early Greek poetry the Homeric poems and the *Shield* correspond to Type A. It is likely that lyric heroic poetry had much in common with Type B, though this cannot be proved from the scanty fragments which have been preserved. At all events tragedy, which probably owed much to it, shows a highly developed form of this type. Type C was well represented in early Greek poetry. The *Instructions of Cheiron* (addressed to Achilles), a poem sometimes attributed to Hesiod, may have been similar to the *Sigrdrífumál*. But the bulk of the didactic heroic poetry was doubtless antiquarian in character. In this body of poetry, however, the heroic elements were combined with theological, aetiological, and other matter; we shall therefore postpone discussion of it until we deal with antiquarian poetry in general.

We may now return to the *Edda* poems. Of the characteristics enumerated on p. 20 ff. the first applies, as we have seen, only to rather less than half of the poems. The second and third may perhaps be said to apply to all the poems except (in part) the Trilogy. But the interest of poems of Type B lies rather in emotional situations arising from adventure than in adventure itself. In the Trilogy the prevailing interest is didactic or informative.

(4) All the poems relate to the Heroic Age—the same period to which the English poems relate.

(5) All the poems are anonymous.

(6) As regards metre the poems of Types A and B show a uniform line, with the exception of one portion of *Helgakviða Hjörvarðssonar* and a single strophe in each of two other poems—*Helgakviða Hundingsbana II* and *Hamðismál*. In the majority of the poems the line is of the kind known as *Fornyrðislag*. In the *Atlamál*, however, it is of the kind known as *Málaháttr*, while the *Atlakviða*, the *Hamðismál* and the *Battle* use an irregular line, sometimes conforming to the *Fornyrðislag*, but more frequently to the *Málaháttr*. Both these metres[1] are probably

[1] These explanations are intended for readers who are not familiar with the Norse terms. We may add that we are far from claiming to speak with any authority upon Norse metres (or those of any other language). But it will be necessary to refer to these terms occasionally in later chapters. Dame B. S. Phillpotts, in *The Elder Edda*, renders *Fornyrðislag* by 'old-lore metre', *Málaháttr* by 'speech-metre', and *Ljóðaháttr* by 'chant-metre'. See also note on p. 63.

derived from the type of line which is used in the Anglo-Saxon and the earliest German poems. In the former the half-line consists of four units, in the latter of five. It would appear therefore that the *Málaháttr* has generalised the longer type of half-line—which is much more frequent in German than in English. The irregular variety found in the *Atlakviða*, etc., seems to be earlier than the fully developed *Málaháttr*.

The poems of the Trilogy (Type C) are for the most part in a totally different metre, the *Ljóðaháttr*, in which a line of the *Fornyrðislag* or *Málaháttr* type alternates with a shorter line. The latter has three accented units, two of which alliterate, but no caesura. The effect is somewhat similar to the Greek elegiac. This metre is the one chiefly used in the mythological speech poems of the *Edda*, as well as in the gnomic *Hávamál*. Sometimes, however, in the same poems we find a related form of metre called *Galdralag* ('Metre of Spells'), in which the longer line is followed by two (or more) of the shorter lines in either the first or second half of the stanza (rarely in both)—which consequently contains five (or more) lines.

The four metres mentioned above—*Fornyrðislag*, *Málaháttr*, *Ljóðaháttr*, *Galdralag*—are practically the only metres found in the *Edda* poems.

(7) All Norse poetry is regarded as stanzaic (strophic). The stanza or strophe usually consists of four lines, except in the *Galdralag*. But five-line stanzas are of very frequent occurrence, especially in the *Atlamál*; and indeed many of the poems with uniform line (*Fornyrðislag* or *Málaháttr*) show great irregularity in the length of their stanzas. These irregularities are ascribed by many editors to textual corruption; but they may be explained as survivals of non-stanzaic poetry.[1] In contrast with Anglo-Saxon poetry the sentence almost always ends at the end of a line. Usually there is a break after every second line.

(8) Speeches occur in all the poems. Generally they occupy a very considerable proportion of the poem. Most of the poems of Type B consist wholly, or almost wholly, of speeches.

(9) The style of the Norse poems presents a striking contrast to the fullness of description found in *Beowulf* and the Homeric poems. Parallels to these are not altogether wanting: we may cite, for example, the account of Hlöðr's arrival at King Heiðrekr's funeral feast in the *Battle*,

[1] We suspect that the four-line stanza is due to the influence of the *Dróttkvætt* metre, in which it is practically universal. This metre is not used in the *Edda* poems. It has internal rhyme (assonance), as well as alliteration, and is perhaps due to foreign influence.

st. 3 ff., or that of Helgi's embarkation and voyage in *H. Hund. I*, 26 ff. But on the whole, though the dialogues are often fairly long, the narrative tends to be concise and even hurried. These remarks apply primarily to poems of Type A.

(10) Static epithets are similar in character to those which are found in the English poems; but they are of much less frequent occurrence. A building is described as 'lofty' (*hár*), a spear as 'whistling' (*gjallandi*), as in English, a stag as 'high-legged' (*hábeinn*), a horse as 'trained to coursing' (*gangtamr*). For a king we find such descriptions as 'lord of men' (*gumna dróttinn*) and 'distributer of treasure' (*baugbroti*, etc.), as in English. Repetitions and recurrent formulae are not infrequent, especially where speeches are introduced.

As regards the length of time covered by the action, Norse heroic narrative poems (Type A) mostly consist of two parts, of which the first is usually the shorter and more or less introductory to the second. In *Helgakviða Hundingsbana I* the first fourteen stanzas give a kind of summary of the hero's life previous to the main action. In *Völundarkviða* and *Sigurðarkviða hin skamma* the first parts are brief narratives of events which cover a considerable length of time. On the other hand in *Atlakviða*, *Atlamál*, *Hamðismál*, and the *Battle* the first part consists of a single scene separated by a short interval—several months in the *Battle*—from the action which follows. In all these poems the second part is limited to a few days at most.

In the Trilogy (Type C) and in those poems of Type B which contain prose narratives these often cover a considerable time. The other poems of Type B consist of one scene only.

In regard to the time of action relative to the poets, the Norse poems frequently show a striking contrast to Greek and Anglo-Saxon heroic poetry. In four cases—*Helgakviða Hundingsbana I*, *Sigurðarkviða hin skamma*, *Guðrúnarkviða I*, and the *Battle*—the poem begins with the word *ár*, 'long ago', while *Oddrúnargrátr* opens with a reference to 'ancient stories'. The beginning of *Hamðismál* emphasises the great length of time which has elapsed since the events related in it took place.

It may be added that the Norse heroic poems—apart from inferences which may be drawn from their language, diction, etc.—furnish no evidence as to the time or region in which they were composed, except that the *Atlakviða* and *Atlamál* are described as belonging to Greenland in the titles under which they stand in the *Codex Regius* of the *Edda*.

In addition to the heroic poems there are a number of prose stories relating to the Heroic Age. Some of these are paraphrases of poems. The *Völsunga Saga* is largely derived from some of the poems discussed above. But the source of the early chapters, which deal with the adventures of Sigmundr, is unknown; and the same is true of nearly the whole of *Hrólfs Saga Kraka* and of several heroic stories preserved in the *Prose Edda* and elsewhere. It is probable that these stories also were ultimately derived from poems. References to some of them occur in works of poets of the ninth century; and it is doubtful whether the cultivation of saga in Norway had begun before this time. A parallel may perhaps be seen in the *Battle*; for the latter part of this poem contains a good deal of prose, which appears to have been paraphrased from lost stanzas, whether by design or through forgetfulness.

There can be no question that a large amount of heroic poetry has perished. The heroic poems of the *Edda* all come from one collection (now represented by only one early MS.), from which also the *Völsunga Saga* is mainly derived. The great majority of these poems are concerned with Sigurðr or his wife Guðrún. The remainder deal with the adventures of (i) Helgi Hjörvarðsson, (ii) Helgi Hundingsbani, and (iii) Hamðir and Sörli. But Helgi Hundingsbani was believed to be a half-brother of Sigurðr, while Hamðir and Sörli are said to be sons of Guðrún, who plays a part in the poems relating to them. The whole collection may therefore be regarded as belonging to one cycle, with the exception of the poem dealing with Helgi Hjörvarðsson, who is said (in the prose) to be a previous incarnation of his namesake. But it is not certain that this group of poems was as a whole more popular than other heroic poetry. References to the story of Hamðir and Sörli are very frequent; but early poets refer less often to the stories of Sigurðr and Helgi than to those of Heðinn and Högni and of Hagbarðr and Signý, which are preserved only in prose paraphrases or by Saxo.

Saxo in his *Danish History* gives many Latin poems which are clearly—in some cases avowedly—translations of vernacular poems. It is from him that we know the *Bjarkamál*, of which only a fragment is preserved in Norse, the story of Hagbarðr and Signý, to which we have merely allusions elsewhere, and that of Ingjaldr (Ingellus) and Starkaðr, of which there is a brief account in *Beowulf* (2024 ff.). Saxo's poems consist wholly of speeches, and it may be that the heroic poems, Danish or Norse, known to him were all of Type B, with the narratives in prose, like *Helgakviða Hjörvarðssonar* and *Helgakviða Hundingsbana II* (cf. p. 27). Indeed many scholars hold that this was the original type of heroic poetry in the North. This, however, is a very doubtful question, to which we shall have to return in a later chapter.

The chief records of the British Heroic Age consist of (i) a considerable number of Welsh poems, most of which are quite short, (ii) a few Welsh sagas, only two of which seem to be of strictly native origin, and (iii) a very large body of foreign medieval literature. To the last we shall only refer incidentally. Mention must also be made of *Triads*, genealogies, and incidental notices in various Latin and Welsh works. These are usually of antiquarian interest, and they will therefore require some discussion in Ch. x. It may be noted here, however, that both the *Triads* and the incidental references sometimes point to the existence of heroic stories which are now lost.

The Welsh heroic poems are almost all contained in the following four MSS.[1]: (1) the *Black Book of Carmarthen*, dating from the twelfth

[1] The poems contained in these Books are all printed and nearly all of them translated in Skene's *Four Ancient Books of Wales* (Edinburgh, 1868)—a work about which it is necessary here to say a few words. Skene's interest lay in early Scottish history, and it was this which led him to undertake the work. He was looking out for references to Scotland, and perhaps he found too many of them. Much more serious is the fact that the translation of the poems was a task beyond the powers of the scholars whom he employed. Welsh philology has made considerable progress since the book was published; and it is now clear that the translators frequently went astray through imperfect knowledge of the old language. But it is also clear, as we shall see in later chapters, that the text of the poems is very frequently ill-preserved in the MSS. In many cases we doubt whether even the best Welsh scholars now would undertake to translate without a liberal use of emendation. Instead of emending or leaving blanks Skene's translators took the course of giving the nearest literal translation they could get, and thereby not unfrequently produced gibberish. The effect of this has been to raise a general feeling of distrust and prejudice against the poems in the minds of those who do not know the language, while Welsh scholars themselves have discarded the translations, though Skene's texts are for the most part still in use.

Our own feeling is that Skene's work has been somewhat unduly disparaged. It was a great undertaking; and his introduction contains a large amount of valuable matter, even if he rode his hobby too hard. We believe that even the translations can be of considerable service, if used with caution. In the great majority of cases—though not always—they give at least an idea of the general drift of a poem; and it appears to us far better to make use of them than to ignore the existence of a very interesting and important collection of literature—which is at present the only alternative for the general reader. But at the same time we would impress upon Welsh scholars the imperative need of producing new translations and commentaries—with no more emendation of the texts than is absolutely necessary. We ourselves have rarely ventured translations of our own, because our knowledge is insufficient for the purpose. But we have given references to more recent translations century; (2) the *Book of Aneirin*, from the middle of the thirteenth century; (3) the *Book of Taliesin*, from the late thirteenth century; and (4) the *Red Book of Hergest*, from about a century later. Of these MSS. the *Book of Aneirin* contains little except heroic poetry. The other three contain also poems on various other subjects, religious and secular, some of which will require discussion in later chapters.

Most of the poems contained in these MSS. are difficult and obscure. Often the language is archaic, and the orthography points to derivation from much earlier originals—sometimes, as e.g. in the 'Appendix' to the *Book of Aneirin*, as early as the tenth century. Indeed many of the poems claim to be works of poets of the sixth century—Taliesin, Aneirin and Llywarch Hen—but the authenticity of this claim has long been a subject of controversy. Here it will be enough to note that if the poems are so old as this they must have undergone a great deal of modernisation.

There are no heroic poems corresponding to the Greek and Teutonic narrative poems discussed on p. 19 ff. Type A is practically unrepresented in Welsh heroic poetry.

On the other hand Type B is represented by several poems. Speech poems relating to the Heroic Age are indeed numerous; but the majority of them are of a didactic or semididactic character. Moreover, in many of them, though they may refer to heroic characters, the interest lies primarily in the speakers themselves, who are famous poets or prophets. Among these we will reserve for discussion in Ch. VI the poems in which Myrddin (Merlin) is the speaker, or one of the speakers. In the same chapter we will also include poems of a didactic character in which the speaker is said to be—or appears to be—Taliesin.

Of the remaining poems we will take first *BBC.* XXXIV—an extremely difficult and obscure piece. It appears to consist of two separate fragments relating to the story of Tristan. In the second and shorter of these the speaker, apparently a woman, is addressing a dwarf. She says that Tristan is furious at his coming; that she has betrayed March for his (the dwarf's) sake in order to obtain vengeance upon *Kyheic*, but that the dwarf's anger has been fatal to her. The first fragment is even

of poems whenever we could find them, except in cases where emendation has been allowed to run riot.

It may be added here that variant texts of a good many poems are to be found in *The Myvyrian Archaiology of Wales*, which is cited from the edition published at Denbigh in 1870. Some of these are derived from early MSS.; but in other cases the MS. source seems to be unknown.

more obscure, though it seems to contain an allusion to the messages which were sent floating down the stream.[1]

A piece somewhat similar to this occurs in *Tal.* XLII; but it relates not to the British but to the Irish Heroic Age—the story of CuRoi and CuChulainn.

Among other dialogue poems we may refer to *BBC.* XXXV, where the speakers are Taliesin and a certain Ugnach, who appears to be a prince. Taliesin is passing on his way through Ugnach's city, and Ugnach invites him to stay with him. Taliesin thanks him but declines. In this case, as in *BBC.* XXXIV above, one cannot help feeling that some kind of introduction is needed to explain the circumstances, as in some of the Norse poems of Type B cited above (p. 27). Or they could be explained even better if originally they formed part of a saga, like the poems contained in the late story *Hanes Taliesin.*

Another dialogue poem, which has something in common with the last, is *BBC.* XXXIII. Here the speakers are Gwyn ap Nudd and Gwyddneu Garanhir. The latter part of the poem consists of a list of battles at which one of the speakers had been present. In form this bears a slight resemblance to the catalogues of *Widsith.*[2]

Next perhaps we ought to mention *BBC.* XXXI,[3] which likewise begins with a dialogue. The speakers are Arthur, who is accompanied by Cai, and the porter Glewlwyd Gafaelfawr. But after the first ten lines the poem becomes a monologue—apparently by Arthur, though he is referred to in the third person—which is entirely occupied with a list of Arthur's heroes and their exploits. This list is obviously the essential part of the poem; the short dialogue at the beginning is intended merely to lead up to it. The poem should therefore be referred to Type C rather than to Type B. It may be noted that here again there is a resemblance to the latter part of *Widsith.*

BBC. I is possibly to be taken with the last poem. It is in the form of a dialogue between the poets Myrddin and Taliesin; but the interest lies apparently not so much in the speakers themselves as in

[1] For a translation and discussion of this poem see Loth, *Rev. Celt.* XXXIII. 403 ff. M. Loth holds that the poem represents an early form of the story, differing in several respects from the later versions, especially in regard to the position of the dwarf.

[2] A much closer analogy to the second and third catalogues of *Widsith* is to be found in *Tal.* XIV. But this poem, although it has heroic interests, is of still greater importance in relation to the poet Taliesin, who is the speaker. We shall discuss it therefore in Ch. VI.

[3] Transl. by Rhys in Malory's *Morte d'Arthur* (Everyman), p. xviii ff.

the heroes and the battles of which they speak. This is another of the cases where one can only deplore the absence of an explanatory context.

Next we come to a group of three monologue poems, *BBC.* XXX, XXXIX, and *RBH.* XI, in which the speaker, who is called Llywarch or Llywarch Hen, bewails the deaths of his sons, killed in battle. The first begins with a long description of winter, and the last with a lamentation over the troubles of old age, several stanzas being addressed to the speaker's crutch. It is known from the royal genealogies—which will be discussed later—that the speaker was a man of princely family and a cousin of Urien, a king who figures prominently in a number of poems soon to be discussed. According to the genealogies Llywarch Hen must have lived in the latter part of the sixth century. The line of kings which ruled in Gwynedd from the ninth century onwards traced their descent from him.

In the preceding cases we have assumed that the poems are speeches in character. The possibility that any of them were actually composed by the speakers or in the circumstances indicated is not worth consideration. But here the case is obviously different. There is no reason why Llywarch should not have composed such elegies upon the deaths of his sons. An analogy may be found in the *Sonatorrek*, an elegy composed by the Icelander Egill Skallagrímsson for his sons—which we shall have to notice in a later chapter. The difficulty is that the language of the poems is that of a period several centuries later than Llywarch. Hence many scholars deny the possibility that the poems can be by him. Yet why should a poet of, say, the eleventh century want to compose such elegies upon people who had died five hundred years before? And what record of them had he? We know hardly anything of Llywarch or his sons except from these poems; but it is possible, of course, that a poet of the eleventh century may have known earlier poems, now lost, from which he may have derived his theme.

These poems, like many others, are composed of three-line stanzas—a form probably derived from Latin hymns.[1] The line commonly contains seven syllables; but there is much irregularity. The condition of the text may be estimated from the fact that half of the stanzas con-

[1] We do not believe that the rhyming metre of these (and other) poems is in any way inconsistent with a sixth century origin. Rhyme presumably became known through Latin hymns in the fifth century. But in Welsh after the loss of final syllables—which seems to have taken place not later than c. 500—the stimulus towards rhyme must have been much greater than in Latin (or any other language) because all words were accented on what had now become the final syllable.

tained in *BBC*. XXXIX occur also either in *BBC*. XXX or in *RBH*. XI. It is impossible to believe that the poems can be preserved in their original form. We shall see later that the evidence points to oral—not written—tradition. But for the present we must leave the question until we meet with other analogous cases. The poems clearly belong to Type B, if they are not the work of Llywarch himself.

Among the speech poems noticed above we have assigned one or two to Type C rather than Type B owing to their predominantly antiquarian interest. They may be conveniently described as CB. There are, however, other poems of antiquarian interest (Type C) which are not in the form of speeches in character.

The obscure poem *Tal*. XXX[1] clearly belongs to Type C. It is full of references to the Heroic Age, especially to Arthur and his ship Prydwen, and to various incidents which occur in the story of Culhwch and Olwen; and the interest, so far as the substance goes, is essentially antiquarian. But this is subordinated, as in some other poems, to a desire for rhetorical effects, which is shown especially in the variation of recurrent sentences. The poem gives the impression of being a 'graduation' exercise of some kind—perhaps composed for the purpose of obtaining the chair of a *Pencerdd*.[2]

Next we come to a large group of poems which differ in character from any of those considered hitherto. They consist partly of elegies upon dead heroes and partly of panegyrics upon princes who are represented as still alive. The former are not of the subjective character which distinguishes the elegies of Llywarch Hen. They are concerned, primarily at least, with the valour and virtues of the heroes whom they celebrate.

We will take the elegies first. Among these we may include the *Gododdin* (*An*. I),[3] the most famous work in early Welsh literature. It celebrates the heroes who fell at 'Catraeth'. Nothing is known of the battle from historical sources, but it is generally believed to have been fought against the Northumbrian English towards the end of the sixth century. The heroes themselves too are almost all unknown, including even the leader, Mynyddawg Mwynfawr. A notable exception is Cynon

[1] Transl. by Rhys in Malory's *Morte d'Arthur* (Everyman), p. xxii ff.

[2] See Ch. XIX.

[3] Transl. by T. Stephens, *The Gododin of Aneurin Gwawdrydd* (ed. by T. Powell); by Sir E. Anwyl, *The Book of Aneirin* in *Trans. of the Hon. Soc. of Cymmrodorion*, 1909–10; by T. Gwynn Jones, *Y Cymmrodor*, XXXII. 1 ff.; and elsewhere. The order of the stanzas is rearranged in some of the translations.

ap Clydno Eidyn,[1] who is perhaps the sole survivor. The heroes are celebrated seriatim—sometimes one stanza, sometimes two or more being devoted to each; sometimes several heroes are celebrated in one stanza. The text, however, appears to be in great disorder. Variants to many of the stanzas have been added in the MS. both at the end of the poem itself and at the end of the book; and in a poem so loosely constructed it would be unwise to assume that all the stanzas originally belonged to it.

Two, or perhaps three, other poems in the same book (*An.* III, IV, V) are elegies upon individual heroes who perished apparently in the same disaster. These also present great difficulty.

The *Book of Taliesin* contains two somewhat similar poems. *Tal.* XLIV[2] is a short elegy on the death of Owein, the son of Urien, commemorating briefly his victories over the Saxons. *Tal.* XLVI seems to be an elegy on the death of Cunedda, a prince of the fifth century, from whom most of the royal families of North Wales traced their descent; but it is extremely difficult and obscure.[3] It claims to be the work of Taliesin himself.

The *Red Book* also contains two elegies (*RBH.* XII, XVI), which resemble one another rather closely; but they differ greatly from those we have been considering. In form they have much more in common with the elegies of Llywarch Hen, discussed above; but they are primarily concerned with the heroes whose deaths they commemorate. The first is an elegy on the death of Urien, whom the poet speaks of (st. 20, 23) as his cousin and lord. In all probability this implies his identity with Llywarch, though the name is not mentioned. The second is an elegy on Cynddylan, an unknown prince of Powys,[4] who has been killed in battle with the Saxons, and whose home and country the poet expects to see ravaged.

The poems which celebrate living heroes are almost confined to the *Book of Taliesin.* Most of them are concerned with Urien, son of Cynfarch; and these may conveniently be divided into two groups.

[1] There seems to be much difference of opinion as to the true form of these names. We have followed Morris-Jones, *Y Cymmrodor*, XXVIII. 77 ff., where the evidence adduced for *Eidyn* seems decisive. The spelling *Clytno* in *BBC.* XIX. 9, 11 points to *Clyddno*; but it is possibly a case of archaic orthography.

[2] Transl. by Morris-Jones, *Y Cymmrodor*, XXVIII. 187 f.

[3] A new interpretation is given by Morris-Jones, *op. cit.* p. 204 ff., where also a translation will be found.

[4] Sometimes identified with the *Condidan* mentioned in the *Sax. Chron.*, ann. 577; but this is quite uncertain. The poem relates to Shropshire.

One group, consisting of *Tal.* XXXII–XXXIV, XXXVI, XXXVII and XXXIX,[1] is occupied with the praise of this hero's prowess in general, his virtues and generosity. The other, consisting of *Tal.* XXXI and XXXV, deals with particular events—battles fought by Urien. The latter approach more nearly to narrative (Type A) than do any other early Welsh poems. Indeed *Tal.* XXXV can hardly be regarded except as a narrative poem, though it is very short. Intermediate between the two groups, but more nearly akin to the former, lies *Tal.* XVIII, which celebrates the martial exploits of Owein, the son of Urien. This poem does not mention Urien by name; but in all the others he is represented as alive and ruling.

It may be observed that *Tal.* XXXIII claims to be the work of Taliesin himself; and the same claim is perhaps implied in *Tal.* XXXVII. As *Tal.* XXXIII ends with a refrain which occurs also in most of the other poems, including XXXI and XXXV, it is not unlikely that they are of the same origin, though the refrain may have been borrowed by some poems from others.

Two poems, *Tal.* XI and XXXVIII, are devoted to the praise of a prince called Gwallawg, the son of Llenawg. The latter shows a general resemblance to the poems of the first group above, while the former has perhaps more in common with *Tal.* XVIII. In both of them the hero is represented as alive and ruling.

Another poem (*Tal.* XXIII) celebrates the generosity of Cynan Garwyn ('Cynan of the white carriage'), son of Brochfael, and the victories won by him and his family in Gwent, Anglesey, Dyfed and elsewhere. This Cynan was king of Powys, perhaps at the time of the battle of Chester (c. 615), at which his son Selyf was killed.[2] The poem is very similar to *Tal.* XI and XVIII, above. The hero seems to be represented as still alive and ruling.

Very different from all these is a poem (*BBC.* XXII, *RBH.* XIV) which celebrates a battle fought by Gereint, son of Erbin, at a place called Llongborth. This poem is of the rhetorical kind, like *Tal.* XXX (cf. p. 37), about half of it being taken up with phrases applied to the hero's horses and repeated over and over again with variations. The poet says

[1] *Tal.* XXXI–XXXIII, XXXV and XXXIX are translated by Morris-Jones, *Y Cymmrodor*, XXVIII. pp. 162, 172, 176, 156, 181.

[2] *Ann. Cambr.* CLXIX (i.e. probably A.D. 614). If the Brochfael (Brocmail) mentioned by Bede in his account of the battle (*Hist. Eccl.* II. 2) was Cynan's father, he must have been a very old man. The name, however, was a common one in the dynasty of Powys. Both Cynan Garwyn and his grandsons, the sons of Selyf, figure in the *Life of St Beuno*.

that he witnessed the battle. This piece is sometimes called an elegy; but it is not clear that Gereint's death is mentioned.[1]

Lastly, reference may be made to some fragmentary pieces. *BBC.* XXXII evidently comes from a poem on Gwallawg. It is in a rhetorical style, somewhat similar to the last piece; but the meaning is obscure to us. *RBH.* XVII seems to have taken its opening and concluding lines from panegyrics upon Urien, like those discussed on p. 38 f. above. But the bulk of the poem belongs to a totally different milieu—not to the Heroic Age at all. To this case we shall have to return in a later chapter. It may be observed here, however, that the concluding lines claim to be the work of Taliesin and speak of Urien as still reigning.[2]

The series of poems, both elegies and panegyrics, which we have been considering in the last few pages, have given rise to much discussion and difference of opinion. Heroic poems of Types B and C may be composed centuries after the Heroic Age has come to an end—in fact as long as sufficient interest is taken in the subjects. But with the poems now under discussion the case is obviously different. It is conceivable that in certain circumstances, e.g. at anniversaries or other commemorations, elegies might be composed in honour of famous men for some considerable time after their death. Such an explanation would perhaps be permissible also for a poem like that on Gereint; for the use of the word *gweleis* ('I saw') may be merely rhetorical. But it is hardly possible to account in this way for the panegyrics upon Urien, Gwallawg and Cynan Garwyn, which represent these heroes as living men. These poems belong to a type which is widespread, as we shall see, among heroic societies and also among societies which are not primarily heroic; but apparently they are always composed within the lifetime of the heroes themselves. The same may be said, in general, with regard to elegies of a subjective character, like those of Llywarch Hen (cf. p. 36).

On the other hand, if these poems really date from the Heroic Age, we have to account for the fact that the language in which they are preserved is that of a very much later period. It is a strange thing too

[1] The *Red Book* text (st. 13) says that he was killed in the battle. But the corresponding passage in the *Black Book* (st. 9) seems to mean that Gereint's brave men from Devon were killed (not the hero himself), and it is clear from the context that this must be the original form of the sentence. *BBC.* has "and before they were slain they made slaughter (of the enemy)", while *RBH.* likewise has the plural here, though the exact meaning is not quite clear to us; cf. Strachan, *Introd. to Early Welsh*, p. 84.

[2] These lines are perhaps disconnected tags; cf. Morris-Jones, *Y Cymmrodor*, XXVIII. 196 f.

that so much should have survived from the Heroic Age when the next five hundred years are almost a blank. Welsh historical poetry begins practically with the twelfth century.

During the past century many scholars have been unwilling to allow that these poems are what they appear to be; and it is still widely believed that they date from much later times than the Heroic Age. In addition to the reasons given above various arguments, both good and bad, have been brought forward against their authenticity. Thus, e.g., the fact that they contain much which is unintelligible—both proper names and other matter—affords no real ground for doubting their antiquity; on the contrary it is what might reasonably be expected if they are very ancient. On the other hand there is no doubt that references to events of the twelfth century occur in some poems which profess to come from the Heroic Age, if not in these poems themselves. A critical attitude is therefore necessary.

It has sometimes been suggested that the persons whom the poems celebrate themselves lived long after the Heroic Age. This suggestion might of course get rid of the difficulties we have noticed; but we are not aware that anyone has seriously attempted to face the problems which such a theory would necessarily raise. There is a large and compact mass of heroic tradition, in which these heroes are deeply embedded. In particular Urien and Llywarch Hen have connections in all directions. It is true that from the thirteenth century onwards we find Welsh records (*Histories*, *Triads*, etc.) which are derived or influenced from Geoffrey of Monmouth. But this element is easily distinguishable. And in point of fact the heroes with whom we are concerned, with the exception of Arthur, are little more than names to Geoffrey, if he mentions them at all. But it would have been far beyond the power of any medieval writer to produce the material with which we have to deal. Moreover there are numerous genealogies and a certain amount of historical material of other kinds which, though not strictly contemporary, yet deserve very serious consideration. These records will require to be examined at length in Ch. VII, when we come to discuss the historical and unhistorical elements in heroic tradition generally.[1]

[1] We may say at once that we cannot undertake to consider suggestions which have been put forward from time to time with regard to the wholesale fabrication of records. Fabrication or falsification of individual records is a well-known phenomenon under certain conditions. But these suggestions apply to practically the whole of the early literature and early records of a nation—many of them preserved in an ancient form of language. The day for theories of this kind has gone by.

At all events we must now recognise the existence of types of poetry other than the three (A, B, C) which we distinguished on p. 28. Elegies and panegyrics may be grouped together under a Type D, as 'celebration' poetry. To this type must be assigned the poems which we have been considering, whatever may be thought as to their date; and further examples are to be found among historical Welsh poems of the twelfth century. Nothing of it survives among the remains of Teutonic and Greek heroic poetry; but it certainly existed in the former. Widsith (99 ff.) says that he sang the praises of Ealhhild; and we shall see later that Greek and Latin writers refer to such poems. We shall find examples also in Greek and Norse poetry (other than heroic), in Irish, and in many other languages. Indeed it is one of the most widely distributed types of poetry.[1]

At the same time it will be convenient to distinguish a fifth type—Type E—which we may call 'personal' poetry or, more specifically, 'poetry relating to the poet's own feelings or experiences, or to persons in immediate relationship with him, or to things which have come under his observation but which are not of general significance'. To this type we may assign the elegies of Llywarch Hen, in view of their subjective character, and also the personal references in *Deor* and *Widsith*—provided that, in each case, these poems are what they profess to be. A reference to the cultivation of poetry of this type in the Teutonic Heroic Age has already been given (p. 26); and numerous examples will be found later—in Greek, Norse, and various other languages.

We may now compare the characteristics of Welsh heroic poetry with those of Greek and Teutonic, according to the analysis proposed on p. 20 ff. (cf. p. 29 ff.) above. The comparison is of course rendered difficult by the fact that most of the Greek and Teutonic poems belong to Type A, which is wanting, or almost wanting, in Welsh; while, on the other hand, Type D is unrepresented in Greek and Teutonic, and more fully represented than any other type in Welsh. Types B and C, however, and perhaps E also, are represented both in Teutonic and in Welsh.

Of the characteristics (1–4) noted on p. 20 the first—that of narrative—is wanting. As regards the second, most of the poems are founded upon incidents of adventure, though this cannot be insisted upon in all cases, e.g. in *BBC.* XIX, XXXV, and some of the panegyrics.

[1] In later chapters we shall extend the application of this type to 'poetry of invocation and exhortation', as well as 'poetry of celebration'.

As regards the third, the poems of Type B were doubtless intended for entertainment, while those of Type C are informative or learned, and those of Types D and E concerned with celebration and reflection respectively. As regards the fourth, all the poems are usually believed to relate to the Heroic Age, though in the case of the panegyrics this view has been questioned.

(5) The fifth characteristic, anonymity, holds good for the poems which belong to Types B and C, and for some of those which belong to Type D. Other poems of this type, however, claim Taliesin as their author, as we have seen; while three—or four, if we include *RBH.* XII—profess to be the work of Llywarch Hen. The title of the *Gododdin* (*An.* I) states that Aneirin was its author; and the same claim seems to be made in two obscure passages in the poem itself. Taliesin is said to have composed *An.* IV in the prose introduction to that poem. He is also claimed as author by some poems of a totally different (non-heroic) character, which we shall have to discuss in Ch. XV. The consideration of these claims may therefore be postponed for the present.

(6) In form the Welsh poems differ greatly from Teutonic and Greek heroic poetry (cf. p. 20 f.). In place of the uniform type of verse seen in the latter they show many varieties of metre, all of which appear to be either modelled upon, or at least influenced by, Latin metres.[1] Rhyme is practically universal; but alliteration, which is presumably of native origin, is also very common.

(7) In place of the unbroken flow of verse found in Greek and, still more, in Anglo-Saxon poetry, the Welsh poems consist of groups of lines, two, three, four, or more in number, connected by rhyme or assonance. In heroic poetry the couplet and the three-line stanza seem to be the most common forms. Sentences rarely extend beyond one stanza, and there is a general tendency towards a break in the sense at the end of each line.

(8) Speech poems, monologue and dialogue, are not uncommon, as we have seen; and even apart from these the first person occurs occasionally. But the introduction of speeches after the manner of Type A (cf. p. 21) is extremely rare. Examples will be found in *Tal.* XXXV, a

[1] It seems hardly necessary to assume that the non-stanzaic metres are of purely Latin origin. But they are presumably affected by Latin influence in the introduction of rhyme and in a tendency to make the lines of approximately equal length. The latter process is far from complete. But we may repeat here that we do not feel ourselves qualified in any way to express opinions on the subject of metre—least of all on Welsh and Irish metres.

poem which may practically be regarded as an example of narrative poetry.

(9) Some poems, especially the *Gododdin* and the poems following it (*An.* I, III–V), show a fullness of description comparable with the normal standard of the Homeric poems. But this applies only to what may be called pictorial descriptions. Narrative, as we have seen, is merely incidental and never given in detailed form, whether in relation to commonplace or exceptional events. On the contrary it is very often so brief as to be extremely obscure—a fact which constitutes one of the great difficulties of the poems. It would seem that the audience was expected to be familiar with the course of events. The poems may, however, have been accompanied by some kind of commentary in prose, which has been lost.

(10) Static epithets are not very common and can hardly be regarded as characteristic of Welsh heroic poetry. On the other hand recurrent formulae and repetitions of various kinds are of very frequent occurrence. They are of a more studied and rhetorical character than those which are found in Greek and English heroic poetry. In poems which consist of stanzas of three or more lines the opening words of one stanza are very commonly repeated in the stanzas—three, four, five, or even more—which immediately follow. Such repetitions occur especially in Type D poems with three-line stanzas, e.g. in the elegies which claim to be by Llywarch Hen. The repetition, as a rule, does not extend to the whole of the first line. Sometimes, though not so frequently, it is found in the second or the third line, instead of the first. In poems of what we have called the rhetorical style, such as *BBC.* XXII, XXXII, repetitions occur in all three lines of each stanza—the result being, of course, a mere waste of words.

The other characteristics discussed on p. 23 scarcely need consideration here. As there is no narrative poetry no question can arise as to the length of time covered by the action. As regards the time of the action relatively to the poet—most of the poems of Type D represent it as present or immediately past. In poems of Type B or Type C no indication is given.

There can be little doubt that heroic saga was cultivated in some form or other from early times; but very little has actually been preserved. Neither the *Mabinogion* proper, i.e. the *Four Branches of the Mabinogi*, nor the stories called *Lludd and Llefelys* and the *Dream of Maxen Wledig* can fairly be regarded as heroic. The former will need consideration in Ch. VI, with the late piece called *Hanes Taliesin*; the latter will be noticed in Ch. X, in connection with antiquarian subjects in general.

There are only two native sagas which can be regarded as definitely heroic—*Culhwch and Olwen*, and the *Dream of Rhonabwy*. Both of them are much nearer to Type C than to Type A of heroic poetry. The narrative in each case is entirely subordinated to antiquarian interest; catalogues and repetitions abound. They may fairly be described as Type CA.[1]

Rhonabwy is said to have been an officer of Madawg, prince of Powys, about the middle of the twelfth century. He dreamed that he encountered Iddawg, one of Arthur's knights, who took him to a place on the Severn, between Montgomery and Welshpool, where Arthur was encamped with all his host. Arthur himself is playing chess with Owein, son of Urien; and the game is constantly interrupted by messengers who say that Arthur's men are fighting with Owein's ravens. Apart from this there is little in the way of incident. The greater part of the *Dream* is occupied with descriptions of the various heroes, their robes and horses.

In the other story Culhwch comes to King Arthur, whose relative he is, and appeals to him and all his knights to assist him in obtaining the hand of Olwen, daughter of the ferocious Yspaddaden Pencawr. The latter names a large number of apparently impossible tasks as the price of his consent; but Arthur and his knights succeed in carrying them out. The chief incident is the hunting of the boar Twrch Trwyth.

Indirect evidence for saga is perhaps to be obtained from the romances, in which names known from native tradition have often been substituted for the French or Breton names. Thus the substitution of Gereint and his Cornish (Devonian) family for Erec, with his Breton connections, may have been due to the existence of similar stories relating to the former. The appearance of the Gododdin hero Cynon, son of Clydno (Eidyn), in place of Calogrenant in the opening scene of the *Lady of the Fountain*, may be due to a similar cause; he may have already figured in such stories of adventure.

Apart from the stories noticed above a few very brief narratives relating to the Heroic Age are preserved in the Laws and elsewhere. One passage describes how Maelgwn secured the supremacy of the kingdom of Gwynedd by means of a throne made of wings, which was

[1] By this we mean a didactic or informative piece in narrative form, whereas we apply the letters CB to didactic or informative poems which consist of speeches in character, like the *Edda* Trilogy.

able to float, and in which he could maintain his position against the incoming tide. Another relates how certain heroes from the north made an expedition against Arfon and how, when a counter-expedition was undertaken from Wales, Rhun, son of Maelgwn, obtained certain privileges for the men of Arfon. These stories are of an explanatory character and belong definitely to Type C.

But the chief source of information is to be found in the *Triads*—a species of compositions, originally perhaps of a mnemonic character, in which heroes (*inter alia*) are grouped together in threes on account of some distinction or peculiarity which they were believed to have in common. It is only from them that one can gather how great a body of heroic tradition must once have existed. Many of the heroes who figure in them are now known otherwise only from genealogies.

As illustrations of the character—and also the difficulties—of the *Triads* we may quote the following examples: 34.[1] "Three loyal retinues of the Island of Britain: The retinue of Cadwallon, son of Cadfan, who were seven years in Ireland with him and asked him for no payment during this time, for fear of being obliged to leave him. And the retinue of Gafran, son of Aeddan, who, when he disappeared, went to sea for their lord. And, third, the retinue of Gwenddoleu, son of Ceidiaw, at Arderydd, who continued the battle for six weeks after their lord was slain. Now the number of men in each of these retinues was a hundred and twenty". 49. "Three shackled[2] retinues of the Island of Britain: 'The retinue of Cadwallon the Long-handed, who bound the shackles (hobbles) of their horses to their feet, each pair of them (together), when they were to fight with Serrigi the Irishman at the Rocks of the Irish in Anglesey. And the retinue of Rhiwallon, son of Urien, when they fought against the Saxons. And the retinue of Belyn of Lleyn, when they fought against Edwin at Bryn Ceneu in Rhos".

The first item in No. 34 is one of the few pieces of evidence for the existence of saga relating to Cadwallon. The third item in No. 49 may come from the same saga or cycle. The second item in No. 34 is obscure. The third relates to one of the most famous events of the Heroic Age, a subject which will require discussion in Ch. VI. In No. 49 the Cadwallon who figures in the first item was an ancestor of his namesake and

[1] These numbers refer to the first of the series of *Triads* contained in *The Myvyrian Archaiology of Wales*, 2 ed. (1870), pp. 388–94.

[2] The practice of binding warriors together by the feet—to prevent any thought of escape—seems to have been not unknown in Ireland. An example occurs in the longer version of the *Battle of Mag Rath* (cf. p. 53, note).

father of Maelgwn. He is known otherwise only from genealogies; but this passage suggests that it was he who drove the Irish out of Anglesey. Rhiwallon, son of Urien, who appears in the second item, seems not to be mentioned in the poems.

It should be noted that the *Triads* vary greatly in age and value. Some are quite late and worthless—derived from Geoffrey of Monmouth and similar sources. But many reflect the same milieu as the poems; very often they relate to persons mentioned in the poems or to near relatives of them. The sagas from which they were derived represented no doubt different strata of tradition, like those which have actually been preserved. Thus in the *Dream of Rhonabwy* we find Rhun, son of Maelgwn, and Owein, son of Urien, among Arthur's heroes. They are missing, however, in *Culhwch and Olwen*, although the list of Arthur's heroes given here is enormous and drawn from foreign, as well as native, sources. The latter saga represents an earlier stage of tradition, in which the different generations of the Heroic Age had not yet been completely fused. Yet it belongs itself to a different world from the historical milieu reflected in many of the poems.

The records of the Heroic Age of Ireland are of a somewhat different character from any of those which we have been considering. There is a considerable amount of heroic poetry, mostly of Types B and C. Type A rarely occurs in early texts. But the poetry is, as a whole, of less importance than the saga, a great body of which has come down from early times—far superior to any of the heroic saga discussed above. Most of the poetry of Type B is contained in sagas in the form of speeches. It will be advisable therefore to consider the saga first.

The records, both saga and poetry, are preserved in a large number of MSS. The most important of these are the *Book of Leinster*, which was written in 1160–70, and the *Yellow Book of Lecan*, written towards the end of the fourteenth century. The oldest important MS. is the *Book of the Dun Cow* (*Lebor na-hUidre*), part of which dates from the early years of the twelfth century. But there is no doubt that these and other MSS. are largely derived from earlier ones, now lost, some of which were written in the eighth and ninth centuries. The earliest MS. containing heroic matter of which there is any trustworthy record—the *Book of Druim Snechta*[1]—is believed to have been written in the first

1 The contents of this book (cf. Thurneysen, *Ir. Heldensage*, p. 17) seem to have been mainly non-heroic sagas of the Heroic Age; but they include some of those noticed above.

half of the eighth century. The written record therefore reaches back practically to the Heroic Age itself.

The Irish Heroic Age without doubt covered a long period, and the stories relate to many different generations. But there is one group or cycle of stories which seems to have been cultivated far more than any of the others at the time when writing was first used for this purpose. This cycle relates to a very remote period, but covers apparently only about one generation. The chief figures are Conchobor, king of Ulster, and his heroes, CuChulainn, Conall Cernach, Fergus mac Roich and others, and also Ailill and Medb, king and queen of Connaught, who are frequently at war with Conchobor. To this cycle belong a large number of stories, only a few of which can be mentioned here.

The longest and most famous of all the heroic stories is the *Táin Bó Cuailnge*[1] ('Cattle Raid of C.'). The subject is a raid made upon Ulster by Ailill and Medb for the purpose of seizing a valuable bull. Advantage is taken of a time when the Ulster heroes are incapacitated by a *ces* or 'infirmity'. But the youthful CuChulainn is not affected by this infirmity, and sets out to resist the invaders. In a series of combats he slays many of Medb's champions and makes great havoc among her forces. He continues his resistance until the Ulster army is able to take the field. A considerable number of poems—nearly all speech-poems of Type B—are contained in the narrative.

The *Tochmarc Ferbe* ('Courtship of Ferb')[2] is one of the very rare cases where the earliest form of the story is a narrative poem (Type A). Conchobor learns in a dream that Maine, a son of Ailill and Medb, is coming to marry Ferb, daughter of a chief named Gerg, apparently in Ulster. He sets off with a large band of warriors and comes upon the wedding party by surprise. Maine and Gerg and most of the combatants on both sides are killed. The story ends with reprisals by Medb, which lead to further fighting.

The story of CuRoi mac Dairi[3] is known in several different forms.

1 Ed. and transl. (German) by Windisch, *Irische Texte* (Extraband); Engl. transl. by Dunn, *The Ancient Irish Epic Tale, Táin Bó Cúalnge*. The references given below are to the lines of Windisch's edition and the pages of Dunn's translation. When the earlier text is cited the references are to the *Yellow Book of Lecan* (*YBL.*), published in a Suppl. to *Ériu*, I–III.

2 Transl. (both poetry and prose) by Leahy, *The Courtship of Ferb* (Nutt).

3 Cf. Thurneysen, *Zeitschr. f. celt. Philol.* IX. 189 ff.; *Ir. Heldensage*, p. 431 ff. We may refer also to the *Aided ConRoi* ('Fate' or 'Tragic Death of CuRoi'), ed. and transl. by Best, *Ériu*, II. 18 ff.

CuChulainn attacks a fort across the sea and carries off a princess and three marvellous cows. The princess is in one version Blathine, daughter of Conchobor; elsewhere she is called Blathnat and appears to be foreign. A disguised man takes part in the raid and is wholly or partly responsible for its success. Afterwards he carries off the booty, and CuChulainn, when he tries to stop him, gets roughly handled. Eventually he is discovered to be CuRoi, a famous king in west Munster. The men of Ulster attack his fort, and he is betrayed to CuChulainn by Blathine (Blathnat), who has stolen his sword. The details of the betrayal vary; in one version she gives the signal by pouring the milk of the cows into a stream. Vengeance is taken upon her by the *fili* ('poet') Ferchertne; but the details again vary.

There are certain poems connected with this story, which are in part preserved independently of the prose narratives. One of them is an early elegy, in which the speaker is Ferchertne, and which we may regard as an example of BD. The story forms the subject also of a difficult Welsh poem of Type B (*Tal.* XLII), which perhaps refers to the incident of the milk.

Next we may take the short saga *Scél Mucce Maic Dathó* ('Story of Mac Datho's Pig').[1] Mac Datho has a valuable dog, which is coveted by Conchobor and also by Ailill and Medb. Not wishing to offend either party he promises it to both, and invites them to come for it with their retinues at the same time. For the entertainment of his visitors he provides a huge pig. The question now arises who is to divide the pig, since this was the privilege of the greatest champion. The Ulster heroes have to give way, one after another, to the Connaught champion Cet mac Matach; but at the last moment Conall Cernach arrives, and to him Cet is obliged to yield. But Conall divides the pig so unfairly that the feast ends in a free fight between the two parties.

Fled Bricrenn ('Bricriu's Feast')[2] resembles the last story in its chief motif. Bricriu Nemthenga ('Poison-tongue'), a chief at Dundrum, builds a great hall and invites Conchobor with all his court to a feast. The invitation is accepted after some hesitation, but owing to Bricriu's mischief-making propensities it is stipulated that he himself shall not be present. He contrives, however, to intercept Laegaire Buadach, Conall Cernach and CuChulainn, and to persuade each of them to demand the 'champion's portion'. Trouble arises therefore as soon as the feast begins; but eventually the combatants are persuaded to refer

[1] Ed. and transl. by N. Kershaw Chadwick, *An Early Irish Reader*.
[2] Ed. and transl. by Henderson (Irish Texts Soc.).

their claims to Ailill and Medb for decision. In the meantime Bricriu persuades the wives of the three heroes each to claim precedence for herself. This leads to a riotous scene, in the course of which CuChulainn pulls down the house. Afterwards the heroes take their claims first to Ailill and Medb, and then to CuRoi mac Dairi, for whom CuChulainn performs some fantastic feats. But the others are unwilling to accept the decisions in favour of CuChulainn until an unknown warrior—said to be CuRoi—enters Conchobor's hall and asks if anyone is brave enough to let him cut off his head—a challenge which only CuChulainn will accept.

Longas mac n-Uislenn ('the Exile of the Sons of Uisliu')[1] is primarily the story of the life of Derdriu, a daughter of Conchobor's story-teller. At her birth the druid Cathbad had prophesied that she would cause great strife in Ulster; but Conchobor had her brought up in secret because of her beauty. When she grew up she induced Noisiu and his brothers—the sons of Uisliu—to carry her off to Britain. The Ulster chiefs are anxious for the heroes to return, and they consent to do so if Fergus, Dubthach and Conchobor's son, Cormac, will guarantee their safety. But the latter are prevented from accompanying them, though Fergus sends his son Fiacha. When they arrive at Conchobor's capital, Noisiu and Fiacha are murdered by Eogan, son of Durthacht; Derdriu is delivered up to Conchobor, and the rest of the party massacred. Fergus and the other securities take up arms, and after some fighting enter the service of Ailill and Medb (in whose army we find them in the *Táin*). Derdriu refuses to be consoled, and is given by Conchobor to Eogan; but she kills herself by leaping out of his chariot.

The story is very briefly told. But the latter part of it—from the return of the heroes—is related at much greater length in a later saga called *Oided Chloinne n-Uisnig* ('the Fate of the Children of Uisnech').[2] Here Conchobor's treachery is greatly accentuated. Derdriu is endowed with second sight and repeatedly warns the heroes, in poems of Type B, against returning. She dies at the burial.

The story of CuChulainn's death[3] is, briefly, as follows: Lugaid,

[1] Transl. by Thurneysen, *Sagen aus dem alten Irland*, p. 11 ff.; Leahy, *Heroic Romances of Ancient Ireland*, I. 87 ff.; Dottin, *L'Épopée Irlandaise*, p. 76 ff.

[2] Ed. and transl. into English by Stokes in Windisch, *Irische Texte*, II. II. p. 109 ff.; also (anonymously) for the Society for the Preservation of the Irish Language (Dublin, 1914).

[3] Cf. Thurneysen, *Ir. Heldensage*, p. 547 ff. The first part of the story is transl. by Dottin, *op. cit.* p. 147 ff. Cf. also Stokes, *Rev. Celt.* III. 175 ff.; Hull, *The Cuchullin Saga*, p. 253 ff.

son of CuRoi, and Erc, son of Cairpre Nia Fer, whose fathers had both been slain by him, led an army against the men of Ulster at the time when the latter were incapacitated by their infirmity. The defence was left to CuChulainn, who set out against the enemy in spite of unfavourable omens. His death was due to certain wizards, sons of Calatin, whose father also had been killed by him. His charioteer Laeg is shot first, then one of his horses, and then the hero himself. Then the army retires, but Lugaid, who is carrying off his head, stays behind to bathe in the Liffey. Here he is overtaken and killed by Conall Cernach, who is under a vow to avenge CuChulainn before sunset on the day on which he is slain. Cuchulainn's favourite horse comes to his wife Emer, and lays its head on her knee; and the story ends with an elegy by her.

We may now take some of the stories which do not belong to the Ulster cycle. *Orgain Dinn Ríg* ('the Destruction of Dinn Rig')[1] is apparently the earliest story—i.e. the story relating to the earliest times—which can properly be called heroic. The genealogies indeed would date it back to a time several centuries before the Christian era. Ugaine the Great, high-king of Ireland, left two sons, Laegaire Lorc and Cobthach Coel Breg, of whom the former succeeded his father as high-king, while the latter was king of Bregia (south of Dundalk). Cobthach wasted away from chagrin at the superior position of his brother and appeared to be dying. He requested Laegaire to arrange for his funeral on the following day, and then apparently died and was laid out in his chariot. But while his brother was bending over his body he stabbed him in the back. Soon afterwards he brought about the murder of Laegaire's son, Ailill, who was king of Leinster, and drove into exile his son Moen, known later as Labraid Loingsech. The latter took refuge with Scoriath, a king in west Munster, whose daughter he married. He had a harper named Craiphtine who was able to lull everyone to sleep, and by his help he succeeded in capturing and sacking the fortress of Dinn Rig; whereupon he became king of Leinster. He then made peace with Cobthach and invited him to a feast. For his reception Labraid had an iron house built in Dinn Rig. Thirty kings were being feasted within it, when it was heated and they were all roasted alive. Labraid's mother gave herself up to perish with them, apparently in order to ensure the success of the plot.

Next, we may perhaps include here the last of the three stories called

[1] Ed. and transl. by Stokes, *Zeitschr. f. celt. Philologie*, III. 1 ff.

Tochmarc Étáine ('the Courtship of Etain').[1] The first of these stories is concerned with gods only, while the second and third belong to a heroic milieu; but it can hardly be assumed that the three stories were originally composed to form a sequence. In the first Etain is the wife of the god Midir; but she is taken away from him and eventually born as a mortal. In the second she becomes the wife of the high-king Eochaid Airem; but after this she is courted by her previous (divine) husband in disguise. In the third story Eochaid finds in Tara to his surprise a young and handsome man, who has entered the fort before the gates were open. The stranger makes known to him that he is Midir and challenges him at chess; and the king, who is a great chess-player, accepts and wins. Here there is a lacuna in the text; but it appears that as a forfeit he compelled his opponent to build a causeway over a certain swamp—a task which was carried out by night and involved great hardship to Midir's followers. But he challenges the king again and wins; and now, as a forfeit, he claims the right to embrace and kiss Etain once. Eochaid asks for a month's delay, and then assembles all his warriors and bars the gates. But Midir appears suddenly in the midst and demands his forfeit. The king is obliged to let him put his arm round his wife; and then he rises with her through the opening in the roof, and they are seen flying away together in the form of two swans. The king then sets out with his troops to break open the elf-hills. At this point the text comes to an end. From later accounts it seems that he recovered his wife, but that the gods afterwards got their revenge and slew him.

A considerable number of stories centre round the famous king Cormac mac Airt, but in many of them non-heroic characteristics predominate. To these we shall have to refer in Ch. VI. Here we may perhaps mention the story called *Cath Chrinna* ('the Battle of Crinna').[2] An attack upon Cormac was planned by Fergus Dubdetach ('Black-tooth'), king of Ulster, who had two brothers also called Fergus. Cormac fled to Munster to seek for help. There he caught a famous hero Lugaid Laga, while he was bathing. To save his own head he had to promise to bring to Cormac that of Fergus Dubdetach. Another famous hero, Tadg, son of Cian, was induced to give his services by the promise that he should have as much land as he could drive round between the close of the battle and sunset on the same day. The valour

[1] Transl. by Leahy, *Heroic Romances of Ireland*, I. 27 ff.; cf. Thurneysen, *Ir. Heldensage*, p. 612 ff.

[2] Ed. and transl. by O'Grady, *Silva Gadelica*, I. 319 ff.; II. 359 ff.

of these two heroes gained the victory for Cormac. Lugaid had to bring the heads of all the three Ferguses, because he did not know which of them was the king. Then he tried to kill Cormac, but the latter had taken the precaution of dressing a druid in his armour and setting him on his throne. Tadg now demanded his reward, but he was so exhausted that he could not keep awake. Cormac therefore ordered his charioteer to turn the horses whenever he went to sleep—with the result that he was able to get round only a small area before sunset.

As may be seen from the above story, Cormac himself is not represented as a hero; he gains his ends by craft, not by his own prowess. Most of the heroic stories relating to his time are concerned with the exploits of Finn mac Cumaill, his son Oissin (Ossian), and their followers, the Fian, of whom perhaps the best known are Cailte and Diarmait. One of the most famous of these stories is that of the *Battle of Gabra*, which tells of the death of Oscar, son of Oissin. Cormac's son, the high-king Cairpre, fell in the same battle. In later times this group of stories became the most popular of all. There are also numerous poems connected with them.

Another group of stories relates to the high-king Eochaid Mugmedon, his wife Mongfinn, and his sons, of whom the most famous was Niall Noigiallach ('Niall of the Nine Hostages'). The best known of these stories is perhaps that of the poisoning of Crimthann, brother of Mongfinn.[1] On the death of Eochaid he had become high-king; but his sister wanted to get the throne for one of her own sons. She therefore offered her brother a poisoned cup. He, being suspicious, insisted upon her drinking first; and they both perished. This story brings us near to the beginning of the historical period; for Niall, the successor of Crimthann, was the father of Laegaire, who was high-king at the time of St Patrick's mission (A.D. 432).

There are a number of stories relating to historical events of the sixth and seventh centuries. Of these perhaps the best known is that of the *Battle of Mag Rath*,[2] which was fought in 637 by the high-king Domnall mac Aeda against the Ulster prince Congal Claen and his allies from Dal Riada in Scotland. The story has only been preserved in late texts, but it shows well-marked heroic features.

[1] Ed. and transl. by O'Grady, *Silva Gadelica*, I. 330 ff., II. 373 ff.; by Stokes, *Rev. Celt.* XXIV. 175 ff.

[2] Ed. and transl. by O'Donovan, *Publ. of the Irish Arch. Soc.*, VII (1822). A shorter and quite different text is ed. and transl. by Marstrander, *Ériu*, V. 232 ff. Congal is here called Congal Caech.

Cath Almaine ('the Battle of Allen')[1] is a story of a different kind, though the milieu at least is heroic. The high-king Fergal, son of Maelduin, invaded Leinster in 722, but was defeated and slain with nearly all his followers at Allen near Kildare. He had taken with him a minstrel and story-teller named DonnBo, who fell at his side. On the evening before the battle DonnBo had been unable to provide any entertainment, but he promised to sing to Fergal on the following night, wherever they might be. His head was cut off in the battle, and one of the Leinstermen afterwards found it singing. He takes it to the house where King Murchad and the Leinster chiefs are feasting; and there turning itself to the wall it sings most beautiful and pathetic music—'for Fergal, not for Murchad'. Afterwards he takes it back to its body, as he had promised; and the minstrel revives and returns home.

Practically all the stories noticed above contain poetry, and the same is true of heroic sagas in general. The majority of the poems, including nearly all those contained in the *Táin Bó Cuailnge*, belong to Type B; but there are also many which are of an informative (antiquarian) character, consisting largely of catalogues, and may be referred to Type C. Some of these indeed are merely quotations from antiquarian poems, of a class which will be noticed in Ch. x.

Of the poems of Type B some are dialogues, some monologues. The latter are sometimes reflections, by one of the characters, on the situation of the moment. Not unfrequently, however, they are prophecies—as in the *Adventure of the Sons of Eochaid Mugmedon*, where the poet Torna prophesies the future greatness of his foster-son Niall Noigiallach, who has been abandoned by his mother through fear of Mongfinn. Another instance, already referred to, is the prophecy of the druid Cathbad relating to Derdriu, in the *Exile of the Sons of Uisliu*. Further examples occur in the *Táin Bó Cuailnge*, and elsewhere. In other cases again the monologue is an elegy. For an example we may refer to the elegy on CuChulainn's death by his wife Emer (cf. p. 51)—which may be compared with the laments of the princesses over Hector at the close of the *Iliad* and with the speech of Guðrún in *Guðrúnarkviða I* (cf. p. 27). Such pieces resemble—and are of course modelled upon—poems (elegies) of Type D; and they may conveniently be described as BD.

Apart from the poetry contained in the sagas there are a number of poems which are found without context in the MSS.—though they sometimes have two or three explanatory sentences in prose prefixed to

[1] Transl. by Stokes, *Rev. Celt.* XXIV. 45 ff.

them. Some of them are of antiquarian character and will be noticed in Ch. x. Others are elegies, similar to those mentioned above; but it is not always easy to distinguish between speech poems in character—of the BD variety—and what may be genuine elegies. We need not hesitate to assign to BD the dialogue elegy upon Niall Noigiallach, in which the speakers are the poet Torna and his son Tuirn.[1] The subject was a very famous king, and one of the speakers was a very famous poet. But the same explanation cannot be given for the elegy of Crede, daughter of Guaire, upon Dinertach.[2] This poem is attributed to the tenth century; but the battle of Carn Conaill, in which Guaire, king of Connaught, was defeated, and in which Dinertach seems to have been killed, took place in 649. Yet neither Crede nor Dinertach appears to be known apart from the poem. How then are we to account for such a composition? Is the poem really three centuries older than the linguistic evidence seems to indicate? Or is it a work of pure fiction? Or, again, was it originally a speech in character contained in a saga? There is a saga on the battle of Carn Conaill; but it is more religious than heroic in character; and neither Crede nor Dinertach is mentioned in it.

It should be observed that besides the complete poems, such as those just noticed, there are in existence also a large number of fragments, both of elegies and of panegyrics upon living princes.[3] Many of them are preserved in metrical tracts, where they are quoted e.g. as illustrations of certain metres, and there is no context. But many others are found in annals, in connection with notices of the princes' deaths. Some of the persons celebrated in them belong to the sixth and seventh centuries. It is generally agreed that from the eighth or ninth century onwards these pieces are for the most part what they profess to be—i.e. contemporary works of Type D. But linguistic and metrical considerations are said to preclude the possibility of this being the case with pieces which celebrate persons of earlier times. This is, it will be seen, practically the same difficulty which we encountered in regard to certain Welsh and Anglo-Saxon poems.

The fragments of elegies preserved in annals are sometimes attributed to a poet whose name is known, sometimes to the dead prince's widow—

1 Ed. and transl. by K. Meyer, *Gaelic Journal*, x. 578 ff.; transl. also in *Ancient Irish Poetry*, p. 69 ff.

2 Ed. and transl. by K. Meyer, *Ériu*, II. 15 ff.; transl. also in *Ancient Irish Poetry*, p. 63 f.

3 See K. Meyer, *Bruchstücke der älteren Lyrik Irlands* (Abh. d. preuss. Akad. 1919, No. 7), pp. 5 ff., 37 ff.

a fact which suggests that they were composed, like Egill's *Sonatorrek*, for the funeral celebrations. We may quote from a fragment attributed to a poet (*éces*) named Ninnine, celebrating the death of a prince called Coning—a son of Aedan mac Gabrain, king of Argyll—who according to the annals was drowned in 621 or 622[1]: "The transparent waves of the sea and the sand have covered them; they have hurled themselves over Coning in his frail little wicker coracle". It seems to us unlikely that such an elegy should be composed a century or more after the event, in memory of a comparatively obscure prince. On the other hand, if they are genuine these elegies are probably the earliest Irish compositions which are capable of precise dating. At all events there can be no doubt that this type of poetry was cultivated during the Heroic Age. Examples survive from the ninth, and probably from the eighth, centuries; and its existence is implied also by the occurrence of BD poems, such as Emer's lament (cf. p. 51), in early texts of the sagas.

We know of no examples of Type E (heroic); but this again must not be taken as implying that such poetry was not then cultivated. Examples from the following centuries will be cited in Ch. XI.

Now if we compare the Irish heroic records in general with the Greek, Teutonic and Welsh, as analysed on pp. 20 ff. and 42 ff., we shall have to take into account the fact that here saga, not poetry, forms what we may call the backbone of the material. It will be convenient to make a brief survey of the records according to the scheme proposed on p. 20 ff.

(1) In contrast with Greek and Teutonic, narrative is almost always in the form of saga. Heroic narrative poetry (Type A) is very rare in early times.

(2) As in Greek and Teutonic, the records, both saga and poetry, are usually—practically always—concerned with adventure or, in the case of poems of Type B, with emotional situations arising therefrom, as in Norse.

[1] *Ann. Ult.* 621; *Chron. Scot.* 622; etc. For *Ann. Tig.* see *Rev. Celt.* XVII. 175. Cf. also K. Meyer, *op. cit.* p. 39. We cannot see how there can be any doubt as to the identity of this Coning, in spite of what is said by Meyer, *l.c.*, and by Pokorny, *Historical Reader of Old Irish*, p. 29 f. The death of one of his sons, named Rigullan, is mentioned shortly afterwards in *Ann. Tig.* (*Rev. celt.* XVII. 180); cf. *Ann. Ult.* 628. Another son, named Ferchar, was king of Argyll about the same time, according to the *Synchronisms* published by Skene, *Chronicles of the Picts and Scots*, p. 19. The obscure reference to *Bile Torten* (perhaps here a kenning for 'prince') can hardly count against the evidence of the historical records.

(3) As in Greek and Teutonic, the object for which most of the records, both saga and poetry, were composed was obviously to provide entertainment. There is, however, a good deal both of poetry and prose which is of a didactic or informative character (Type C). Indeed even the sagas, as we have them, often contain a certain amount of informative matter, e.g. explanations of the origin of place-names. But these antiquarian elements cannot be said to constitute the primary interest of the sagas any more than the didactic elements in such poems as *Beowulf* constitute the primary interest in them. The question whether these elements are intrusive, in both cases, will require to be noticed later. There are, however, sagas—relating in part to the Heroic Age—in which the antiquarian interest is primary; but these will be considered in Ch. x.

(4) The sagas and poems discussed above all relate to the Heroic Age; but this period appears to be longer, and its lower limit to be less clearly marked, than elsewhere.

(5) Both sagas and poems are anonymous. As exceptions we may note a few poems of Type D (elegies), belonging to the seventh century, if they are really what they profess to be (cf. p. 55 f.); and also a number of antiquarian poems, most of which date from later times.

(6) In contrast with the uniform line of Greek and Teutonic, Irish heroic poetry, like Welsh, shows a considerable variety of metres. These metres, as we have seen, fall into two quite distinct classes. One has rhyme (assonance) and a fixed number of syllables in each line; sometimes also it shows alliteration, like certain Welsh poems. The other class, known as 'rhetorics', has neither rhyme nor a fixed number of syllables, but usually has alliteration. This is without doubt the older type; but whether it is of native origin or not is a question upon which opinion is divided. Some scholars[1] derive it from rhythmical Latin prose—an explanation which is naturally suggested by the Irish name—*retoric*, from Lat. *rhetorica* (*ars*). The later type is derived, like some of the Welsh metres, from Latin religious poetry. There are a few

[1] Cf. K. Meyer, *Learning in Ireland in the Fifth Century*, p. 16. On the other hand Thurneysen, *Ir. Heldensage*, p. 55, points out that the Irish rhetorics differ from this style of Latin in the construction of the sentences, and also that they are very often used in prophecies. He suggests that this was their primary origin, though he seems to admit Latin influence (*ib.* p. 54). We would call attention in particular to their use in spells—in which Latin influence is improbable. We think the Latin derivation requires to be proved. The use of the word *retoric* may mean no more than that Latin scholars and scribes were struck by a—perhaps merely superficial—resemblance to Latin rhetorical prose.

poems which show a transitional form—with rhyme and alliteration, but without a fixed number of syllables—suggesting that the influence of the Latin hymns made itself felt gradually.

(7) In contrast with Greek and English, the later type of poetry is entirely stanzaic. This applies to the rare poems of Type A, as well as to those of the other types. The four-line stanza, as in Norse, is by far the most common, though the three-line form, so frequent in Welsh, is not very rare. As in Norse and Welsh, the sentence usually ends at the end of a stanza, and there is a tendency towards a break at the end of the line. On the other hand the rhetorics are not stanzaic—or at least they cannot be divided into stanzas of any regular form. They are distinguishable from prose only by their diction and to a certain extent by repetition and alliteration. There are, however, a few pieces which show transitional forms—four-line stanzas without fixed number of syllables in the line, and sometimes entirely without rhyme.

The transitional forms noted above, both those with and those without rhyme, seem to occur only in antiquarian and religious poetry—not in heroic sagas. The poetry found in the sagas consists partly of rhetorics and partly of the later rhyming type; but the latter is by far the more common. There appears to be no difference in usage. Rhetorics are used e.g. for the dialogue between Cet and Conall Cernach in the story of Mac Datho's Pig (cf. p. 49), and for Emer's elegy in the story of CuChulainn's death (cf. p. 51); and the later metres are used in similar cases. The difference indeed seems to be merely chronological. Rhetorics occur only in the older sagas, and they are probably to be regarded as survivals of an earlier usage. The language is generally very difficult and archaic. How old the type is may be gathered from the fact that the transitional form with rhyme is attributed to the seventh, and that without rhyme to the sixth, centuries.

(8) Speeches are extremely numerous in the sagas and form a considerable proportion of the matter. The vast majority of them are in prose; and in general they are shorter than the speeches in the Greek and Anglo-Saxon epics. But speeches in verse, i.e. poems of Type B, are by no means rare. Usually they are chosen for more or less solemn pronouncements, such as prophecies, visions, elegies and reflections; but we meet with them also not unfrequently in dialogues, e.g. between combatants on the field of battle.

(9) Fullness of description is a well-marked feature of Irish heroic saga. It is not quite the same as in Greek and Anglo-Saxon heroic poetry. Combats are often described in great detail, just as there; but

the ordinary, familiar scenes of life are not depicted so fully. On the other hand, we frequently meet with long and minute descriptions not only of the armour of heroes, as in Greek and Anglo-Saxon, but also of their clothes and their personal appearance, though as a rule these descriptions conform to a few familiar and strictly conventional types. The same remarks apply to the descriptions of heroines and other women.

(10) Static epithets are not frequent or striking in either poetry or saga. Repetitions or refrains occur in the poems, though not to the same extent as in Welsh poetry. In sagas the most striking feature of this kind is the frequent recurrence of the conventional descriptions—to which we have just alluded—of the appearance and dress of heroes and heroines. For an extreme example we may refer to the description of Etain at the opening of the *Destruction of Da Derga's Hall.*[1]

(11) The length of time covered by the action varies greatly from saga to saga. The period covered by the *Táin Bó Cuailnge* runs to several months, of which three are occupied by CuChulainn's activities before the arrival of the Ulster army. The *Story of Mac Datho's Pig* consists of two scenes, separated by an interval which does not seem to be long. The *Exile of the Sons of Uisliu* extends over the whole of Derdriu's life. It falls practically into four scenes, of which the first relates her birth and the last her death. The story of the *Destruction of Dinn Rig* covers three generations. In the *Battle of Allen* the action is practically limited to two days.

(12) The sagas always represent the events related in them as having happened in the past; but they rarely, if ever, give any indication of the length of time which has elapsed since they took place. It is to be remembered, however, that most of the heroes belonged to families whose genealogies were widely known.

It will be convenient now to make a brief comparative survey of the various heroic records. The Irish records are by far the most extensive, owing to the very large amount of saga (Type A) which has been preserved and which serves as a backbone for this Heroic Age as a whole. For the British Heroic Age unfortunately no such backbone exists. Type A here is practically unrepresented, whether in poetry or saga, and for our knowledge of this Heroic Age we are dependent upon a limited number of poems of Types B, D and E, and a considerable amount of antiquarian matter (Type C), both verse and prose. The

[1] *Rev. Celt.* XXII. 13 ff.

Greek Heroic Age is represented by two narrative poems, which are very full, the Teutonic Heroic Age by a larger number, which are not so full, as well as by a few Norse poems of Type B; but these supply us with only a very limited number of stories. Apart from them we are practically dependent upon antiquarian records, which in Greece were extremely numerous and seem to have been drawn largely from early poems of Type C.

It will be seen that the distribution of the types is very uneven. Type A (narrative poetry) is represented in Greek and Teutonic, and to a very small extent, and not very early, in Irish. Type A (saga) is represented in Irish and, in a late and debased form, in Norse; the Welsh sagas belong rather to Type C (CA). Type B (the speech-poem in character) is represented in Norse, Welsh and Irish; in the last it is incorporated in the sagas. Type C (the didactic and informative type) is found everywhere, in one form or another. Type D (the elegy and panegyric) is found in Welsh and perhaps in Irish. Type E (personal or occasional poetry) certainly existed in Teutonic, and appears to be preserved in English and Welsh. Some scholars, however, refuse to allow that any of the surviving poems of Types D and E are genuine.

Next we may take the list of characteristics discussed on pp. 20 ff., 29 ff., 42 ff., and 56 ff., above. This list was originally drawn up for Greek and English narrative poetry. We must now see how it applies to the heroic records in general.

(1) The distribution of narrative poetry and saga of Type A has just been noted. There seems to be some narrative poetry or saga of Type C almost everywhere; but this may be treated more conveniently in Ch. x.

(2) Adventure seems to be involved everywhere, though in Type C it tends to fall into the background.

(3) Type A, both poetry and saga, and Type B seem to be intended for entertainment everywhere. Type C is didactic or at least informative. Type D is intended for celebration. Type E comes under none of these heads, and we may perhaps defer consideration of its purpose until we meet with further examples.

(4) All records relate to the Heroic Age.

(5) Type A, poetry and saga, and Type B seem always to be anonymous. In Types C and D there is variation; but the absence of the author's name in poems of Type D may perhaps be merely accidental. Poems of Type E are of course only recognisable as such if the author is known.

(6), (7) In regard to metre the poetry of the two Celtic languages shows a striking contrast to early Teutonic and the earliest Greek poetry. In the former we find multiformity, stanza or couplet, and rhyme; in the latter uniformity and a tendency to an unbroken flow of speech. These characteristics are not in either case confined to heroic poetry. But it is to be noted (i) that Greek uniformity disappears in the seventh century—the couplet and the stanza make their appearance; (ii) that neither stanza (or couplet) nor rhyme occurs in the earliest Irish poetry, whatever its origin; (iii) that Norse poetry seems to be in course of transition from the Teutonic to the Celtic type; even heroic poetry is stanzaic and not uniform, while post-heroic poetry of Types D and E shows both rhyme and much variety in other respects. Lastly, it is to be remembered that rhyme in both Welsh and Irish seems to be derived from Latin. Hence the features noted above as common to Welsh and Irish poetry cannot be founded upon any peculiarly Celtic characteristics.

A question of greater importance is whether the resemblance between Greek and Teutonic may be due to the existence in both of heroic narrative poetry. The metres in question are not confined to such poetry; but it is highly probable that this was in early times the dominating influence in the poetry of both peoples. Moreover it may be noted (i) that the two Anglo-Saxon heroic poems which are not narrative show end-stops (cf. p. 25), and (ii) that traces of a non-uniform-line metre occur in Anglo-Saxon gnomic poetry.

(8) Speeches are a constant feature of poetry and saga of Type A, and they usually occupy a large proportion of the matter. This is true also of the Welsh (CA) sagas. In the other types the occurrence of speeches is exceptional.

(9) Fullness of description and leisurely narrative are characteristic of the Greek and English poems of Type A; but in the corresponding Norse poems they appear rarely. In a slightly different form they also characterise Irish saga. This specialises in descriptions of personal appearance and clothes—a feature which is shared by the *Dream of Rhonabwy*. Fullness of description characterises also many Norse, Welsh and Irish poems of Types B, D and E; but this is of quite a different character—emotional or (in certain Welsh D poems) laudatory.

(10) Static epithets are a conspicuous feature of Greek and English heroic poetry, and they occur also, though less frequently, in Norse heroic poetry, where they may have a common origin with the English.

Repetitions are of frequent occurrence in the heroic poetry of all these languages. In Greek, English and Norse they consist largely of static formulae. But in Welsh poetry—and to some extent also in Irish, where they seem to be less frequent—they are of a more rhetorical character—refrains rather than mere repetitions. These differences are doubtless due in part to the fact that the Greek, English and Norse poems belong mainly to Type A, whereas most of the Welsh poems belong to Type D. It may be observed that the English poem *Deor*, which has a refrain (cf. p. 25), does not belong to Type A.

(11) Consideration of the length of time covered by the action applies practically only to poetry and saga of Type A. The action of the Greek and English poems extends over only a few weeks, or less, apart from the long interval between the two parts of *Beowulf*. The Norse poems tend to fall into two scenes, separated from each other usually by no great interval. Irish sagas vary greatly—from a few days to many years, and even generations.

(12) Poems and sagas of Type A as a rule merely speak of the action as past. Norse poems, however, frequently emphasise the great length of time which has elapsed since the events took place; and something similar is implied in the *Dream of Rhonabwy*. Poems of Types E and D profess to be contemporary—with a possible reservation in the case of certain elegies.

It need hardly be pointed out that the analysis of the heroic records into types (A, B, C, D, E), adopted above, is merely for convenience; the distinctions must not be pressed too rigidly. Thus, one could cut out from the *Iliad* a passage which in itself would be similar in all respects to *Guðrúnarkviða I*. Indeed the attraction of Type A, at least to a modern reader, depends largely upon the extent to which it approximates to Type B. Again, it may seem arbitrary to refer *Culhwch and Olwen* to Type C, when Irish sagas which contain much informative matter are given under Type A. We suspect, however, that in the latter this element is largely secondary. We have had more hesitation in refusing to admit *Tal.* xxxv as a Welsh example of Type A; for it is practically a narrative poem and contains three speeches. This is indeed clearly a case of transition from D to A. Lastly, it must be borne in mind that if the poems referred to Types D and E are not admitted to be genuine, they must all be assigned to Type B.

Our analysis raises several questions, which will need consideration in later chapters:

(1) The question alluded to in the last sentence—Are the poems which we have referred to Types D and E really what they profess to be or not?

(2) No such question will arise with reference to Types A, B and C. But here we are faced with other questions: How, when, and by whom were these poems and sagas produced?

(3) Is the use of poetry and prose in heroic records governed by any general principles? We have spoken of prose (saga) only in relation to Types A and C—not because we believe its use to be impossible in the other types, but because we have not actually met with it in them. Again, it is often suggested that the Irish form of heroic narrative—saga interspersed with speech poems (Type B)—represents an earlier stage than the narrative poetry of Greek and Teutonic. Is there any reason for believing this to be true?

(4) What is it which constitutes a heroic story? This is not the same question as the one raised at the end of Ch. II—What is it which constitutes a Heroic Age? For we shall see in Ch. VI that there can be non-heroic stories relating to a Heroic Age. It is hoped that the discussion in the next three chapters will enable an answer to be given to this question.

NOTE. An admirable account of early Norse metres (cf. p. 29 f.) and of the Edda poems generally will be found in *Edda and Saga* (Home University Library) by B. S. Phillpotts (the late Dame B. S. Newall), which has been published since this book went to Press.

CHAPTER IV

THE HEROIC MILIEU

IN this chapter we propose to discuss certain features which appear to be characteristic of the life portrayed in the heroic stories. They may conveniently be classified under the following headings: (1) The social standing of the personnel—the characters who figure in heroic poetry and saga; (2) the scenes of the stories; (3) the accessories of heroic life; (4) the social standards and conventions observed in heroic poetry and saga.

(1) The personnel of the *Iliad* consists almost wholly of princes and their military followers. The latter themselves sometimes belong to princely families, as in the case of Achilles' followers, Patroclos and Phoinix. The few remaining persons include several priests, such as Chryses, Dares and Dolopion, and seers, such as Calchas and Helenos. But some of these are of princely birth; Helenos is a son of Priam. There are also a few heralds, like Talthybios, Eurybates, Idaios and Dolon. These appear to be personal servants of princes, though Dolon declares that he is wealthy. An incidental reference to a shield-maker, Tychios, occurs in VII. 220. Various other references of a general character to persons engaged both in handicrafts and in agriculture are to be found, especially in similes; but these persons are never named. Lastly, there is the abusive orator Thersites, a character who will require discussion in Ch. VIII.

In the *Odyssey* the range is somewhat wider. Penelope's suitors are said to be of princely rank—a fact which seems to indicate that the princely class was very numerous. Mention is made of several other inhabitants of Ithaca, who may belong to the same class. There are also a number of Phaeacians, mostly athletes, whose rank is not stated; their names show them to be fictitious characters created for the occasion. Besides these we find a priest, Maron, minstrels like Phemios and Demodocos, and heralds, such as Medon. The seers mentioned seem to be princes. There are occasional references to handicraftsmen (III. 425, XIX. 57). Two passages deal with Phoenician merchants (unnamed), who are presented in a very unfavourable light; and another passage (VIII. 161 ff.) contains a derogatory reference to merchants in general. Certain slaves belonging to Odysseus' family—Eumaios,

Philoitios, Melanthios, Dolios, Eurycleia and Melantho—figure prominently, especially in the latter part of the poem; and even a beggar, whom the suitors call Iros, is introduced.

Taking the evidence of the two poems as a whole, it may be said that the interest is concentrated exclusively upon persons of princely rank and their households. Even the servants come in for a share of notice. But the merchant, the farmer, and the artisan are practically ignored.

In *Beowulf* all persons mentioned by name, whether in the main action or in episodes, appear to be members either of royal families or of the courts or military retinues of princes. To the former class belong the hero himself and presumably his relative Wiglaf, as well as the other princes of the Geatas, the Danes and the Swedes. The other persons mentioned by name are as follows: Wulfgar, King Hrothgar's herald—described as *Wendla leod*, which probably means that he is an aristocrat; Hunferth, the same king's 'spokesman' (*þyle*),[1] who lends Beowulf his sword; Aeschere—with his brother Yrmenlaf—Hrothgar's old councillor and former comrade in arms; Hondscio, a member of Beowulf's retinue; Eofor and Wulf, two brothers who slay the Swedish king Ongentheow—the former subsequently marries King Hygelac's daughter. Probably all the characters mentioned in the episodes belong to the same classes. In addition to these there are speeches by five persons, whose names are not given: the officer who guards the Danish coast, Hrothgar's minstrel, Wiglaf's messenger, the man who (in a past age) buried the treasure, and the old warrior—known in Scandinavian tradition as Starkaðr—who incites Ingeld to revenge. There is practically no reference in the poem to any person of a rank inferior to those enumerated above, with the exception of the unfortunate man who first discovered the dragon's hoard. He is described probably[2] as the 'slave of someone or other of the sons of heroes' (2223 f.). Later (2406 ff.), when he has to act as guide, his plight is referred to with scorn rather than pity.

What has been said of Beowulf appears to be true also of the other English heroic poems. All the characters mentioned by name seem to be either princes or members of princes' retinues. Among the latter may be included the court minstrels Deor and Widsith. There are no references to persons of humbler rank.

The same remarks apply to the Norse heroic poems. In these the

[1] The meaning of this term will be discussed in Ch. XIX.

[2] The text is injured at this point.

personnel is much less numerous; and nearly all the characters belong to princely families. The few exceptions appear to be military followers or servants. Such is the case with Knéfröðr or Vingi, the messenger of Atli, and presumably with the cowardly Hjalli of the *Atlakviða*, who in the *Atlamál* is called a scullion. Among liegemen of more distinguished rank we may mention Ormarr—the Wyrmhere of *Widsith*—and the aged Gizurr in the *Battle of the Goths and Huns*.

It is clear also that most of the leading characters of the British Heroic Age were of princely rank. Maelgwn and his descendant Cadwallon were kings of Gwynedd. Cynan Garwyn was king of Powys, and Rhydderch Hael king of Dumbarton. Urien and Gwallawg reigned over districts which cannot be identified with certainty. In the *Gododdin* poems Mynyddawg Mwynfawr, leader of the ill-fated expedition, was evidently a king, though his genealogy has not been preserved. Gwenddoleu was probably a king, like his cousin Dunawd. Arthur and Gereint appear as kings in later records. The poet Llywarch Hen is a cousin of Urien.

Most of the other persons mentioned in the poems appear to be military followers of princes, similar to those who figure in the English poems. Such no doubt are the heroes celebrated in the *Gododdin* poems, in so far as they are not princes themselves, like Cynon, son of Clydno Eidyn, who belongs to the same family as Gwenddoleu and Dunawd. The same may be said of Cai, Bedwyr, and the other warriors associated with Arthur. Indeed it is not clear that persons of any other class are mentioned, except perhaps the poets themselves. Myrddin is made to say that he had been an honoured military follower of Gwenddoleu. Taliesin, whatever may have been his origin, is clearly a court poet—at first in the service of Elphin.

The Irish evidence is in general similar to the rest. The number of persons who figure in the sagas is of course very much greater, but with comparatively few exceptions they belong either to princely families or to the military retinues of princes. The latter class is most fully represented in sagas of the Ulster cycle, where the personnel is more numerous than elsewhere. But the two classes are not easily distinguished. CuChulainn and Conall Cernach are sons of King Conchobor's sisters, and the latter belongs on his father's side also to the Clann Rudraige, the royal house of Ulster—as do many more of Conchobor's warriors. Stories relating to later times, which are less detailed, usually deal with high-kings and kings of provinces, but many minor chiefs are often mentioned.

Of persons not belonging to these classes the most distinguished are the druids, who are hardly inferior to kings. Cathbad, the Ulster druid, is King Conchobor's father in the older records. Some stories represent him as a warrior in earlier life. *Filid*, a class which will require notice in Ch. XIX, were also highly honoured. Sometimes they are attached to princes, as Ferchertne to CuRoi. Amorgein, the father of Conall Cernach, is a warrior as well as a *fili*. We hear also of smiths who were distinguished and wealthy. Amorgein's father, Ecet Salach, is a smith. Another smith, Caulann, is able to entertain King Conchobor and part of his retinue; he cannot afford to provide for the whole, as he is not a landowner. But Da Choca has a hall (*bruiden*) at cross-roads, at which everyone is entitled to receive hospitality. Other halls of the same kind are owned by Forgoll, the father of Emer, Da Derga, Mac Datho, and Blai. Of these Mac Datho is a king of Leinster; but Blai is merely a wealthy landowner, while the rank of the others is apparently not stated.

Among persons who probably belong to a somewhat humbler station mention may be made of Fedlimid, Conchobor's saga-teller. He is evidently in the king's service; but DonnBo and perhaps also Ua Maiglinni, the saga-tellers who figure in the *Battle of Allen*—a story of much later times—appear to be independent persons. Lastly, a curious figure who enters into many stories is Leborcham, a slave-woman belonging to Conchobor. She is deformed,[1] but extremely swift of foot and intelligent, and is employed by the king as his messenger.

There are sagas and poems (non-heroic) relating to *filid*, which will be noticed later. But in the heroic stories themselves the Irish evidence presents little or nothing that is exceptional. Da Choca's hall is the scene of a sanguinary fight; but he himself plays practically no part in the story, and the other owners of similar halls are hardly more prominent. In Ireland, as elsewhere, the interest of heroic stories is centred in members of princely families. Military followers and even slaves of the princes may come in for a share of attention. Priests and minstrels may be noticed. But the remainder of the population is virtually ignored.

(2) In the *Iliad* the scene is laid sometimes in or among the tents of the Achaean leaders, sometimes on the field of battle, less frequently in the palaces of Troy. In the *Odyssey* it is much more varied. Much of

[1] Her knees are turned backwards. This kind of deformity is found in other cases, and seems to be generally associated with fleetness of foot.

the action takes place at Odysseus' home; but at other times the scene is laid at various places in the island of Ithaca, in the land of the Phaeacians, at the courts of Nestor and Menelaos, and elsewhere. One scene is in the swineherd's hut.[1]

As heroic stories are primarily concerned with princes, the court scenes are naturally what may be called the normal scenes, the others are usually the scenes of adventures. It may be observed that the poets seem to take a certain pleasure in dwelling on the formalities of court life—the reception of visitors, banquets, and even the movements of royal persons about their palaces. For an illustration of the first we may refer to *Od.* IV. 20 ff., where Telemachos and Peisistratos arrive at the palace of Menelaos. In Odysseus' own home such formalities are not observed; but on Mentes' arrival (I. 118 ff.) Telemachos recognises and apologises for the lack of them. As examples of the last we may cite I. 328 ff., where Penelope comes to hear the minstrel, and IV. 121 ff., where Helen's movements are described. Even in the camp life of the *Iliad* we find a good deal of formality, as, e.g., in IX. 192 ff., where Odysseus and Aias are received by Achilles.

In the Teutonic poems also the scenes may be divided into court scenes and scenes of adventure, though adventures sometimes take place also in the former. In the first part of *Beowulf* the scene is laid partly in the Danish king's palace and partly at Grendel's lair. The last scene is in Hygelac's palace, on Beowulf's return home. In the second part the action takes place in the neighbourhood of the dragon's barrow. In the court scenes much attention is paid to formalities, especially in the reception of visitors. The account of Beowulf's reception at the Danish court occupies eighty lines before the hero begins to declare his mission. It includes four speeches by the king's herald, one by the king himself and one by Beowulf, before the latter enters the king's presence. Note is made (358 f.) of the correct attitude taken by the herald in addressing the king. Again, the movements of the king and queen are rather carefully described, e.g. (920 ff.) their formal entry into the hall with their retinues on the morning after the fight with Grendel. So also when the queen or a princess passes round the hall with a tankard, as is done by Hrothgar's queen in 612 ff., 2016 ff., by his daughter in 2020 ff., and by Hygd, the wife of Hygelac, in 1980 ff.

In the Norse poems, where all prolixity is avoided, these lengthy

[1] It is noteworthy that the similes of the *Iliad* usually relate to scenes of humbler life. This is a point which will require notice later.

descriptions of formalities are naturally not to be found. If a court scene is described at any length some tragic situation or a debate on some question of importance is involved. Such scenes in point of fact occupy by far the greater part of the poems; but ceremonies and things which belong to the ordinary routine of court life are dismissed in a few words. Probably the nearest approach to the usage of *Beowulf* is in the *Battle of the Goths and Huns*, st. 3 ff., where Hlöðr arrives at the funeral feast of Heiðrekr.

In Welsh heroic poetry, which is mostly of Type D (cf. p. 42), the scene, if so it can be called, lies almost always either at the hero's court or on the battle-field. Very often it shifts from one to the other —or passages dealing with one contain references to the other. Of the panegyrics some are chiefly occupied with the hero's geniality and generosity in his hall, others with his achievements in battle. The *Gododdin* poems are primarily concerned with the latter, but contain many references to the former. Perhaps the most interesting poem for our present purpose is Llywarch Hen's elegy on Urien (*RBH.* XII), especially from st. 46 to the end. The poet here draws a contrast between the festive life of which Urien's hall has been the scene, and its condition in the future, when it will lie ruined and overgrown with brambles. Somewhat similar pictures are to be found in the elegy on Cynddylan (*RBH.* XVI).

In Irish heroic sagas of the Ulster cycle the variety of scene is as great as in the Homeric poems. In the *Táin Bó Cuailnge* it is usually laid either in the camp of Ailill and Medb or at the various places where CuChulainn encounters their warriors. In other sagas the action takes place at Conchobor's court or that of Ailill and Medb, or at CuChulainn's home—and many other places. Not unfrequently the scene is the house of some great man, to which the king and his retinue have come either by invitation or to seek hospitality. In stories dealing with later times the scene is most commonly either a king's court or a field of battle.

A special characteristic of the Irish sagas is the minute description of the appearance and dress of royal persons, both men and women. We may refer, for example, to the description of Etain at the well at the beginning of the *Destruction of Da Derga's Hall*, and of CuChulainn and other heroes in *Bricriu's Feast*, cap. 45 ff.; but examples are numerous. Such descriptions usually follow conventional lines; sometimes indeed different sagas have them in almost identical form. For instances of ceremonial receptions we may refer to the *Táin Bó Fraich*, cap. 2, and the next passage in *Bricriu's Feast* (cap. 54 f.)—but for these again there are many parallels. The sagas give the impression that the life of the Irish courts was full of ceremonial, perhaps of a somewhat barbaric kind. But what they most like to depict is not, as in the Greek and the English poems, the ordinary course of the ceremonial, but the occasions when it breaks down. A good example occurs in *Mac Datho's Pig*, cap. 6 ff. The custom was that the most distinguished warrior present should carve the pig; but a dispute arises, first as to who is entitled to this honour, and then as to the fairness of the distribution; and the banquet eventually becomes a brawl (cf. p. 49). In *Bricriu's Feast*, cap. 14 ff., a similar dispute arises. When the heroes have been pacified, their wives each claim the honour of entering the hall first. They race for the door; the race becomes a scramble, and the result again is a general brawl. In spite of the abundance of ceremonial, the picture which the records suggest is that of a very youthful and unsophisticated society, in which the attraction of a rough and tumble mêlée often proves too much for the dignity of even the most distinguished heroes.

(3) Warfare in one form or other seems to be an essential rather than an accessory of heroic life. On the special features of heroic warfare something will have to be said in the course of the next chapter.

It may be questioned whether feasting does not come under the same head; but we may mention it here. Banquets are frequently spoken of in the Homeric poems, especially at the reception of visitors. Indeed it has often been remarked that the amount of feasting recorded as taking place in the Achaean camp in the *Iliad* is astonishing. Banquets in kings' palaces are usually accompanied by minstrelsy, whether in Ithaca, among the Phaeacians, or at the palace of Menelaos (*Od.* IV. 17 f.). But minstrelsy is found at other hours also. It is evidently the intellectual occupation of the courts; and it is cultivated by princes, as well as by professionals. Achilles is singing heroic poetry to his lyre (*Il.* IX. 186 ff.), when Odysseus and Aias come to his tent.

The possessions which heroes seem to value most highly are their horses and armour. In the *Iliad* desperate adventures are undertaken for the sake of such booty. We may instance the raid made on the Thracian camp by Odysseus and Diomedes for the horses of Rhesos. Aineias' horses, which also are captured by Diomedes (*Il.* V. 323 ff.), are said to be of supernatural origin (*ib.* XX. 223 ff.)—descended from Boreas (the North Wind). Achilles' horses, Xanthos and Balios, are the offspring of Zephyros (the West Wind) and the Harpy Podarge, and are themselves immortal (*ib.* XVI. 148 ff.). Xanthos once speaks (*ib.* XIX. 404 ff.), and prophesies his master's death. In armour the articles most valued appear to be the shield and breastplate. Achilles' new shield, which was made for him by the god Hephaistos, is described at length in *Il.* XVIII. 478 ff. Agamemnon's breastplate, described in XI. 19 ff., is also an elaborate work of art.

This breastplate was a gift from Cinyres of Cyprus. Costly gifts like this from one prince to another, but especially to guests, are recorded on several occasions. When Telemachos bids farewell to Menelaos and Helen, they present him with a silver mixing-bowl, a cup and a costly robe (*Od.* XV. 101 ff.). Odysseus receives lavish presents from Alcinoos and his court. As prizes in the funeral games of Patroclos, Achilles gives to his friends a great variety of things, including slave-women, horses, silver and bronze vessels, and weapons.

In the Teutonic poems, both English and Norse, feasting is much in evidence. But it is not the meal itself—of which little or nothing is said—but the drinking which follows it. This time of drinking occupies the greater portion of the first part of *Beowulf*. It so dominates the indoor life of the courts that this is commonly described by terms for drinking. Whenever there is occasion to mention the relations of a king with the members of his court the reference usually takes the form of an allusion either to the mead, wine or ale, with which he regaled them or the gifts which he bestowed upon them. The drinking is commonly accompanied with minstrelsy. In *Beowulf* we find both professional minstrels and others; even King Hrothgar himself (2105 ff.) takes his turn in reciting to the harp.

The articles most valued by the hero are his weapons and armour. Both the sword and the helmet are of more account than in the Homeric poems, and they are sometimes carefully described. Swords have personal names, such as Naegling, Hrunting, Mimming. But the mail coat is the most valued of all. Beowulf (452 ff.) begs Hrothgar to send his mail coat back to Hygelac, if he is killed by Grendel. It was made by Weland, and has belonged to Hygelac's father. Waldhere trusts in the loyalty of his mail coat—which has belonged to his father—when he is assailed by faithless kinsmen.

Presentations are often mentioned; usually they take place at the feast, i.e. the drinking. As a reward for his fight with Grendel, Hrothgar presents Beowulf with a golden standard, a helmet, mail coat and sword, and eight horses, one of which was the king's war-horse, with all its harness complete. Similar presents are given to him after slaying Grendel's mother. The queen gives him a magnificent golden necklet, which he presents to Hygd, Hygelac's queen, on his return home. Beowulf at his death gives to Wiglaf the gold necklet, helmet and mail coat which he is wearing. Widsith is presented by Eormenric and other princes with gold armlets or bracelets as a reward for his minstrelsy. The presentation of such articles by a king to his military followers is a commonplace.

The Norse evidence is very similar to the English, though not quite so broadcast. We may quote the *Battle of the Goths and Huns*, st. 20, where Angantýr, before the beginning of the battle, says: "When we were drinking mead we were a great host, but now when we should be many our numbers are few". In the same poem, st. 2, it is stated that "Hlöðr was born in the land of the Huns...with cutlass and with sword, with ample coat of mail, with treasure-decked helmet, with keen blade, and with well-trained steed". The *Hervarar Saga*, in which this poem is preserved, adds in explanation of the passage that it refers to the weapons which were being forged at the time the man was born; also to any horses or other animals that were born about the same time.[1] Perhaps the most distinctive feature in Norse is the greater prominence given to horses. We may refer especially to *Guðrúnarkviða II*, 4 ff., where Sigurðr's horse, Grani, comes to make his death known to Guðrún. It does not speak; but it lowers its head to the ground at her feet. 'The horse knew that his owner was lifeless.' According to the *Völsunga Saga*, cap. 13, Grani had been given to Sigurðr when he was a child by Othin; it was sprung from Othin's horse Sleipnir.

The Welsh evidence also is very similar to the English, though it is expressed in a different form. References to feasting occur everywhere, but it is almost always the mead or wine, not the food, which is mentioned. The picture constantly brought before us in the poems is that of a festive company—the hearth, the flowing mead and the minstrel. In the *Gododdin* the mead is over and over again said to have been the cause of the disaster. Mynyddawg had treated his company so generously that they embarked on a desperate enterprise while they were not in complete possession of their senses. Parallels may be found both in *Beowulf* (480 ff.) and in the *Iliad* (xx. 83 ff.).

References to warriors' arms—especially the spear, sword and shield—are very frequent; but no details are given, though it is clear

[1] Cf. Kershaw, *Anglo-Saxon and Norse Poems*, pp. 148 f., 201; *Stories and Ballads of the Far Past*, p. 128.

from other sources[1] that Welsh princes valued their weapons as highly as did the English. Little is said about the giving of arms or treasure, except to minstrels; but the custom is probably implied by the frequent references to the gold necklets worn by the heroes. The generosity of Owein in giving horses is recorded in the elegy on his death (*Tal.* XLIV. 10); and the horses of heroes are often mentioned in other connections. Lists of famous horses are given in *Tal.* XXV and in the Triads in *BBC.* VIII. Other *Triads* attribute marvellous feats to the horses of certain heroes.

In Irish heroic sagas we find feasting everywhere. It has already been mentioned that in several sagas the scene is laid in the house of some wealthy man where Conchobor and his court are feasting. There are references to the food as well as the drink; pork appears to be the food most valued, as may be seen from the story of *Mac Datho's Pig*. But the drinking is the main thing; enormous quantities are said to be provided. The extreme case is perhaps the story called *Mesca Ulad*, or the 'Intoxication of the Ulstermen'. CuChulainn and another chief named Fintan have invited Conchobor and his court to feasts on the same night. Neither of them will give way to the other, and so it is settled that they shall go first to Fintan's until midnight, and then move on to CuChulainn's. But by midnight Fintan has treated them so well that they completely lose their way, and arrive in front of CuRoi's fortress before they know where they are. As regards normal times, it is stated in the story of CuChulainn's childhood in the *Táin Bó Cuailnge*[2] that Conchobor spends one-third of each day in eating and drinking until he and all his musicians and entertainers fall asleep. In addition to saga-telling and minstrelsy, the favourite indoor amusement of the heroes is a game called *fidchell*—apparently something like chess—which is very frequently mentioned.

Weapons are often referred to, especially the sword, spear and shield. The most famous are Fergus' sword Caladcolc and an instrument of obscure character, called *Gaebulga*—perhaps a forked spear—belonging to CuChulainn. In his boyhood CuChulainn obtains weapons and a chariot from Conchobor. But presents to grown-up

[1] We may refer to the *Life of St Cadoc*, cap. 59 (transl. by Rees, *Lives of the Cambro-British Saints*, p. 387 f.), where a certain Guengarth, a foster-son of King Morcant, presents to the Saint's church a sword called Hipiclaur of the value of seventy cows, together with a donation of land. The whole passage is very interesting for the light it throws on the life of Welsh princes about the close of the seventh century.

[2] Windisch, 872 f.; Dunn, p. 46.

heroes seem more usually to be in the form of precious vessels. Horses play a great part in the stories. When Conall Cernach fights with Lugaid, his horse comes to his rescue and disables his opponent. CuChulainn's horses appear to be of supernatural origin. In the older version of the *Conception of CuChulainn* they are foaled in the phantom house during the night when the child is born, which is reborn as CuChulainn (cf. p. 216). When he is grown up they always draw his chariot. But in *Bricriu's Feast*, cap. 31, they come from two different lochs and have just been caught. At his death they flee to their lochs; but one of them returns and defends his body, and afterwards makes its way home to his wife.[1] It lays its head on Emer's lap, to let her know what has happened—a rather striking parallel to the incident in *Guðrúnarkviða II*, 4, noted above (p. 72).

(4) Express statements of social standards are of rare occurrence in heroic poetry and saga, except in *Beowulf*, where they are quite frequent. We will therefore begin with the English evidence.

Briefly summarised the cardinal virtues of a hero are courage, loyalty and generosity. Courage seems to be bound up with physical strength; it is never found without the latter. Loyalty is purely personal; the references are usually to the relations of a prince with his personal followers. It involves the duty of vengeance, as well as protection—'it is better to avenge a friend than to give way to grief'. Generosity likewise is usually referred to in connection with a prince's treatment of his followers. Sometimes, however, as in *Widsith*, there is special reference to the treatment of minstrels. In such cases the expression 'winning praise' has come to be equivalent to 'showing generosity to minstrels'. The vices which receive censure are the antitheses of the virtues mentioned above—cowardice, disloyalty and meanness—together with avarice, arrogance, violence towards one's own household, and disregard of oaths. In *Beow.* 2864 ff. Wiglaf bitterly upbraids Beowulf's retinue for deserting him in the hour of danger. Heremod's undoing was due to his meanness and his violence towards his followers (1718 ff.).

In some passages we find reference to a different set of standards—of a definitely Christian character. As a rule these are easily distinguishable; but occasionally an attempt to present them seems to go astray. Thus a passage (1739 ff.) apparently inspired by some Christian homiletic discourse leads to nothing except a denunciation of meanness and arrogance. A more interesting question is raised by the fact that the

[1] *Book of Leinster*, fol. 123 *a*; cf. Thurneysen, *Ir. Heldensage*, p. 556.

hero's kindheartedness is emphasised, especially in the closing lines of the poem. It is held by many scholars that this must be due to Christian influence. But we are not at all sure that the poet is thinking of anything more than Beowulf's attitude towards his immediate followers. We think that in the first part of the poem Hrothgar and Beowulf are to be taken as more or less ideal pictures of the old king and the young prince of heathen times.

Reference has already been made (p. 68) to the love of court ceremony and etiquette shown in the poem. It may be added that an air of good manners prevails throughout, so far as the human beings are concerned. The only exceptions occur in Hunferth's address to Beowulf, where the references to the hero's past exploits are offensive, and Beowulf's reply, which in places strikes us as very rude. But there is no obscenity even here; and the disputants are quickly reconciled. It is to be observed that, apart from details of slaughter, there is nothing throughout the poem which could offend the most fastidious taste.

Norse heroic poetry, unlike English, contains few express statements of heroic standards. Those which occur, e.g. in the *Atlakviða*, st. 19 and 32, relate to courage. It is clear that both courage and loyalty are expected from a hero. Generosity is rarely mentioned, again in contrast with English usage; but it is implied in certain static epithets applied to princes in general. There are no references to professional minstrels. Gunnarr and Högni are charged with disloyalty and the violation of oaths in the murder of Sigurðr; but the crime is brought about by Brynhildr, who has herself been treated with treachery. The death of Gunnarr and Högni—whose courage largely retrieves their reputation—is due to the avarice of Atli, which is followed by his own ruin. It is the avarice and arrogance of Hlöðr which leads to the tragedy of the *Battle of the Goths and Huns*.

The standard of decorum is not the same as in English heroic poetry. Atli would hardly have been allowed to eat his children in the latter; and we doubt if the shrieking coward Hjalli could have made his appearance. But the standard is much higher than in poems relating to the gods. The heroes are never made ridiculous; and obscenity is found only in abusive dialogues in the three *Helgi* poems.

Welsh heroic poetry also rarely gives express statements of social standards, though they occur frequently enough in gnomic poems. The inferential evidence points to much the same standards as in English. The courage and generosity of heroes are often celebrated, the latter especially in relation to minstrels. References to loyalty are rare;

but this is perhaps due to the fact that the poems are exclusively concerned with princes, and hardly mention their followers. We may refer to the *Triad* on the 'loyal retinues', quoted on p. 46, which indicates the recognition of standards very similar to those found in *Beowulf*. As an illustration of courage or warlike ardour we may cite an expression used of certain heroes in the *Gododdin* (*An.* I. 1, 5), that they were more ready to have their blood poured on the ground and to become the prey of wolves and ravens than to go to the marriage feast and the altar. A very similar description is given of Hervör, the sister of Angantýr, in the *Battle of the Goths and Huns*, st. 19.

On the other points noticed above the Welsh poems yield little more than negative evidence. Some dreadful and absurd things are said of Gwenddoleu and other heroes in the *Triads*, while *Culhwch and Olwen* revels in the grotesque; but the poems are serious, dignified and fastidious.

In the Homeric poems, again, standards are rarely stated. An expression of moral judgment is hardly to be seen in the remark (*Il.* XXIII. 176) that Achilles devised evil deeds in his heart—the slaying of Trojan prisoners at Patroclos' pyre—for the same phrase occurs elsewhere without moral significance; and it seems to mean no more than 'evil for the victims'. But it is not difficult to distinguish the characteristics which meet with approval and disapproval. Of the former by far the most important is courage—which is usually combined with physical strength; personal appearance also counts for a good deal. Loyalty and generosity are comparatively seldom noticed. The latter is expected from a prince when he is visited by another prince, and perhaps especially when the visitor is in distress. Indeed it is clear, especially from *Od.* VII. 159 ff., that princes were expected to show generosity to suppliants. But there is little definite evidence for generosity either to personal followers or to minstrels (cf. *Od.* VIII. 477 ff.). For loyalty perhaps the most definite evidence is that of Patroclos' speech to the Myrmidons (*Il.* XVI. 269 ff.). The paucity of such evidence may be due to the fact that the *Iliad* is almost wholly concerned with princes; their followers are not often mentioned. Loyalty is not a striking characteristic of Odysseus' followers in *Od.* IX–XII—a narrative which contrasts in many respects with the rest of the *Odyssey* and the *Iliad*. Among princes themselves it may perhaps be said to be wanting in the case of Achilles in the *Iliad*. But Achilles appears to be rather an ally than a subordinate of Agamemnon.

Of vices the most frequent appears to be arrogance (ὕβρις)—the tendency of a powerful man, trusting in *force majeure*, to trample upon the rights of others. Examples occur in Agamemnon's conduct, first to the priest and then to Achilles, at the beginning of the *Iliad*. In the *Odyssey* we have the picture of a large number of idle aristocrats quartering themselves on the household of an absent king and eating up his property. Perhaps the worst offence is the violation of oaths, as in the case of Pandaros. The treachery of Clytaimnestra and Aigisthos is also strongly condemned. On the other hand, the treatment of Helen is usually sympathetic, except in speeches which make her responsible for the troubles of the war.

The behaviour of the heroes often strikes the reader as childish or brutal. This is especially true in the case of Achilles, who seems indeed to be hardly civilised. Odysseus is not an attractive character in either poem. The old Nestor is perhaps the most pleasing of the heroes; but he is much inferior to Hrothgar. In the funeral games several heroes lose their temper in a rather foolish way, and Antilochos' behaviour is contemptible. But, except perhaps in the last case—where the hero seems to be only a boy—it is not clear that any disrespect is intended by the poets. The treatment is dignified throughout, and fastidious except in details of slaughter. These qualities, however, are wanting in certain scenes and stories relating to the gods, a fact which will require notice in Ch. IX.

In Irish saga also statements of heroic standards are rare. There are some 'Instructions to Princes'—collections of maxims addressed to princes who have just been appointed to the kingship—attributed to CuChulainn, Conall Cernach and other heroes. But it is at least doubtful whether these belong to an early phase of heroic saga—so we shall reserve them for discussion in Ch. XII.

It is clear enough from the narratives that courage was the quality most esteemed in a hero. Sometimes, especially in the case of Cu-Chulainn, it takes the form of frenzy. Loyalty and generosity are rarely referred to, though it would perhaps be unwise to infer from this that they were not valued. The most notable case of the former is that of Ferchertne—a *fili*, not a warrior—who avenges his master CuRoi by seizing his faithless wife Blathnat in the presence of the Ulster heroes and throwing himself with her over a precipice.[1] Elsewhere loyalty appears

[1] *Aided ConRoi* (ed. and transl. by Best, *Ériu*, II. 18 ff.), cap. 14 (*ib.* p. 30 f.). In the earlier version of the story, ed. and transl. by Thurneysen, *Zeitschr. f. celt. Philol.* IX. 190 ff., cap. 12 (*ib.* pp. 192 f., 196), there seems to be a double vengeance. Ferchertne stabs the lady; but Luach, CuRoi's charioteer, leaps into the chariot of Coirpre, son of Conchobor, and drives it over a cliff, whereby they both perish.

chiefly in the relations of one hero to another. We may refer to the instant vengeance taken by Conall Cernach for the death of CuChulainn.[1] Much value is attached to personal appearance. Even CuChulainn's beauty is emphasised, although he is small and dark.

Disapprobation is rarely expressed. The *fili* Athirne is evidently regarded with aversion on account of his pitiless avarice; yet he is supported by the men of his own province (Ulster). The conduct of Conchobor to the sons of Uisnech leads to hostilities with his own son Cormac and two other great nobles, who desert him with all their followers. Yet it seems that the desertion was due not to the atrociousness of the king's conduct—for which it would be difficult to find a parallel in any heroic story—but to the fact that they had been guarantors for the safety of the murdered heroes, and consequently their honour had been impaired by the treachery. In the *Destruction of Dinn Rig* no blame is attached to Labraid Loingsech for taking vengeance upon Cobthach, while he is entertaining him as his guest. Cormac mac Airt is frequently guilty of crafty and dishonourable conduct; but the stories relating to him are perhaps not properly to be regarded as heroic (cf. p. 52 f.).

The dignified and fastidious tone which prevails in Teutonic and Greek heroic poetry is not generally characteristic of Irish heroic saga. It is to be found in certain stories, especially the (third) *Courtship of Etain*; but more frequently the love of the grotesque and the fantastic and of rough horseplay throws all sense of dignity to the winds. For the modern reader this want of restraint is apt to spoil the interest of the Irish heroic stories; and it tends also to obscure the fact that the younger heroes, especially CuChulainn, compare very favourably with their Greek counterparts. On the other hand one must confess that the portraiture of the older people, especially the sovereigns, such as Conchobor, Ailill and Medb, is neither dignified nor attractive, though the grotesque elements here are wanting. Stories of a thoroughly savage and disgusting character are not unknown. We may cite in particular the *Fate of Lugaid and Derbforgaill*,[2] which is on a level with the crudest folk-tales.

In the course of this chapter we have seen that in all the cases we have considered heroic poetry and saga are concerned primarily with

[1] This passage (from the *Brislech mór Maige Muirtheimne*) is printed and transl. by Stokes, *Rev. Celt.* III. 183 ff.

[2] Ed. and transl. by Marstrander, *Ériu*, v. 201 ff.

persons of princely rank. Military followers and household servants of princes are sometimes introduced, and so also minstrels, seers and priests, but they never play more than a subordinate part. The peasant hero of folk-tales never appears, so far as we know. As might be expected from such a personnel, the scene is normally laid in a king's court, except when the action takes place on the battle-field or other place of adventure. The poets generally seem to take pleasure in describing the splendour and the etiquette of court life. The life of the heroes, their interests and pastimes, are quite in accordance with this milieu. We hear everywhere of feasting, which is often accompanied or followed by minstrelsy. As regards outdoor pastimes we may add that falconry and hunting the stag with hounds are referred to in English and Welsh heroic poetry, the former also in Norse.[1] The hero's chief pride is in his weapons or armour and in his horses. Heroic standards of conduct are seldom expressly stated, except in English. But courage, combined with physical strength, is recognised everywhere; loyalty and generosity are emphasised in English, the latter also in Welsh. Dignity and decorum prevail almost without exception in English and Welsh, both in the conduct of the heroes and in the poets' treatment of their subjects. In Greek it is rare, though not unknown, for heroes to lose their dignity, while in Norse horrors are occasionally introduced; but in both cases the treatment is dignified. It is only in Irish that we find any considerable body of evidence at variance with the norm. Here the behaviour of heroes is often crude and boorish and the treatment grotesque. There are, however, Irish heroic sagas to which this characterisation does not apply in any marked degree; and in general Irish heroes are represented as strongly resenting any infraction of their dignity.

In all cases, therefore, the heroic milieu is aristocratic. In later chapters we shall see that this is generally true of the Heroic Age in other countries. But exceptions do occur. In Vol. II it will be seen that heroic life and heroic poetry can exist in very poor communities, to which the term 'aristocratic' could not properly be applied.

[1] E.g. *Beow.* 1368 ff., 2263 f.; *An.* I. 87; *RBH.* XII. 27 f., 47; *Guðrúnarkviða II*, 19, 44.

CHAPTER V

INDIVIDUALISM IN THE HEROIC STORIES

THIS subject may conveniently be divided as follows: (1) Individualism and nationality; (2) Heroic warfare.

(1) It has often been remarked as strange that the Anglo-Saxon poems which have come down to us contain very few references to persons of English nationality and make no mention of Britain. There is no evidence for the existence of heroic poems dealing with English heroes in this country, though the invasion of Britain took place long before the close of the Heroic Age. The only heroic story which is certainly concerned with English heroes is that of Offa, who 'ruled over Angel' perhaps a century before the invasion of Britain; and even to this story we have only two references, amounting to ten lines in *Widsith* and about thirty in *Beowulf*. We know far more of the story from Danish sources. Perhaps the only other case—and this is uncertain—is that of the Hengest who figures in the story of Finn, if he is to be identified with the Hengest who conquered Kent.

In *Beowulf* the hero belongs to the Geatas (Gautar) of southern Sweden. The scene is laid partly in Denmark and partly in Sweden; and the poem is almost wholly concerned with persons belonging to those countries. In *Waldhere* the hero belongs apparently to some Teutonic community settled in Gaul, while his opponents are Burgundians. Finn is king of the Frisians. In *Deor* and *Widsith* references to Gothic heroes predominate. The latter poem, however, also contains passages relating to the Burgundians, the Lombards (in Italy), the Danes and other peoples, as well as to the English, and references to princes of many other nations. Altogether about a hundred and thirty persons are mentioned by name in the poems; and of these hardly more than half a dozen can be English.

The German heroic poems are concerned mainly with heroes of the Burgundians and the Goths—nations which had disappeared before the time even of the *Hildebrandeslied*, and many centuries before that of the *Nibelungenlied* and the other poems. Siegfried seems to be a Frank; but no emphasis is laid on this. It is remembered that Etzel (Attila) was king of the Huns. Hetele (Heðinn) is placed in Denmark, and his father-in-law Hagene (Högni) in Ireland.

The Norse heroic poems also are chiefly concerned with Burgundian and Gothic heroes. But the nationalities are not clearly remembered; indeed the name 'Burgundian' occurs only once. The Huns figure in the *Battle of the Goths and Huns*, as well as in the story of Atli. Sigurðr appears as a Dane, though his later adventures are placed 'to the south of the Rhine'. Heroic poems dealing with Danish and Swedish heroes must once have existed; but we know these stories only from Danish (Latin) histories and Norse sagas and antiquarian poems, which are doubtless ultimately derived from them. The Danish historians also preserve the story of the English hero Offa, who here appears as a Dane. The story of Heðinn and Högni is located partly in the southern Baltic—doubtless its original home—and (in Norse) partly in the Orkneys. The scene of the Helgi poems is difficult to determine; but the evidence seems to point to the south-west of the Baltic. There appear to be no Norse heroes.

It will be clear from this brief summary that nationality plays no part in stories of the Teutonic Heroic Age—apart from the fact that the heroes are all Teutonic. As regards the latter point Attila and the Huns are perhaps hardly to be regarded as constituting an exception. In the poems it is never recognised that they are of alien nationality; and historically it is probable that they were largely Teutonised in the times to which the stories relate. *Widsith* mentions a few non-Teutonic princes, but gives no further information about them than, e.g., that 'Casere (i.e. Caesar) ruled the Greeks'.

It is clear, further, that many of the stories had an international currency. The stories of Eormenric, of Weland, and of Heðinn and Högni were known in England, Germany and the North. The story of Sigurðr, the Burgundians and Attila is celebrated both in Norse and German poetry. The stories of Widia and of Waldhere were familiar both in England and in Germany, the stories of Offa, of Ingeld, of Sighere and various other heroes both in England and in the North. Among the latter of course we may include the Danish and Swedish princes mentioned in *Beowulf*.

The interest of the poems is centred not in nationality but in the individual. It may be extended in such a way as to include the ancestry of the chief characters—as in *Beowulf*, which begins with an account of the early kings of the Danes. These, however, are introduced in order to lead up to Hrothgar; and it is the glory of the family rather than of the Danish nation which is emphasised. Again, Hrothgar is frequently spoken of as 'Scylding' or 'lord of the Scyldingas' (the family name), and similarly the national name 'Geat' is sometimes used for the hero himself. But these are merely variations employed in order to avoid constant repetition of the individual name.

In almost every story there is one character whose adventures form the chief subject of interest. He is made to perform feats of great—sometimes superhuman—prowess, and in consequence of these he is held up to admiration. His nationality appears to be a matter of no importance; but the sympathy of the reader or listener is enlisted on the side to which he belongs.

This sympathy, however, does not necessarily involve the blackening of the characters of his opponents, if they are human beings. In the Norse poems, though not in the *Nibelungenlied*, Attila is represented as treacherous. In the *Nibelungenlied*, though not in the Norse poems, Hagen (Högni) is represented as fierce and cruel. The disagreement suggests that in the original form of the story neither character was wholly unsympathetic; and in the latter case this inference is borne out by the evidence of *Waltharius*. Indeed there is no character who appears uniformly in an unfavourable light. The most extreme case is that of Eormenric; but even of him *Widsith*—apart from the prologue—notes nothing but his generosity.

There are even stories which can be told from different points of view—i.e. with the sympathy on either side. The story of Ingeld is told in *Beowulf* from the point of view of the hero's enemies, though his own case is put quite fairly. But Saxo (p. 244 ff.) tells the same story at length from Ingeld's side; and from one of Alcuin's letters[1] it appears that in England also heroic poems were current in which he figured as the leading hero. Both in the German *Kudrun* and in Snorri's account[2] of the story of Heðinn and Högni the sympathy inclines to the side of Heðinn (Hetele); but it is easy to see—especially from the *Sörla þáttr*—that the opposite side could equally well have been presented. The mortal quarrel of Brynhildr and Guðrún is a favourite subject in Norse poetry; but the sympathy is not uniformly on one side.

How far can the principles noted above be said to hold good in the case of the Greek heroic stories? At first sight the *Iliad* seems to constitute an exception. The war with which it deals gives the impression of being a national struggle more than any of those which supply the subjects of Teutonic heroic poetry. The army of the Achaeans consists

[1] Mon. Germ., *Epist. Carol.* II. 124; cf. Chadwick, *Heroic Age*, p. 41 f.

[2] *Skaldskaparmál*, cap. 49 (transl. by Brodeur, *Prose Edda*, p. 188 f.); cf. *Sörla þáttr*, cap. 5 ff. (transl. by Kershaw, *Stories and Ballads of the Far Past*, p. 49 ff.).

wholly of Greek forces, whereas the Trojan army is drawn from various foreign peoples. Hence it is not surprising that the story is told from the Achaean point of view. It is true that the treatment of the Trojans is often far from unsympathetic. Indeed to the modern reader Hector is a more attractive figure than any of the Achaean heroes. Yet the sympathies of the poem are clearly Achaean. In combat the Achaean heroes are usually victorious over their opponents; and any successes gained by the latter are due as a rule to accidental circumstances or to the interposition of deities. Usually also the scene is laid on the Achaean side of the battle front.

Yet, curiously enough, it is never noted that the Trojans are foreigners. No hint is given that they speak a different language from the Achaeans—although this is stated of their allies the Carians, while in the *Odyssey* expressions denoting the use of a foreign language are applied to the Egyptians and the Sinties of Lemnos. Whatever may have been the case historically, it would seem that in Greek heroic tradition the Trojans were regarded as no more alien than the Huns in Teutonic tradition. Indeed if we may compare small things with great, the *Battle of the Goths and Huns* affords a rather close parallel to the *Iliad* in this respect. Humli, king of the Huns, denounces the suggestion that violence should be offered to the Gothic herald—as doubtless Priam or Hector would have been made to do in similar circumstances.

Within the Achaean area itself the sympathies of the poems are not confined to any particular district or city. So wholly wanting is the spirit of patriotism in the narrower sense that in later times it was much disputed what city, and even what part of the Greek world, 'Homer' belonged to. Seven cities—and more—claimed the honour of being his birthplace. There is no trace in the poems of any strong feeling for or against any of the various contingents in Agamemnon's host. If the Myrmidons sometimes receive exceptionally high praise, it is probably because Achilles, the chief hero, belongs to them. The leading heroes in general come from widely different districts, and several of them from districts which were quite unimportant in historical times. All of them are represented as distinguishing themselves in feats of arms in one portion or another of the *Iliad*, and it is by their individual prowess and that of the Trojan heroes that the fortunes of war are swayed. The rank and file count for nothing in the fighting.

In the episodes contained in the *Iliad* and throughout the *Odyssey*, both in the main story and in the episodes, the interest is wholly centred in individuals. The same would seem to have been the case in the lost poems, such as those dealing with the Theban wars. Indeed the same remark may be applied to all Greek heroic stories of which we have any knowledge.

Love of home and patriotism of the practical kind are of course by no means unknown in the Homeric poems. We may quote *Il.* XII. 243, where Hector says that 'the best of all omens is to fight in defence of our country'. For other examples reference may be made, e.g., to XV. 494 ff., XXIV. 499 f. But it is to the Trojans, who are defending their city and homes, that such passages usually apply. The Achaean heroes do not pretend to have been led to embark on the expedition from any national feeling. The absence of any such feeling is well illustrated by the story of Achilles' quarrel with Agamemnon—where the chief hero retires from the war owing to a personal affront from the commander-in-chief. We may refer especially to the speech of the former in *Il.* I. 149 ff. Diomedes treats Agamemnon with much greater respect (IV. 401 ff.), possibly because he is more immediately dependent upon him; yet in one rather striking passage (VI. 119 ff.) he and the Lycian chief Glaucos fraternise and exchange armour in the midst of the battle, when they discover that a guest-friendship had existed between their ancestors.

In the *Odyssey*, where the heroes are represented as living at peace, we find them depicted, especially Nestor and Menelaos, in attractive colours; but it is always as individuals, not as rulers. Of relations between one state and another we hear nothing at all. In XXIV. 114 ff. it seems to be implied that, when Agamemnon desired to obtain Odysseus' aid in the expedition to Troy, he secured an introduction from one of the dependent princes of Ithaca.

The Welsh evidence is on the whole very similar to the Greek and Teutonic, although the poems themselves mostly belong to Type D and are therefore of quite a different character. Many of the poems relate to war with the English; and one might have expected that in the case of a long continued warfare like this references to nationality would occur frequently. But such is not the case. In the panegyrics upon Urien, Gwallawg and Cynan Garwyn we have noted only two instances of the name *Brython* and two of *Cymry*; in the *Gododdin* poems four instances of the former name and one of the latter. Examples of *Bedydd*, 'the Christians' (lit. 'baptism'), are hardly more frequent. The interest is wholly personal and individual. It may be observed that none of these names occurs in the elegies upon Urien and Cynddylan (*RBH.* XII, XVI), although the latter is said to have been killed by the Saxons.

The grief described by the poet is his own and that of the hero's immediate entourage. He does not refer to any loss sustained by the nation. It is also to be remembered that the total number of personal names recorded in these various poems is very considerable. But the references are purely personal—they are mentioned as friends or opponents of the heroes. The same remarks apply to the small group of poems belonging to Type B (cf. p. 34 ff.)—in which national names do not occur.

The significance of these characteristics may be seen by a comparison with antiquarian and predictive poetry. Thus the name *Cymry* (or the sing. *Cymro*) occurs fifteen times in the antiquarian poem *RBH.* I, and the same number of times in the predictive poem *Tal.* VI. In poems of the latter class personal names other than those of the revenants Cadwaladr and Cynon are rarely mentioned. The interest here is not individual but national.

In one respect the Welsh evidence does seem to contrast with the Greek. The numerous persons mentioned whether as friends or foes of the heroes are apparently Britons, almost without exception. In *An.* I. 89 (cf. 78) there is a reference to the death of Dyfnwal Frych, presumably the Scottish king Domnall Brecc who was slain by the Britons in 642. The name Fflamddwyn in *Tal.* XXXV and XLIV seems to denote some English leader; but apparently no English names occur. It would appear that enemies of alien nationality were regarded collectively.

On the Irish evidence little need be said. For the feeling of nationality in the wider sense the heroic stories afford hardly any scope, for external enemies seem to have been practically unknown before the Viking Age. As regards nationality in the narrower sense, as between one province or kingdom and another, the stories which centre round Conchobor and CuChulainn are almost invariably told from an Ulster point of view—much in the same way as the *Iliad* is related from the Achaean side. Stories of later times also often evince sympathies which show where they originated. But in general the feeling for nationality in this sense is not particularly striking. The dominating note throughout the stories is definitely personal and individual.

(2) The individualism of the heroic stories—and of the society which produced them—is reflected very clearly in the nature of the warfare which they describe. This is everywhere apt to take the form of single combats between the leading men.

In the *Iliad* we hear of two combats which are arranged beforehand, viz. those of Paris and Menelaos and of Hector and Aias, which form the subjects of the third and the sixth books respectively. These are carried out with certain formalities, and the general fighting is in each case suspended while they are in progress. But even during the general actions the fighting which is actually described consists of a series of duels. It is as warriors rather than as commanders—in the modern sense—that the leaders are expected to distinguish themselves.

The same remarks hold good for the Teutonic stories. In the battles noticed in *Beowulf* attention is generally concentrated on combats between individual heroes, e.g. the combats between Beowulf himself and Daeghraefn in 2501 ff., between Weohstan and Eanmund in 2611 ff., between Ongentheow and the brothers Eofor and Wulf in 2961 ff. In the story of Offa the hero's single combat is the central feature. In both the Danish and the later English versions of the story it is a prearranged affair, fought against two opponents. A single combat is likewise the subject of the story of *Hildebrand*, while the story of *Waldhere* consists in the main of a series of single combats fought by the hero. The *Hamðismál* describes the mortal struggle of two heroes against overwhelming numbers.

The Welsh evidence in this respect is exceptional. References to single combats are quite rare in the heroic poems. Probable instances occur in, e.g., *BBC.* XXXIX. 8, *Tal.* XLIV, *RBH.* XII. 36 ff.; but there are no descriptions of such contests—perhaps owing to the absence of narrative in the poems. The romances of course abound with descriptions of such encounters, while two examples occur in the *Mabinogion* proper—between Pwyll and Hafgan in the story of Pwyll, and between Gwydion and Pryderi in the story of Math.

In Irish heroic sagas descriptions of single combats are extremely frequent; indeed nearly all the fighting is of this character—in pitched battles as well as in isolated encounters. A large part of the *Táin Bó Cuailnge* is taken up with a series of combats between CuChulainn and champions of Medb's army. It is agreed that he shall encounter one champion each day; but he is not informed beforehand who the champions are. In the *Battle of Crinna* the Munster champion Lugaid Laga brings to Cormac mac Airt the heads of three Ulster princes in succession—those of the king, Fergus Dubdetach, and his two brothers.

In single combats, whether they take place in the course of general engagements or arise from private feuds, heroes are usually expected to show a chivalrous spirit, which will prevent them from taking advantage of any disability on the part of their opponents. Yet, strangely enough, even the greatest heroes sometimes win their most notable triumphs by means which appear to us to be unfair—especially by the intervention of deities or animals on their behalf. Thus in the two most important combats in the *Iliad*, between Hector and Patroclos in XVI. 731 ff. and between Achilles and Hector in XXII. 226 ff., the issue is decided by the intervention of deities, Apollo and Athena, whose behaviour seems to us outrageous.

In *Beowulf* the hero shows chivalry even in his encounters with demons. Before the combat with Grendel he says (679 ff.) he will not use his sword, because his opponent is ignorant of the use of weapons—though elsewhere (804 f.) it is stated that Grendel had cast a spell upon all weapons, so as to render them useless against him. In another passage (2518 ff.) Beowulf excuses himself for going in full armour to attack the dragon, on the ground that he does not know how otherwise it is possible to deal with such a creature. In the account of the slaying of Ongentheow by the two brothers Eofor and Wulf (*ib.* 2961 ff.) the poem gives no hint of disapprobation. But Saxo (p. 136 ff.) in his description of a very similar incident, the slaying of Athislus by the brothers Keto and Wigo, states that the action of the latter, though profitable to the Danes, was regarded as discreditable; and he adds that Offa's undertaking to fight two opponents at once was due to a desire to wipe out the disgrace which his nation had incurred thereby.

In Irish heroic sagas instances of chivalrous conduct are frequent. Yet here again we sometimes find even the greatest heroes owing their triumphs to conditions which are hardly those of fair fight. For an example of the former we may refer to the *Battle of Mag Rath*[1] (cf. p. 53), where the high-king Domnall, hearing that his opponent Congal has lost his horse and weapons, sends him first his own horse, then his shield, and then his sword. In the *Táin Bó Cuailnge* CuChulainn's conduct to his opponents is uniformly chivalrous. He spares the life of Fraech in his first encounter, and will not attack Nad-Cranntail, who has come against him without proper weapons. He frequently declares that he will not slay charioteers, messengers and persons unarmed. Yet the same hero in the story of CuRoi's death (cf. p. 48 f.) triumphs by unworthy means; his opponent is betrayed to him by his own wife. But perhaps the most striking example is to be found in the story of CuChulainn's death, or the *Slaughter of Mag Murtheimne* (cf. p. 50 f.). Lugaid, son of CuRoi, has slain CuChulainn but has lost a hand in the

[1] Ed. and transl. by Marstrander, *Ériu*, V. 226 ff.

fight. He is overtaken by Conall Cernach, who has sworn to avenge the hero. Lugaid appeals to Conall to fight fairly, and the latter consents to have one of his own hands bound.[1] The fight is for a long time indecisive, until Conall's horse—apparently at a signal from its master—attacks and wounds Lugaid. Lugaid protests that this is not fair fighting; but Conall replies that he has given his word only for himself, not for animals which are without understanding. He then takes Lugaid's head.

As we have seen above, it is not for generalship or skill in warfare, but for personal courage that heroes are usually famed. Not unfrequently we hear of vows—sometimes made in a state of intoxication. In *Beow.* 636 ff. the hero, before his encounter with Grendel, says to the queen: "I am resolved to perform a deed of knightly prowess or to meet with my life's end in this mead-hall". In *Il.* xx. 83 ff. Apollo in disguise taunts Aineias as follows: "Aineias, thou counsellor of the Trojans, where now is thy boasting, in which thou didst vow to the princes of the Trojans, when quaffing thy wine, that thou wouldst try thy strength in open battle against Achilles, son of Peleus?" We may compare also *Beow.* 480 ff.: "Often enough have scions of combat vowed over the ale-cup, when drunken with beer, that they would abide Grendel's onset in the hall with their terrible swords". In the *Gododdin* poems the disaster of Catraeth is repeatedly said to have been due to the mead supplied to the heroes by Mynyddawg.

In this connection we may also refer to passages where heroes boast of their own achievements or the glories of their ancestors. Examples are of frequent occurrence, especially in challenges to combat. A typical instance is *Finn*, 24 ff., where one of the heroes challenges his opponents as follows: "Sigeferth is my name. I am a prince of the Secgan and a rover known far and wide. Many hardships and stern encounters have I endured. Here too thou shalt have for certain whichever course (i.e. war or peace) thou dost prefer to take with me". We may compare *Beow.* 2511 ff., where the hero, before his fight with the dragon, says: "Many valiant deeds did I venture upon in my youth. Now that I am the venerable guardian of the nation, I will once more essay a combat and carry it out with glory". In *Il.* vi. 127 ff., when

[1] The same incident recurs in the fight between Conall and MesGegra in the *Battle of Howth* (ed. and transl. by Stokes, *Rev. Celt.* viii. 47 ff.), where it is believed to have been taken from the story cited above; cf. Thurneysen, *Ir. Heldensage*, p. 510, note.

Diomedes meets Glaucos in the battle and is in some doubt whether his opponent is a man or a god, he says: "Unhappy are they whose sons offer resistance to my prowess....If thou art a mortal come near, and soon shalt thou find thyself in the toils of destruction". In XIII. 448 ff. Idomeneus makes himself known to the Trojan prince Deiphobos: "Now stand forth thyself to face me, that thou mayest know what sort of a scion of Zeus is here. First Zeus begat Minos to be ruler of Crete, and Minos again begat the blameless Deucalion; and Deucalion begat me to be lord over many men in broad Crete. But now have ships brought me hither with consequences evil to thee and to thy father and the rest of the Trojans". Irish heroic sagas supply many parallels. In the *Story of Mac Datho's Pig* the contest between the heroes of Ulster and Connaught for the 'champion's portion' is decided by boasting. We may quote Conall Cernach's speech in cap. 16: "I swear what my people swear, that since I took a spear in my hand I have not often slept without the head of a Connaught man under my head, and without having wounded a man every single day and every single night". Here also we may note what Diodoros, v. 29, says of the ancient Gauls: "When armies are drawn up in battle array, it is their custom to rush out in front of the line and challenge the bravest of the enemy to single combat, brandishing their arms and trying to strike terror into their foes. And whenever anyone will listen to their challenges, they begin to glorify the valour of their forefathers and to boast of their own prowess; and at the same time they deride and belittle their opponent, and try by their speeches to rob him of all the courage he has in his heart".

Thirst for fame, especially the desire to leave a glorious name after death, appears to be the governing principle of the ideal hero. In *Il.* VII. 85 ff. Hector, before his combat with Aias, says that if he is victorious he will give up his opponent's body to the Achaeans for burial, and they shall construct for him a memorial barrow by the broad Hellespont. "So shall it be said in time to come by some one who lives in after days, when he sails his many-oared ship over the dark sea: 'This is the memorial of a man who died long ago, who once upon a time was slain in his prowess by glorious Hector'. So shall it be said in time to come; and my fame shall never perish". We may compare *Beow.* 2802 ff., where the dying hero gives instructions for his funeral: "After the pyre is consumed command my famous warriors to construct a splendid grave-chamber where the headland juts into the sea. It shall tower aloft on Hrones Naes as a memorial for my people—so that in after days the name of Beowulf's Barrow shall be familiar to mariners who ply their tall ships from afar over the dark waters". Waldhere (I. 8 ff.) is exhorted by his lady as follows: "O son of Aelfhere, a day is come which without doubt has in store for thee one or other of two issues—either to lose thy life or to possess lasting glory among mortals". In Irish sagas we find the heroic gnome: "Fame is more lasting than life".[1] In the *Táin Bó Cuailnge*[2] CuChulainn, when he first receives arms in his boyhood, says: "Excellent would be the value if I should be in the world only for a single day and a single night, if only the stories of me and my exploits survive me". We may compare the *Hamðismál*, st. 31: "We have made a good fight. We stand on the slaughtered bodies of the Goths, like eagles on a branch. Good fame have we won, even if we must die now or tomorrow. No one can live a single night beyond the decision of the Norns".

Some of the adventures for which heroes are famed are of a reckless and indeed hopeless character. Such is the case with the attack of Hamðir and Sörli upon Jörmunrekr and his warriors, which forms the subject of the poem last quoted. A not uncommon feature is the disregard of warnings and of omens which forbode disaster. We may instance Gunnarr's disregard of the warning message sent him by Guðrún in the *Atlakviða* and the treatment by the same hero and Högni of the ominous dreams related to them by their wives in the *Atlamál*. Still more striking is the series of warnings and portents which lead up to the death of CuChulainn in the *Slaughter of Mag Murtheimne*.

Next we may consider briefly the nature of the causes which in heroic stories are said to lead to wars and quarrels. In view of the importance attached to personal honour and glory, as noted above, it is not surprising to find that personal wrongs, especially insults and outrages to dignity, are among the most prolific sources of strife. Such is the case not only with the quarrel between Achilles and Agamemnon, which forms the subject of the *Iliad*, but also with the siege of Troy itself. Noteworthy Teutonic examples of the same kind are to be found in the stories of Heðinn and Högni and of Angantýr and Hlöðr. Most commonly in Teutonic stories war seems to arise out of quarrels between relations in law. Such is the case, for example, in the stories of Finn, Ingeld, Sigurðr and Atli—though in some of these cases the motif of vengeance is also involved. It may be noted that historical records

[1] Cf. *The Martial Career of Conghal Clairinghneach*, ed. and transl. by P. M. Macsweeney, p. 52 f.

[2] Windisch, 1111 ff.; Dunn, p. 62.

amply confirm the testimony of the poems that the strifes of the Heroic Age were largely of personal origin. We may refer, for example, to the frequent quarrels of the Merovingian princes, both among themselves and with their neighbours, and more particularly to the story of the war between the Angli and the Warni recorded by Procopios (*Goth.* IV. 20), which was due to a breach of promise of marriage.

Similar causes of strife are commonly found in the Irish stories. We may instance the *Battle of Cnucha*,[1] which arises out of an incident similar to the cause of the siege of Troy—the abduction by Cumall of Murni Muncaim, daughter of the druid Tadg. The expedition of CuChulainn against CuRoi is due to the love of the former for Blathnat, CuRoi's wife. It is apparently for the sake of Derdriu that Noisiu and his brothers are slain—an event which leads to the revolt of Fergus and other important heroes of Ulster. Sometimes very trivial incidents are alleged to be the causes of great battles. The battle of Mag Rath (cf. p. 53) is said to have arisen out of a quarrel at a feast given by the high-king Domnall. Congal Caech helps himself to an egg before he is served by the king, and the latter calls him a thief.[2]

Another frequent cause of strife is the desire of plunder. The *Iliad* refers to many plundering raids, especially cattle raids. We may instance the sacking of Thebe, Lyrnessos and other Asiatic cities by Achilles (VI. 414 ff., XX. 90 ff.) and the great cattle raid made by the men of Pylos against Elis in Nestor's youth (XI. 671 ff.). Reference may also be made to the plundering of the women and the cattle of the Cicones by Odysseus on his homeward journey from Troy (*Od.* IX. 40 ff.). Hesiod (*W.D.* 161 f.) seems to regard the expedition of the Seven against Thebes as a raid of this kind.

Cattle raids are among the most frequent incidents of Irish heroic sagas. In the lists of sagas *Táin Bó*—, 'Raiding of the Cattle of—', is one of the commonest titles. The most famous example of course is the *Táin Bó Cuailnge*, though in this case the primary object of the raid is to capture a certain bull. Other stories of raids are connected with this. In the *Táin Bó Regamain* the cattle are carried off in order to provide the army of Ailill and Medb with food on their expedition. The *Táin Bó Fraich* and the *Táin Bó Dartada* are concerned with adventures undertaken for the sake of cattle required for the same purpose. In addition to the stories called *Táin* there are others to which the title *Togail* (or *Orgain*), 'Destruction', is applied. Some of these, e.g. the

[1] Ed. and transl. by Hennessy, *Rev. Celt.* II. 86 ff.

[2] Cf. *Ériu*, V. 234 f., and p. 53, note, above.

Destruction of Da Derga's Hall, are examples of brigandage on a big scale.

In Welsh and Teutonic heroic poetry references to plundering raids—as such—are not frequent. Cattle raids are mentioned in *Tal.* XVIII, while raiding of a general character seems to be meant in *Beow.* 2475 ff. The final attack upon Finn is a *togail*, which is prompted by desire for vengeance, but ends with plunder (*ib.* 1154 ff.). The evidence of the Frankish historians[1] shows that the expedition—frequently mentioned in *Beowulf*—in which Hygelac lost his life, was in reality a great plundering raid. From other Latin historical works (e.g. Jordanes, cap. 53) it is clear that cattle raiding was widely practised in the Teutonic Heroic Age.

We shall see in a later chapter that plundering raids appear to be a characteristic feature of the Heroic Age everywhere—indeed, we may say, an essential feature. The booty derived therefrom enabled active and ambitious princes to attract to themselves and to maintain large bodies of followers, without which they were at the mercy of their neighbours. We know from historical records of Teutonic kings who were forced into aggressive warfare against their will by their followers. Such was the case with the Frankish king Hlothhari (Lothair I), who about the year 556 was forced into a campaign against the Saxons, although the latter are said to have offered him more than half their property to purchase peace.[2] A very similar story is told by Procopios (*Goth.* II. 14) of Hrothulf, king of the Heruli, who—about half a century earlier—was forced into an unprovoked attack upon the Lombards.

The plunder taken on the battle-field itself is not to be ignored. Indeed the desire to capture the arms and ornaments of a slain foe—both for their own sake and for the distinction which they conferred—was one of the chief incentives to heroism. Numerous examples are to be found in the *Iliad*, where much of the fiercest fighting takes place over the bodies of slain heroes. Teutonic parallels are not rare. We may refer, for example, to the slaying of Eanmund by Weohstan related in *Beow.* 2611 ff., which shows that it was customary for a knight to present the captured spoils to his lord. Reference may also be made to *Hildebrand*, 60 ff. and to *Waldhere*, 16 ff. In both these cases, as in the *Iliad*, the corselet seems to be the article most prized.

Homeric warriors fight not only for the armour but also for the body of a slain hero. But they do not appear to have been head-hunters, as

[1] Gregory of Tours, III. 3; *Gesta Regum Franc.* cap. 19.

[2] Gregory of Tours, IV. 14.

the heroes of the northern peoples were. In Irish heroic sagas we meet with this practice everywhere. In the *Story of Mac Datho's Pig*, cap. 16, Conall Cernach boasts that he has not often slept without the head of a Connaught man under his head, and produces on the spot that of their greatest champion, whom he has just slain. In the *Slaughter of Mag Murtheimne* Lugaid cuts off CuChulainn's head. He is subsequently overtaken by Conall Cernach, who cuts off his head and carries it off with him. In another version of the same story[1] Conall cuts off the heads of many more of CuChulainn's enemies and affixes them to a rod. In the *Táin Bó Cuailnge*,[2] when Conchobor arrives to take part in the war, he and Celtchair cut off eight score heads of the enemy at their first attack.

It is stated in the story of Conchobor's death[3] that the men of Ulster used to take the brains out of the heads of their slain enemies, mix them with lime and make them into balls. These balls were kept and could be produced whenever the slayer's prowess was called in question. On one such occasion the brain of MesGegra, king of Leinster, who has been slain by Conall Cernach, is brought out. While Conchobor's jesters are playing with it, it is seized by the Connaught champion Cet. Later, he uses it as a missile against Conchobor and inflicts a wound which ultimately causes his death.

Similar practices are known to have prevailed among the ancient Gauls. According to Diodoros (v. 29) "when they have slain their enemies they cut off their heads and fasten them to the necks of their horses; and they hand the bloodstained spoils over to their pages and carry them off as booty, shouting triumphantly and singing songs of victory. And they nail these trophies up on the walls of their houses, just as hunters do with wild beasts they have killed. But the heads of their most distinguished enemies they preserve and keep carefully in a box, and show them to visitors, glorying in the fact that they or their fathers or one of their ancestors have been offered a large sum of money for such and such a head, and have refused the offer".

In Welsh heroic poetry we know of no direct evidence for head-hunting. But it is likely that the practice was known. Later poems (*Tal.* I. 23; *BBC.* XVII. st. 1) refer to 'playing at ball with the heads of

[1] Cf. Thurneysen, *Ir. Heldensage*, p. 565 f. (for the earlier version *ib.* p. 554 ff.; cf. also Stokes, *Rev. Celt.* III. 185; Hull, *The Cuchullin Saga*, p. 263).

[2] Windisch, 4946 f.; Dunn, p. 305.

[3] Frequently translated, e.g. in Hull, *The Cuchullin Saga*, p. 265 ff.; cf. Thurneysen, *Ir. Heldensage*, p. 534 ff.

Saxons'. A passage in Llywarch Hen's elegy upon Urien (*RBH.* XII. 6 ff.) perhaps suggests that it was customary for a slain hero's head to be cut off and carried away by his own friends, if they were afraid that it would fall into the hands of his enemies. The same custom is found in other countries, as we shall see later.

There can be little doubt that head-hunting was practised to some extent by the Teutonic peoples, though here again the evidence to be found in heroic poetry is very slight and unsatisfactory. Beowulf cuts off Grendel's head and brings it back in triumph; but in this case the analogy may possibly be with hunting rather than with warfare. But there can be no question with regard to the story of Alboin (Aelfwine), king of the Lombards, who cut off the head of his enemy Cunimund, king of the Gepidae, and made a drinking vessel out of his skull.[1] At a feast, when he was drunk, he called upon Cunimund's daughter Rosamunda, whom he had married, to drink from this—an incident which cost him his life (c. 571). In England the custom of cutting off the heads of distinguished enemies was known in the seventh century. Oswald's head and arms were cut off by Penda in 642. When Edwin was defeated and killed by Cadwallon in 633, his head was carried off apparently by his own men and buried at York—presumably to save it from falling into the hands of his enemies. In the North the practice continued in use much later. In the *Saga of Harold the Fairhaired* (*Heimskr.*), cap. 22, it is related that Sigurðr I, earl of Orkney (c. 880), slew a Scottish earl named Melbrigði and cut off his head, which he fastened to his saddle. Unfortunately he tore his leg on the dead man's teeth, and blood-poisoning set in, from which he died. The head of Byrhtnoth, earl of Essex—who was defeated and killed by a host of Vikings at Maldon in 991—was cut off and carried away by the enemy, according to the *Book of Ely*, II. 6. In *Grettis Saga*, cap. 82, the hero's head is cut off by his slayers and preserved in salt. Yet it can hardly be said that instances are sufficiently numerous to justify the conclusion that head-hunting was a general custom, either in England or in the North. The Norse practice was perhaps derived from Ireland.

In the course of this chapter we have seen that feeling for nationality is of no account in heroic poetry and saga. Love of home and the duty of defending it are of course recognised. But the interest of the poet or saga-teller is always concentrated upon the doings or experiences of

[1] Paulus Diaconus, *Hist. Langobard.* I. 27; cf. II. 28.

individuals. In later chapters we shall see that this is a constant feature of heroic stories everywhere.

This individualism is reflected in the warfare described in the records. The fighting is apt to take the form of single combats between the leading heroes. The hero boasts of his own achievements, both past and future. To gain personal glory is the goal of his ambition. Wars and quarrels arise partly from personal wrongs and insults, partly from the desire of acquiring plunder and trophies. Plunder is a necessity for the hero who wishes to maintain an active force of armed followers. Trophies, which consist usually of the accoutrements or the heads of his foes, are valued as evidence of his prowess. For all these features we shall find parallels elsewhere. In details there is of course some variation between one country and another. But the prominence—indeed we may say the dominance—of the individual appears to be an essential characteristic of heroic stories and of the Heroic Age itself.

CHAPTER VI

NON-HEROIC STORIES RELATING TO THE HEROIC AGE

WE have now to notice certain stories which chronologically belong to the Heroic Age, but which show characteristics different from those of heroic stories, and often have little or nothing in common with the latter. To one class of such stories we have already had occasion to refer—namely stories which deal with the origin and history of nations and communities. Such stories as those of the Desi, the sons of Cunedda, the Heracleidai, and the Lombards could be treated here, in so far as they relate to the Heroic Age. We should then refer them to Type C, as their antiquarian interest is strongly pronounced. But in view of the fact that they belong to a larger class of stories which extend far beyond the Heroic Age it will be more convenient to treat them in Ch. x as a part of this larger class, and in connection with aetiological and antiquarian matter in general. We shall therefore confine our attention here to stories relating to individuals.

Within these we may conveniently distinguish three classes of stories:

(1) Stories relating to Christian saints.

(2) Stories relating to prophets, wizards, and persons, other than ecclesiastics, who are credited with abnormal or supernatural powers and knowledge.

(3) Stories relating to persons not included in either of these categories.

For stories of this kind the Irish evidence is on the whole the fullest and most satisfactory, and we will therefore begin with it.

(1) Stories of the first class are hardly to be found, within the limits of the Heroic Age, except in Ireland and Britain. In the former country especially they are abundant, and consist usually of narratives of miracles and prophecies. Most of the 'Lives' of Irish saints seem, it is true, to be late in their present form; but very similar stories occur in quite early works, e.g. in Adamnan's *Life of St Columba*, which was written within about a century of the saint's death. This work is divided into three main sections, of which the first contains stories of his prophecies, the second of his miracles, the third of visions of angels relating to him.

There can be no question that such stories were very widely cultivated in the early Irish Church. To many of them parallels may be found in other Christian lands during the same period; and these are probably of ecclesiastical derivation. But there are others which seem to have their origin in native beliefs. We may refer, for example, to the story of the storm (II. 22)[1] which the Saint raises by his prayers, and which brings about the death of certain raiders. In later works, e.g. the Lives of St Ciaran of Seirkieran, we hear of treasures or cattle presented by saints to kings, which disappear as soon as the saint has departed.[2] Welsh parallels will be noticed later.

(2) As a specimen of the second class we may take the story of the *Colloquy of the Two Sages*,[3] which relates to the times of the Ulster cycle. Adna, the chief poet and sage of Ireland, has a son called Nede, who goes to Scotland to study. One day he learns, by casting a spell upon the sea, that his father is dead and that his chair has been taken by a poet named Ferchertne. He sets off home, and on his arrival meets the mischievous Bricriu, who incites him to take his seat in his father's chair. When he has done so, Bricriu informs Ferchertne and stirs him up to defend his position. The result is a contest between the two in wisdom and prophecy, which will require to be noticed in a later chapter. In the end Nede confesses himself to be worsted, and withdraws from the chair. The scene is laid at Emain Macha, Conchobor's capital.

In another story[4] Nede is beloved by the wife of Caier, king of Connaught, his uncle, and persuaded by her to demand from him a certain knife which it was taboo (*ges*) to him to part with. On his refusal Nede curses him. The king then is disfigured and disgraced, and gives up the throne to Nede. After a time Nede repents of his behaviour, and goes to see Caier; but the latter at sight of him dies from shame.

In explanation of this story it should be mentioned that the word *fili*, usually translated 'poet', originally meant 'seer'; and that a *fili* had power by his curses to injure a person, especially by raising blisters on his face, and even to cause his death. Further, it was not allowed to refuse a demand made by a *fili*. But Caier, like many other Irish heroes,

[1] Cap. 23 in Reeves' edition.

[2] Numerous references to incidents of this kind—in which saints seem to have taken over the attributes of druids—will be found in Plummer, *Vitae Sanctorum Hiberniae*, I. CLXVII ff.

[3] Ed. and transl. by Stokes, *Rev. Celt.* XXVI. 4 ff.

[4] Preserved in the later version of *Cormac's Glossary*, contained in the *Yellow Book of Lecan*; cf. Thurneysen, *Ir. Heldensage*, p. 523 f.

was subject to certain taboos or special prohibitions, which it was likewise impossible for him to violate. He was therefore placed in a hopeless position.

In the *Siege of Howth*[1] the Ulster *fili* Athirne makes a progress round Ireland, demanding the wives and treasures of his hosts. On one occasion he visits a one-eyed prince and demands his eye. He is refused nothing, but the Leinstermen afterwards take up arms to recover their property. The same *fili* figures also in other stories, generally in an unfavourable light. He is said to have been the most inhospitable of men.

Next we may take a story which relates to much later times.[2] Mongan, an Ulster king who according to the Annals died in 625, is said to have had a violent altercation with his *fili*, named Forgoll, upon a question of antiquarian lore. The king asserts that it was at the place where they were residing—in Co. Antrim—that Fothad Airgthech, high-king of Ireland, had been killed by Cailte, the follower of Finn mac Cumaill; but the *fili* maintains that the event took place near Wexford. So hot becomes the contention that the king stakes all his possessions and even his person on being able to prove his point within the next three days. But he takes no steps, and as the hours wear on the queen and the court are thrown into the deepest distress. At last, on the third day, he begins to comfort his weeping wife, saying that he can hear the feet of a deliverer wading through various streams—first in the south-west of Co. Kerry, and then gradually nearer—on his way to the palace. The *fili* is demanding his forfeit when an unknown warrior appears, carrying a headless spear. He announces himself to be Cailte and points out, not far from the palace, the place where Fothad was buried. Nearby he finds the spearhead which had been broken off in the battle. It may be noted that Cailte addresses Mongan as Finn; he has come to the rescue of his old master who is now re-incarnate.

(3) The last story could have been given under this heading also, since it concerns the king as much as the *fili*. But we will take here cases in which no persons of this kind are involved.

The most important is the story of the *Destruction of Da Derga's Hall*.[3] This is commonly regarded as a heroic story; but the heroic

[1] Ed. and transl. by Stokes, *Rev. Celt.* VIII. 49–63; cf. also Hull, *Cuchullin Saga*, p. 85 ff.

[2] Ed. and transl. by K. Meyer, *The Voyage of Bran*, I. 45 ff.

[3] Ed. and transl. by Stokes, *Rev. Celt.* XXII. 9 ff., 165 ff., etc.; also republished in book form, Paris, 1902.

elements are slight and unessential. Conaire Mor's ancestry and upbringing are full of marvels; he is the great-grandson of Eochaid and Etain, whose story was given above (p. 52). At the time when he is appointed to the high-kingship he is chasing birds in the direction of the sea. When they reach the water they assume human form, and one of them imposes upon him a number of taboos. Among these are that he shall not travel with Tara on his right and Bregia on his left, that he must never be absent from Tara for more than eight nights, and that he must never be preceded by three 'reds' on his way to the house of a 'red' (*derg*). His reign is blessed with profound peace, and he banishes even his own foster-brothers for raiding. They make a pact with a British pirate named Ingcel Caech, that either party shall support the other in any enterprise upon which they decide.

Now it happens once that—against one of his taboos—Conaire goes to stop a quarrel between two of his subjects, and on his return journey all his taboos are violated. He determines to stay for the night at the hall of Da Derga, near Dublin, but he cannot prevent three horsemen in red—supernatural beings—from riding there in front of his cavalcade. The pirates happen to be in the neighbourhood, and Ingcel compels his comrades to join him in raiding the hall. But first he goes to reconnoitre, and the greater part of the story is taken up with his account of the occupants of the various rooms. His Irish allies identify everybody from his descriptions—Da Derga himself, the king and various members of his retinue, certain Ulster heroes who are visiting him, including Conall Cernach and Cormac, son of Conchobor, and also several supernatural beings. Ingcel insists upon making an attack, and sets fire to the hall. The king makes a brave defence, but his chief hero, Mac Cecht, has to go to seek water for him to slake his thirst. When he returns he finds Conaire himself and nearly all the combatants dead.

The Ulster heroes play no important part in the story and probably did not enter into it in its original form. Indeed it differs a good deal from the Ulster stories in its extreme love of the catalogue form and in the excessive number of formal repetitions—features which refer it to Type C rather than to Type A. But the most essential point is the stress laid on the violation of the taboos as the cause of Conaire's disaster. It will be seen in a later chapter that this is significant for the milieu in which the story was produced. Its utilisation for purposes of general entertainment has not greatly obscured its original character—which points to 'prophetic' rather than heroic circles.

Next we will take a story of a somewhat different character, known as the *Adventure of Cormac mac Airt*, or *Cormac's Adventure in the Land of Promise*.[1] The *Battle of Crinna*, noticed above (p. 52 f.), represents Cormac as a man of resource and cunning, of not too honourable a character, and various details which we omitted merely strengthen this impression. But in Irish tradition as a whole he is famed for wisdom of all kinds—he stands for intellectual as against heroic activities.

The story of the *Adventure* is as follows: One day in Tara Cormac saw an unknown warrior carrying a silver branch with three golden apples. When the branch was shaken it produced delightful music, which sent to sleep all those who were in pain or trouble. Cormac desired the branch so greatly that he consented to pay any price for it; and the man claimed and took first his daughter, then his son, and then his wife. Cormac shook the branch each time to soothe the grief of the court; but after losing his wife he set out to look for her. He became enveloped in a mist, and after various experiences he arrived at a palace where a pig was being prepared for dinner. The owner of the palace told Cormac that a quarter of the pig was cooked whenever a true story was related; and he asked him to take his turn. Cormac described how he lost his wife and children, and the truth of his story was proved by the cooking. Then the man sent him to sleep, and when he awoke he found his wife and children there beside him. Then the man gave him a gold cup, which he kept till the end of his life, and which had the peculiarity that, if three false words were spoken under it, it broke into three pieces; but if three true statements were then made under it, it became whole again. He then announced that he was Manannan mac Lir, king of the Land of Promise; and sent Cormac home with his wife and children.

It can hardly be doubted that this story also originated in intellectual, rather than in heroic, circles. This is indicated most clearly perhaps by one of Cormac's experiences on his journey. He saw a body of horsemen roofing a house with feathers. But they had not a sufficient supply to complete their work; and while they were away collecting more feathers those which were already in position were blown away. Manannan explained to Cormac that these horsemen were the men of learning (*aes dána*) in Ireland, collecting wealth which passes away. He also explained that a fountain which Cormac had seen, with five streams running out of it, was the Fountain of Knowledge, and that the five streams were the five senses through which knowledge was obtained.

[1] Ed. and transl. by Stokes, *Irische Texte*, III. 183 ff.

Many other stories relating to Cormac belong to this category. One of the longest of these is the *Siege of Druim Damgaire*, which is preserved only in a late text.[1] Cormac is warned by Oengus mac Óc that a disastrous murrain of cattle will befall him in the course of his reign, and receives from him certain advice, which later he disregards. When the disaster comes, Cormac is advised by his steward to recoup himself by claiming a double tribute from Munster. Fiacha Muillethan, king of Munster, refuses to admit the legality of the claim; and Cormac, against the advice of his druids, decides to exact the tribute by force. While hunting, he meets with a damsel from the shee-mounds, who encourages him in his enterprise, and gives him two (supernatural) druids and three druidesses, the latter in the form of sheep. Cormac sets out with his army; and his supernatural assistants soon reduce the enemy to a desperate pass. Eventually, however, they procure the aid of a druid called Mog Ruith, who, by means of a magic eel and three magic dogs, enables the Munstermen to destroy the druidical beings who are helping Cormac. The army of the latter is then put to rout, and the expedition ends in disaster. It is to be observed that in this story the warriors count for practically nothing. Everything is decided by the powers of the druids employed on either side.

It may be observed that the examples given above all belong to Type A (and CA). But this category is not entirely confined to narratives. In the *Colloquy of the Two Sages* (cf. p. 97) the narrative is merely introductory to the colloquy itself, which is a dialogue in character. The subject-matter is didactic or prophetic, and the interest is general rather than particular, so it will be noticed in Ch. xv more fittingly than here; but the form is that of Type B—or rather CB. To the same Type belong the *Instructions of King Cormac*, a collection of gnomes in the form of a dialogue in character between Cormac mac Airt and his son Cairbre. A similar but shorter collection is in the form of a dialogue between Cormac's judge, Fithal, and his son. Both of these may be compared with the *Sigrdrífumál*; and with it they will require notice in Ch. xii. It is merely the framework to which we refer here.

It is no accident that these character pieces belong to CB rather than to B—that is, that they are didactic and general, rather than personal; for in this chapter we are dealing mainly with prophets and sages. But there are exceptions. One curious case is the dialogue poem mentioned on p. 55. In form this poem belongs to the present chapter, for it is a dialogue in character (Type B) between two learned poets,

[1] Ed. and transl. by Sjoestedt, *Rev. Celt.* xliii (1 ff.).

Torna and Tuirn; but the subject is heroic—an elegy upon King Niall Noigiallach. The *Eulogy of St Columba* also, if it is not really[1] an example of Type D, must be regarded as a speech poem in character (Type B), put into the mouth of a famous poet.

The British evidence is also abundant, though much of it is difficult to understand. There is more resemblance to the Irish here than in the heroic category.

(1) Stories relating to saints are numerous, though late. The earlier Lives are mostly in Latin. We may take a case[2] from the *Life of St Cadoc*, which is believed to date from about 1075. A certain chief, named Ligesawg, had killed three of Arthur's warriors and fled for refuge to St Cadoc, with whom he remained in concealment for seven years. Then Arthur got news of him and brought a troop of warriors to the River Usk. St Cadoc summoned a gathering of ecclesiastics and others—St David among them—to meet him; and Arthur agreed to accept a payment in cattle in settlement of his case. But he stipulated that the cattle must be red in front and white behind; and St Cadoc's people were completely at a loss where to find such beasts. The saint, however, told them to get the proper number of cattle, whatever colour they might be. When they were brought to the gathering they were transformed into the colours required. Then St Cadoc led them down into the river, opposite to where Arthur and his warriors were waiting to receive them. Cai and Bedwyr came forward and eagerly laid hold of them; but they immediately changed into bundles of ferns. Later, they were found safe in their owner's field. Arthur was so impressed with the miracle that he begged the saint for forgiveness and granted privileges of asylum to his sanctuary. The story must be referred to Type C, as it seeks to explain both privileges and place-names. As regards the chronology, Arthur can hardly have been a contemporary of St Cadoc, still less of St David.

Another example may be taken from Jocelin's *Life of St Kentigern*[3] (cap. 21), written between 1175 and 1199. The saint, during the earlier part of his episcopate, met with much opposition from a king named Morken (Morcant). On one occasion his monastery was in distress through want of food, and he begged the king to let him have some corn

1 Ed. and transl. by Stokes, *Rev. Celt.* XX. 30 ff., 132 ff., etc.

2 Cf. Rees, *Lives of the Cambro-British Saints*, pp. 48 ff., 340 ff.

3 Published in Forbes, *Lives of S. Ninian and S. Kentigern* (Historians of Scotland, V); Edinburgh, 1874.

from his supplies. But the king replied he could only have it if he could get it removed from his barns to the monastery without human hands. Then, in answer to the saint's prayers, the Clyde rose in flood and carried away the king's barns, but deposited them uninjured beside the monastery in Glasgow. The king, infuriated at what had happened, kicked the saint and threw him down; but he died of gout shortly afterwards, because of his sins.

(2) Among stories relating to prophets, wizards, etc. we will first take the *Hanes Taliesin*, which has been preserved only in a very late form—dating perhaps from the sixteenth century. A man called Tegid Foel and his wife Caridwen have an ugly son named Afagddu. For him his mother keeps a 'cauldron of inspiration' boiling for a whole year. While she is out gathering herbs for the cauldron, she employs a man called Gwion Bach to stir it. One day three drops fly out of the cauldron and fall upon Gwion's finger; and immediately the cauldron breaks, and all the contents are wasted. Gwion's finger is scalded, and he puts it in his mouth; and thereupon he acquires knowledge of the future. He takes to flight, but Caridwen on her return sets off in pursuit of him. Both of them transform themselves into various animals and birds; but at last Gwion, who has turned into a grain of wheat, is swallowed by Caridwen, who has become a hen. Nine months later she bears him as a child, and throws him into the sea in a leather bag. This is washed into the weir of Gwyddno Garanhir, whose home is said to be between Aberystwyth and the Dyfi. Gwyddno's son Elphin goes to fish in the weir and finds the child. He takes it home and calls it Taliesin. The child at once begins to sing poems.

Thirteen years later Elphin goes to visit King Maelgwn, his uncle, at Deganwy. While he is there the guests say that no one is so well off in all respects as Maelgwn, and in particular that no one has so virtuous a wife or such skilful bards. But Elphin challenges these statements—at which the king becomes much enraged and puts him in prison until he can prove his case. Then he sends his son Rhun to test the virtue of Elphin's wife; but she by the advice of Taliesin, who has second sight, disguises herself, and when Rhun returns home Elphin is able to show that he has been cheated. Then Taliesin himself sets off to Maelgwn's court and bewitches the bards, so that when they come to perform before the king they can do nothing but make mouths at him. The king charges them with being drunk, but they plead that their helplessness is due to the presence of a spirit in the form of the boy Taliesin. The king then sends for the boy and asks him who he is. He replies in poetry that he is Elphin's bard, and charges the king's bards with incompetence—to which they are still unable to reply. He then recites further poetry, and finally raises a great storm, which threatens to throw down the castle. At this the king falls into a panic and releases Elphin. Further incidents follow, including a horse-race, and Taliesin recites more poetry; but the text breaks off incomplete.

The early poems, especially those in the *Book of Taliesin*, contain a number of references to this story, though they seem to have known it in a somewhat different form. Ceridwen (Caridwen) is mentioned in *Tal.* IX. 4, XIV. 11, as well as in *BBC.* III. 3, IV. 1. In the last three passages the term *Gogyrwen* or *Ogyrwen* (of uncertain meaning) is applied to her, while in two cases (*Tal.* IX. 2, *BBC.* III. 1) the word *awen*, 'inspiration', occurs. In *Tal.* VII. 74, XV. 36 the word *awen* is again found in connection with *Ogyrwen*; the latter passage speaks of three *awen* coming from a cauldron. *Tal.* XIV. 11 mentions the cauldron of Ceridwen. *Tal.* XVI is a monologue poem of Type B, in which Ceridwen is the speaker. In it she speaks of her cauldron, as well as of her chair and her laws (*l.* 24); also (*l.* 9 ff.) she speaks of her son Afagddu as an accomplished poet. The latter is mentioned also in *Tal.* VII. 10, XLVIII. 27.[1] These passages, taken together, clearly suggest that Ceridwen is a mythical being—apparently a goddess of poetry or poetic inspiration. In *Tal.* VII. 220 ff., a poem of Type B or CB, in which the speaker is Taliesin, there is a long list of what might be transformations, each expressed by the word *bum*, 'I have been' (a dog, etc.). This passage must be connected with the *Hanes*, for in 234 ff. the speaker says that he has been a grain and has been swallowed by a hen and rested nine nights in her womb. But similar catalogues with the *bum* formula occur in *Tal.* VIII. 1–23, 205–8, XXV. 58–68, where this interpretation is at least improbable. We may also compare certain catalogues with the formula *wyf*, 'I am', especially *Tal.* III. 9–13, 25 f. These catalogues—which have Irish analogies—will require notice in Ch. XV. For the present it is sufficient to note that much of the matter contained in the story of Taliesin's birth is traceable in much earlier times. We do not know of any reference to the weir in the poems.

The poems contain references also to the second part of the story. Elphin is frequently mentioned. In *Tal.* XIV, a poem of Type B, the speaker, who is clearly Taliesin, says (*l.* 23 ff.) that he came to Deganwy to strive with Maelgwn, and that he liberated his lord Elphin. *Tal.* XIX,

[1] A reference to Gwion occurs perhaps in *RBH.* XXIII. 87; cf. also *Tal.* VII. 13, XIII. 66. But all these passages are obscure.

another poem of Type B, speaks of Maelgwn with respect, and represents Elphin as still in prison. This poem must have been composed for a definite point in the story—rather earlier than the point where it has been introduced by Lady Charlotte Guest, and perhaps before Taliesin's arrival at Deganwy. It is hardly conceivable that such a poem could be composed, except in connection with a narrative. We may conclude therefore either that the *Hanes* is a good deal older than its present form seems to indicate or that it has taken the place of an earlier story on the same subject—which may of course never have been written down. It may be observed that there are at least two other poems (*Tal.* III and VII) which appear to have been designed for a contest with bards, and may have been composed for this story—though that can hardly be proved. No poem, however, refers to Elphin's wife; so the incident relating to her may not have formed part of the original story.

Our view is that a number of these poems originally belonged to a story which told of the imprisonment of Elphin by Maelgwn and his release, but was in other respects similar to the Irish *Colloquy of the Two Sages*; and that the *Hanes* is descended, however indirectly, from this story. It may not be out of place here to refer to the story told in the *Historia Brittonum*, cap. 42, of the boy Ambrosius who, like the Taliesin of the *Hanes*, had no father, and who contended successfully in divination with the *magi* of King Guorthigirn at a place not so very many miles from Deganwy. Even if there be no connection between the two stories, the Ambrosius incident tends to confirm the evidence of the *Hanes* as to the existence of contests in wisdom here, just as in Ireland—and in many other countries. The obscure reference to *praecones* in Gildas' attack upon Maelgwn (cap. 34) suggests that in point of fact bardism was cultivated at his court.

Next we may take the prophet Myrddin (Merlin). In this case we have no vernacular story, like the *Hanes Taliesin*. The story is told in the *Vita Merlini*, which is now, we believe, generally accepted as the work of Geoffrey of Monmouth, and which in any case is worthless for historical purposes. Much is said about Merlin also in Geoffrey's *History*, which is likewise worthless, and in various medieval romances, where he is treated in the style of imaginative fiction. Yet the story is of considerable importance in connection with this class of literature. We shall therefore have to treat it at greater length than usual.[1] We will first take the vernacular records, which consist of poems and *Triads*.

[1] This is the more necessary because some most judicious and careful scholars have expressed the opinion that Merlin was invented by Geoffrey.

The poems are all dialogues or monologues of Type B (or CB), and probably all belong to the twelfth century in their present form.

BBC. I is a very obscure poem in the form of a dialogue between Myrddin and Taliesin. They bewail disastrous battles and the slaughter of heroes. It is worth noting that, among other names, we hear of Maelgwn and the sons of Eliffer, and of the battle of Arderydd. *BBC.* XVII is a monologue poem, commonly known as *Afallenau*, or the 'Apple-Trees'. It contains ten stanzas; but there are other texts[1] which have these, in a different order, and twelve or thirteen more. This poem will require notice in a later chapter (XVII); but we may note here that in it Myrddin speaks of the wood of Celyddon, in which he slept, of his joy in the apple-trees there, of the liberality with which he had been treated by Gwenddoleu, who is evidently dead, of Rhydderch, of Gwendydd, whose son he has slain, and of the spirits in the woods, among whom he has wandered for fifty years. He speaks of himself as miserable, without clothes and without honour, although in the battle of Arderydd he had worn a golden torque. But, along with all this, he refers frequently to persons and events of the twelfth century; and once also (st. 7—not in the *BBC.* text) to the story of Arthur. *BBC.* XVIII, commonly called *Hoianau*, is very similar, and shows the same combination of subjects (except the last). Indeed it is clearly modelled on the *Afallenau*. *RBH.* I, commonly called *Cyfoesi*, 'Conversation' (or perhaps 'Synchronism'), is a long dialogue poem between Myrddin and his sister Gwendydd. It begins with a description of the power of King Rhydderch Hael, who has all the Cymry under him; but Myrddin adds that he will die the day after tomorrow. Then, in answer to Gwendydd's questions, he says that Morcant will succeed him, then Urien, then Maelgwn. Then he goes through the list of Maelgwn's descendants and the principal kings of Gwynedd down to Howel the Good (d. 950). Then follow a number of names which are difficult to identify; but there are references to the 'Son of Henry', i.e. apparently Robert, earl of Gloucester (d. 1147), and probably to Owein Gwynedd (d. 1170) and his father Gruffydd—perhaps also to even later princes. We hear too of the city of the bards in the land of the Clyde, of the death of Gwenddoleu in the slaughter of Arderydd, and of the loss of Myrddin's reason through the spirits of the mountain. In st. 11 Gwendydd addresses him (probably) as 'fosterer of poetry at the stream of

[1] *Myv. Arch.* (1870), p. 115 ff.; Stephens, *Literature of the Kymry*, p. 212 ff. These two texts also differ from one another considerably in the order of the stanzas.

Clyde'; while in st. 3 she calls him *llallogan*, and in many other passages *llallawc*—terms of unknown meaning.

The other poems need not detain us long. *RBH.* II is a monologue by Myrddin now dead, addressed from his grave to Gwendydd. It is mainly concerned with events about the year 1163, especially Henry II's invasion of South Wales and his quarrel with Thomas à Becket, and has little to say about the speaker himself. St. 7 contains the prophecy with regard to the ford of Pencarn, near Newport, which, according to Giraldus Cambrensis, *Itin. Cambriae*, I. 6, was believed by the Welsh to be fulfilled at the king's arrival, and which took the heart out of their resistance. In *Tal.* VI the expression 'Myrddin foretells' occurs merely as a variation of '*Awen* ('Inspiration' or 'the Muse') foretells'. There is no reference to Myrddin's own story.

The *Triads* are of importance chiefly for the information which they give with regard to the death of Gwenddoleu and the battle of Arderydd. The most interesting passage perhaps is one which has already been quoted (p. 46): the third of the loyal retinues was that 'of Gwenddoleu son of Ceidiaw, at Arderydd, who continued the battle for six weeks after their lord was slain'. We may also refer to the next *Triad*,[1] which gives among the 'disloyal retinues' that 'of Gwrgi and Peredur, who deserted their lords at Caer Greu, and they had to fight on the morrow with Eda Glinmawr, and they were both killed there'. Another *Triad*[2] mentions among 'burdens of horses' that 'of Cornan, the horse of the sons of Eliffer of the Great Bodyguard, which carried Gwrgi and Peredur on its back...(it also carried) Dunawd, son of Pabo, and Cynfelyn Drwsgyl to see the slaughtered host of Gwenddoleu at Arderydd'. Many other *Triads* refer to the same heroes and also to Rhydderch Hael.

It may be mentioned here that according to the genealogies[3] Gwenddoleu was first cousin to his opponents, Gwrgi and Peredur, the sons of Eliffer. Ceidiaw, the father of Gwenddoleu, Eliffer and Pabo were all brothers; and in one text Morfryn, the father of Myrddin, is their first cousin. In the *Annales Cambriae* the following dates are given: 574 for the battle of Arderydd (*Armterid*); 581 for the death of Gwrgi and

[1] I. 35; *Myv. Arch.* (1870), p. 390.

[2] II. 11; *Myv. Arch.* (1870), p. 396; cf. *Trioedd y Meirch*, I (*ib.* p. 394).

[3] The most important text is the *Genealogy of the Men of the North* (*Bonhed Gwyr y Gogled*), published by Skene, *Four Ancient Books of Wales*, II. 454, from MS. Hengwrt 536. Myrddin's genealogy is known to us only from Stephens, *The Gododin of Aneurin Gwawdrydd*, p. 173, note, the source of which is not given. Morfryn, the father of Myrddin, is mentioned in *RBH.* I. 112, II. 2.

Peredur; 596 for that of Dunawd. Rhydderch is not mentioned in the Annals, but there is no doubt (cf. p. 144) that he was king of Dumbarton about this time—before 597. It is clear then that in such poems as *BBC.* XVII, XVIII, *RBH.* II, we have to deal with two totally different sets of persons and events, one belonging to the latter part of the sixth century and the other to the twelfth century. The same is true of *RBH.* I, though in this case the gap is to some extent bridged over by the list of kings.

We must now notice briefly the works of Geoffrey of Monmouth, which give the earliest connected account of the story of Myrddin—or rather Merlin (*Merlinus*). Here we have to distinguish between the *History*, including the *Prophecies* in Book VII, and the *Vita Merlini.* In the former Merlin has little in common with the Myrddin of the poems beyond the fact that he is a prophet. But with the *Vita* the case is different. There is certainly some relationship between this work and the Welsh poems discussed above, though the relationship is differently interpreted by different scholars. For reasons which are given in the Excursus at the end of this chapter we are convinced that Geoffrey had some knowledge of three of these poems, viz. *BBC.* I, XVII, and *RBH.* I. He had also other sources of information for the story of Merlin. Some of these are known, and will be discussed in the following paragraphs. Apparently he had also one or more sources which are now lost. We doubt, however, whether any evidence of much value for the story is to be derived from his works.

The records of St Kentigern require to be discussed more fully. In the *Life* of the saint by Jocelin,[1] which was written between 1175 and 1199, much is said about a king Rederich, who is certainly to be identified with Rhydderch Hael. He reigned during the latter part of St Kentigern's career, and was his chief supporter. In the last chapter of the *Life* it is stated that he kept at his court a madman called Laloecen. After St Kentigern's death this man gave himself up to extreme grief, and said that Rederech and another of the chief men would die within the same year.

Jocelin, in the Preface to the *Life*, says that he knew two previous *Lives* of the saint—one which was actually in use at the church of Glasgow, and another, presumably earlier, which he had discovered, and which he describes as *stilo Scottico dictatum.* Now in MS. Cott. Titus A. XIX. fol. 76–80, the Preface and first eight chapters of the former

[1] Published in Forbes, *Lives of S. Ninian and S. Kentigern* (Historians of Scotland, V).

Life are preserved.[1] The Preface states that it was written for Herbert, bishop of Glasgow 1147–1164. In the same MS. on fol. 74, 75, there is a story which is obviously taken from a *Life of St Kentigern*, probably the one just mentioned. Part of this story is also preserved in Bower's *Scotichronicon* (III. 31). In the intervening space (fol. 75, 75*b*) between this extract and the Preface there is another story not known elsewhere. We may call these two extracts *a* and *b* respectively.[2]

In extract *a* St Kentigern sees a naked hairy madman in a lonely wood. In answer to the saint's questions the madman tells him that he had been present at a very famous battle which was fought between the Liddel and *Carwannok* (for which the *Scotichronicon* reads *Carwanolow*). During the battle he had heard a voice from the sky, like a tremendous roar, saying to him: "Lailoken, Lailoken! since thou alone art guilty of the blood of all those who are slain here, thou alone shalt pay for the sins of them all; for, committed to the angels of Satan, thou shalt have thy abode among the beasts of the forest until the day of thy death". And looking up at the sound, he saw a vision of intolerable brightness—countless troops of warriors in the sky brandishing their spears at him. Then an evil spirit seized him and drove him to the forest. When he had told this story to the saint, he fled to the woods.

At a much later date, apparently, the same madman used to come and sit on a rock over the stream Mellodonor—now called Molendinar—in the north of Glasgow and interrupt the services of St Kentigern's clergy by shouting prophecies; but his prophecies were never consistent with one another. One day he demanded the sacrament, saying that he was going to die. The saint sent three times to him to ask how he was going to die. The first time he replied that he would be stoned and beaten to death; the second time that he would be pierced by a stake; the third time that he would be drowned. But when the saint recognised that he was the same man who had spoken to him long before, he pitied him and gave him the sacrament. Then the madman repeated that he was going to die that day, and added that the noblest of the kings of Britain, the holiest of the bishops, and the most distinguished of the nobles would follow him in the same year. Having said this, he set off to the woods; but on the same day he was caught and beaten to death by King Meldred's shepherds, near Dunmeller (now Drumelzier)

[1] Published by Forbes, *op. cit.* p. 243 ff. (transl. p. 123 ff.).

[2] Both extracts (together with the passage in the *Scotichronicon*) are published by Ward, *Romania*, XXII. 504 ff.

on the Tweed. As he was dying he fell into the river and was pierced by a stake, which was fixed upright in it.

In extract *b* Lailoken is captured by a prince (*regulus*) Meldred and imprisoned by him in his fortress Dunmeller. The prince wished to get a prophecy from him, but he would not speak. One day he saw the prince pick a leaf out of his wife's hair and gave a loud laugh. When the prince asked him why he did so he answered at first in riddles, but eventually promised to explain if he was released. He also said that he was going to die in a few days by a triple death; and got the prince to promise to bury him near the burial-ground of Dunmeller, close to where the stream *Passales* (Pausayl) runs into the Tweed. A very obscure prophecy follows. As soon as he was set free he explained his riddles. The prince's wife had been guilty of adultery in the garden, and the leaf was a witness to her deeds. She, in order to defend herself from the charge, said that her husband should not believe the word of a madman, and reminded him of Lailoken's absurd prophecy that he was to die three times; but Meldred is unconvinced. She then determined to get Lailoken put to death; and after some years, on the day he had received the sacrament, while he was passing near Dunmeller at sunset, he was killed in the way he had foretold by some shepherds who were acting under her orders.

The origin of this extract (*b*) is unknown. There are discrepancies between it and the previous extract (*a*) which show that it cannot have belonged to the same work, though a few passages, especially near the end, suggest that the man who made the extract had tried to bring it into conformity with *a*. This may also be the explanation of the discrepancy in the extract itself between 'days' and 'years', if it is not due to mere carelessness. The style is hardly incompatible with the idea that the extract comes from the earlier *Life* described by Jocelin as *stilo Scottico dictatum*; but if it has been edited, as we have suggested, there is nothing to show that it is derived from any *Life of St Kentigern*.

It may be mentioned that both the extracts discussed above, and also the passage in the *Scotichronicon*, contain references which identify Lailoken with Merlin (Myrddin). But the references in *a* and the *Scotichronicon* are independent of one another; and it is generally agreed that both of them, and also the reference in *b*, are additions to the original texts.

We have no doubt, however, that the identifications are correct, and that Lailoken is the same person as the Myrddin of the poems. In both cases the subject is a madman[1] endowed with prophecy, who lives in forests. The district in which he lives seems to be the same in both cases. We are not aware that Myrddin's home, the *Coed Celyddon*, has been identified with certainty, although it is mentioned alsewhere—e.g. in the *Historia Brittonum*, cap. 56, where it is the scene of one of Arthur's battles. But there are other names which point to the south of Scotland (cf. p. 106 f.).[2] Again, both prophets belong to the same time—the reign of Rhydderch, king of Dumbarton, in the latter part of the sixth century; and both of them prophesy this king's death. Both of them also appear to have lost their reason through the same battle. There is no reference to a vision in the poems; but Myrddin is haunted by the ghosts of those who were slain in the battle of Arderydd—which is generally identified with Arthuret[3] (Longtown). The locality specified in extract *a* is about 3–5 miles east of Longtown, and immediately adjacent to the parish of Arthuret.[4] Lastly, the resemblance between the name Lailoken (Laloecen) and the terms *Llallawc*, *Llallogan* applied to Myrddin in *RBH*. I can hardly be due to coincidence.[5] Similar names occur elsewhere, *Lalloc* in Ireland and *Lallocan*(*t*) in Brittany,[6] but they seem to be quite rare.

Next we may quote a passage from Giraldus Cambrensis, *Itin. Kambriae*, II. 8: "There were two Merlins: one who was also called Ambrosius—for he had two names—and prophesied in the reign of Vortigern. He was begotten by an incubus, and discovered at Carmarthen—whence also the place derives its name, Carmarthen, i.e. 'city of Merlin', from the fact that he was found there. The other, however, belonged to Scotland (*de Albania oriundus*). He is also called Celidonius from the *Celidonia silua* in which he prophesied, and

[1] For Myrddin's madness cf. *BBC*. XVII. 7; *RBH*. I. 20 f.

[2] Apart from these there are cases where it is doubtful whether a place-name is intended; thus, e.g., it has been proposed to take *llanerch* in *BBC*. XVII. 5, line 1, as 'Lanark'.

[3] Cf. Skene, *op. cit.* I. 65 f.; Lloyd, *History of Wales*, p. 166, note 20.

[4] The present boundary of Arthuret seems to be the Carwinley Beck (*Carwanolow*, cf. p. 109). The early forms of *Carwinley* favour Skene's derivation of the name from Caer Gwenddoleu; cf. Lloyd, *op. cit.* p. 167, note 22; Sedgefield, *Place-Names of Cumberland*, p. 33.

[5] F. Lot (*Ann. de Bretagne*, XV. 518 f.) insists that the word *llallogan* (*RBH*. I. 3) must be an adjective and, consequently, that it cannot have anything to do with *Lailoken*, etc. We fear that the text of this poem—and the same, unfortunately, is true of very many other early Welsh poems—is by no means in such a condition as to justify arguments of this kind being based upon it.

[6] Cf. Ward, *Romania*, XXII. 511, and Phillimore, *Y Cymmrodor*, XI. 48.

Silvester because—when he had taken up his position in a line of battle and, looking up into the sky, saw an exceedingly terrible portent—his mind became deranged, and he fled to the forest, and led a forest life (*siluestrem uitam*) down to his death. Now this Merlin belonged to the time of Arthur, and is said to have prophesied far more fully and more openly than the other".

Here the first Merlin is clearly derived from Geoffrey's *History*. The second, however, owes nothing but the form of his name to Geoffrey. It is clear from other passages in Giraldus' works (cf. p. 129) that what he means by *Merlinus Siluester* is the Myrddin of Welsh prophetic poems which were carried on mainly by oral tradition. The first Merlin comes ultimately no doubt from the same source—through Geoffrey—but this was apparently not recognised by Giraldus. It may be observed that for the forest he uses the form *Celidon-*, like the poems (*Coed Celyddon*), not *Calidon-*, as in the *Vita Merlini*. On the other hand, although all authorities agree in representing the madness as the result of a certain battle, it is only Giraldus' account and the anonymous *Life of St Kentigern* (extract *a*) which record the vision. The account in the *Vita Merlini* supplies a totally different motif, while the Welsh poems are silent. Lastly, Giraldus' statement that Merlin Silvester belonged to the time of Arthur is hardly in accord with any of the other authorities. In the *Vita Merlini* Arthur's reign does fall within the range of Merlin's prolonged existence; but the two are not associated.

It is in the Romances that we find Merlin associated with Arthur; yet of those which deal with this subject none are believed to be earlier than 1188, the date of Giraldus' work. In the Romances Merlin appears chiefly as a magician. Here also we meet with the story of Viviane, who induced him to impart to her his magic arts, and then utilised the knowledge thus gained to bring about his undoing. Geoffrey and the other authorities know nothing of this story, though there seem to be allusions in *BBC*. XVII to a courtship of long ago. But the Welsh poems occasionally use a word *hwimleian* (*chwibleian*), 'Sibyl', or rather 'Inspiration' personified (similar to *awen*, cf. p. 107)—which shows a curious resemblance to the name *Viviane*, as was pointed out long ago.[1]

The possibility of deliberate fiction is of course to be taken seriously into account in the last category, although we believe that its scope in general has been greatly exaggerated by many scholars. The existence of a traditional story, or collection of stories, of some kind is without doubt involved both by the Welsh poems—which, it must be re-

[1] Cf. Skene, *Four Ancient Books of Wales*, II. 336 f.

membered, are in the form of speeches in character—and by the Glasgow records. The chief difficulty lies in determining the relations of the two extracts in MS. Cott. Titus XIX to one another and to Geoffrey and Giraldus. Did the two latter derive their information from the extracts, or from Glasgow at all? Neither of them refers to St Kentigern. Yet Giraldus' statement corresponds to *a*, which clearly comes from a *Life* of the saint. The origin of *b*, as we have seen, is not so obvious. And it is not to be forgotten that a story which is at variance with the rest occurs in Jocelin's *Life* (cf. p. 108).

The natural conclusion seems to be that a number of stories relating to the mad prophet—partly, but not wholly, in connection with St Kentigern—were current in the church of Glasgow at the time when the Scottish Church was reorganised, early in the twelfth century. The introduction of Anglo-Norman ecclesiastics gained for these stories a wider circulation, in England as well as Scotland, not merely through the written *Lives* of the saint, but also orally and no doubt through correspondence. The stories also, probably at a much earlier date, made their way to Wales; but this can only be stated with confidence, of course, for such incidents as happen to be referred to in the poems. We do not know whether the story of the vision was current there. All that can be said with certainty is that, wherever Giraldus acquired it, he evidently had no doubt—any more than Geoffrey had—that the mad prophet of Strathclyde was the same person as Merlin (Myrddin). On the other hand the poems contain some features which do not appear in the Glasgow records, but may yet quite possibly be ancient. Thus it is at least implied in *RBH*. I that the prophet was regarded with a certain honour in spite of his madness and his wretched mode of life.

It may be noted here that the story as a whole contains various features which point quite definitely to its antiquity. Thus the incident of a warrior going mad in the course of a battle is of not infrequent occurrence in Irish stories relating to the seventh and following centuries.[1] Such persons are not regarded as prophets; but they are credited with the supernatural power of flying. Sometimes they make their way to the woods and live there. Again, the prophecy of death in a triple or complex form belongs to the same period or slightly earlier.

[1] Cf. *The Adventures of Suibhne Geilt*, ed. and transl. by J. G. O'Keefe (Irish Texts Soc. XII), p. 14 ff.; *The Battle of Allen* (cf. esp. *Rev. Celt.* XXIV. 55 and note 1, with the references there given); *Speculum Regale* (cf. K. Meyer, *Ériu*, IV. 11 f.). We may also refer to the *Hávamál*, st. 129, where both the word *gjalti* and the idea seem to be of Irish derivation.

An analogy to Lailoken's prophecy is to be found in Adamnan's *Life of St Columba*, I. 36,[1] where the saint prophesies a somewhat similar fate for the Ulster prince Aed Dub, who in the year 565 had killed the high-king Diarmait mac Cerbaill. Irish stories relating to the death of Diarmait himself present a still closer parallel; for the death prophesied for him by the seer Bec mac De is definitely of a triple character.[2] Moreover, the milieu of the story is that of the sixth and seventh centuries rather than of any subsequent period. It was then more than at any other time that saints and other people were in the habit of retiring into solitudes to live the life of hermits.

The contrast between the two figures, Taliesin and Myrddin, whom we have been considering, is as great as possible. The former is a sage, a magician, and a composer of panegyrics. The latter represents the emotional side of poetry and the ecstatic form of prophecy. We know from Giraldus (cf. p. 129) that prophetic ecstasy was not uncommon among the Welsh of his day; and it is a phenomenon for which we shall find parallels among various barbaric peoples. The really remarkable fact is that the Welsh of the twelfth century should have used as the chief vehicle of their political and national propaganda the story of an insane man who had lived in a distant region some five or six hundred years before. There is no reason indeed for supposing that the story was then new to them; but it had probably gained in popularity.

Next we may take the *Mabinogion*. These stories are often regarded as mythological, and some of the characters have been identified with Irish deities. Thus the children of Llyr are commonly connected with the Irish children of Ler, and the children of Don with the Irish *Tuatha De Danann*, or 'Peoples of the goddess Danu'. In particular Manawyddan, son of Llyr, is identified with the god Manannan mac Lir. Yet the two names, though related, are not identical, and the two characters themselves and their adventures have little in common. The other children of Llyr have no Irish counterparts, while the resemblances between the children of Don and their suggested Irish equivalents are negligible. Indeed it is very doubtful whether the Irish expression had in early times the meaning given to it above.[3]

1 Cap. 29 in Reeves' edition.

2 Cf. O'Grady, *Silva Gadelica*, II. 85 ff. (also 74f., 79 f.). The meeting of Bec mac De and St Columba described here may be compared with the last meeting of Lailoken and St Kentigern (cf. p. 109). Bec mac De's name, like Myrddin's, was used as a vehicle for prophecies in later times.

3 Cf. Thurneysen, *Irische Heldensage*, p. 63.

At all events it is clear that, whatever their origin, the characters of the *Mabinogion* are not represented as other than human beings in the texts as we have them. Apart from the stories themselves and a few references to them in early poems, these characters are little known. Manawyddan, however, is mentioned apparently among Arthur's heroes in *BBC.* XXXI, and the occurrence of his name in the catalogue in *Culhwch and Olwen* may possibly be due to a reminiscence of the same connection. For the rest we know of no references which point clearly to a non-human character. We shall therefore treat them as human, without regard to the question whether their origin is to be sought in history, mythology or fiction.

It will be sufficient to take two of the stories—*Pwyll, Prince of Dyfed*, and *Math, son of Mathonwy*. These appear to be free from the learned and the Irish influences which are generally suspected in *Branwen, daughter of Llyr*. The stories are so well known[1] that it is unnecessary to give an abstract of them here.

The character of Pwyll differs little from that of a typical heroic prince of the better sort. He is brave, generous, and honourable. He is credited with no supernatural or magical powers. Yet we cannot regard his story as heroic. Almost all the experiences and adventures through which he is made to pass are of abnormal character; he himself either plays a purely passive rôle or acts as he is directed. His story therefore belongs obviously to the third of the classes distinguished at the beginning of the chapter. It has something in common with the story of Conaire Mor (the *Destruction of Da Derga's Hall*). But, unlike this, it is not tragic. On the whole Pwyll experiences more good than bad fortune. The didactic elements too are negligible in this case. It is purely a story of entertainment (Type A).

The story of Math,[2] on the other hand, belongs to Class 2 of the scheme set forth on p. 96. The leading characters belong to the ruling family of Gwynedd; and both Math himself, the actual ruler, and his nephew Gwydion are warriors. But the heroic element is secondary. Both of them are primarily wizards, and most of the events in the story are governed by their skill in magic. Math is superior to Gwydion as a

[1] Transl. by Lady Charlotte Guest ('Everyman'); by Ellis and Lloyd (Oxford, 1929); and by J. Loth, *Les Mabinogion* (Paris, 1913). The last is of great importance, owing to the full notes and Appendices which it contains.

[2] For an elaborate discussion of the origins of this story (with text and translation) the reader may be referred to Gruffydd, *Math vab Mathonwy*. The subject, however, lies beyond the scope of our work.

magician; but the latter also is an expert. The fact that Gwynedd is ruled by a family of magicians—a family too who evidently inherit through the female line—is peculiar; for neither feature seems to occur in Wales during the historical period. We may note in passing that Pwyll is succeeded by his son Pryderi, neither of whom is credited with knowledge of magic. Like *Pwyll*, this story clearly belongs to Type A. Didactic or informative elements are not wanting; but they are slight and probably secondary. Early poems contain a number of references to the story. The most specific is *Tal.* XVI. 14 ff., where Ceridwen is made to speak of Gwydion's exploits in creating Blodeuwedd out of flowers and in cheating Pryderi of his pigs by means of the sham horses which he had made out of fungus.

In conclusion we may perhaps refer here to a very obscure story which forms the subject of a poem in the *Black Book* (No. XXXVIII).[1] The first stanza is addressed to a certain Seithenhin, calling upon him to see that Gwyddneu's plain has been flooded by the sea. The next two stanzas curse a girl, unnamed, who is said to be responsible for the catastrophe. The rest of the poem consists of reflections; but each stanza refers to the cries of a madman. An analogy to the story has been found in a short Irish saga called the 'Fate of Eochaid son of Mairid',[2] in which the main features recur. The madman here foretells the flood—which is said to have given rise to Lough Neagh. Later Welsh speculation located the flooded region in Cardigan Bay. But the interest of this poem is emotional, not antiquarian.[3]

In Greek stories belonging to Cl. 2 and 3 of this category are numerous. But not one of them is told at length in any early work now existing. Neither have we any early poems of Types B or C relating to such stories. The material consists of notices relating to lost works, and a few references to stories of this kind in early works which still exist.

The *Melampodeia*, a poem often attributed to Hesiod, seems to have contained a collection of stories of this kind. One fragment relates to a kind of contest in mantic skill between two seers, Calchas and Mopsos.

1 Discussed at length by Loth, *Rev. Celt.* XXIV. 349 ff. (transl. p. 362 f.). For later developments of the story see Lloyd, *History of Wales*, p. 25 f.

2 Transl. by O'Grady, *Silva Gadelica*, II. 265 ff. (text, I. 233 ff.). A somewhat similar story is known in Brittany; cf. Loth, *l.c.*

3 The last stanza, which speaks of Seithenhin's grave, occurs also in *BBC.* XIX (st. 6), from which it is perhaps derived.

It may be compared with the dialogue between Ferchertne and Nede (cf. p. 97). Mopsos guesses correctly the number of figs on a certain tree, and Calchas being overcome dies. Other fragments deal with the stories of Melampus, Teiresias, Amphilochos, and other seers. References to some of these, especially Melampus, occur in the Homeric poems, and there is no doubt that their stories were widely known. The same applies to Amphiaraos and others. Calchas of course takes part in the action of the *Iliad*. In the lost *Nostoi* he seems to have figured somewhat more prominently.

Another poem sometimes attributed to Hesiod was the *Instructions of Cheiron to Achilles*, of which one or two fragments are preserved. It may perhaps have had something in common with the *Sigrdrífumál* (cf. p. 27 f.). Cheiron is mentioned in a number of stories relating to the Heroic Age, especially as an educator of young heroes.

Reference may also be made here to a number of legendary Thracian poets, who were apparently believed to have lived in the Heroic Age. One of these, Thamyris, is mentioned in the *Iliad* (II. 594 ff.), the rest —Orpheus, Philammon, Musaios, Eumolpos and others—only in later works. Certain poems, now wholly lost, were attributed to them by the ancients. These seem to have been partly hymns and other poems of a religious character, and partly prophecies. What is said by Herodotos (VII. 6, VIII. 96, IX. 43) about the prophecies of Musaios rather suggests that they may have been adapted, like the Myrddin poems, to the political exigencies of the hour, although according to the first of these passages the poet Onomacritos was banished (c. 520) for interpolating compositions of his own among them. The stories of these prophets and religious poets are preserved only in late form.

The instances given above all belong to Cl. 2. Examples of Cl. 3 are perhaps still more numerous; but since these also are known only from secondary and late authorities, they are often difficult to distinguish from Heroic, Type C, and from stories of primarily antiquarian character.

The story of Oidipus probably belongs to our present category. References occur to an epic poem called *Oidipodeia*, which presumably dealt with this story, and which was sometimes attributed to the early poet Cinaithon. But practically nothing is known of this poem, and it is uncertain whether the story as given by Sophocles and other later writers is derived from it. The story has much in common with that of Conaire Mor (cf. p. 98 f.); but the prohibitions, the transgression of which brings Oidipus to ruin, are social laws of general application, not special taboos applicable to one specific individual only, as in the case of Conaire.

References to stories of this class occur even in the *Iliad*. Such is the passage relating to Niobe in XXIV. 602 ff. The much longer passage in which Phoinix tells the story of Meleagros (IX. 528 ff.) is perhaps not so clear a case; but at all events it has much in common with the class under consideration.[1] Later works relating to the Heroic Age are full of examples. Thus, for example, most of the stories of Theseus and Heracles belong here, though in the former antiquarian elements are also very prominent. Indeed there can be little doubt that in the course of time the non-heroic tended largely to encroach upon the heroic. This may be seen, for example, in the differences between the Homeric poems and Attic drama in the treatment of the story of the Atreidai. The dramas are in the main doubtless derived ultimately from heroic tradition, and most of them may be regarded as highly developed specimens of Heroic Type B; but non-heroic elements are generally prominent, especially in references to the past.

We know of no stories of Cl. 1 which can properly be called Teutonic and which relate to the Heroic Age. Teutonic examples of Cl. 2 also seem to be extremely rare. This is all the more remarkable because the chief god Othin (Woden) is represented as a wizard.

An example—not very satisfactory—of Cl. 2 is to be found in the first part of the *Reginsmál*. The story is also told by Snorri in his *Skaldskaparmál*, cap. 39. The gods Othin, Hoenir and Loki killed an otter and took it with them to the house of a certain Hreiðmarr, from whom they asked for quarters for the night. Hreiðmarr arrested them, said that the otter was his son, and demanded compensation. Loki was sent to get the ransom, and robbed a dwarf named Andvari of all his gold, including a ring upon which Andvari imposed a curse. The gods were then released; but Fáfnir, son of Hreiðmarr, demanded a share of the compensation from his father, and on his refusal murdered him. Then Reginn, another son, demanded his share; but Fáfnir refused and drove him away. Reginn attached himself to the youthful Sigurðr, and eventually induced him to kill Fáfnir, who had turned into a dragon and

[1] Non-heroic elements seem to have been more prominent in the lost Cyclic poems, if we may judge from the extant summaries. Prophecies apparently were frequent; and there seems to have been a tendency to bring out supernatural causes for events, e.g. (in the *Cypria*) the story of Peleus' marriage and the 'judgment of Paris'. Other non-heroic features will be noted in later chapters.

lay upon the gold. Reginn is said to be both a smith and a wizard, and Fáfnir also would seem to have something of the latter element in him. Perhaps the whole family were regarded as wizards.

Here also we may perhaps take the story of Weland (Völundr), which is told most fully in the *Völundarkviða*—how Völundr was captured by Níðuðr, hamstrung and forced to do goldsmith's work for him, and how he revenged himself upon Níðuðr's children and then escaped by flying. The same story is implied in *Deor*, while references to Weland as a smith occur in various English and German poems. His story therefore was widely known. He is of course primarily a smith; and there is no definite statement, as there is in Reginn's case, that he is also a wizard. But at all events he possesses abnormal powers.

For an instance of the prophetic variety we may refer to the dialogue poem *Grípisspá*, or 'Prophecy of Grípir'. Sigurðr comes to his mother's brother Grípir, who is endowed with knowledge of the future; and in answer to his questions Grípir prophesies to him in detail the course of his life. The poem is generally believed to be very late—perhaps twelfth century.

Examples of Cl. 3 are somewhat more frequent; but they are seldom connected with heroic stories, and it is sometimes doubtful to what times they relate. Such is the case with the story which forms the introduction to the *Grímnismál*. Othin prides himself on the prosperity of his foster-son Geirröðr, who is now king—perhaps of the island Gotland. Frigg says that he is inhospitable, a charge which Othin denies and determines to put to the test by visiting him in disguise. Frigg, however, sends her handmaid Fulla, who advises Geirröðr to arrest any unknown visitor whom dogs will not attack. Accordingly, when Othin arrives he is arrested. He gives his name as Grímnir, but refuses to answer any questions about himself. In order to find out who he is Geirröðr tortures him by setting him between two fires and keeping him without food for eight days. Then Othin recites the *Grímnismál*, thus gradually revealing his identity. When Geirröðr discovers who he is he springs up to release him; but in doing so he stumbles and falls upon his sword, and is killed.

Somewhat similar to this is the story of Gestumblindi in *Hervarar Saga*, cap. 10f.[1] Heiðrekr, king of the Goths, had a great reputation for wisdom; and he allowed accused men to ask him riddles as an alternative

[1] Transl. by Kershaw, *Stories and Ballads*, p. 113 ff. The name seems to owe its existence to a scribal error, originating in the acc. case, *Gest inn blinda*, 'the blind stranger'. Othin, on other occasions, when disguised, adopts the name Gestr.

to trial. This course was taken by a certain Gestumblindi, who really was Othin in disguise. Gestumblindi put to the king a long series of riddles, all of which he solved. At last he asked him what was the secret which Othin told Balder at his funeral. Then Heiðrekr recognised him and attacked him with his sword. Othin flew away in the shape of a falcon; but the king was slain by his slaves the same night. It is to be remarked that the saga in which this story occurs is of complex origin. In the early part of Heiðrekr's career the milieu appears to be that of the Viking Age. But his death is immediately followed by a story of the Heroic Age—that of the *Battle of the Goths and Huns* (cf. p. 26).

Perhaps the most interesting story of this class is one which is told in the *Ynglinga Saga*, cap. 17, 22. Vísburr, one of the earliest kings of the Swedes, divorced his wife and deprived her of the bridal gifts (*mundr*) which he had given her, and among which was a gold necklet. The divorced wife had recourse to witchcraft. When her sons were growing up she sent them to their father to demand the bridal gifts; but he refused. Then they declared that the necklet would prove the death of the noblest of his descendants. Again recourse was had to witchcraft, by means of which they were enabled to slay their father; while misfortune and death were brought about for his successor Dómaldi, their half-brother. Dómaldi's descendant in the fourth generation was a famous king named Agni, who defeated and slew the king of the Finns (Lapps) and carried off his daughter Skjalf. At her request he made a great funeral feast for her father. When he was drunk she told him to take care of his gold necklet; so he fastened it securely round his neck before he went to sleep. Then she attached a rope to it and her men hanged him thereby on a tree beneath which he was sleeping.

The way in which a heroic story may assume non-heroic character may be illustrated from the longer, and probably later, version of the story of Heðinn and Högni—found in the *Sörla þáttr*. In the shorter version—found in the *Skaldskaparmál*, cap. 49—Heðinn is a free agent; he raids Högni's land and carries off his daughter Hildr. In view of its resemblance to the German account (in *Kudrun*) this is in all probability the original form of the story.[1] But in the longer version Heðinn is the blind instrument of supernatural powers.[2] Freyja has promised Othin

[1] Not necessarily, of course, in all respects. The account given by Saxo, p. 195 ff. (158 ff.), which is earlier than the *Skaldskaparmál*, agrees with the *Sörla þáttr* in representing Heðinn and Högni as being friends before Hildr was carried off.

[2] A close parallel is to be found in the story of the 'judgment of Paris', which is introduced in the *Cypria* and later works in order to account for the abduction of Helen and the Trojan War.

to bring two mighty kings into everlasting strife; and all Heðinn's doings are instigated by the Valkyrie Göndul, whom Freyja sends to him from time to time. The change of motif may probably be traced in part to the Heðinn of *Helgakviða Hjörvarðssonar*—a different person—who at the instigation of an ogress pledges himself to marry his brother's betrothed.

The Teutonic examples of this category are few in number and, with one exception, their antiquity is doubtful. The story of Weland was certainly both ancient and widely known; but it stands rather by itself, since Weland is primarily a smith. The story of Heðinn and Högni was also ancient and widespread, but apparently only as a heroic story. It cannot be stated with confidence that the non-heroic elements in any of these stories, except that of Weland, date from the Heroic Age. And account must be taken of the fact that second sight and supernatural agencies and events of various kinds figure prominently in stories of the Viking Age.

In Greek also, as we have seen, there was a tendency for non-heroic elements to encroach. Yet a number of stories of non-heroic character are referred to in the *Iliad*; and we are not justified in assuming that such stories are necessarily later than the Heroic Age.

In Irish the case is similar but clearer. In late versions of heroic sagas, such as the *Fate of the Children of Uisnech* (cf. p. 50), non-heroic elements tend to become more prominent. But there can be no doubt that non-heroic stories frequently go back to the Heroic Age. Several such stories are known to have been included in the *Book of Druim Snechta*, which is believed to have been written in the first half of the eighth century, i.e. about the close of the Heroic Age (cf. p. 47 f.). In some stories, e.g. the *Destruction of Da Derga's Hall*, the milieu is so definitely heathen that it is difficult to date them even as late as the seventh century.

The difference then between heroic and non-heroic is not necessarily due to chronology. Moreover it is not due to geography, for heroic and non-heroic stories are found among the same peoples and in the same localities. We must seek for it therefore in the conditions and circumstances or in the circles in which the stories and poems were composed. Now we have seen that heroic stories are primarily concerned with adventure and with the prowess of heroes, whereas in non-heroic stories the interest lies in the doings of persons who are credited with the possession of supernatural or abnormal powers, or in the fortunes of those who have incurred the wrath—or gained the favour—of supernatural beings or transgressed laws or taboos of a vital character. Non-heroic stories have something in common with stories of the gods, such as will be discussed in Ch. IX, and also with stories of mythical characters which owe their origin to antiquarian speculation, like those of Prometheus and his family, and which will be treated in Ch. X. We do not know of any non-heroic stories—i.e. of any stories other than heroic—relating to the Greek, Teutonic, British or Irish Heroic Ages, which do not come within the description given above.

There are cases where one may hesitate whether to regard a story or poem as heroic or non-heroic. Such cases are chiefly stories or poems of a didactic character (Type C). The principle we have followed is to treat such a piece as heroic if the chief character occurs as a hero in other (heroic) stories; otherwise we treat it as non-heroic. Thus we should have taken the *Destruction of Da Derga's Hall* as a heroic story (Type C) if Conaire Mor had been familiar as a hero in other stories.

Sometimes heroic and non-heroic elements are found in the same story or poem. One element or the other may be merely incidental and derived from another story, as, for example, the references to Thamyris and Niobe in the *Iliad*. But there are cases where the combination of the two elements is more important. We have treated the Norse Trilogy—*Reginsmál*, *Fáfnismál* and *Sigrdrífumál*—as an example of Heroic Type C, because (1) the chief character is the famous hero Sigurðr, and (2) the substance is predominantly didactic. But the first part of the *Reginsmál* cannot be regarded as either heroic or didactic; it is an example of Non-heroic Type A, like *Math, son of Mathonwy*, though combined with poetry of Type B. This shows clearly that Heroic Type C and Non-heroic sometimes belong to the same milieu.

It is perhaps not an accident that poems belonging to this category were connected by the Greeks with Hesiod rather than with Homer. The *Instructions of Cheiron* were presumably a didactic poem; and though they may well have resembled the *Sigrdrífumál*, the central figure was probably Cheiron rather than Achilles. But it is not clear that the *Melampodeia* was didactic; it seems to have contained narrative as well as speeches. At all events the extant poems attributed to Hesiod have something in common with our category.

In a later chapter it will be seen that two distinct classes of poets or authors were to be found practically everywhere in early times. One class consisted of court-entertainers, who were occupied mainly with heroic poetry. The other class was concerned with didactic and speculative work in theology, moral and natural philosophy, and antiquarian lore, which was often combined with prophecy. In course of time this second class generally tended to encroach upon the sphere of the other. Especially was this the case among the Celtic peoples; in Ireland the *filid* ('seers'; cf. p. 97) became the chief repositories of heroic saga, while in Wales the two classes were completely merged.

It is to the second of these classes that we have in all probability to look for the origin of non-heroic poetry and saga, as well as for the didactic treatment of heroic stories. We do not mean, of course, to suggest that the two classes were at any time absolutely cut off from and uninfluenced by one another. Poets and saga-tellers of the first class were no doubt open from the beginning to non-heroic influence, e.g. in the form of antiquarian lore, as in Irish, or moral reflection, as in Anglo-Saxon, while those of the second class probably always drew their subjects largely from heroic stories or heroic life. But it would seem that in course of time—whether at the end of the Heroic Age or later—the influence of the non-heroic class usually tended to prevail over that of the heroic.

EXCURSUS I

MERLIN IN THE WORKS OF GEOFFREY OF MONMOUTH

In the preceding chapter we have made little use of Geoffrey's works, because we do not regard his evidence here as trustworthy any more than in other stories. There are, however, a number of scholars who, while they would not dissent from this estimate of Geoffrey's trustworthiness, regard the case of Merlin as somewhat apart from the rest—holding either that he was invented by Geoffrey, or at least that the existing poems and stories relating to him, together with his prophetic character, owe their origin to Geoffrey's influence. It is necessary therefore to go into this question in some detail.

It has been mentioned above (p. 108) that the Merlin of Geoffrey's *History*, including the *Prophecies* in Book VII, has little in common with the Myrddin of the Welsh poems beyond the fact that he is a prophet. He is identified with the boy Ambrosius of the *Historia Brittonum* (Nennius), cap. 41 f. (cf. p. 111 f.), and consequently belongs to an earlier period than the latter. His activities extend from the time of Vortigernus (Guorthigirnus) to the birth of Arthur, at which point he disappears from the story. There is no reference to the persons—Gwenddoleu, Rhydderch, Gwendydd and the rest—who figure in the poems. Nor is there much more resemblance in the prophecies themselves. The coming of Cadwaladr and Cynan is once referred to (VII. 3)—as also in the *Vita* (967 f.)—but this is a regular feature of Welsh predictive poetry, which will require notice in Ch. XV; it is by no means confined to the Myrddin poems. In general the prophecies in the *History*, so far as they are specific at all, relate either to the early history of the Britons, from the fifth to the seventh centuries, or to English history of Geoffrey's own time, whereas Myrddin's prophecies relate as a rule to Welsh history of the twelfth century.

The prophecies in the *Vita*[1] are like those in the *History* and show no more resemblance than they do to the prophecies in the Myrddin poems. But with the story itself the case is different. Merlin is made to say in his retrospect (982 ff.) that he remembers the time of Vortigern, and in another passage (681 ff.) he speaks of his prophecies to that king —thus connecting the *Vita* with the *History*—but he has lived on into a later age; even Arthur himself now belongs to the past (929 ff., 1122 ff.). The actual personnel of the story is that of the Myrddin poems. Merlin, who is said to be king of Dyfed (19 ff.), goes to war, along with Peredurus, prince of Gwynedd, and Rodarchus, king of the Cumbri, against Guennolous, king of Scotland. The Scots are defeated, but Merlin's mind gives way at seeing the slaughter, and especially because of the fall of three brothers—apparently his own; and soon afterwards he betakes himself to the woods. Rodarchus, who is married to Ganieda, Merlin's sister, sends a minstrel, who sings of the grief of Ganieda and of Guendoloena, Merlin's wife, and thus persuades him to come back (165 ff.). He laughs when he sees Rodarchus taking a leaf out of Ganieda's hair, and when asked why he does so explains that she had been among the bushes with a lover (254 ff.). The queen, in order to discredit the charge, gets Merlin to prophesy the death of a certain boy, whom she brings before him in three different disguises. Merlin prophesies three different forms of death—first by falling from a rock, then by dying in a tree, and then in a river—and the king then believes in his wife's innocence (303 ff.). Merlin insists on going back to the woods, and gives his wife leave to marry again; but on the wedding day he comes and kills the bridegroom (347 ff.). Ganieda builds him a house in the woods and, strangely enough, often goes to see him. He prophesies

[1] The references are to the edition by J. J. Parry, *The Vita Merlini*, in the *University of Illinois Studies in Language and Literature*, X (1925).

to her the death of Rodarchus and the course of British and English history, including the Danish and Norman invasions (565 ff.). Ganieda on her return home finds her husband dead, and buries him. Then she decides to go and live with her brother in the woods (689 ff.). Telgesinus comes to see Merlin, and discourses on natural history (732 ff.). Merlin replies with a long retrospect of British history (958 ff.). A new spring now bursts out. Merlin drinks of it and is cured of his madness (1136 ff.). His subjects ask him to return to the throne, but he refuses on the ground of age (1259 ff.). Further discourses follow, and another madman is cured (1292 ff.). Finally Ganieda prophesies certain events in the reign of Stephen (1469 ff.). The poem concludes with a remark by Merlin that the spirit seems to have passed from him to her (1521 ff.).

It is obvious that in this story Rodarchus, Guennolous, Ganieda and Telgesinus correspond to the Rhydderch, Gwenddoleu, Gwendydd and Taliesin of the poems respectively, and Peredurus to the Peredur of the *Triads*. Moreover the *Calidonis silua*, where Merlin has gone to live, is clearly the *Coed Celyddon* (*Keliton*) of *BBC*. XVII. The apple-trees are mentioned in the *Vita* (90 ff.), as well as in the latter poem. But there are important differences. Gwenddoleu, whom Myrddin is constantly calling to mind as his generous lord, is only once mentioned in the *Vita*—and then as an enemy; it is not even stated that he was killed in the battle. On the other hand Merlin is provided with a wife—unknown to the Welsh poems—whose name (Guendoloena) bears a suspicious resemblance to his. Again, Myrddin in the Welsh poems frequently refers to Rhydderch; and in *RBH*. I. 8 he foretells his death to Gwendydd, as in the *Vita* (596, 684). But it is not stated that Gwendydd is his wife; and, further, neither the poems nor the *Triads* represent him as taking part in the battle of Arderydd. The *Vita* does not name the battle, and gives no hint that Merlin has killed Ganieda's son; while the Welsh poems know nothing of Myrddin's healing or of his ceasing to prophesy. On the contrary in *RBH*. II he prophesies in his grave. It may be added that the poems (*RBH*. I and II) mention Myrddin's father, Morfryn; but in the *Vita* there is no reference to such a person—necessarily, of course, since in the *History* (VI. 17 f.) Merlin is said to have had no human father.

Similar resemblances are to be found between the *Vita* and the Glasgow records discussed on p. 108 ff. Thus, for example, the prophecy of the king's death, and the incidents of the faithless queen and the leaf and of the triple death occur in both; but it is to be observed that the two latter incidents are related of different persons. In the *Vita* the faithless queen is Rodarchus' wife and Merlin's own sister; while the triple death is told not of Merlin himself, but of another man. Nothing is said of Merlin's own death; nor is there any mention of the name Lailoken, or of St Kentigern.

It is generally agreed that Geoffrey borrowed from the Glasgow records. But many scholars hold that the Welsh poems are derived from the *Vita*, not vice versa. This means of course that there is no connection between the poems and the Glasgow records except through the *Vita*; and consequently any connection between the names *Llallogan* (*Llallawc*) and *Lailoken* (*Laloecen*) is impossible. Lailoken was not the same man as Merlin, though Geoffrey transferred incidents from his story to the *Vita*.

The view under consideration is obviously open to two very serious objections: (1) In deriving his prophet from Carmarthen (Caerfyrddin, *Hist.* VI. 17) Geoffrey must have been aware of the existence of a Welsh prophet called Myrddin. (2) The story is connected with a large body of Welsh tradition, some elements of which are recorded in the *Annales Cambriae*, which were compiled c. 960, or earlier (cf. p. 146 ff.). The poems frequently allude to these traditions, especially to the famous battle of Arderydd, and their allusions are never at variance with what we know of them from other sources. Geoffrey's allusions are much less frequent and precise. Thus he mentions the battle, but neither gives it a name nor indicates where it was fought. Sometimes his statements are definitely in conflict with tradition, e.g. when he makes Peredurus a prince of Gwynedd and Guennolous a king of Scotland (*Albania*)—presumably the old kingdom of Alban, since Rodarchus is (correctly) represented as king of the Cumbri. We may add that the forms of the names are correctly given in the poems, whereas in the *Vita* they are often corrupt.

To graft a fictitious story upon this body of tradition, making all the corrections involved, would have required a genius as constructive as Geoffrey himself. But why should the precise be derived from the vague and the correct from the incorrect? And why should the authors of the poems be at such trouble to represent Myrddin's grief for his lord Gwenddoleu, when this person is mentioned only once—and then as an enemy—in the original?

So far as we are aware, this extreme view has not been endorsed by any scholars who have made a study of the Welsh evidence—indeed we do not think this would be possible—though it is expressed not unfrequently by those whose interest lies exclusively in Geoffrey and the Romances. There is, however, a modified form of the same theory which has received such endorsement, and consequently deserves somewhat more consideration. According to this view[1] the poems which now survive are derived from the *Vita*, but there were earlier poems or stories relating to Myrddin, now lost, to which Geoffrey had access. It is due to these also that the names, perhaps too the relationships of the characters, appear in a more correct form in the Welsh poems than in the *Vita*. Myrddin was known previously, but perhaps not as a prophet.

We cannot assent to the reservation in the last sentence. If Myrddin was not already a prophet, what reason had Geoffrey for identifying him with the prophetic boy Ambrosius, whom he took over from the *Historia Brittonum* (cf. p. 123)? The *History* indeed reveals no knowledge of Myrddin and his story except the fact that he was a prophet. For the rest, we do not doubt that, when he wrote the *Vita*, Geoffrey had acquired some knowledge of a story of Myrddin; and he may also have known some poems which are now lost. At all events he had learned from somewhere that one of the enemies of Gwenddoleu was Peredur[2]—who happens not to be mentioned in any of the Myrddin poems now existing. But the theory that the existing poems are later than and derived from the *Vita* needs careful examination.

First, it may be noted that the reference to the apple-trees in the *Vita*, 90 ff., indicates a literary relationship with the *Afallenau* (*BBC*. XVII). Next, there can be little doubt of a similar relationship between *RBH*. I and Merlin's prophecy in the *Vita*, 580 ff. Both prophecies are addressed to the prophet's sister. Both foretell the death of Rhydderch, and in both cases this prophecy is followed by others which cover several centuries of history, though the details have nothing in common. Again, it can hardly be an accident that conversations between Myrddin and Taliesin occur both in *BBC*. I and in the *Vita*, though here also the speeches have nothing in common.

Against these parallels we have to set a striking contrast in the representation of the prophet and in the general character of the works. In the Welsh poems we have the picture of an unhappy and deranged prophet, constantly lamenting for his lord Gwenddoleu, and haunted by the ghosts of his old comrades. The dominant characteristics of the

[1] For a full statement of this view see F. Lot, *Annales de Bretagne*, XV. 505 ff. (cf. also p. 520 ff.).

[2] It is rightly pointed out by Lot, *op. cit.* p. 530, that the term *Largus* applied to Rodarchus in his epitaph in the *Vita* (730) is a translation of *hael*. But the latter epithet is applied to Rhydderch in *RBH*. I. 4 ff., as well as in the *Triads*.

poems are emotion and pathos. In the *Vita* also the prophet is deranged—until his cure, near the end of the story—but he delights in his sylvan Arcadia, which is depicted as seen through the eyes of a sophisticated townsman. Gwenddoleu is mentioned only once, and then as his enemy. As a whole the *Vita* is a typical production of a literary dilettante who is writing in a more or less light-hearted vein, but at the same time is anxious to display his learning. It would be nothing remarkable if such a writer had borrowed the incidents and motifs noted above from the Welsh poems—with which he need not have had more than a very superficial acquaintance. But it would be one of the strangest freaks in literary history if these poems owed their existence to such a work as the *Vita*.

Yet in spite of this it is contended by some scholars that these poems must be derived from the *Vita*, because they contain references to events later than the date of its composition. Thus, *RBH.* I contains a number of (obscure) references to events which may be later than 1154, while somewhat clearer references to such events occur in the longer texts of the *Afallenau* (cf. p. 106)—though not in *BBC.* XVII.[1] Still more definite references to later events are to be found in other Myrddin poems, especially *BBC.* XVIII and *RBH.* II. There can be no doubt therefore that in their present form some of these poems are later than the *Vita*.

It is to be remembered, however, that the Myrddin poems are works of Type B, i.e. speeches in character, and that the speaker—or chief speaker—is a prophet. We have to distinguish between two different elements in each case, one of which is concerned with the prophet himself and his circumstances, and the other with the subjects of his prophecies. The most characteristic feature of the poems is that these two elements are combined in a peculiar way. A stanza dealing with the first element may be followed by one dealing with the second; and sometimes both elements occur in the same stanza.

It is with the first element—which supplies what we may call the framework of the poems—that we are concerned here. If it could be shown that the poems were fixed and invariable from the time of their first composition, we should be justified in inferring a date for the framework from the prophecies. But this is not the case. Of the *Afallenau*, as we have seen (p. 106), there are three texts. One of these (*BBC.* XVII) contains ten stanzas, the others twenty-two or twenty-

[1] We cannot assent to the interpretation of *BBC.* XVII. 3 given in *Annales de Bretagne*, XV. 507.

three; and there is hardly any agreement between the shorter and the longer texts in the order of the ten stanzas which are common to them all. The references to times later than the appearance of the *Vita* occur only in stanzas which are wanting in the *BBC.* text. Again, the text of *RBH.* I is in great disorder. There are obvious omissions and transpositions of stanzas; and the references in the latter part of the poem are mostly obscure.

There can be no doubt that prophecies like those of the *Afallenau* were used for political purposes—e.g. to advance the interests of an aspiring prince, or to rouse up opposition to the English—and it would seem that additions were made to them from time to time. But we have no reason for supposing that the genus was new—or the framework in which the prophecies are set.

Giraldus Cambrensis in his *Descriptio Kambriae*, I. 16, clearly regards *Merlinus Siluester* as belonging to the *Awenithion*, or 'persons inspired', *quasi mente ductos*, of whom, he says, there are a good number in Wales, and whose ecstasies he describes. It is evident from his account that these persons were very similar to the prophets whom we find among other barbaric peoples. In later chapters we shall have occasion to notice the influence which they possessed in stirring up popular feeling. It would be absurd to suppose that this class owed their origin to the literary activities of Geoffrey of Monmouth.

The same writer in his work *De Vaticiniis*,[1] of which only the opening has been preserved, again mentions *Merlinus Siluester*, whom he here calls also *Celidonius* and whom he distinguishes, as elsewhere (cf. p. 111), from Merlinus Ambrosius. He says that the former "has remained little known down to our times, not yet having got rid of his *Britannica barbaries*".[2] This means that he was known only in Welsh, as appears from what follows. A little later he says: "Until now it was only by report that Celidonius Siluester was famous everywhere. But the memory of his prophecies had been preserved (i.e. his prophecies had been preserved by memory) by the British 'bards', as they call their poets, orally among very many, but in writing among very few". Giraldus goes on to say that he sought throughout Wales for a copy of the prophecies, and at length found one "in a most remote district of Gwynedd which is called Lein (Lleyn)". It had been put away long ago, and had been treated with a kind of reverence. He set to work to translate

[1] Rolls Series, Vol. v, p. 401.

[2] Nondum...Britannicam exutus barbariem usque ad haec tempora latuit parum agnitus.

it with the help of men who knew the British language. Again a little later he observes that in these works, as in others, the bardic profession has shown itself to be malicious and addicted to falsification, and has added to the true (prophecies) many things of its own in the form of prophecies.[1]

It is incomprehensible to us how this passage can have been understood to apply to any works derived from Geoffrey's *Vita Merlini*. The *Vita* was written between 1148 and 1154. Giraldus discovered the MS. at Nevin during his journey through Wales with Archbishop Baldwin, in 1188,[2] and he says that the prophecies which it contained were carried on by oral tradition by a large number of bards. It has already been mentioned (p. 107) that a stanza in *RBH*. II is quoted by the same writer (*Itin. Kambriae*, I. 6) as a prophecy of *Merlinus Siluester*; he says that the Welsh were discouraged by it in their resistance to Henry II. This happened in 1162, near Newport, at the other end of Wales.

Whether Giraldus knew the *Vita Merlini* or not, it is plain that what he means by *Merlinus Siluester* or *Celidonius* in all the passages cited above is a traditional character, of whom saga in some form or other was current, and who was regarded as the author of a body of prophetic poetry which was widely known among the bards by oral tradition, but rarely committed to writing. His words also show that additions were made to these prophecies; but that as a whole this body of literature was by no means of recent origin. This is indicated not only by the words *libellum... ab antiquo repositum*, but also by such expressions as *usque ad haec tempora latuit*, and *memoria retenta fuerat*. It is only the name *Merlinus* which Giraldus has taken from Geoffrey. The works which he means are the Myrddin poems, including no doubt some of those which have come down to us, but also others which are now lost.

We have no hesitation therefore in subscribing to the view that the *Vita* is derived from the Welsh poems, not vice versa. The story of Geoffrey's activities now becomes clear enough.[3] We have to distinguish two phases, separated from one another by many years. In the earlier phase Geoffrey had learnt of the existence of prophetic poetry in Wales, and that it was attributed to a prophet called Myrddin, whose name he changed into *Merlinus*. He did not know who Myrddin was, but con-

[1] Sicut in aliis, sic in istis bardorum ars inuida, naturam adulterans, multa de suis tamquam prophetica ueris adiecit.

[2] *Itin. Kambriae*, II. 6.

[3] Cf. Parry, *The Vita Merlini*, p. 16.

jecturally identified him with the boy Ambrosius in the *Hist. Britt.* cap. 41 f., who also was a prophet. As he was ignorant of Welsh, his knowledge of the contents of the prophecies was limited to a very few details, such as the coming of Cadwaladr and Cynan; but he was clever enough to see that in these prophecies he had struck a vein which might be made to appeal to the reading public in England. This phase is represented by the Merlin of the *History*, including the *Prophecies* in Book VII.

Later, when he came to write the *Vita Merlini*, Geoffrey had found out a good deal more about Myrddin. He had learnt that there was a poem which consisted of a dialogue between Myrddin and Taliesin; but of the contents of this he could make nothing—as one might expect. He had also discovered the poem consisting of the dialogue between Myrddin and Gwendydd; from which he got the prophecy of the death of Rhydderch and the idea of following it up with a retrospect of history in the form of prophecy. He had also got to know something of the *Afallenau*, from which is derived not only the specific reference in the *Vita* (90 ff.), but also, to some extent at least, the general setting of this work. Some other information must have reached him, probably in the form of a story, from which he got the name *Peredurus*. The Lailoken story also, from which he derived certain incidents (cf. p. 124 f.), must have been known to him in some form or other. These incidents are not to be regarded as extraneous matter, like the quotations from Isidore, of which the speeches in the *Vita* are largely composed; for there is no reason for doubting that Lailoken and Myrddin were the same person from the beginning (cf. p. 110 f.). We have seen that the incident of the vision, which is not mentioned by Geoffrey, is recorded by Giraldus (cf. p. 111 f.) as happening to *Merlinus Siluester*, i.e. Myrddin. We do not know whether the name *Myrddin* occurred either in Giraldus' sources or in Geoffrey's; but both writers evidently knew that the person credited with these experiences was Myrddin.

It must have become plain to Geoffrey, when he got all this new information, that he had made a bad shot in identifying Myrddin with the boy Ambrosius. But, not being willing to go back upon this, he made his hero live on into a new age, i.e. into the age to which tradition assigned him. The earlier work involved him also in geographical difficulties. In the *History* Merlin had belonged to Dyfed; and so in the *Vita* Geoffrey makes him king of Dyfed. But he was probably conscious of the fact that the actual scene of the story, the *Calidonis Silua*, lay in the south of Scotland. Hence the geographical indications are—necessarily—given as vaguely as possible.

Since Geoffrey evidently had some source or sources of information which are now lost, it is not impossible that the *Vita* may contain elements of fact or ancient tradition even where confirmatory evidence from other sources is wanting. Thus it is possible that Rhydderch did take part in the battle against Gwenddoleu, and again that Gwendydd was the wife of this king—although Jocelin gives a different name to his queen. But we do not feel inclined to attach any importance to such evidence.

CHAPTER VII

HISTORICAL ELEMENTS IN STORIES OF THE HEROIC AGE

THERE is no doubt that many of the persons and events celebrated in stories of the Teutonic, British and Irish Heroic Ages are historical. Their existence is proved by contemporary documents or monuments. But there are many other cases where no such evidence is available. The greater part of the Irish Heroic Age is prehistoric; and the same is true of the whole of the Greek Heroic Age. Even in the Teutonic and the British Heroic Ages the great majority of the persons and events are not mentioned in contemporary records. As to the historicity of these much difference of opinion exists. Half a century ago it was generally believed that heroic poetry and saga were derived from mythology; and consequently there was a tendency to regard as mythological all persons and events which could not be identified from historical records. Now opinion has greatly changed; but widely divergent views are still held.

It is not to be regarded as an unfortunate accident that so small a proportion of the matter contained in heroic tradition can be verified from historical records. In later chapters we shall see that the Heroic Age is a widespread phenomenon in the history of society; but that it is rarely or never accompanied by the keeping of such records. The most the historian can hope for is that within or in the neighbourhood of a heroic society there may be communities or individuals in a different phase of civilisation, to which the keeping of historical records is natural, and that information relating to the heroic society may be preserved thereby.

The evidence available for demonstrating the existence of historical elements in heroic stories may conveniently be classified as follows:

(*a*) Contemporary native historical records.

(*b*) Foreign historical records. This evidence is valid even when not strictly contemporary, provided that it can be shown to be free from the influence of the heroic tradition.

(*c*) The existence of independent traditions in different regions.

(*d*) The existence of independent traditions in the same region.

(*e*) The consistency of heroic tradition.

The first two of these stand, of course, apart from the rest. But the evidence of (*c*) may be almost as good if it can be shown that the two traditions have been independent from the beginning. But if the interruption of communication between the two regions has not taken place until long after the time to which the stories relate, the value of the evidence is proportionately reduced. The evidence of (*d*)—the existence of a non-heroic (ecclesiastical or other) tradition beside the heroic in the same region—can only be used with great caution; for there are many openings for the influence of the latter upon the former. Yet this class of evidence may have a certain value, e.g. when there are divergences in details. Even the existence of a consistent heroic tradition (*e*) by itself, without supplementary evidence, may be not without value, especially if it has wide ramifications. This may perhaps best be appreciated by a comparison of heroic tradition with the stories of the gods current in the same community.

In addition to the above there are three other classes of evidence which sometimes deserve consideration:

(*f*) Archaeological evidence can demonstrate the existence of the conditions required by a heroic story at a given place and time, though it can supply no names, unless writing is found. The excavations at Troy have contributed materially to a change of view as to the story of the *Iliad*, though they have yielded no evidence in regard to the names of the persons who lived and fought there. Evidence for obsolete political geography may also be taken into account in this connection.

(*g*) The use of a heroic name, if it is of an unfamiliar type, may sometimes be taken as evidence that a heroic story was known at the time. Thus when we find a bishop at Dorchester in the latter part of the seventh century bearing the name *Aetla*, which is not of English origin, we may infer that stories relating to Attila were current in England about the middle of that century or earlier.

(*h*) The occurrence of heroic names in place-names is the least secure form of evidence, owing to the almost universal prevalence of antiquarian speculation. One may refer, e.g., to the numerous examples of Arthur's name in various parts of this country, and the Ossianic place-names in Scotland. Yet place-names may occasionally preserve a true historical record, especially when a hero's name has been forgotten long ago—perhaps through a change of nationality in the district. A probable case of this kind is the preservation of the name *Gwenddoleu* in *Carwinley* (cf. p. 111, note); for the district came into English hands doubtless in the early part of the seventh century.

We will take the Teutonic evidence first, since on the whole this seems to be the most satisfactory. It is doubtful, however, whether there is any evidence here which properly comes under (*a*). Information bearing upon our subject occurs in Latin works written under Teutonic government before the end of the Heroic Age, and among the writers were men of Teutonic nationality like Jordanes; yet the sources of the latter, except for ancient times, appear to have been Roman, and the evidence as a whole can hardly be separated from that which naturally comes under (*b*). Moreover, though the Teutonic peoples of the Heroic Age were acquainted with the art of writing, and inscriptions containing personal names are not very rare in the North, none of these names can be identified with certainty with characters of heroic stories.

Evidence from Roman (Latin and Greek) sources (*b*) is comparatively abundant and usually allows us to identify with confidence at least one character in each of those heroic stories which relate to the more southern of the Teutonic peoples. Thus we know from strictly contemporary authorities that Ermenrichus (Eormenric, Jörmunrekr, Ermenrich), king of the Goths, died about 370, Gunthaharius (Guthhere, Gunnarr, Gunther), king of the Burgundians, in 437, Attila (Aetla, Atli, Etzel), king of the Huns, in 453, and Theodericus (Theodric, Þjóðrekr, Dietrich), king of the Ostrogoths, in 526; and it is from these and other dates that we are able to determine the times to which the heroic stories relate.

For stories dealing with the more northern peoples such evidence is naturally more difficult to obtain; for these peoples lay practically beyond the horizon of the Roman historians. In the story of *Beowulf*, however, there is one clear case. The poem frequently mentions the hero's uncle, Hygelac, king of the Geatas, and refers more than once to a disastrous expedition against the Franks and Frisians, in which he lost his life. Now this expedition is recorded by Gregory of Tours, *Hist. Franc.* III. 3, and later Frankish documents. The date was evidently about 520–530, i.e. some ten or fifteen years before Gregory was born. It is clear, however, that his information was derived from contemporary Frankish sources and not from any (Scandinavian or other) heroic poem.

A great deal more evidence comes under (*c*)—i.e. from a comparison of the heroic traditions of different Teutonic peoples. The English poems, especially *Beowulf* and *Widsith*, record the names of many Northern princes, and the former gives a detailed account of the royal families of the Danes, the Geatas and the Swedes. Now many of these persons, including the Danish and Swedish princes—though not those of the Geatas—are mentioned also in early Norse and Danish authorities; and in general—though with noteworthy exceptions—they bear the same relationship to one another as in *Beowulf*.

For the purpose of comparison it may be of interest to give the genealogy of the Danish royal family (Scyldingas, Skjöldungar) as it is found in *Beowulf* and in the Northern records. The genealogy in *Beowulf* is as follows:

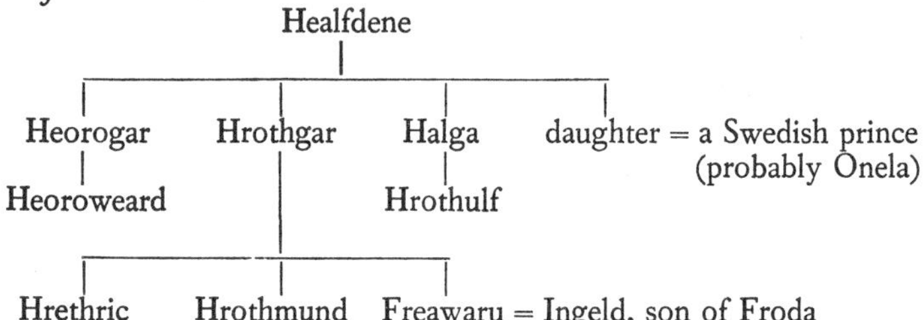

Healfdene, Heorogar, and apparently Halga also, are dead. The reigning kings are Hrothgar, who is very old, and Hrothulf, son of one of his brothers (probably Halga, though this is not actually stated). Hrethric and Hrothmund are very young. The name of Healfdene's daughter and part of her husband's name are lost through a lacuna in the MS. Froda and Ingeld belong to a people or dynasty called Heathobeardan. They are not Danes.

Hrothgar's hall is called Heorot; but no localities are mentioned.

In Northern records the genealogy is as follows:

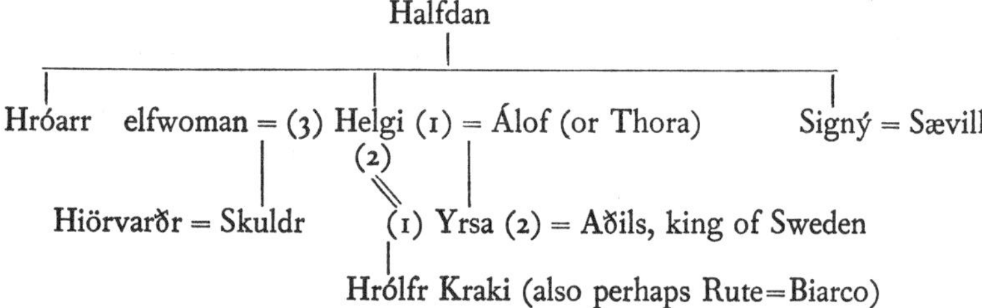

The Northern versions of the story differ a good deal from one another. Names from Saxo are given in brackets. It will be seen that there are no names corresponding to Heorogar, Hrethric, Hrothmund, or Freawaru. The names Hróarr, Helgi, Hrólfr and Hiörvarðr correspond regularly to Hrothgar, Halga, Hrothulf and Heoroweard; but here Hiörvarðr is a stranger. Fróði and Ingjaldr are kings of the Danes, and never appear in the relationship to the above which is indicated in *Beowulf*. In Saxo they belong to a much later period. In other records Fróði is the name of Halfdan's father or brother.

Leire, in Denmark, is always the scene of the story.

The ancestry of Healfdene (Halfdan) has nothing in common in the two traditions except the eponymous Scyld (Skjöldr), who is his grandfather in *Beowulf*, but in the Scandinavian versions is separated from him by a varying but greater number of generations.

It is instructive to notice that the chief characters are the same and stand in the same relationships to one another in the two traditions, while the minor characters either appear only in one tradition, or stand in different relationships. The story of incest, however—between Helgi and his daughter—can hardly be reconciled with the picture of the family given in *Beowulf*, where Hrothulf (Hrólfr) is evidently much older than the sons of Hrothgar.

It is not permissible to suppose that the story of these persons was borrowed by English poetry from Northern sources, or vice versa, in late times. Had that been the case, the forms of the names would have resembled one another more closely than they do. There would have been traces of Northern phonetic change in the names given in the English poems, or vice versa—just as in records of the ninth century we find similar Northern names represented in English works in true Northern form. The two languages had without doubt begun to show marked divergences from one another before the end of the sixth century; and the linguistic evidence clearly indicates that these names were preserved by tradition independently in the two languages from that period. This conclusion accords with the fact that we have very little evidence for any knowledge of Northern lands or persons of Northern nationality in England between the *Beowulf* story and the ninth century.[1]

But if these persons and their adventures were known both in England and in the North in the sixth century, the evidence is practically equivalent to a contemporary record; for several of them belong to a younger generation than Hygelac, whose death took place not earlier than c. 520–530, as we have seen. It is the general view therefore of all

[1] A Danish king named Ongendus in mentioned by Alcuin, *Vita Willebrordi*, cap. 9; but it is in connection with the saint's missionary journeys in the region about the mouth of the Elbe—early in the eighth century. Bede, *Hist. Eccl.* v. 9, speaks of the *Danai* as one of the heathen peoples of 'Germany', whom the English missionaries set out to evangelise; but the spelling suggests that the name was unfamiliar to him. For a reference by the same author to communication with 'Thyle' (perhaps Norway) see Chadwick, *Origin of the English Nation*, p. 19.

who have written on the subject in recent years that these persons are to be regarded as historical, though reservations are sometimes made in certain cases, especially that of the hero Beowulf himself.[1] Further, in cases where English and Northern tradition differs in regard to the position and relationships of various persons, the general tendency is to follow the English authorities, as being by several centuries the earlier. We have no doubt that these views are substantially correct.

The same remarks apply in general to other stories which are preserved in both English and Northern tradition. It is to be observed, however, that most of them seem to relate to earlier times than the *Beowulf* story. Thus the story of the English kings Wermund and Offa, which is preserved in both English and Danish tradition, relates to the fourth century according to the genealogies; while various other stories probably belong to the fifth century. In such cases the existence of the double tradition cannot be said to be equivalent to a contemporary record, though it carries the evidence back to within a century or two of the heroes. Much the same may be said with regard to stories which are preserved in both Scandinavian and German tradition, though it is less clear at what date these traditions became independent of one another. For the purpose of comparative study it may be of interest to set out the family relations of the heroes who figure in the most famous of these stories.

In the *Nibelungenlied* the royal family of the Burgundians is as follows:

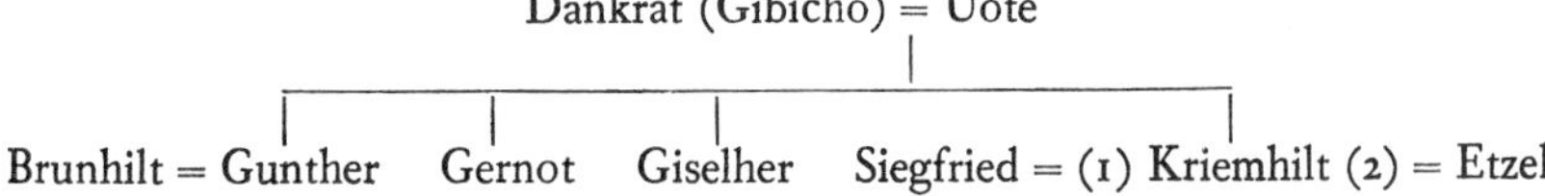

Dankrat is the name of the father in the *Nibelungenlied*, but Gibicho in *Waltharius Manu Fortis*, and similar forms in other sources.

Apart from the family itself the most important character in the story is Hagen, a vassal of the kings but apparently not related to them. The death of the three brothers and of Hagen at the hands of the Huns is due to Kriemhilt, who desires to exact vengeance for the murder of Siegfried, not to Etzel, who is opposed to it. The story ends with the slaying of Kriemhilt by Hildebrand, the follower of Dietrich. Etzel remains alive.

The scene of the first part of the story is laid at Worms. Siegfried

[1] Such cases will be noticed in the next chapter.

comes from the lower Rhine—Xanten. The scene of the second part is laid in the land of the Huns, on the Danube.

In the Norse records the family is as follows:

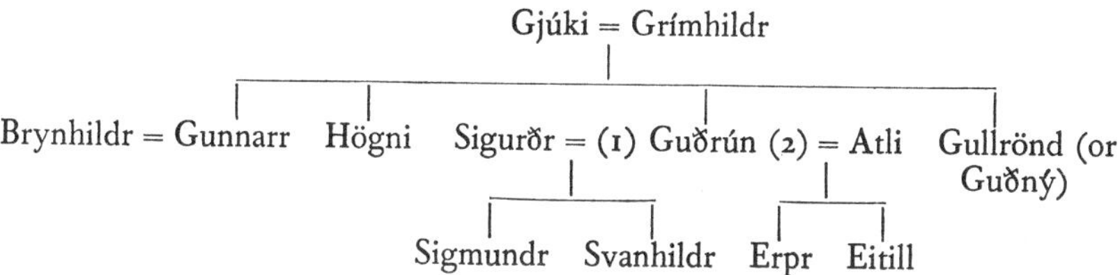

Here the names Gjúki, Gunnarr, Brynhildr, Högni, Sigurðr and Atli correspond to Gibicho, Gunther, Brunhilt, Hagen, Siegfried and Etzel respectively. The name Grímhildr can hardly be dissociated from Kriemhilt, but the place of the latter in the story is taken by Guðrún. Gullrönd appears only in *Guðrúnarkviða I*, Guðný in the *Skaldskaparmál*. In *Guðrúnarkviða I* Gjúki has a sister called Gjaflaug. In the *Atlamál* Gunnarr has a second wife called Glaumvör, while Högni has a wife called Kostbera and a son called Hniflungr. Högni is always a brother of Gunnarr and Guðrún. Gotthormr, the actual slayer of Sigurðr, is according to some authorities a stepson of Gjúki. The death of Gunnarr and Högni is due to Atli, not to Guðrún, who tries to save them. She avenges her brothers by killing her sons Erpr and Eitill, and giving their flesh to Atli (their father) to eat, and then by murdering Atli himself. She survives, and eventually marries a third husband called Jónakr.

The scene of the first part of the story is 'to the south of the Rhine'. Sigurðr comes from Denmark. The nationality of Gunnarr and his family is practically forgotten. The name 'Burgundian' occurs only once. They are sometimes called 'Goths', more frequently Hniflungar or Gjúkungar. The scene of the second part of the story is laid in the land of the Huns, which is sometimes regarded as over the sea. Northern features, e.g. glaciers, sometimes occur in the topography.

In this story again it will be seen that the chief characters and their relationships to one another are in general the same in both the German and the Norse traditions—with the exception that in the latter Högni is represented as a member of the family. There is also a difference in the name of the wife of Sigurðr and Atli. In the minor characters there is a good deal of variation between the two traditions, just as in the story of the Scyldingas.

As regards the relationship between the two traditions there can be no doubt that the story went to the North from Germany. The forms of the names show that this must have taken place by the eighth century, and probably not later than the seventh. It will be seen that the local and national names are much better preserved in the German tradition than in the Norse, although the latter has come down to us in earlier works.

This story is not found in English sources. Gifeca and Guthhere are, however, mentioned in *Widsith* as kings of the Burgundians, while Guthhere and Hagena appear in the *Waldhere* fragments, without any indication of the nature of the relationship existing between them. It has already been mentioned that Atli (Etzel) and Gunnarr (Gunther) are well-known historical characters. The latter was slain by the Huns in 437. Gundobad, who became king of the Burgundians in 474, in his *Lex Burdungionum* refers to Gibica, Godomares, Gislaharius and Gundaharius among his predecessors.

There are other stories for which no historical evidence is available and for which we are entirely, or almost entirely, dependent on a comparative study of the traditions. Such is the case, for example, with the story of Heðinn and Högni, which was apparently one of the most widely known of all the Teutonic heroic stories.

As the evidence under (*b*) and (*c*) is comparatively abundant, it is hardly necessary to enter into (*d*), which is rather doubtful, except in Norse. In regard to (*e*) it may be said that in general heroic tradition is consistent—more so of course within each of the areas than between one area and another, as in the examples given above. Discrepancies and anachronisms, however, are not rare, especially in late works. Instances will be noticed in the following chapter.

As regards (*f*) much valuable evidence is afforded by the English poems, e.g. with respect to weapons and heathen rites. In particular it may be noted that swords are frequently described as damascened. Many such swords have been found in the peat bogs of Denmark and Sleswick, dating from the fourth and following centuries; but no examples earlier than the Viking Age have been discovered in this country, so far as we are aware.

Further, the political geography of the stories is in general that of the times to which they relate. This again is most true in the case of the English poems, whereas in Norse records the names of ancient peoples tend to disappear or become confused. The catalogues of *Widsith* show a geography, which—excluding of course the Biblical additions—goes back to the fifth century, and in some items apparently still earlier; and there can hardly be any doubt that, at least in the main, these catalogues are derived from heroic stories.

The value of this evidence may be illustrated by one or two examples. The story of Heðinn and Högni was known in England, Germany and the North; but it is one of the cases for which no strictly historical evidence is available.[1] The geography of the different traditions of the story varies greatly. The German account places Hagen in Ireland and Hetel in Denmark. In the Norse records the story begins apparently in the Baltic and ends in the Orkneys, while Saxo speaks only of Denmark and the Baltic. But *Widsith*, which is older by several centuries than any of the other authorities, states that Hagena (Högni) was king of the Holmryge, a people who are known to have occupied the coast of Pomerania in early times.[2] Now if, as we may presume, *Widsith* derived this information from the story—naturally a much earlier form of the story than any of those which survive—it would seem that the story came into existence while the Holmryge were still known. But there can hardly be any doubt that the whole of eastern Germany had become Slavonic before the end of the fifth century, and that the only Holmryge or Rugi who then remained were those who had settled in Austria. The early disappearance of the nation is probably responsible for the varying geography of the existing forms of the story.

Another case for which no historical evidence is available is that of the *Battle of the Goths and Huns*. This story is preserved only in Norse, but *Widsith* refers to several of the characters. Among other localities, which cannot be identified, the Norse poem gives the name of the Dnieper—which was possibly misunderstood—and also the name Myrkviðr, which in other Norse heroic poems is applied to a forest region in the land of the Huns.[3] But *Widsith* (119 ff.), referring to the same battle, says that the Goths were defending their ancient home against the Huns 'around the forest of the Vistula'. It is clear then that the scene of the story was laid in Poland—perhaps also in the Ukraine. In point of fact this region was the ancient home of the Goths; but they had disappeared from it before the middle of the fifth century at the

[1] For the reference in *Deor* cf. p. 25 f.

[2] Cf. Tacitus, *Germ.* 43; Jordanes, *Get.* 4. In the former they are called Rugii, in the latter Ulmerugi (for *Holm-*). Their name survives in Rügenwalde and probably in Rügen.

[3] It is worth noting that in a fragment of verse quoted in the saga, just before the poem, Heiðrekr is said to have perished *und Harvaða fjöllum* ('below the mountains of H.'), an expression which may preserve an early Teutonic form of the name of the Carpathians; cf. Kershaw, *Anglo-Saxon and Norse Poems*, p. 145.

latest. Here again therefore, as in the last case, we find a political geography, long obsolete, which must have served as the framework of the story and could hardly have been preserved without it. This consideration does not actually prove the stories to be historical, but it raises a strong presumption in favour of that view.

Personal names (*g*), especially if they are of unusual types, may supply valuable evidence for a knowledge of heroic stories (cf. p. 134). Thus the occurrence of the names *Widsith* and *Beowulf* (*Biuuulf*) in the Durham *Liber Vitae*—in sections where the names are apparently those of persons belonging to the seventh century—shows that these characters were already known in England. But it is rarely, if ever, possible to find such names at a date sufficiently early to prove the historicity of the characters from whom they are taken. The Frankish duke Chedinus (Heðinn), who lived in the latter part of the sixth century, may well have got his name from the story noticed above; but we do not know how long the story had then been in circulation.[1] A better case perhaps is that of the Gothic general Sarus, who was serving in Italy during the early years of the fifth century. He may have taken his name from the Sarus who with his brother Ammius (Sörli and Hamðir) made the famous attack upon Eormenric (cf. Jord. 24). If this was a historical event it must have taken place not long before 370. But it is possible that the name was current among the Goths before this. Again, the Burgundian king Sigismund, son of Gundobad, had a grown-up family when he was killed, c. 524; he must therefore have been born before 480. As his name is the only one in the dynasty, so far as we know, which has not initial *G*-, one is strongly tempted to derive it from Sigmundr (Siegmund), the father of Sigurðr (Siegfried), who is represented as living about fifty years before.[2] But not one of these cases can be regarded as conclusive.

For the British Heroic Age[3] there is a little evidence which must certainly be included among contemporary native records (*a*). Gildas,

[1] The name (*Heðinn*) is rare. There is another Heðinn, who figures in *Helgakviða Hjörvarðssonar*, a brother of the hero; but he is not mentioned except in this poem.

[2] In some of the Norse records Sigurðr has also an infant son called Sigmundr, who is killed with him.

[3] Prof. F. Lot in his paper "Bretons et Anglais aux Ve et VIe Siècles" (*Proc. Brit. Acad.*, 1930) allows little value to the historical records available for the period under discussion. He makes no charge of wholesale and deliberate fabrication, as some writers on this side of the Channel have done; his attitude is purely negative. It would be out of place here to discuss his opinion at length, more especially as he is

cap. 27 ff., writing apparently not long before the middle of the sixth century, attacks several of the kings of his time for their vices, and among them (cap. 33 ff.) *Maglocunus*, i.e. Maelgwn, king of Gwynedd, who is frequently mentioned in the poems and other records of the Heroic Age, and who according to the *Annales Cambriae* died in 548. Gildas charges him with various crimes, but recognises his pre-eminent position. Another passage in the same work (cap. 26) refers to the siege of *Badonicus Mons*, which in the *Historia Brittonum* (see below) is one of Arthur's battles; but Gildas mentions no personal name in this connection.

Under (*a*) we may also doubtless include some monumental evidence. In the church of Llangadwaladr, near Aberffraw, in the south of Anglesey, there is the monument—now built into the north wall of the nave—of *Catamanus Rex*, i.e. Cadfan, a descendant of Maelgwn and father of the famous Cadwallon. The date of Cadfan's death is unknown, but in all probability it was within the first quarter of the seventh century. Another monument, found near Yarrow Kirk in Selkirkshire, is not wholly legible, but seems to mark the grave of two sons of *Nodus* (or *Nudus*) *Liberalis*. This person is probably to be identified with Nudd Hael,[1] a prince who is occasionally mentioned in records of the Heroic Age. According to a genealogy given by Skene, *Four Ancient Books*, I. p. 169, he was first cousin to Rhydderch Hael. In a story contained in the Welsh Laws, *Ven.* II. ii. 1 (cf. p. 46), he is said to have made an attack upon Arfon (Carnarvonshire) along with other 'Men of the North'—Clydno Eidyn, Rhydderch Hael and Mordaf

chiefly concerned with the fifth century, which lies outside our scope. We are in agreement with much (not all) that he says about the early entries in the Saxon Chronicle. But his treatment of the British evidence seems to us to go much too far on the negative side. Our view is (1) that if one admits only evidence which is strictly first class—i.e. our (*a*) and perhaps contemporary (*b*)—and rejects all late or indirect evidence and that of records preserved by oral tradition, one cannot but get an entirely erroneous impression of the British—or any other—Heroic Age; and (2) that fictitious elements require to be demonstrated just as much as historical elements. We confess therefore that we must identify ourselves with the charlatan depicted on the last page of M. Lot's paper; and so we will now proceed with the production of the counterfeit guinea.

[1] This is the interpretation given by Rhŷs, *Academy*, 29 Aug. 1891. A different interpretation is given by Diack, *Scottish Gaelic Studies*, II. 221 ff., who takes *nudi* to be Gaelic ('grave'). But is not the inscription, like that of Llangadwaladr, an attempt—not very successful—at hexameter verse? It may be observed that the word *hael*, 'generous', is applied as a kind of surname to more than one of Nudd's relatives, as well as to himself.

Hael. He is also mentioned in at least one of the panegyrics upon Urien (*Tal.* XXXVII), as well as in the *Triads*. He was evidently a contemporary of Rhydderch Hael, and therefore lived presumably in the latter part of the sixth century (see below).

The *Annales Cambriae* and the *Historia Brittonum* contain a certain number of notices which may properly belong here; but in view of the uncertainty prevailing as to the history of these works it will be preferable to treat their evidence as a whole under (*d*) below.

Independent foreign evidence is limited in amount but valuable. Adamnan, *Life of St Columba*, I. 15[1] (which was written about the end of the seventh century), states that the saint was once consulted by Rodercus son of Tothail, who reigned upon the 'Rock of the Clyde' (i.e. Dumbarton), and who wished to know whether he would be slain by his enemies. The reply was that he would die at home in his bed; and so it came to pass eventually. This prince is certainly identical with Rhydderch Hael (son of Tudwal), who has been mentioned frequently above; and the passage shows that Rhydderch must have been reigning before 597, when St Columba died. Another passage in the same work (I. 1) records the battle in which *Catlon* (i.e. Cadwallon, king of Gwynedd) was defeated and slain by Oswald.

The wars carried on by *Caedualla* (Cadwallon) in the north of England are described briefly by Bede, *Hist. Eccl.* II. 20–III. 2. It is clear that they took place in the years 633–4. Apart from this Bede gives us little information bearing upon the British Heroic Age. He records the battle of Chester (*ib.* II. 2), which was fought about 614–15; but the only British name he mentions in connection with it is that of *Brocmail* (Brochfael), who was in charge of the monks of Bangor. It is just possible that this is the Brochfael, king of Powys, celebrated in *Tal.* XIV. 7 f.—the father of Cynan Garwyn (cf. p. 39), whose son Selyf was killed in the battle (see below); but the name *Brochfael* seems to have been a favourite one in this family. Other early English authorities add practically nothing. In the *Saxon Chronicle*, ann. 577, three British kings are said to have been killed in a battle at Dyrham, near Bath; and one of them, called Condidan, has been identified by some writers with the Cynddylan celebrated in *RBH.* XVI (cf. p. 38).

The evidence of traditions preserved independently in different regions (*c*) is somewhat doubtful in the case of the British Heroic Age. From the close of this period—early in the seventh century—the surviving British territories were cut off from contact with one another

[1] Cap. 8 in Reeves' edition.

by land. But the Britons of Strathclyde were to some extent in communication with Wales in the ninth century, and perhaps even later. For Cornwall and Brittany there are no satisfactory early records. Consequently, although British heroic stories were evidently much cultivated in Brittany—from whence they became known to the French—it is uncertain at what point the tradition ceased to be in touch with that of Wales. In view of certain unhistorical associations, e.g. that of Owein, son of Urien, with Arthur, which appears both in the Welsh *Dream of Rhonabwy* and in Chrestien de Troyes, though not in the Welsh poems, it would seem that communication did not cease very early—indeed the severance may never have been complete. On the other hand, the Breton tradition may well have developed special features; but the evidence here is so complex that we are not prepared to deal with it.

Under (*d*)—evidence from independent traditions within the same community—we may consider the information contained in Lives of the Saints. Here—i.e. under (*d*) rather than (*c*)—we should perhaps include the saints of the North, if we are right in believing that Strathclyde was in communication with Wales for two or three centuries after the close of the Heroic Age.

The value of this class of evidence again is difficult to estimate. There seems, however, to be no reasonable ground for doubting that much of the information contained in the Lives of St Kentigern is independent of heroic tradition. Such is the case, for example, with what is said about Rederech (Rhydderch) and Morken (Morcant) in Jocelin's *Life*. But one would like to know the origin of the story in the earlier *Life*, dedicated to Bp. Herbert (cf. p. 108 f.), cap. 1 f., that Owein, the son of Urien, was St Kentigern's father. One is naturally inclined to treat this as an idle tale, arising from the desire to connect the saint with a famous hero.[1] But the form of Urien's name (*Erwegende*) is against a late derivation of the story. Moreover, it is clear from cap. 3 that a sequel to it was contained in the later chapters (now lost)—in the form of an interview between St Kentigern and Owein. There is some reason therefore for thinking that, whether true or not, the story may be derived from early ecclesiastical tradition.[2] The dates are not impossible,

[1] The sentence next after that which first mentions Owein adds: *in gestis historiarum uocatur Ewen filius regis Ulien*; but this is evidently a late gloss.

[2] In various Genealogies of the Saints (*Myv. Arch.* pp. 415, 421) St Kentigern is sometimes son, sometimes grandson of Owein, son of Urien. In later Scottish records Eugenius (i.e. Owein) is his father.

as we shall see below, if St Kentigern died a comparatively young man.

In the *Lives* of Welsh saints heroes who belonged to Gwynedd and Powys figure frequently. Sometimes they are represented as treating the saints generously, sometimes as oppressing them. In the latter case a miracle usually follows, and the hero sometimes repents and is forgiven. The incidents themselves are rarely connected with anything which we know from heroic poetry or saga, and show as a rule no trace of derivation or influence from this quarter. Maelgwn is perhaps the hero who appears most often, generally in a more or less unfavourable light. Among his descendants Cadfan and Cadwallon are also mentioned. Of heroes belonging to Powys, Cynan Garwyn figures in the *Life of St Cadoc*, cap. 41, and in that of *St Beuno*,[1] and Selyf, son of Cynan, also in the latter. In stories relating to the south-east of Wales we sometimes meet with Arthur and his heroes Cai and Bedwyr. What is said of Arthur is not always much to his credit. We may instance the scene in the Prologue to the Life of St Cadoc, where he is inclined to waylay a fugitive and take his wife.

The *Lives* are not preserved in early form—in no case earlier than the eleventh century. This leaves an interval of at least four centuries, during which they were known probably by oral tradition only. The same remark applies to the Genealogies of the Saints, of which the earliest texts are still later. Giraldus Cambrensis, *Descr. Kambriae*, I. 17, says that the Welsh of his time—the twelfth century—paid such attention to genealogies that even commoners could trace their ancestry back to the sixth or seventh generation. But in the Genealogies of the Saints we have to reckon with a period about three times as long; so caution is obviously necessary. The number of heroes who figure as fathers or ancestors of saints is considerable, and they come from all parts of the country. In the south-west we find saints who are said to be sons of Gereint, son of Erbin.

More important is the evidence of the *Annales Cambriae* in MS. Harl. 3859, the genealogies which immediately follow in the same MS., and the *Historia Brittonum*, one of the best texts of which is likewise preserved in this MS. The origin of the *Annales* is unknown. The last entry relates to c. 955, and there is no reason for doubting that the text in its present form dates from about that time, although the MS. itself was written about a century and a half later. But it cannot have

[1] Rees, *Lives of the Cambro-British Saints*, pp. 79, 15, 17 (transl. pp. 375, 302, 304).

been originally composed at that time. Many events in the seventh and following centuries, and some even in the sixth, are dated with approximate correctness—which at least shows the extensive use of earlier materials, often unknown to us. Moreover, from its primitive character and from the fact that it frequently betrays the influence of an obsolete system of chronology[1] we may infer with confidence that it has a long history of its own behind it. Many of the earliest entries relate to Irish affairs, including those of Iona and the kingdom of the Scots in Argyll; and consequently it is commonly held that the *Annales Cambriae* are derived from an Irish collection of annals. There is certainly a connection of some kind in the early entries—down to the beginning of the eighth century; but we are not satisfied that this explanation is quite correct.[2] The British and Irish churches were without doubt in communication with one another in the sixth century, and very probably down to the time (c. 718) when the last (Columban) Irish monasteries conformed to Roman usage. Such communication would naturally lead to the interchange of information and of documents of the 'calendar' type between Irish and British monasteries; and it is to this interchange, rather than to the borrowing of an Irish chronicle, that we would attribute the references to Irish events.

This explanation is favoured not only by the extreme meagreness of the Welsh annals, as compared with the Irish, but also by the fact that the borrowing is not all on one side. It is true that for the fifth and sixth centuries there is little or nothing in the Irish annals to set against the references to Irish affairs in the Welsh. In the early part of the seventh century, however, the Irish annals contain a number of references to

[1] It seems to be derived ultimately from the Paschal Tables of Victorius of Aquitaine, which were adopted by Pope Leo I in 457. The first entry in the *Annales* relates to this event, though it is not correctly dated. The first year (blank) of the *Annales* is probably 446 (not 444), i.e. the initial year of the 19-year cycle current at the time when the new reckoning was adopted. It may also be noted that in the brief *Calculi* which immediately precede the *Annales* in the MS., but which properly, as in many other MSS., form the conclusion of the *Historia Brittonum*, two of the dates selected are the Consulship of Constantinus and Rufus (A.D. 457) and that of the two Gemini, Rufus and Rubellius (A.D. 29). The latter date is that of the Passion, the starting point of Victorius' cycles. From other references in the *Hist. Brittonum* it is clear that this scheme of chronology was well known in Wales.

[2] Victorius and his Paschal Cycle are frequently mentioned by early Irish authorities; cf. *Ann. Ult.* 455 and Hennessy's note *ad loc.* (*Annals of Ulster*, I. 16). But we do not know of any Irish chronicles which show signs of being based thereupon. Moreover, the Irish chronicles are so full, even for the seventh century and earlier, that it is difficult to believe that so meagre a record as the *Annales Cambriae* can be derived from them.

British affairs, which correspond to entries in the *Annales Cambriae*, and which are not derived from English sources, as the later references to Britain evidently are. This fact is important; for there is no doubt that the notices to which we refer were contained in an Irish chronicle written very early in the eighth century. They are good evidence therefore for the existence of written records in Britain during the seventh century. The evidence is not sufficient to show that anything which can properly be called a chronicle was in existence so early; but it is clear that some of the matter incorporated in the *Annales Cambriae* goes back to this time.

There need be no hesitation in regarding as historical such notices of British affairs as occur both in the *Annales Cambriae* and in the Irish annals. Among these we may include the reference to the death of Selyf, son of Cynan (Garwyn), at the battle of Chester in 614. The Irish authorities here are more detailed, especially the *Annals of Tigernach*.[1] Another example is the notice of the slaying of Iudris (probably king of Meirionydd) in 633. The references to Cadwallon's battles in 631 and 632 may also be examples; but here the question is complicated by the existence of a literary connection between these entries and the *Historia Brittonum*. On the other hand, there are about the same time several entries relating to Welsh affairs, which do not appear in the Irish annals. We are inclined to believe that these, as well as the entries noticed above, come from contemporary records—and consequently fall under (*a*)—but this cannot be proved.

Between the middle of the seventh century and the middle of the eighth the *Annales Cambriae* contain apparently only four entries relating to Wales (including Cornwall). Then, after an interval of more than thirty years, they begin again in 755. Soon after 800 they become so frequent that we are justified in assuming the existence of a real chronicle of some kind.

In the intervening period, 650–750, most of the references to Britain relate to the affairs of the North Britons, the Northumbrians and the Picts. These notices actually begin in 574 and cover a period of just over two centuries. They point clearly to the existence of a brief chronicle, or at least of written records of some kind, among the North Britons (Strathclyde) during the latter part of the eighth century. The entries which concern us here are the earliest of the series: 574 the battle of *Armterid* (Arderydd), 581 the death of Gwrgi and Peredur, 596 the death of King Dunawd, 613 the death of St Kentigern. These entries

[1] *Rev. Celt.* XVII. 171.

cannot be proved to come under (*a*), though we suspect this to be true at least for the last of them. The other three are at all events rather early examples of (*d*). It may be observed that Dunawd is not a prominent figure in the poems, though he is mentioned in *RBH.* XII. 37, as well as occasionally in the *Triads*.

Three entries remain to be considered: 517 and 538 the references to Arthur's battles, *Bellum Badonis* and Camlann, and 548 the plague in which Maelgwn died. The source of the two former is unknown. In the first there is a discrepancy with the *Hist. Brittonum* as to the battle in which Arthur carried the cross, while Camlann is not mentioned in the latter work. The third entry in part corresponds verbally to the Irish annals[1] and may be derived from them; but the Irish annals do not mention Maelgwn. He was a contemporary of Gildas (cf. p. 143) and certainly lived about this time; and since non-heroic tradition[2] represents him as dying of the 'yellow plague' the notice, whatever may be its origin, is probably correct. As for the other notices one would like to know when and from whence they found their way into the *Annales*. If an obscure passage of Gildas, cap. 26, is rightly interpreted to mean that the siege of the *Badonicus Mons* took place forty-four years before the time at which he was writing, there is a chronological error either in 517 or in 548; for Gildas speaks of Maelgwn as still alive.

The *Annales Cambriae* are immediately followed in the MS. by a series of genealogies thirty-one in number—not counting the list of Cunedda's sons, which comes at the end. Most of these genealogies are found also in other MSS., of which the most important are Jesus College (Oxford) 20 and Hengwrt 536. According to Loth, *Les Mabinogion*, II. 326, 349, both of these date from the fourteenth century. The Hengwrt MS. gives only the genealogies of the 'Men of the North'. The language in both cases is modernised, whereas that of the Harl. text is of the oldest type.

The connection of the genealogies with the annals in Harl. 3859 is not due to mere accident. The first two genealogies give the paternal and maternal descent of Owein, son of Howel the Good. Owein reigned in the south-west of Wales (Dyfed and Seisyllwg) from c. 950 to 988, and it is in the early years of his reign that the annals come to an end. There can be little doubt therefore that the original MS.—both of the annals and the genealogies—from which Harl. 3859 is derived, was written at this time. But this MS. was 'original' only for

[1] *Mortalitas magna in qua paus-*, etc., *Ann. Ult.* 548; cf. *Rev. Celt.* XVII. 140.

[2] Cf. Lloyd, *History of Wales*, p. 131, and the references there cited.

the text in its final form. The genealogies, like the annals, have a history behind them. Only the genealogies of Owein and perhaps one other (Dunoding) come down to the tenth century. Of the remainder at least seven extend to the ninth century, while most of the others[1] come to an end in earlier times. Even the genealogy of the kings of Gwynedd contemporary with Owein is wanting.

An explanation of these facts may be obtained by consulting the Jesus genealogies. This text contains a number of later genealogies; but the lines which correspond to the longer Harleian genealogies usually stop at about the same point.[2] Here, however, the centre-point is not Owein, son of Howel, but his great-grandfather, Rhodri the Great (r. 844–877). Four lines of this king's ancestry are given, besides a list of his sons and the genealogy of his wife. The other long genealogies are those of his contemporaries; and the common source of the Harleian and Jesus texts must have been drawn up in his reign. This explanation will account for the curious inclusion in the former of a line (No. IV) which ends c. 750; in Jesus (No. XIX) it is one of Rhodri's lines of ancestry. It is curious, but presumably due to accident, that Rhodri's direct paternal ancestry—from Llywarch Hen—is omitted, though it is preserved in Jesus (No. XVII).

The shorter lines in the Harleian text are partly collateral branches of the longer ones. Thus to the line of Powys (No. XXVII) four collateral branches (Nos. XXII, XXIII, XXX, XXXI) are given. The rest, so far as they can be identified, belong to the series of the 'Men of the North'. Six of these (Nos. VI–XII)[3] come together in a group, after the genealogy of Strathclyde (No. V), while another, a collateral of No. XI, is introduced later (No. XIX). Now it can hardly be an accident that the four

[1] All except five, which we have not been able to identify, viz. XVI, XX, XXI, XXIV, XXV. The first and possibly also the last of these might reach to the ninth century, judging from their length. The other three are quite short—five, two and eight names respectively. According to Phillimore, *Cymmr.* IX. 145, note, XXV is Damnonian. In XVI the genealogy is traced back to a long list of Roman emperors.

[2] The lines of (non-insular) Gwynedd and Meirionydd (Harl. III, XVIII; Jes. XXXIX, XLI) end with the same names. In place of the last Cardigan king in Harl. XXVI, Jes. XXI gives his sister Angharad, wife of Rhodri. In Dunoding Harl. XVII adds one name to the list of Jes. XL. On the other hand, Jes. IX has a later (collateral) line for Morgannwg-Gwent in place of Harl. XXX (which ends in 848) and XXXI (a generation later).

[3] We think that No. VII was originally not a separate genealogy but an unhappy correction of No. VI by someone who had Clydno Eidyn in his mind (cf. Hengwrt, No. III).

names with which the first four genealogies (VI, VIII–X) begin occur also as a group in the *Historia Brittonum*, cap. 63. There the order of the names is Urien (*Urbgen*), Rhydderch Hen, Gwallawg, Morcant. In the genealogies it is the same, except that Rhydderch Hen comes first, presumably because it was seen that his genealogy was a collateral of the immediately preceding (Strathclyde) line. We may note also that in both cases Rhydderch is called *Hen*, 'old, ancient', not *Hael*, 'generous', the epithet which he usually bears in the poems.

The two following genealogies (Nos. XI, XII) are those of Dunawd and of Gwrgi and Peredur. Again, it can hardly be an accident that these are the heroes whose deaths are recorded in the annals (596, 581; cf. p. 148) —the only northern heroes mentioned in that work. Yet we have seen that Dunawd is not a prominent figure in heroic story. Here then we have another connection between the genealogies and the annals.

The connection between the northern genealogies in Harl. 3859 on the one hand and the annals and the *Historia Brittonum* on the other may perhaps best be appreciated by a reference to the genealogies of the 'Men of the North' in Hengwrt 536. The latter text gives eleven genealogies, of which only four (those of Urien, Rhydderch, Dunawd, and Gwrgi-Peredur) occur in Harl. 3859, while the genealogies of Gwallawg and Morcant are wanting. It may be noted that Rhydderch bears the epithet *Hael* here, as in the poems. On the other hand, those genealogies which are found in both texts begin at the same point. Urien's sons are not mentioned in either, though Owein is scarcely less famous than his father. In the same way Hengwrt III, which is wanting in the other text, begins with Clydno Eidyn, ignoring his more famous son, Cynon. Lastly, it may be observed that the first names in all these genealogies—in both texts—stand either in the fifth or sixth generation from a certain Coel or in the second, third or fourth generation from a certain Dyfnwal Hen. Dunawd, Gwrgi and Peredur belong to the former series, and Rhydderch to the latter; and as these are all said to have lived at the same time—towards the close of the sixth century—it follows that the persons with whom all these genealogies begin were all more or less contemporary. The period to which they belonged is separated by more than two centuries and a half from the reign of Rhodri the Great.

As regards the question how far the genealogies are to be trusted, we have the following data. The Irish story of the 'Expulsion of the Deisi',[1] cap. 11, contains the genealogy of Dyfed in a form derived from a text

[1] Ed. and transl. by K. Meyer, *Y Cymmrodor*, XIV (p. 112).

written during the reign of Tewdos, the father of Maredudd who died in 796. This text agrees with the genealogy of Dyfed given in Harl. 3859 (No. II) as far back as the fifth century, though the earliest names in the genealogy differ,[1] and the origin of the family is traced not to Maxen Gwledig, but to an Irish source. Again, the king belonging to this dynasty mentioned by Gildas (*Vortiporius*, *Guortepir*) comes at approximately the right place in the genealogy; and the same is true of the king called *Cuneglasus* (*Cynlas* in the line of Gwynedd) recorded by the same author. Further, in the genealogy of Strathclyde (Harl. No. v) Beli, Tewdwr and Dyfnwal, who according to the annals died in 722, 750 and 760 respectively, are in the sixth, seventh and eighth generations from Dyfnwal Hen,[2] while Rhydderch, who lived towards the close of the sixth century (cf. p. 144), is in the third generation, by a collateral line, from the same man. Again, Dyfnwal Hen himself is grandson of Ceredig Gwledig (*Ceretic Guletic*), who is in all probability to be identified with the king Coroticus, to whose soldiers St Patrick addressed his *Epistle* (c. 440–460).[3] All this tends to show that the royal genealogies[4] are generally trustworthy at least as far back as the beginning of the sixth century—which covers the period with which

[1] It may be observed that the genealogy of Dyfed in Jes. 20 differs widely from the Harl. text from the point at which the agreement with the Irish ceases. The first name beyond this point is in Jes. 20 *Ewein vreisc*, in the Irish *Aed(a) Brosc*. No name resembling these occurs in the Harl. text. This is one of the cases in which the Jes. text preserves earlier readings.

[2] The king called *Hoan*, mentioned in *Ann. Ult.* 641 (also called *Auin* in 693) is probably to be identified with *Eugein*, who stands in the fourth generation from Dyfnwal Hen.

[3] Coroticus is described as *Coirthech regem Aloo* in the Table of Contents to Muirchu's *Life of St Patrick*. *Aloo* is presumably *Alcluith* (Dumbarton). Cf. Stokes, *Tripartite Life*, pp. 271, 498; Bury, *Life of St Patrick*, p. 314.

[4] The genealogies of the saints cannot be regarded with the same confidence. Most of the saints are represented as belonging to well-known royal families; but in some cases this may be due to mere speculation. The numerous progeny attributed to Brychan is doubtless mainly of this origin. Of course even the royal genealogies not unfrequently omit one or more generations, as may be seen by comparing the texts; and late texts sometimes show much larger lacunae. For an example of this one may refer to the genealogies of certain Carmarthenshire families published by G. P. Jones, *Y Cymmrodor*, xxxv. 117 ff. These genealogies are traced back to Pascent, a son of Urien, and the generations when counted up would make the latter live in the early part of the tenth century. The author of the article infers from them that Urien actually did live at this time and that he was a Norse Viking ruling in the valley of the Tywi (Towy). It is indeed remarkable how such an interpretation could be put upon the poems and traditions relating to Urien, especially if one bears in mind that at the time specified this district was under the immediate rule of

we are concerned—though in regard to earlier times antiquarian speculation was already busy in the ninth century. It may be noted that no genealogy is traced to Arthur, though his ancestry is given in one text.[1]

The *Historia Brittonum* is a work with a complicated literary history, and preserved in a number of widely differing texts. It is much disputed whether these different texts represent successive editions of a work by one author, Nennius, whose name is borne by the Prologus and the Apologia, or whether this man merely edited and added to works which were in existence before—perhaps long before—his time.[2] Into this

Howel the Good, and not very many miles distant from the place where he held his famous assembly. But the theory has to rest upon what is for many generations a single line of genealogy. No support is really afforded by the reference (*ib.* p. 129) to a genealogy (No. XXXIII) in Jes. Coll. 20. It is there stated that Ellelw, wife of Llywelyn of Builth (who was born c. 1050), was descended in the sixth generation from a certain Gwgawn, who was—according to the emendation proposed—a grandson of Pascent, son of Urien. This Gwgawn then ,according to the genealogy, must have lived c. 900 or somewhat earlier; and the following sentence, which makes him slain at Abergwili with Llywelyn son of Seissyll—who fought at Abergwili in 1022 and died in 1023—must be corrupt. It seems to us that this section (XXXIII) of the Jesus text has incorrectly incorporated (marginal) notes from an earlier MS., and consequently that the emendation which would connect the genealogy with the family of Urien is extremely doubtful. We think that all that can be inferred from the other genealogies is that in the Middle Ages (and later) there were in Ystrad Tywi families which, rightly or wrongly, claimed to be descended from Pascent, son of Urien. If this claim was not a mere invention a considerable, though varying, number of steps must have been lost in the genealogies.

A more serious difficulty is presented by the fact that in all the genealogical texts known to us Cadwallon, who died in 634, is represented as in the fifth generation from Maelgwn, who died in 548—which is hardly credible. It is unlikely that any of the intervening names are fictitious; all of them, except Rhun, occur in historical records (cf. *Ann. Cambr.* 613). More probably either two brothers have come to be represented as father and son, or two of the names originally belonged to one man. Was *Iago* (*Iacob*) originally an alternative name of Cadfan? In any case the mistake suggests that the various texts of this genealogy had a common origin, perhaps in the ninth century.

[1] Cf. Anscombe, *Arch. f. celt. Lexikographie*, II. 157.

[2] The former view was strongly advocated by Liebermann in *Essays in Mediaeval History presented to T. F. Tout*, p. 32 f. with his customary learning and care; but we think that he did not fully appreciate the milieu in which the *Hist. Brittonum* was produced. It cannot fairly be compared with the work of Bede, a scholar who had all the Latin learning of the time at his disposal, but whose interests lay almost exclusively in ecclesiastical things. The general (Latin) learning of the writer or writers of the *Hist. Brittonum* was far inferior, as were also doubtless their libraries; they had only recently, and probably to a very slight degree, come into touch with the learned world beyond their borders. But their interests were not the same as Bede's; they lay in the national traditions. The object of their aspirations was to bring these traditions into relation with what they knew of general history.

question we cannot enter, though we think that, if the former view is correct, the author must have either incorporated or made very extensive use of earlier works, including a Life of St German. Nennius in his Apologia describes himself as a disciple of St Elfodd, who according to the annals discussed above died as archbishop of Gwynedd in 809, while in the Prologus he says that he was writing in the reign of Merfyn[1]—who was king of Gwynedd from 816 or 825[2] to 844. It is generally agreed that both the Harleian text and the (later) Cambridge text date from about this time, or at least from the period c. 800–860.

The interest of the *Historia* is essentially antiquarian. It deals with the origin of the Britons and the Irish, and incidentally refers to the origin of several British dynasties. To traditions and speculations of this kind, which evidently were widely current among the Welsh of the ninth century, we shall have to return later (Ch. x). References to stories and persons of the Heroic Age are less frequent and practically confined to cap. 56–65.[3]

Cap. 56 is occupied with a list of twelve battles fought by Arthur. Among these are the battle of *Tribruit*, mentioned in *BBC.* XXXI, and that of *Mons Badonis*, recorded—though without mention of Arthur—by Gildas. There is no reference to Camlann or to Arthur's death; and it is not at *Mons Badonis* but in another battle that Arthur carries

[1] The text actually specifies the date as the year 858 of the Incarnation and the twenty-fourth year of King Merfyn. Cap. 16, where the same date seems to be intended, gives the fourth year of Merfyn. But Merfyn died c. 844. We are inclined to trust the writer for the regnal years of Merfyn rather than for the years of the Incarnation. But the chronology of the *Hist. Brittonum* is a tangled skein.

[2] According to Lloyd, *Hist. of Wales*, p. 231 (cf. p. 244, note) Merfyn did not become king until 825—and consequently reigned less than twenty years. He holds that Merfyn's predecessor (grandfather) Cynan and his opponent Howel were brothers—presumably owing to the words *y brawt* in the *Bruts*; but this may have been taken over from the preceding line through a scribal error. Is it very likely that two brothers would fall into so desperate a quarrel sixty years after their father's death? Is it not more probable that this Howel was the son of Caradoc and last king of non-insular Gwynedd, and that he took advantage of his neighbour's old age to invade Anglesey? In that case Merfyn became king of Anglesey on Cynan's death in 816, and of the rest of Gwynedd (perhaps by conquest) on Howel's death in 825. We are therefore inclined to the view that the date claimed for the *Hist. Brittonum* is 839–40.

[3] Cap. 56 is found in all the complete MSS. Cap. 57–65 are found in MSS. of the Harleian group; but those of the Cambridge group have in their place a statement that "since the genealogies of the Saxons and other nations seemed useless to my teacher, that is Beulan the priest, I have been unwilling to write them out, but have written about the cities and the marvels of the Island of Britain, as other writers before me have written".

the cross. Consequently, there is no evidence for a connection between this passage and the *Annales Cambriae* (cf. p. 149). The source of cap. 56 is in all probability to be sought in a catalogue poem similar to *RBH.* xv, which gives a list of the places where Cadwallon pitched his camp.

The groundwork of cap. 57–65 is derived from an English document consisting of the genealogies of various English dynasties and lists of Northumbrian and Mercian kings with the length of their reigns, and dating from about the close of the eighth century.[1] It is preserved in MS. CCCC. 183 and the *Textus Roffensis*, while traces of its use may be seen in the *Saxon Chronicle* and various other works. In the *Historia Brittonum* this matter has been expanded by the inclusion of a considerable number of notes. A few of these may be of English origin, but most of them are British. They relate to Northumbrian and British history. In the latter case they are concerned partly with Gwynedd and partly with the Britons of the north.

The most important passages are the following: In cap. 62, immediately after a brief notice of Ida, the founder of the Bernician kingdom, we find: "Then Dutigirn at that time fought bravely against the nation of the English. Then Talhaern Tat Aguen (i.e. 'father of the Awen') shone in poetry; and Neiren (Aneirin?) and Taliessin and Bluchbard and Cian who is called *Gueinthguaut* shone all together at one time in British poetry. A great king, Mailcunus (Maelgwn), reigned among the Britons, that is in the land of Gwynedd; for his great-grandfather, namely Cunedag, with his sons the number of whom was eight, had come previously from the North, namely from the land which is called Manau Guotodin, a hundred and forty-six years before the reign of Mailcun. And they expelled the Scots from those lands with a most huge slaughter; and they never returned again to occupy them".

Next follow the reigns of Ida's successors—Adda, Aethelric, Theodric, Frithuwald and Hussa; and then comes the second important insertion: "Against them four kings, Urbgen (Urien) and Riderch Hen and Guallanc (i.e. Gwallawg) and Morcant fought bravely. Deodric (i.e. Theodric) with his sons fought bravely against that

[1] Van Hamel in Hoops' *Reallexikon d. germ. Altertumskunde*, s.v. *Nennius*, §§ 5, 7, separates these two elements, holding that the lists of kings were included in the earliest form of the *Hist. Brit.* (which he dates 687–705), while the genealogies were introduced by Nennius between 820 and 859. It is true that the two elements are sometimes found separately (e.g. Sweet, *Oldest English Texts*, pp. 148, 169 ff.), and also that only the earlier parts of the lists of kings appear in the *Hist. Brit.*; but we doubt if it is safe to build on these facts.

Urbgen. At that time sometimes the enemy, sometimes the men of the country (*ciues*) were conquered. And he beleaguered them for three days and three nights in the island Metcaud (Lindisfarne). And while he was campaigning he was slain at the instigation of Morcant through jealousy, because he possessed above all kings the greatest valour in the waging of battle".

Of Dutigirn nothing is known. Aneirin claims to be the author of the Gododdin (*An.* I). Taliesin has been discussed above (p. 103 ff.). Talhaern and Cian are mentioned in *Tal.* VII, though no extant poems claim their authorship. Maelgwn has been frequently mentioned. The list of Cunedda's sons is given in the Harleian genealogies, No. XXXII, and elsewhere. The four British kings recorded in cap. 63 are those whose genealogies occur in the same text, Nos. VI–X (cf. p. 150 f.). They all figure also in heroic poetry, though the events here related of them are not mentioned in the poems. According to *RBH.* XII. 45 and *Triad* 38 in Hengwrt 536 Urien was slain by a certain Llofan Llawddino (or *Lawdifro*). The two records do not of course necessarily exclude one another, especially since in *RBH.* XII. 40 Morcant appears as an opponent of Urien. But it is clear that the notices in the *Historia Brittonum* are not derived from any heroic records known to us.

Acquaintance with Taliesin and other early poets is shown in cap. 62. Knowledge of heroic story is shown also by a note in cap. 61, where in a Northumbrian genealogy the name of Eata, father of King Eadberht and Archbp Ecgberht is followed by the comment *ipse est Eata Glinmaur*—i.e. he is identified, no doubt erroneously, with the hero Eda Glinmawr,[1] by whom Gwrgi and Peredur were slain (Hengwrt *Triad* 35). But in general the notes do not convey the impression of being derived from heroic saga or poetry. They are clearly connected with the Harleian genealogies; and it has been observed above (p. 151) that in both documents alike Rhydderch bears the title 'old, ancient' instead of 'generous' which is regularly applied to him in the poems. The reason for this may be seen by referring to the genealogy of Strathclyde (Harl. No. V), where it appears that there was a second king called Rhydderch reigning c. 800.[2]

It seems then that some of these notes are due to information

[1] For the genealogy of this person see Anscombe, *Arch. f. celt. Lexikographie*, II. 154, 157. From this he would seem to have been regarded as English.

[2] Similarly, Rhydderch's ancestor, Dyfnwal *Hen* ('the ancient'), probably owes his title to the desire to distinguish him from his descendant Dyfnwal who died in 760.

obtained—probably in written form[1]—from Strathclyde about the beginning of the ninth century. This may well be connected with the Strathclyde annals noted above (p. 148) in the *Annales Cambriae*. Further evidence for such northern information is supplied by a note in cap. 57, which states that Ecgfrith made war against his cousin called Birdei, king of the Picts, and was slain in a battle called *Gueith Linn Garan*. Moreover, such evidence is not confined to these chapters. A good example occurs in cap. 23 (Cambridge text)—the description of the Roman wall between the Forth and the Clyde—which shows intimate local knowledge, and cannot possibly be derived from Bede, as has sometimes been suggested.[2]

From this northern source may well come also the much discussed statement, which is found both in cap. 63 and in the *Annales Cambriae* (627), that the Northumbrian king Edwin was baptised by Rhun, son of Urbgen. In the later texts Paulinus, archbishop of York, takes the place of this Rhun, in accordance with Bede, *Hist. Eccl.* III. 14; and in one case[3] St Elfodd and a bishop named Renchidius are cited as authorities for Paulinus. Now, according to *Ann. Cambr.* 768, it was St Elfodd who brought the Welsh church into conformity on the Easter question; he must therefore have been acquainted with Bede's works. We may conclude then that the story of Rhun is derived from earlier British sources. Again, the same name recurs in cap. 57 as that of the grandfather of Riemmilth (Raegnmaeld in the Durham *Liber Vitae*), the first wife of King Oswio. As *Rhun* is not a man's name in English, it is generally agreed that this is probably the same person—in which case he will have taken orders not very early in life. Lastly, the same person may be traceable also in the title of the earliest (Chartres) text of the *Historia Brittonum* which has been preserved. The title, though unfortunately corrupt,[4] seems to mean that the work (or an important element in it) was obtained by 'a son of Urbgen' from a Life of St German.

[1] This is suggested by the archaic form of the name *Urbgen*.

[2] Note in particular the description of the circular building near Carron ascribed to Carausius. This was evidently the structure known as 'Arthur's Oven', near Falkirk, destroyed in 1743. We are not prepared to deny the influence of Bede in this section of the *Hist. Brit.* (cap. 21 ff.)—which is wanting in the Chartres text—but other sources of information have also been used.

[3] After cap. 56 in the texts (Cambridge, etc.) which do not contain the genealogies.

[4] *Incipiunt. exberta. fiiurbaoen* (or *urbacen*) *de libro sci germani. inuenta*, etc. The name of the 'son of Urbgen' seems to have fallen out.

It is held by many scholars[1] that all these passages relate to the same person, a son of the famous Urien who figures in cap. 63, and who is the subject of so many heroic poems (cf. p. 38 ff.). The name appears to have been a rare one in early times;[2] and the dates are entirely favourable to the identification. Theodric, the opponent of Urien, reigned c. 572–579 according to the best tradition. Urien then was probably born not much before 520–530. Taliesin, who celebrates his praises (cf. p. 39), had visited Maelgwn—as a boy according to the legend. A son of Urien born c. 560 may well have had a granddaughter of an age suitable to marry Oswio, who was born in 613, and may himself have taken part—as an old man—in the conversion of Edwin in 627.[3] Urien is not definitely stated to have had a son called Rhun in the poems or the *Triads*. But in the Elegy on Urien (*RBH.* XII) there is a passage (st. 32 ff.) celebrating the generosity and prowess of a certain Rhun who may well have been the hero's son. It comes between the passage relating to Eurddyl, Urien's sister—the mother of Gwrgi and Peredur—and those which celebrate the prowess of Owein and other sons of Urien.

If the title of the Chartres text has been correctly interpreted we may probably regard it as almost equivalent to contemporary evidence (class *a*; cf. p. 133). The remaining evidence may most properly be treated under (*d*). The *Historia Brittonum*, the earlier part of the (Harleian) *Annales Cambriae* and the Harleian Genealogies represent the antiquarian activities of Welsh scholars in the reigns of Merfyn and Rhodri the Great—i.e. between 816 (?) and 877.[4] In addition to the

[1] Cf. Thurneysen, *Zeitschr. f. deutsche Philologie*, XXVIII. 83; van Hamel in Hoops' *Reallexikon d. germ. Altertumskunde*, s.v. *Nennius*.

[2] An Urien, son of Llywarch Hen, is mentioned in *BBC.* XXXIX. 3, and another, a great-grandson of Llywarch Hen, in the *Genealogies of the Saints*. These belong to the same family and may well have taken the name from their famous relative. In later times the name is not very rare.

[3] Too much, we think, has been made of the discrepancy between Bede and the *Hist. Brittonum* on this point. More than one person may have taken part in the conversion of the Northumbrians. If there was a British ecclesiastic present—one who belonged to a famous royal family—British tradition would naturally attribute it to him, whereas Bede, or the tradition followed by him, might be expected to ignore the part played by such a person. It has not been sufficiently appreciated that the anti-British feeling so frequently displayed in the *Hist. Eccl.* is primarily odium theologicum; there is no reason for supposing that such feelings were generally shared by the princes on either side.

[4] We believe that the three works are closely connected. The *Hist. Brit.* was presumably in existence before 839–40, since the 'edition' dated in that year (cf. p. 154, note) is a revision. We think that the materials for the genealogies were

work of the 'son of Urbgen', they had at their disposal no doubt other records in written form, perhaps mainly from Strathclyde (cf. p. 157). But we do not know how old these records were. And much may have been added in Wales from oral tradition, e.g. some of the notices relating to Gwynedd in the last chapters of the *Historia*.

It may be observed that even if the written records were no earlier than c. 800, this date carries us back four or five centuries beyond the time of the extant MSS. of the poems. Moreover, the evidence is independent of any heroic tradition which has come down to us. This remark applies to the case of Arthur among the rest, though the account of his battles may have been committed to writing first by Nennius himself. To his case we shall have to return shortly. Here we may note that the references to Maelgwn and Rhydderch Hen are in accord with evidence, noticed above (p. 143 f.), which is beyond dispute. There is no reasonable ground for doubting that the other characters—not only Urien, but also Gwallawg, Morcant, and the poets—were historical persons of the sixth century.[1]

After what has been said above under (*a–d*) it is scarcely necessary to discuss at length the evidence which falls under (*e*)—the consistency of heroic tradition. In general the heroic poems seem to contain little or nothing which can be put down with confidence to inconsistency. A few exceptions, which are due, we believe, to additions or to the incorporation of alien matter, will be noticed in the next chapter. The same consistency is observable in the *Triads*, except of course those which are under the influence of Geoffrey and other foreign sources. The evidence of the *Triads* in this case is particularly useful because, like the later genealogies, they contain many notices of marriages between royal families. To verify the historical truth of these is generally beyond our power; but the evidence is invaluable as representing an apparently consistent 'corpus' of heroic tradition existing before Geoffrey's fantasies came into operation. The *Triads* which are due to Geoffrey's influence, together with the Romances and other late works, are of course full of unhistorical situations—some of which will be noticed in the next chapter.

likewise collected during Merfyn's reign. This view is favoured especially by the preservation of his grandfather's paternal and maternal ancestry (in Jes. 20. XVII, XIX).

[1] One can hardly take seriously the strange theory that Taliesin lived in the reign of Owein Gwynedd (1137–1170), and that *Urien* is the name which he applied to that prince. The remarkable thing is that such a theory should have been produced by a scholar who was pre-eminent in his own line of work.

Non-heroic tradition, even when fairly early, seems to be less consistent. The *Four Branches of Mabinogi* form a world of their own, seldom connected with other stories and apparently consistent in itself. But Taliesin figures in *Branwen, daughter of Llyr*, and, though he plays practically no part in the story, his connection with it is referred to in *Tal.* XIV. 4, 31. Yet in the same poem he is associated with Maelgwn and Urien, as elsewhere, and also with Brochfael of Powys, presumably the father of Cynan Garwyn, who was no doubt a contemporary of Urien. It may be that the world of the *Mabinogion* is an imaginary world into which historical characters were only occasionally drawn. To this question we shall have to return in the next chapter. All that need be said here is that none of the chief characters can be identified historically. There is, however, one other remarkable exception to the general isolation of this cycle—Manawyddan or Manawyd, son of Llyr, who in *BBC.* XXXI appears as one of Arthur's heroes.

There remains one story, very different from the *Mabinogion* and definitely heroic in character, for which we are practically dependent upon evidence of class (*e*)—the story of the battle of *Catraeth*, which forms the subject of the great *Gododdin* poem (*An.* I). There is nothing here which suggests a creation of the imagination; yet not one of the numerous heroes mentioned can be identified historically with any confidence—not even the leader of the ill-fated army, Mynyddawg Mwynfawr. Unfortunately the text of the poem is hopelessly corrupt, as may be seen from the number of stanzas which are in reality mere textual variants.[1] It appears too that stanzas—perhaps many stanzas—relating to quite different events have been added to the original poem. Thus st. 89, with its variant st. 78, contains a reference to the death of the Scottish king Domnall Brecc, who was defeated and slain by the Britons c. 641. Other stanzas seem to relate to Wales and Welsh heroes. But the nucleus and probably the greater part of the poem is evidently concerned with a disastrous battle fought against the English of Bernicia and Deira—apparently at a somewhat earlier date.

Although none of the heroes can be identified historically, there is at least one whose connections and approximate date are open to no doubt. Cynon, son of Clydno, is frequently mentioned in the poem; he appears to have been one of the very few heroes, possibly the only one, who survived the slaughter. His name occurs also in other poems, especially the *Verses of the Graves* (*BBC.* XIX) and in *Triads*; and he

[1] These will be noticed in Ch. XVII, below. Variants will be found not only in *An.* I but also in the Addenda to *An.* V.

figures—at Arthur's court and in association with Owein, son of Urien—in the *Lady of the Fountain*. His father, Clydno Eidyn, is one of the northern heroes who (with Rhydderch Hael) are said to have raided North Wales, in a story noticed on p. 143. The genealogy of the family is given among the genealogies of the 'Men of the North' in Hengwrt 536, from which it appears that Clydno's father Cynwyd was first cousin to Gwenddoleu, Dunawd, Gwrgi and Peredur. Again, in Hengwrt *Triad* 53 Cynon himself is one of the three 'enamoured ones' of the Isle of Britain, the object of his affections being Morwydd, daughter of Urien. It is clear therefore that Welsh tradition regarded him as belonging to the generation of heroes who lived towards the close of the sixth century. We may therefore infer with probability that it was some event about this period which formed the original subject of the poem.[1]

Archaeological evidence (*f*) for this period is practically wanting, apart from a few inscribed stones (cf. p. 143). It is not even known whether any Roman buildings or sites were still occupied. Of small objects (metal, etc.) only a few are known, and these probably of ecclesiastical origin. The civilisation of this period is the most remarkable blank in our history.

For Arthur we have not been able to find any contemporary, or indeed any very early direct evidence. The *Historia Brittonum* shows that he was famous in the first half of the ninth century. The entries in the *Annales Cambriae* (517, 538) are independent of this, but their antiquity cannot be proved; and the same may be said of certain references in the poems. But indirect evidence in the form of personal names (*g*) carries us back much further. Aedan, king of the Scots of Argyll, had a son called Arthur (*Arturius*) who was killed in battle before the death of St Columba[2] (597). In the genealogy of Dyfed the same name is borne by a man who must have lived early in the seventh century. About 625, according to the *Annals of Tigernach*,[3] the Ulster king Mongan was killed in Cantire *ab Artuir filio Bicoir*—a Briton. There is evidence for the use of the name in Ireland about the same time.[4] It would seem then that by the end of the sixth century the name was familiar throughout

[1] The title of the poem attributes it to Aneirin—doubtless the poet (*Neiren*) who in the *Hist. Brit.*, cap. 62, is said to have flourished in the sixth century—and in st. 45 the poet speaks of himself by this name, though the context is far from clear. In several other passages the poet says that he was present at the battle; but this is possibly a literary convention.

[2] Adamnan, *Life of St Columba*, I. 9 (I. 8, Reeves).

[3] *Rev. Celt.* XVII. 178; cf. *Ann. Ult.* 624.

[4] Cf. Chambers, *Arthur of Britain*, p. 169.

the Celtic parts of the British Isles. Yet before the sixth century it is practically unknown.[1] It is clearly Roman (*Artorius*), and presumably derived from some Roman official settled in this country. There is therefore good reason for believing that its wide currency towards the end of the sixth century must have been due to some famous person of that name in the near past. This would agree well enough with the dates given to Arthur in the annals.[2]

The evidence of place-names is less reliable, as we have seen (p. 134). Since the twelfth century, owing to the popularity of Geoffrey's *History* and the Romances, speculation has been active in identifying Arthurian localities and the hero's name has been applied broadcast to places and objects in various parts of the country. Actually to determine the scene of Arthur's activities seems to be a difficult matter. The earliest evidence points to the valley of the Wye and neighbouring districts. Such is the case with the references to Arthur in the *Mirabilia*[3] attached to the *Historia Brittonum*, which can hardly be much later than the beginning of the ninth century. But in the *Hist. Brittonum* itself, cap. 56, the scene of one battle at least—that *in Silua Celidonis, id est Cat Coit Celidon*—must clearly be sought in Scotland (cf. p. 111); and some of the other sites may also be there. On the other hand, *Urbs Legionis* (in the same catalogue) is presumably either Caerleon or Chester; and Mons Badonis is not likely to have been in the north. Consequently, if we are to believe the record, we must suppose that Arthur's activities extended over a very large area. That in itself is not impossible; for in 634 Cadwallon, who came from Anglesey, was killed in the neighbourhood of Hexham. But there are other difficulties. It is not very likely that Saxons would be encountered in Arthur's time at Caerleon or Chester, and most improbable that they had penetrated to the forest of Celyddon by then. We cannot, therefore, with confidence treat this list as a historical record of battles against the English. And the possibility has to be taken into account that not all the battles were originally connected with Arthur.

[1] In Irish Fenian stories (cf. O'Grady, *Silva Gadelica*, I. 98 ff., II. 105 ff.) Beinne the Briton—the ally of MacCon—has a son Artur. But the evidence can hardly be regarded as of historical value.

[2] A somewhat earlier date is favoured by the Latin name. Latin names are very frequent in the earlier stages of the genealogies, especially for persons whose births would seem to fall in the fourth century and the first half of the fifth. After 450 they seem to have become much less common.

[3] The references here are to Builth and Archenfield. The passages are transl. by Chambers, *Arthur of Britain*, p. 6 f.

Unfortunately, geographical uncertainty is by no means limited to the story of Arthur. It applies indeed to nearly all the stories and poems except those relating to Wales. We know that Rhydderch Hael belonged to Dumbarton, and that he was descended from the same ancestor (Dyfnwal Hen) as the later kings of Strathclyde (cf. p. 152), while another branch of the same family, represented by Nudd Hael, would seem to have been settled in Yarrow, Selkirkshire (cf. p. 143). But of the numerous heroes descended from Coel Hen there is only one who can be located with any confidence, viz. Gwenddoleu, who in all probability belonged to the neighbourhood of Longtown, on the Border (cf. p. 111). It is likely enough that his opponents, Gwrgi and Peredur, lived not far away, while Morcant, who was sprung from a distant branch of the same family, must likewise have belonged to Scotland or the Border,[1] if he is rightly identified with the opponent of St Kentigern. The evidence available, therefore, for this family also[2]—i.e. for all the 'Men of the North'—points to the same region. But there remain a number of important princes, including Urien, Gwallawg, Dunawd, Llywarch Hen and Cynon, the son of Clydno Eidyn,[3] whose dominions or homes cannot be determined with certainty.

In the poems which celebrate some of these princes there is no lack of what appear to be place-names. But some of these (e.g. *Aeron*) are names which occur in various parts of England, Scotland and Wales, while others—the majority—are not to be found on the map. On the strength of names of the former class the heroes have been located by some scholars in England, by others in Scotland, by others again in Wales. The last identification is by far the least probable. If the heroes had really belonged to Wales, their families could hardly have all

[1] Jocelin's *Life*, cap. 21, locates Morken at Glasgow, but this was surely within the dominions of the other (Rhydderch's) family. The story is probably derived ultimately from saga; and Jocelin's evidence is always to be treated with caution. We may refer, for example, to the arbitrary manner in which he deals with the story of St Kentigern's birth. The episode relating to the Saint's sojourn in Wales (cap. 23–31) is hardly credible; and if he was really invited to 'return' by Rhydderch it is unlikely that he would have established his see so far away as Hoddom—about five miles from the Solway. The truth may be that Hoddom was his first headquarters, and that he moved from there to Glasgow at Rhydderch's invitation. Morken possibly belonged to the former district.

[2] A less important prince, named Cadrawd, brother of Clydno Eidyn, belongs to a place called *Calchfynydd*, which is generally identified with Kelso (cf. Skene, *Four Ancient Books*, I. 172 f.).

[3] Eidyn is identified by many scholars with Edinburgh; cf. Watson, *Place-Names of Scotland*, p. 340 f.

disappeared; yet none of the numerous royal families of Wales, so far as we know, traced their descent from Coel Hen.[1] Moreover, in that case the large number of unidentifiable place-names would be inexplicable. It is less easy to decide between England and Scotland. But it is to be borne in mind (1) that down to the end of the sixth century not more than one-third of the north of England seems to have been in English hands—i.e. that an area larger probably than either modern Wales or the part of Scotland which comes into account was still British territory; (2) that this area must have borne the worst, if not the whole, of the warfare with the English, which is frequently referred to in the poems; (3) that within the next generation (after 600) British rule seems to have been finally destroyed throughout the whole of this area—which sufficiently accounts for the disappearance both of the dynasties and of the place-names—whereas a considerable part of Scotland remained British until much later times. It is difficult therefore to avoid the conclusion that some at least of these heroes must have belonged to the region between the Border and the southern boundaries of Lancashire and Yorkshire.[2]

[1] Except of course the later dynasty of Gwynedd, beginning with Merfyn (d. 844; cf. p. 154), whose paternal ancestry goes back to Llywarch Hen. But Merfyn's claim to Gwynedd (Anglesey) was through his mother. His father, Gwriad, belonged either to the Isle of Man or to Scotland (cf. Lloyd, *History of Wales*, p. 323 f.). In later times there were families (not royal) in South Wales which claimed to be descended from Urien (cf. p. 152, note), but there is no evidence worth consideration that he himself belonged to that region. *Dyfed* and *Deheubarth* occur in a panegyric on Owein (*Tal.* XXXV)—as also 'the men of Gwent', though this is perhaps ambiguous; but the context is obscure and the text perhaps corrupt. The same poem also contains references to places in Scotland.

[2] It is impossible here to discuss the identifications of *Reged* (the home of Urien), *Catraeth*, and other places, which have been proposed by various scholars. Reference must, however, be made to an article by Loth, *Rev. Celt.* XXI. 328 ff., by which a number of later writers seem to have been greatly influenced. The author rightly points out that the *Gododdin* poems contain earlier and later strata—a subject to which we shall have to return in Ch. XVII. But it should not have been assumed that the names *Brennych* and *Deivyr* in these poems mean enemies in general. There is no instance of such usage in any of the poems discussed in this book, except perhaps in the very late poem *BBC.* XVIII (st. 15), where the reference is to the story of Myrddin. These names date from the seventh century, in the course of which the kingdoms—Bernicia and Deira—ceased to exist as such; and there is no valid reason for doubting that in the *Gododdin* poems the names have this meaning and that they belong to the earliest stratum—which, it is admitted, may go back to the seventh century. But there is not the slightest ground for supposing that the story of the *Gododdin* had anything to do with the wars of Cadwallon, Penda and Oswio, none of whom is mentioned in the poems. The frequent references in them to Cynon

The Heroic Age of Ireland was without doubt of very long duration, and the evidence available for the different periods of it varies greatly in character.

(*a*) For stories relating to the seventh and eighth centuries, such as the *Battle of Mag Rath* and the *Battle of Allen* (cf. p. 53 f.), a good deal of native historical evidence is available in the Annals, especially the *Annals of Tigernach* and the *Annals of Ulster*, the common elements of which are believed to be derived from a chronicle composed in the

(cf. p. 161 f.) show that they relate to an earlier generation; and in view of these the allusion to the death of Domnall Brecc (cf. p. 160) must be regarded as a subsequent addition—suggesting that the poems were preserved in Strathclyde for a time, before they found their way to Wales. Again, it should not have been assumed that such names as *Aeron*, *Elfed* and *Llwyfein* must refer to localities in Wales; for the same names were borne by localities in the north of England. Indeed there is a striking uniformity in Celtic nomenclature everywhere, even as far back as Roman times. There are references in the *Gododdin* poems to Gwynedd and occasionally to other localities in Wales; but since the poems were preserved orally in Wales—probably for a long period—these may well belong to the later strata. Both Urien and his vassal Llywarch Hen seem to have relations with Powys—which rather suggest that Lancashire may have been their home.

It is possible that the name *Rheged* was at one time applied to a district in Wales—perhaps the basin of the Towy—as well as to Urien's kingdom in the North. If so it would help to explain the claim to descent from the hero made by certain families in this district in later times (cf. p. 152, note). But the evidence is far from conclusive. And there was a general tendency of Welsh antiquarian speculation to locate the 'Men of the North' in Wales. Thus we find Llywarch Hen located in Penllyn (cf. Lloyd, *Hist Wales*, p. 246), Gwyddno Garanhir and Taliesin near Aberystwyth, and Myrddin at Carmarthen. On the same principle various Teutonic heroes came to be located in England, e.g. Wermund, the father of Offa, at Warwick.

With regard to *Catraeth*, the objection raised to the identification of this place with *Cataracta*, i.e. Catterick on the Swale, cannot stand. Many scholars hold that the phonetic correspondence of the two names is regular (cf. I. Williams, *Y Beirniad*, I. 76 f.; Ekwall, *English River-Names*, p. lxxii, note). But even if this be not the case—if *Catraeth* must represent an earlier *Cat-traeth* ('shore of battle')—it must be remembered, firstly, that the difficulty applies to the English name just as much as to the Welsh, and secondly, that there is a common tendency in place-names to transform unfamiliar into familiar elements. Examples are extremely numerous in English, e.g. *-ton* for *-don*, *-hall* for *-hale*, *-ford* for *-worth*. We may refer also to such cases as *Auckland* for earlier *Alclit*, Benwell (in Newcastle) for earlier *Bynnewalle*, 'within the Wall' (cf. Mawer, *Place-Names of Northumberland*, pp. 7, 18). It may be observed that there was probably no place in the north of England of greater strategic importance than Catterick at the time when the east and the west were in different hands. Apart from the fact that it commanded the fork of the two great roads to the north, its possession to allied forces co-operating from Bernicia and Deira was obviously vital. We may note that in Edwin's time it seems to have been an important royal residence (cf. Bede, *Hist. Eccl.* II. 14).

eighth century.[1] This evidence may therefore be regarded as practically contemporary. A number of contemporary poems are also preserved in the Annals and elsewhere, while in a few cases references occur in early ecclesiastical works, e.g. Adamnan's *Life of St Columba*, which was written shortly before the end of the seventh century. It is true that most of the stories contain unhistorical elements—which will require notice in the next chapter—but there can be no doubt that the battles and the princes with which they are concerned belong to history.

For the sixth century, and indeed from c. 450 onwards, the Annals yield evidence which is similar in kind, though less full. There can be no doubt that they are derived largely from earlier records, presumably of ecclesiastical origin. One of these is believed to have been an Irish (Latin) continuation of Eusebius, concluded in 607.[2] The Annals also often refer to a lost *Book of Cuanu*, while the frequent occurrence of alternative dates, sometimes with the addition of *secundum alios* or *ut alii dicunt*, shows that they had yet other authorities. A few poems or fragments of poems may also perhaps date from the close of this period, though they were probably not written down until later. There is no evidence, however, even for ecclesiastical records before c. 450—the time of St Patrick; and for times anterior to 400 it may safely be assumed that evidence belonging to class (*a*) does not exist.

Since the historical elements in sagas relating to the seventh and eighth centuries are more or less fully substantiated by the Annals, and those which relate to the fifth and sixth are comparatively unimportant, we shall confine our attention in the following to stories of the earlier periods—anterior to the beginning of the fifth century.

(*b*) We know of no foreign historical evidence for times before c. 400. Stories relating to Niall Noigiallach, whose reign was dated c. 378–405 (see below), speak of raiding expeditions carried out by him and other princes in Britain and elsewhere; and this is in accord with the frequent references to the piratical activities of the Irish (*Scotti*) contained in Roman works of the same period. It was in one of these expeditions that St Patrick was carried off, apparently c. 402–5. Mention may also be made of a passage in the story of the *Expulsion of the Desi*,[3] where the genealogy of the kings of Dyfed is traced to a prince of that people who fled from Ireland to Wales in the time of Cormac mac Airt.

[1] Cf. MacNeill, *Ériu*, VII. 73 ff., where it is suggested that this chronicle was compiled in 712.

[2] Cf. *Ann. Ult.* 609; MacNeill, *Ériu*, VII. 62 ff.

[3] Cf. K. Meyer, *Y Cymmrodor*, XIV. 112.

The genealogy dates apparently from c. 750,[1] but the number of generations—fourteen—reckoned back to the founder of the dynasty does not agree very well with the date (c. 250) assigned to Cormac by Irish chronologists.

(*c*) The question whether we have any independent traditions from different areas must be deferred for the moment. It may be noted here merely that Welsh tradition speaks of the presence of *Gwyddyl* or *Scotti*, in various parts of Wales, from whence, according to the *Historia Brittonum*, cap. 14, they were expelled by Cunedda and his sons (cf. p. 155). If these *Scotti* were invaders from Ireland—and there can be little doubt that such was the case at least in part—their arrival is probably to be dated about the end of the fourth century; for until this time the greater part of Wales, including Carnarvon, was controlled by Roman garrisons. It is possible of course that small settlements were made in earlier times. The genealogy of Dyfed is traced in Welsh records not to the Desi but to an obviously fictitious origin. But the *Historia Brittonum*, cap. 14, speaks of a settlement of the *filii Lethan* in Dyfed, Kidwelly and Gower; and the Ui Liathain were conterminous, though not identical, with the Desi who were settled in Co. Waterford.[2] The context, however, suggests that the passage is partly of Irish origin. On the whole therefore the Welsh evidence does not amount to much.[3] On the other hand, we shall see later that there are grounds for believing that the traditions current in different parts of Ireland itself were to some extent independent of one another.

(*d*) The evidence available for comparison with the stories—heroic and non-heroic—under this head consists of Annals and other antiquarian records, in prose and verse, including local ('tribal') traditions, such as the story of the *Expulsion of the Desi*. Some of these latter seem to have been committed to writing as early as the eighth century, while a few of the antiquarian poems are believed to have been composed—hardly written—in the seventh and even before the close of the sixth century. By far the fullest and most important evidence, however, is that of the Annals, which record the succession of the high-kings of Ireland from the earliest times, together with their dates, the length of

[1] The genealogy begins (ascending) from Tewdos, whose son Maredudd (*Morgetiud*) died in 796 (*Ann. Cambr.*).

[2] *Cormac's Glossary*, s.v. *Mogheime*, mentions a stronghold of the 'son of Lethan' (*dind map Lethain...i. dún maic Liathain*) situated apparently in Cornwall (*i tírib Bretan Cornn*).

[3] For Brychan, the legendary founder of Brecknock, see Lloyd, *History of Wales*, p. 270 f.

their reigns and the manner of their deaths. Incidentally they refer also to the achievements and deaths of many other famous heroes. In short they provide a chronological framework for early Irish tradition as a whole.

A few examples will be sufficient. They date the reign of Niall Noigiallach c. 378–405—a period which is probably not far from the truth. About fifty years before the former date they record the destruction of Emain Macha by three brothers named Colla, cousins to the high-king Muredach, Niall's grandfather. The reign of Cormac mac Airt, Muredach's great-grandfather, is dated c. 215–255; that of Cormac's grandfather, Conn Cetcathach, shortly before the middle of the second century, and that of Conn's grandfather, Tuathal Techtmar, about half a century earlier. The *Revolt of the Vassals* takes place at the death of Tuathal's father, or grandfather Fiacha. The time of Conchobor, king of Ulster, and his heroes CuChulainn, Conall Cernach, and the rest, with their opponents, Ailill and Medb, king and queen of Connaught, is placed about the beginning of the Christian era, or a trifle earlier. The story of Eochaid Airem (cf. p. 52) belongs to the next previous generation, for Eochaid is Medb's uncle. The story of the *Destruction of Dinn Rig* (cf. p. 51), which was perhaps regarded as the earliest of the heroic stories,[1] is assigned to a much more remote period.

The period covered by the stories is therefore extraordinarily long. Conchobor is placed more than four centuries before the time of St Patrick, the beginning of the historical period; and heroic stories continue for nearly three centuries after the latter date. The slaughter of Dinn Rig is placed some six centuries before Conchobor.

There can be no doubt that this chronology is derived partly from native antiquarian traditions and speculations and partly from Latin learning. To the latter of course is due the chronological scheme itself—the synchronising of Irish tradition with universal history as arranged by Eusebius, and beginning with the Book of Genesis. On the other hand, the arrangement—the systemisation—of the traditional material must be due, to a large extent at least, to native learning. It represents without doubt the activities of the *filid* or learned poets.

With the origin and character of this class of persons we shall have

[1] At least we know of no earlier story which can properly be called heroic. In the *Battle of Allen*, cap. 8 (*Rev. Celt.* XXIV. 50 f.) it is said that before the battle Hua Maiglinni began reciting the battles of Conn's Half and Leinster from the *Destruction of Dinn Rig* down to that time. There may of course have been earlier stories of battles between other combatants.

to deal in a later chapter. Here it may be noted that as one of their qualifications they were required to know—and to be able to recite—a very large number of sagas, heroic and unheroic—between which no distinction is recognised. But they were by no means mere entertainers. The *Book of Leinster* contains a list of sagas which were required to be known, and it adds at the end: "He is no poet (*fili*) who does not synchronize and harmonize all the stories".[1] This statement dates of course from Christian times; but it is clear from many other passages that the *filid* were concerned with antiquarian lore, including genealogies and, probably, lists of kings. Some sort of systemisation, therefore, was doubtless in use before Latin learning became known. It may be noted that the chronicles usually state how, or by whom each king was slain.[2]

Antiquarian studies must have been well developed before the seventh century. In poems[3] dating from that century we already find the genealogies of Leinster and Cashel carried back to Eremon and Eber, the sons of Mil, and through them after long lists of names, partly of native, and partly of Classical origin, to the genealogies of the patriarchs in Genesis. It is obvious that Latin learning was already cultivated by some of the *filid*; but the great abundance of names in the native parts of the genealogies points to the existence of antiquarian speculation on an ambitious scale before the foreign elements were introduced.

It cannot safely be assumed, however, that the native elements are always derived from ancient tradition. Additions seem to have been made to the lists of kings, and probably to the genealogies also, in literary times. Thus the *Annals of Tigernach* give—no doubt from the eighth-century chronicle mentioned above (p. 165 f.)—a list of high-kings in Tara who follow one another in a direct genealogical line, from father to son, from the reign of Lugaid Reoderg, who is represented as contemporary with Claudius Caesar. But later chronicles intersperse this line with names of kings from Ulster, Leinster and Munster, who are represented as reigning, usually for very short periods, in the intervals between the kings of the regular line. In most cases the alien king obtains the throne by slaying his predecessor, and in turn he is himself slain by the son of the latter. The same principles are

[1] Cf. O'Curry, *MS. Materials*, p. 583; MacNeill, *Celtic Ireland*, p. 37.

[2] Analogies from various countries will be noticed later. In particular we may refer to the Norse poem *Ynglingatal* and the *Ynglinga Saga* (cf. pp. 271, 295).

[3] Cf. K. Meyer, *Über die älteste irische Dichtung* (Abh. d. k. preuss. Akademie d. Wissenschaften, 1913), I. pp. 27 ff., 39 ff., 53 ff.

followed in the long list of high-kings who precede Lugaid, and who are not mentioned in the *Annals of Tigernach*.

Somewhat similar difficulties are presented by the genealogies. This subject is too big and too complicated to be discussed here; for Irish genealogies are numerous and of very great length, and many of them have never been published. It may be stated, however, that on the whole they give an impression of antiquity. Yet different texts of the same genealogy sometimes show important discrepancies, while the numbers of generations assigned to different lines are often wholly irreconcilable. Note may also be taken of the fact that names of deities occur at times quite late in the pedigrees.[1]

The list of high-kings from Lugaid Reoderg, contained in the *Annals of Tigernach*, coincides almost entirely[2] with the genealogy of the same family—the ancestors of Niall Noigiallach. One is naturally inclined to suspect that the list is derived from the genealogy,[3] though the dates given in the *Annals* to Lugaid and his successors are later than what would be inferred from the genealogy.[4] But the genealogies of the other kingdoms do not fit in well with the scheme; they are either too long or too short. In particular the Ulster genealogies agree neither among themselves nor with that of the high-kings, nor again with the series of the kings of Ulster (Emain Macha) contained in the *Annals of Tigernach*. This last, however, gives a chronology which is not incompatible with the genealogy of the high-kings—a fact which is of some interest, as it is not a mere genealogy converted into a list of kings, as the series of high-kings seems to be, but shows frequent breaks in the succession.

[1] Cf. MacNeill, *Celtic Ireland*, p. 47 ff.

[2] The only departure from the direct line is the case of Colla Uais, who slew and took the place of his uncle, Fiacha.

[3] Cf. MacNeill, *Phases of Irish History*, p. 115: "It is a succession from father to son, which is contrary to the known custom of all the insular Celts, in Ireland, Wales, and Scotland". One is tempted to ask how the chroniclers came to apply such an alien system to Ireland. But the statement is too strong. In Wales and Strathclyde at least, as in pre-Roman Britain, succession from father to son seems to be the normal, though not exclusive, type—so far as the kingship is concerned.

[4] Lugaid figures in the *Sickbed of CuChulainn*; but CuChulainn and his contemporaries are placed by the *Annals of Tigernach* about fifty years before Lugaid's accession. The passage is generally believed to be a late addition to the saga, and perhaps rightly. But the synchronism involved is implied elsewhere, e.g. in Lugaid's relationship to Medb. The *Ann. Tig.* themselves make Iriel, son of Conall Cernach, to be slain by Crimthann, son of Lugaid (*Rev. Celt.* XVI. 415). It is not unlikely therefore that the original reckoning of Lugaid's date was in accordance with the genealogies.

(*e*) As regards agreement between different sagas it may be said that this prevails as much as could be expected in such a body of literature. Discrepancies are of frequent occurrence, but they rarely affect the essentials of a story; nor is the personnel of different cycles confused to any great extent—apart from certain stock figures, such as Ferchertne the *fili*. We may suspect that Lugaid Reoderg had originally nothing to do with the *Sickbed of CuChulainn* and that Conall Cernach was not one of the company in Da Derga's Hall in the original form of that story; but neither hero really affects the course of events. There are no instances of confusion so great as we find in medieval German poetry, e.g. when Eormenric and Theodric (Dietrich) are brought together. Conchobor's heroes are never introduced into stories of Cormac and his times.

The case which presents the greatest difficulties in this respect is the (non-heroic) story of the *Revolt of the Vassals*. In the later form of this story Fiacha, the high-king slain by the rebels, is son of Feradach, while his child who avenges him is Tuathal Techtmar. But in the older version[1]—sometimes called *Mac Dareo's Hall*—some texts of which quote an earlier poem, Feradach is the son and avenger of Fiacha. The chronicles, including the *Annals of Tigernach*, agree with the relationship stated in the former version. The rest of the names, including Tipraide Tirech, the Ulster child and avenger, are identical in both. But according to the chronicles, including *Tigernach*, this Tipraide was the slayer of Conn, the grandson of Tuathal, while Tuathal himself is slain by Mal, an ancestor in the third or fourth generation of Tipraide.[2] The *Annals of Tigernach* mention all these princes, as noted above, but they know nothing of the *Revolt*.[3] On the contrary, they contain a number of entries which seem to be incompatible with the story. Feradach is succeeded by his son Fiacha, who is slain by Elim, king of Ulster[4] (a grandson of Fergus mac Roich).

[1] Ed. and transl. by Thurneysen, *Zeitschr. f. celt. Philol.* XI. 56 ff.; cf. MacNeill, *Celtic Ireland*, p. 65 ff. The text ed. by Craigie, *Rev. Celt.* XX. 335 ff. is inconsistent.

[2] In the list of kings of Ulster contained in the Rawlinson Genealogies (*Zeitschr. f. celt. Philol.* VIII. 326 f.) Tipraide is the son of Mal; but in an Ulster genealogy which follows in the same document (*ib.* p. 335) there are three intervening generations.

[3] Except a reference to the reign of Cairbre Cenn Cait, which appears to have been inserted by a later hand (*Rev. Celt.* XVI. 416). It occurs in the middle of Feradach's reign.

[4] In later versions of the story Elim succeeds Cairbre Cenn Cait as high-king (of the Vassals) and as such is slain by Tuathal. In a note at the end of the poem in the *Book of Fermoy* Feradach (here the son of Fiacha) is slain by Elim, king of Ulster, and by the kings of Leinster, Connaught and Munster.

Three years later Tuathal Techtmar, son of Fiacha, becomes king and—whether before or after is not stated—slays Elim in revenge for his father. Tuathal is eventually killed by Mal, king of Ulster. Mal is succeeded by Bresal,[1] and the latter by Tipraide Tirech, who slays Conn, the grandson of Tuathal. It is plain that in place of the *Revolt of the Vassals* we have here quite a different story—the story of a long-standing feud between the kings of Tara (the high-kings) and those of Ulster. The story of the *Revolt*, whatever its origin, cannot have been universally known or accepted.

Now, after consideration of the evidence for (*d*) and (*e*) we may return to the question (cf. p. 167) whether (*c*) is represented. It seems at least highly probable that such is the case. In the first place the stories of the Ulster cycle—relating to Conchobor and his times—represent a totally different point of view from those of the high-kings. In the former the centre of interest lies in Ulster, in the latter in Tara and its dynasty. The former indeed do not recognise the existence of a high-kingship, except in one or two passages. They represent Tara as ruled not by the family with which we have been dealing, but by kings, Cairbre Nia Fer and his son Erc, who belong to the dynasty of Leinster. Secondly, we have seen that stories relating to later times, which affect both Ulster and the high-kings, show discrepancies which cannot be accounted for except by the existence of different traditions. One of these belonged presumably to Tara; and there can be little doubt that the other—represented by the *Annals of Tigernach*—came from Ulster; for it is only the kings of Emain Macha and of Tara whose succession is given in the annals during this period. We may add that these annals contain a list of kings of Emain Macha from the most remote times—a list which is found elsewhere also and comes evidently from the Irish Eusebius. This list has hardly anything in common with the traditions or speculations which elsewhere are centred in the high-kingship, and nothing is known about most of the persons mentioned in it. But it testifies to the age of antiquarian speculation in Ulster.

It is not to be supposed that the two traditions remained wholly independent of one another. The stories of the high-kings may well have absorbed elements from Ulster and elsewhere. In the Ulster cycle

[1] Called *mac Briuin*. Bresal (or Bres) mac Feirb is the king of Ulster killed by the Vassals. In the Ulster genealogy given in the Rawlinson Genealogies (cf. p. 171, note) the names Bresal and Ferb appear between Tipraide and Mal. It is to be suspected that they are taken from the story.

we find Lugaid Reoderg in the *Sickbed of CuChulainn.*[1] But the rareness of such cases is remarkable and seems to show that the broad lines of the Ulster stories were fixed before they were influenced from Tara. The significance of this may be realised if one bears in mind the antiquity of the genealogies from the sons of Mil, as pointed out on p. 169 above. Such genealogies must have been preceded by a long period of antiquarian study—and surely not less at Tara than elsewhere.

(*f*) Archaeological evidence is abundant, though not as a rule entirely satisfactory. Great numbers of raths or earthen fortresses, usually more or less circular, still exist, and very many of them are mentioned in stories of the Heroic Age. The difficulty of fixing the scene of an event, which is so continually present in stories of the British Heroic Age, rarely occurs in Ireland. It is true that some of the fortresses mentioned in the sagas, e.g. Dun Delgan (Dundalk), the home of CuChulainn, are now believed to be of medieval date; but they may be reconstructions on earlier sites. Many others date without doubt from much earlier times. Gold torques and other objects of the La Tène period are said to have been found at Tara, and though the evidence is not quite so precise as one could wish, it is now believed that the occupation of this site goes back to this period and probably even to the Bronze Age.[2] Brooches of the La Tène period are said to have been found at Emain Macha.[3]

One of the most important sites is that of the 'Banqueting Hall' at Tara, which is attributed by tradition to Cormac mac Airt. It has been suggested that this is a copy, on a huge scale, of a Roman Basilica.[4] Most, if not all, of the Roman cities in Britain contained buildings of this type, and the date assigned by tradition to Cormac—the middle of the third century—falls well within the times when such buildings were most likely to be copied. The inference is strengthened by the existence of another tradition which attributes to the same king the establishment of a permanent standing army—the *Fiana*—which may likewise have been due to Roman influence. We see nothing improbable in the suggestion

[1] Edited by Windisch, *Irische Texte*, I. 197 ff.; transl. by Leahy, *Heroic Romances*, I. 51 ff.; cf. also Thurneysen, *Irische Heldensage*, p. 413 ff. The passage relating to Lugaid is generally regarded as an interpolation.

[2] Cf. Macalister, *Archaeology of Ireland*, p. 180 f.

[3] Cf. Ridgeway, *Early Age of Greece*, I. 581 ff. Wilde, *Catalogue of Irish Antiquities*, fig. 473, gives a brooch resembling an Etruscan 'leech-brooch', which is said to have been found at the same site (p. 568).

[4] Cf. Macalister, *op. cit.* p. 21; *Proceedings of the R. Ir. Academy*, XXXIV. C. 281 (cf. 262 ff. and Pl. IX); *Tara: a Pagan Sanctuary*, p. 60 ff.

that a powerful and active-minded king sought to copy the institutions of a more advanced civilisation which he knew to be in active operation in a neighbouring country.

Another important monument which requires notice is the Black Pig's Dyke, a great earthwork which stretches across Ireland from west to east—from Bundoran, at the southern boundary of Co. Donegal, to near the head of Carlingford Lough. It faces southwards[1] and consequently must have been constructed as a defence of Ulster against attacks from that quarter. For this work also Roman influence is believed to be responsible.[2] It is indeed difficult to doubt that the idea of a fortification stretching from sea to sea was inspired by the Walls between the Clyde and the Forth and between the Solway and the mouth of the Tyne.

The Black Pig's Dyke is perhaps of special importance historically, because it seems to imply the existence of a political unity to the north—a kingdom of Ulster—at the time of its construction.[3] This kingdom of course is the centre of the early stories and figures largely in the stories of the high-kings; but in historical times it was a thing of the past. From the fifth century onwards practically the whole province, except the counties of Down and Antrim, was divided among families belonging to the dynasty of Tara. According to tradition the kingdom was broken up and its capital, Emain Macha, destroyed by Colla Uais and his brothers, who were cousins to Muredach, the grandfather of Niall Noigiallach; and from thenceforth only the lands to the east of Lough Neagh remained in the possession of the Ulidians. The date indicated falls in the first half of the fourth century. On the other hand, it is to be noted that the *Táin Bó Cuailnge* and other early sagas relating to Conchobor and his times never mention the Dyke,[4] although they deal very largely with events in its neighbourhood. This silence is in full conformity with the fact that they represent Conchobor's kingdom as extending much further south—to the Blackwater and the lower

[1] Cf. Dobbs, *Zeitschr. f. celt. Phil.* VIII. 339; Kane, *Proc. R. Ir. Acad.* XXXIII. 549.

[2] Cf. Macalister, *Archaeology of Ireland*, p. 177.

[3] Cf. MacNeill, *Phases of Irish History*, p. 131, whose explanation we follow. But the direction taken by the line at its eastern end raises some difficulty (cf. the map in *Proc. R. Ir. Acad.* XXXIII. Pl. XLVIII). Why is Co. Louth—and apparently also part of Co. Down—excluded?

[4] It is pointed out by Miss Dobbs, *Zeitschr. f. celt. Phil.* VIII. 340 ff., that the route taken by Medb's army seems to avoid the line of the Dyke. But the explanation may be that the reciters of a later day, when the Dyke was an existing and effective barrier, knew only the roads which avoided it.

Boyne. It would seem then from the traditions that the time when the Dyke was constructed must have been subsequent to the age to which these stories relate, though anterior to the destruction of the kingdom of Ulster. But we have seen that in the intervening period traditions speak of a longstanding feud between Ulster and the high-kings—which may well account for the construction of the barrier. This period, if we are to attach any value to the genealogies, would cover the times when the Walls in Britain were built.

It is of importance to notice that the political geography of the traditions is by no means uniform. Three periods must be distinguished. Stories relating to the fifth and following centuries show a political geography which can be verified from historical sources. Thus the greater part of Ulster is held by families from Tara and Connaught, as mentioned above. Only the eastern part, Antrim and Down, remains under native dynasties—the kingdoms of Dal Riada, Dal Fiatach and Dal Araide—together with the Conaille of Murthemne, a small community in Co. Louth. The name *Ulaid* (Ulidians) is frequently applied to the Dal Fiatach, while the Dal Araide and Conaille of Murthemne are commonly known as Cruithni (Picts). In the next preceding period—extending from the first century to the fourth, according to the chronicles—there is, as later, a high-kingship at Tara. But there is also a kingdom of Ulster, embracing apparently the whole province and frequently at war with the high-kings. The kings of Ulster are not all of one line. The majority, including all those mentioned in the last few pages, belong to what is later the dynasty of Dal Araide, while the rest, including Fergus Dubdetach who fought against Cormac mac Airt, belong to Dal Fiatach. Lastly, in stories relating to the times of Conchobor there is a kingdom of Ulster governed by this king and extending considerably to the south of the later province. But, apart from exceptional passages, there is no high-kingship of Ireland. On the contrary, we hear regularly of the five 'Provinces' (*Coicid*, lit. 'Fifths') as sovereign and apparently equal powers.

The term 'Province' or 'Fifth' never went out of use; but in the light of these stories it is believed to have originated before the establishment of the high-kingship and when the 'Fifths' were supreme. Yet there is some discrepancy as to what was the fifth 'Fifth'. The prevailing view[1] now is that in the earliest form of the stories Leinster contained two 'Fifths', the more northern of which had its capital at Tara, though it extended a good deal to the south of the later Meath. In the stories the

[1] Cf. MacNeill, *Phases of Irish History*, p. 102 ff.

king of this region is Cairbre Nia Fer, who is succeeded by his son Erc. These kings do not belong to the family which later—from Lugaid Reoderg onwards—rule as high-kings at Tara, but to the dynasty of (southern) Leinster. Cairbre is a brother of the king of Leinster, Finn Fili. Consequently, if the two Leinster Fifths were ancient divisions, a change of dynasty is involved for the northern one. This district may previously have been under the ancestors of its later owners, or it may have belonged to a different family, e.g. perhaps the line of Conaire Mor. The important point is that the early stories do not recognise a high-kingship—at least not as a regular institution. In Conchobor's time there is no high-king; and though high-kings figure in some stories relating to earlier times the references do not necessarily imply more than a temporary supremacy.[1]

Another remarkable feature of the stories of the Ulster cycle is that they know nothing of the ancestors of the dynasty which ruled over the Ulaid in historical times. We have seen that in stories of what may be called the later prehistoric period some of the kings of Ulster belong to this dynasty, the Dal Fiatach, while others—the majority—are ancestors of the Dal Araide. This latter line claim descent from Conall Cernach, an ancestry which is claimed also for the Conaille of Murthemne (cf. p. 175) and other families which are known as Cruithni. Now Conall Cernach is son of Finnchaem, sister of Conchobor, whose own descendants have died out; and his father, Amorgin, also belongs to the same stock, the Clann Rudraige, from which most of the ancient Ulster heroes seem to be sprung. In the list of Ulster kings Conall's son Iriel comes to the throne on the death of the last son of Conchobor. It seems clear to us, therefore, that the line of Dal Araide were regarded as the legitimate successors of Conchobor's line.[2]

[1] Several stories, as well as the later chronicles, speak of Eochaid Feidlech (Lugaid's grandfather) and his brother Eochaid Airem as high-kings; but their immediate ancestors are never represented as holding this position. It is likely enough that the permanent high-kingship was preceded by a period of temporary supremacies, as in Saxon Britain.

[2] We regret that in this point we are obliged to disagree with MacNeill, *Celtic Ireland*, p. 13 (and passim). Prof. MacNeill himself admits (*ib.* note) that "there is one fact for which I know no adequate explanation in tradition or otherwise. The historical kings of the Ulâid, the Dál Fiatach line, make no genealogical claim to be Ulidians", etc. But surely this fact, together with the positive evidence given above, is enough to show that they were not the legitimate successors of Conchobor's line. The early stories use the provincial name or (less frequently) the family name (Clann Rudraige), not that of the ruling state in the province. But it is possible that the name *Cruithni* was used only by aliens.

On the other hand the ancestors of the Dal Fiatach are never mentioned, so far as we are aware, in stories relating to the times of Conchobor. Fiatach Finn, the founder of the dynasty, appears in the list after Conall's grandson. The previous history of the family is unknown; but they are always connected in the genealogies with the Erainn, the stock to which Conaire Mor belongs, and usually, though more distantly, with the line of the high-kings at Tara and with that of Leinster. The genealogical relations of the lines may be expressed as follows:

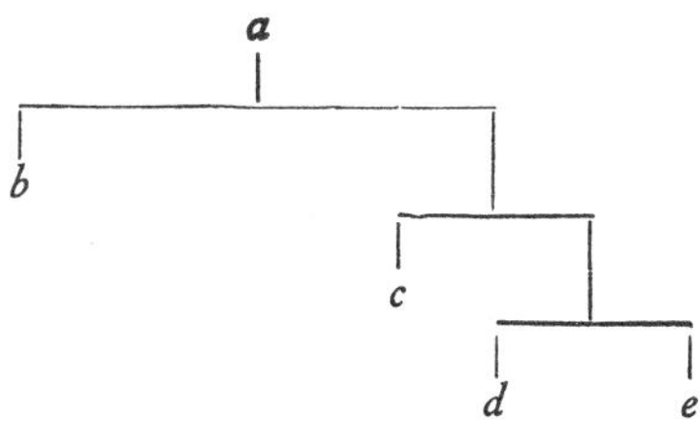

In this table *a* denotes the line of Eremon down to Ugaine Mor, *b* the line of Leinster, *c* the line of the high-kings at Tara, *d* the line of Conaire Mor, including the Dal Riada, and *e* the Dal Fiatach. The stock as a whole extends over all parts of Ireland and includes most of the kingly lines, though those of Dal Araide and Cashel, as well as some of the minor lines, are excepted. We do not know how old the genealogy is, but it was certainly recognised, at least in part, in the seventh century, and there is no reason for supposing that it was then new. It was suggested, presumably, by conditions, political or other, which prevailed at some time. It does not appear to be recognised in the ancient Ulster stories.

What has been said will probably be sufficient to illustrate the antiquity of Irish genealogical lore and the fact that different strata are to be distinguished in it. The genealogies doubtless contain many mythical and fictitious names—which are not confined to very early times. But the fact that the leading house in Ulster in historical times made no claim to be descended from the ancient kings of Ulster, whose fame was celebrated over the whole country, shows that certain traditions had become fixed at a very early date.

It is not only in political conditions that the ancient Ulster stories present us with a picture of things long passed away. The same is true also in the case of family relationships. It is remarkable that some of the leading heroes are frequently—not invariably—called after their mothers, e.g. Conchobor (mac Nessa), Fergus (mac Roich), Ailill (mac Magach or Mata), CuChulainn (mac Dechtire). With this usage is probably to be connected the variation in the statements as to the paternity of these heroes. Thus Conchobor is sometimes said to be son of the druid Cathbad, sometimes of a previous king Fachtna Fathach; CuChulainn is sometimes son of Sualdaim, sometimes of the god Lug. Ailill is usually said to be son of Rus Ruad, king of Leinster; but Mata is sometimes apparently the name of his father. Again, the throne appears to be obtained occasionally by marriage—a remarkable fact since as a rule the kingdom was regarded as the property of the native royal family. Ailill is said to have acquired the kingdom of Connaught by his marriage with Medb. One of his brothers is king of Leinster and another of Tara—which again points to some irregular form of succession.

The evidence as to family relationships noted above is by no means consistent. Some heroes regularly bear surnames from their fathers, e.g. Celtchar mac Uthidir (or Uthechair). Conchobor is succeeded by his sons, one after another, and Cairbre by his son Erc. And though some allowance must be made for changes in the long course of tradition, it would be arbitrary to assume that all such cases are non-original. But the fact remains that the descriptions and the relations of the leading characters show features which are unknown in later Irish tradition and history, though they have been and still are found among many peoples in other parts of the world—wherever relationship is reckoned, solely or chiefly, through the female line. We have already met with them in one Welsh story (p. 116), and in the kingdom of the Cruithni (Picts) in Scotland[1] a somewhat similar system survived, apparently unmodified, down to the eighth century. Taken as it stands the evidence of the Ulster stories points without doubt to the existence of a social system in a state of transition between this type and the type found in historical times.[2]

[1] We think it highly probable that the Clann Rudraige, from whom all the Irish Cruithni—i.e. their reigning families—appear to have claimed descent, had come over from Scotland, perhaps in not very remote times. It is possible, though by no means clear, that the system of kinship through the mother preserved its vitality among them longer than among the native Irish. But we have no belief in the dogma that the Picts are proved by this system to be the aboriginal pre-Celtic inhabitants of the British Isles. On the contrary the system can be traced in Greece, Italy, among the Teutonic peoples, and throughout the west of Europe, though naturally it survived longest in the most remote regions.

[2] It should be observed that the existence of such a transitional system may account for some of the unexplained changes of dynasty, noticed above.

We may now sum up the Irish evidence. There is no doubt that stories which relate to the sixth and following centuries rest upon historical foundations, whatever unhistorical elements they may contain. For stories relating to times before St Patrick no proof is possible owing to the absence of contemporary documents, native or foreign. But there are abundant traditional records, which in part seem to be independent of one another, and their testimony is supported in various important points either by archaeological evidence or by a consideration of the political conditions which they depict.

Owing partly to the archaeological evidence and the evidence as to political conditions and partly to the general reaction against the mythological interpretation of heroic stories which prevailed last century, a marked change of opinion on this subject has taken place during the last twenty or thirty years. Many scholars formerly regarded Cormac mac Airt as a mythological character; but we believe he is now usually held to have been a real man. We have no doubt that this change of opinion is fully justified. But at the same time it is to be noted that the characters in regard to whom opinion has changed are those whose stories are of the heroic Type C (i.e. more or less didactic) or non-heroic. It is to stories of the heroic Type A, i.e. to stories composed solely or chiefly for the purpose of entertainment, that we would rather call attention.

There can be no doubt that the early Ulster stories were originally of this type, as indeed many of them still are, in spite of 'informing' additions. Now these stories, as we have seen, depict political and social conditions unknown in the Ireland of the earliest historical times, and quite foreign even to the stories relating to Cormac. Yet in the light of the evidence noted above it is clear that they must once have existed. But these conditions are merely the framework of stories designed for entertainment, and as such they must have been a reality familiar at the time when the stories assumed a fixed form. Consequently, as the framework indicates a period anterior to Cormac, we must infer that the stories themselves had taken shape before his time. This brings us back to within a few generations of the time when, according to the genealogies, the heroes lived; and therefore the probability that they were real persons is at least greatly increased. In the next chapter it will be seen that the unhistorical elements which the stories obviously contain are not of a character incompatible with this conclusion.[1]

[1] We have not thought it necessary to enter into the evidence of personal names, because its value in this case seems to us somewhat doubtful. Probably the best

The evidence available for the Heroic Age of Greece is on the whole very similar in character to that which we have been discussing for the earlier part of the Irish Heroic Age. Contemporary native records (*a*) are entirely wanting. Evidence from early foreign records (*b*) may be available in the future—e.g. from Cretan documents, when these are deciphered, or from Hittite sources; but we are not convinced that any definite results have yet been obtained, except perhaps for one—very early—period.[1] For the present the most important categories of

case is *Gwenhwyfar* (*Guinevere*), the name of Arthur's wife, which is identical with *Finnabair*, the name of Medb's daughter. But even if it be allowed (i) that this really was the name of the historical Arthur's wife—it does not occur in any early records —and (ii) that it was necessarily derived from Irish heroic saga—a rather hazardous assumption—it would prove no more than that Irish heroic saga was known in the fifth century. But in the light of the evidence discussed above there can be no doubt that it existed long before that time.

[1] By far the most convincing of the identifications which have been proposed is that of Tavagalavas, son of Antaravas, in Hittite records of c. 1330, with Eteocles, son of Andreus, of Orchomenos. Tavagalavas is described as Ayavalas, and represented as attacking a place called Laaspa—names which it is proposed to identify with Aiolos and Lesbos respectively. Unfortunately little is known of the history or traditions of Orchomenos, though its importance in early times was generally recognised by the ancients. According to Pausanias, IX. 34 ff., our chief authority, it was founded by Andreus. Eteocles left no children, and was succeeded by descendants of Aiolos, whose history Pausanias traces for seven generations, down to the Trojan War. Eteocles therefore belongs to very remote times. There are eponymoi (Minyas, Orchomenos) among his successors; but what is said about him himself does not suggest myth.

Another widely accepted identification is that of Attarissyas, like Tavagalavas a ruler of Ahhiyava, with Atreus, father of Agamemnon. The records which mention Attarissyas date from c. 1250–1225; and his activities relate to the south of Asia Minor, apparently Pamphylia, and a country called Alasya—a name which elsewhere is connected with Cyprus and the opposite mainland. Atreus belongs to a period which is much better known from tradition than that of Eteocles; but we do not know of any tradition which connects him with these regions. A more serious difficulty lies in the names. It is hardly credible that *Atreus* can be represented by *Attarissyas* and *Andreus* by *Antaravas* in the same language, even allowing for the difference of a century between them. *Attarissyas* must surely represent a name in *-ios*. An identification with Acrisios would, we think, be less open to objection, if the latter represents an earlier form *Akrissios*; and, though we are not inclined to attach much importance to such an identification, a connection in Greek tradition might then be found in the story of Bellerophon, the scene of which is laid in the same or neighbouring regions. Alasya may well be the πεδίον τὸ Ἀλήιον of *Il.* VI. 201—identified in later times with the plain of eastern Cilicia. Bellerophon's story is bound up with that of Proitos, the brother of Acrisios. Proitos' wife is a Lycian, and it is from that country, according to Strabo, VIII. vi. 11, that he obtains the Cyclopes, who build his castle at Tiryns.

evidence are *c*, *d*, and *f* (cf. p. 133 f.)—as in the case of prehistoric Ireland.

There is a great body of evidence relating to the Heroic Age which appears to come from tradition. The first question we have to consider is to what extent this evidence is independent of the Homeric poems. In so far as it is independent it is probably to be treated under (*c*) rather than under (*d*), i.e. as coming from a different area rather than merely from a different social or intellectual milieu; for its home appears to be in European Greece, whereas the Homeric poems are generally believed to have originated on the Asiatic coast. The question of a difference of milieu also is by no means to be disregarded. But the chief question is: Can it be shown that there are two (or more) independent groups of traditions, belonging to different areas—just as traditions of the Teutonic Heroic Age are preserved independently in England, Germany and the North?

In point of fact stories relating to the Heroic Age are so numerous and so widely distributed that it would probably not be easy to find in all Greece a place of any importance which did not claim connection with one or other of the heroes. Moreover, not a few of these stories conflict with the evidence of the Homeric poems. But one must not assume, as is too often done, that such stories are necessarily of independent origin. Indeed there can hardly be any question that many of them are due to the popularity of the poems. Very frequently the immediate source is to be found in antiquarian speculation, which flourished in Greece from very early times. Scope for this was afforded by the obsolete place-names which occur rather frequently in the poems, and also by the tendency to connect identical or similar names, both local and personal. Most commonly no doubt the speculation was based on local stories; but some even of these may have been derived ultimately from the poems.

It is unfortunate that practically nothing is left of the works of the early antiquarian poets, except Hesiod. The earliest of them, such as Eumelos and Cinaithon, are said to have lived in the eighth century. There remain a certain number of fragments ascribed to Hesiod and later poets of the same type, and also some fragments of lyric poems relating to the Heroic Age. But the earliest surviving works, apart from the Homeric poems, which treat heroic stories in detail, date from the fifth century—the Odes of Pindar and Bacchylides and the Athenian dramas. To the same period belong the earliest prose accounts, contained in Herodotos' *History* and in fragments of earlier writers. But the great bulk of our information comes from poems, treatises, scholia and various other records dating from the Alexandrian and Roman periods. Perhaps the most important source of all is the *Description of Greece* by the antiquarian traveller Pausanias, who lived in the second century A.D.

From these sources we hear of many stories of which nothing or practically nothing is known from the Homeric poems, or from any similar poems of which we have record. Such are the stories of the early kings of Athens, to which the Homeric poems contain only one or two references—and these in passages which Alexandrian critics regarded as spurious. The stories of the early kings of Argolis are still more famous; and to these also the Homeric poems refer quite rarely. The longest passage (*Il.* VI. 152 ff.) suggests a different form of the genealogy from that which was known in later times. Another striking case is that of the Iamidai, a family whose origin is treated at some length by Pindar (*Ol.* VI. 28 ff.). This family is not mentioned in the Homeric poems, except in a passing reference to a locality in the 'Catalogue of Ships' (*Il.* II. 604).

These and many other stories are clearly independent of the Homeric poems. For the most part, however, they either relate to times anterior to those with which the poems are concerned, or else they are definitely antiquarian or non-heroic in character. But if we turn to the characters and events with which the poems are primarily concerned we find that, though the main outlines of the stories are the same here and later, there are not inconsiderable divergences in details. We may take as an example the family of the Pelopidai, which is represented as the most powerful of all the families of the period. The Homeric genealogy of this family is as follows:

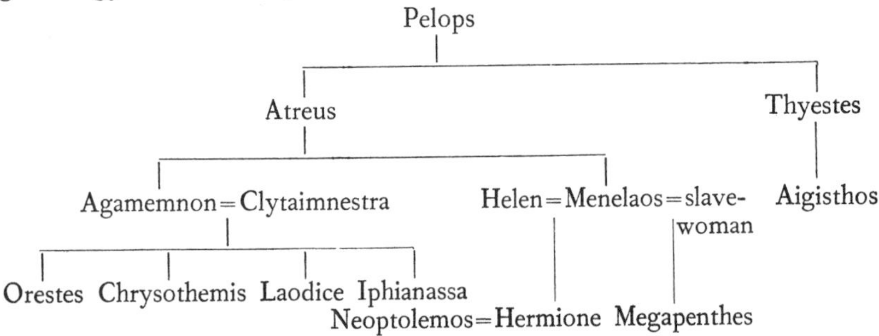

Pelops is succeeded by Atreus, Atreus by Thyestes, and Thyestes by Agamemnon (*Il.* II. 104 ff.). It is not stated where Pelops and Atreus resided, but Agamemnon's home is Mycenai. According to *Il.* II. 569 ff. his dominions include also the cities on the north coast of the Peloponnesos, and according to IX. 291 ff. various cities in Messenia. Menelaos' home is Lacedaimon. Thyestes resides at an unspecified locality, perhaps on the east coast of the Peloponnesos, and is succeeded there by Aigisthos. The latter gains the favour of Clytaimnestra, and on Agamemnon's return murders him with her assistance. The murder takes place at a banquet at Aigisthos' house—which apparently is not far from Agamemnon's home (*Od.* IV. 528 ff.). Aigisthos then rules Mycenai for seven years. But eventually Orestes returns from Athens and slays him (*ib.* III. 306 ff.). It is not stated specifically that he also killed his mother; but this is perhaps implied, since he celebrates her funeral rites with those of Aigisthos.

Later authorities show marked divergences from this story, both in the genealogy and in other respects. There is a good deal of disagreement, but the following is probably the earliest (non-Homeric) form of the genealogy:

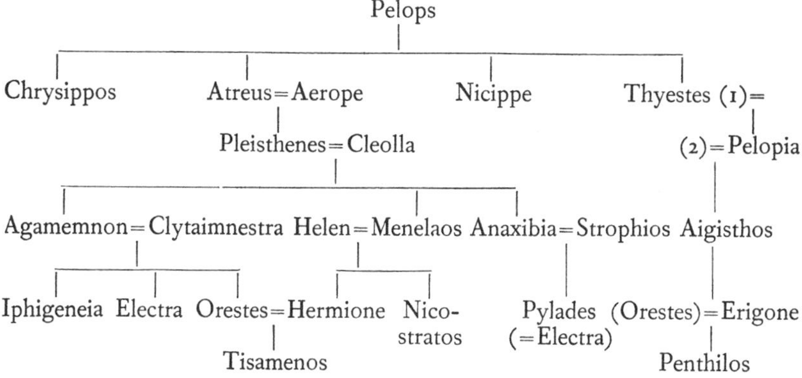

Pelops is said to have come from Lydia or Phrygia; Tantalos is his father, and Niobe his sister. He becomes king of Pisa by causing the death of Oinomaos (in a chariot race) and marrying his daughter Hippodameia. His sons Atreus and Thyestes murder their half-brother Chrysippos and flee to Mycenai, where the king, Eurystheus, marries their sister Nicippe. On Eurystheus' death Atreus becomes king. Agamemnon and Menelaos are not sons of Atreus, but of his son Pleisthenes. Pleisthenes, instigated by Thyestes, attempts to slay his father, but is killed by him. Thyestes also seduces Atreus' wife. Atreus in revenge kills two of Thyestes' sons and gives them to him to eat at a banquet. The history of the family is indeed little more than a catalogue of crimes committed by one member of it against another.

Most of the names and relationships given in the above genealogy can be traced back to the antiquarian poetry of the eighth and seventh centuries. Nicostratos, Erigone, Tisamenos and Penthilos are cited from Cinaithon;[1] Nicippe, Aerope, Pleisthenes, Cleolla, Anaxibia, and Nicostratos from Hesiod's *Catalogos*.[2] The story of the sacrifice of Iphigeneia and her rescue by Artemis was contained in the *Cypria*,[3] which also seems to have known Tantalos as father of Pelops. Pylades appeared with Orestes at the vengeance in the *Nostoi*.[4] Electra is first mentioned apparently by Xanthos, a lyric poet of the seventh century; but the reference[5] implies that her name was already known. On the other hand frequent discrepancies occur in the works of later poets, chiefly through the introduction of names and relationships from the Homeric poems. Thus, Sophocles has a daughter of Agamemnon called Chrysothemis—presumably from the *Iliad* (IX. 145)—while various poets describe the same king as a son of Atreus. It may be due to the same cause that several authorities represent Hermione as married first to Neoptolemos, and then, after his death, to Orestes; sometimes he is killed by Orestes.

It is not unlikely that the speculations of antiquarian poets may be responsible for some items in the genealogy. But there is no justification for assuming that all the non-Homeric elements are due to such web-spinning. They are not mere amplifications of the Homeric account; sometimes they definitely contradict it—and that not only in the case of Pleisthenes and in the names of minor characters. Thus, the *Odyssey* (IV. 12 ff.) states that Menelaos had no son by his queen; Hermione was Helen's only child. But both Cinaithon and Hesiod's *Catalogos* give Nicostratos as son of Helen. Again, in *Od.* III. 306 f. Orestes comes from Athens to avenge his father; but later tradition gives a circumstantial account of his doings. According to this he was brought up in

[1] Fragm. 3, 4 (Kinkel).

[2] Fragm. 115–17 (Kinkel). It is possible that Hesiod is not responsible for all the names given in fragm. 116, since other authorities are mentioned with him; but the case of Pleisthenes can hardly be in dispute.

[3] For Iphigeneia see the epitome in Proclos' *Chrestomathy* (Kinkel, *Epic. Graec. Fragmenta*, p. 19); cf. Hesiod, fragm. 118 (*ib.*). Pelops is called Tantalides in Cypr., fragm. 9 (*ib.*).

[4] See the epitome, *ad fin.* (Kinkel, *op. cit.* p. 53); cf. also Asios, fragm. 5 (*op. cit.* p. 204).

[5] Aelian, *Historical Miscellany*, IV. 26 (cf. Edmonds, *Lyra Graeca*, II. p. 12 f.). Xanthos appears to have identified Electra with the Laodice of the *Iliad*.

Phocis by Strophios, the husband of Anaxibia, his father's sister; and it was from there he set out, accompanied by his cousin Pylades, who subsequently married his sister Electra. Moreover there are differences in the setting and connections—what may be called the traditional political geography—of the two versions. There seems to be a discrepancy as to the scene of Agamemnon's death, and perhaps also as to the seat of his government; but to this question we shall have to return later. It may be mentioned here, however, that in the 'Catalogue of Ships' (*Il.* II. 574 f.) this king has under his immediate sway a group of cities on the north coast of the Peloponnesos—a district later known as Achaia. But according to the tradition regularly accepted in later times these cities had belonged to the Ionians down to the 'Return of the Heracleidai', when they were conquered by the Achaeans under Tisamenos who had been expelled from Argos.

Now if the Greek genealogies which we have been discussing be compared with the Teutonic genealogies given on p. 136 f. and p. 138 f., it will be seen that the resemblances and differences between the different versions in each case are in general of a similar character. The more important persons and their relationships with one another are for the most part identical in both versions, and this is generally true also of the outstanding incidents in the stories. In the minor characters there is a considerable amount of variation. The greater abundance of names in the later Greek genealogy may be due in part to learned speculation; but, whatever its cause, the Norse version of the Burgundian genealogy is to a certain extent parallel.

Other parallels between the Norse and the later Greek versions may be seen in the stories of incest between a father and daughter—unwitting in both cases—and in the banquets at which a father is maliciously made to eat the flesh of his infant children—again in ignorance. Of the incestuous origin of Hrothulf (Hrólfr Kraki) there is no hint in *Beowulf*; indeed his age, as we have seen (p. 137), seems practically to exclude the possibility of the story. Again, the banquet given to Atli (Attila) goes with the story of his death (cf. p. 139), the history of which can to some extent be traced. It is known from the contemporary account of Priscus[1] that Attila died a natural death (from the bursting of a blood vessel) on the night following his marriage with a girl called Hildico. Eighty years later, however, we find the Roman chronicler Marcellinus Comes recording that he was murdered by night by a woman. This may well come from a contemporary rumour, since the circumstances

[1] Quoted by Jordanes, *Get.* 49.

described by Priscus were obviously such as to rouse suspicion. But the woman can hardly be any other than the bride. We do not know from any historical source that Attila married a sister of Guntharius, though this feature is common to both versions of the story and in itself is in no way improbable. But if this sister was Hildico, the alleged murderess—as is assumed by many scholars—there can hardly have been any children ready for him to eat.

The milieu in which such motifs as these could flourish must clearly have been different from that which produced *Beowulf* or the Homeric poems. In Greece, as in the North, heroic poetry must have passed from the court, with its reticence and decorum, to circles of cruder tastes. The story of Thyestes is to be taken in connection with those of Iason and Medeia, Pentheus, Oidipus, the Minotaur, and other similar horrors—all of which show characteristics more in accordance with folk-tale than with heroic story.

It is not to be supposed that these horrors were introduced into the stories in late times. The dramatists of the fifth century seem rarely to have taken their subjects from the Homeric poems; but when they did so they appear to have kept fairly close to the stories. No new characters are introduced in the *Rhesos*[1] or even in the *Cyclops*, except supernatural beings. Even in the imaginative continuations of the *Odyssey*, which were composed in the two previous centuries, the new matter apparently did not conflict with the old; the scene was laid mostly in unknown lands. The prestige enjoyed by the Homeric poems was too great to allow of innovations except in purely imaginative spheres. We know of only one definite departure from their authority—the story invented by Stesichoros in his *Palinoidia* that it was not Helen herself but only a phantom or semblance of her which went to Troy. But this experiment belongs itself rather to the imaginative than to the heroic sphere, for it was not denied that Helen appeared to be in Troy; and it was remarkable enough to give rise to a kind of myth relating to the poet himself.

We see no reason therefore for doubting that the two versions of the story of the Pelopidai were as independent of one another as those of the story of the Scyldingas. It may very well be that the origin of the non-Homeric traditions is to be traced to heroic poetry (or saga)—which is doubtless true to some extent of the (Northern) story of the Scyldingas —but if so this poetry must have been different from anything we can

[1] In the tragedy (279 and passim) Rhesos is said to be son of the Strymon, whereas according to *Il.* x. 435 his father's name is Eioneus. Possibly the tragedian took this to be the name of the river.

properly call Homeric. The elements common to the two versions must be regarded as more or less contemporary records.

The two versions of the story of the Burgundian kings do not provide so good an analogy. It is not known at what date they became independent of one another; and neither of them bears any close resemblance to the Homeric poems. But in *Beowulf* we have a work similar in character to the latter and arising out of very similar conditions. In both cases we have heroic epic poems which became crystallised in form at a comparatively early date, but the origin of which is to be sought in records, perhaps in poetic form, carried over the sea to a new land—in one case probably by the settlers themselves, in the other through communication between the home land and the land which had been occupied not long before. In both cases also we find records of the same events surviving in the home lands or countries adjacent thereto. But these records, instead of becoming crystallised, have passed through a process of disintegration, and consequently, as records of the past, are far inferior to those which have been preserved in the new lands.

The Scandinavian version of the story of the Scyldingas is known both from Danish and Icelandic sources. The Icelandic tradition came, at least mainly, from Norway. Between the two there are not inconsiderable differences, and even among the various Norse accounts and references we find no complete uniformity. The same is true also of the later Greek version, though here the influence of the Homeric poems is no doubt largely responsible for variations. But although there is no necessity for believing that all the post-Homeric traditions of the Pelopidai came from the same centre, yet a good deal of evidence points to one particular locality as the chief source of information. This is the neighbourhood of Sparta, and especially Amyclai.

The Spartans appear to have regarded Agamemnon as one of their own kings. This is implied in the speech attributed by Herodotos (VII. 159) to the envoys sent to Syracuse in 480, just before the great Persian invasion; and later writers give evidence to the same effect. Thus, Clement of Alexandria[1] states that the Spartans worshipped a Zeus Agamemnon, and Pausanias (III. 19. 6) says that they had a tomb of Agamemnon and Cassandra at Amyclai. This last piece of evidence is in accord with the statement of Pindar (*Pyth.* XI. 31 f.) that Amyclai was the scene of Agamemnon's death. Stesichoros and Simonides placed his royal residence 'in Lacedaimon'.[2] In another passage Pindar

[1] Clement of Alexandria, *Protr.* II. 38.

[2] Cf. Edmonds, *Lyra Graeca*, p. 54 f., from the scholiast on Euripides, *Orestes* 46.

(*Nem.* XI. 34) speaks of Amyclai as the home of Orestes, while in *Pyth.* XI. 16 he describes the same hero as a Laconian.

Amyclai is not mentioned in the Homeric poems, except in one passage in the 'Catalogue of Ships' (*Il.* II. 584), where it is included among the cities governed by Menelaos; and in historical times it was never a place of any great importance. But, although it is less than three miles distant from Sparta, it is said[1] to have remained in Achaean hands at the time of the Dorian invasion, and not to have been conquered by the Spartans until the reign of Teleclos, about the middle of the eighth century. This place would seem therefore well fitted to preserve traditions of the earlier period. It may be recalled (cf. p. 184) that the earliest references to the non-Homeric genealogy of the Pelopidai come from fragments of Cinaithon, a Spartan poet who is said to have lived in the eighth century.

We have treated the story of the Pelopidai at some length because the evidence for this is by far the fullest and most satisfactory. Of the other heroes who figure most prominently in the Homeric poems non-Homeric records have comparatively little to say; and in some cases it is doubtful whether even this comes from genuine tradition. Most of them, it may be observed, belong to localities which were of little or no importance in later times. But the true explanation may be that these heroes have acquired fame only in connection with the siege of Troy. The cases of Odysseus, Achilles, Neoptolemos, Diomedes and Idomeneus will require notice in the next chapter. Diomedes certainly played a part in the story of the fall of Thebes; but it is doubtful whether the (non-Homeric) adventures recorded of the others come from early heroic poetry. In regard to Idomeneus it may be remarked that though non-Homeric records have little to say about the hero himself, they supply a good number of stories relating to Minos and other members of his family.

Reference, however, may be made here to the case of Meleagros, whose story is told—incidentally—at some length in *Il.* IX. 529 ff. The account given here differs in some noticeable features from the story as told in later times. There is no mention of Atalante or of the Moirai, and it seems to be implied that Meleagros' death is due to the Erinys invoked by his mother. We do not know how far back the later story can be traced; but it has a special interest because it seems to be derived from a poem (or saga) of Type A, rather than from antiquarian poetry. It may be observed that according to the Hesiodic

[1] Pausanias, III. 2.

Eoiai[1] Meleagros' death was due to Apollo, who was defending the Curetes. This is at variance with both versions of the story.

We have not taken into account the evidence of the forms of heroic proper names, because such evidence seems to us to be not free from ambiguity. Such a name as *Wekaba* (Hecabe), which occurs on early vases depicting Trojan scenes, might of course come from non-Homeric tradition; but as a Trojan name it is obviously much more likely to be of Homeric origin. It is well known that the Homeric poems were recited in various parts of Greece, perhaps everywhere, and we see no grounds for assuming that the Ionicised form of language, in which they have come down to us, was employed for such recitations in, say, Doric cities. On the other hand there are a number of variants such as *Agamedmon* for Agamemnon, and *Olysseus* for Odysseus, which are not of a purely phonetic character; and it seems to us very likely that some of these may come from non-Homeric tradition. More than this can hardly be said with confidence. Some peculiarities of heroic nomenclature will be noticed later.

From what has been said above it will be seen that there is good evidence for (*c*)—i.e. the existence of independent traditions in different regions. Evidence for (*d*) need hardly be discussed. As regards (*e*)—the consistency of heroic tradition—it may be said that the Homeric poems, the *Iliad* and *Odyssey*, rarely show any inconsistencies; and the same seems to be true of some of the lost Cyclic poems, so far as one can judge. On the other hand the Homeric evidence is frequently at variance with non-Homeric tradition, though perhaps not often on points of fundamental importance. For the character of the *Cypria* it is instructive to notice that, if we may trust the epitome given by Proclos, this poem made the Achaean fleet to set out twice from Aulis. The first account seems to have been taken from the *Iliad* (II. 303 ff.), while the second, which described the sacrifice of Iphigeneia, was in accord with non-Homeric tradition.

The archaeological evidence (*f*) has been so frequently treated that we need not enter into any detailed discussion of this subject here. It will be sufficient to note briefly a few of the chief features which characterise the civilisation depicted in the Homeric poems, and which enable us to determine the position of this civilisation in the chronological scheme which has been established as a result of archaeological investigation.

The great prehistoric fortresses of Troy and Mycenai, and perhaps

[1] Fragm. 159 (Kinkel).

also the palace of Cnossos, are represented as still occupied. No detailed descriptions of these are given; but the account of the—probably imaginary—palace of Alcinoos in the *Odyssey* suggests that decorations of the Mycenean period were familiar to the poet. Iron is known, but weapons are regularly said to be of bronze. The sword is used for striking as well as for thrusting, and would therefore seem to be of the type—usually leaf-shaped—characteristic of the late Bronze Age in western Europe, which appears only at the very end of the Mycenean period. Brooches, which are first found in late Mycenean graves, seem now to be in more general use. The horse is always used for driving, though one or two passages perhaps suggest that riding was not absolutely unknown. The disposal of the dead is by cremation, a custom apparently not practised in the Mycenean period. The only detailed description of a funeral—that of Patroclos—is of a barbaric type, similar to those described in *Beowulf*, though with the addition of human victims, as in *Sigurðarkviða hin skamma*, st. 70. The construction of the barrow, both in form and purpose, is entirely in accord with northern custom.

The 'Catalogue of Ships' gives a detailed political geography of Greece, which is not altogether in harmony with the indications contained elsewhere in the *Iliad*. But both alike show features which are quite unknown to the Greece of even the earliest historical times. Several of the leading heroes come from districts—Pylos, Malis, Salamis, and Ithaca—which were never of any importance in the historical period. The Ionians and the Dorians, the chief national groups of historical times, are barely mentioned, and even then the names are applied to the inhabitants of particular localities, and not as collective terms. There are no Greek settlements on the Asiatic coast; in the Trojan Catalogue (*Il.* II. 867 f.) Miletos is a Carian city. The Phrygians are located in 'Lesser Phrygia', to the south of the Marmara. On the other hand there is no trace of any knowledge of the Hittite empire. Maritime activity and commerce are in the hands of the Phoenicians, who are also famous for metal working, especially the production of silver vessels. In the *Odyssey*, the western Mediterranean is a region of mystery, though not absolutely unknown from report.

This evidence is not entirely uniform, though the discrepancies are not very important. The constant and governing elements—we may instance the regular use of bronze weapons and the absence of Greek settlements in Asia Minor—cannot represent conditions later than the tenth century at the latest. On the other hand there are some items, such as Achilles' new shield, Odysseus' brooch, and Helen's wheeled workbox, which may have been suggested by novelties of the eighth century. The last date does not seem to us quite certain; for concentric zone decoration and wheeled bijoux had a long history before they found their way into Etruscan graves. But in any case these later elements are quite exceptional; the general picture of civilisation and political geography contained in the poem cannot have been true even for the ninth century.

It is essential to bear in mind here, as in the Teutonic, British, and Irish heroic stories, that these pictures of civilisation and political geography form merely the setting and framework of the stories, without which they could not have come into existence. This has too often been overlooked. Theories have been put forward, e.g. that the *Iliad* is founded upon a tradition that some (nameless) king of Mycenai had once led an expedition against Troy. But all such theories are due to a fundamental misconception of the character of heroic story—the interest of which is essentially personal. The object of the Homeric poets was to relate stories of adventure, not to reconstruct the prehistoric civilisation of Greece. The civilisation and political geography described in the poems must represent what actually existed at—or very shortly before—the time when the stories took shape. In other words the stories must date substantially from the tenth century or earlier.

As regards the upper limit, it is to be observed that the civilisation depicted in the poems does not correspond to that of the late Mycenean period ('Late Minoan III'), as revealed by archaeological investigation. There are many important differences in details, e.g. with regard to the disposal of the dead, and as a whole the civilisation of the poems seems to be on a decidedly lower level—more barbaric—than the other. We may note also the absence of any knowledge of the Hittites and the fact that Sidon, not Crete, is the centre of maritime activity and trade. The Hittite empire in Asia Minor is known to have been destroyed just before 1200, and it is believed that the Cretan-Mycenean civilisation was shattered or at least transformed about the same time or not long afterwards.[1] Articles of later types have been found at Mycenai and at

[1] The archaeological evidence at present available for the Greek mainland seems to point not to a single catastrophe, but to a decadence accompanied by external (barbaric) influences. The analogy of Rome suggests a series of barbaric irruptions and conquests. But it is apparently still difficult to assign fixed dates to the various phases of the decadence; and the same may be said with regard to the substitution of iron for bronze in weapons. When did the iron sword come into general use in Greece?

some of the old Cretan sites, but these are in general more like the Homeric things. We may therefore probably fix the twelfth century as the upper limit. But in view of the fact that the poems show no knowledge of any catastrophes, such as would undoubtedly attend the downfall of a higher civilisation, it would be unwise to carry the history of the poems back beyond the eleventh at the earliest. The fact that the reigning families are represented as having held their power for two or three generations points to the same conclusion.

There is of course a natural inclination to connect the detailed picture of Heroic Greece given by the poems with the splendour of the Mycenean period, rather than with the dark and practically unknown age which followed; and in spite of the discrepancies observable in the two civilisations many scholars are unable to resist the temptation to do so. It is doubtless more attractive to visualise Agamemnon with his quasi-imperial position reigning as a Constantine in a still unconquered Rome than as a Gothic king settled amidst its decay. And, moreover, it was the attempt to trace the history of Agamemnon which first led to the discovery of the Mycenean civilisation. A way out of the difficulty is therefore sought by distinguishing sharply between the times in which the poems were composed and those to which the stories relate. The Heroic Age is identified with the Mycenean period—say, the thirteenth century and earlier—while the poems and the civilisation which they depict are referred to much later times.

This is a theory which finds much favour at present. No evidence in support of it is to be obtained from the poems themselves, but it is in accordance with the calculations of the ancient historians and chronologists. The chronology generally accepted in later times was that of Eratosthenes (shortly before 200 B.C.), which dated the fall of Troy in 1183. The Parian Marble (half a century earlier) gives 1209 for the same event. Herodotos (II. 145) places the Trojan War eight hundred, and (II. 53) the time of Hesiod and Homer four hundred, years before his own time (c. 440). The grounds upon which the last statement is based are not known. Many scholars are disposed to accept it for Homer, though not for Hesiod; but it will hardly account, for example, for the bronze weapons. If the civilisation is that of 'Homer's' time he must be dated at least a century farther back. But even then the political geography is that not of his time but of the Heroic Age—which is said to be two or three centuries earlier.

Whatever may be the origin of Herodotos' date for Homer, the other dates given above are not mere random guesses but items in a scheme of chronology, which was based on genealogies. Herodotos and other writers of his time do not apply dates in our sense to the Heroic Age, but they have a conventional reckoning of forty years to a generation, which enables them to state in numbers of years the distance at which a person of the far past stands removed from their own times. From various passages, especially VII. 204 and VIII. 131, compared with II. 145, it is clear that when Herodotos reckons eight hundred years from his own time to the Trojan War, he means twenty generations.[1] The Alexandrian chronologists made a step forward, fixing definite dates for various events, e.g. 1183 for the fall of Troy, and 1104 for the 'Return of the Heracleidai'. But the principle on which these dates are based was taken over by them from their predecessors, i.e. forty years per generation—not only for the Heroic Age but also for all the early period, down to the seventh century.

It is only by those who are willing to allow an average of forty years per generation that any value can be attached to these dates.[2] Those who, like ourselves, are unwilling to allow this must reduce the figures by about 25 per cent. in order to arrive at the dates really indicated by the genealogies. Then the Trojan War will fall six hundred years before Herodotos' time, i.e. some time after 1050, and the end of the Heroic Age (the 'Return of the Heracleidai') some time in the first half of the tenth century. It is without doubt to these dates that the evidence of Greek tradition points. Unfortunately no genealogies except those of the Spartan royal families have been preserved complete. But there is some evidence with regard to other genealogies which points to the same conclusion.[3]

The Spartan genealogies carry us back to the end of the Heroic Age eight generations before Theopompos (c. 720), with whom the historical period begins. The Trojan War falls about two generations earlier, i.e. about three centuries in all. If we accept this, the only evidence available, the history of Greek heroic poetry becomes clear enough. According to tradition, the 'Return of the Heracleidai' and the first settlement in Asia (the 'Aeolic Migration') took place about the same

[1] There are a few exceptional cases, especially the calculation of the date of Dionysos' birth (II. 145) and the duration of the rule of the Heracleidai in Lydia (I. 7), which can hardly be explained, we think, except as early scribal errors, perhaps through the use of numerals.

[2] This view has recently been defended. The question is discussed in the note at the end of this chapter.

[3] We may refer especially to the Arcadian genealogy recorded by Pausanias, VIII. 4 f. For other genealogies cf. Chadwick, *Heroic Age*, p. 182 f.

time. One of the leaders in the latter movement was Penthilos, son of Orestes, from whom the noblest family in Mytilene claimed descent. We need not hesitate to believe that poems relating to the Trojan War, as well as to other events of the Heroic Age, were already current by this time, and that they were carried over to Asia by the settlers. There they formed the nucleus from which the Homeric poems grew in the course of the next few generations. In the homeland remains of the same early poetry seem to have survived, more or less disintegrated, and perhaps only in the form of saga, until the time of the antiquarian poets.

Evidence for the use of heroic names (*g*) does not amount to much, owing to the fact that very few names have been preserved from the long period between the Heroic Age and the seventh century. There was an Agamemnon reigning in Cyme towards the end of the eighth century, and a Hector in Chios not much later. But there can be no doubt that by this time the Homeric poems were widely known in Asia, if not in European Greece also. Hesiod's brother Perses bears a heroic name; but it is clear from the *Works and Days* (160 ff.) that Hesiod was familiar with Homeric poetry. Their father had come from Cyme. It is perhaps of somewhat more importance that the name Menelaos appears among the early kings of Sparta, though it does not occur in Herodotos' genealogy (VII. 204). The king bearing this name would seem to have lived about the beginning of the eighth century. But in view of the evidence discussed above we have little doubt that Menelaos was always known at Sparta—especially perhaps in connection with the temple of Helen at Therapne, between Sparta and Amyclai.

In heroic names, however, there is another feature which deserves attention. If the Homeric and non-Homeric genealogies of the Pelopidai given on p. 182 f. above be compared, it will be seen that the names common to the two, i.e. the essential names in the story, are not of Greek—at least not specifically Greek—origin. *Pelops* and *Menelaos* may be Greek. The former is an ethnic name of the type borne by some peoples in the north of Greece, e.g. *Dolopes*, *Dryopes*. But similar names occur also in Macedonia and elsewhere, e.g. *Deuriopes*. Names in *-lawos* are Phrygian, as well as Greek. None of the other names appear to be Greek. Two (*Thyestes* and *Orestes*) are ethnic names taken from peoples (*Dyestai*, *Orestai*) in Illyria and Macedonia. Some of the names which occur only in the non-Homeric genealogy also seem to be doubtful. *Aeropos* is the name of one of the brothers in a Macedonian story related by Herodotos (VIII. 137); the others have native names. It is also the name of a later king. *Penthilos* does not appear to be Greek. One is tempted to connect it with the goddess Bendis (the Thracian Artemis).

According to non-Homeric tradition Pelops was a foreigner who had come from Phrygia or Lydia. The names noted above suggest that the connections of the family lay in a different direction. But there is no doubt that the Phrygians (*Phryges*) were an offshoot from the Bryges or Brygoi, a people of Macedonia, and that with various other peoples they had passed over into Asia from the Balkan Peninsula. In the Heroic Age the difference in sound between the two names had not yet come into existence. It is likely therefore that the localisation of Pelops in Asia was due to a misunderstanding. At the same time it is to be noted that names of non-Greek appearance are by no means confined to this family; *Nestor*, *Achilleus*, *Aias*, and many others are quite as strange. It would seem indeed as if there was a numerous and dominant foreign element in Greece during the Heroic Age.

It is important to notice that the later forms of some of the names mentioned above (*Bryges*, *Dyestai*, *Bendi-*) show different sounds from those which appear in the heroic names. This is due to a sound-change characteristic of the Greek language, through which the original sounds *bh*, *dh*, *gh* became *ph*, *th*, *ch*. The heroic names show this change, but the foreign names learned by the Greeks in later times have *b*, *d*, *g*.[1] Other examples are *Berecyntes*, the name of a Phrygian people, which is apparently identical with *Phorcys*, the name of the leader of the Phrygians in the *Iliad*, and *Baiace*, the name of a 'city' in Chaonia, according to Hecataios, which is probably to be connected with the *Phaieces* (Phaeacians) of the *Odyssey*. It is to be observed that names in Asia Minor derived from Phrygian or Mysian rarely if ever show *ph*, *th*, *ch* unless they are found in the *Iliad*. Usually such names have *b*, *d*, *g*, as in *Berecyntes* or *Germe* (related to Greek *Therme*). It would seem therefore that this sound-change had ceased to operate at—or soon after—the time of the Greek settlement of Asia Minor. This means that the heroic names given above, both of peoples and persons, date from the Heroic Age itself.

The results of our discussion may now be summarised briefly as

[1] The heroic names of peoples which remained in contact with the Greek world, like the Phrygians, were of course preserved. The Bryges, being an inland people, may have been unknown to the Greeks for centuries after the Heroic Age. They seem to be mentioned first in the *Telegony*, which is ascribed to the early sixth century. The name was evidently not derived from heroic tradition.

follows: (i) Traditions of the Heroic Age were preserved independently in Europe and Asia; (ii) The civilisation and political geography which serve as a framework to the Homeric poems and owe their preservation to this fact, represent substantially the conditions of the Heroic Age; (iii) Some at least of the names, both of persons and peoples, contained in the poems date from the same period. From this evidence we may infer with confidence that the Greek Heroic Age was no mere creation of literature, but an epoch of history parallel to the other Heroic Ages discussed above—in spite of its antiquity and the length of time by which it is separated from the strictly historical period. The records indeed are more satisfactory than those for the early part of the Irish Heroic Age. Unhistorical elements abound, as we shall see in the next chapter; but there can be no reasonable doubt that some at least of the stories have a historical basis.

NOTE. The credibility of the reckoning of forty years to a generation in the Spartan royal genealogies, upon which Alexandrian chronology seems to have been largely based, has been defended recently by Myres, *Who were the Greeks?* p. 304. Speaking of the pedigree of Leotychides (Herod. VIII. 131) he says that "it has to be observed first, that in this list we are not dealing with generations but with reigns, and secondly that the Spartans postponed legal marriage till the age of forty".

We do not see how the first statement can be correct. Herodotos gives the list quite definitely as a genealogy—"Leotychides, son of Menares, son of Hegesileos", etc. He adds that all these, except the two mentioned first after Leotychides (i.e. Leotychides' father and grandfather), had been kings of Sparta. It is commonly held, we believe, that 'two' here is due to a scribal error for 'seven', since Leotychides' seven immediate ancestors are all wanting in the list of kings of this line (the Eurypontidai) given by Pausanias, III. 7. But, whether this be so or not, the genealogy of Leotychides cannot possibly be regarded as a list of the Eurypontid kings. Herodotos himself mentions three predecessors of Leotychides who do not appear in it, and Pausanias adds three more.

The source of the second statement—that the Spartans postponed legal marriage till the age of forty—is not known to us. We think it must come from a theoretical writer. It may represent a Spartan ideal; but in practice it is quite irreconcilable with the succession of Spartan kings in the fifth century—when first we have detailed information from Herodotos, Thucydides, etc. In Herodotos, VII. 3, Demaratos is represented as saying that at Sparta the right of succession belonged to a king's son who was born after his father's accession—not to those who had been born previously. If this custom was rigidly observed, it might reasonably be expected that the length of a generation in the Spartan royal families would be somewhat above the average; but in point of fact this does not seem to be borne out by the records for the fifth, fourth and third centuries. It may be added that we hear—not unfrequently and in various periods—of kings (Zeuxidemos, Leotychides, Pleistoanax, etc.) whose fathers never reigned.

Even if the statement as to the prohibition of marriage under forty applies only to the period before the fifth century, we shall still have difficulties to face. Leotychides was grown up (cf. Herod. VI. 65) when he became king in 491; he cannot have been born later than 510. Then his eighth ancestor Theopompos—the first name in the genealogy which we can identify—must have been born not later than 840–830, if marriage under forty was illegal. Theopompos was the king who conquered Messenia—for which the date given by Pausanias (IV. 13) is 724. To meet the requirements of a forty-year generation scheme we shall have to carry back not only this event but also the second Messenian War and the activities of Tyrtaios to dates far earlier than those which are generally accepted.

In the same work, p. 577, note 8, Prof. Myres says that the abnormal length of the generations extends only to the sons of Aristodemos, and that from Aristodemos we have generations of normal length back to Heracles, whom he dates c. 1230 B.C. But it is clear that Herodotos made no distinction of this kind. In VII. 204 and VIII. 131, he traces the genealogies of Leonides and Leotychides back to Eurysthenes and Procles (the sons of Aristodemos) in the fifteenth and to Heracles in the twentieth generation. The births of Leonides and Leotychides may be dated with confidence c. 530–510. Again, in II. 145 he says that Heracles was born about nine hundred years before his own time (c. 450–440), i.e. c. 1350–1340. He cannot therefore have regarded the five earliest generations as shorter.

Similar evidence is to be found elsewhere. Eusebius and the Parian Marble, though they give different dates, both assume an interval of three hundred years between the arrival of Danaos with his daughters and the fall of Troy. This interval is doubtless derived from earlier authorities, and based ultimately upon genealogies. Presumably the starting point is the birth of Abas, whose descendants in the Trojan War—Tlepolemos, son of Heracles, of the line of Acrisios, and Sthenelos, son of Capaneus, of the line of Proitos (cf. Pausan. II. 18)—are descended from him in the seventh generation. Again, we may take the ancestry of the kings of Cyrene, whose genealogy, though not preserved in detail, covers both the Spartan and pre-Spartan periods. According to Pindar, *Pyth.* IV *ad init.*, Battos I, the founder of the dynasty, is descended in the seventeenth (i.e. sixteenth) generation from Euphemos—one of the Argonauts, and a contemporary of Heracles. Battos is said to have founded Cyrene c. 630, i.e. about a century (or slightly more) before the births of Leonides and Leotychides, who stand in the twentieth generation from Heracles. We may also compare the Arcadian genealogy recorded by Pausanias, VIII. 4 f., which comes down only to the second Messenian War—about 650 B.C. From the last king, Aristocrates II, persons concerned with the voyage of the Argo and with Heracles stand in the fourteenth and fifteenth generations. Holaias, brother-in-law of Cresphontes, the brother of Aristodemos, stands in the tenth generation from the same king. The Spartan kings Anaxandros and Anaxidemos, who according to Pausanias, III. 3, 7, reigned during the second Messenian War, stand in the twelfth and eleventh generations from Aristodemos.

It is quite clear therefore that the ancients did not regard the Spartan generations as of exceptional length. The abnormality lies not in the length of the Spartan generations but in an erroneous estimate of the length of generations in general. There seems indeed to be some evidence that the error was detected by some of the Alexandrian scholars, e.g. Callimachos. But this is a question which must be left to experts in Greek chronology. All that we are concerned with here is to make clear that Greek dates, whether they come from Alexandrian writers or from Herodotos or Hecataios, are in themselves of no value. They form no part of tradition, and they are based on erroneous calculations. They ought never to be quoted, except as illustrating the growth of historical research.

With genealogies, as with traditional matter in general, the case is of course quite different. We cannot share the robust faith shown by some recent writers. These records, before they came into the hands of the chronologists, had had a long life, during which they had been exposed to errors of all kinds, arising both from forgetfulness and from antiquarian speculation. Thus, to take a single example, Proitos and Bellerophon belong to the same story, as contemporaries; yet the former is in the sixth, the latter only in the second generation from heroes of the Trojan War. Eponymoi and other suspicious names are not uncommon. On the other hand still less can we share the robust 'scepticism' (so called) of the last century—which in reality assumed that the traditions were all myths or fictions. On this road no progress can be made. Myth and fiction require to be demonstrated just as much as fact.

The Spartan genealogies, which we have been considering, present no features which can fairly be called suspicious, in spite of one or two discrepancies, e.g. the presence or absence of the name *Soos*, which (following Herodotos) we have—perhaps wrongly—ignored. We are inclined to think they are genuine. But we are not prepared to embark upon a discussion of the origin of the dual kingship.

CHAPTER VIII

UNHISTORICAL ELEMENTS IN STORIES OF THE HEROIC AGE

IN poetry and saga relating to the Heroic Age one meets almost everywhere with incidents and scenes which appear to be of an unhistorical character. The evidence afforded by the various Heroic Ages is in general very similar and conforms to certain well-marked types. It will be convenient therefore in this case to treat the matter collectively and to arrange it according to these types.

Three main types may be distinguished: I. Incidents and situations which are in conflict (*a*) with reliable historical evidence or (*b*) with other heroic stories. II. Incidents and situations which are in themselves incredible. III. Matter of various kinds which is neither in conflict with other evidence nor yet in itself incredible, but which, at least in its context, is certainly or probably to be regarded as unhistorical. The invention of characters and motifs will be treated in connection with the last of these sections.

I. Incidents and situations in conflict with good historical evidence occur frequently in the later versions (German and Norse) of the Teutonic heroic stories. In the *Nibelungenlied* we find Dietrich von Berne, i.e. Theodric the Ostrogoth, and his men at the court of Etzel, i.e. Attila, although Theodric was not born until a year or two after Attila's death. In other medieval German poems the confusion is carried much farther, for Dietrich, who died in 526, is made to be nephew of Ermenrich (Eormenric), who died c. 370 and was in reality his remote ancestor. Banished by his uncle, he takes refuge with Etzel, who died in 453. The result of this confusion is that the same characters are associated with Dietrich and Ermenrich, and indeed come upon the scene in most of the heroic stories.

It is to be observed that this confusion does not appear in the early German *Hildebrandeslied.* Here Dietrich's enemy is not Ermenrich but Otachar, i.e. Odoacer, who actually was a contemporary and enemy of Theodric. But the relations of the two even here are not in accordance with history. Dietrich has fled from Otachar's hostility, has lost his friends and spent thirty years in exile. It is to be suspected that these features have been taken over from another story (cf. p. 201). In reality Theodric came in contact with Odoacer when he invaded Italy in 489, and killed him in 493.

In the Norse heroic poems, which are earlier in date than the German—except the last mentioned—similar anachronisms occur, though not quite to the same extent. Þjóðrekr (Theodric) is brought into association with Atli only in *Guðrúnarkviða III*,[1] a poem concerned with a story which is otherwise unknown either in Norse or German heroic literature. On the other hand Jörmunrekr (Eormenric) is everywhere made contemporary with Atli, but he comes into the story only in one special connection. He is never brought into relations with either Atli or Þjóðrekr; but Svanhildr, who is his wife in the Norse version of the story, is the daughter of Guðrún, the widow of Sigurðr and Atli. It is worth noting that this feature seems to be unknown to Saxo, who includes Jörmunrekr among his Danish kings, but makes no reference to the Norse version[2] of the stories of Sigurðr and Atli. In his account Guðrún is merely a sorceress, who assists the brothers of Svanhildr in their attack upon Jörmunrekr.

It should be observed that although anachronisms occur in both Norse and German, they are not in reference to the same relations. This seems to show that they did not occur in the earlier forms of the stories, from which both versions are descended.

In the English poems anachronisms of this kind seem to be limited to *Widsith* and *Waldhere*. One of the fragments of the latter poem refers to Theodric in association with Widia. In medieval German poems Widia (Wittich) is frequently associated with both Dietrich and Ermenrich; but he seems originally to have belonged to the latter. At all events he is mentioned as a hero of the past by Priscus[3] about 446, before Theodric was born. The reference in *Waldhere* may therefore indicate that the confusion of the Theodric and Eormenric stories was already known; but this inference is not quite certain (see below).

In *Widsith* the speaker, who is a minstrel, says that he has visited a number of famous kings, including Eormenric, who died c. 370, Guthhere, who died in 437, and Aelfwine, king of the Lombards, who

[1] Also in the prose introduction to *Guðr. II*; but there is no reference to him in the poem itself, and the passage is doubtless due to *Guðr. III*. Curiously enough in *Guðr. III* Þjóðrekr is once called Þjóðmarr. This is the name of Theodric's father—who is known to have been in Attila's service. Is it possible that the story was originally told of him?

[2] There is an incidental allusion to the German version of the story in Bk. XIII (p. 427, Holder). There is no reference to Siegfried or Etzel.

[3] Jordanes, *Get.* 34.

died c. 570. But these kings are not associated with one another. Later in the poem (v. 109 ff.) he says that he visited the household retinue of Eormenric; and then he gives a list of heroes whom he visited. Some of these apparently belonged to later, and one at least to earlier times than those of Eormenric. The list is perhaps intended as a catalogue of early Gothic heroes.

The English evidence, as usual, represents an earlier phase than the Norse and German. The passage in *Waldhere* is perhaps capable of a special explanation. From the association of Theodric with Widia here and in German poems, and from the unhistorical experiences with which the former is credited even in the *Hildebrandeslied* and the resemblance of these experiences to those of Wolfdietrich, one is tempted to suspect that Theodric was confused with an earlier hero of the same name.[1] Apart from this case we have only the anachronisms of *Widsith*, which are of a different kind. Characters belonging to different ages are visited by the same minstrel, but are not associated with one another. This earlier form of anachronism shows merely that the minstrels did not carry any scheme of chronology in their heads. They did not think of Eormenric and Aelfwine as belonging to different periods of time, but rather as characters who did not enter into the same stories. Anachronisms in the stories themselves belong to a later phase.

Unhistorical elements other than wrong associations seem to occur earlier than these. We may instance the references to Theodric in the *Hildebrandeslied*, whatever may be the explanation of them. There are even cases where an unhistorical incident may be traced to more or less contemporary sources, as pointed out above (p. 185) in reference to the story of Attila's death. But it is hardly conceivable that wrong associations like those which we have been discussing could have arisen until long after the time of the persons affected.

We may next take the case of discrepancies between different accounts of an event or situation for which no good historical evidence is available. It is obvious that one of the accounts must be unhistorical, while the other may or may not be in accordance with fact. Numerous examples of such discrepancies occur in the different versions of heroic stories. We may refer to the genealogies given on p. 136 ff. and the paragraphs which follow. In general the earlier records are those which inspire most confidence. Thus the account of the Scyldingas given in *Beowulf* has a greater appearance of verisimilitude than the accounts of the same family in Norse and Danish records. But there are exceptions.

[1] This suggestion was put forward in *The Heroic Age*, p. 154 ff.

According to all Scandinavian records Bjarki (Beowulf) remains in Denmark in the service of Hrólfr Kraki, and marries his sister. Eventually he is slain in the attack made upon that king by Hjörvarðr. This story has at least the advantage of being possible. In the poem Beowulf becomes king of the Geatas and, after reigning fifty years, falls in combat with a dragon. Even if we deduct the dragon, it is rather curious that Beowulf's long reign is practically a blank, while references to earlier events are frequent.

In regard to the relations of persons belonging to the British Heroic Age there is much discrepancy between the earlier and later records. Records of the later period tend to bring heroes into association with Arthur. Thus in the *Dream of Rhonabwy* we find Rhun, son of Maelgwn, acting as judge at the court of Arthur. But early records give no hint of any connection between Arthur and this family; and in spite of the date (538) assigned to Camlann in the *Annales Cambriae* (cf. p. 149) it is unlikely that Arthur was alive when Maelgwn reigned. Again, in the same piece, as well as in the Romances, we find Owein, son of Urien, at Arthur's court; and in the *Lady of the Fountain* his cousin Cynon, son of Clydno Eidyn, is there with him. But we have seen (p. 38 f.) that there are a considerable number of early poems—panegyrics and elegies—relating to Urien and Owein; and in not one of these is there any reference to Arthur. A passage in the *Historia Brittonum* (cf. p. 155 f.) states that Urien was flourishing c. 572–579, and this date agrees well enough with the indications contained in the poems. But Arthur must have been dead long before this. Cynon is a prominent figure in the *Gododdin* (*An.* I), which relates to an event probably about the close of the sixth century.

In the early heroic poems discrepancies of this kind are hardly to be found. In *An.* I. 89, cf. 787, mention is made of the death of Domnall Brecc (king of Dal Riada), which took place in 642, whereas the disaster which is the subject of the poem would seem to have happened some half a century earlier. But the text of the poem is so corrupt and confused, as we shall see in a later chapter, that no argument can safely be based upon this.

In non-heroic poems and sagas, anachronisms appear to be more frequent. In *Tal.* XIV, a poem which in part bears much resemblance to *Widsith*, the speaker, who is obviously Taliesin, is made to say that he has sung in the presence of Urien and of Brochfael of Powys. Then he speaks of his visit to Maelgwn—which is not incompatible with the previous statements, since, according to the *Hanes Taliesin*, he was very young when this took place. But, later in the same poem, he says that he has been in Ireland with Bran—and in the *Mabinogi* of *Branwen*, he is one of the party which returns from Ireland, though he plays practically no part in the story. It is difficult to believe that there can be any historical basis for this fantastic tale; but if there is it must surely relate to times long before those of Taliesin. In this connection we may refer also to Manawyddan, brother of Bran, who figures both in this *Mabinogi* and in the one which bears his own name. In *BBC.* XXXI he appears as one of Arthur's knights.

In stories relating to the Irish Heroic Age discrepancies are frequent enough, though in stories of the Ulster Cycle they are as a rule not very serious. The most serious cases occur in stories of the early high-kings, before Cormac mac Airt. The different versions of the *Revolt of the Vassals* show many discrepancies, as we have seen (p. 171), though this story is properly to be regarded as non-heroic. One of the versions at least must be largely unhistorical, and probably this is true of the story as a whole.

Great discrepancies occur also in regard to the relations between the family of the high-king Conn Cetchathach, grandfather of Cormac mac Airt, and the kings of Leinster. Conn is said to have had a brother named Eochaid Finn, who in alliance with CuChorb, king of Leinster, made successful war upon Munster and, as a reward for his services, was granted the districts called Fotharta in Leinster.[1] But CuChorb in the genealogies is the fourth ancestor of Cathair Mor, who is said to have preceded Conn in the high-kingship.[2] A discrepancy of several generations is therefore involved; and it cannot be put down to a mere mistake in the name of the Leinster king, for a son of Conall Cernach, named Laigsech Cennmor, is associated with Eochaid in the story and receives the province of Leix as a reward. There can be little doubt that the origin of the story is to be traced to family traditions; and it may be taken as an illustration of the discrepancies which prevail between these traditions and the stories of the high-kings. Many scholars hold that Conn himself is not a historical character. This, however, is a point to which we shall have to refer later.

Perhaps the greatest discrepancies are those which affect non-heroic characters, at least in proportion to the amount which is related of them. Ferchertne, the *fili*, is sometimes in the service of CuRoi, and visits Ulster only to exact vengeance for his master's death. But in

[1] This story is ed. and transl. by Dobbs, *Zeitschr. f. celt. Philol.* XVI. 395 ff.

[2] Cf. the *Battle of Cnucha*, ed. and transl. by Hennessy, *Rev. Celt.* II. 86 ff.

other stories he appears to be a member of Conchobor's court. He is found also in the *Destruction of Dinn Rig*, which relates to quite a different period.[1] Again, the judge Morann sometimes belongs to the time of the Ulster heroes. In one version of the story of *CuChulainn's Birth* he is called upon to decide who is to have the fosterage of the child. But elsewhere he lives in the time of the *Revolt of the Vassals*. In the earliest account of this story he is the son of Cairbre Cenn Cait (cf. p. 171). It may also be noted that Craiphtine, the harper of the *Destruction of Dinn Rig*, appears again in the *Destruction of Da Choca's Hall*, one of the Ulster stories. It would seem that Ferchertne, Morann and Craiphtine were on the way to becoming stock characters or types of their professions.

As regards the Heroic Age of Greece the discrepancies between the Homeric poems and non-Homeric tradition in the story of the Pelopidai have already been noticed (p. 182 ff.). We may also refer to the story of Meleagros (cf. p. 188 f.), in which case an important discrepancy appears among the non-Homeric accounts themselves. In later authorities many heroes have associations, both personal and local, which seem to be quite unknown to the Homeric poems; but in such cases it is of course often difficult to speak with confidence. In heroic stories which are not found in the Homeric poems discrepant accounts are common enough.

II. Incidents and situations in themselves incredible fall mostly into several well-marked categories, which it will be convenient to treat separately.

(*a*) The introduction of supernatural beings is a very common occurrence in heroic poetry and saga. In the Homeric poems gods play a large part in the action. Sometimes the scene is laid amongst the gods themselves in their common home on Mount Olympos, where they meet together and from whence they go to their special sanctuaries in various parts of the Greek world and elsewhere. Sometimes again they visit men in disguise. On such occasions they not unfrequently reveal themselves, and the revelation causes no very great surprise. In *Il.* VI. 119 ff., when Diomedes encounters Glaucos resplendent in golden armour, he expresses doubt as to whether the latter is a man or a god; if he is a god he would prefer not to fight with him. Frequently the gods are present during the fighting, though it is only on rare occasions, as in

[1] One catalogue text makes three different persons called Ferchertne out of these three cases; cf. Stokes, *Zeitschr. f. celt. Philol.* III. 16; Thurneysen, *Ir. Heldensage*, p. 520.

Il. v. 842 ff., that they actually strike a blow. In this passage also Diomedes wounds Ares, with the help of the goddess Athene. More often they merely exhort and advise their favourites and place their opponents at a disadvantage by various stratagems.

Goddesses can transform themselves into birds, as in *Od.* III. 371 f., where this is done by Athene before a concourse of people. More than once in the *Odyssey* the same goddess acts like a witch, transforming the hero in appearance and clothes by a stroke of her wand. The supernatural witch Circe changes men into pigs.

Monsters figure little in the Homeric poems, except in Odysseus' account of his adventures (*Od.* IX–XII). In *Il.* VI. 179 ff., however, there is a reference to Bellerophon's fight with the Chimaira. It is not quite clear whether the boar of Calydon (*Il.* IX. 538 ff.) belongs to this category, though it is sent by the goddess Artemis. In non-Homeric tradition monsters are much more prominent; we may cite, for example, the stories of Perseus, Heracles and Theseus. It may be observed that in most of these adventures the hero is unaccompanied, that the scene is often laid in distant lands, and that they all relate to times anterior to the siege of Troy.

Several of the leading characters in the poems are children of deities. Sarpedon is a son and Helen a daughter of Zeus. Aineias is a son of Aphrodite, and Achilles of the mermaid (Nereid) Thetis. According to non-Homeric tradition most of the chief heroic families are descended from deities.

The Irish evidence is very similar to the Greek. Deities visit the heroes, and there are even amatory relations between them. In the *Táin Bó Cuailnge*[1] when CuChulainn is exhausted with his long struggle, an unknown warrior comes to him and offers to take his place while he rests. In some texts he gives his name as Lug mac Ethlenn. The subject of the *Sickbed of CuChulainn*[2] is an illness brought upon the hero by two divine women, one of whom is Fann, the wife of Manannan mac Lir. She has been deserted by her husband and is in love with CuChulainn. A year later she sends for him, and he goes and brings her to his home. Here trouble arises with Emer, the hero's wife; and eventually Manannan comes to reclaim his wife, and takes her back. Again, in the *Táin Bó Fraich*[3] the hero (Fraech) is son of a supernatural

[1] Windisch, 2448 ff.; Dunn's transl. p. 181 f.

[2] Transl. by Dottin, *L'Épopée Irlandaise*, p. 123 ff.

[3] Ed. and transl. by Anderson, *Rev. Celt.* XXIV. 127 ff., and elsewhere; cf. Thurneysen, *Ir. Heldensage*, p. 285 ff.

woman Befinn, sister of Boann, goddess of the Boyne. When he comes to court Finnabair, daughter of Medb, Boann supplies him with a magnificent equipment. He is injured in a struggle with a water-monster, and his mother with a numerous body of supernatural women carries him off to an elf-hill. On the following day they bring him back cured of his wounds. In the *Táin Bó Cuailnge*[1] the same hero is killed by CuChulainn, and his body is carried away by supernatural women to an elf-hill, which was afterwards called Sid Froich. A still more striking story is that of the god Midir and Etain, the wife of Eochaid Airem, a short account of which was given on p. 52. Another story[2] is that of the high-king Conn Cetchathach, who sees a horseman approaching him in a dense mist. He invites the king to his palace, the splendour of which is described, and gives his name as Lug mac Ethlenn. He prophesies to Conn the course of his reign and those of his successors. This story may be compared with that of Cormac's visit to Manannan mac Lir, a summary of which was given on p. 100.

These cases all belong to prehistoric times. But there is one similar story, the *Conception of Mongan*,[3] which relates to historical persons of a much later period. When Aedan mac Gabrain, king of Dal Riada (in Scotland) invaded England in 603, to fight against the Northumbrian king Aethelfrith, he is said to have been accompanied by Fiachna Lurgan, king of Ulster. On the evening before the battle an unknown man arrived at Fiachna's palace and made advances to his wife. She consented only when he declared that he would save her husband's life on the morrow. On leaving he gave his name as Manannan mac Lir; and he carried out his promise on the field of battle. The child born of this union was Mongan—of whom another story was given on p. 98 above.

In stories relating to earlier times also divine parentage is by no means unknown. The case of Fraech has already been mentioned above. CuChulainn is in some accounts son of the god Lug.[4] Mes-Buachalla, the mother of Conaire Mor, comes from the elf-hill of Bri

[1] Dunn's transl. p. 80 f.; *YBL.* 755 ff. (*Ériu*, i. Suppl., p. 29).

[2] *Baile in Scáil*; ed. and transl. by O'Curry, *MS. Materials*, p. 618 ff.; also transl. by d'Arbois de Jubainville, *Le Cycle Mythologique Irlandais*, p. 301 ff.

[3] This story, which comes from the very early *Book of Druim Snechta* (cf. p. 47 f.), has been ed. and transl. by K. Meyer in the *Voyage of Bran*, I. p. 42 ff. Cf. also d'Arbois de Jubainville, *op. cit.* p. 333 ff.

[4] The story is told in one version of the *Conception of CuChulainn*, a very early text; cf. Thurneysen, *Ir. Heldensage*, p. 269 f.

Leith and is partly of divine origin.[1] The warriors by whose aid she obtains the throne for her son are divine, not human. Moreover it has been pointed out[2] that most of the royal genealogies contain the names of gods, usually Lug or Nuadu, or both.

Transformations of supernatural beings are not uncommon. In the story of the *Two Swineherds*[3] a series of such transformations takes place. In the *Vision of Aengus*[4] Caer, the daughter of Ethal Anbuail, and her companions are seen in the form of swans; but similar transformations are found also in the case of human princesses. Bodb (or Badb), who is somewhat similar to the Valkyries (see below), assumes various disguises; sometimes she appears in the form of a crow.

Monsters play no great part in early heroic stories. The story of the death of Fergus mac Lete[5] bears a rather close resemblance to the last adventure of Beowulf. The hero loses his life in combat with a monster (*sinech*) which haunts the waters of Loch Rudraige (the inner Dundrum Bay). This Fergus is mentioned not unfrequently in stories of the Ulster cycle, generally as a man of the near past. In the *Annals of Tigernach* he is Conchobor's predecessor in the kingship. But the story is supposed to be not earlier than the eleventh century and to have arisen out of a false reading in a passage in the Laws (*Senchas Mor*).[6] An earlier and undoubted example occurs in *Bricriu's Feast*, where the three heroes, Laegaire, Conall Cernach and CuChulainn go to CuRoi mac Dairi to have their courage tested. Among CuChulainn's adventures is (cap. 85 ff.) an attack by a huge monster which rises out of the loch. When he has disposed of this he is assailed by an enormous giant, who has already overthrown both his competitors. Some of the (anthropomorphic) supernatural figures which appear in the *Destruction of Da Derga's Hall* may perhaps be included in this category. Giants, like Goll and Garb slain by CuChulainn, belong chiefly to later stories; and in much later times monsters of various kinds become more frequent.

In the remains of Teutonic heroic poetry which have come down to

[1] Cf. Gwynn, *Ériu*, VI. 130 ff.; Thurneysen, *op. cit.* p. 619 ff.

[2] MacNeill, *Celtic Ireland*, p. 52 ff.

[3] Cf. Nutt, *The Voyage of Bran*, II. p. 58 ff.; Thurneysen, *op. cit.* p. 277 ff.

[4] Ed. and transl. by Müller, *Rev. Celt.* III. 344 ff.; cf. Thurneysen, *op. cit.* p. 601 ff.

[5] Ed. and transl. by O'Grady, *Silva Gadelica*, I. p. 238 ff., II. p. 269 ff.; cf. Thurneysen, *op. cit.* p. 539 ff.

[6] Cf. d'Arbois de Jubainville, *Zeitschr. f. celt. Philol.* IV. 456 ff.; Thurneysen, *op. cit.* p. 539 ff. The explanation is certainly very ingenious. But is the passage in *Ann. Tigern.* (*Fergus mac Leti, qui conflixit contra bestiam hi Loch Rudraige*, etc.; *Rev. Celt.* XVI. 404) really so late as the eleventh century?

us gods appear only in the *Reginsmál*, the first poem of the Trilogy noticed on pp. 27 f., 118. Here the first scene is laid in a supernatural milieu, while later in the poem Othin visits Sigurðr in disguise and gives him gnomic advice. It is to be observed that this Trilogy belongs to Type C, not to Type A. The setting is heroic, but the substance is mainly didactic.

It would be hasty, however, to assume from the silence of the other poems that the introduction of gods was unknown or even unusual in Norse heroic poetry. In the form of the *Hamðismál* known both to the *Völsunga Saga* and to Saxo[1] Othin arrived during the fighting, and it was he who gave the advice (cf. st. 27) to stone the assailants. Moreover there can be little doubt that the story of Sigmundr contained in the *Völsunga Saga* is derived in part from heroic poems; and here Othin appears twice—first (cap. 3) at the wedding feast when he brings the sword, and again (cap. 11) when he meets the hero in his last battle, and the sword is shattered by the touch of his spear. We may also refer to a passage in the *Bjarkamál*,[2] where Bjarki suspects that the same god is riding among the enemy and declares that he will lay him low if he can catch sight of him.

No heroes are said to be sons of deities in Norse heroic poetry, but here again the *Völsunga Saga* supplies evidence. The wife of Völsungr and mother of Sigmundr is (cap. 2) the supernatural Valkyrie Hljóð, daughter of the giant Hrímnnir, while Völsungr himself is a great-grandson of Othin. In *Hervarar Saga*, cap. 2, we hear of a king named Sigrlami, who is said to be a son of Othin, though nothing more is recorded of him. It may be observed that the Norwegian royal family of later times traced their ancestry, through the early kings of the Swedes, to the god Frey.

In *Helgakviða Hundingsbana I* (*ad init.*) the Norns appear at the hero's birth and cast their threads to determine his future fame. The Valkyries who figure in heroic poetry are human and will be noticed in the next section, though supernatural Valkyries are often mentioned elsewhere. The Valkyrie Hljóð in the *Völsunga Saga* is first sent by Othin in the form of a crow. Elsewhere Valkyries appear as swans. The only monster is the dragon (or serpent) Fáfnir, slain by Sigurðr; but this has been a man.

In the English heroic poems gods are not mentioned. It is possible that they may have been eliminated through ecclesiastical influence, for

1 Cf. *Völsunga Saga*, cap. 42; Saxo, p. 338, Elton (281, Holder).

2 Saxo, p. 80 (66).

most of the English royal families claimed descent from Woden. Wermund, the father of Offa, stands in the fourth generation from this god. The only supernatural beings which figure in the poems are monsters. Grendel and his mother seem to be partly anthropomorphic,[1] though they do not speak. The theriomorphic element is represented by the dragon of *Beowulf*, and also by another dragon, slain by Sigemund—a story told incidentally in *Beowulf* (884 ff.), which is presumably identical in origin with the slaying of Fáfnir by Sigurðr.

In German heroic poetry also no gods are mentioned; but nearly all these poems date from a period six or seven centuries after the adoption of Christianity. Both Wodan and Fria are introduced in the story of the origin of the Lombards—which will require notice in Ch. x. It is remarkable that other supernatural anthropomorphic beings appear not unfrequently. Such are the river-maidens encountered by Hagen in the *Nibelungenlied* (1533 ff.), and the Nibelunge, whose treasure Siegfried acquires. In the *Rabenschlacht* (964 ff.) Witege, pursued by Dietrich, gallops into the sea, where he is rescued by the mermaid Wachilt. This mermaid is perhaps to be identified with the one mentioned in *Þiðreks Saga af Bern*, cap. 23—who is the mother of Witege's grandfather. Encounters with giants supply Dietrich with various other adventures. Theriomorphic monsters are little in evidence. The slaying of the dragon by Siegfried is referred to in the *Nibelungenlied* (st. 100, etc.), and it is stated that he has become invulnerable, except in one spot, by bathing in its blood (st. 902). But the story is related only in later ballads.

In stories of the British Heroic Age also gods as such are not mentioned; and no hero is credited with divine descent. The question whether any of the characters in the *Mabinogion* and other stories were originally deities will be noticed later.[2] In the early heroic poems supernatural beings do not appear at all. Probably the earliest examples are to be found in *BBC*. xxxi. 78 ff., which refers to the nine witches[3]

[1] Cf. *Beow.* 1349 ff. Grendel's arm (cf. 984 ff.) is that of a wild beast, probably a bear; but in 2085 ff. he has what seems to be a bag of some kind. The mother in 1545 ff. uses a knife, and in general the scene below the water suggests human conditions more than the encounter in the hall. Perhaps two different conceptions have been combined.

[2] Arawn and Hafgan, the rival kings of Annwfn in the *Mabinogi* of *Pwyll*, appear to be supernatural beings. The milieu seems to be similar to that of the *Sickbed of CuChulainn*, Annwfn corresponding to Mag Mell.

[3] Rhys (in his Preface to *Morte d'Arthur*, p. xx) refers in this connection to the nine witches of Gloucester, who figure in the story of Peredur.

and the cat Palug destroyed by Cai. In *Culhwch and Olwen* and in the Romances monsters of various kinds, both anthropomorphic and theriomorphic,[1] are common.

Taking the evidence as a whole it seems likely that in heathen times the attribution of divine parentage or ancestry to heroes and the participation of deities in human affairs were more or less regular features of heroic tradition. The British Heroic Age does not come into account here, since it falls wholly within the Christian period. But the absence of deities in English and German heroic poetry may well be due to their elimination through the influence of the Church. It may be observed that in Irish the use of the word 'god' (*dia*) for these characters is avoided. The word generally applied to them is *side*, 'people of the *sid*' ('elf-hills' or 'shee-mounds'). The same remarks apply to such supernatural beings as mermaids and 'swan-maidens', who are distinguished from gods among the Teutonic peoples—though not in Greece—and consequently have been allowed to remain in German heroic poetry. Monsters are found everywhere, even in Welsh; but they occur most frequently either in late stories or in stories relating to adventures in distant lands.

It has been held by many scholars, especially with reference to the *Iliad*, that events in which deities take an active part are *ipso facto* proved to be unhistorical. But this view is erroneous. It appears to be a widespread convention in imaginative oral poetry to represent deities as intervening in human affairs, even with reference to contemporary events. The *Hákonarmál* is an elegy on Haakon I, king of Norway, who was killed at the battle of Fitje in 960. It consists of two scenes. In the first Haakon converses with two Valkyries on the field of battle. In the second he enters Valhöll, where he is greeted by Othin and heroes of ancient times. Yet there can be no doubt that the poem was composed within a few years of the king's death. The author, Eyvindr Finnsson, was present at the battle. So in modern Serbian heroic poems relating to historical events of the nineteenth century Vile or elves of the mountains are frequently introduced. Some of these poems were written down and published within a few years of the events; probably they were composed immediately after them. Usually the

[1] Among the latter we may refer especially to the pig Twrch Trwyth, the story of which is told in *Culhwch and Olwen*. There are references to this story in the *Mirabilia Britanniae*, which dates from the beginning of the ninth century or earlier (cf. p. 154, note 3) and also in *Cormac's Glossary*. It may be compared with the story of the boar of Calydon.

function of the Vila is to warn or rouse those whom she favours; and this is the part she plays as a rule in poems relating to the reign of Prince Danilo (1851–60). But poems relating to earlier times provide analogies for practically all the activities attributed to the Homeric goddesses. The great hero Kraljević Marko, who died in 1394, is even represented as marrying a Vila and keeping her at his home for some time, though eventually she flew away.

Such conventions must of course ultimately have some foundation in actual belief. It is said that the belief in Vile is still—or was until very recently—pretty general in the more backward districts of Yugoslavia; and very many people claim to have seen them. So also in the Viking Age —when St Ansgar visited Sweden not long after 850, he found that the success of his mission was seriously endangered. A man had come to Björkö, where the king, Olaf, was residing, and stated that he had been present at an assembly of the gods, who had sent him to deliver a message to the king and nation.[1] Much more striking cases have been known to occur in the excitement of battle. According to Plutarch (*Theseus*, cap. 35) many of the Athenians at the battle of Marathon (B.C. 490) believed that they saw the hero Theseus leading them. This story need not be dismissed as a fabrication of later times.[2] An exact parallel occurred during the war of 1912 in Macedonia. When the castle of Prilip, which once had belonged to Kraljević Marko, was captured, a whole brigade believed that they saw Marko leading the charge.[3]

We have seen that the chronological mistakes and unhistorical situations discussed on p. 199 ff. are such as could not have arisen until long after the time of the persons concerned. With the unhistorical elements which we are now considering the case is different. The inventions of the *Iliad* are for the most part such as occur in contemporary poetry; we doubt whether there are any which could not have been produced within the next two generations. The same remark applies to some of the Irish and Norse examples. In point of fact the written record for the story of Mongan goes back to within a century or so of his death.[4]

(*b*) Next we may take the attribution of supernatural (or super-

[1] Cf. Rimbertus, *Vita Anskarii*, cap. 26.

[2] A number of parallels, ancient and modern, are cited by Frazer in his note to Pausanias, x. 23. 2.

[3] Cf. Petrovitch, *Hero-Tales and Legends of the Serbians*, p. 64 f., note.

[4] Cf. p. 206 and note. Mongan was killed in Cantire in 625 according to the annals, i.e. about a century before the *Book of Druim Snechta* was written.

human) powers to human beings, or occasionally to animals. This category is well represented in Norse heroic stories by Valkyries who are said to be of mortal origin, though they are sometimes employed by Othin on his errands. Such is the case with Brynhildr. In several records, especially the poem *Helreið Brynhildar*, she is identified with the Valkyrie Sigrdrífa (cf. p. 27 f.), who has disobeyed Othin by giving victory to the wrong hero. He has declared that she shall no longer bring victory in battle but shall marry. Sometimes these human Valkyries have the power of riding through the air and over the sea. Such is the case with Sváfa, the beloved of Helgi Hjörvarðsson, and with Sigrún, the beloved of Helgi Hundingsbani. Kára,[1] the beloved of Helgi Haddingjaskati, transforms herself into a swan in *Hrómundar Saga Greipssonar*, cap. 6 f., which is probably derived from the lost poem *Káruljóð*. Here also we may refer to the three swan-maidens in *Völundarkviða*, who take up their abode for eight years with Völundr and his brothers and then fly away. In the prose introduction they are called Valkyries, and a human parentage is assigned to them.

No exact parallels are to be found in English or German heroic poetry. Brunhilt may have been a Valkyrie in an earlier form of the story, but in the *Nibelungenlied*, as we have it, she is merely an athlete and Amazon. It may be observed that Valkyries who appear to be human beings—presumably witches—are mentioned in Anglo-Saxon historical works of later times.[2]

Similar features are found, though less frequently, in the case of men. Sigurðr is able to exchange forms with Gunnarr; and in the *Nibelungenlied* the same hero (Siegfried) can render himself invisible by means of the cloak Tarnkappe. Perhaps a better example occurs in *Hrólfs Saga Kraka*, cap. 50, where a bear fights beside the king while Bjarki is asleep. When Bjarki is roused and comes out to fight the bear disappears. This incident is not found in the other records; but it has often been remarked that Beowulf's method of fighting is sometimes similar to that of a bear.

A much more usual and prominent feature of heroes is that they are endowed with superhuman strength and prowess. Beowulf has the strength of thirty men and can swim over long stretches of open sea. Siegfried slays twenty-nine men in one attack, and on another occasion

[1] These three ladies are re-incarnations of one another. The same is the case with their husbands, each of whom is called Helgi.

[2] Examples may be found in the sermons of Wulfstan, Abp. of York (1002–1023), e.g. in his famous *Sermo ad Anglos*. Elsewhere the word seems to be used for supernatural beings.

overcomes seven hundred knights single-handed. In such cases of course the incredibility of the statements lies not in the quality but in the extent of the powers attributed to the hero.

Irish heroic saga furnishes examples of women who can transform themselves. In the story of CuChulainn's death[1] Badb, the daughter of Calatin, who is a witch, takes the form of a crow and also a human form different from her own. In one version of the *Conception of CuChulainn*[2] Dechtire, sister of Conchobor, disappears for three years with her fifty maidens. They return in the form of birds and eat up all the corn in the neighbourhood of Emain Macha.

Filid are credited with various supernatural powers. For an illustration reference may be made to p. 97.

In descriptions of the deeds of heroes the sagas abound with superhuman feats and extravagancies of every kind. The youthful CuChulainn single-handed defends Ulster from the combined forces of the other four provinces for three months. He performs numerous incredible feats of valour; perhaps the most fantastic descriptions are those of his battle-frenzy. In the *Destruction of Da Derga's Hall* each of the chief heroes goes out to encounter the enemy and slays three or six hundred of them. As in other sagas the figures mean nothing. In the same story Mac Cecht goes the round of the rivers and lakes of Ireland in one night to get a drink for Conaire Mor. It would no doubt be a mistake to take all these descriptions too seriously. Often they are intended as much to amuse as to impress. But the humour is primitive; and it is no doubt largely due to this unrestrained extravagance that the Irish sagas, in spite of their pathos and picturesqueness, do not enjoy greater popularity.

We do not know of any satisfactory Greek examples of human beings endowed with definitely supernatural powers, like those of Valkyries. Witches, like Medeia, and prophets, such as Melampus and Teiresias, are hardly to be included here. Better analogies perhaps are to be found in Thetis and Circe; but these are goddesses. The flying horse Pegasos is likewise of divine origin, and Achilles' horse Xanthos, which speaks on one occasion,[3] is also immortal.

1 Cf. Thurneysen, *Ir. Heldensage*, p. 560 f. This incident occurs only in the later version. The beginning of the earlier version is lost.

2 Cf. Thurneysen, *op. cit.* p. 271. A brief synopsis of the two versions will be found in Ch. XVII, below.

3 Birds speak in Norse poetry, but only the privileged can tell what they say. Procopios (*Goth.* IV. 20) records that Irmingisl, king of the Warni, was warned by a bird that he would die in forty days. This story deals with events which must have happened only a few years before Procopios wrote.

On the other hand we do find heroes endowed with superhuman strength and prowess, just as in the Teutonic and Irish Heroic Ages. Such is the case with Achilles in the *Iliad*. His attack is irresistible, and his very shout makes his enemies take to flight. Odysseus in the *Odyssey* is credited with strength, endurance and resourcefulness beyond all other men. In non-Homeric stories Heracles is irresistible.

As regards the British Heroic Age no evidence for purely supernatural powers is to be found in the early poetry, so far as we are aware. Later records yield a good deal. The nine witches of Gloucester, who figure in the Romance of *Peredur*, may perhaps be compared with Valkyries, though no transformation is recorded of them. In other stories, especially that of Math, transformation into beasts and birds is common; but it is effected not by the persons themselves but by wizards. In the story of Pwyll the hero exchanges forms with Arawn, but the transformation is the work of the latter, who evidently has magical powers, and is probably a supernatural being. Apart from transformations illusions of various kinds occur in the *Mabinogion*; sometimes they are due to wizards.

The late *Hanes Taliesin* (cf. p. 103) contains a remarkable story of self-transformation. Gwion is pursued by the witch Caridwen, and each of them takes a number of different forms in succession, until finally Caridwen in the form of a hen swallows Gwion in the form of a grain of wheat. Later, she bears Taliesin. An earlier form of this story seems to be implied in *Tal.* VII. 234 ff., a poem of Type B, in which Taliesin is the speaker. The passage follows a list of what appear to be transformations (or possibly 'incarnations'), parallels to which occur in *Tal.* VIII. 3 ff. and XXV. 58 ff. To these passages we shall have to return in a later chapter; but they rather suggest that the bards were credited with the power of self-transformation.

Superhuman prowess on the part of heroes is perhaps less in evidence here than elsewhere; but it is not entirely wanting even in the early poems. In the *Gododdin* poem (*An.* I) more than one hero is credited with an impossible amount of slaughter. The Romances consist in the main of strings of combats, in which the hero is uniformly victorious; but these follow French models.

Taking the evidence as a whole we have to distinguish between (i) supernatural powers which in general may be brought under the head of witchcraft, and (ii) superhuman strength and prowess on the part of heroes. The former are no doubt to be explained on the same principles as the intervention of supernatural beings, treated under (*a*) above.

They represent poetic conventions, which are themselves based upon real beliefs of the time or of former times. The conventional Valkyrie, perhaps the most striking figure of this group, can largely be explained from what is known of the early Teutonic and Celtic peoples. Women and girls frequently accompanied the armies; and it is likely enough that they sometimes fought[1] and sometimes were employed as messengers, like Leborcham. We know also that they were credited with prophetic power. What remains, especially the power of transformation, seems strange enough to us; but it is no more than what was universally believed in down to the seventeenth century.

The superhuman prowess attributed to heroes is another convention, but due to other causes—hero-worship, in the modern sense, and the tendency to exaggeration stimulated thereby. It is to be compared, we believe, to conventional descriptions of the beloved of heroes, and not to be taken more literally than these. As a rule there is not more than one hero in a story to whom superhuman powers are attributed. Odysseus in the *Odyssey* has superhuman endurance and resourcefulness; but in the *Iliad*—where Achilles is the favoured hero—he is merely a shrewd counsellor and stubborn fighter. Now it may be observed that the outstanding heroes of some Teutonic stories, e.g. Beowulf and Siegfried, are not mentioned in any historical records, though they may be associated with persons, whose historical existence is well authenticated. From this fact the inference has been drawn by various scholars that the chief figures of heroic stories—such as Achilles, Odysseus, CuChulainn, and the two just mentioned—must necessarily be products of myth or fiction, even if their associates are real persons. Such inferences, however, are without justification. Historical references even to the characters of Teutonic heroic stories are always meagre; and the persons mentioned are almost always kings. It is their power which attracts the notice of the historian. But the hero *par excellence* is in a subordinate position; or he carries out his exploits alone or with only a few companions. We know of no great hero who is represented as commander-in-chief of a powerful army. The two things are probably incompatible. It is physical strength, gallantry, and other personal qualities which attract the poet and the saga-teller.

[1] In the *Conception of Conchobor* Nes, the mother of Conchobor, before her marriage commands a band of warriors, with whom she tries to obtain vengeance for the murder of her foster-fathers. We may compare the story of the elder Hervör in *Hervarar Saga*, who is chief of a band of pirates. This case seems to be analogous to that of an Albanian heiress who has lost all her male relatives in vendetta and lives and dresses as a man.

(*c*) Stories relating to the birth and childhood of heroes or sages of the Heroic Age are found everywhere, and frequently they have common elements. It will be convenient therefore to treat them together here as a separate group.

Irish saga is especially rich in stories of this kind. There are two very different—but both early—versions of the *Conception of CuChulainn*, as well as a *Conception of Conchobor*; and there are known to have been *Conceptions* of other heroes. Among other noteworthy features it may be mentioned that the births of CuChulainn (in Version I), of Conchobor and of Conall Cernach were all due to their mothers swallowing worms in water. With this may be compared the story of Etain, the wife of Eochaid Airem (cf. p. 52), who was originally divine but fell—apparently in the form of a butterfly—into the cup of the woman who became her mother. In both versions of the CuChulainn story there is a phantom house, in which Conchobor and his heroes are entertained. In Version I (the older) a child and two foals are born during the night. The child is tended by Deichtine, Conchobor's daughter, but soon dies. Then the owner of the phantom house appears to her in a vision, gives his name as Lug mac Ethnenn, and says that she shall herself bear a child by him in its place. The foals are the famous horses which draw CuChulainn's chariot throughout his life. The child is given to the smith Caulann (Culann) to bring up. He kills the smith's dog, and afterwards does duty for it—whence his name ('Culann's Dog'). Further adventures of CuChulainn's boyhood are related at great length in the *Táin Bó Cuailnge*.

In Norse heroic poetry we know of only one story of this kind—the scene at the beginning of *Helgakviða Hundingsbana I*, where the Norns come and weave or spin the destiny of the new-born hero. English and German heroic poetry add nothing. Later Norse and German works, however, from the thirteenth century onwards, contain a number of examples. In the *Völsunga Saga*, cap. 1 f., the birth of Völsungr is due to an apple brought by Hljóð from Frigg to his parents in answer to their prayer for offspring. In *þiðreks Saga af Bern*, cap. 159 ff., the wife of Sigmundr is accused of unfaithfulness and taken to a forest. Her accusers fight with one another; but she dies in giving birth to Sigurðr, who is eventually found and suckled for a year by a hind. Then he is adopted by Mimir the smith, who rears him until he breaks his anvil. Thereupon he sends him into the forest, expecting that the dragon will kill him; but he destroys it. This is believed to be a North German version of the story. In the true Norse version Sigurðr is a posthumous son of Sigmundr, brought up by his stepfather Hjalprekr; but Reginn, who is both smith and sage, is a kind of foster-father to him later. Othin gives him the horse Grani. In the other German versions Siegfried has both father and mother living. In the *Nibelungenlied* he remains with them till manhood; but in the Ballad he leaves them and joins a smith, whose anvil he breaks and who consequently sends him against a dragon. All the German versions, but not the Norse, record that he made himself invulnerable, except in one spot, by bathing in (or smearing himself with) the dragon's blood. Though the different versions are not wholly independent of one another, it seems probable that a smith played some part in the original story; perhaps he was connected with the dragon.[1] But it is not clear that anything else is ancient[2] except the names of the father and son.

Mention must also be made of the origin of Bjarki (Beowulf), as described in *Hrólfs Saga Kraka*, cap. 17 ff., and—in a somewhat different form—in the *Bjarkarímur*. Both these works are late—hardly earlier than the close of the fourteenth century. A Norwegian king called Hringr has a son named Björn ('Bear'). His wife dies, and he marries a woman called Hvít, who by witchcraft transforms her stepson Björn into a bear. He retires to a cave, where he is a man by night; but in the daytime he is a bear. His beloved, who is called Bera ('She-bear') but is entirely human, recognises him and visits him. Eventually he is killed by the king's hunters. Bera soon afterwards brings forth triplets, one of whom is Bjarki. He takes vengeance later by killing the queen. This story is not referred to by Saxo or any earlier Norse authorities. In *Beowulf* itself there is no mystery about the hero's origin. His father is a famous noble of the Geatas, who has married King Hrethel's daughter, and from the age of seven he is brought up at his grandfather's court. It is probable that the origin of the story is to be sought in an attempt to account for the name *Bjarki*, which is a derivative of the word 'bear'. We may refer also to the transformation story in the same saga, cited on p. 212 above.

Not much information on this subject is to be found in the Homeric

[1] The smith and the dragon are brothers both in the Trilogy and in *þiðreks Saga*. But the scribe of the latter (which calls the dragon Reginn) evidently knew the Norse version.

[2] The cleaving of the anvil is found in the Norse prose accounts, as well as in the two later German versions. It is possible also that Sigurðr's lying answer to Fáfnir in *Fáfn.* 2 implies a form of the story more like that of *þiðreks Saga*. But against all these connections it is to be remembered that in *Beowulf* the slayer of the dragon is Sigemund.

poems; but non-Homeric sources supply a good deal. Thus in the *Iliad* Achilles is said to be son of a goddess, the mermaid Thetis; and he is often befriended by her. But no details of his birth or childhood are given, except that he has been instructed by the Centaur Cheiron. The marriage of Peleus and Thetis was treated in the *Cypria* and the Hesiodic Catalogue, but the story as a whole is known only from later works. Thetis, in order to escape from Peleus, transformed herself into various shapes, and it was only with the aid of Cheiron that he succeeded in catching her. The gods were present at the marriage and presented Peleus with arms and other gifts. Poseidon gave him the immortal horses which afterwards drew Achilles' chariot. After Achilles' birth Thetis left Peleus because he had discovered her putting the child in the fire—perhaps to make him immortal. She also dipped him in the water of the Styx, which rendered him invulnerable, except in the heel by which she held him. It may be observed that other stories are told of Peleus, e.g. his adventures with Acastos, which are unconnected with Thetis and Achilles and may have been preserved by independent tradition. But Achilles, apart from the incidents noted above, is known only in connection with the expedition to Troy. The Scyros story may have arisen out of references to Neoptolemos in the Cyclic poems.

There is one motif which is as common in non-Homeric stories of this kind as the swallowing of the worm is in Irish. This is the case of twins of which one is the child of a god and the other the child of a human father. It is very likely that such stories, like the Irish ones, reflect the popular belief of some past age. Well-known examples are the births of Heracles and Iphicles, of Polydeuces and Castor. Sometimes the hero child performs feats in its cradle, as when the infant Heracles destroys the snakes sent against him by Hera. On the other hand snakes lick the ears of the future seer, so that he can understand the language of birds.

In the non-Homeric story of Meleagros' birth the Moirai come to determine the destiny of the new-born child, just as in *Helgakviða Hundingsbana I* (cf. p. 216). A much closer parallel, however, to the story is to be found in *Nornagests Saga*, cap. 11.[1]

We know of practically no birth-stories of heroes belonging to the British Heroic Age. The story at the beginning of *Culhwch and Olwen* is hardly worth mentioning, while the case of the boy Ambrosius in the *Historia Brittonum*, cap. 41 f., is not quite clear—he seems here to be a

[1] Transl. by Kershaw, *Stories and Ballads of the Far Past*, p. 35 f.

seer rather than a hero, though there is doubtless some reminiscence of Ambrosius Aurelianus. An interesting example, however, relating to the poet-sage Taliesin occurs in the late story cited above (p. 103). Caridwen had swallowed Gwion in the form of a grain of wheat. Nine months later she bore a child, which she put into a bag and threw into a weir belonging to Gwyddno Garanhir, which is said to be situated on the shore between the Dyfi and Aberystwyth. Elphin, son of Gwyddno, came to the weir expecting to get a great haul of fish, but he found nothing except the new-born child, which he carried home with him. On the way the child produced a 'Consolation' and other poems. Elphin brought him up; and when he was imprisoned by Maelgwn, Taliesin, now twelve years old, obtained his release by a contest with the king's bards, in which he deprived them of the power of speech. It has been mentioned above (p. 104) that, although the story is late as we have it, something similar seems to be implied in certain early poems. Allusions to the liberation of Elphin are frequent.

Taking the evidence as a whole it may be observed that there are a good number of recurrent features, although the actual circumstances of the conception or birth assume different forms in different countries. The hero (or sage) is sometimes the child of a deity, sometimes a hero (or sage) reincarnate. Sometimes he is presented with horses, and perhaps arms, by a deity. Sometimes the goddesses of Fate come to visit him in his cradle. Often he exhibits his prowess or wisdom at an abnormally early age—even in infancy. Sometimes he is brought up or instructed by a smith or sage, or by a smith who is also a sage. Sometimes he is invulnerable except in one spot.

Some of these features are not necessarily incredible, if allowance be made for popular belief, especially in regard to customs which have passed out of use. The goddesses of Fate are probably reflections in popular belief of prophetesses who in actual life did visit new-born children to tell their fortune; for the foretelling and shaping of destiny were not clearly distinguished, as we shall see in a later chapter. In the part played by the smith or sage there is nothing remarkable apart from the personality of the instructor. It is not strange that a king's child should hang about his father's smithy, just as loafers did about the village smithy in Hesiod's time. This is not peculiar to birth-stories; we find it, e.g., in the story of Weland. As for the gifts of the gods some light on the story of CuChulainn, and perhaps on that of Achilles, is afforded by the custom of presenting a child with any colt which was foaled or any weapon which was forged at the time of his birth.[1] The invulnerability of the hero may mean no more than that he never received a wound before the one which proved his death.

But though various elements in the stories are capable of explanation, it must not be supposed that they are in any sense historical records. There is probably no other class of stories in which the element of fiction is so great. They owe their origin to the fame acquired by the hero in later life, or even after his death; and they are products partly of rumour and partly of speculation. Definite information not being available, they draw upon the floating store of material preserved in folktales.

It is quite possible that some of these stories began to be current while the heroes were yet alive. But others clearly did not come into existence until much later times. The story of Bjarki's birth cannot have been invented until his family and the kingdom of the Gautar (Geatas) had been forgotten. It belongs evidently to the same milieu as the stories of descent from bears which were told of several prominent men of the eleventh century,[2] and is no doubt connected in some way with the widespread folktale of the 'Bear's Son'. Some of the stories of Siegfried's birth and childhood may be older; but the absence of agreement between the different versions points to no very great antiquity. In view of the agreement between the *Nibelungenlied* and the *Edda* poems of Type A, especially *Sigurðarkviða hin Skamma*, there can be little doubt that the original heroic poems relating to him began with his arrival at the Burgundian court. The various stories of his childhood may, as in other similar cases, be due to the tendency to expand a story of adventure into a biography. At the same time they served—at least in Norse, and perhaps in German also originally—to connect his story with that of Sigmundr. The stories of Achilles' birth and childhood may have originated at a relatively earlier stage, for some elements occur in the *Iliad*. But later authorities add a good deal of information—indeed this is practically all that we know of the hero apart from Homeric poetry. It may therefore probably be taken as an illustration of the growth of legend.

It is hardly necessary to discuss other categories. Mention, however, may be made of poetry relating to heroes after their deaths. Such poetry falls into two classes. The first describes the visit of a living

[1] We may refer especially to the *Battle of the Goths and the Huns*, st. 2, quoted on p. 72, above.

[2] Cf. Chadwick, *Heroic Age*, p. 120 and note.

person to the dead; the second is concerned with the dead alone. Both classes are represented in the *Odyssey*.

The first class is represented by Odysseus' visit to the 'House of Hades' in Bk. xi. He goes there to consult the seer Teiresias; but incidentally he converses with his mother and various old comrades. We know of no true analogy to this scene in the other early literatures which we are discussing. Saxo describes more than one visit to the region of the dead; but no heroes are introduced. Parallels are, however, to be found elsewhere. A very striking example occurs in a story[1] relating to Tchaka, king of the Zulus, who died in 1828. A man described to the king a visit which he had made to the region of the dead, where he had seen "all the old people who had been killed in war, and those who had died at home". They sent a message by him to the king.

The other class is represented by the opening scene in Bk. xxiv. Agamemnon and Achilles are discussing the circumstances of their deaths, when the suitors slain by Odysseus arrive and explain how they have been deprived of life. A Teutonic analogy is to be found in the Norse poem *Helreið Brynhildar*, where the dead Brynhildr is driving to Hell. An ogress assails her with reproaches; and in reply she describes and defends the course of her life. Better parallels, however, occur in the Norse poems *Eiríksmál* and *Hákonarmál*,[2] which belong to a more or less heroic milieu, though they are not connected with the Teutonic Heroic Age. In each poem the king is represented as entering Valhöll and being greeted there by Othin and heroes of the past. We may also refer to a Serbian poem[3] composed on the funeral of Prince Danilo (in 1861), in the last part of which the prince is welcomed in Paradise by Dušan, Lazar, Miloš Obilić and other national heroes. All poems of this class seem to belong to Type B or Type DB.

III. We have now to consider elements which appear to be unhistorical, although they are not necessarily incredible in themselves[4] nor yet in conflict with other evidence. Under this head we shall treat incidents, motifs and characters which seem to be either (*a*) taken from some other story, or (*b*) invented or adapted from some idea or sequence of ideas which cannot be regarded as a story in the ordinary sense of the word.

[1] Cf. J. Shooter, *The Kafirs of Natal* (London, 1857), p. 270 f.

[2] Transl. by Kershaw, *Anglo-Saxon and Norse Poems*, pp. 97 f., 105 ff.

[3] *Srpske Narodne Pjesme*, ed. by Vuk St. Karadžić, Vol. v (1865), p. 530 ff.

[4] In point of fact some of the incidents noticed below are incredible in themselves and might consequently have been included under II. But they are treated here for the sake of convenience.

(*a*) A good example of the borrowing of incidents (and motifs) may be found in the later Norse account of the story of Heðinn and Högni, contained in the *Sörla þáttr*.[1] In this account Heðinn does not raid Högni's kingdom. He is received there and entertained by Högni as a friend. But during Högni's absence he not only carries off his daughter but also puts to death his wife. His conduct is instigated by a witch (the Valkyrie Göndul), whom he encounters repeatedly in forests. Both the meetings with the witch and the motif are unknown to the other versions of the story; and there can be little doubt that they are derived from the story of Helgi Hjörvarðsson, where another Heðinn, the brother of Helgi, is incited by a witch to claim the hand of Sváva, the beloved of Helgi.

In this case the borrowing both of incidents and motif is due evidently to identity of name. It is to be suspected that this is a fruitful source of confusion in heroic stories. As a probable instance we may refer to the stories of Dietrich von Bern and Wolfdietrich, which show certain remarkable resemblances. Both heroes have the misfortune to lose all their men and to be driven into exile for thirty years—incidents which are at variance with historical evidence in the case of the former.[2]

Next we may take a somewhat different case. In *Hervarar Saga*, cap. 6,[3] Heiðrekr appeals to his father Höfundr, who is a sage, for (gnomic) advice, and obtains from him a number of maxims. One of these is that he should not undertake to bring up the son of a man more powerful than himself. Another is that he should not tell secrets to his mistress. He resolves to put these maxims to the test, and so undertakes to foster a son of King Hrollaugr. Then he visits the king and, while he is there, conceals the child. His mistress asks him where the child is, and he tells her that he has killed him—a secret which the mistress soon betrays to the queen. Practically the same story[4] is told of Flaithri, the son of Fithal, who was a judge and sage under Cormac mac Airt. He obtains similar maxims from Fithal, and then undertakes the fosterage of a son of Cormac—with the same *dénouement*. It is uncertain whether the Norse story is derived from the Irish or vice versa—or even whether the two are immediately connected. There is a widespread folktale—

[1] Transl. by Kershaw, *Stories and Ballads of the Far Past*, p. 49 ff.

[2] In the case of the latter too, if Wolfdietrich is really to be identified with Theodberht, king of the Franks. But this seems to us very doubtful; cf. Chadwick, *Heroic Age*, pp. 23, 155.

[3] Transl. by Kershaw, *Stories and Ballads of the Far Past*, pp. 103 f., 109.

[4] Keating, *History of Ireland*, I. 46. We do not know Keating's source for this story. Other *Instructions of Fithal* will require consideration in Ch. XII.

known even to some of the Bantu peoples of South Africa—which in varying forms contains the essential elements of the story.

The adventure with the Cyclops narrated in Bk. IX of the *Odyssey* is derived from another widespread folktale;[1] and it is more than likely that other adventures described in the following Books, especially the incident with Circe, are adapted from similar sources. Indeed the whole narrative contained in Bks. IX–XII is more in accordance with folktale than with heroic story. It is not by his valour, nor even by his resourcefulness, that the hero overcomes his difficulties here. Like heroes of folktale he owes everything to the guidance of superior powers.

A more interesting case occurs in Bk. XXI of the same poem. Penelope produces Odysseus' bow and declares that she will marry whichever of the suitors can string the bow and penetrate a certain mark. Not one of the suitors can bend the bow; but Odysseus himself, who has returned home disguised as a ragged beggar, successfully accomplishes the whole task. Then he attacks the suitors. The affinities of this story seem to be Oriental rather than Greek. It is possible that the svayamvara—the ceremony at which a bride selects a husband from the assembled suitors—may once have been known in Greece, though the evidence for it is very slight.[2] But we do not know any other Greek examples of the stringing of a bow employed as a test, whereas in India and Turkestan this is a familiar feature of the svayamvara. The description of the svayamvara of Draupadi in the *Mahabharata*[3] presents a curious parallel to the story in the *Odyssey*. Not one of the assembled princes—apart from the disqualified Karna—is able to string the bow; but the hero Arjuna, who has come disguised as a Brahman and accompanied by Brahmans, both strings the bow and hits the mark. The princes, furious at a Brahman's success, attack the king, and Arjuna comes to defend him; but the fight is stopped by Kršna. It would seem therefore that this incident in the *Odyssey* is derived from some Eastern source—possibly the very story we have cited, though derivation from a folktale is perhaps more likely. In Tartar stories, as we shall see in a later chapter, the hero occasionally arrives disguised as a beggar.

[1] Cf. Macculloch, *Childhood of Fiction*, p. 279 ff.

[2] Something of the kind seems to be implied (in the case of Helen) in Hesiod's Catalogue, fragm. 94 (Rzach). In later times we may compare the story of Cleisthenes, given by Herodotos, VI. 126 ff.

[3] Bk. I. 187 ff. An abbreviated account of the incident will be found in R. Dutt, *The Ramayana and the Mahabharata*, p. 218 ff.

The adventures of Beowulf have been so often discussed that it is unnecessary here to deal with them in detail.[1] The adventures with Grendel and his mother obviously bear a close relationship to the story told in *Grettis Saga*, cap. 64–66, of the outlaw Grettir, who died in Iceland in 1031. They also show a resemblance—which is less close and only partial, but can hardly be altogether accidental—to the folktale called 'Bear's Son'. Now it may be observed that the story of Bjarki's origin contained in *Hrólfs Saga Kraka* and the *Bjarkarímur* (cf. p. 217) has features connected with the same folktale. But the account given by these authorities of Bjarki's adventure with the monster or monsters—which cannot properly be separated from Beowulf's adventure with Grendel—shows no resemblance to the folktale. It would seem therefore that the stories of Beowulf and of Bjarki, though originally identical, were influenced independently by the same folktale. The impetus to this influence may have been supplied by the names *Bjarki* (cf. p. 217) and *Beowulf*, if the latter was really recognised to be a term (kenning) for 'bear'.[2] But the adventure with the monsters itself may well have originated in an encounter with a bear, as related by Saxo.

The story of Beowulf's fight with the dragon and death may have had a somewhat similar history. We think, however, that this story has been transferred from another character of the same name,[3] like the incident of Heðinn and the witch, discussed on p. 222 above.

Another story which has given rise to much discussion is the first adventure in *Yvain* and *The Lady of the Fountain*. In Chrestien's poem the scene is laid in the Forest of Broceliande, which is in Brittany; but such evidence as is available points perhaps as much to something in the nature of a folktale as to a local legend. The nearest analogy is to be found in the Irish story called *The Pursuit of the Gilla Dacker*,[4] where

[1] Cf. Chadwick, *Heroic Age*, p. 116 ff.; Chambers, *Beowulf: An Introduction*, pp. 41–68, and 365 ff. Cf. also Ch. XIV, below.

[2] Lit. 'wolf (i.e. enemy) of bees', owing to the animal's predilection for honey; cf. Chambers, *op. cit.* p. 365 f. The explanation seems likely, though there are no very close early parallels. It would serve to explain why the hero came later (in Scandinavian lands) to be called *Bjarki*, which probably meant 'Little Bear'.

[3] The ancestor of the Danish kings mentioned in *Beow.* 18, 53 (cf. *The Heroic Age*, p. 122 ff.). In the genealogies he is called Beaw, Beo, etc. Reference may also be made to the dragon story given by Chambers, *Beowulf*, p. 192 ff., which shows some striking analogies to the story in *Beowulf*. It is curious that this story is placed in the time of Gram, who, like the earlier Beowulf, is the son of Skjöldr (Scyld).

[4] Transl. by O'Grady, *Silva Gadelica*, p. 301 f.; by Joyce, *Old Celtic Romances*, p. 247 ff.

the hero Dermot comes alone to a well beneath a magnificent tree. Beside the spring stands a pillar-stone, on which lies a drinking horn; and Dermot, who is thirsty, fills it from the well and drinks. Then a wizard arrives in armour, and they fight together till evening, when the wizard dives into the well. The same proceedings are repeated on the next two days. But on the third evening Dermot grips the wizard, and they go down together; and at the bottom Dermot finds himself in a new country. It seems probable that the scene both here and in *Yvain* is derived from heathen sanctuaries. In one text of the *Pursuit* the tree and well are surrounded with a stone circle; while in *Yvain* there is a 'chapel' by the well, and Lunet is to be burned to death near by. In other respects *Yvain* and the *Lady of the Fountain* suggest a sanctuary with customs comparable with those of Nemi. But in any case, whether the story is a folktale which has come down from heathen times or a local legend of Brittany, it can hardly have been told originally of the hero, Owein the son of Urien, who belonged to the Christian period and lived in the north of England or Scotland.

It is unnecessary here to give instances of the borrowing of characters by one heroic story from another. The principle is sufficiently illustrated by the examples of unhistorical situations and discrepancies given on p. 199 ff., above. It may be observed that confusions of this kind seem to be most frequent in the late German stories and in the Arthurian Romances. In the latter there is a strong tendency everywhere to attract into Arthur's circle characters which belonged to later generations, such as Urien and his son Owein, Rhun son of Maelgwn, Cynon son of Clydno Eidyn, and Myrddin.

No instances, however, of the borrowing of characters from stories of the gods have been given as yet. We have discussed (p. 204 ff.) the introduction of gods as gods in Greek, Irish and Norse heroic stories. But we refer here to characters who are represented in the stories as human beings, but who in reality appear to be divine.

A probable example occurs in *Hrómundar Saga Greipssonar*,[1] where the king Ólafr has in his service two brothers called Bildr and Voli. The latter at least is a wizard. The hero Hrómundr, who is their enemy, possesses a sword called Mistilteinn ('Mistletoe'). It seems likely that these names are taken from the gods Baldr and Váli, who are also brothers, although the description of them has little in common with the story of Baldr. It may be observed that this saga, which is said to

[1] Transl. by Kershaw, *Stories and Ballads of the Far Past*, p. 62 ff.

have been composed in 1119,[1] belongs to the class called *lygisögur* or 'fictitious stories'. The characters belong partly to the Viking Age and partly to the Heroic Age, and it borrows a whole episode from another story, as will be seen below.

It is commonly held that some of the characters of the *Mabinogion* were originally deities. Thus Manawyddan fab Lyr is identified with Manannan mac Lir, and Llew Llaw Gyffes with Lug mac Ethnenn. Such a derivation is in itself by no means impossible. The *Mabinogion* in their present form cannot go back beyond the eleventh century at the earliest; and though there are references to these persons in poems which are doubtless earlier, they do not give us much information about them. As Wales had been Christian for six centuries or more by this time, it is likely enough that any stories of the gods which might survive would tend to have their character obscured. But the identifications are not quite convincing. *Manawyddan* and *Manannan* are not the same name, though both may be derived from the name of the Isle of Man. The two characters also have little in common, except that they are both apparently skilled in magic—which, however, Manawyddan rarely practises. Moreover, Manawyddan has a brother and sister, Bran and Branwen, who are unknown in Ireland. Llew has nothing beyond his name—assuming that this stands for *Lleu*—in common with Lug.

In the case of Manawyddan some borrowing would seem to have taken place, for in *BBC.* XXXI he appears among Arthur's heroes. The heroes who were later affiliated to Arthur—Owein and the rest—do not appear in this poem. Moreover he is here connected with a battle (*Trywruid*) which is mentioned (as *Tribruit*) in the list of Arthur's battles contained in the *Historia Brittonum*, cap. 56. A reminiscence of this association may be preserved in *Culhwch and Olwen*, where Manawyddan appears in the long list of Arthur's heroes. On the other hand he is associated with Pryderi in *Tal.* XIV. 47, as in the *Mabinogion*. Did he originally belong to Pryderi or to Arthur? This is a question we are not prepared to answer. The absence of reference to him in *Pwyll* and *Math*, which we are inclined to regard as the oldest or most conservative of the *Mabinogion*, is possibly an argument for the latter.

The witch Caridwen, who appears in the *Hanes Taliesin* as the poet's mother, is clearly a mythological being. She is no doubt identical with Ceridwen, who is mentioned fairly often in the poems in connection

[1] Cf. the *Saga of Thorgils and Hafliði*, cap. 10. The passage is transl. by Kershaw, *op. cit.* p. 58.

with poetic inspiration (cf. p. 104). She seems to be a goddess of poetry. But the milieu in which she appears in the opening scene of the *Hanes* is obscure. The story bears a remarkable resemblance to that of the theft of the poetic mead by Othin; and consequently we think it best to treat both of them in the next chapter, although the characters are all represented as human in the *Hanes*, as we have it.[1]

All the stories noticed above were either composed in Christian times or at least preserved—doubtless not without considerable change—through many centuries of Christianity. A different problem is presented when we come to consider Greek and early Irish and Norse stories, where gods and men are brought before us as different classes of beings. It has often been held that various heroes of the Greek, Teutonic and Irish Heroic Ages are 'faded' gods; but this theory no longer meets with the same general favour which it enjoyed formerly. The weakness of the evidence was well pointed out by the late Dr W. Leaf in *Homer and History*, p. 10 ff.—to which the reader may be referred for a full discussion of the subject.

Lastly, we have to take the case where both incidents and characters, even whole episodes, are transferred from one story to another. A good example occurs in *Hrómundar Saga Greipssonar*, cap. 8, which is obviously taken from *Helgakviða Hundingsbana II*. The hero Hrómundr is sheltered by a man called Hagall and disguised as a grinding-maid when the king's messengers under Blindr come to hunt for him. Here the names Hagall and Blindr are borrowed, together with the incident itself. Hrómundr takes the place of Helgi, and Haddingr (the king) that of Hundingr. The whole passage is instructive in showing how the 'fictitious sagas' (cf. p. 225 f.) were built up.[2]

We have seen that in Romances of the twelfth and following centuries, and even in the Welsh *Dream of Rhonabwy*, heroes belonging to different generations are attracted into the circle of Arthur. It is likely enough that some of the adventures with which these heroes are credited were told of them before they were associated with Arthur; for as a rule he does not enter much into the action. The same may perhaps be said in the case of the prophet Myrddin (Merlin), although what is recorded of him in the Romances has not much in common with what we know of him from Welsh and Strathclyde tradition.

[1] The introduction of Arawn and Hafgan in the *Mabinogi* of *Pwyll* (cf. p. 209, note) is not quite analogous, though they are not said to be non-human.

[2] The course of the narrative bears some resemblance to *Eyrbyggja Saga*, cap. 20, and is possibly modelled upon this.

Again, the view has often been put forward that various incidents and episodes in the *Iliad* were originally independent stories bearing no relation to the story of the siege of Troy, with which they were brought into connection only at a later time. This case is of course not analogous to either of the two which we have just noticed. Stories like *Hrómundar Saga Greipssonar* were known as 'fictitious stories' (*lygisögur*), to distinguish them from stories derived from old tradition; but Greek opinion constantly regarded the Homeric stories as coming under the latter description. As for the French Romances, which deal with the British Heroic Age some six centuries before, we see no reason for believing that any such great lapse of time or change of milieu took place in the course of Homeric tradition. To appreciate the essential difference between the two classes of records one need only note the comparative poverty of the personnel and the almost complete absence of precise localisation in the Romances. These objections do not apply to the *Dream of Rhonabwy*. But the character of this piece is to be borne in mind. It is a *tour de force* of Type C, in which the author sets out to display his knowledge of legendary lore, as well as his power of description. It has little in common with the *Iliad*.

In itself the hypothesis that the *Iliad* has absorbed independent stories is not unreasonable—especially if one bears in mind the very great number of persons and incidents contained in the poem. But satisfactory evidence for such transferences is difficult, if not impossible, to obtain. One of the most plausible cases occurs in *Il.* v. 628 ff., where Tlepolemos of Rhodes encounters Sarpedon of Lycia. Since Rhodes and Lycia are neighbouring lands, and both of them are far from Troy, it is suggested that the fight between the two heroes had originally nothing to do with Troy but took place in Rhodes or Lycia. This may be so; but there is no evidence for such a fight, so far as we are aware. Moreover, Sarpedon fights with other heroes in the *Iliad*, besides Tlepolemos. He is slain by Patroclos, a hero from Opus, who is in command of warriors from Malis and Phthia—all of them lands remote from Lycia.

In any case we do not believe that such transferences are responsible for any considerable element in the *Iliad*. We know of no other fights between neighbours; and the other evidence which has been adduced in support of the theory is even less convincing. Most of it may be due to mistaken identifications and speculation of various kinds based on the poem itself. The important fact, as pointed out above (p. 188), is that little or nothing is known of most of the heroes apart from the siege of

Troy. If the *Iliad* were really a congeries of stories relating to different generations of the Heroic Age, we should certainly have found famous heroes like Perseus, Heracles, Minos, Theseus and Iason figuring in it. Something of the kind seems actually to have been done in poems on the voyage of the Argo; and it is in these, not in the *Iliad*, that we may see Greek counterparts of the *Dream of Rhonabwy*.

(*b*) We have yet to consider the evidence for incidents and characters which appear to have been invented, or to have been adapted from some idea, or from some sequence of ideas which cannot properly be called a story.

The invention of incidents is essential to heroic narrative poetry, and indeed probably to almost all kinds of narrative poetry. The only question is to what extent it is permitted. Such incidents as meetings and conversations are doubtless invented everywhere; and in poems relating to warfare, like the *Iliad*, we may probably allow for the invention of a good deal of fighting. The heroic poet is not a mere recorder. He adheres, we believe, more or less to the facts which he knows; but he fills up the details of his pictures, whether of life or warfare, according to his view—the standard view of his circle—of what ought to be.

It has been mentioned above (p. 201) that sometimes we meet with serious discrepancies between two accounts of the same event. Thus in the Norse version of the Burgundian story Atli is killed by his wife, who remains alive at the end, while in the German version Etzel (Atli) remains alive and his wife is killed. In such cases deliberate invention may often be involved. But other factors have also to be taken into account; and consequently we have preferred to treat them—as discrepancies rather than inventions—at the beginning of this chapter.

Invention can perhaps best be illustrated from series of adventures in which the same motif is repeated. Many examples are to be found in the Romances; but the principle is most easily to be traced in *Bricriu's Feast*, where palaeographical and linguistic evidence make it possible to trace the growth of the story. Laegaire, Conall Cernach and CuChulainn are all in turn incited by Bricriu to claim the 'champion's portion'; and a great tumult arises in consequence. It is decided to refer the question to Ailill, who sets three demon cats on the heroes and gives his award in favour of CuChulainn as a result of the adventure. The others will not accept the decision, and consequently they all go to CuRoi, who also decides for CuChulainn. Again they will not give way, until a giant comes to the court at Emain and offers to have his head cut off by any hero who will engage to let him cut off his head on the following day. All those present, except CuChulainn, either refuse or subsequently draw back; and the giant awards the championship to CuChulainn. This is the story as told in the original text; but the later texts add five or six more adventures, all animated by the same motif. CuChulainn succeeds in each test, while the other competitors fail. It should, however, be remarked that the last of these additions is a mere doublet of the adventure with the giant, while some of the others ought perhaps to be put down to transference rather than to invention. The original story itself may well be a product of fiction—representing what might be expected to happen under the given circumstances, rather than what actually did happen.

Turning now to the invention of characters, we may first take cases where invention is shown by the character of the names. A good illustration occurs in the list of Phaeacian athletes given in *Od.* VIII. 111 ff. They are thirteen in number, and all the names, like those of most of the Phaeacians, are formed from words meaning 'sea', 'ship', 'oar', etc. Some of the names are not unknown in actual use, but others must have been coined for the occasion, like *Anabesineos* ('Embark-on-a-ship'). An analogous list of names is that of the Nereids given in *Il.* XVIII. 49 ff., which will be noticed in Ch. X.

Names of this type, as applied to mortals, are not very common elsewhere in the Homeric poems. A probable example is Dolon, son of Eumedes (perhaps 'Crafty', son of 'Well-advised'), the Trojan spy in Bk. X of the *Iliad.* The minstrel Phemios Terpiades may also belong here, if the former name is connected with the idea of 'speech' and the latter with that of 'delight'. And there are a few other, more or less probable, examples in both poems. The principle is illustrated by the false account which Odysseus gives of himself in *Od.* XXIV. 304 f. He says that he is a son of Apheidas Polypemonides from Alybas, which we take to mean 'Unstinting, son of Very-wealthy, from Silverland'.

A somewhat different case is the abusive orator Thersites in *Il.* II. 212 ff. We take this name to be a synonym of Ares,[1] the war-god, and to be applied here on the same principle as the name *Iros* is applied in *Od.* XVIII. 6 f. to the beggar whom the suitors of Penelope use as a messenger—from Iris, the messenger of the gods. Nothing is said of Thersites' family, and the passage in the *Iliad* distinctly suggests that he is a character created for the moment, like Dolon and the Phaeacian

[1] Ares was worshipped under this name (*Theritas*) at Sparta; cf. Pausanias, III. 19.

athletes. It is surprising therefore to find that he is said to have figured again in the *Aithiopis*,[1] where his death at the hands of Achilles was apparently treated as a matter of some consequence. One is inclined to suspect that this story was built up out of hints contained in the passage in the *Iliad*, the character of which was misunderstood. But if so, the poem can hardly have originated in a truly Homeric milieu.

In Irish heroic sagas the invention of characters is probably very widespread. A number of examples are to be found among CuChulainn's opponents in the *Táin Bó Cuailnge*. A pretty clear case is that of Lethan, who is killed at a ford called Ath Lethan,[2] said to be named after him; but the name means 'Broad Ford'. It is held that some of the more important heroes, such as Ferdiad and Fraech, are of similar origin; but the connection between a place-name and a hero's name may arise in more than one way, as we shall see later. A different principle of invention may be seen in the name of Ailill's messenger, Traigthen, son of Traiglethan,[3] i.e. 'Swift-foot, son of Broad-foot'. When we find in the *Exile of the Sons of Uisliu* that this person is one of those slain by Fergus in revenge for the death of Noisiu, we are inclined to suspect an analogy to the introduction of Thersites in the *Aithiopis*. Here also we may refer to Conchobor's woman messenger, whose name seems to mean 'Long Bent' or 'Long Crooked'. There is no reason for supposing that fictitious characters are limited to cases where the origin of the name is more or less apparent.

In Teutonic heroic stories fictitious characters with names of this type are rare. The name *Widsith* ('Far-travelled') occurs only in the introduction to the poem which may well be later than the rest of it. The body of the poem, which is in the first person, may have been in existence—at least a considerable part of it—before the name was coined. Unferth ('Not-peace'), the name of the Danish king's 'spokesman' in *Beowulf*, may be an earlier case; he is said to have killed his own brothers. But names with the negative prefix, though rare, are not unknown in Anglo-Saxon; and the man's father bears a name (*Ecglaf*), which is of an ordinary type and occurs elsewhere. In Norse we have found fictitious names of this kind only in late (prose) works. Thus in *Völsunga Saga*, cap. 23, Brynhildr has a sister who is called Bekkhildr (from *bekkr*, 'couch'), because she stays at home and does not go to war.

1 Kinkel, *Epicorum Graec. Fragmenta*, p. 33.
2 Windisch, 1439 ff.; p. 86 in Dunn's translation.
3 P. 166 in Dunn's translation; cf. Thurneysen, *Ir. Heldensage*, p. 240.

One case of this kind dates from much earlier times—the legendary smith Weland (Völundr), if we are right in believing that the name had a meaning, such as 'artificer' or 'contriver'. But the character cannot have been created for any of the works which have come down to us, unless the history of the *Völundarkviða* is to be traced back to a much greater antiquity than is generally supposed. The story, non-heroic as it is, was probably current among most of the Teutonic peoples even during the Heroic Age.[1]

Fictitious characters without appropriate names, like those above, are much more difficult, if not indeed quite impossible, to identify. One naturally assumes that most of the characters who are introduced in the battle scenes of the *Iliad* merely to serve as victims for the greater heroes were created for this very purpose; but we know no way of proving this. The same remarks apply perhaps in some degree to the suitors of Penelope, of whom fifteen are mentioned by name. Some of these names are probably required for the existence of the story, for leading characters are rarely, if ever, nameless in heroic poetry; but one is naturally reluctant to allow that so many can have been preserved by genuine tradition. Yet here again no positive evidence is available.

In Teutonic and Celtic heroic stories the minor characters are usually not so numerous. But they present similar problems. To take a case from *Beowulf*, a certain Aeschere, described as a trusted councillor of the Danish king and as 'elder brother of Yrmenlaf', is introduced merely to be eaten by Grendel's mother. His credentials for historicity then are not convincing. He may be a creation of the poet's imagination—in which case the brother's name is added to give verisimilitude to the incident. But on the other hand he may of course have figured originally in some other connection.

In the Norse poem *Guðrúnarkviða I* we find several characters who are unknown elsewhere: Gjaflaug, a sister of Gjúki, Gullrönd, a daughter of the same king, and Herborg, 'queen of Húnaland', who is addressed by Gullrönd as 'foster-mother'. The probability is that they are new creations. It may be observed, however, that the two former names have initial *G*-, like the rest of the Burgundian royal family—which indicates that they were not invented at a very late date, indeed hardly after 850.

Thus far we have dealt only with minor characters. The essential characters must of course be considered in connection with the story or episode to which they belong.

[1] The origin of the story is discussed in *The Heroic Age*, p. 132 ff.

First let us take the 'Doloneia', Bk. x of the *Iliad.* The first part consists of preliminary matter, a debate of the Achaean leaders. The action proper begins at 273, where Diomedes and Odysseus set off by night in the direction of the enemy's lines. They capture the Trojan spy Dolon, son of Eumedes, who has been sent by Hector to reconnoitre, and kill him after he has told them of the arrival of the Thracian king Rhesos with his valuable horses. Then they kill Rhesos, carry off his horses and chariot, and return to the Achaean camp. The episode is complete in itself and has no bearing on the story of the *Iliad* as a whole. The essential characters are Diomedes and Odysseus, who belong to the whole story, and Dolon and Rhesos, who appear only here. In the action itself no one else takes part, except the goddess Athene and a Thracian called Hippocoon. We have seen (p. 230) that *Dolon* and *Eumedes* appear to be fictitious names. The same is probably true of *Rhesos*, which may be the Thracian word for 'king',[1] while *Hippocoon*, lit. 'one who has care of horses', is a specially fitting name to give to a Thracian. There can be little doubt therefore that the episode is a work of fiction.

Next take the story of Odysseus' revenge. We have seen that the names of the suitors do not betray themselves as fictitious, though it is curious that so many of them are recorded. But the motif of the stringing of the bow, combined with the svayamvara and the arrival of the hero in rags, appears to be derived from some Eastern story. This, however, cannot be held to prove that the whole story of the vengeance is fictitious. The motif is not essential to the vengeance. Moreover there are not wanting indications that the plot of the *Odyssey* has undergone considerable change. It is difficult to believe that the journey of Telemachos, and more especially the ambush set by Antinoos, were intended from the beginning to lead to nothing. In our opinion the introduction of the Oriental motif in the *Odyssey* is analogous to the adventures with Grendel and his mother in *Beowulf*. All the Northern authorities—Saxo, *Hrólfs Saga Kraka* and the *Bjarkarímur*—credit Bjarki (Beowulf) with an adventure with a monster or bear at the same place and the same time, though the details differ; but it is only in *Beowulf* that we find the monster taking the form of Grendel and his mother, a form which is known elsewhere in quite different connections. The story of Odysseus' vengeance may have been affected in a similar way.

Fiction in the ordinary sense is of course by no means unknown in the *Odyssey*. The principle is recognised in the false accounts which the

[1] Possibly related to A.S. *rice*, Lat. *regius*—in the sense of 'royal' (person).

hero gives of himself on more than one occasion. For clear examples, however, we must turn to the first half of the poem—the story of the hero's adventures among the Phaeacians and the account which he gives of his experiences in Bks. IX–XII. Both afford good examples of fiction, though they represent different varieties of it. The latter consists of a series of stories akin to folktales, which will require notice in Ch. XIV. The former belongs to what we should like to call 'romantic fiction'. The milieu is not that of folktales; but neither is it that of the heroic world. The name 'Phaeacian' appears to be derived from heroic tradition (cf. p. 195), and the same origin may perhaps be allowed for two or three of the chief characters. But there is no evidence that either the country or the personnel of the story was known intimately. The poet would seem to have given free play to his imagination; and the picture he has drawn is not that of a rude and backward community, such as we should expect in the far west, but rather that of a wealthy city and court which preserved traces of Mycenean splendour. Again, both these forms of fiction differ from what we find in the 'Telemachy'. Here probably all the incidents are fictitious, including Telemachos' visits to Nestor and Menelaos, though the fiction is of a kind which might be found in any narrative poem; but the milieu and the personnel belong to the heroic world.

There can be little doubt, however, that all the first half of the poem is of secondary origin and that the original story—which gave birth to the rest—was that of the return and vengeance of Odysseus. This latter part of the poem also, as we have it, contains much which looks like imaginative fiction. But we see no reason for doubting that the main structure represents heroic tradition.

Another probable example of fiction is to be seen in the Norse poem *Oddrúnargrátr*. Borgný, daughter of Heiðrekr, is in the throes of childbirth, and Oddrún, sister of Atli, comes to her assistance with spells. Later, in reply to a taunt from Borgný, Oddrún tells the story of her love for Gunnarr, and gives an account of his death which contains various particulars unknown elsewhere. There is a reference to Oddrún and her love for Gunnarr in *Sigurðarkviða Sk.* 58, which may be taken from this poem; but she does not belong to the recognised personnel of the story. The other characters mentioned in the poem, Borgný, her lover Vilmundr, and her father Heiðrekr, are not known from other sources, unless the last named is to be identified with Heiðrekr, the father of Angantýr, in the *Battle of the Goths and Huns*.

It was formerly an accepted article of faith and is still apparently believed by many scholars that Sigurðr (Siegfried) and Brynhildr themselves were products of fiction, though not fiction in the ordinary (modern) sense of the word. They were believed to have originated in personifications of light, who meet with their doom in conflict with powers of darkness typified in the (H)Niflungar (Nibelunge). The evidence for this theory is derived from the later elements in the story, and even in these a large amount of arbitrary change is required if they are to bear the interpretation which is desired. The theory, however, has been so much discussed that it is unnecessary to enter into details here.[1] A similar origin has been claimed for the stories of Achilles, CuChulainn, and other heroes, though in the case of the former we believe that it is now generally abandoned, at least in this country. All these claims in our opinion spring from a fundamental misconception of the nature of heroic poetry and saga. The characters on whose behalf they are made are essentially and primarily heroic; but the claims are based on secondary works composed in later times in a more or less non-heroic milieu. These, however, are questions which will need consideration in a later chapter.

If it be urged that Sigurðr and Brynhildr[2] may be products of fiction in the ordinary sense, that is a different matter; the same objections do not hold. But we do not think such an explanation is likely. Where fiction can be traced more or less clearly is in secondary stories, like the 'Doloneia' and *Oddrúnargrátr*. But it will hardly be suggested that the story of Sigurðr may belong to this category. Our belief is that primary heroic stories are contemporary, i.e. that the first stories which celebrate a hero's exploits are composed within living memory of the events. Such stories may contain fictitious elements, such as e.g. the introduction of supernatural beings, if this is a recognised convention of the times. But we do not know any examples of heroic poetry or saga relating to recent events, in which the leading characters are

[1] The theory is discussed in *The Heroic Age*, p. 139 ff. Perhaps the most significant fact is that in all versions of the story the hero is killed by the Burgundians, who are incited thereto by Brynhildr herself. This is the central feature of the story everywhere.

[2] According to one recent theory Brynhildr is a late addition to the story, introduced into the North from Germany in the eleventh century. In order to substantiate this a very late date is assigned to certain poems, while in others the references to Brynhildr are treated as interpolations—a process by which it is easy to make out a case for this—or any similar—theory. Incidentally of course the central motif of the story—Brynhildr's jealousy—disappears from it in its original form.

fictitious. Messengers are of course excluded, however long their speeches.

CuChulainn unluckily has no historically authenticated brother-in-law, as Sigurðr has; and consequently we cannot hope to get our feet planted on *terra firma* when we are discussing his story. But we have seen (p. 174 ff.) that the general conditions described in the sagas are such as may well have prevailed in the times to which tradition assigns the story, but did not prevail in later times. We have also seen (p. 179) that it is only as a framework to the sagas, especially the *Táin Bó Cuailnge*, that these conditions can have been remembered. We may add that the *Táin Bó Cuailnge*—and other sagas—cannot have existed without CuChulainn. Conchobor, Medb, Ailill and some other characters are also essential. We see no reason therefore for regarding these persons as products of fiction, much less for seeking their origin in celestial phenomena. It is to be feared that, like other heroic communities, the ancient Irish were less interested in the 'perennial conflict of light and darkness' than in the almost equally perennial conflicts arising from cattle-raiding, which touched them more closely.

Fictitious stories of a secondary character are by no means unknown in early Irish. Among these we may probably reckon not only the 'Conceptions' (cf. p. 216), in which hardly any new (human) characters are introduced, but also a number of stories which are loosely connected with the *Táin Bó Cuailnge*. The characters are in part such as are known in this work, and in part peculiar to the stories themselves. Thus in the *Táin Bó Fraich*, the *Táin Bó Dartada* and the *Táin Bó Regamain* we find on the one hand Ailill and Medb, and perhaps some of their children—in one case also Conall Cernach—on the other certain characters which are wholly or almost wholly unknown outside the story in which they appear. It is of course possible that in some of these cases fiction has been assumed too readily, and that in reality it is not the story itself but the association with Ailill and Medb which is secondary; but as to the existence of the class there can hardly be any doubt. Examples are doubtless to be found in the *Táin Bó Cuailnge* itself. In later times fictitious stories connected with Finn became very popular.

We do not mean to suggest that a hero can originally have figured in only one story—that would be absurd, as we shall see later from modern examples—but there can be no doubt that, when a hero has acquired great popularity, adventures come to be attributed to him, which are either invented or transferred from other heroes. Odysseus,

CuChulainn and Beowulf furnish abundant examples, while in Romances of the Arthurian cycle the process is developed *ad nauseam*. The growth of fiction in this last case is difficult to trace owing to the loss of these stories in their native form; but with the French poets fiction was doubtless the dominant element from the beginning. Some impression of its working may perhaps be obtained from the story of Merlin and Viviane (Niniane). No satisfactory trace of this story is to be found in native records; and enough is known of Myrddin from early Welsh poetry and from the Glasgow records (cf. p. 108 ff.) to make it improbable that such a story existed in this country. Its origin, apart from the *Vita Merlini*, may perhaps be traced partly to poetry dealing with Gwendydd and her enquiries, and partly to the *hwimleian* or 'Inspiration' (personified) which is sometimes mentioned in the Myrddin poems (cf. p. 112).

The history of the Romances is so obscure that, although we have no doubt as to the extensive use of fiction, there is always the possibility that elements of early British tradition may be preserved where they are least expected. We have seen (p. 224 f.) that the first part of *Yvain* and the *Lady of the Fountain* appears to be derived from a folktale or local legend. It is quite in accordance with such a derivation that no name is given to the lady in the Welsh story. But in *Yvain* she is once named (21 f.)—Laudine de Landuc, daughter of Duke Laudunet. These names show a curious resemblance to the description of the father of Thaney (*Denu*, *Thenoi*, etc.), the mother of St Kentigern. In the anonymous *Vita Kentegerni* dedicated to Bishop Herbert of Glasgow (cf. p. 108 f.), cap. 1, he is called *Leudonus* and his kingdom *Leudonia*. In the Genealogies of the Saints he appears as *Leudyn Luydauc* (*Lewddun Luyddawg*, etc.) 'of the fortress of Eidyn in the North'.[1] It is to be remembered that the story of St Kentigern's birth and the *Lady of the Fountain* both relate to love adventures of the same man—Owein, the son of Urien.[2] In the narratives themselves there is little enough resemblance, as one might expect—one being hagiology and the other romance. But common features are not wanting. In both the lady is

[1] *Myvyrian Archaiology*, pp. 415, 421; cf. Anscombe, *Arch. f. celt. Lexikographie*, II. 150, 152.

[2] It is noteworthy that no disapprobation of Owein's conduct is expressed in the *Life*. On the contrary some pride seems to be felt in the fact that the Saint had so distinguished a father. The same inference may be drawn from the frequent occurrence of his pedigree (through Owein) in the Genealogies. Incidentally it may be noted that the Genealogies represent Thaney as the mother of several other saints, though by a different father. This suggests a somewhat different form of the story from that contained in the *Life*.

unwilling and the man faithless, and in both the meeting is brought about by a woman intermediary. A fountain is mentioned in the *Life*, though it plays no part in the story. On the whole it seems by no means impossible that the legend in the *Life* may have been derived from an earlier form of the story—before the folktale was introduced. The cruel treatment which Thaney suffers in the *Life* was perhaps originally inflicted upon the intermediary, as in the Romance.

We may now briefly summarise the results of our discussion. The unhistorical elements found in stories of the Heroic Age are of various kinds and make their appearance at different stages in the history of the stories. It would be premature to try to formulate any rules as to the stages at which they appear until we have considered evidence from countries where heroic stories are found in their infancy. But we have seen that certain fictitious elements, such as the introduction of supernatural beings, may be found in contemporary poems, whereas others, such as anachronisms and associations of persons who lived in different periods, cannot have come into existence until long after the times of the persons concerned. Such associations are characteristic of works which belong to the later stages of heroic stories, e.g. as the medieval German poems, *þiðreks Saga af Bern*, the Arthurian Romances, and late poems on the voyage of the Argo.

The most characteristic feature of heroic story in this direction is the tendency to attribute exaggerated and even superhuman prowess to the hero. There is no reason to doubt that this tendency is present from the beginning. But if the hero gains in popularity—which is perhaps due in the main to poets—he may come before very long to be credited with new exploits, which seem chiefly to be borrowed from folktales and stories of earlier heroes, presumably because this was the material most ready to hand. As may be seen from the case of Kraljević Marko, this process may in course of time be carried to such an extreme length that a popular hero becomes credited with any exploits which may seem appropriate to him. As examples we may cite the stories of Heracles and some of those relating to Dietrich von Berne. We suspect, however, that it is only in communities where heroic story has been largely cultivated in peasant circles that these extreme cases occur. Where it remains in favour with the upper classes the tendency to magnify the hero is controlled by interest in the story as a whole—which is of course antagonistic to the wholesale use of material so essentially detached as folktales. Here we find attention given to the secondary characters, as in the *Iliad*, the heroic poems of the *Edda* and sagas of the Ulster cycle; and at times we meet with new characters and incidents, as in the 'Doloneia' and *Oddrúnargrátr*, which are unconnected with the chief hero.

We have given more attention in this chapter to heroic than to non-heroic stories, because more evidence is available for the former. We have little doubt, however, that unhistorical elements are more prevalent in the latter.[1] The object of the non-heroic poet or saga-teller was not so much to entertain as to instruct; and where no genuine information was available he had to have recourse to speculation. Heroic stories were not excluded from his province, for there can be no doubt that he is responsible for heroic poetry and saga of Type C—such works as the Norse Trilogy. But it was not until the fame of a hero had become widespread and all direct remembrance of him had come to an end that the learned were called upon to provide particulars of his life, especially his birth and childhood, which were not already recorded in poetry or saga. Hence these stories are always secondary and based on speculation. No significance need be attached to the fact that the Irish 'Conception' stories are sometimes preserved in very early texts; for there can be no doubt that stories of CuChulainn and Conchobor had been in existence for several centuries before the earliest texts which have come down to us were written. In Ireland, however, as in post-Homeric Greece, the non-heroic saga-teller (poet) tended to encroach upon and displace the heroic, as we shall see in a later chapter.

In tracing the growth of fiction in heroic stories perhaps the most difficult thing to understand is how the hero came to have adventures transferred to him from folktales and other stories. One source of confusion has been noted above (p. 222)—the case where a story is transferred from one hero to another of the same name. But this explanation will of course apply only to exceptional cases. An explanation which will apply more generally is suggested by a passage in *Beowulf* (867 ff.), which occurs in the description of the rejoicings after Grendel's death: "Now one of the king's squires, a man full of grandiloquent

[1] Many non-heroic stories are regarded, we believe, by all scholars as essentially unhistorical—though opinions may vary as to whether their origin is to be found in mythology, folktale or deliberate fiction. Such is the case with the four *Mabinogion*. This view may be correct; at all events there is nothing to prove the contrary. But it is equally possible that the 'folklore' elements—we refer in particular to elements common to, for example, Welsh and Irish stories—may be secondary. Few would have suspected that Mongan was a real person, if his existence had not been authenticated by early historical records.

phrases and intent on poetry, who remembered a very great number of stories of the past—(wherein) one expression (or 'illustration'?) led to another in due sequence—this man in his turn proceeded to describe Beowulf's adventure in skilful style, declaiming with success a well constructed narrative, with varied phraseology. He related everything that he had heard told of Sigemund and his deeds of prowess". Then he goes on to speak in general terms of Sigemund's encounters with monsters, ending with a short account of his fight with a dragon.

This passage is of interest as showing that the composition of heroic narrative poems was expected to begin immediately after the events which they commemorated, just as in modern Serbian. But why is Sigemund introduced? In other passages in the poem where characters of the past are introduced, it is for the sake of comparison with the hero or some other character; and we need not doubt that such is the case here. Unfortunately we know the story of Sigemund only in a late and probably ill-preserved form—from the *Völsunga Saga*, cap. 3–12. But his adventures would seem to belong largely to the supernatural sphere. In *Beowulf* 883 f. it is said that he and his nephew Fitela had laid low with their swords a vast number of the race of monsters. He was therefore by no means an unsuitable character to choose for comparison with Beowulf. In point of fact one incident related in the saga—the adventure with the she-wolf in cap. 5—bears a curious resemblance to the adventure with Grendel. But apart from all details we would suggest that the transference of incidents from one story to another—or to speak more precisely the transformation of one hero's adventures on the model of adventures previously recorded of another hero—was materially facilitated by the use of such comparisons.

We have confined our attention in this chapter to unhistorical elements of a positive character. A story may of course be practically unhistorical through its omissions; and it is to be suspected that this is often the case with heroic stories. Attention is concentrated upon one or two individuals, while the part played by others may be ignored. A good example occurs in the *Battle of Mag Rath* (cf. p. 53), where Congal Claen and his animosity to the high-king are made responsible for the battle and form the centre of interest throughout. But in reality[1] the leader of the army seems to have been Domnall Brecc, king of the Scottish Dal Riada, who plays but little part in the saga; in the shorter version indeed he is not mentioned.

[1] Cf. MacNeill, *Phases of Irish History*, p. 199.

CHAPTER IX

POETRY AND SAGA RELATING TO DEITIES

IN poetry belonging to this category four of the Types specified above (pp. 28, 42), viz. A, B, C and D, are represented, while in saga Types A and C are found. In view of the Greek evidence it will be convenient in this case to begin with Type D, which comprises hymns and invocations.

Invocations and prayers to deities occur in the Homeric poems, but as a rule they are quite short. Both poems begin with appeals to the Muse to sing or tell of what follows. But perhaps the most striking example is Achilles' prayer to Zeus in *Il.* XVI. 233 ff. for the success and safe return of Patroclos. Mention may also be made of invocations in oaths, as in *Il.* III. 276 ff.

Hesiod's *Works and Days* begins with an invocation to the Muses to sing of Zeus and the various fortunes which he deals out to mankind. The *Theogony* opens with the sentence, 'Let us begin our poem with the Muses of Helicon'; and several invocations to the Muses occur later.

Such invocations are found regularly also in the *Homeric Hymns*, an anonymous collection of poems in hexameter metre and in a form of language which is practically identical with that of the Homeric poems. These *Hymns* vary greatly in length. They appear to have been composed as introductions[1] to the recitation of epic poetry at festivals; and many of them consist of nothing more than an invocation to a deity, followed by a few lines relating to his attributes, parentage and sanctuaries. But in some hymns this introductory matter is followed by an account of one or more adventures of the deity, which occasionally are described at considerable length.

The *Hymns* usually begin with some such formula as 'I will sing of...', or 'Sing, O Muse, of...'. The forms of the second person are frequently used, especially in the shorter *Hymns*, in both verbs and pronouns referring to the deity to whom the hymn is addressed. But

[1] The original name for these Hymns was προοίμιον, which may mean either 'introduction' or 'invocation' (followed by the name of a deity in the genitive). It is disputed whether this term denoted properly the whole poem or only the invocation at the beginning. Thucydides (III. 104) uses it in the former sense, in reference to *Hymn I*; but we are inclined to think that the latter was the original meaning (cf. p. 244 f., below).

in the narratives the third person is more usual. The Hymns often conclude with a brief prayer for blessings from the deity, which is followed by some formula such as 'Having begun with thee I will pass on to another lay', or 'I will remember thee and another poem'—which seems to have the same meaning. The narratives, which occupy the greater part of the longer Hymns, will be noticed below.

Invocations occur rather frequently in fragments of early lyric and elegiac poems. Sometimes they appear to be the beginnings of hymns, as in Terpandros, fragm. 1: 'O Zeus, beginning of all, leader of all'. But poems of other kinds may begin with an invocation of the Muses. We may instance Solon's gnomic poem (fragm. 40): 'Ye Muses of Pieria, glorious children of Mnemosyne and Olympian Zeus, hear my prayer! Grant me prosperity from the blessed gods', etc. The most famous example, however, is the poem—a prayer rather than a hymn—in which Sappho (fragm. 1) appeals to Aphrodite to help her in her distress. Other fragments of her poems contain invocations of Hera, the Charites, the Nereids and other goddesses, as well as Aphrodite. The poems seem to have been of a personal and emotional character, mythology apparently being more or less disregarded.

Very little early Norse poetry of this type has been preserved. There are poems composed in honour of deities, such as the *Thórsdrápa* of Eilífr Guðrúnarson; but they take the form of narratives in the third person, as in some of the *Edda* poems, which we shall have to consider shortly. Poems containing invocations and addresses to deities—in the second person—were certainly composed in heathen times, but only one or two very short fragments of such poems have survived.[1] Some idea as to their character may perhaps be obtained from the opening of the *Hyndluljóð*, where Freyja goes to visit the giantess Hyndla; but the poem itself belongs, in its framework, to Type B. Freyja asks the giantess to accompany her to the sanctuary of Valhöll, and then proceeds: "Let us beseech the Father of Hosts to keep us in his favour. He gives rewards and gifts to his followers. He gave to Hermóðr a helmet and coat of mail", etc.

Invocations sometimes occur in oaths, as in the solemn oath which according to the heathen law of Iceland was to be sworn upon the sacred bracelet: "May Frey and Njörðr and the all-powerful god (Thor)

[1] By the poets Vetrliði and Thorbjörn Dísarskald. The fragments, which celebrate Thor's deeds in the second person ('Thou didst', etc.), are preserved in the *Skaldskaparmál*, cap. 4. They are published also, with translation, by Vigfusson and Powell, *Corpus Poeticum Boreale*, II. 27.

help me, provided that", etc.[1] As an example of imprecations we may quote from *Egils Saga Skallagrímssonar*, cap. 56 (ad fin.) a stanza which Egill is said to have uttered against Eric Blood-Axe, king of Norway (930–935). The king's men had broken up a court which was listening with evident favour to a claim made by Egill to certain property. "May Othin and the deities be wroth! May the Powers drive the king from his territories—thus may the gods requite him for despoiling me of my property. O god of the land! make the tyrant to fly from the country. May Frey and Njörðr be estranged from the public foe, who violates sanctuaries!" The last words refer to the sanctity of the law-courts.

Among the Christian peoples, the English, Welsh and Irish, practically nothing of this kind has been preserved except in spells, which will be noticed later. An Anglo-Saxon spell for the fertilisation of the fields[2] contains an invocation to 'Erce, Mother of Earth'. This expression may well be equivalent to 'Mother Earth'; but the name *Erce* is unknown elsewhere.

The remaining Types, A, B and C, may be considered together.

We have seen that gods are very frequently introduced in the Homeric poems. Sometimes the scene is laid among the gods themselves on Mt Olympos or elsewhere; sometimes gods are represented as visiting men in disguise. With one exception all these scenes are connected with the main themes of the poems—the siege of Troy and the wanderings of Odysseus—and are incidental to the general course of the narratives, although allusion is made not unfrequently to the domestic life of the gods themselves, their loves and quarrels.

The exceptional case is the story recited by the minstrel Demodocos in the account of Odysseus' visit to the Phaeacians (*Od.* VIII. 266 ff.). The subject of the story is the clandestine visit paid by Ares to Aphrodite during the absence of her husband Hephaistos, the stratagem by which the latter contrives to entrap the guilty pair, and the glee with which he calls Poseidon, Apollo and Hermes in to view the spectacle.

Other stories of the gods occur, as we have seen, in the *Homeric Hymns*. In certain cases these stories are connected with the foundation of sanctuaries, presumably the sanctuaries at which the recitations were given. Thus Hymn I describes the birth of Apollo at Delos and seems

[1] *Landnámabók* (*Hauksbók*), cap. 268 (ed. F. Jónsson, p. 96).

[2] Publ. in Grein-Wülcker, *Bibliothek d. ags. Poesie*, I. 314 f.; Wyatt, *Anglo-Saxon Reader*, p. 129.

clearly to have been designed for recitation at festivals in that island. Hymn II describes the establishment of the priesthood at Delphoi, and may well have been designed for use there. Hymn V recounts the wanderings and the sorrows of Demeter, when she had lost her daughter Persephone, and concludes with her injunctions for the institution of the Mysteries at Eleusis. It is clearly connected with that festival. All these are to be taken as examples of Type C, or perhaps DC.[1] They are intended for instruction at least as much as for entertainment; and their connection with the festival or sanctuary is no doubt primary.

There are other Hymns, however, which likewise appear to have been recited at festivals, if we may judge from the opening and concluding sentences, but which betray no sign of a local origin. Such are Hymn III (to Hermes) and Hymn IV (to Aphrodite). The former relates briefly the birth of Hermes and how, as a new-born child, he killed a tortoise and made the first lyre out of its shell. Then it describes at length how he stole Apollo's cattle, how Apollo tracked him to his cradle, how he denied the theft, and finally appeased Apollo's wrath by producing the lyre. Hymn IV, after a short account of Aphrodite's attributes, relates how she appeared before Anchises, declaring herself to be the daughter of a Phrygian king. They retire to bed together, and Anchises falls asleep. Then she awakens him and manifests her divine nature; and declares how in course of time he will find their son Aineias.

The didactic element is not wholly wanting in these poems. In No. III it may be seen in the references to the lyre, while in No. IV it is obvious enough, at least in the introductory part. But in neither case is it the main interest of the poem. The primary object of both is to provide entertainment. Hymn III, which is near akin to comedy, belongs properly to Type A, apart from the opening lines. Hymn IV contains very little action. It is rather a poem of situation and approaches more nearly to Type B than any other piece of early Greek poetry. We may classify it under AB or BA.

These Hymns seem to us to be—to some extent—of composite origin. The opening and closing lines may be regarded as detachable. Thus the beginning of Hymn III (1–9) is a mere variant of Hymn XVIII,[2] which contains nothing more, except the closing formula. It

[1] Hymn I largely preserves the form of a hymn (in the modern sense)—address alternating with narrative. The same is true of the opening portion of Hymn II.

[2] As to the precise relationship between the two Hymns we are not prepared to speculate. Reference may also be made to Hymn XXV, as compared with Hesiod, *Theog.* 94 ff. The influence of one poem upon another is always to be taken into account. But we believe the principle, as stated above, to be correct.

would appear that there were certain recognised formulae appropriate to the festivals—or perhaps to the praise generally—of certain deities. The shorter Hymns consist merely of these formulae, whereas in the longer ones they are prefixed and appended to the recitations. The recitations themselves are not all of the same origin. The didactic Hymns, I, II and V, were evidently composed for use at festivals, but Hymns like III and IV are, we think, taken from a different source. From *Od.* I. 337 f. and VIII. 266 ff. it is clear that in early times stories of deities were included in the repertoire of minstrels for entertainment on secular occasions; and we see no reason for doubting that these Hymns were derived from the same milieu as the heroic stories, which also came to be recited at religious festivals. They may have been modified to a certain extent, to fit them for such use. This is suggested by the slightly didactic tone of certain passages, as noticed above. But it is evident, not only from a comparison of Hymns III and XVIII, but also from Hymn I, 146 ff., as compared with the parallel text given by Thucydides III. 104, that such poems as these were not preserved by a strictly verbal tradition. This is a point which will require notice in a later chapter.

The scenes which are laid among the gods in the Homeric poems not unfrequently contain allusions to incidents which may have formed the subjects of narrative poems in early times. Some of the stories also which are found only in later works may have had a similar origin. At all events there is no reason for supposing that the stories of the gods which were known to minstrels like Phemios and Demodocos were limited to a small number.

Stories of the gods, whether in the *Hymns* or the *Odyssey*, are told in much the same form as heroic stories and like them are interspersed with frequent speeches. But there is a remarkable difference in tone, which shows itself also in the scenes which are laid among the gods, both in the *Iliad* and the *Odyssey*. Princes are never treated otherwise than with respect by the poets, even when their arrogance forfeits our sympathy. But gods, though they are assumed to be more powerful than princes, are often treated with familiarity, and sometimes made to behave in a rude, unseemly or contemptible way. Their appearance and their dwellings are said to be of greater splendour than would be found among mankind; but actually their standard of life is on a lower plane than that of princes. The pictures given of them, especially in the *Iliad*, are decidedly human—more true to life, we may suspect, than those of the heroes; but it is not the life of the highest class. Their behaviour frequently gives the impression of boorishness and occasionally even of brutality. Nothing could be more unseemly than the story of Ares and Aphrodite—not merely the conduct of the principals themselves, including Hephaistos, but perhaps even more the mirth with which the incident is treated by the other gods present. In the *Iliad* Ares is little better than a brutal rough, while Aphrodite is more than once made to cut a poor figure. And these are not the only deities who are treated with disrespect. In *Il.* XXI. 489 ff. Artemis is held up to ridicule without apparent reason. And the daily relations of the chief god Zeus himself with his wife Hera are depicted in a way which is lifelike enough, but which in modern literature is generally reserved for more or less humorous sketches of bourgeois life.

We have taken our examples chiefly from the *Iliad*, where the material is most abundant. But the treatment of the gods in Hymn III is just as familiar, though more playful. The crude sense of humour with which the gods are credited may be illustrated from 294 ff., which is not very remote from *Od.* VIII. 325 ff. or *Il.* I. 599 f. or XXI. 388 ff., and is indeed such as might be expected from the boisterous and rather ill-bred family depicted in these passages. But the tone of the Hymns which belong to Type C, Nos. I, II and V, is quite different. The treatment of the gods here is reverential.

The note of familiarity is wanting also in Hymn IV. Aphrodite here is not made contemptible, though she deceives her lover. The treatment is parallel to what we find in the *Iliad* and *Odyssey*, when the scene is laid not among the gods themselves but between a deity and one or more mortals. In such cases the deities are usually treated with respect, not with familiarity or ridicule; but their dealings with heroes are characterised by extreme partiality or spitefulness. In the *Iliad*, when they interfere in the action, their conduct frequently strikes us as unfair. Notable instances may be found in the accounts of the deaths of Patroclos and Hector. In the *Odyssey* the vicissitudes in the hero's fortunes are largely governed by the spite felt towards him by Poseidon and the favour shown him by Athena.

Types A, B and C are all fairly well represented in Norse poetry relating to the gods, especially in the anonymous *Edda* collection (cf. p. 19). It will be convenient, however, to reserve for discussion in the next chapter a number of poems of essentially antiquarian interest, which properly belong to Type C. Among these we include the *Völuspá*, *Vafþrúðnismál* and *Grímnismál*, which in subject-matter are somewhat parallel to Hesiod's *Theogony*, the *Hyndluljóð* which has much in common with the Hesiodic Catalogue, and the *Alvíssmál* and *Rígsþula*, which have no close parallels in early Greek poetry. In form the first five of these poems consist of speeches in character; and they may therefore be classed as CB. The *Rígsþula*, which will require notice in Ch. XIII, may be classed as CA, though it is descriptive, rather than narrative, in form.

Of the poems which remain we will take first the small narrative group (Type A). In the *Hymiskviða* the giant Aegir, who is entertaining the gods, requests Thor to bring him a cauldron big enough for the feast. Týr tells him that his father, the giant Hymir, has such a cauldron, and they go to seek it. Thor eats two of the giant's oxen for supper. Then they go fishing, and Thor hooks the Miðgarðsormr (the 'World-serpent'), while Hymir is catching whales. Afterwards Thor breaks a stone jar on the giant's head, and eventually succeeds in carrying off the cauldron.

In the *Thrymskviða* the giant Thrymr has stolen Thor's hammer, without which the gods are defenceless. Loki borrows Freyja's 'feather-form',[1] and flies off to look for it. He finds that Thrymr has got it; but the giant refuses to give it up, unless he obtains Freyja in marriage. Freyja indignantly refuses; and, at the suggestion of Heimdallr, Thor himself, in spite of his protests, is dressed up in her clothes and sent off as a bride to Thrymr's home. Loki accompanies him, dressed as a handmaid; and a great feast is prepared by the giants for their welcome. Thrymr is rather taken aback by the bride's appetite and by the look in her eyes when he lifts the veil to kiss her; but Loki is ready with a satisfactory explanation, that Freyja has been unable to eat or sleep, owing to her passionate eagerness for the marriage. Then the hammer is brought in for the marriage ceremony, and laid on the bride's knees. As soon as Thor gets hold of it he makes short work of the giants. This poem is a masterpiece of light comedy.

The *Vegtamskviða* (or 'Balder's Dreams') is a short poem, beginning with the anxiety felt by the gods at the ill-boding dreams with which Balder was troubled. Othin rides off to Hell, to the grave of a witch, whom he rouses by a necromantic spell. She foretells to him the death of Balder and the birth of a child (Váli) to Othin, who will avenge him. Othin calls himself Vegtamr, but she discovers his identity at the close

[1] We do not know how to translate the word *hamr*, which means a change, not merely of dress, but of shape—into an animal or bird. In this case Loki is probably turned into a falcon.

of the poem. Some scholars have doubted the antiquity of this poem, but hardly on sufficient grounds. It presupposes a version of the story of Balder different from what is found in the *Prose Edda*.

The three poems just noticed are all in the uniform line metre (*Fornyrðislag*), which is used in the majority of the heroic poems (cf. p. 29 f.) and identical in origin with Anglo-Saxon metre, except that it is stanzaic. The following poems, except the *Hárbarðsljóð*, are in a different metre (*Ljóðaháttr*), in which long and short lines alternate, as in the Greek elegiac. The metre of the *Hárbarðsljóð* is irregular, prevailingly *Málaháttr* (cf. p. 29 f.). All these poems belong to Type B and consist wholly of speeches, though the text adds a few explanatory sentences in prose.

In the *Skírnismál* Frey's parents notice that he is in distress and send his page Skírnir to find out what is wrong. Frey replies that he has lost his heart at sight of the beauty of Gerðr, daughter of the giant Gymir; and he promises to give Skírnir his marvellous horse and sword if he can get her for him. After a speech to his horse, Skírnir next appears before Gymir's house. He finds Gerðr and offers her priceless treasures if she will grant Frey his desire; but Gerðr, whose brother has been killed by Frey, refuses the offers. Then he threatens to cut off her head; but she still holds out, saying that Gymir will be ready to encounter him. Finally, Skírnir pronounces against her a long and elaborate spell or curse, which we shall have to notice in a later chapter. At the ghastly prospect described in the spell Gerðr gives way; and Skírnir then exacts from her a promise to meet Frey in a certain grove. As a work of art—especially in the way it leads up to a climax—this poem is not inferior to the *Thrymskviða*.

In the *Lokasenna* ('Loki's Abusive Speeches') the gods are feasting in Aegir's hall, when Loki arrives and demands a place. He enters into an angry altercation with the various gods and goddesses, charging them all in turn with disgraceful acts or humiliating experiences. At length Thor arrives, whereupon Loki, after reviling him and cursing Aegir, retires in fear for his life. This poem and the next are not without a certain didactic—or rather informative—element.

The *Hárbarðsljóð* consists of a dialogue between Thor and a ferryman called Hárbarðr ('Greybeard'), who appears to be Othin in disguise. Thor wants to be ferried across a strait; but the ferryman after a long altercation refuses to take him. Each of them in turn prides himself on his achievements—Thor on his victorious encounters with giants, and the other on his gallantries and successes in witchcraft. This poem has something in common with the last, but the dialogue is much less virulent—more raillery than abuse.

The *Hávamál*[1] as a whole does not come in for consideration here; for, although Othin is the speaker throughout, the matter is essentially gnomic, and as such will require consideration in Ch. XII. Properly speaking the poem consists of two gnomic collections, st. 1–110 and st. 111 to the end, the connection between which is very slight. The only portions which interest us here are the accounts of certain experiences of the speaker, which are introduced at the end of the first part and in the course of the second.

The first passage is introduced as an illustration of the maxim (st. 94) that love turns wise men into fools. He became passionately enamoured of a 'daughter of Billingr', whose name is not given. The young lady invited him to visit her alone in the dark; but each time he made the attempt he found people with torches or savage dogs ready for him—and he had to retire humiliated.

The next passage illustrates the advantages to be gained by cultivating the art of fluent and persuasive speaking (st. 103). The incident here introduced was very famous—how Othin acquired Óðrerir, the mead of poetic inspiration. Probably no story in Norse mythology is more frequently alluded to by the poets. The mead had come into the possession of the giant Suttungr, who had committed it to the charge of his daughter Gunnlöð. "I have visited the old giant and have just come back. It was not by silence I succeeded there. Many a speech did I utter to my advantage in the halls of Suttungr. Gunnlöð on her golden throne gave me a draught of the precious mead. It was a poor recompense I made to her for her true feelings and for her anxious heart....Clever people generally succeed. I got beauty at a good bargain and made good use of it, for Óðrerir has now arrived at the abodes of men. (But) I doubt whether I should have come back from the courts of the giants, if I had not made use of Gunnlöð, the good lady whom I took in my arms. The Frost-giants set off next day to seek the counsel of the High One in the hall of the High One. They enquired after Bölverkr[2]—whether he had made his way to the gods, or whether Suttungr had slain him. I expect Othin swore a solemn

[1] Cf. *The Hávamál*, ed. and transl. by D. E. Martin Clarke, especially pp. 66 f., 68 ff., 78 ff.

[2] The name assumed by Othin on his visit to Suttungr. Hávi, 'the High One', is also a name—probably a ritual name—of Othin, whence the poem takes its name.

oath.[1] How can his word be trusted? He managed to defraud Suttungr of his mead, and left Gunnlöð in tears." In the *Skaldskaparmál*, cap. 1, where this story is told in a somewhat different form, Othin, after drinking the mead, flies off in the form of an eagle. Suttungr pursues him, also in the form of an eagle, but fails to catch him.

The sardonic humour of these passages is to be taken in connection with the fact that the gnomic collection to which they are appended has largely been converted into an instrument of entertainment, as we shall see in Ch. XII. In the second collection, beginning at st. 111, no such change has taken place; the gnomes are to be understood seriously. After these gnomes comes a passage (st. 138) which transports us into an atmosphere very different from that of the stories noticed above. "I know that I hung for nine long days on Vingi's tree, pierced by a spear and given to Othin, myself to myself—on a tree of which no one knows from the roots of what (tree) it springs. They revived me neither with bread nor with drink. I peered downwards. I took up runes; screaming I took them. Thereupon I fell back." This passage is obscure not only in various details,[2] but even in its general application. Is it a sacrifice of the god which is described, or merely a kind of initiation ceremony?[3] The latter interpretation seems to be favoured by the following verses, which relate that the speaker now began to progress in knowledge and eloquence. But in any case there can be no doubt that the passage is to be taken seriously; and most probably it has some ritual significance. Perhaps therefore it should be regarded as an example of Type C (CB), rather than of Type B.

Apart from the *Edda* the chief early poem dealing with stories of the gods is the *Haustlöng* by Thjóðolfr of Hvín (about 900), which describes the adventures of Othin and other gods with the giant Thjazi, the abduction by Thjazi of the goddess Iðunn with the apples of rejuve-

[1] Lit. 'oath on the (sacred) bracelet', the most solemn oath known in the North in heathen times. It is not quite clear who is the speaker here. We are inclined to think it is still Othin himself; but it may be a reflection by the poet.

[2] Thus, does *Vinga meiði á* mean 'on Vingi's tree', as above, or 'on a windy (windswept) tree'? Is the reference to a gallows or to Yggdrasill's Ash, the 'Tree of Fate' of the gods? What is the meaning of 'I took up runes'? The last line of st. 139 has no alliteration and seems to be corrupt.

[3] It is the ritual of a sacrifice to Othin which is described (cf. Chadwick, *Cult of Othin*, pp. 4, 14 ff.). But it seems to us possible that at one time those who wished to claim special sanctity or godhead may have gone through such rites to the limit of human endurance. Austerities hardly less severe are still practised in the East, though nearer analogies were perhaps to be found among the Red Indians a century ago.

nescence, and Thor's fight with the giant Hrungnir. The subjects are taken from pictures on a shield. Mention must also be made of the *Thórsdrápa* by Eilífr Guðrúnarson—about three quarters of a century later—which describes Thor's visit to the giant Geirröðr. Both these poems are in the *Dróttkvaett* metre; but neither of them is preserved complete. Many other short fragments of poetry contain allusions to stories of the gods.

The largest collection, however, of these stories is to be found in the *Prose Edda* of Snorri Sturluson (1178–1241). They are derived in part from the poems which we have discussed above, including those of Thjóðolfr and Eilífr, while others are evidently based on poems of which little or nothing remains. Some stories of the gods are also preserved in the *Ynglinga Saga* and other prose works. We may refer to the story which serves as an introduction to the *Grímnismál* (cf. p. 119). Other stories of this kind have been incorporated by Saxo in his *Danish History*.

Now if the Norse evidence as a whole be compared with the Greek, it will be seen that here, as there, examples of a serious and indeed reverential attitude to deities are not wanting. Such is the case in the last passage from the *Hávamál* (st. 138 f.) quoted above, and generally in the antiquarian poems which will be noticed in the next chapter. In the *Hyndluljóð*, st. 10, Freyja prides herself on the devotion of Óttarr. In sagas this attitude is much more frequently in evidence. We may instance the devotion of Thórolfr of Mostr to Thor in the *Eyrbyggja Saga*, that of Hrafnkell to Frey in *Hrafnkels Saga*, and above all that of Earl Haakon the Great to Thorgerðr Hölgabrúðr. In various stories devotion to Othin is represented as taking a fanatical form. But the prevailing attitude towards the gods in most of the poems which we have been considering is quite as familiar as that of the Homeric poems. The tone of the *Thrymskviða* is playful, that of the *Lokasenna* scurrilous and even contemptuous.

Again, the representation of the life of the gods bears a somewhat striking resemblance to its Greek counterpart. It is assumed in both cases that the gods are greater and more powerful than men; and in the Norse poems there are passages which speak of their abodes as splendid and ablaze with gold. But the general impression given by the poems suggests the picture of a farmer's household rather than that of a king. In intelligence and morals they are often inferior to men. Thor is well-meaning but stupid and blustering, a heavy eater, flying into fury without provocation, and quite helpless when deprived of his hammer.

Othin is a still less attractive character, priding himself on his skill in amorous adventures—generally discreditable—trusting entirely to cunning and magic, and yet obliged to have recourse to the help of witches. Frey is represented as hopelessly love-sick, while his sister, Freyja, is very similar to the Homeric Aphrodite. If we are to credit the *Lokasenna*, not one of the chief goddesses has a stainless reputation.

The relations of the gods with one another and with mankind are much the same as in Greek. The marriage of Njörðr and Skaði is no great success—in fact they are a discontented couple. The relations of Othin and Frigg seem to be not unlike those of Zeus and Hera. In the introduction to the *Grímnismál* (cf. p. 119) Frigg by a mean trick contrives to get her husband into a very painful situation. The character of Othin himself in relation to the other deities is hardly more distinctive than that of Zeus, though he is perhaps even more uxorious. Towards human beings, however, even those who have been his votaries and protégés, he is often cruel, treacherous and vindictive.[1]

It is of course to be remembered (cf. p. 75) that Norse heroic poetry does not show the standard of decorum which is observed in Greek and Anglo-Saxon. Ugly and barbaric incidents are not very rare. Yet on the whole the life and conduct of the heroes even here are on a higher plane than what we find in the stories of the gods.

As regards features in which the Norse stories differ from the Greek, the most distinctive figure in the former is Loki. He is not of divine parentage, but he is usually associated with the gods. He is clever and amusing, but also malicious. Sometimes he is able to get the gods out of difficulties by his superior cunning. But at other times he works irremediable mischief; and in the end he helps to bring about their destruction.

Another feature which distinguishes the Norse gods in general is their helplessness. An illustration of this has been seen in the case of Frey in the *Skírnismál*. But it is in their relations with the giants that this feature is most noticeable. Situations frequently arise in which the gods are all but overcome by their adversaries; and they have to look forward in the future to a disastrous encounter, in which all the leading gods will perish. The Greek gods are more fortunate; all their demonic adversaries have been crushed. It may be remarked that these latter seem to differ from the gods more than their Norse counterparts.

[1] These characteristics are due in part to the fact that he is the god of the dead—those slain in battle—as well as the giver of victory (cf. Chadwick, *Cult of Othin*, p. 7 ff.).

Indeed the distinction between god and giant[1] is not very easy to define in Norse, apart from a kind of 'political' organisation. Several leading members of the Norse pantheon, including Týr, Loki and Skaði, are giants by parentage. There are, indeed, certain theriomorphic giants, the Miðgarðsormr and the Fenrisulfr, said to be children of Loki, who play a great part in the final overthrow of the gods; but they do not figure much in other stories.

The chief difference, however, between the Greek and the Norse pantheons is one which hardly affects stories of the kind which we have mainly been considering. The homes of the Greek gods are real places. Collectively their home is on Mount Olympos in Thessaly; individually they possess homes in various parts of the Greek world—where they had sanctuaries. On the other hand Ásgarðr, the collective home of the Norse gods, is evidently an imaginary place, and the same appears to be true of the homes of the individual gods, named in the *Grímnismál* and elsewhere. Such also is the case with Yggdrasill's Ash, the Tree of Fate, to which the gods ride for the purpose of holding their meetings, and which plays a great part in their life. In one or two passages it is even represented as comprehending the whole world; but these are exceptional.

This difference seems to explain why we have no Norse poems parallel to the Hymns to Apollo of Delos and Apollo of Delphoi, or to the Hymn to Demeter, which is bound up with Eleusis. Yet we doubt if the difference in this respect is really fundamental. It is clear from sagas and other early records that Frey was intimately connected with the Swedish national sanctuary at Upsala, which was believed to have been founded by him. In the same way the goddess Gefjon was probably connected with the island of Sjælland; according to a fragment of the very early poet Bragi Boddason she had created it with her plough. Associations of other deities with various localities may be inferred from place-names and other evidence. We suspect therefore that the absence

[1] The Norse Jötnar—for which 'giants' is a time-honoured but entirely unsatisfactory translation—are mostly anthropomorphic beings, differing little from the gods, though they were not worshipped. They live in different communities, usually hostile to the gods. Frequently, but not always, they are represented as backward in civilisation and ferocious. But several of the gods have wives from them. It would seem as if Thrymr was a kind of counterpart of Thor, for his name is probably to be connected with *þruma*, 'clap of thunder'. In *Hversu Noregr Bygðist* (cf. p. 306 f.) the ancestry of the family of Guðbrandr of Guðbrandsdalir is traced to a daughter of Thrymr. They were great highland chiefs and probably the most important worshippers of Thor in Norway.

of local associations of the gods in the *Edda* poems is due to some secondary cause. The fact that our texts come exclusively from Iceland—far from the ancient sanctuaries—must be taken into account. On the other hand we are not inclined to deny that the imaginary localities, such as Ásgarðr and Valhöll, may have had a rather long history; and the existence of such conceptions may be regarded as an important difference between Norse and Greek mythology.

Among the other Teutonic peoples references to mythology have rarely been preserved, though it is clear from the names of the days of the week and various other items of evidence that a number of the same deities were known. An obscure Anglo-Saxon spell[1] speaks of Woden's skill in magic, while a German spell[2] relates how he cured by his spells a horse which had put its leg out of joint. The latter spell mentions also the names of several goddesses.

But the only story which is worth noticing here is one which is contained in the *Origo Gentis Langobardorum*, an anonymous tract dating from the latter part of the seventh century.[3] According to this story the Lombards came originally from Scandinavia and were called Winniles. Soon after their emigration they came into conflict with the Vandals. The object of the story is to explain how they acquired the name *Langobardi*, which is interpreted as 'Long-beards'. Ambri and Assi, the leaders of the Vandals, asked Wodan (*Godan*) to give them victory over the Winniles. Wodan replied, saying: "Whomsoever I shall first look upon, when the sun rises, to them will I give victory". Then Gambara with her two sons Ibor and Aio, who were chiefs over the Winniles, asked Fria (*Frea*), the wife of Wodan, to be gracious to the Winniles. Fria then gave counsel that the Winniles should come when the sun rose, and that their women should let down their hair about their faces after the fashion of a beard and should come with their husbands. Then, as it was becoming light, while the sun was rising, Fria turned the bed on which Wodan lay and put his face to the east and wakened him. And he looked and saw the Winniles and their women with their hair let down about their faces, and said: "Who are those long-beards"? And Fria said to Wodan: "As thou hast given them a name, give them also victory". And he gave them victory, etc. The relations between

[1] Grein-Wülcker, *Bibl. d. ags. Poesie*, I. 322.

[2] Publ. in Braune, *Althochdeutsches Lesebuch* (p. 81), and various other works.

[3] Pertz, *Mon. Germ., Script. Rerum Langobard.* p. 2 f.; cf. Paulus Diaconus, *Hist. Lang.* I. 8.

Wodan and Fria (i.e. Othin and Frigg) here are evidently much the same as in the introduction to the *Grímnismál.*

Several Irish stories in which gods figure were noticed in the last chapter. We have now to consider stories which are wholly or mainly concerned with deities. It may be observed here that the word 'god' (*dia*) is hardly ever applied to these beings. The usual term is *side* (pl.), which may be translated 'elves' (from *sid*, 'elf-hill', 'shee-mound'). But there is no doubt that they were the gods of heathen times.

The stories are preserved in the form of saga, just like heroic stories, and sometimes they are closely connected with these. They contain a number of speech-poems (Type B). Poetry of Type C also is not uncommon; but most, if not all, of it seems to date from the period of written literature, and falls therefore outside our province. Traces of various lost stories are preserved in the *Dinnšenchas*—collections of speculations upon place-names, which we shall have to notice in the next chapter.

The *Vision of Aengus*[1] relates how Aengus, also called Mac Oc ('Young Boy'), dreams every night that he sees a fair maiden unknown to him. From love of her he falls ill, but the cause of his malady remains a secret until he confesses it to a famous doctor, who has made a correct diagnosis. The doctor then summons Aengus' mother Boann, who sends in all directions to search for the girl—but without success. He next summons the Dagda, Aengus' father, who applies for help to Bodb, king of the elves of Munster. The latter discovers that the girl is Caer, daughter of Ethal Anbuail, an elf-chief in Connaught. The Dagda now applies for help to Ailill and Medb. Ailill replies that he has no authority over Ethal, but at the Dagda's request sends his steward to summon him. Ethal refuses to obey; and then the combined forces of Ailill and the Dagda capture the elf-hill and its owner, and kill sixty of his men. Caer is not found there; but Ethal, when Ailill threatens to kill him, declares that at Samuin[2] she will be at Loch Bel Dracon (in Co. Tipperary) with her girl attendants in the form of swans. Aengus is brought to the lake, and calls to her to come to him in her human form. She consents on condition that she is allowed to return to the lake. Then they both assume the form of swans and sleep together; after which they

[1] Ed. and transl. by Müller, *Rev. Celt.* III. 344 ff.; cf. Thurneysen, *Ir. Heldensage*, p. 300 ff.

[2] The autumn festival (1 November).

fly over the lake—to fulfil the promise—and then to Aengus' home at Brug na Boinne, where Caer remains.

The *Courtship of Etain*[1] consists of a rather long and loosely connected series of adventures. Properly speaking, there are three 'Courtships of Etain',[2] one in her first life and two in her second, while the introduction to the first of them is not concerned with her at all, but with the birth of Aengus (Mac Oc). The beginning of the story is as follows: The Dagda is enamoured of Boann, wife of the elf ('shee') Elcmar. In order to gratify his desire, he sends Elcmar on a mission to Bres mac Elathan in Lecale (Co. Down) and contrives by various artifices to get him detained there for a considerable time. Meanwhile Boann bears a son, and recovers before her husband's return. The child, Aengus, is brought up by the shee Midir of Bri Leith, in ignorance of his parentage. But in course of time Midir takes him to the Dagda, who acknowledges him, and asks him to provide him with a home. The Dagda advises him to get possession of Brug na Boinne—the great prehistoric cemetery north of the Boyne, between Slane and Drogheda—which belonged to Elcmar. Following the Dagda's instructions, Aengus surprises Elcmar in the 'hill of the Brug' (perhaps New Grange), to which he has come unarmed at the festival of Samuin. To save his life Elcmar has to promise to give the Brug to Aengus for '(a) day and (a) night'; but Aengus refuses to restore it on the ground that 'day and night' means 'for ever'. The matter is referred to the Dagda, who decides in favour of Aengus.

At this point the text is damaged, but it appears that both Midir and Aengus were suitors for Etain Echraide, daughter of a certain Ailill, and that a quarrel had taken place between them. She becomes Midir's wife, but is bewitched by another wife named Fuamnach, out of jealousy, and reduced to such a state that she is blown away by a puff of wind. Then she is found by Aengus and kept by him in what seems to be a kind of pavilion. Fuamnach, hearing of this, advises Midir to invite Aengus; but as soon as Etain is left alone she causes her to be blown away again. When Aengus finds out what has happened he kills Fuamnach. But Etain eventually falls into the cup of the wife of an Ulster warrior called Etar. She is swallowed by her, and born again as her daughter.

[1] Transl. by Leahy, *Heroic Romances of Ireland*, I. 7 ff.; cf. Thurneysen, *op. cit.* p. 598 ff.

[2] They follow one another immediately in the *Lebor na h-Uidre* (fol. 129 ff.), apparently the only MS. which contains the whole series.

In the story of the second courtship[1] Etain has grown up and become the wife of the high-king Eochaid Airem. But Eochaid's brother Ailill Anguba falls secretly in love with her to such an extent that he seems to be dying. The king has to leave home, and entrusts his brother to Etain's care. He soon begins to recover, and makes an assignation with Etain; but when the appointed time comes he is asleep, and in his place Etain meets with a man exactly like him. The same thing happens a second time. On the third occasion the stranger declares himself to be Midir, who had been her husband in her former life; and he admits that he had caused both the illness and the sleep of her brother-in-law. He asks her to come back to him; but she has apparently no recollection of him and refuses, though eventually she agrees to do so if her (present) husband should consent. The third courtship, which follows, has already been noticed (p. 51 f.).

Here we may refer again to the *Sickbed of CuChulainn* (cf. p. 205). It is as much concerned with mortal as with divine beings, but the latter supply the governing motif. The hero's illness is due to a dream, in which two women appear to him and beat him with a whip till he is nearly dead. He lies speechless for a year. Then Fann, the wife of Manannan mac Lir, sends messages to him, first by her brother and then by her sister, summoning him to her home, Mag Mell ('Plain of Delight'). The sister, Li Ban, promises that her husband, Labraid Luath, will give Fann to CuChulainn if he will help him to overcome his enemies. CuChulainn first sends Laeg, his charioteer, and then goes himself to the home of Fann, the splendours of which are described. He slaughters Labraid's enemies and remains a month with Fann. After his return to his own home Fann comes to him; but this arouses the jealousy of his wife Emer, who tries to kill her. CuChulainn intervenes, and an altercation takes place. Then Fann gives way and bewails her plight; but at this point Manannan arrives and reclaims his wife.

It may be observed that this story contains no reference to shee-mounds. The situation of the localities mentioned—except of course CuChulainn's home—is not very clear; but Fann's home seems to be situated on an island. At the end of the story Manannan comes riding over the sea. The story contains a large amount of poetry of Type B.

The three stories noticed above all belong to Type A. Next we may

[1] Transl. by Leahy, *op. cit.* p. 23 ff., cf. Thurneysen, *op. cit.* p. 610 ff. A different and later text of this story is ed. and transl. by Müller, *Rev. Celt.* III. 350 ff. In one passage in this, taken from the beginning of the *Destruction of Da Derga's Hall*, Etain knows her divine origin.

take, as representative of Type C (CA), the *Second Battle of Moytura*,[1] a story in which the informative element is predominant, and which in form may be compared with the story of *Culhwch and Olwen* (cf. p. 45). It is not free from Latin influence; its framework is the 'Invasion' story, which we shall have to notice in the next chapter. The gods, who here are called Tuatha De (Danann), or 'Tribes of the Goddess (Danu)', come to Ireland as invaders. They defeat the Firbolg, who are in possession of the country, but their king Nuadu loses a hand in the battle.[2] A silver hand is eventually made for him; but in the meantime they choose as king a certain Bres, whose mother belongs to the Tuatha De. His father Elathan, however, belongs to the Fomori, who are represented as living beyond the sea, apparently to the north or north-east. Bres' reign is a miserable time owing to his miserliness and the exactions of his Fomorian relatives. Even the Dagda is forced to work and receives insufficient food. At length Bres is compelled to retire, and Nuadu re-appointed in his place. Bres makes his way to the Fomori and rouses them to avenge his wrongs.

While the Tuatha De are anxiously awaiting their enemies, Lug arrives and makes himself known. His father Cian is one of the Tuatha De, but his mother Ethne is a daughter of Balor, king of the Fomori. Owing to his many accomplishments he is made commander-in-chief. The Dagda, who is represented as an enormous eater, is sent to delay the enemy, and elaborate preparations are made. When the battle has begun, Nuadu is killed by Balor; but the latter is disabled by Lug, and eventually the Fomori are completely defeated. The story ends by relating how the Dagda recovered his harp.

The *Fate of the Children of Tuirenn*[3] may be taken as an example of Type A; for the interest in the narrative is dominant, though there is a rather large informative element. The story is only preserved in a very late form, much affected by foreign influence. The subject is closely related to that of the last piece. The stewards of the Fomori are exacting tribute, when Lug, who has the horse and armour of Manannan, arrives and slays them. Balor, king of the Fomori, sends his son Bres to take vengeance, and Lug assembles an army against him; but the king, Nuadu Argetlam ('Silver-hand'), is afraid to support him. His father

[1] Ed. and transl. by Stokes, *Rev. Celt.* XII. 56 ff.

[2] This battle is the subject of the *First Battle of Moytura*, a late work, ed. and transl. by Fraser, *Ériu*, VIII. 4 ff.

[3] Ed. and transl. by R. J. O'Duffy (Society for the Preservation of the Irish Language).

Cian sets out to gather reinforcements, but meets Brian, Iucharba and Iuchar, the sons of Tuirenn, with whom he is at feud. He turns himself into a pig, to escape from them, but they succeed in identifying him, and stone him to death. Then the battle takes place, and Lug is victorious. He now begins to search for his father, and finds his mangled body. Then he charges the sons of Tuirenn with the murder; and the king agrees to the terms of compensation which he proposes to exact from them. The terms appear to be absurdly light—they are to obtain for him three apples, a pig's skin and various other trifles. But when they have agreed to them—not without misgivings—Lug declares that the apples he requires are the Apples of the Hesperides. The pig's skin is one which will heal all wounds; it belongs to the king of Greece, and the Greeks will never part with it. And the other things are equally difficult to obtain. The sons of Tuirenn set out, and after terrible struggles succeed in obtaining everything; but they return to Ireland exhausted and mortally wounded. They ask to have their wounds healed by the pig's skin; but Lug refuses, and they die.

The earliest of these stories were not committed to writing until Ireland had been a Christian country for some centuries. But, apart from the avoidance of the word 'god', they do not appear to have been affected by Christian doctrine or feeling, though the two last have certainly been influenced by Christian learning. A reservation is probably to be made with regard to the poems which they contain, especially those relating to Mag Mell. Christian references occur, e.g. in the poem in which Midir summons Etain to come to him and also in the description which Laeg gives to CuChulainn of the home of Fann.[1] In the former case the description of Mag Mell is hardly in place, and it would seem that this subject, whatever its origin, was one of growing popularity. It is a favourite theme in poetry as far back as the seventh or eighth century.[2] But the narratives seem to be little affected by it.

One difference between the first three and the last two stories given above is obviously due to Christian learning. In the latter the gods are represented as people of the remote past—long before the earliest times to which any of the heroic stories relate. But in the first three stories the gods are contemporary with the heroes, though their sphere of existence is distinct from that of men. They are not immortal; but, unless they are killed, they seem to be regarded as living on from age to age. Thus,

[1] Cf. Leahy, *op. cit.* I. 26 f., 74 f.; Dottin, *op. cit.* p. 132 ff.

[2] Cf. Nutt and Meyer, *Voyage of Bran*, I. 4 ff., 16 ff., and xvi; Meyer, *Ancient Irish Poetry*, pp. 3–8.

Manannan appears in stories of CuChulainn, of Cormac mac Airt in the third century, and of Mongan at the close of the sixth century. This doubtless represents the belief of heathen times.

The local associations of the gods are clearly shown in the first two stories and elsewhere. Aengus belongs to the Brug na Boinne (cf. p. 256). His mother Boann appears to be a personification of the Boyne, as will be seen in the next chapter. Midir belongs to Bri Leith, near Ardagh, Co. Longford. Bodb's home is the Sid ar Femen in Co. Tipperary. We are not aware that Lug is precisely located; but his mother Ethniu (*Ethlenn*, *Ethne*) seems to be a personification of the Inny, Co. West-Meath, while his foster-mother Tailtiu is buried at Telltown, Co. Meath. From the 'Vision of Aengus' it would seem that Bres was originally located in Lecale, Co. Down.

The gods are organised politically like men. There is a high-king, the Dagda, in Meath, and provincial kings in the other provinces. Bodb, king of Munster, figures in the *Vision*; and kings of the other provinces appear in the story of the *Two Swineherds* (cf. p. 207), where we find Bodb at war with the gods of Connaught. But most of our stories are concerned with the gods of Meath. There seems to have been a tendency to bring all the gods into relationship with one another. Thus, in the *Lebor Gabála*, cap. 115, Bodb is great-grandson of Bres; and the latter is according to one genealogy (cap. 106) a brother of the Dagda, while another (*ib.*)—probably older—genealogy gives him a totally different ancestry. Again, Manannan (cap. 113) is made a son of Elloth (not Ler), a brother of the Dagda; yet in early stories his home is beyond the sea, usually in the Isle of Man. It is questionable therefore how far these genealogies and relationships go back to heathen times.

Most of the supernatural beings who appear in *CuChulainn's Sickbed* are not mentioned elsewhere. Several of them have names with an obvious meaning; and they may have been invented for this story. It is to be borne in mind, however, that nearly all the surviving stories of the gods relate to those of Meath.

A difference, which is striking at first sight, between the Irish and the Norse gods lies in the fact that the stories of the former are always concerned either with deities only or with deities and human beings. 'Giants' play little or no part in the Irish stories. Some scholars indeed regard the Fomori as 'demonic' beings;[1] but the evidence is unsatis-

[1] Cf. Thurneysen, *Ir. Heldensage*, p. 64, as against K. Meyer (*Abh. d. k. pr. Akad.* 1913, No. 10, p. 6), who took them to be (originally) a historical people. The Fomori are mentioned not unfrequently in heroic stories. We suspect them to be the

factory. On the other hand, as we pointed out above, the difference between the Norse 'giants' and gods is not easy to define—beyond the fact that the giants do not belong to the community or political organisation of the gods. If this is the only essential difference—a question which we shall have to notice shortly—the relations between giants and gods in the North may be compared with those between different communities of gods in Ireland.

In their relations with one another and with human beings the Irish gods closely resemble their Greek and Norse counterparts. Perhaps their most striking characteristic is their want of power. They are scarcely more than a match for great kings and heroes. The Dagda has to call Ailill to his assistance against Ethal Anbuail; and his success in the end is chiefly due to his human ally. Labraid Luath is in great dread of his foes; but CuChulainn, when he comes to his assistance, soon disposes of them.[1] Midir and Eochaid Airem wage a long struggle for the possession of Etain. In the *Third Courtship of Etain* Midir carries her off from Eochaid's court (cf. p. 52); but Eochaid destroys one shee-mound after another relentlessly until he has rescued her. From references in other stories it appears that vengeance was taken upon him by Sigmall, a descendant of Midir; but there seems to have been a retribution even for this.

In other respects the dealings of the gods with human beings are much the same as in Greek and Norse. In the *Táin Bó Cuailnge* Lug protects CuChulainn, who is perhaps his son (cf. p. 205 f.). Manannan shows favour to Cormac mac Airt, after first playing a very trying trick upon him (cf. p. 100). The amorous side may be illustrated by Fann's appeals to CuChulainn and by Manannan's visit to the mother of Mongan (cf. p. 206). Midir shows a good deal of cunning, as well as amorousness, in his courtship of Etain, although he prides himself on the straightforwardness of his conduct.

The same appears to be true in general of the relations of the gods with one another. One feature indeed seems to be wanting. There is no Irish parallel to the relations of Zeus and Hera or of Othin and Frigg. The Dagda appears to have no legal wife. In other respects, however,

broch-builders, presumably Picts of the islands, a people whose existence has been strangely ignored by the historians of both Ireland and England. There can be no doubt that in the early centuries of our era they were most formidable pirates; and their forts are found as far south as Galloway. It is perhaps worth noting that the name Fomor is borne by an ancestor of the Clann Rudraige (cf. p. 178, note).

[1] This case does not stand alone; cf. d'Arbois de Jubainville, *Le Cycle Mythologique Irlandais*, p. 356 ff.

the stories have much in common. The helpless lovesick Aengus is closely parallel to the helpless lovesick Frey. The relations of the Dagda with Boann are not unlike those of Ares with Aphrodite. The spitefulness of Fuamnach towards the first Etain is very similar to the behaviour of Hera to Semele and other rivals.

In the *Second Battle of Moytura* and the *Fate of the Children of Tuirenn* certain gods appear in a very unfavourable light. In the latter Lug's desire for vengeance becomes mere heartless cruelty. In the former the Dagda is little more than a glutton and buffoon. But we are not disposed to place a very high value on these stories as evidence for the ideas of heathen times. The *Vision* and the introduction to the *Courtship of Etain* doubtless give a truer picture of the Dagda as he was then thought of—a voluptuous and shifty, but not unkindly, character. In general the attitude of the early stories towards the gods is familiar, but not unfriendly or even contemptuous. Midir's case in his struggle with Eochaid Airem is stated fully and quite sympathetically.

Unfortunately, owing to the absence of poetry of Types C and D and saga of Type C, dating from heathen times, we know nothing certain of the more serious side of Irish theology. It is incredible that serious theological poetry did not exist, especially in view of the activities of the Gaulish Druids, which we shall have to notice in the next chapter. But it is only in the poems relating to Mag Mell that this side is represented, and we do not know how far these are affected by Latin influence. Mag Mell is not only an abode of deities, but also a Paradise to which human beings can, sometimes at least, attain. But Norse evidence shows that the conception of a distant Paradise can exist side by side with a conception of immortality which is bound up with shee-mounds. Frey himself was a shee according to the *Ynglinga Saga*, cap. 12; he was believed to live in a great barrow at Old Upsala. This is in full accordance with the belief in immortality usually found in the sagas, especially those relating to Iceland. But beside this belief we find also, especially in poetry, the doctrine of a Paradise (Valhöll) far away, which seems to us quite incompatible with it. The doctrine of Mag Mell may therefore have existed alongside of the belief in shee-mounds[1] as the abodes of the gods—perhaps originally in connection with a different set of deities.

Some features in the descriptions of Mag Mell may well be ancient. The joyous life of the warriors has something in common with Valhöll;

[1] In the texts which have come down to us the two conceptions are often confused. Laeg applies the word *sid* ('shee-mound') to Labraid's home.

and in particular the 'Tree of Victory'—presumably the same as the silver tree which stands at the gate of Labraid's dwelling—may be compared with the tree called Glasir, which 'stands with golden foliage before the abode of the God of Victory'.[1] But the theme was probably developed during the period of transition—the sixth and following centuries—when the old learning was becoming permeated by the new. Owing to the resemblance which it presented to the descriptions of Paradise in Christian Latin poetry, it was one of the very few features in the old religion which were able to maintain their position.

Very little satisfactory material is to be found in Welsh sources, for the traditions rarely, if ever, go back to heathen times. One clear case, however, occurs, curiously enough in the introduction to the very late story of Taliesin noticed on p. 103. There can be no doubt that the woman Caridwen with her 'cauldron of inspiration' is identical with Ceridwen, a being who is mentioned not unfrequently in early poetry and who appears to have been a goddess of poetic inspiration. In *Tal.* XVI. a monologue poem of Type B (or CB), she is the speaker. She refers to the accomplishments of her son Afagddu in poetry and to the achievements of Gwydion, son of Don—which are related in the story of *Math* (cf. p. 115). She mentions also her chair, her cauldron and her laws. Her cauldron is again referred to in *Tal.* XIV. 11, where Taliesin is the speaker; and an obscure passage in *Tal.* XV. (35 f.) seems to contain an allusion to the three drops—here called *awen* (cf. p. 104)—which came from it.

There can be little doubt that the story in the *Hanes Taliesin* has been somewhat obscured in the course of time. The liquid which Caridwen is boiling is clearly that of poetic inspiration; and the story is to be compared with that of the stealing of Óðrerir by Othin (cf. p. 249)—though in this case the pursuer catches the fugitive. The point of the story is that Taliesin is the reincarnation of the person who swallowed the liquid of poetic inspiration, though we know nothing of this person (Gwion) apart from the story. For this liquid, and even for the stealing of it, we shall find parallels in other mythologies. In the meantime it is of interest to note that the goddess of poetry—alone of the deities—was able to maintain her position to a certain extent in Christian times.

Another story which suggests a mythological origin occurs in the *Mabinogi* of *Pwyll* (cf. p. 115). Pwyll, while engaged in hunting,

[1] A fragment quoted in *Skaldskaparmál*, cap. 34. Glasir is probably the same as Yggdrasill's Ash.

unintentionally shows discourtesy to an unknown knight, who gives his name as Arawn, king of Annwn. To make up for the discourtesy, he promises to comply with a request which Arawn makes to him. They are to exchange places and forms for a year. Pwyll takes Arawn's place in Annwn, and Arawn Pwyll's place in Dyfed. At the end of the year Pwyll has to encounter an enemy of Arawn, named Hafgan. He gives Hafgan a mortal wound with his first blow. Then Hafgan asks him to finish him off; but Arawn had warned him against this, and Hafgan is carried away to die. Pwyll now annexes Hafgan's kingdom to Arawn's, and again meets Arawn, as they had arranged. They return, each to his own form and place, united in the closest friendship. In the *Mabinogi* of *Math*, Pryderi, son of Pwyll, has received from Arawn a present of pigs—the first ever seen in Britain. We know nothing more of Arawn, except that he is said to have fought against Amaethon, son of Don, at the Cad Goddeu—where the latter was apparently successful through the cleverness of his brother Gwydion.[1] But the name *Annwn* (*Annwfn*) means 'Underworld', and consequently there is some ground for suspecting that Pwyll's adventure is similar to CuChulainn's visit to Mag Mell—apart from the love motif in the latter. It has been proposed[2] to read the name *Hafgan* in *Tal.* XIV. 48—in a passage describing a place which bears some resemblance to Mag Mell.

Many other characters and incidents in the *Mabinogion* are commonly held to be derived from mythology. Thus, Manawyddan, son of Llyr, is identified with the Irish Manannan mac Lir, and the children of Don with the Irish sons of Danu (cf. p. 258).[3] But we are not convinced that these identifications are correct (cf. p. 226); the stories have hardly anything in common. We do not doubt, however, that names from the ancient mythology may have survived, perhaps without any clear remembrance of their associations. A very probable case is Lludd Llawereint ('Silver-hand'). We know nothing of this person beyond what is said in *Culhwch and Olwen* about the deadly quarrel which took place between the suitors of his daughter Creiddylad. But his

[1] This is narrated in the prose introduction to a short fragment of poetry published in the *Myvyr. Arch.* I. 127. There is no reference to the incident in the account of the Cad Goddeu given in *Tal.* VIII.

[2] Cf. Sir J. Morris-Jones, *Y Cymmrodor*, XXVIII. 236 (reading *amcan* for *am tan*).

[3] So also Llew Llaw Gyffes (or Llawgyffes) is generally identified with the Irish god Lug Lamfada ('Long-hand'). The first names seem to be identical; for the verses have *Lleu* for *Llew*, and this is presumably the earlier form. But the word *-gyffes* (*cyffes*) has not been satisfactorily explained, and the resemblances between the story of Llew and what is recorded of Lug are at least by no means obvious.

name is surely identical with the Irish Nuadu Argetlam (cf. p. 258)—with assimilation of the initial of the first name to that of the surname. This is one of the few Irish deities whose names can be traced back to ancient times. The origin of both the Irish and the Welsh names is to be found in the god Nodons (Nodens), who in the Roman period had an important sanctuary at Lydney on the Severn.

In the course of this chapter we have seen that remarkable differences in tone are to be found in poetry and saga relating to the gods. In Types C and D the attitude is serious and reverential, whereas in Types A and B it is commonly marked by familiarity, which not rarely tends to burlesque. The Greek evidence indicates that in early times Type A belonged to a different milieu from Types C and D. The former provided themes for entertainment at secular gatherings, while the latter were bound up with religious festivals and sanctuaries. In a later chapter we shall see reason for believing that they are the work of different sets of poets—indeed, we may perhaps say, of poets belonging to different 'professions'. In Greece Type A was cultivated by the same minstrels who cultivated heroic poetry of Type A.

It is true that in Greece of the historical period heroic poetry and serious theological poetry seem to have been recited on the same occasions and by the same persons. But we doubt if this was in accordance with ancient custom. The heroic minstrel of the Homeric type appears to have died out. In Ireland we find the *filid*, who were originally seers, encroaching upon the province of the Bards. In the North too, as also in Wales, changes had certainly taken place, though they may not have been exactly the same. As an illustration of the changes which might result from the transference of a poem from one milieu to another, we may cite the first part of the *Hávamál*, where a collection of gnomic poetry has been converted into an instrument of entertainment. The stories of Othin's love adventures, which follow, have probably had a similar history.

The difference of tone depends to a certain extent on the setting of the stories. It is in stories relating to gods only that the lighter, familiar attitude prevails. Exceptions in this case are rare. The relations of Demeter with the other gods are treated seriously in Hymn V; but it is the relations of the goddess with human beings which form the primary interest of this Hymn. On the other hand the familiar treatment of relations between gods and giants seems to be peculiar to certain Norse stories. Elsewhere the treatment of such relations is serious

(Type C). The treatment of relations between gods and men is rarely, if ever, familiar; but it often presents the deities in an unfavourable light. Their doings are often governed by amorousness, while in other cases they are characterised by favouritism or spite, to gratify which very unfair means are sometimes used. Both the Irish and the Norse gods are rather helpless beings. The former are hardly more powerful than kings or heroes, while the latter can barely cope with the giants.

It is beyond the scope of our work, even if it were possible, to attempt any systematic explanation of these phenomena. Some of the stories may be as old as the deities themselves, and indeed bound up with their origin. This, again, was clearly not uniform. Some of them were doubtless at first personifications of natural phenomena; others may have been vegetation spirits; others may originally have been human beings, whether individuals or types of men—magicians or kings. The origin of a very large proportion of them is wholly uncertain. Some of the stories, e.g. those which relate to encounters with theriomorphic demons, may have 'grown up' with the gods, and have been preserved perhaps through some kind of ritual use. From the absence of such stories in Ireland, together with the prevailing belief in barrows as the homes of the gods, it is a likely inference that the cult of the dead was responsible for the largest element in the Irish pantheon. The influence of souterrains, however, must not be forgotten.

But the stories and the pictures of the gods which have come down to us must often be remote from the original myths. It is clear that Zeus was originally a personification of the sky; and his association with the thunderbolt was never forgotten. But the picture which the Homeric poems give of him is entirely human—an elderly man, indolent and amorous, with an ill-tempered wife and a troublesome family. In the case of Njörðr we find—what is more remarkable—a change of sex; but the stories related of him preserve no remembrance of this.

Perhaps the most instructive case is that of Thor; for the evidence here is abundant and free from doubt. The god's name is identical with our word 'thunder', and in Sweden his connection with the thunder was never forgotten.[1] But in Norse poetry and saga hardly a trace of this connection is to be found. He is entirely human—a well-meaning and exceedingly strong man, but rough, stupid and voracious. In general the picture which the stories suggest is that of a rough, uncultured backwoodsman, on whose strong arm one could rely for protection

[1] Cf. Adam of Bremen, IV. 26 (referring to the temple at Upsala): *Thor...qui tonitrus est....*

against savages. In Norway and Iceland he was more worshipped than any other deity, and names compounded with *þór*—implying a kind of dedication—are of the greatest frequency. It is significant, however, that they are hardly ever found in the royal families, and there is very little evidence for his worship by this class. Thor's non-aristocratic associations are indeed emphasised in the *Hárbarðsljóð*.

The fact that some deities, whatever their ultimate origin, have plebeian associations may be partly responsible for the phenomena noted above. It is not true of every case; Othin's associations are with the royal class, though he is himself a magician, not a king. But when the deities came to be united in one community, the plebeian character of some of them may have affected the conception of the community as a whole. But we do not mean to suggest that this—or any other one cause—is solely responsible. Chronological and other considerations have to be taken into account. It is unlikely that the pantheons came into existence complete. Presumably they were built up gradually; and it is reasonable to expect that deities may preserve traces of the more primitive or more advanced conditions under which they first came to be known. Thor seems to be a very ancient, as well as a plebeian, god. He has no horse. In the *Grímnismál*, st. 29 f. (cf. *Gylfaginning*, cap. 15), when the other gods ride to Yggdrasill's Ash to hold their court, Thor has to walk—though in some stories he has a goat-carriage. It would seem that his habits had become stereotyped before riding was generally known.

We have taken our examples from Norse because the Norse pantheon is less homogeneous than either the Greek or the Irish. Yet differences may be observed in the two latter also. Among the more prominent deities in the *Iliad* Apollo and Athena, whatever may be their origin, are more dignified figures and usually behave with more decorum than Ares and Aphrodite, although they are conspicuously unfair in their dealings with heroes. Midir is a more dignified figure than the Dagda.

Some light upon the questions we have been discussing may perhaps be obtained from a consideration of the theological poetry of other peoples. In the meantime we would emphasise that in Greek the same poems deal with both gods and heroes, that the gods behave towards one another with less dignity and decorum than do the heroes, and that their conduct towards heroes is less fair than that of one hero towards another. We may add that when comic relief is required it is supplied from stories and scenes of the life of the gods. The same features recur in the poems of the *Edda*, though these are of a more heterogeneous character than the Homeric poems. When a hero has been guilty of faithlessness, like Sigurðr in his relations with Brynhildr, the greatest care is taken to cover the matter up. But Othin's faithlessness in his amorous adventures is openly vaunted. Here also comedy occurs only in stories of the gods. In Irish records on the other hand the difference between heroic and divine standards is far less noticeable; for here, as we have seen (p. 78), the former are usually on a lower plane and cruder than elsewhere.

One remark may be added. In the treatment of the stories of the gods, whatever their origin—whether they have plebeian associations or not—the work of the poets shows no less care or skill than in narratives and scenes from heroic life. In construction and in the vividness of the narrative the story of Ares and Aphrodite will compare favourably with almost any passage in the *Odyssey*. The *Thrymskviða* is perhaps even better, while the *Skírnismál*—in a different way—is hardly inferior. It would seem that the poets took a peculiar pleasure in these stories, perhaps owing to the scope which they allowed for the exercise of their imaginative powers. Stories of the gods probably played an important part in the development of fiction.

CHAPTER X

ANTIQUARIAN LEARNING

IN the preceding chapters an attempt has been made to distinguish various types of early poetry and saga. The greater part of the discussion has necessarily been devoted to those types which were primarily intended for entertainment—Types A and B in poetry and Type A in saga—because these are as a rule by far the most fully represented. Next we have to consider compositions of various kinds, both poetry and prose, the object of which is primarily didactic. In the present chapter we propose to discuss such didactic compositions as are concerned with the past, and especially with the origin of specific names, peoples, institutions, etc. In the following chapter we shall have to consider didactic compositions of general application, relating to timeless social and natural phenomena. Examples of both categories have been noticed incidentally in the preceding chapters, in connection with poetry and saga of Type C, but here they will require to be discussed more fully.

The primary object of these compositions was not so much to entertain as to impart information, whether antiquarian or general. In antiquarian compositions, with which we are now concerned, much of the information was derived from tradition in various forms, poetry, saga, etc.; but a good deal is obviously due to speculation, by the author himself or his predecessors. No distinction, however, is made in the presentation of the matter; whether its source is really tradition or speculation, it is stated as fact.

Antiquarian interest finds expression in various forms. Even heroic narrative poetry (Type A) is not always entirely free from it, though here it is generally limited to a few short genealogies and catalogues, which may be thought necessary to explain the story. In Irish heroic saga it is much more prominent; sometimes indeed it constitutes the primary interest, as also in the Welsh *Culhwch and Olwen* and the *Dream of Rhonabwy*. To such stories, as also to some of the Homeric Hymns, it will be convenient to apply the term CA. More important perhaps are a number of monologue and dialogue poems in Norse and Welsh, which are antiquarian in substance but have the form of Type B. They may be described as CB. The same description may be applied to *Widsith*, although we think it originated in a personal poem of Type E.

Apart from works referable to Type C in the categories already discussed there are in Greek, Norse, Welsh and Irish a large number of catalogue and genealogical poems which are essentially antiquarian in interest, though they are connected with stories of heroes and deities. The more important of these will be noticed in the following pages. Genealogies and antiquarian catalogues are also frequently found in texts by themselves or incorporated in Latin works. With these we may class the Welsh (antiquarian) *Triads*, which bring together various heroes and incidents of the past in groups of three, on account of some characteristic which they have in common. Here also mention may be made of Irish works, in verse and prose, the object of which is to explain the names of places and persons. Lastly, a large amount of antiquarian lore is preserved in historical works of later times. This is especially important in Greek, owing to the fact that little of the early antiquarian poetry has been preserved except in fragments.

It will be convenient to divide the material as follows: I. Genealogies. II. Other catalogues. III. The origins of place-names and personal names. IV. The origins of customs and institutions. V. The origins of places and buildings. VI. The origins of nations. VII. The origin of mankind and the world.

I. Genealogies of families, especially royal families, are one of the most widespread forms of antiquarian learning. As a rule they are derived from genuine tradition for a number of generations; but the beginnings are supplied by speculation, either from gods or from mythical eponymoi. Here we are concerned only with genealogies of families. Genealogies which embrace whole nations will be considered later under VI, genealogies of the gods under VII.

In heroic poetry and saga genealogies are not often found, and when they do occur they are usually quite short. In the Homeric poems they are seldom given for more than three generations. The longest are those of Aineias (*Il.* XX. 215 ff.), which contains eight generations, and that of Glaucos (*ib.* VI. 153 ff.), which contains six, counting the hero himself in each case. But the former includes Zeus and three or four generations of national eponymoi.

Greek antiquarian poets of the eighth and following centuries were very largely occupied with genealogical lore. Hesiod's *Theogony* gives a genealogy of the gods, and the Catalogue contained a genealogy of national eponymoi, with much other genealogical matter. But in form at least this work, with others of the same period, was a catalogue (in our sense) rather than a genealogy, and as such will be noticed below. It is known that many families in the historical period traced their descent from heroes and gods. Indeed, this is probably true of the nobility in general. But very few of these genealogies have been preserved. The most satisfactory examples are those of the two Spartan royal families recorded by Herodotos (VII. 204; VIII. 131).

In Teutonic heroic poetry genealogies can hardly be said to occur except in the opening passage of *Beowulf*. This is of definitely antiquarian character, giving the ancestry of the Danish kings. Even here the genealogy contains only five[1] generations, of which one is a mythical eponymos and only two can be regarded as ordinary mortals. A parallel to the Hesiodic catalogue is to be found in the Norse genealogical catalogue poem *Hyndluljóð*, which will be noticed below. In Norse, however, we find also true genealogical poetry. The *Ynglingatal*, which is preserved almost complete, traces the ancestry of the Norwegian royal family from the god Frey and his descendants, the early kings of the Swedes—including Óttarr and Aðils, the Ohthere and Eadgils of *Beowulf*. It was composed by Thjóðolfr of Hvín, court poet of Harold the Fair-haired (who reigned c. 860–930), in honour of a prince named Rögnvaldr, a cousin of Harold. Each prince mentioned in the genealogy has from four to eight lines devoted to him; usually the circumstances of his death are noticed. Of similar character was the *Háleygjatal*, of which only fragments remain. It was composed, perhaps in imitation of the above, by Eyvindr Finnsson for Earl Haakon the Great, who reigned from 975 to 995, and traced his descent from Othin and Skaði, through the ancient kings of Hálogaland.

The genealogies of most of the English royal families are either preserved in texts by themselves—sometimes with other catalogue matter—or incorporated in historical works. Several of them are given by Bede, and it is probable that many of them were committed to writing in the seventh century. The later generations are historical, while the earlier may be presumed to be due to speculation. Names known from heroic stories occur in the Mercian and West Saxon[2]

[1] Counting *Scyld Scefing* as two, on the same principle as *Sisyphos Aiolides*. Sceaf actually figures in some later genealogies; but the context is rather against taking Scefing as a patronymic here.

[2] There is no reason for doubting the claim of the Mercian royal family to be descended from Wermund and Offa, the ancient kings of Angel. But the presence of

genealogies, national eponymoi in the West Saxon and Bernician. All the genealogies are traced back to gods—all except one (Essex) to Woden. In the earlier genealogies Woden's ancestry is carried back for five generations. In later texts this element is greatly expanded, partly (apparently) by combining different genealogies, and partly by adding to these the genealogy from the Book of Genesis.

Genealogies of considerable length were in vogue among the Teutonic peoples of the Continent even in the Heroic Age. We may refer to the genealogy of the Gothic kings given by Jordanes, cap. 14, while the early traditions of the Lombards[1] consist practically of genealogies. Both these instances probably contain mythical as well as historical elements; but no descent from a deity is stated in the latter, while the earliest Gothic names are hopelessly corrupt.

In Norse sagas relating to the Viking Age genealogies are of very frequent occurrence. The 'Book of the Colonisation of Iceland' (*Íslands Landnámabók*) contains a very large number—those of all the more important colonists. By means of these one is able to reconstruct to some extent the early history of Norway, though speculative elements are common enough in the early portions of the genealogies.

Irish heroic sagas rarely, if ever, contain genealogies. Genealogical catalogue poetry, however, was widely cultivated from early times. Some poems still extant, tracing the ancestry of the Leinster and Munster royal families, are believed to date from the seventh century.[2] They are catalogues rather than genealogies in form, but, in general, they agree with the genealogies. It is noteworthy that even at this early date the genealogy from the Book of Genesis is brought into connection with the native records. Classical and other national names from Latin sources are also introduced.

Collections of genealogies are numerous; there are said to be many still unpublished. Some of them date from early times; the collection known as the Laud genealogies[3] comes from a text of the eighth century, though additions have been made to it in later times. But there

British names late in the West Saxon genealogy renders it highly improbable that this is genuine, though it contains heroic names (Wig, Freawine), as well as an eponymos (Gewis). Most probably the family was British in origin, but had appropriated the genealogy of an English family, with which they may have been intermarried.

1 *Origo Gentis Langobardorum* (Mon. Germ., Script. Rer. Langobard. p. 2 ff.); Paulus Diaconus, *Hist. Langobard.* I. 3 ff.

2 Edited by K. Meyer, *Abhandl. d. preuss. Akad. d. Wissenschaften*, 1913, No. 6.

3 Published by K. Meyer, *Zeitschr. f. celt. Philologie*, VIII. 291 ff.

can be no doubt that many of the genealogies were in existence orally long before this time. It was presumably upon them that the Irish schemes of chronology, which were drawn up in the seventh century,[1] were based. We believe that in some cases, at least in that of the high-kings, the genealogies are more or less trustworthy as far back as the third century, if not further. From that date we find nearly fifty generations back to the 'Milesian' invasion; and even before that there are a number of generations with Irish names, until we reach the patriarchs of the Book of Genesis. The great bulk of this matter must be due to speculation. In most of the genealogies we find a few names of deities, especially Nuadu and Lug; but the origin of most of the names is unknown. The object of extending the genealogies to such a length was presumably to fill up the blank in the Eusebian scheme between the patriarchs and the beginnings of the native tradition. It may be that lists of heroes have been converted into genealogies. In any case the process seems to have operated—perhaps in a tentative way[2]—in the seventh century, at the time when the Irish Eusebius was drawn up.

For the British Heroic Age the only evidence available is contained in genealogical texts and in genealogies incorporated in historical works. The most important of the former, Harl. 3859, which is attached to a text of the *Historia Brittonum*, has already been discussed (p. 149 ff.). The MS. is derived from a text which was written soon after the middle of the tenth century, but nearly all the matter was collected about a century earlier. It is very likely that some of the genealogies—those of the 'Men of the North', most of which end not long before or after A.D. 600—are derived from much earlier texts. The *Historia Brittonum* itself (cap. 49) contains one genealogy, that of Builth, while an earlier text of the genealogy of Dyfed, dating from c. 750, is preserved in the Irish *Expulsion of the Desi* (cf. p. 151 f.). On the other hand, many genealogies, including even the direct paternal ancestry of the kings of Gwynedd from c. 816, are preserved only in collections of much later date.

[1] For the Irish Eusebius and the Irish chronicle based partly upon it, reference should be made to MacNeill, *Ériu*, VII. 53 ff., 73 ff.

[2] This is suggested by the rather large number of discrepancies. It is not clear that the Milesian and other invasions were mentioned in the Irish Eusebius; cf. MacNeill, *Celtic Ireland*, p. 28 ff. The first Irish event recorded in *Ann. Tigern.* seems to be the slaughter of Dinn Rig. It may be that the extension of the genealogies and of Irish history generally into the far past was a consequence of the Eusebius. The extension had, at all events, taken place when the genealogical catalogue poems noticed above were composed.

We believe that, in general, the genealogies represent trustworthy tradition as far back as the fifth century (cf. p. 151 f.), beyond which date no evidence is available. Three of Cunedda's sons, who would seem to fall within the latter half of the fifth century, serve as eponymoi; but, as we shall see later (p. 309 ff.), it is not clear that they are necessarily mythical. With much greater confidence can this be claimed for *Dimet* (i.e. Dyfed),[1] who appears in the Harleian genealogy of Dyfed in a position which would date him to the fourth century. The name, significantly, is wanting in the earlier genealogy, contained in the *Expulsion of the Desi*. Other ancient mythical elements, such as gods, may be present; but we cannot identify them. It is of interest, however, to note the appearance of what may be called a new mythology, arising out of speculations relating to the Roman period and Church legends. In the Harleian genealogy of Dyfed, *Dimet* is son of *Maxim Guletic*, i.e. the Emperor Magnus Maximus (d. 388), whose ancestry is traced to Constantine (the Great) and Helena. Maxim Guletic is also the ancestor of another line (Harl. No. IV; cf. p. 150), while a third (*ib.* No. XVI), that of Caratauc map Cinbelin, is traced to a long list of Roman emperors—from Constans to Octavianus (Augustus Caesar)—which has been converted into a genealogy. In the same text two other lines, Nos. I (the old line of Gwynedd, or rather Anglesey) and X, are traced to a certain Beli and Anna, the latter of whom is said to be a sister of the Virgin Mary.

This new mythological element can, to a certain extent, be seen growing. In the Harleian Genealogies (No. V) the line of Strathclyde is traced back to a certain *Dumnagual* (Dyfnwal) *Hen map Cinuit map Ceretic Guletic*—in all probability the *Coroticus* of St Patrick's Epistle—followed by a series of unknown names. But in the genealogies of the 'Men of the North', contained in the much later fourteenth-century MS. Hengwrt 536, this Dyfnwal Hen is said to be *ab Idnyvet ab Maxen Wledic*—i.e. the old genealogy is displaced for Maximus.[2] Again, we have seen that in the Harleian Genealogies the line of Dyfed is traced to *Dimet map Maxim Guletic*. But in the earlier genealogy contained in the *Expulsion of the Desi* these names do not appear; the line is traced

[1] The name (*Demetai*) is found as that of a people in the same district in Ptolemy's *Geography* (second century).

[2] Possibly through the influence of the genealogy (Harl. No. IV) mentioned above, in which Maximus appears even earlier. We cannot locate this genealogy, but we suspect it belongs to the northern series. The first name (*Iudgual*) is that of a brother of Merfyn's grandfather's mother; cf. Jes. 20. XIX.

back to an Irish source.[1] We have little doubt that the introduction into the genealogies of Maximus and the other Roman and ecclesiastical elements is due to the wave of antiquarian activity which produced the *Historia Brittonum* and other documents which we shall have to consider shortly. But it must not be assumed that such transformations could only take place through Latin influence. Antiquarian speculation can be traced very frequently, as we shall see, where no such influence can be suspected.

Perhaps the most interesting of the speculative genealogies is that of Gereint, son of Erbin, which is preserved in a number of late texts. In one case the genealogy starts from Arthur, Gereint's cousin. The first (i.e. latest) few names are not of a character to arouse suspicion. At least three of them are found connected with Damnonia (Cornwall, etc.) elsewhere, though the persons themselves are unknown. But in the sixth generation from Gereint (or Arthur) we find Gadeon (Kadiawn, etc.), son of Cynan, son of Eudaf. These names belong to the *Dream of Maxen Wledig*, though here Adeon (Gadeon) is a brother of Cynan and Elen, and son of Eudaf. In most of the texts Eudaf is son of Caradoc, son of Bran, son of Llyr. These are characters in the *Mabinogi* of *Branwen, daughter of Llyr*, Bran being Branwen's brother. In Jes. Coll. 20 Eudaf is said to be son of *Custenin*, son of *Maxen*, whose ancestry is traced to Constantine, Constantius and Elen; this passage, however, occurs not in the genealogy of Gereint (Sect. XI), but in a different connection. It would be interesting to know how old the genealogy is. It was evidently known in part to Geoffrey of Monmouth;[2] for he makes (VI. 4) a brother of Constantine (the grandfather of Gereint and Arthur) to be fourth in succession from Conan, the son of Octauius (i.e. Eudaf). He also knows the story of Conan's conquest of Armorica (V. 13 f.), which is related in the *Dream*. It is true that he makes no mention of Eudaf's ancestry, or of his daughter Elen, or even of the cutting out of the Armorican women's tongues, though the last incident is referred to in some texts of the *Historia Brittonum* (cap. 27); but no conclusions can safely be drawn from his silence. The

[1] The last six names are as follows: (*maic*) *Alchoil maic Trestin maic Aeda Brosc maic Corath maic Echach Almuir maic Artchuirp*. The Harl. text has in the corresponding place: (*map*) *Aircol map Triphun map Clotri map Cloitguin* (*Gloitguin*) *map Nimet map Dimet map Maxim Guletic*.

[2] The alternative view—that the genealogies here (and the *Dream*) have borrowed from Geoffrey—seems to us most improbable. Elen may originally have been taken from a story relating to Constantius; but what is said of her in the *Dream* has nothing in common with Geoffrey's account.

passages cited above (p. 274) from the Harleian Genealogies of the tenth (ninth) century show that speculations relating to the Roman period, and to Maximus in particular, had long been cultivated.

II. Catalogues are not a usual characteristic of heroic narrative poetry or saga (Type A). In the Homeric poems the longest examples are the catalogues of the Achaean and Trojan forces in *Il.* II. 494 ff., 816 ff. A short catalogue of the same character is that of the Myrmidons in XVI. 168 ff. In XVIII. 39 ff. there is a list of mermaids, of whom thirty-three are named. Short lists of slain warriors also occur from time to time in the battle scenes. The *Odyssey* has in VIII. 111 ff. a list of Phaeacian athletes and in XI. 235 ff. a list of distinguished women whom Odysseus encounters in Hades.

The Phaeacian list, as we have seen (p. 230), consists of a series of names made up from nautical terms and was obviously composed—not without a touch of humour—for the place which it occupies in the poem. But the same cannot be said of the list of Nereids, which is clearly parallel to the similar list contained in the *Theogony* (243 ff.), as we shall see in a later chapter (XVII). The latter comes among a series of catalogues of the same kind and would seem to be more in place. Again, the list of distinguished women is evidently a composition of the same kind as the lists of women in the Hesiodic Catalogue (see below), while in the *Odyssey* it bears no relation to the context. In these two cases therefore we see an encroachment of antiquarian interest upon the heroic story. The catalogues of forces are likewise of an informative character; and from the prominence given to the Boeotians and various other details it is likely that they are additions to the poem. Indeed the Trojan catalogue is said to have been given also in the *Cypria*—for which it may originally have been composed. But the connection with the story is much closer than in the lists of Nereids and distinguished women. In contrast with the latter they may be regarded as necessary or at least desirable for the explanation of the course of events. It will be seen below that parallels are to be found in Irish and Norse; and there can be little doubt that such catalogues as these are among the earliest informative elements in heroic story.

In post-Homeric poetry catalogues are of far more frequent occurrence; indeed the poems of the eighth and seventh centuries seem to have consisted very largely of information conveyed in this form. Thus in Hesiod's *Theogony* we find lists of Muses (77 ff.), of the children of Uranos (133 ff.), Night (211 ff.) and Strife (226 ff.), of Nereids (243 ff.), of Rivers (337 ff.), of Water-nymphs (349 ff.), and many other mythological beings and personifications—ending (967 ff.) with a list of goddesses who entered into wedlock with men. The 'Catalogue', of which only fragments survive, consisted apparently of a long list of women of the Heroic Age, with stories relating to each of them. The *Eoiai* seems to have been a work of similar character. Each example was introduced with the words 'Or such (woman) as...'[1] These poems in the course of time were apparently combined so as to form a kind of Corpus of mythology and tradition. The last four lines of the *Theogony* are really an introduction to the Catalogue, while the *Eoiai* is believed to have been attached to the latter. One section of the *Eoiai* is preserved as an introduction to the 'Shield of Heracles'—which again illustrates the way in which the poetry of this age was transmitted. It is not quite clear why the poets were so much concerned with women of the Heroic Age; but some light is perhaps thrown on the question by the Norse poem *Hyndluljóð*, which we shall have to consider shortly.

A somewhat different kind of antiquarian catalogue appears in the *Works and Days*; but this will require notice under VII, below. The catalogue form was also much in favour for gnomic poetry during the same period, as we shall see in the next chapter.

Antiquarian catalogues can hardly be said to occur in the heroic narrative poetry of the Teutonic peoples. Perhaps the best example one can produce is the brief catalogue of rulers (four in number) in the *Battle of the Goths and Huns*, st. 1, and it is disputed whether this properly belongs to the poem. On the other hand, three catalogues are contained in *Widsith*, which may practically be regarded as heroic Type C (CB), though we believe it to have originated in Type E (cf. p. 42). The first (18–35) gives a list of famous kings with the nations which they ruled, precisely similar to that in the *Battle*, but much longer. The second (57–87) enumerates the peoples visited by the poet, with some incidental remarks. It may be observed that this list contains, towards the end, a group of names derived from Biblical learning—which shows how such lists can be expanded. The third list (112–124) gives the names of a number of famous heroes visited by the poet and described as 'Eormenric's household force' (cf. p. 201). The references in *Deor* to stories of trouble may also be described as a catalogue.

There can be little doubt that similar catalogue poetry was known among the Teutonic peoples of the Continent. The remains of early

[1] ἢ οἵη... The name of the poem is a plural made out of this—like *Afallenau*, *Gnodiau*, etc.

German poetry are indeed too meagre to yield much evidence on such a question; yet reference may be made to the list of deities enumerated in one of the Merseburg spells.[1] A parallel to the second list in *Widsith*, however, is to be traced in the list of peoples conquered by Eormenric, as recorded by Jordanes, cap. 23—which is evidently derived from Gothic tradition, presumably in poetic form. Similar poetic catalogues are perhaps to be traced in the description of the inhabitants of Scandinavia given in cap. 3 of the same work.

Although catalogues can hardly be said to occur in Norse heroic narrative poetry or in sagas derived therefrom, good parallels to the catalogues of forces in the *Iliad* are to be found in a story which relates to the early part of the Viking Age, but differs in no respect from heroic standards. The story is told in one of the fragments of the *Skjöldunga Saga* (cap. 8) and also by Saxo, p. 309 ff. (257 ff.), whose account seems to be derived from an earlier form of the saga. It is concerned with the battle of Brávík, fought between Haraldr Hilditönn and Sigurðr Hringr, probably about the beginning of the ninth century. The warriors engaged and the contingents they brought from various countries are described as fully as in the *Iliad*.

In some of the Norse mythological poems catalogues are almost as frequent as in Hesiod's *Theogony*. Thus the *Grímnismál* (cf. p. 321) gives a descriptive list of the homes of the gods (st. 4 ff.), lists of (chiefly mythological) rivers (27 ff.), of the horses of the gods (st. 31), of mythological snakes (st. 35), of Valkyries (st. 37), of names of Othin (st. 47 ff.), and various other short lists. In st. 44 we find even a list of the best things of their kinds: "Yggdrasill's Ash is the noblest of trees and Skíðblaðnir of ships, Othin of gods and Sleipnir of steeds, Bifröst of bridges and Bragi of poets, Hábrók of falcons and Garmr of hounds". The *Völuspá*, after relating the creation of the dwarfs (st. 9 f.), gives a long list of them (st. 11–15), which is very similar to the lists of mermaids in the *Iliad* and the *Theogony*. We may also refer here to the long series of questions and answers on mythological lore contained in the *Vafþrúðnismál* (cf. p. 321). The *Prose Edda*[2] quotes fragments of lost poems which give lists of the horses belonging to gods and heroes, and also of oxen.

Lastly, we may consider here the poem *Hyndluljóð* (cf. p. 242). In reply to Freyja's request Hyndla (st. 15 ff.) recites the ancestry of

[1] Published in Braune, *Althochdeutsches Lesebuch*, p. 81, and various other works.

[2] *Skaldskaparmál*, cap. 57, from the lost *Thorgrimsþula* and *Kalfsvísa*; transl. by Brodeur, *The Prose Edda*, p. 210 ff.

Óttarr, both paternal and maternal, for a few generations. Then she goes on to enumerate various heroes and famous families of the past, adding in each case the words 'All this is thy ancestry'. St. 33 ff. give genealogies of gods and other supernatural beings; but this part is generally believed to be interpolated. The important point to notice is that Óttarr requires the knowledge of his ancestry to support his claim to family property. The genealogy seems to be equivalent to a title-deed. When Hyndla has finished speaking, Freyja asks for 'ale of remembrance' to be given to her favourite, so that he may be able to remember the genealogy when he comes to meet the rival claimant.

This poem perhaps throws some light on the origin of Greek genealogical catalogue poetry. Hesiod's Catalogue appears to have been a Corpus of antiquarian lore, as we have seen. But if descent in Greece was at one time reckoned through women—a hypothesis which has a good deal of evidence in its favour[1]—the type may have had its origin in practical considerations such as are illustrated in the *Hyndluljóð*.[2]

In poems of the British Heroic Age, catalogues are not very rare. These poems, it is to be remembered, are of Type D (panegyrics and elegies), not Type A. A long list of battles occurs in *Tal.* XI, a panegyric upon Gwallawg and similar but shorter lists in *Tal.* XVIII and XXXVI, which are panegyrics upon Urien. Examples are also to be found in the elegies. The framework of the *Gododdin* poem (*An.* I) is in the form of a catalogue, and short catalogues occur in it incidentally, e.g. st. 30 f.

In poems which are of a definitely antiquarian character and belong no doubt to a later period catalogues are far more frequent. Such is the case with the *Stanzas of the Graves* (*BBC.* XIX), a poem describing briefly a long list of graves, many of which are those of characters of the Heroic Age and of the *Mabinogion.* As a general rule one stanza is devoted to each grave, but sometimes two or more graves are combined in one stanza, and occasionally a hero is celebrated in more than one stanza. To this poem we shall have to return later (under V, below). Here also we may mention *RBH.* XV, though the meaning of the last two stanzas is not clear to us. The greater part of the poem consists of a list of the places at which Cadwallon pitched his camp on his expeditions. The list of battles fought by Arthur given in the *Historia Brittonum*, cap. 154 f. would seem to be derived from such a piece as this.

1 Cf. Chadwick, *Heroic Age*, p. 357 ff. (especially p. 359, note 2).

2 Analogies are to be found in other parts of the world. The subject will come up for discussion again in connection with Polynesian antiquarian lore.

Another poem (*Tal.* xxv) contains a list of horses, mostly unnamed, belonging to various persons, including Arthur, Taliesin and Lleu; but the context is obscure. With this may be compared the *Triads* contained in *BBC.* VIII,[1] which give the names of the horses of various famous heroes—a catalogue similar in character to those in the Norse fragments cited above. Indeed the whole body of 'historical' Triads may be included here, since they consist of antiquarian lore epitomised for mnemonic purposes.

Two poems (*Tal.* XIV and *BBC.* XXXIII) show a certain resemblance to the second and third catalogues in *Widsith* (cf. p. 277). In the former the speaker, who is clearly meant to be Taliesin, says that he has visited and sung before various princes, including Brochfael of Powys and Urien. As in the case of *Widsith*, it is quite possible that this may be derived ultimately from a poem of Type E. But later in the poem he claims (31 f.) that he has been in Ireland with Bran, as in the *Mabinogi* of *Branwen*, and taken part in various other unhistorical events. In *BBC.* XXXIII (cf. p. 35) one of the speakers, Gwyddno or Gwyn ap Nudd, says (st. 15 ff.) that he has been present on the occasions when Gwenddoleu and others were killed, and adds (st. 19) that he was not present when Gwallawg was slain.

Culhwch and Olwen contains a very long catalogue of the members of Arthur's court who are invoked by the hero. The names are drawn not only from native tradition but also from Irish and even Continental sources. Other catalogues occur in the same story, e.g. the long list of tasks which the hero undertakes to perform for Yspaddaden Pencawr. The *Dream of Rhonabwy* has a long list of Arthur's councillors. On the other hand, in the Romances, both French and Welsh, catalogues are rare, though not altogether wanting. In the earlier Romances perhaps the longest are the lists of Arthur's knights in *Erec et Enide* and in *Gereint son of Erbin*.

The dating of Welsh antiquarian poetry and native saga is a difficult problem; but it must not be assumed that catalogues are necessarily

[1] These are the earliest datable *Triads*, for this part of the MS. was written about the middle of the twelfth century. The two last Triads—there are four in all—cannot be much earlier than this, since they include Gilbert, son of Cadgyffro, presumably Gilbert FitzRichard (ancestor of the Clare family), who did not attain power in Wales until 1110. The other names which appear in these two Triads are such as usually figure in later works—Cai, Gwalchmai, Caradawg and Caswallawn. The last Triad is incomplete. The series affords another probable example of the tendency to expansion which is found everywhere in catalogue poetry; for the two first Triads may well be earlier.

late. Reference has already been made to the list of Arthur's battles in the *Historia Brittonum*, cap. 56. The lists of the Cities and Marvels of Britain, which are attached to several MSS. of the same work, appear to have been in existence before the time of Nennius.[1] Indeed it is a question whether Gildas had not the former in his mind when he wrote (cap. 1) that there were twenty-eight cities in Britain. We suspect that several of the catalogues noticed above may have a long history. Compositions of this kind cannot safely be dated by the latest item.

In Irish sagas relating to the Heroic Age catalogues are by no means rare, and sometimes they run to a considerable length. The most remarkable case is the (non-heroic) story of the *Destruction of Da Derga's Hall*. A large part of this story (sect. 75–140)[2] consists of a dialogue between the British pirate Ingcel and his Irish confederates, in which the former, who has been to reconnoitre the Hall, describes the occupants of the various rooms, and the others identify them from his description. This form of dialogue seems to be a recognised convention in such cases. In the *Táin Bó Cuailnge*[3] there is a long description of the muster of the Ulster army, which affords an interesting parallel to the catalogues of the Achaean and Trojan forces in the *Iliad*, though the description of the warriors here is much more detailed. The whole passage is in the form of a dialogue between Ailill, his spy Mac Roth and the Ulster hero Fergus. Mac Roth describes each of the warriors, and Fergus, in reply to Ailill's questions, identifies them.

The cases given above are examples of descriptive catalogues. Catalogues which consist wholly or almost wholly of names are more frequent. The *Táin Bó Cuailnge*,[4] shortly before the last passage, gives a long list of the heroes summoned by Conchobor to the muster.[5] In *Bricriu's Feast* we find similar lists—in cap. 2 of the heroes invited to the feast, and in cap. 4 of their wives. Such lists are indeed of frequent occurrence in Irish sagas, whenever there is occasion to describe an expedition or any event in which many heroes take part. For an instance

1 In the Cambridge text, after cap. 56 (p. 207 in Mommsen's ed.) the writer—apparently Nennius—says: *de ciuitatibus et mirabilibus Britanniae insulae, ut alii scriptores ante me scripsere, scripsi.*

2 *Rev. Celt.* XXII. 174 ff., 282 ff. (text and transl. by Stokes).

3 P. 316 ff. in Dunn's translation; Windisch, 5159 ff.

4 P. 302 ff. in Dunn's translation; Windisch, 4771 ff.

5 A somewhat similar list—contained in 'rhetorics'—occurs in Emer's Lament for CuChulainn (*Book of Leinster*, facsim., fol. 123 *b*). It is a list of the heroes who ought to have been present to support CuChulainn, when he was slain.

relating to an event towards the close of the Heroic Age we may refer to the list of princes killed in the *Battle of Allen.*[1]

A characteristic feature of Irish sagas is to be found in the long lists of places through which an army or even a single hero passes in the course of a journey. As an example we may cite the detailed itinerary of Medb and Ailill with their army, given in the *Táin Bó Cuailnge.*[2] This feature is doubtless connected with the highly developed topographical interest of Irish antiquarianism, which we shall have to notice in the next section. Short lists of various kinds also occur frequently. In some late sagas, e.g. the later *Táin Bó Flidais*, the 'catalogue' element assumes considerable proportions.

In early Irish poetry catalogues of various kinds are far more prominent than in the sagas. Some of the earliest poems in existence are genealogical catalogues, as we have seen (p. 272). Similar elements figure largely in the poetry of the 'synthetic historians', from the ninth century onwards.[3] For an example we may refer to a poem ascribed to Kenneth O'Hartigan (d. 984) on the *Deaths of some Irish Heroes*, which describes the deaths and often the graves of various heroes from Fergus mac Lete down to the battle of Allen or later.[4] The poem is continued by Find, bishop of Kildare (d. 1160), and others down to the twelfth century. It has analogies on the one side to the Norse *Ynglingatal* (cf. p. 271) and on the other to the Welsh *Stanzas of the Graves.* Another parallel to the latter may be found in a poem[5] ascribed to Torna Eces, a poet of the fifth century, though in reality it is no doubt much later. This gives a list of the kings buried at Relic na Rig ('Cemetery of the Kings') near Cruachan, including Dathi (Nath-I), the successor of Niall Noigiallach, Eochaid Feidlech and Eochaid Airem and their family, Labraid Loingsech, and even some of the Tuatha De Danann.

The above examples are all taken from poems of a definitely antiquarian character. Short catalogues, more or less rhetorical, occur also in poems of Type D. They bear a general resemblance to the lists of battles mentioned in the panegyrics upon Gwallawg and Urien

[1] Cf. *Rev. Celt.* XXIV. 52 ff.

[2] Windisch, 300 ff.; p. 19 f. in Dunn's translation.

[3] Cf. Hull, *Text-book of Irish Literature*, Part I, (Note on) Chronology (p. 5 f.) and p. 172 ff.; MacNeill, *Celtic Ireland*, p. 39.

[4] Ed. and transl. by Stokes, *Rev. Celt.* XXIII. 304 ff. Two of the three texts claim Kenneth O'Hartigan as author; but most scholars believe the poem to have been composed in the eleventh century.

[5] Transl. by O'Curry, *Manners and Customs*, II. 71 f.

(cf. p. 39). As an example we may cite a poem[1] addressed to the sword of Cerball, king of Leinster (d. 909), which celebrates a number of battles, in which it had fought. The poem is quite in the heroic style.

Reviewing the evidence for catalogues as a whole it must be repeated that they are not always of antiquarian origin. The lists of battles which occur in panegyric poetry are intended to emphasise the glory of the hero whose praise is celebrated. The catalogues of warriors found in narrative poetry and saga are of an informative but not necessarily antiquarian character. They may be explained as helps to the narrative; but in point of fact they generally give a good deal more information than is required, and often they seem to be additions to the story, due to antiquarian interest in the personnel. In most of the other cases the antiquarian interest is present from the beginning.

III. Speculation upon the origin of names, especially place-names, is one of the most widespread, and apparently one of the earliest, forms of antiquarian activity. Examples are to be found in all the early literatures with which we are concerned; but it is only in Ireland that we find what may be called a systematic study of the subject.

The word *dinnšenchas*, which properly means 'story of a place', is applied to short stories in verse or prose which explain the origins of the names of places.[2] A collection of over a hundred such poems, together with a few prose pieces, is preserved in the *Book of Leinster*. A number of them are ascribed to known poets of the ninth, tenth and eleventh centuries, but the majority are anonymous. The name *Dinnšenchas* is also applied to the whole collection, as well as to two later collections which are largely derived from it. In these later collections the stories are given mainly in prose, usually with one four-line stanza. For an example we may take the origin of the name *Rath Cruachan* (Medb's capital) as explained in the older collection.[3] When Etain, the wife of Eochaid Airem, was carried off by the god Midir (cf. p. 52), she was accompanied—according to this story—by her maid Crochen or Cruachu. They arrived at a certain elf-hill, and Crochen asked Midir if it was his home. When he said it was not, she asked him if her name

[1] Ed. and transl. by K. Meyer, *Rev. Celt.* XX. 7 ff.; transl. also in *Ancient Irish Poetry*, p. 72 ff.

[2] Cf. Thurneysen, *Irische Heldensage*, p. 36 ff.

[3] Cf. E. Gwynn, *The Metrical Dindshenchas*, III. 348; Thurneysen, *op. cit.* p. 616.

could be given to it. He agreed, and also presented her with the place as a reward for the journey.[1]

The prose collections frequently give alternative etymologies. Thus the latest collection,[2] which is believed to date from about 1200, gives three explanations of the name *Temair* (Tara), of which two are founded on native speculations and the third on a Greek etymology. These are followed by a detailed list of the sites and monuments at Tara—in the style of a guide-book.[3] Three explanations are also given for *Ard Macha* (Armagh).[4] Two at least of these can be traced to earlier sources, and were framed originally for Emain Macha, the ancient capital of Ulster, three miles from Armagh. In each case Macha is the name of a woman. In the first she is the wife of Nemed and belongs to the story of the 'Invasions', which we shall have to notice under VI, below. In the second she is the daughter of the ancient king Aed Ruad and foundress of Emain Macha, which she 'marked out' with a brooch. This story is known from Cormac's Glossary and other sources. Sometimes she is said to be the wife of Cimbaeth, with whom according to the Annals—apparently from the Irish Eusebius (cf. p. 273)—reliable history begins.[5] In the third explanation she is the wife of an Ulsterman called Cruinn or Cronn, and daughter of Midir (cf. p. 256f.). She is forced to race against Conchobor's horses, when she is with child. She wins the race and immediately brings forth twins. Her death follows, but first she curses the men of Ulster, imposing upon them the weakness of childbed when need should befall them. This story also is known from various other sources,[6] in which the husband is sometimes called Crunnchu or Crunniuc. It may be observed that some of the other sources connect the name *Emain* with words for either 'brooch' or 'twins'.[7] These speculations are omitted in the *Dinnšenchas* owing to the fact that the stories have been transferred from Emain Macha to Armagh.

Mention may also be made of a work called *Cóir Anmann* or 'the correct (interpretation) of names', which contains speculations on a large number of names of persons—also a few communities—known from

[1] In other sources the name is derived from Crochan, the wife of Eochaid Feidlech (E. Airem's brother) and mother of Medb.

[2] Ed. and transl. by Stokes, *Rev. Celt.* xv. f., from the Rennes MS.

[3] Cf. Stokes, *Rev. Celt.* xv. 277 ff.

[4] Cf. Stokes, *Rev. Celt.* xvi. 44 ff. The first two lines on p. 45 should be transferred to the foot of the page.

[5] (*Ann. Tig.*) *Rev. Celt.* xvi. 394.

[6] Cf. Thurneysen, *Ir. Heldensage*, p. 360 ff.

[7] Cf. *emuin*, 'twins', *eó*, 'brooch' (with *muin*, 'neck'—taken as 'neck-brooch').

saga and early history. It is preserved in two very different forms; but there appears to be much difference of opinion as to its antiquity.[1]

Apart from these works the sagas themselves contain numerous remarks on the origins of names.[2] In the story of Mac Datho's Pig,[3] cap. 19, the plain of Ailbe is said to take its name from the dog Ailbe, which was killed there, as it was pursuing Ailill's chariot. It had mounted on the pole when the driver cut off its head—which remained behind when the body fell off. In the next chapter, Ailill continues his flight over the 'Ford of the Dog's Head' (*Ath Chind Chon*), where the dog's head fell from the chariot.

The *Táin Bó Cuailnge* supplies numerous examples of such etymologies. Indeed it is probable that in this—as in other sagas—many incidents owe their origin to speculations on place-names. Thus one passage[4] relates that CuChulainn fought with a hero called Lethan at a ford called *Ath Lethan for Nith*, that the chariots were broken at another ford close by, called *Ath Carpat*, and that Lethan's charioteer Mulcha was killed in a ravine called *Guala* ('ravine') *Mulchai*, between the two fords. The name of the first ford means 'the broad ford on the Nith', that of the second 'ford of chariots'—so it is very likely that both the warriors themselves and their adventure are products of speculation on the names. At present, we think, there is a tendency to overestimate the effects of the operation of this principle. When we find a hero called Fraech and a ford called *Ath Froich* (Fraech's Ford) it is not necessary to infer that the hero was invented to account for the name of the ford. Weland certainly did not owe his existence to the megalithic monument called Wayland Smith's Cave in Berkshire. Neither was Wada created out of Wade's Causeway, nor Arthur out of the numerous places which bear his name. They were all well-known characters before they were associated with these places, and it was partly owing to their being well known that they were associated with them. There is no reason for doubting the operation of the same principle in the case of Irish heroic story. The heroes were well known, and places came to be called after them. But there seem to be a number of cases, like the one noted above, where heroes have been created out of place-names.

[1] According to Dobbs, *Sidelights on the Táin Age*, p. 57 ff., the earlier text has had a long history, reaching back to c. 700; but Thurneysen, *Ir. Heldensage*, p. 48 ff., holds it to be not older than the thirteenth century.

[2] For conversations on place-names see the (late) *Martial Career of Conghal Clairinghneach*, cap. 12; also Hull, *Text-book of Irish Literature*, I. 176 f.

[3] Ed. and transl. by Chadwick, *An Early Irish Reader*.

[4] P. 86 in Dunn's translation; Windisch, 1439 ff.

Explanations of personal names are by no means so frequent; but they are not rare. As an example we may take the name *CúChulainn*, which is interpreted as 'Culann's Dog' (*cú*). In the *Táin Bó Cuailnge*[1] the name is explained by an adventure of the hero's childhood. He is said to have killed the dog of a smith called Culann, and then to have taken its place as watchman.

In early Teutonic records speculation of this kind is by no means so ubiquitous. Examples seem not to occur in English or Norse heroic poetry, except in the invention of such names as *Widsith* and possibly *Unferth*, which have already been noticed (p. 231), and older national and dynastic names, like *Scyld*, which will require discussion under VI, below. Elsewhere cases occur sporadically. We have little doubt that by a careful search it would be possible to collect a considerable amount of evidence.

An interesting example is to be found in the story quoted above (p. 254) from the *Origo Gentis Langobardorum*, the object of which is to explain how the Langobardi acquired their name—which is interpreted to mean 'Long-beards'. A somewhat similar case occurs in Jordanes, cap. 17. The Goths are said to have come from Scandza in three ships, of which one, containing the Gepidae, was slower than the others. "This is said to have given the nation its name; for in their language *gepanta* is the word for 'slow'."

In Widukind, *Res Gestae Saxonicae*, I. 6 f., a story is told which, according to some, explains how the Saxons—the Old Saxons of the Continent—acquired their name. The Saxons had agreed to come to a conference with the Thuringians, both sides being unarmed. But the Saxons had big knives concealed under their cloaks, and with these they massacred their enemies. The word for the big knife of ancient times was *sahs*. Practically the same story is told in the *Historia Brittonum*, cap. 46, of Hengest and the Britons. Hengest and his men, who are called *Saxones*, had treacherously concealed knives (*saxas*) in their boots when they came to the conference. The story here is not used for the purpose of explaining the name 'Saxon', but in view of its parallelism to the Old Saxon story we strongly suspect that its origin is to be sought in an early speculation on the national name.

In the *Saxon Chronicle* antiquarian activity may be traced especially in the account of the West Saxon invasion, from *ann.* 495 onwards. Thus Cerdic is associated with *Cerdices Ora*, *Cerdices Ford* and *Cerdices Leah*, Port with *Portes Muþa*, Wihtgar with *Wihtgares Burh*, etc. Genuine tradition may of course be preserved in one or other of these cases.

[1] P. 57 f. in Dunn's translation; Windisch, 1019 ff.

But in the first three examples at least speculation is much more probable; for it is extremely doubtful whether a Teutonic invader of the fifth century could have had such a name as *Cerdic*. In the fourth also it may be suspected that Port owes his existence to the Latin word *portus*, 'harbour'. It is true that this story as we have it may never have existed in the form of oral tradition; it may largely be the creation of the man who first wrote it down, presumably in Latin. But there is no need to doubt that he was working on time-honoured native lines.

In the 'Book of the Colonisation of Iceland' (*Íslands Landnámabók*) explanations of this kind are extremely numerous. There are stories which give the various early names of the country, and how they originated, and very many stories relating how settlers or their descendants gave their names to localities. Other stories again offer explanations of names which are not derived from personal names. As examples of the last type we may refer to some places which are said to have received their names from incidents connected with the landing of Queen Auðr of Dublin (II. 16)—'Breakfast Headland', where she and her party had breakfast, 'Comb Headland', where she lost her comb, 'Cross Hills', where she used to retire for prayer. There is no reason to doubt that many of these names have been preserved from the beginning by genuine tradition; for Iceland was to all intents an uninhabited country before the Norse colonisation. But many others are probably due to speculation.

Sagas often explain the origins of place-names, not only in Iceland but also in Norway and other lands. In *Ólafs Saga Tryggvasonar* (*Heimskr.*), cap. 71, we find Othin in disguise explaining to the king the origin of the name *Ögvaldsnes*, the place where he was staying, not very far from Stavanger. In *Ynglinga Saga*, cap. 22, Agnafit, a place near Stockholm, is said to derive its name from an ancient king called Agni, who met with a tragic death there.

An interesting case of speculation arising out of a personal name is to be found in the same saga, cap. 25, where the description of King Hugleikr seems to be entirely derived from his name. He is said to have been no warrior, but to have kept at his court all kinds of players, harpers and fiddlers. The name seems to have been interpreted as 'one whose mind (*hugr*) is devoted to play (*leikr*)'. But he is probably to be identified with Hygelac, the uncle of Beowulf, who was a great warrior. Apparently nothing was remembered of him in Norse tradition, except that he had lost his life in a great disaster. The kingdom of the Gautar (Geatas), to which he really belonged, had long disappeared, and his family was completely forgotten.

The Greek evidence is very similar to the Teutonic. The Homeric poems seem to contain little or nothing which properly comes under this head. On the other hand, speculations of this kind occur very frequently in later literature, especially in antiquarian and historical works; and there can be little doubt that many of them are derived from oral tradition. As a fairly early example we may cite the explanation of the name *Delphoi* given in the *Hymn to the Pythian Apollo*, especially 315 ff. The god boards a Cretan ship in the form of a dolphin and guides it to Crissa, the port of Delphoi. Then assuming human form he leads the crew to his shrine and establishes them there as its guardians. The idea was no doubt suggested by the resemblance of the word *delphis* (δελφίς), 'dolphin', to the name *Delphoi*.[1]

As typical explanations of place-names recorded by Strabo, Pausanias and other antiquarian writers we may cite that of the Saronic Gulf, from a king named Saron who was drowned there; of Naupactos, from the building of ships[2] there by the Heracleidai, when they crossed over to the Peloponnesos; of Harma, a place in Boeotia, from an accident to a chariot (ἅρμα), which took place there during the campaign of the Seven Heroes against Thebes. In the last case it was disputed whether the hero whom the accident befell was Amphiaraos or Adrastos.[3]

Explanations of this kind are not limited to stories of gods or of characters of the Heroic Age. We may refer, e.g., to the account given by Herodotos, v. 92, of Cypselos, who was ruler of Corinth c. 655–625. An oracle had foretold that he would overthrow the reigning family of Corinth, and shortly after his birth emissaries were sent to put him to death. His mother saved his life by concealing him in a chest (κυψέλη), from which he is said to have taken his name.

The early Welsh evidence for speculations of this kind appears to be limited; but this is no doubt due to the character of the records. In heroic poetry we have not noticed any examples.

A parallel to the last chapters of 'Mac Datho's Pig' (cf. p. 285) is to be

1 Names with *Delphin-* were associated with Apollo elsewhere. His temple at Athens was called *Delphinion*.

2 From ναυπηγέω, 'to build ships'.

3 In *Il.* vi. 37 ff. another Adrastos, a Trojan, is thrown from his chariot. It is not unlikely that a confused reminiscence of this passage may have led to the substitution of Adrastos for Amphiaraos in the local story. Some scholars, however, contend that the Trojan Adrastos has been transferred from the Theban story; and this also is quite possible. His father's name is not given; but it may be observed that the adventure costs him his life, whereas the more famous Adrastos survives the expedition to Thebes.

found in the *Mabinogi* of *Math*. When Gwydion has cheated Pryderi and carried off his pigs, the various places at which he stops for the night are said to have received their names from the occasion. Three of them are called *Mochdref* or 'homestead of swine', and the fourth *Mochnant* or 'valley of swine'. Finally he pens them up at a place called *Creuwyrion*, which is evidently regarded as a derivative of *creu* (*crau*), 'pigsty'. In a Triad contained in Hengwrt 536 and in the *Red Book*[1] the name *Maes Gwenith* ('Field of Wheat') in Gwent is explained by the story of a sow which dropped wheat there.

Speculative explanations of place-names from the names of famous characters occur in Welsh records, as elsewhere, and in later times are very common. As an example we may take the name Traeth Maelgwn ('Maelgwn's Strand'), at the mouth of the Dovey, respecting which a story is told in certain MSS. of the Laws.[2] At a meeting of princes here Maelgwn's supremacy was recognised because he was able to maintain his position against the incoming tide—by means of a floating chair made of wings which he had had constructed. Again, Carmarthen (Caerfyrddin), a name which can be traced back to Roman times (*Moridunum*), was interpreted, at least by the twelfth century (cf. p. 111), as 'city of Myrddin'. Places bearing Arthur's name are of course widely distributed over England, Wales and Scotland.

A far-fetched explanation dating from much earlier times is to be found in some texts[3] of the *Historia Brittonum*, cap. 27. The Britons who went over sea with Maximus are said to have massacred all the male inhabitants of western Gaul. Then they appropriated their wives and daughters and cut out their tongues, in order to prevent the children from learning the language of their mothers. "Whence also in our language we call them *Letewicion*, i.e. *semitacentes*, because they speak confusedly." Evidently the idea is to derive this name[4]—the early British name for the Bretons—from the words *lled*, 'half', and *tewi*, 'to be silent'.

IV. Next we have to take traditions and speculations relating to the origin of institutions, customs and ceremonies. Greek records contain numerous examples. Often they are preserved only by late authorities;

1 *Myv. Arch.*, pp. 390 (No. 30), 398 (No. 56).

2 Cf. Skene, *Four Ancient Books*, I. p. 64 f. (transl.); Lloyd, *History of Wales*, p. 129.

3 Cf. Mommsen's ed., p. 167, note 1.

4 Lat. *Letavici*, Anglo-Saxon (Dat.) *Lidwiccum*, *Lidwicingum*, from Lat. *Letavia*, mod. W. *Llydaw*.

but there can be little doubt that many even of these are derived from early antiquarian poetry or saga.

The most familiar case is the double kingship at Sparta, the origin of which is traced to the twin sons of Aristodemos. It may be observed that this story, as told by Herodotos, VI. 52 (cf. IV. 147), is well supplied with details, which imply a somewhat elaborate form of saga. The same author, I. 147, notes that among the Ionians it was customary for women to eat separately from men. In this case he makes merely a general statement—no doubt derived from antiquarian tradition—that the original women were Carians, whose husbands and fathers had been killed by the first Greek invaders. Again, from references in various authorities, mostly late,[1] there would seem to have been a story which explained the origin of the Locrian custom of devoting girls of the nobility to serve at the sanctuary of Athena at Troy. As an example of speculation relating to a more general custom we may cite the passage in Hesiod, *Theogony*, 535 ff., which explains the Greek practice of devoting the bones of victims to the gods by the story of Prometheus' sacrifice.

The numerous festivals which were held in all parts of Greece frequently had stories connected with them, which explained their origin. Sometimes they were said to have been established by the gods themselves, as in the Homeric *Hymn to Demeter*, 473 ff.—with which may be compared the *Hymn to the Pythian Apollo*, 353 ff.—and sometimes by famous heroes. One of the most curious of these stories was that which described the origin of the Nemean Games. These were said to have been instituted by the Seven Heroes who were marching against Thebes, and were to commemorate the death of the child Opheltes or Archemoros, whom they buried at Nemea.[2] It is not necessary, however, to suppose that such stories were all pure inventions. The Olympian festival is said to have been established by a certain Iphitos, king of Elis. This person evidently lived before the beginning of the historical period—perhaps in the ninth century—and nothing further seems to be known of him. We see no reason for regarding the tradition as incredible. Even in this case, however, there were other stories, according to which Iphitos merely re-established a festival which had been instituted long before, by Pelops or Heracles or still earlier heroes.

Early Irish evidence also is fairly abundant. One of the most peculiar features in the Ulster stories is the *ces* or 'weakness of childbed', to which the warriors of Ulster are subject. In some accounts it lasts only

[1] Cf. Brückner, *Troja und Ilion*, p. 557 ff.

[2] Cf. Pausanias, II. 15, with Frazer's note *ad loc.*

nine half-days, i.e. four days and a half; but in the *Táin Bó Cuailnge* they are incapacitated by it throughout the winter, and Medb takes advantage of this fact by starting on her raid at the beginning of November. One explanation of the *ces* has been referred to above (p. 284)—that it was due to the curse imposed on the men of Ulster by the shee-woman Macha, when she had to race in her pregnancy with Conchobor's horses. This story is given in many sources and seems to have been the usual explanation. There was, however, another story, which is preserved in only one text.[1] The shee Elcmaire broke Cu-Chulainn's chariot, and the hero in revenge cut off his thumbs and great toes and carried off his wife Fedelm. At the end of a year Fedelm showed herself naked to the men of Ulster, and this brought upon them the *ces*.

For another example we may refer to the tribute (*boraime*, *boramha*), which was claimed from Leinster by the high-kings. Almost every high-king down to the time of Finsnechta (d. 694) attempted to enforce it; but it was frequently resisted, and many great battles are said to have been due to this cause. According to one story[2] the tribute was imposed by Tuathal Techtmar because of an insult done to him by Eochaid Ainchenn, king of Leinster. Eochaid had married one of Tuathal's daughters; but later, thinking he had made a bad choice, he shut her up, giving out that she was dead, and married her sister. When the second wife on her arrival found her sister living, she died from shame, and thereupon the first wife died from grief.

Bede (*Hist. Eccles.* I. I) tells a story relating to the Picts which is probably of Irish origin, though we do not know it from any Irish sources. He says that the Picts first came to Ireland and asked for permission to settle there. The Irish refused but advised them to settle in Britain, which they did. But they had no women with them, and therefore they begged the Irish to give them wives. The Irish granted this request on condition that whenever a question of succession arose, they should choose their king by his maternal, rather than paternal, ancestry—a custom which, he adds, is observed by the Picts down to the present

[1] Cf. Thurneysen, *Ir. Heldensage*, p. 359 f.

[2] Ed. and transl. (from the Book of Leinster) by Stokes, *Rev. Celt.* XIII. 32 ff.; O'Grady, *Silva Gadelica*, I. 359 ff., II. 401 ff. A shorter version of the story (also from the Book of Leinster) is ed. and transl. by Owen, *Journal of the Ivernian Soc.*, VII. 211 ff. Cf. also O'Curry, *MS. Materials*, p. 230 (and p. 585, note 129). We gather from MacNeill, *Phases of Irish History*, p. 238, that there is another story, which gives a different explanation of the origin of this tribute; but we do not know where it is preserved.

day. The object of this story obviously is to explain the Pictish law of succession, according to which descent was reckoned through the female line, down to the time of Bede and apparently for about a century later. For this custom there is evidence from other sources; the few fathers of kings who can be identified are foreigners—Britons or English. Moreover, somewhat similar phenomena can be traced in Ireland from stories of the Ulster cycle (cf. p. 177 f.) and in Wales from the *Mabinogi* of *Math* (cf. p. 116). But it was only among the Picts of Scotland that the custom persisted into historical times—whence it came to be regarded as an anomaly requiring explanation.

The festivals of heathen Ireland, many of which survived in later times as fairs, were provided with stories explaining their origin, like those of the ancient Greeks. Several of them are ascribed to Tuathal Techtmar, the high-king mentioned above, who, coming as he does just after the 'Revolt of the Vassals', is represented as a great founder or re-founder of institutions. But others are said to have been instituted by gods. Thus the famous festival and games of Tailtiu (Teltown, Co. Meath) are said to have been established by Lug in honour of his foster-mother Tailtiu, daughter of Magmor, who had declared her desire to have a festival at her grave. In historical times this fair was regularly held by the high-king.[1]

In early Teutonic records we cannot recall any evidence which properly comes under this section. In the *Ynglinga Saga*, cap. 8, certain funeral practices are said to have been instituted by Othin—cremation, the burying of treasure (for use in the next life) and the erection of memorial stones. Saxo, p. 36 f. (29 f.), ascribes the establishment of the festival of Frey—apparently the great Swedish festival—to a legendary king Hadingus, who had been advised to propitiate the gods, because he had killed a sea-monster. In another passage, p. 90 (74 f.), Frey himself is said to have instituted human sacrifices at Upsala. To this sanctuary, however, we shall have to return in the next section.

In early Welsh records also we know of hardly any evidence. In certain texts of the Laws some stories are introduced to account for the existence of privileges. The story relating to Maelgwn cited on p. 289 is introduced to account for the privileged position of the king of Aberffraw (Anglesey). The object of another story[2] is, apparently, to justify the claim of the men of Arfon to lead the van in the army of Gwynedd.

[1] For references see Stokes, *Rev. Celt.* XVI. 51. Cf. also O'Curry, *MS. Materials*, p. 478, note.

[2] *Myv. Arch.*, pp. 977, 1030; cf. Skene, *Four Ancient Books*, I. p. 174 f. (transl.).

The story relates that Rhun, son of Maelgwn, led an army to the north against certain princes, including Clydno Eidyn and Rhydderch Hael, and that during the expedition a dispute arose as to which section of the army was entitled to the privilege of leading the van.

V. Next we may take traditions and speculations relating to ancient buildings, graves, sanctuaries, and localities in general.

This type also is well represented in Greek. Many of the great castles and palaces of the Bronze Age seem to have had stories attached to them. Tiryns is said to have been built by Proitos, Mycenai by Perseus. Most of these stories are known only from later times; but even in the *Odyssey* Cnossos is associated with Minos, the grandfather of Idomeneus, one of the leaders of the expedition against Troy. In the *Iliad*, XXIV. 614 ff., the unfortunate Niobe, who had been turned into stone, is identified with an ancient (Hittite) monument on Mount Sipylos—not very far from Smyrna—or perhaps with a peculiarly shaped natural rock in the neighbourhood.

Similar explanations were given for prehistoric tombs. The shaft-graves in the grave-circle at Mycenai, which date from cent. XVII–XVI B.C.—the existence of which was still known in Pausanias' time, though they had never been opened—were believed to be the tombs of Agamemnon and his entourage. The great domed tombs in the lower city were held to be the treasure-houses of the same family. Examples are to be found even in the *Iliad*. More than one reference occurs to the tomb—apparently a barrow—of Ilos Dardanides, who in XI. 372 is described as an ancient leader of the people. He is perhaps to be identified with the Ilos, son of Tros, mentioned in XX. 231 f., and to be regarded as an eponymos of the city (Ilios), although in XX. 236 f. he is said to be Priam's grandfather. Again, in II. 604 there is a reference to the tomb of Aipytos (in Arcadia), from whom the famous family of seers called Iamidai claimed to be descended.

The origins of certain sanctuaries are related in the Homeric Hymns. Thus Hymn I celebrates Delos as the birthplace of Apollo. In Hymn II the same god is described as travelling in search of a sanctuary and eventually establishing himself at Delphoi. In Hymn V Demeter chooses Eleusis as her sanctuary, owing to the kindly welcome she received there in her distress. Later works recount the origins of very many other sanctuaries. Sometimes it is not easy to distinguish early tradition or speculation from the observations of the writer himself, especially if he be a traveller like Herodotos; but there is no doubt that even writers of much later times give a large amount of information from genuine local sources.

In the North, where ancient buildings did not exist, antiquarian speculation of this kind was confined in the main to tombs and sanctuaries, but in regard to these it seems to have been almost as active as in Greece. For an example we may refer to a passage (cited above, p. 287) in *Ólafs Saga Tryggvasonar* (*Heimskr.*), cap. 71, where Othin visits the king in disguise and, in answer to his question why the place was called Ögvaldsnes, tells him the story of a king Ögvaldr, whose barrow and memorial stones were to be seen close by. The tombs of famous men of the past—even those of the Heroic Age—were often known, whether from tradition or conjecture; and sagas contain stories of tomb-robbers who plundered them. We may refer, e.g., to *Þórðar Saga Hreðu*, cap. 3, where it is stated that an Icelander named Skeggi, who lived in the latter part of the tenth century, made a voyage to Sjælland, where he broke into the tomb of Hrólfr Kraki. He secured Hrólfr's sword and Hjalti's axe, but failed to get Bjarki's sword away from him. An extraordinary example of the persistence of tradition seems to be shown by the name 'King Óttarr's Barrow'[1] borne in the seventeenth and eighteenth centuries by a barrow near Vendel, to the north of Upsala. This explains the name *Vendilkráka* applied in Norse tradition to Óttarr, the father of the famous Swedish king Aðils. In *Beowulf* he is mentioned as Ohthere, the father of Eadgils. Recent examination of the barrow has shown that it dates from the time (c. 500) indicated for Ohthere by *Beowulf*; it contained, *inter alia*, a gold coin of 477–8.

For Denmark Saxo sometimes supplies evidence which is almost as interesting as that of the sagas. He refers not only to burial-places but also occasionally to the precise scenes of certain events, which would seem to have been fixed by tradition or early speculation. In particular we may notice the incidental reference in Book XII (p. 402) to the place where Uffo (Offa) fought his famous combat—an island in the Eider, at Rendsburg. It is of interest also to note that he seems to know the burial-place of Balder; for he records, p. 94 (77 f.), that an attempt to break into it was made in his own time.

The chief sanctuaries of the North were those of Gamla Upsala in Sweden and of Leire, not far from Roskilde, in Sjælland. The former place was also the chief abode of the Swedish kings and the latter that of

[1] *Kong Ottars Hög* in a work published in 1725, *Utters högen* in a document of 1675, etc. Cf. Chambers, *Introduction to Beowulf*, pp. 343 f., 356 f., where an account is given of the barrow with references bearing on the question.

the Danish kings in heathen times. There is no doubt that both places were great centres of antiquarian tradition and speculation, although we know it only from Icelandic sources and—to a limited extent—from Saxo. The traditions of Upsala are given in the *Ynglinga Saga*, which is derived in part from the *Ynglingatal*, a genealogical poem (cf. p. 271) by the Norse poet Thjóðolfr of Hvín, who lived towards the close of the ninth century. Both the Saga and Saxo state that the sanctuary was founded by the god Frey, and that the Swedish kings and the nobility of the district were descended from him.[1] Unfortunately the *Skjöldunga Saga*, which doubtless contained the traditions of Leire, is lost, apart from a few fragments; and consequently we are dependent on a short Latin epitome and on references in other authorities. There can be little doubt, however, that Skjöldr, the eponymos of the Danish royal stock, was connected with Leire;[2] and the same is probably true of Gefjon, the goddess who created Sjælland with her plough. According to the *Ynglinga Saga*, cap. 5, she was the wife of Skjöldr.

German travellers in the Middle Ages attributed the chief buildings of ancient Rome, such as the Castle of St Angelo, the Colosseum and the Baths of Caracalla, to Dietrich von Berne. It is true that these associations are due to popular rather than to learned speculation; but this remark may apply to most cases of the kind in their initial stages. The attribution, e.g., of Cnossos and Mycenai to ancient Achaean heroes may have begun in popular speculation, though it was accepted by the learned. The tendency would seem to be to attribute ancient buildings to the most ancient characters who were well known, at least if there was any ground for believing that they were connected with the locality or country—as Dietrich was with Italy and Minos with Crete. But they were usually characters known from national tradition. German tradition knew only Teutonic heroes, not the native emperors of Rome.

In England the true origin of Roman buildings and structures was known, at least to the clergy, as far back as the seventh century. An early example of antiquarian interest of this kind, relating to the year 685, is to be found in Bede's *Life of St Cuthbert*, cap. 27, where the saint is taken to view the Roman fountain and the walls of Carlisle. But the names applied to Roman and prehistoric structures were not given by persons acquainted with Roman history, except when they are

[1] Cf. *Ynglinga Saga*, cap. 12 ff.; Saxo, p. 90 (74 f.), 228 (185), 313 (260).

[2] Skjöldr and Gefjon dwell at Leire in *Yngl. Saga*, cap. 5; for the creation of Sjælland, cf. *Gylfaginning*, cap. 1 (from the early poet Bragi).

comparatively modern; antiquarian speculation had doubtless begun long before the return of Latin learning. Procopios, *Goth.* IV. 20, writing about 550, gives a wonderful account of Britain. He knows that the ancients had built a great wall across the island, but as a reason for it he states that the country beyond was uninhabitable owing to its wildness—it was impossible even to enter it because of poisonous snakes. There can be little doubt that this is derived, however indirectly, from English speculation.

The attribution of ancient structures to individuals seems to have been unusual in this country in early times. To the god Woden were attributed the post-Roman earthwork Wansdyke (*Wodnes dic*) and a Long Barrow near Alton Priors, now called Adam's Grave, but formerly *Wodnes beorh.*[1] We may also mention Wayland's Smithy, a megalithic tomb near Lambourne, and Wade's Causeway, a Roman road near Pickering. The latter name comes doubtless from Wada, who figures in various Teutonic stories and in *þiðreks Saga af Bern* is said to be father of Weland. More frequently personal names appear to have been made out of native place-names, e.g. *Andredesceaster* (apparently Pevensey) from *Anderida*, and in all probability such cases as *Wintanceaster* (Winchester) from *Venta.* The more usual type, however, is plural. Such was perhaps originally the case with *Hunsbury*, as well as *Wandlebury*—names derived from peoples famous in Teutonic heroic poetry. This type also sometimes arises out of native place-names, e.g. *Verlamacaestir* (an English name for St Albans, according to Bede) from *Verolamium.* Not unfrequently it may be suspected that a name may be due to antiquarian speculation, even when its origin is unknown, as in *Waetlingaceaster* (St Albans) and the Roman roads Watling Street, Ermine Street and Icknield.

The usual Anglo-Saxon term for Roman structures is (*eald*) *enta geweorc*, '(old) structures (handiwork) of giants'. It occurs at the beginning of the Cottonian Gnomic Verses:[2] "'Chesters' are visible from afar, skilful structures of giants which are in this land, marvellous constructions of masonry". The same expression appears again in *The Wanderer* (87) and *The Ruin* (at the beginning), where ruined buildings, evidently of the Roman period, are described,[3] and also in imaginary

[1] Cf. Crawford, *Introduction to the Survey of English Place-names*, p. 157.

[2] Prefixed to MS. C of the Saxon Chronicle (Cott. Tib. B. I), and published in Earle and Plummer, *Two Saxon Chronicles*, I. p. 280 ff.

[3] Both poems ed. and transl. by Kershaw, *Anglo-Saxon and Norse Poems*, pp. 8 ff., 54 ff.

descriptions of Roman roads and Roman ruins in foreign lands, e.g. *Andreas* 1235, 1495. Moreover, in *Beowulf* we find it applied not only to the dragon's lair, which seems to be a megalithic chamber-tomb, but also to various metal vessels and weapons, which were believed to be ancient. It was evidently thought that the world had previously been occupied by a superhuman race—an idea founded on the perfectly correct observation that the buildings and artefacts of the past were far superior to anything which could be produced in the poets' own day. Attributions to the Devil seem to belong to much later times.

The Britons were never entirely without Latin learning; and some knowledge of the Roman period seems always to have been preserved in one or other of their monasteries. In certain texts of the *Historia Brittonum*, cap. 23, it is stated that the round building—now destroyed (cf. p. 157)—on the Carron, not far from Falkirk, was a triumphal arch erected by the emperor Carutius (presumably Carausius), from whom the river (Carun) derived its name. These are doubtless erroneous speculations, the latter perhaps even absurd; but they testify to a knowledge of the past which could hardly arise except through Latin learning. We may refer also to cap. 27 of the same work, where it is stated: *in ueteri traditione ueterum nostrorum, ut legimus, vii imperatores fuerunt a Romanis in Britannia; Romani autem dicunt ix fuisse.* In point of fact all texts of the *Historia*, except one, give an account of nine emperors. The only exception is the Chartres text, probably the earliest of all, which gives a much briefer account of seven emperors—presumably from the *uetus traditio.*

In later times Arthur's name was given to many ancient structures, as well as natural features (hills, rocks, etc.) in Scotland, Wales, and various parts of England. Thus the round building near Falkirk, just mentioned, was called Arthur's Oven, while a dolmen not far from Barmouth is known as Coeten Arthur ('Arthur's Quoit'), and another, in Gower, as Arthur's Stone.[1] It is doubtful whether any of these names go back beyond the twelfth century—the beginning of the Romances. To the same class probably belong some names derived from Arthur's knights, though these are less frequent. An example is Caer Gai, a Roman fort near the Lake of Bala, which seems to be called after Cai. The earliest instances occur in the list of *Mirabilia* attached to certain MSS. of the *Historia Brittonum* and belong to the valley of the Wye.

[1] For other examples see Lloyd, *History of Wales*, p. 10 f. The name Coeten Arthur seems to have been applied to many dolmens. A long list of Arthurian place-names will be found in Chambers, *Arthur of Britain*, p. 184 ff.

With these examples may be compared 'Taliesin's Grave', a megalithic tomb not far to the south of the estuary of the Dovey. This name seems to be connected with a group of speculations relating to the central coast district of Wales. Close by is Tref Taliesin. In the late *Hanes Taliesin* (cf. p. 103) Gwyddno's home is in this district. Moreover, the Cantref y Gwaelod, or 'Lowland Hundred'—interpreted as 'Submerged Hundred'—which belonged to the same prince, was identified with Cardigan Bay, or a portion of it, and eventually the line of rocks known as Sarn Badrig ('St Patrick's Causeway') came to be regarded as remnants of the barrier which the drunken Seithennin allowed to be pierced by the sea (cf. p. 116). The last idea is known to have grown up in the course of the past three centuries,[1] and it is at least doubtful whether any of these identifications go back to very early times. Gwyddno belonged to the 'Men of the North'.

There are, however, other traditions and speculations of this kind, which are of much greater antiquity. The fortifications on Moel Fenlli, which date from the Roman period, though the site was clearly not Roman, are probably to be connected with the wicked king called Benli, who in the *Historia Brittonum*, cap. 32 ff., is said to have been destroyed with his fortress on account of his treatment of St German. The Life of St German from which this story is derived seems to have been an early work (cf. p. 157 f.); and it is by no means impossible that the name may have been preserved by genuine tradition. A parallel case is Carwinley, near Longtown, which is generally believed to be derived from Caer (G)wenddoleu (cf. p. 111). The fort here has long been forgotten,[2] but the name attaches to a beck and hamlet.

From the *Historia Brittonum* it would seem that forts and other places as far apart as Dyfed and Cumberland derived their names from Gwrtheyrn as their founder. Speculation with regard to this king was evidently very active in early times, though in one case at least—the district called Gwerthrynion (*Guorthigirniaun*) on the upper Wye, where the local dynasty claimed to be descended from him—the name may be due to historical tradition. A good instance of antiquarian speculation is to be found in cap. 40 ff., if the *arx* referred to is the hill-fort now called Dinas Emrys, near Beddgelert, Carnarvonshire. But we do not know how far back this name can be traced; possibly it may be taken from this passage. The antiquity of names in Merioneth commemorating

[1] Cf. Lloyd, *History of Wales*, p. 25 f.

[2] Perhaps it was the important Roman cavalry station (Castra Exploratorum), now called Netherby, close to Carwinley.

Idris is also unknown to us. We may refer especially to the menhir called Llech Idris, near Dolgelly. This person is presumably the king of Merioneth killed in 630 (cf. p. 148); but he is said to have become a giant or wizard in the folklore of the district. Still more widespread than any of these is the name Sarn Helen, applied to various Roman roads in Wales. This can be traced back to the beginning of the thirteenth century in the *Dream of Maxen Wledig*, and may possibly be much older; but ultimately it must surely be of learned origin.

We do not know whether Roman ruins were ever attributed to giants, as among the English; but this is certainly the case with prehistoric remains, both in Wales itself and also in Cumberland, Cornwall, and the districts on the Welsh border. A good example is Tre 'r Ceri, 'abode of the giants', the name of a large ruined village with massive fortifications, on the Rivals, not far from Nevin. It is a native work, whether of the Roman period or earlier.

It has already been mentioned (p. 279) that the graves of various heroes form the subject of a long catalogue poem (*BBC.* XIX). In many cases it is the heroes themselves rather than their graves which the poet or poets have in mind. One obscure passage (st. 29) seems to mean that the grave of Arthur was not to be found.[1] But other passages are obviously suggested by the graves themselves and are of a more or less descriptive character. St. 44 is concerned with certain graves of unknown persons, perhaps prehistoric tombs.

For traditions or speculations relating to pre-Christian sanctuaries there is no early evidence, so far as we are aware. The Heroic Age falls within the Christian period.

In Ireland there appears to have been much less of a break with the past than in any of the other countries under consideration. Ancient structures, especially prehistoric tombs and enclosures with earthen fortifications—usually circular and known as *rath*, *dun*, *liss*, etc.—have been less interfered with than elsewhere by agricultural or industrial operations, and are still preserved in very great numbers. Moreover, most of these structures have their own stories; and these stories are not, as is so often the case in Britain, mere attributions to giants and devils, or adaptations of later romances or stories from overseas, or products of modern folklore. In a large number of cases they are connected with ancient stories of well-known individuals, some of whom were doubtless historical persons, while others owed their

[1] The literal translation of the words (*anoeth bid*) is disputed; cf. Rhys' Preface to the 'Everyman' edition of Malory, *Le Morte d'Arthur*, p. xiv.

origin to speculations of pre-Christian times. Ireland indeed is unrivalled as a museum of both monuments and traditions of ancient times.

There can be no reasonable doubt that the traditions relating to many fortified sites are largely of a historical character. Such is the case with Emain Macha (Navan Fort, near Armagh), the capital of the ancient kings of Ulster, and with the hill of Tara, the ancient residence of the high-kings. It has already been mentioned (p. 284) that we have a detailed account of the antiquities at the latter place as they existed at the end of the twelfth century. The origins of the various raths, mounds, graves and other monuments on the hill, as explained in this work, are doubtless products of antiquarian speculation for the most part; but many of these speculations may be very old. The antiquity and importance of the site as a whole is not to be questioned.

Difficulty is sometimes caused by the fact that the existing remains date from times much later than those to which the stories relate. As an example we may take the place which is usually—though not in the *Táin Bó Cuailnge*—represented as CuChulainn's home, Dun Delga (Dundalk) or the Moat of Castletown, two or three miles to the west of Dundalk. The fortifications here belong to a type which is believed to be not older than the eleventh century at the earliest. Yet Dun Delga is mentioned in texts which must have been in existence long before this time, e.g. in Emer's Lament for CuChulainn—the 'rhetorics' at the close of the *Great Slaughter of Mag Murtheimne*.[1] It would seem then that, as in many other cases, the existing fortifications were superimposed upon earlier ones.[2] But we cannot infer with certainty that even this earlier fort was CuChulainn's home from the beginning; for the silence of the *Táin Bó Cuailnge* on the point suggests that in the original form of the story the hero had no fortified home.[3]

The site of Dundrum Castle appears to have been the subject of interesting speculations in very early times. The castle is believed to have

[1] *Book of Leinster*, facsim., fol. 123 *b*.

[2] For the continuous or repeated use of the same sites we may compare the moat at Greenmount in the same county, where there were found among other things a polished stone axe and part of the hilt of a Viking sword with a Runic inscription (cf. Macalister, *Archaeology of Ireland*, p. 354). The occupation of Tara itself is believed to date from the Bronze Age (pp. 180, 70, 154 ff.).

[3] Cf. Thurneysen, *Ir. Heldensage*, p. 90. It is, however, to be borne in mind that in the *Táin B.C.* CuChulainn is a mere boy and unmarried. The stories which mention Dun Delga represent him as a married man, living there with his wife.

been built early in the thirteenth century on the base of an earthen castle erected in John de Courcy's time (1177–1203); but here again there had been an earlier fortified residence, Dun Rudraige, on the same site—to which some of the existing earthworks perhaps belonged. In *Bricriu's Feast* (cf. p. 49 f.), which dates from the eighth century, or not much later, this place is Bricriu's home and the scene of the first part of the story. It is mentioned also incidentally in other stories; and the bay, close by, is the scene of Fergus mac Lete's fatal adventure with the monster (cf. p. 207). More interesting, however, is the fact that the Ulster princely families of the earliest period were known collectively as Clann Rudraige. Their genealogies are traced to a king called Rudraige,[1] but this person is probably an eponymos. It is believed that the name is derived from Dun Rudraige[2]—which means that this place was thought to be the ancestral home of the Clann.

Traditions and speculations relating to graves are numerous; and poetry similar to the Welsh *Stanzas of the Graves* is not wanting. The most famous of these poems is one on *Relic na Rig*, or the 'Cemetery of the Kings', near Cruachan—to which we have already referred (p. 282). A closer resemblance to the Welsh poem is shown by incidental references to graves in the poem on the *Deaths of some Irish Heroes*, attributed to Kenneth O'Hartigan (cf. p. 282), e.g. st. 10, 12 f., 25 f., 28, 36. But the main concern of the poems is with the deaths, rather than the graves, of heroes.

Speculations relating to the barrows of earlier times, especially the great chamber-tombs of the Bronze Age, are more interesting and evidently much older, though they are preserved only incidentally in sagas or in works of later date, like the *Dinnšenchas* (cf. p. 283). Barrows were known as *side* ('shee-mounds' or 'elf-hills') and were believed to be the homes of the Tuatha De Danann. According to some authorities they had retired to these when they found themselves unable to resist the sons of Milid; but it is not at all likely that this represents a belief of heathen times. The idea may have been suggested by souterrains, which are known to have been in use even in the Christian period and which doubtless often served as refuges in times of danger. In point of fact such later chambers are occasionally found in prehistoric barrows, as e.g. in the hill of Dowth. The great chambers themselves may have been regarded as souterrains of the gods before the

[1] This seems to be the only form (usually genitive) which occurs in early texts.

[2] Cf. Thurneysen, *Ir. Heldensage*, p. 92.

'invasion' theory was invented. It is at all events to be suspected that they were sanctuaries in heathen times.[1]

The most important of these localities was the great prehistoric cemetery known as Brug na Boinne, within which lie the barrows of Dowth, New Grange and Knowth, in the angle of the Boyne, about five miles west of Drogheda. According to the story, which is preserved in several variant forms,[2] this land originally belonged to a shee—i.e. probably a god (cf. p. 255)—called Elcmar, whose wife (or sister), by an intrigue with the Dagda, became the mother of Aengus (Mac Oc). The latter was brought up by Midir; and eventually by the counsel of the Dagda surprised Elcmar unarmed in the 'Hill of the Brug' (possibly New Grange).[3] Elcmar was then compelled to grant him possession of the Brug for ever, as related on p. 256, above. It may be remarked that if Aengus' mother was Elcmar's sister Boann (the goddess of the Boyne), as stated in one—not the earliest authenticated—account,[4] the story would seem to have originated in local speculation. In the days when descent was reckoned through the female line (cf. p. 178), Aengus would be Elcmar's legitimate successor.

Another story, relating to the hill of Knowth, is known only from late references.[5] Aengus was in love with Englicc, daughter of Elcmar; but during the autumn festival (Samuin) she was carried off by a rival—Midir in one account—from this hill. The records seek to derive the name *Cnogba* (Knowth) from *cno*, 'nut', and *guba*, 'lament'—because Englicc's disappearance was lamented here by her companions or Aengus. Those who took part in the festival lived on nuts.

Side in other parts of Ireland also are frequently mentioned. The *sid* of Bri Leith, near Ardagh in Co. Longford, is the home of Midir; and it is to this place according to most of the accounts that he carries off Etain, the wife of Eochaid Airem (cf. p. 52). Eochaid subsequently

[1] In the ninth century the 'caves' of the Brug were plundered by the Norse kings of Dublin (*Ann. Ult.* 862). They were therefore presumably repositories of treasure. But it is difficult to believe that 'heathen gold' can have remained untouched through three or four centuries of Christianity. Perhaps the people of the Viking Age concealed their treasures there.

[2] For the variant forms of the story cf. Thurneysen, *Ir. Heldensage*, p. 598 ff.

[3] It has often been thought that Uam Achaid Aldai (*Ann. Ult.* 862) was the proper name of New Grange; but we know of no stories attaching to this name. We cannot identify any of the monuments of the Brug enumerated in the *Dinnšenchas* (*Rev. Celt.* xv. 292 f.).

[4] It is stated also in the *Dream of Aengus* (a fairly early text) that Boann is brought to attend her son Aengus in his sickness.

[5] Cf. Thurneysen, *Ir. Heldensage*, p. 603 f.

destroys the *sid* with his warriors, and rescues his wife. The *sid* of Cruachan[1] is referred to in various stories, more especially in the *Adventure of Nera*. Another elf-hill in Connaught, Sid Uamain, is destroyed, in the *Dream of Aengus*, by the combined forces of the Dagda and the (human king) Ailill, because the elf-king Ethal Anbuail, to whom it belongs, has refused to give up his daughter to the lovesick Aengus. Mention may also be made of the Sid ar Femen—said to be in Co. Tipperary—which sometimes belongs to Midir, but more often to Bodb, king of the elves (shee) of Munster.[2] We do not know whether any of these barrows have been identified.

The ancient sanctuaries of Ireland can hardly be dissociated from the festivals held at them (cf. p. 292). We may refer, e.g., to the origin of Tailtiu (Teltown). It is believed[3] that some of the great royal residences, such as Tara and Emain Macha, were originally sanctuaries; but such stories as we have relating to their origin are as a rule merely speculations on the names.[4] There can be no doubt, however, as to the existence of other sanctuaries, especially the *side* and the sources of rivers. We may instance the story of the origin of the Boyne, which is preserved in somewhat varying forms.[5] Nechtan, the husband of Boann, had in his *sid* a spring at which no one was allowed to look, except his three cup-bearers. Boann, either out of presumption or in order to clear herself from the charge of relations with the Dagda, ventured to walk round the spring, and thereupon lost the use of one eye, one arm and one leg. She tried to make her way to the sea, but the water of the spring broke loose, and pursued and overwhelmed her. Sid Nechtain is said to be the source of the Boyne; but we do not know whether the barrow has been identified. The source of the Shannon was also perhaps a sanctuary; but this will require notice in a later chapter.

The antiquarian speculations of early Ireland can be traced in many other directions. We may refer, e.g., to the story of Midir and Etain (cf. p. 52), where the elves are compelled to build for Eochaid Airem a causeway over a swamp called Lamraige; and again, where it is stated that the Irish learned from these elves a new way of yoking oxen. We do not know whether these questions have been investigated.

[1] This is a natural cave, but the entrance is artificially built up; cf. Macalister, *Archaeology of Ireland*, p. 179.

[2] E.g. in the story of the *Two Swineherds* (cf. Thurneysen, *op. cit.* p. 276 ff.).

[3] Cf. Macalister, *Archaeology of Ireland*, pp. 93, 180, etc.

[4] For Tara the *Dinnšenchas* (*Rev. Celt.* XV. 277 ff.) also gives much detailed information.

[5] Cf. Thurneysen, *Ir. Heldensage*, p. 605 ff.

Reference may also be made to the story of Mongan (cf. p. 98), where a purely antiquarian discussion between this king and his *fili* is conducted with such vehemence that the king stakes all his possessions on the truth of his speculations.

VI. Traditions and speculations relating to the origin of nations are usually connected on one side with the genealogies of royal houses—which have been noticed under I, above—and on the other with speculations on the origin of mankind, which will require notice in the next section.

A large amount of speculation relating to the origin of the various peoples and states of Greece is to be found in ancient records. Reference has already been made (p. 270 f.) to the genealogy, first found in the Hesiodic Catalogue, in which the eponymos Hellen is made the ancestor of the various branches of the Greek (Hellenic) nation through his three sons, Aiolos, Xuthos and Doros. In other fragments of the Catalogue Magnes and Macedon, the eponymoi of the Magnetes and Macedonians, are said to be sons of a sister of Hellen, while another eponymos, Graicos, belongs to the same family.[1] Hellen himself is the son of Deucalion, the survivor of the great flood; and he again is the son of Prometheus, who instituted sacrifices and acquired fire for mankind. Prometheus and his ancestors are treated in the *Theogony*; to them we shall have to return in the next section.

It is clear, however, that many Greek states had local traditions which were incompatible with the genealogy of the sons of Hellen. Xuthos appears in Attic traditions, but not in the very earliest generations. The traditions of Argos, Thebes, and many other states know nothing of Hellen or his sons. Usually the founder of the state is the son of one of the great deities or of a river-god or other local deity. The Homeric poems also know nothing of the family; for there is no indication that Aiolos Hippotades, the 'keeper of the winds' (*Od.* x. 21), is to be identified with Aiolos, the son of Hellen. Indeed the genealogy, as we have it, may not have been of any very great antiquity. But the principle was certainly old. A somewhat similar genealogy, full of eponymoi, is given for the Trojan royal house in *Il.* xx. 215 ff.

The origin of the state was usually bound up with the genealogy of the early kings. Probably the only exceptions were the colonies founded in comparatively recent times, like the cities in Italy and Sicily; but the traditions relating to these would seem to have been of a more or less

[1] Fragm. 22 f. (Kinkel).

historical character. The traditions of the Greek states in Asia Minor—which were considerably older—appear to have conformed to the usual type. Thus the poet Mimnermos of Colophon says in one of the fragments of his poems:[1] "We left the lofty citadel of Pylos (in the Peloponnesos) and came in ships to the coveted (land of) Asia. Through the overwhelming force which we possessed we occupied lovely Colophon". The explanation of this is to be found in a lost passage of the same poem cited by Strabo, XIV. 1. 3, according to which Andraimon, the founder of Colophon, came from Pylos. In general, however, the Ionians claimed to have come from Athens under the sons of Codros, who according to legend was the last king of that city. Strabo (*l.c.*) says that at Ephesos in his time certain privileges of royalty were still enjoyed by the descendants of the founder, Androclos son of Codros. The same writer (XIII. 1. 3) relates that Penthilos, son of Orestes, was the leader of an expedition which, under his descendants, settled in Lesbos; and the poet Alcaios (fragm. 70, 75) speaks of a family in Mytilene which was regarded with special honour owing to its descent from Penthilos and Atreus.

Similar traditions were not unknown in European Greece. The most famous of them was that of the 'Return of the Heracleidai', a movement which affected the greater part of the Peloponnesos. This tradition also was connected with royal genealogies, several of which are preserved either wholly, as at Sparta and Corinth, or in part. The invasion of a new and alien people, the Dorians, is led by the descendants of a dispossessed native family. As in the case of the Ionic invasion of Asia, it is very difficult to determine where tradition ends and speculation begins. The presence of Dorians in the Peloponnesos, however, is unknown to the Homeric poems; and they seem always to have been regarded as invaders.

The Teutonic evidence is very similar to the Greek. Every royal family doubtless had its genealogy, and many of these are still preserved, as we have seen. In England these genealogies are regularly traced back to gods; and the same is true of some at least of the Northern genealogies. Mythical eponymous names also occur not unfrequently.

The earliest Teutonic genealogy which we possess is given in Tacitus' *Germania*, cap. 2, and bears a close resemblance to that of Hellen. "They proclaim in ancient poems...that the god Tuisto, born of Earth, and his son Mannus were the origin and founders of the race. To Mannus they attribute three sons, from whose names those (peoples) who are nearest to the Ocean are called Ingaeuones, those in the centre

[1] Fragm. 9 (Bergk).

Hermiones, and the rest Istaeuones. Some, in accordance with the uncertainties of ancient tradition, adduce a more numerous offspring of the god and a larger number of national names—Marsi, Gambriuii, Sueui, Vandilii." It is remarkable that these three brothers recur in a genealogical document,[1] apparently of Frankish origin, some four or five centuries later, though Tuisto and Mannus are forgotten. The names of the brothers are given here as Ermenus, Inguo and Istio; and from them thirteen chief peoples of the West are said to be descended. The genealogy, therefore, would seem to have had a long life. But we would specially call attention to its antiquity. Tacitus' information is derived from poems which were believed to be old even in his day. Antiquarian speculation of this kind had evidently a long history among the Teutonic peoples. Indeed this is probably the earliest Teutonic intellectual production of which we have any record.

For several Teutonic peoples we possess accounts of their origin and early history which are evidently derived from native tradition and speculation. The fullest of these is the account of the early history of the Goths given by Jordanes, cap. 4–24. This contains, it is true, a very large amount of matter—e.g. the chapters relating to the Getae—derived from Roman learning; but the latter element is easily distinguishable. The story of the Lombards is given, also at considerable length, in the *Origo Gentis Langobardorum* (cf. p. 254) and, still more fully, in Paulus Diaconus' *Historia Langobardorum* (I. 2, 7 ff.).

The stories of the Goths and the Lombards consist in the main of a series of movements from one region to another. Each movement is associated with a king. The first movement is in both cases a migration from Scandinavia. A similar origin is claimed for the Burgundians in the *Vita S. Sigismundi*, and perhaps also, elsewhere,[2] for the Old Saxons and other Teutonic peoples of the Continent. Modern opinion is much divided as to the credibility of the claim.

The origin of the Norwegians is treated in a short document called *Hversu Noregr Bygðist* ('How Norway was Settled'), part of which occurs also under the name *Fundinn Noregr* ('Discovery of Norway') as an introduction to the *Orkneyinga Saga*. Both texts are preserved in the *Flateyjarbók*. In this document the genealogies of a number of the leading families are traced back to eponymous and other apparently

[1] Müllenhoff, *Deutsche Altertumskunde*, III. p. 325 ff.; cf. Chadwick, *Origin of the English Nation*, p. 208.

[2] Cf. Widukind, *Res Gest. Saxon.* I. 2; Hrabanus Maurus, *De Inuentione Linguarum* (in Goldast, *Script. Rer. Alem.* II. i. p. 67).

mythical ancestors. The progenitors of these are Nórr and Górr, two brothers who are represented as coming to the country from the north or north-east in search of their sister Gói. Their ancestors bear names which in part are personifications of nature—'Sea', 'Ice', 'Snow', etc. The later generations are found also to a considerable extent in the poem *Hyndluljóð* (cf. p. 278 f.).

The aristocracy of the Uppland Swedes traced their descent from the god Frey. The genealogy of the early kings is given in the poem *Ynglingatal* (cf. p. 271) and in the *Ynglinga Saga*. In the latter the gods are represented as living and dying in Sweden, having come there from the south. The story as we have it is by no means free from Latin influence, but it seems to contain elements derived from native tradition or speculation—and these are probably not limited to the account of Frey. The other gods are said to return at their deaths to their old home, and in cap. 15 Svegðir, one of the early kings, sets out to find this place. For this motif an interesting analogy is to be found in Central Africa, as will be seen in a later chapter.

Whatever may be the explanation of this case, it will be seen that most of the stories noticed above are concerned with movements of peoples, like the Greek stories cited on p. 305. The later movements of the Goths and the Lombards are historically authenticated, and it is likely enough that records of earlier movements may have been preserved by tradition. But the stories of migration from Scandinavia can hardly be explained except as products of antiquarian speculation; for these nations were settled in their Continental homes at the beginning of the Christian era—the time when we first obtain detailed information of the Teutonic peoples. It is highly probable[1] that at all times small parties of adventurers—princes with military followers—were in the habit of crossing the Baltic, seeking their fortunes in the service of famous kings; and traditions relating to such adventurers may have become incorporated among the national traditions, if they or their descendants eventually attained to power, through royal marriages or otherwise. This is the explanation which we are inclined to favour.

In any case it would be rash to assume that all Teutonic peoples possessed traditions in which they were represented as incomers. According to Tacitus, *Germ.* 39, the Semnones, who claimed to be the most ancient and noble of the Sueui, held festivals in a sacred grove, to which all peoples of the same stock sent delegates. Special reverence

1 Such incidents occur in Norse legendary sagas, e.g. *Hervarar Saga*, cap. 6 f.; cf. *Völsunga Saga*, cap. 1.

was paid to the grove as the cradle of the nation and the abode of the god who ruled over them all. The whole passage implies that the Semnones were believed to have been settled in the same place from time immemorial.

The speculations which trace the origin of the Britons to Brutus are obviously of learned (Latin) origin, though they appear to be very old. In the *Historia Brittonum* they are found in different forms, which suggest derivation from different sources. In one form (cap. 17 f.) Brutus is said to be son of Hessitio (*Ysition*, etc.), i.e. the Istio of the Frankish genealogy (cf. p. 306), while the ancestry of the Frankish brothers is traced to Aeneas and the Trojan genealogy of the *Iliad* (cf. p. 270), and from thence to Noah. In the other (cap. 10 f.), the various texts differ a good deal among themselves, but the Frankish element does not appear.

Bede was apparently acquainted with some speculation on the origin of the Britons which has not come down to us; for he states (*Hist. Eccl.* I. 1) that they are said to have come originally from Armorica. This speculation perhaps belonged to the Britons of the North; for the genealogy of Strathclyde in MS. Harl. 3859 (No. v; cf. p. 152) contains an obscure statement relating to the founder of the family, which has been interpreted to mean that he came from Brittany. It is conceivable that this speculation was connected with the Frankish genealogy, for in the latter the Brittones (Bretons) are one of the peoples descended from Istio; but this must be regarded as quite uncertain.

There are traces of other traditions or speculations relating to very ancient times, which do not appear to be wholly of Latin origin. Such is the case with the stories of Beli (Bellinus), son of Mynogan (Minocanus) and his family. In the *Mabinogion* and elsewhere Beli has a son Caswallawn, who has the same name as Cassiuellaunus, the opponent of Julius Caesar, though he does not play the part of Cassiuellaunus. In the *Historia Brittonum*, cap. 19, Bellinus himself is king of the Britons in Caesar's time. Other stories and poems have much to say of Lludd, son of Beli, and his brothers; but the origin of the cycle is obscure. It may be observed that in the Harleian Genealogies (Nos. I and x) the ancestry of Cunedda and of Coel Hen is carried back to Beli Magnus, who is said to be the husband of Anna, the sister of the Virgin Mary. If this is the same person, which we see no reason to doubt, the speculations relating to him have probably had a long history.

In the *Historia Brittonum*, cap. 49, the ancestry of the kings of Builth is traced to Gwrtheyrn, and through him to a certain *Gloui*, who is said to have built Gloucester. We see no reason for doubting the later part of the genealogy. Gwrtheyrn was hardly so popular a character that fictitious pedigrees would be traced to him. Of the earlier part of the genealogy we know nothing. *Gloui* is presumably an eponymos; but the passage suggests the existence of a tradition that the family belonged to that part of the country.[1]

The origin of the royal family of Powys is given in the *Historia Brittonum*, cap. 35. The founder of the line, Cadell Durnlwg, is there said to be a slave of a tyrant called Benli. When Benli's castle is destroyed by fire with all its inhabitants, Cadell and his family are preserved owing to the kindness he had shown to St German; and the saint declares that he and his offspring shall be kings from that day forward. The story is strange; but such turns of fortune may have occurred in the fifth century. There is some ground for believing that the *Book of St German* (cf. p. 157), from which this story is presumably taken, was an early work—of the sixth or early seventh century; but in any case it would be difficult to account for the acceptance of a story of servile origin for the dynasty, if it were fictitious. The earlier genealogies do not profess to know Cadell's ancestry.

In the genealogy of Dyfed (cf. p. 274) the early stages, as given in the Harleian Genealogies (No. II), are clearly fictitious. The ancestry of the family is here carried back to *Maxim Guletic*, i.e. Magnus Maximus, and through him to Constantine the Great. But a much earlier form of this genealogy is preserved in an Irish source (cf. p. 151 f.)—from which it appears that in the eighth century the family claimed to be of Irish origin.

A large part of North Wales, together with Cardiganshire, was ruled by families which, as we have seen, claimed to be descended from a certain Cunedda. In the *Historia Brittonum*, cap. 62, this man is said to have come with his eight sons from the North, from a region called Manau Guotodin, a hundred and forty-six years before the reign of Maelgwn, and to have expelled the Scots from Gwynedd and elsewhere. A similar notice occurs in the Harleian Genealogies (No. XXXII), and here the names of the sons—nine in all—are given. The eldest son is said to have died in Manau Guotodin, but his son shared with his uncles in the division of territory. It may be observed that the names of two of the sons, Dunaut and Ceretic, and of the grandson, Meriaun, coincide

[1] William of Malmesbury (*Gesta Regum*, I. 23) applies the name *Wirtgernesburg* apparently to Bradford-on-Avon. Place-names containing *Gwrtheyrn* occur in various parts of Wales, but may be due to the story in *Hist. Brit.* cap. 40 ff.

with those of the kingdoms over which their descendants rule, Dunoding, Ceredigion (Cardigan) and Meirionydd. Moreover the names of four of the other sons can be traced in the names of districts—cantrefs or commotes—which in the historical period were included in the territories of larger kingdoms.[1] It is a natural inference therefore that these persons were mythical eponymoi, invented in rather early times.

Yet Cunedda and his movement from the North are commonly held to be historical; and the reasons for this belief—apart from the date, which seems to us incredible[2]—are undeniably strong. His immediate ancestors bear names which are not of a mythical type, but Roman: Aetern(us), Patern(us), Tacit(us). Patern has the surname *Pesrud*, i.e. *peisrudd*, 'of the Red Robe' (suggestive of a Roman dignitary). *Manau*, i.e. *Manaw* (Gaelic *Manann*), is the name of the Isle of Man. But there was another district on the Pictish border,[3] in the neighbourhood of the Forth, which also was called Manann in Gaelic, and of which the name is preserved in Slamannan, in south-east Stirlingshire, and perhaps in Clackmannan. This is probably the district referred to in the story, especially since the name Guotodin seems to be a reminiscence of the Otadinoi (presumably for *Wotadinoi*), who are located in the south-east of Scotland by Ptolemy. Again, Cunedda's genealogy is traced ultimately to a certain Aballach, and through him[4] to Beli and Anna (cf. p. 274). These are the same names which head the ancestry of Coel Hen, whose descendants, so far as they can be traced with confidence, belonged to the south of Scotland and the north of England. In the intervening stages, immediately after Tacit, we find three peculiar pairs of names: Cein, Guorcein, Doli, Guordoli, Dumn, Gurdumn. These have never been explained; but they are clearly to be connected with the series of fifteen similar pairs of names in the list of ancient

[1] The cantref of Rhufoniog and the commotes of Dogfeiling, Edeyrnion and Aflogion; cf. Lloyd, *History of Wales*, pp. 117 f., 240 f., 245.

[2] Cunedda was a grandfather when the expedition took place, so 146 years can hardly have elapsed between that event and the accession of his great-grandson (Maelgwn). The latter died in the great plague of 548; but we do not know when he began to reign. If we allow twenty years to his reign the 146 preceding years will reach back to a time when North Wales was still occupied by Roman garrisons; for there is evidence that the fortress at Carnarvon was held as late as 385 (cf. *Antiquaries Journal*, 1922, p. 63). Possibly *cxlvi* may be a corruption of *xlvi*—which would give a much more likely date; but we are entirely in the dark as to the origin of the statement.

[3] Cf. *Ann. Ult.* 710. The reference to the same event in the *Saxon Chronicle* points to the neighbourhood of Falkirk as the scene.

[4] The intervening name Amalech is possibly only a doublet of Aballach.

Pictish kings contained in the Pictish Chronicle: Brude Pant, Brude Urpant, etc.[1] The evidence therefore, taken as a whole, points distinctly to the existence of a tradition that Cunedda's family were Picts or northern Britons with Pictish affinities, who had come under strong Roman influence—such as might be expected in that region in the fourth century.

It would seem then that the story of Cunedda[2] is derived from tradition rather than from speculation, and belongs to the twilight of history rather than to mythology. This does not prove of course that he really had seven sons who gave their names to seven districts of Wales. Indeed it is worth noting that the most important kingdoms held by his descendants, those of Gwynedd and Anglesey, have no eponymoi. But there is no need to conclude that the derivations are all necessarily fictitious. A king of Cardigan named Seisyll in the eighth century conquered Ystrad Tywi (part of Carmarthenshire), and the enlarged kingdom was known thenceforth as Seisyllwg.[3] The kingdom of Morgannwg derived its name from a historical king Morgan.[4] Analogies may be found in other countries—we may refer, e.g., to Loth(a)ringen (Lorraine), which took its name from the emperor Lothaire (840–855). The Welsh names may be compared with those of English dynasties—Oiscingas, Ic(e)lingas, Wuffingas. We cannot prove the historical existence of Icel or Wuffa, who are recorded only in genealogies, nor even of Oisc (Aesc), who is mentioned in the *Saxon Chronicle*; but we see no adequate reason for doubting it. In the same way we are inclined to the view that some of Cunedda's sons may come from genuine tradition, while others may have been invented, on the analogy of these, by families who wished to claim a distinguished ancestry.

The value of the British evidence lies largely in the fact that it approaches more nearly to the origins than any of the other cases which we have to discuss. Here, as elsewhere, we find dynasties which are said to have obtained their thrones by invasion. The invaders, although they must have had military followers, are clearly represented as families rather than peoples; and the kingdoms come into existence as the property of these families. Except in the north most of the kingdoms

[1] Published by Skene, *Chronicles of the Picts and Scots* (p. 5).

[2] There is a poem (*Tal.* XLVI) which has usually been interpreted as an elegy on Cunedda, but it is so obscure that we have not been able to make any use of it. The reader may be referred to Morris-Jones, *Y Cymmrodor*, XXVIII. 202 ff., where a new interpretation is given.

[3] Cf. Lloyd, *History of Wales*, p. 257.

[4] *Ib.* p. 274.

seem to date from the fifth century, i.e. very soon after the connection with the central government at Rome had come to an end. The eponymous and other speculative elements are mostly confined to the ancestries of the families which then obtained power, though they are probably not wanting in the generation which represents the actual period of reconstruction. To a certain extent the growth of this speculation can be seen. Thus in the Harleian Genealogies, which date from the tenth—or more probably the ninth—century (cf. p. 150), the line of Dyfed is carried back to the emperor Maximus; but in another source (cf. p. 151 f.), which dates apparently from the eighth century, the same line is traced to an Irish origin. It may be noted that the same phenomenon recurs later in the genealogy of Strathclyde. In the Harleian Genealogies this line is traced back to the doubtless historical *Ceretic Guletic* (cf. p. 152); but in the fourteenth century MS. Hengwrt 536 Maximus (*Maxen Wledic*) has taken the place of Ceredig.

It is unfortunately beyond our power to deal adequately with the Irish evidence bearing upon this subject. Genealogies and other materials exist in such abundance that it would require several years' special study to obtain a command of them; and much of the material is still unpublished. We shall therefore have to be content with selecting a few cases, which we shall deal with to the best of our ability, though briefly. But we would warn the reader that even in these cases evidence may exist which we do not know and which may to some extent impair the value of our observations.

From the seventh century onwards Irish scholars were active in constructing a history of Ireland and the Irish people from the earliest times. The scheme was probably suggested by the *Chronicle* of Eusebius (cf. p. 168 f.); but early native traditions and speculations were doubtless utilised, and it is sometimes difficult to distinguish between the Latin (Biblical and Classical) and the native elements. The early stages of the history are mainly occupied with a series of invasions, the last of which is led by the sons of Milid. From three of these sons, Eremon, Eber and Ir, nearly all the chief families of Ireland are made to be descended, though the ancestry of one family which occasionally attained to the high-kingship is traced to a certain Ith, son of Bregan, a brother of Milid. Milid, Eremon and Eber are mentioned in genealogical poems of the seventh century, and we see no reason for doubting that the main features of the story were then known. But its origin is far from clear. It is generally held that the name Milid is taken from Lat. *miles*; but no satisfactory explanation of the other names has yet been offered, as far as we know.[1] The three sons of Milid may have been suggested by the three sons of Noah or by the three Frankish brothers; but parallels are so widespread that it is hardly safe to assume that they cannot be products of independent native speculation.

It has been suggested above (p. 273) that the amazing length of the genealogies was due to the desire to fill up the interval between the times of the Biblical Patriarchs and the beginning of Irish history—calculated according to the chronological scheme of Eusebius. If so, it is a product of Latin rather than native speculation. Note may be taken of the fact that no ramifications are recorded until many generations after the time of the three brothers. It is only when the ramifications appear that the presence of native speculation can be detected with any confidence. These ramifications occur much earlier among the descendants of Eremon than in the other lines. And here it may be noted that Eremon's descendants are far more numerous and widespread than the others. To them belong the ruling families of Tara, Connaught and Leinster, as well as some of the leading families of Ulster and Munster. On the other hand, Eber's descendants are represented as belonging in early times exclusively to Munster, while the descendants of Ir are all traced back to a few of Conchobor's heroes.

The origin of the first ramification among Eremon's descendants—between the line of Leinster and that of the high-kings (Tara)—is traceable to the story of the *Destruction of Dinn Rig* (cf. p. 51), in which the progenitors of the two lines are brothers. It is therefore of native origin. In the *Annals of Tigernach*[2]—presumably from the Irish Eusebius—this story is synchronised with the times of Romulus and Hezekiah, i.e. the latter part of the eighth century B.C. Now it is only the genealogy of Leinster which contains a sufficient number of generations to reach back to this date; the genealogy of the high-kings (Tara) is much too short.[3] We may infer then that the calculation was

1 The explanation given by van Hammel, *Zeitschr. f. celt. Phil.* x. 168, note, seems to us incredible.

2 *Rev. Celt.* XVI. 378.

3 We are reckoning from Cathair Mor and his successor Conn Cetchathach, who in the same Annals (*Rev. Celt.* XVII. 7) are placed about the middle of the second century A.D. Conn is in the twenty-second generation from Cobthach, and in the twenty-third from Ugaine Mor (Cobthach's father). Cathair is in the twenty-seventh generation from Labraid Loingsech (Cobthach's great-nephew), and in the thirtieth from Ugaine Mor. Among Conn's descendants about thirty years or slightly more seem to be reckoned to a generation; so the calculation of c. 950 years from these two kings to their common ancestor (Ugaine Mor) is evidently based on the longer genealogy.

based on the former genealogy. It may be noted that even in the story itself the Leinster family seems to be represented as the senior line. At all events Loegaire Lorc, its progenitor, reigns as high-king before his brother Cobthach. Indeed a genealogical poem of the seventh century[1] appears to claim the high-kingship for this line continuously from the time of Labraid Loingsech to that of Cathair Mor. But we do not know how the Leinster genealogy came to be built up, any more than that of the rival line. It is incredible to us that the story of Dinn Rig can relate to such remote times.

The next ramifications appear in the seventh generation from Cobthach and in the fifteenth from Labraid. In the latter case the line of Ossory separates from that of Leinster. In the former the progeny of Cobthach divides on the one side into the line of the high-kings (Tara), often known as 'descendants (*sil*, *clann*) of Conn', and on the other into a line commonly called Erainn. There are traces of a story, evidently mythical, relating to the origin of the latter. This line again divides in the tenth generation—one branch being represented later by the Erainn of Munster, to whom Conaire Mor belonged, the Dal Riada of Ulster, and various other families, while the other survives in the Ulaid or true Ulstermen, properly known as Dal Fiatach (cf. p. 177).

In all these cases—which, it should be observed, relate to times anterior to the beginning of the Christian era—the element of (native) speculation is doubtless very large, though the reasons for the relationships stated are generally obscure. The case of Conn Cetchathach, who belongs to a later period (cf. p. 168), is somewhat different. He is the grandfather of Cormac mac Airt, a doubtless historical person, and there are stories relating to him and his immediate family which do not give the impression of myth. Yet his ancestors, as well as his descendants —in fact all this branch of the stock of Eremon—are frequently called *Sil Cuinn* or 'Progeny of Conn'; and even if this name arose in later times, the name *Connachta* (Connaught), which is said to have much the same meaning, is certainly very ancient. Again, the northern half of Ireland is often called *Leth Cuinn*, while the name *Leth Moga* is applied to the southern half. There is a story which relates how Mog (Mug) Nuadat, king of Munster, made war against Conn with the result that eventually they divided the country between them. But it has often been remarked that literally *Leth Cuinn* means 'the freeman's half', and *Leth Moga* 'the slave's half'. On the whole perhaps the most likely

[1] Cf. K. Meyer, *Abhandl. d. k. pr. Akad. d. Wiss.* 1913, *phil.-hist. Cl.*, No. 6, p. 14 ff.

explanation is that Conn was a real man, who lived at the time to which tradition assigns him, that he bore a name which was also applied to his clan generically[1] and that—in consequence of this—he was made responsible by later speculation for things which had come to pass before his time.

The progeny of Ir is represented in ancient times by the Clann Rudraige, the royal family of Ulster, to which belong Conchobor, Conall Cernach and the other Ulster heroes of their time. This line is less than half as long as even the shorter line from Eremon to the same point—six or seven generations before Conn. It would seem to have been framed to fit a different scheme of chronology. The *Annals of Tigernach* contain entries of the kings of Emain, i.e. Emain Macha, from Cimbaeth, son of Finten, who is stated to have become king in 307 B.C. and who elsewhere is said to be the husband of Macha, the eponymous foundress of Emain Macha. The entry[2] which gives this date indicates the existence of two systems of chronology which differed from one another by nearly five centuries. As the entries of the kings of Emain belong to the shorter system, this probably originated in Ulster. The succession of kings recorded in the Annals is not from father to son—which is in harmony with the genealogies. For the latter contain a number of ramifications even in the early stages; and

[1] This is a rare occurrence, but examples are not unknown. It is unlikely that the Gothic king Ostrogotha (Eastgota) recorded by Cassiodorus, *Var.* XI. 1, Jordanes, cap. 16 f. and *Widsith* 113, was a mythical eponymos.

[2] *Rev. Celt.* XVI. 394. The entry is as follows: *In anno xviii Ptolomei fuit initiatus regnare in Emain Cimbaed filius Fintain, qui regnauit xxuiii annis. Tunc Echu Buadach pater Ugaine in Temoria regnase ab aliis fertur, liquet* (i.e. *licet*) *praescripsimus ollim Ugaine imperasse. Omnia monimenta Scottorum usque Cimbaed incerta erant.* The last sentence seems to have been misunderstood by some modern scholars. Starting from a (rather doubtful) etymology of the name *Finten* or *Fintan* (from *finn*, 'white', and *tan*, 'time') it has been ingeniously proposed that the meaning is that Cimbaeth was the beginning of all things, because he was the son of 'Blank Time'. But the context clearly shows that the writer is referring to a discrepancy in his authorities in regard to the date of Ugaine (Mor). Some say that Ugaine lived at this time—which is in accord with the story that Ugaine was brought up by Cimbaeth—but he has already entered Ugaine's reign at a different date. The only previous mention of Ugaine is in the entry relating to the story of *Dinn Rig* (cf. p. 313, note), in which his son Cobthach is the chief character. This entry is more than four centuries earlier than the other. More probably, however, the reference is to some entry in the early part of the Annals, which is lost. The fragment extant begins just before the birth of Romulus. We suspect that the early annals, like some later works which are probably derived from them, gave widely discrepant dates for the coming of the sons of Milid.

though these seem not to continue beyond two generations, there are traces of stories attached to some of the names. Both the genealogy and the Annals therefore suggest the existence of a good deal of native speculation.

The royal family of the Ulaid or true Ulstermen in later times traced their descent from a certain Fiatach Finn, from whom the kingdom is known as Dal Fiatach. His ancestry is traced—many generations back—to the same source as that of the Erainn of Munster (cf. p. 177), and comes ultimately from Eremon. But the ancient Clann Rudraige, from Ir, is represented by the kings of Dal Araide, who traced their descent from Conall Cernach. The same ancestry was claimed by the kings of Leix, in Leinster, and other families, all of which—including Dal Araide—seem to have belonged to communities known as Cruithni or Picts. It is commonly assumed that the Cruithni were the aboriginal inhabitants of Ireland, though we know of no evidence worth consideration in support of this view. But it has never been explained, so far as we are aware, why the Cruithni should claim descent from Conall. The evidence of tradition is clear, so far as it goes. The Dal Araide claimed to be the legitimate descendants of the Clann Rudraige. No such claim was ever put forward by the Ulaid (Dal Fiatach), though they would surely have claimed the more distinguished ancestry, if there had been any justification for doing so. The claim of Leix is explained by a story which relates that a son of Conall called Laigsech Cennmor took service with CuChorp, king of Leinster, an ancestor of Cathair Mor in the fifth generation, and on his behalf expelled the men of Munster from Leix—for which he was rewarded with the kingdom. Laigsech seems to have got his name from Leix (Laigis), though he plays some part also in other stories. In other communities, such as the Conaille of Murthemne, Conall himself figures as an eponymos. A good deal of speculation therefore is involved. But it is speculation on the origin of families, and founded on the movements, real or imaginary, of individual princes. It would seem that the people of Leix were regarded as Cruithni because their royal family claimed to be an offshoot from the Cruithni of Ulster.

From the examples given above it will be evident that in Ireland a large amount of Latin learning and speculation has been grafted upon a still larger body of native tradition and speculation. The latter has been made to fit into a scheme supplied by the former, and consequently the two are sometimes by no means easy to disentangle. The native element is concerned with individuals and families; the national genealogies, as elsewhere, are properly those of the royal families and may be traced back to strangers, as in the case of Leix. But it can rarely, if ever, be determined where genuine tradition ends and speculation begins. If we are right in believing (cf. p. 177 f.) that in the age of the Ulster heroes succession was through the female, at least in some parts of Ireland, the genuineness of the genealogies, which are always paternal, cannot of course be maintained beyond that point. It may be that in some cases different genealogies have been strung together. This is rather suggested by the recurrence of the name of the god Lug—perhaps also the name Nuadu—at various stages in the genealogies.

The two most important features which are in doubt are (1) the three ancestral brothers, and (2) the invasion motif in general. The former may, as we have seen, be of Latin origin; but analogies are widespread. In addition to the Greek and early Teutonic examples noticed above we may refer, e.g., to the Scythian story given by Herodotos IV. 5 f. The invasion story, as we have it, is obviously inspired from Biblical and Classical sources. But here again analogies are so numerous that we need not suppose it to have been entirely without native foundation. It is indeed much to be doubted whether native tradition preserved any memory of the great invasion or series of invasions which introduced the Gaelic language into Ireland. But movements by bodies of adventurers on a smaller scale may have taken place in much later times; and we think it not unlikely that the invasion doctrine was in part suggested or furthered by traditions of such movements.

VII. Lastly, we have to consider speculations upon the origin of mankind in general, the gods and the world.

Greek poetry of the Hesiodic type seems to have treated the whole of this subject systematically in genealogical form. In the Catalogue, as we have seen (p. 304), the eponymous Hellen was said to be son of Deucalion, and the latter to be son of Prometheus. Beyond this point the genealogy is given in Hesiod's *Theogony*. Prometheus is son of Iapetos, a brother of Cronos, the father of Zeus. Cronos and Iapetos have other brothers and sisters—Hyperion, Theia, Oceanos, etc.—while Hyperion and Theia are the father and mother of Helios (the Sun) and Selene (the Moon). The whole family are children of Gaia (Earth) and Uranos (Heaven); but Gaia had herself given birth to Uranos, as well as to the Mountains and the Sea (Pontos).

It will be seen that the whole genealogy, beginning with Uranos, amounts to only three generations down to Prometheus and Zeus, or four down to Deucalion and the children of Zeus. The first human beings are first or second cousins to the gods. It is not quite clear whether Prometheus himself is human, but there seems to be no doubt about his son Deucalion. Again, Zeus and his children, though not human, are doubtless thought of as anthropomorphic, in accordance with the usual Greek conceptions of these deities. But other members of the family are primarily elemental, and their elemental character is not forgotten or obscured.[1] To this type belong all the members of the first generation, and several of those in the second and third. There are also a number of monstrous beings, theriomorphic and half-theriomorphic, and mostly maleficent. The majority of these are descended from the union of Pontos and Gaia.

Beside this family the *Theogony* gives another. Gaia was not the first being to come into existence. First came Chaos, then Gaia[2] and Eros (Love). The relationship of the three is not stated, and no genealogy is traced from Eros. From Chaos, however, come Erebos (Darkness) and Nyx (Night). From Nyx and Erebos come Aither (Bright Sky, perhaps originally Daylight) and Hemera (Day). Later (211 ff.), Night is said to have given birth to Doom (Moros), Fate, Death, Sleep, the Fates (Keres), Woe, and other abstract beings, including Nemesis and Strife. Strife in turn gives birth to other abstract beings of a troublous and criminal character, and also to Ruin (Ate) and Oath[3] (Horcos). It may be observed that this abstract family is separated from Aither and Hemera, the elemental children of Nyx (124 f.), and comes as an interruption in the history of Gaia's progeny, which begins at 126—a fact which suggests that it did not belong to the original structure of the poem.

Horcos is personified also in the *Works and Days* (217), where also we find personifications of Justice and other abstract qualities. In regard to the beginnings of human history the *Works and Days* has in common with the *Theogony* the story of Prometheus and Pandora—the origin of human troubles. But this is followed (109 ff.) by another account of human history—the story of the five races, who are said to have followed one another in succession (cf. p. 13). Both the first, or golden, race

[1] We are speaking here of the Hesiodic—and the ordinary Greek—conception of Zeus. Linguistic evidence (Skr. *Dyaus*, etc.) shows of course that Zeus himself was originally elemental, and equivalent to Uranos.

[2] With Gaia is mentioned Tartara; but this is hardly personified.

[3] In Hesiod's poems Horcos is properly a personification of Calamity which befalls those who swear false oaths.

and the second, or silver, race are said to have been created by the gods—those who possess the homes of Olympos. The Golden Race lived in the time of Cronos. The Silver Race was much inferior to this, and the third, or Bronze, race again much inferior to the silver. With the fourth race—the heroes who fought at Thebes and Troy—the descending scale is interrupted; but it is resumed again with the fifth race or Race of Iron—the people of the poet's own time, who are represented as the worst of all. The third and fourth races are said to have been created by Zeus; but the creation of the fifth race is not specified. It will be seen that the first, second, third and fifth races are called from metals; in the account of the two latter there are clear reminiscences of the transition from the Bronze Age to the Iron Age. In this respect also the sequence is interrupted by the fourth race, which does not get its name from a metal; and in a later chapter we shall see reason for believing that this race did not find a place in the original scheme.

To Hesiod[1] is also attributed another story of creation, according to which Prometheus formed the human race out of earth, while Minerva (Athena) infused breath (*spiritus*) into them. The context is unknown; but later writers who give varieties of the story place this creation sometimes before, sometimes after, the flood of Deucalion. Since Deucalion himself appears to be a man, the latter form of the story is possibly more in accordance with Hesiodic ideas. It is perhaps a form of how the earth was replenished after the flood.

In the Homeric poems also personifications both of nature and of abstract conceptions are not uncommon. The sun, the dawn, etc. are regularly described as deities; and we find also personifications of Night, Sleep, Dreams, Strife, etc. No genealogy of these is given—nor indeed of the gods themselves, though their relationships to one another are often referred to. It is not at all clear that the Hesiodic genealogy as a whole was known to the Homeric world. Heaven and earth seem not to be personified. In two passages, *Il.* XIV. 201 (cf. 302) and 245 f., Oceanos is described as the 'origin' (γένεσις) of the gods. Yet in the former passage at least he is clearly personified.

There seems to be little or no material available for bridging over the interval between this early mythological cosmology and the speculations of the philosophers of the sixth century. Certain expressions[2] occur which suggest that by some Zeus was regarded as the originator of all things. But the absence of context makes it impossible to speak with confidence.

[1] Fragm. 21 (Kinkel). The authorities are Latin.

[2] E.g. Terpandros, fragm. 1: Ζεῦ πάντων ἀρχά.

The earliest 'rationalistic' speculations known are those of Thales of Miletos, in the first half of the sixth century. He held that water was the substance from which all things arose and of which they consist, and that the earth floats upon water. This doctrine does not seem to be so very far removed from the Homeric expression noticed above. Personifications, however, and genealogies are abandoned; and Thales' ideas are probably not to be regarded as a mere development of native speculation, since he is said to have studied mathematics and astronomy in Phoenicia and Egypt—countries where the history of civilisation had been long and uninterrupted. He is believed not to have committed his speculations to writing.

The speculations of Thales' younger contemporary Anaximandros fall outside the scope of our work; for he is known to have written scientific treatises, though these have perished. It may be noted, however, that he is said to have regarded as the origin of all things 'the infinite'—apparently an unlimited mass of matter, which was always in process of motion. This motion led first to the separation of the warm from the cold. From these two arose the damp; and from the damp were separated the earth, the air, and the encircling fire, which appears to us as the heavenly bodies. He is also said to have believed in periodic alternations of renewal and destruction of the world. Parallels to some of these ideas are to be found elsewhere, as we shall see below.

A good deal of speculation upon these subjects is preserved in early Norse poetry and prose records; but the material available from other Teutonic lands is very meagre. We will therefore begin with the former.

The chief sources of information are the three early anonymous poems *Völuspá*, *Vafþrúðnismál* and *Grímnismál*, and the first part of the *Prose Edda*, called *Gylfaginning*, or the 'Hallucination of Gylfi'. The former date no doubt from heathen times; but the *Prose Edda* was written by the Icelandic scholar and statesman Snorri Sturluson early in the thirteenth century, at a time when Iceland had been Christian for more than two centuries. The three poems just mentioned were his chief sources here; but he gives also a good deal of information, apparently from tradition, which is not preserved elsewhere. The peculiar framework in which the *Gylfaginning* is set—a kind of didactic dialogue—will require notice in a later chapter. It will be sufficient here to note that the material is to some extent systematised and presented in a more coherent form than is to be found in the poems.

The *Völuspá*, or 'Prophecy of the Witch' (or Seeress), is in the form of a monologue delivered, at least in part, to Othin by a witch (*völva*).

After a short preamble, the poem describes briefly the origin of the world (st. 3–6); then it relates the creation of the dwarfs and various incidents in the history of the gods, including the war with the Vanir and the death of Balder. At st. 43 the seeress begins to speak of *Ragnarök*, the impending doom of the gods, and proceeds to describe the coming of Surtr and the other hostile powers and their conflicts with the deities. At st. 58 she passes on to the resuscitation of the world under those of the gods who have survived the struggle. The text is in a very confused state, and there are great differences between the two extant MSS.

The passage which chiefly interests us is as follows (st. 3 ff.): "It was in the beginning of the ages—where Ymir dwelt there was no sand or sea, nor cool waves. The earth did not exist at all, nor the heaven above. There was a yawning abyss, but nowhere was there vegetation—until the lands were raised by the sons of Borr (i.e. Othin and his brothers), who formed glorious Miðgarðr. The Sun shone from the south upon a world of stone.[1] Then was the surface of the earth grown over with green herbs. The Sun, with her comrade, the Moon, waved her right hand[2] from the south along the border of heaven. The Sun knew not where her abode was; the Moon knew not what power he had; the stars knew not where their places were. The deities, the gods most holy, all went to their seats of judgment and held debate. They gave names to night and the new moons; they named morning and mid-day, forenoon and afternoon, for the counting of the years".

The *Vafþrúðnismál* is a dialogue between Othin and the wise giant Vafþrúðnir. It is a typical specimen of the 'contest between two sages' —a not uncommon form of literature, which we shall have to notice in a later chapter. The subjects of the contest are natural phenomena, the origin of the world, the life of the gods, and *Ragnarök*. The *Grímnismál* is a monologue in which Othin gradually reveals his identity to King Geirröðr, who is torturing him (cf. p. 119). The greater part of this poem is occupied with a description of the homes of the gods; but natural phenomena and the origin of the world are also treated incidentally.

For the origin of the world we may quote *Grímn.* 41 f. (cf. *Vafþr.* 21): "The earth was formed from Ymir's flesh, and the sea from his blood; the cliffs from his bones, the trees from his hair, and the sky from his skull. And from his eyelids the gracious deities made Miðgarðr for the sons of men; and from his brains were formed all the cruel storm-clouds". As examples of references to natural phenomena we

[1] Lit. 'stones of the habitation', i.e. earth.

[2] Perhaps the allusion is to the driving of the Sun's chariot.

may take *Vafþr.* 12 and 14, where Othin has been asked to give the names of the horses which draw (the chariots of) Day and Night: "Glittering Mane is the name of him who draws bright Day over the sons of the host. Among the Hreiðgotar he is reputed to be the best of horses. Light constantly radiates from the steed's mane....Frosty Mane is the name of him who draws each Night over the gracious deities. Every morning he sheds drops of foam. From them comes dew throughout the valleys". In st. 25 Day is said to be son of Dellingr and Night to be daughter of Nörr, while in st. 23 the Sun and the Moon are called children of Mundilfoeri, but nothing more is said of these persons, and the genealogies are not carried further. The Sun and the Moon are pursued on their travels by wolves, who will catch and destroy them at *Ragnarök*.[1] In st. 46 Othin asks: "Whence will there come a Sun into the smooth heaven when Fenrir has destroyed this one?" Vafþrúðnir replies: "A daughter will be born by Elfgleam (the Sun), before Fenrir destroys her. This daughter shall drive along her mother's path, when the deities die".

In the *Gylfaginning* cap. 4–9[2] are devoted to the origin of the world and of various kinds of beings, cap. 10–13 to natural phenomena, cap. 14–50 to descriptions of the homes of the gods and of the gods themselves, and stories of their adventures, cap. 51–53 to Ragnarökr[3] and the recovery of the world. As mentioned above, the treatment of our subjects is more systematic here than in the poems. Details are given which may have been known to the ancient poets, but are not recorded by them. In some cases the additions seem to reflect a later phase of thought.

In *Vafþr.* 28 Othin asks who was the first of the gods or of Ymir's stock (i.e. the giants) to come into existence. Vafþrúðnir's answer implies that Aurgelmir was the first; and Othin then asks whence he came. The reply is as follows (st. 31): "Freezing drops fell from the Elivágar,[4] and the growth produced thereby ultimately became a giant.[5] In him

[1] From analogies in other regions it would seem that this motif originated in an eclipse myth, which has been incorporated in the story of *Ragnarök*.

[2] Cap. 3 gives a cosmology which is at variance with the account contained in the following chapters. Othin here is eternal, as well as omnipotent. Possibly this chapter is derived ultimately from some attempt to recast the national religion in the last phase of the struggle with Christianity.

[3] A later term for Ragnarök—with the substitution of *rökr*, 'darkness', for *rök*.

[4] The name is supposed to mean properly the half-frozen waves of the Arctic Ocean.

[5] Lit. 'it grew (impers.) until a giant arose therefrom'.

all our genealogies meet. That is why it (our stock) is all very fierce". Then he goes on to describe how the giant generated children by means of his own feet. In *Gylf.* 4 f. the obscure reference to Elivágar is interpreted as follows: *Ginnunga Gap*, the 'Yawning Abyss' of *Völ.* 3, (cf. p. 321), is bounded on the south by a world of heat and fire called *Múspell*[1] or *Múspellsheimr*, where Surtr dwells, and on the north by *Niflheimr* ('Mist-World'), which is completely cold. The abyss is affected both by sparks from the south and by ice from the north; and it was from the moisture produced by the hot air from the south playing upon the ice that Aurgelmir—who is here identified with Ymir—grew. This primeval being is still regarded as anthropomorphic; but in other respects the account would seem to point to rationalistic speculation—not so very remote from that of Anaximandros (cf. p. 320).

The formation of the world as it actually exists is treated in *Gylf.* 7 f., which seems to be taken from a combination of *Völ.* 4 (cf. p. 321) with *Grímn.* 40 f. (*Vafþr.* 21; *ib.*). Ymir is killed by the sons of Borr (i.e. Othin and his brothers), who make the earth out of his body, the sea from his blood, etc. The flood motif is introduced in connection with the latter.

The origin of the gods themselves is not mentioned in any poem which has come down to us; but *Gylf.* 6 gives an account which seems primitive enough. Ymir lived on the milk of a cow, which had grown out of the ice. From the ice-blocks which the cow licked there arose gradually a man called Buri. His son was Borr, the father of Othin. Nothing further is known of either Buri or Borr; but Othin's mother Bestla is said to be the daughter of a giant called Bölþorn. Othin himself has brothers and sons, among the latter being Thor and Balder. In other cases the relationship is not always clear. Ullr is son of Sif, the wife of Thor, but his father's name is not recorded. The gods collectively are known as *Aesir*, and their home as *Ásgarðr*. They were once at war with another tribe of gods called Vanir, of whose origin nothing is recorded, and the war was terminated by an exchange of hostages. The hostages given by the Vanir were Njörðr and his children, Frey and Freyja, all of whom are among the chief deities. To the Vanir also probably belongs Heimdallr, who is said to be the son of nine sisters;

1 This name occurs in poetry only in the phrase 'sons of Múspell', applied to Surtr and his followers. It is no doubt connected with the name *Muspilli*, 'Day of Judgment', in a Bavarian religious poem of the ninth century. It is commonly believed to be of foreign origin; but no satisfactory explanation has yet been given, so far as we know.

but, again, no father is mentioned. Lastly, it may be noted that the relations of the gods with the giants are normally, though not invariably, hostile. Several of the gods, both Aesir and Vanir, have wives from the giants.

As regards the origin of mankind we may quote the following obscure passage from the *Völuspá* (st. 16 f.): "Three mighty and gracious gods...found Askr and Embla on the shore, without power and with destiny unfixed. They had neither breath (i.e. life) nor intelligence, nor blood nor voice nor the right hues (sc. of life). Othin gave them breath, Hoenir gave them intelligence, and Lóðurr gave them blood and the right hues". In *Gylf.* 9 this passage is interpreted as follows: "When Borr's sons were walking along the shore, they found two logs and lifted them up and made men of them. The first gave them breath and life, the second intelligence and movement, the third (human) appearance, speech, hearing and sight. They gave them clothes and names; the man was called Askr and the woman Embla. And from them was sprung the human race, to whom the dwelling-place beneath Miðgarðr was given". We see no reason for doubting that the passage in the *Völuspá* also means the progenitors of mankind; but Askr and Embla[1] are not mentioned elsewhere, and no genealogies are traced to them.

In treating of Norse cosmology it is impossible to omit notice of Yggdrasill's Ash, which is perhaps its most striking conception. There can be no doubt that the conception originated in the sacred or 'guardian' trees, which in the North, as in many other lands, used to stand in the neighbourhood of farms and villages, and upon which the welfare of the local community was believed to depend. Yggdrasill's Ash is properly—and indeed usually—the sacred tree or 'Tree of Fate' of the divine community.[2] In *Völ.* 18 it stands over the Spring of Fate. But in *Grímn.* 31 it has come to be represented as a 'World Tree', covering and sheltering all kinds of beings. Here we hear that "Beneath Yggdrasill's Ash three roots[3] stretch in different directions; Hel dwells beneath one, the frost-giants beneath the second, human beings beneath the third". The poem then goes on to describe the animal life in the tree. In *Gylf.* 15 the picture is developed and expanded.

The references to cosmology contained in poems other than those discussed above, e.g. the *Fáfnismál* and the *Fjölsvinnsmál*, need not be

[1] *Askr* means 'ash' (tree), but the meaning of *Embla* is unknown.

[2] Cf. Chadwick, *Cult of Othin*, p. 75 ff.

[3] Perhaps a trifurcated trunk is meant. Trees of such growth are regarded as sacred in some countries.

treated here; but a word must be said with regard to the *Rígsþula*. This poem describes how a certain Rígr visits in succession the homes of three couples called respectively Great-grandfather and Great-grandmother, Grandfather and Grandmother, and Father and Mother. He sleeps with them and thereby becomes the progenitor of the three classes of society—the slaves, the free, and the noble. The interest of the poem is descriptive rather than antiquarian, for it gives detailed pictures of the life and characteristics of the three classes. But the antiquarian element is not entirely wanting—at least if the prose introduction is correct in identifying Rígr with the god Heimdallr. In *Völ.* 1 the seeress begins her prophecy with an appeal to 'all the holy kindreds, the greater and the lesser sons of Heimdallr'—which suggests the existence of some story in which Heimdallr figured as the progenitor of mankind.

Very little record has been preserved of the cosmological speculations of the other Teutonic peoples. We have already (p. 305 f.) quoted the genealogy which Tacitus, *Germ.* 2, gives as coming from ancient poems. Here Mannus, the father of the three ancestral brothers, presumably represents the first human being. His father is a god, Tuisto, who is son of Earth. In *Germ.* 40 the term Terra Mater is used for the goddess Nerthus, whose name is identical with the Norse Njörðr, though the latter deity is male. This fact throws light on the origin of the Vanir. But Tacitus' two notices relate to different regions—the first probably to the Rhineland, the second doubtless to Denmark—and it cannot safely be assumed either that the genealogy of Mannus was known in the latter region[1] or that Nerthus is the deity meant by *Terra* in *Germ.* 2.

For speculations on the genealogies of the gods current in later times there is evidence in a letter[2] from Bishop Daniel of Winchester (709–44) to St Boniface. The reference is doubtless to the heathen Frisians and Old Saxons, whom St Boniface was striving to convert; but it is likely enough that reminiscences of English heathenism—which was not extinct in his childhood—were present in the bishop's mind. He advises his friend not to proceed with a direct denunciation of the genealogy of the gods, but to put awkward questions to the heathen: "Do they imagine that gods and goddesses are still generating other gods and goddesses? Or, if they are not now generating them, when and

[1] Frey was also called Yngvi, a name which is identical with Inguo, the name of one of the ancestral brothers in the Frankish genealogy (whence Tacitus' *Inguaeones*). But Frey is son, not grandson, of Njörðr.

[2] Publ. by Jaffé, *Bibliotheca Rerum Germ.* III. 71 ff.

why did they cease from begetting and bearing offspring? But if they are still generating, the number of the gods must now have become infinite", etc. It is not likely that cosmological problems would be excluded from such speculations as are here referred to.

It would probably not be difficult to collect a fair amount of indirect evidence for cosmological speculations. The Irminsul, the sacred pillar of the Old Saxons, seems to have had some significance of this kind attached to it[1]—perhaps analogous to the conception of the 'world-tree' in the *Grímnismál*. Linguistic evidence may also be taken into account. Thus, all Teutonic languages have a word for the inhabited earth which properly means 'central enclosure' or 'enclosure in the centre',[2] implying the existence of an outer zone—which in Norse mythology is the abode of hostile beings. But all such evidence presents problems which cannot be discussed here.

In Britain and Ireland the cosmological speculations of heathen times can hardly be traced; for they were displaced at an early date by the Bible and the *Chronicle* of Eusebius. As regards Britain nothing more need be said. In the case of Ireland, however, mention must be made of the great fabric of imaginative history which was built up to cover the interval between the times of the Patriarchs and the beginnings of native tradition. This history centres round a number of invasions—three in the original form of the story, to which two others were added later.[3] It can hardly be doubted—especially in view of the Gaulish evidence to be considered shortly—that these invasions have taken the place of the cosmological speculations found in other lands. But the evidence seems to point to a substitution of new learning for the old, rather than to a transformation of the latter, at least in the first place.

The fourth invasion is that of the Tuatha De, usually called Tuatha De Danann, which seems to mean 'Peoples of the Goddess (Danu)'. The story relates their wanderings, their genealogies, their arrival in Ireland, and their conflict with the previous invaders, called Fir Bolg,

[1] *Irminsul...uniuersalis columna quasi sustinens omnia* (*Translatio S. Alexandri*, cap. 3).

[2] Goth. *midjungards* (οἰκουμένη), Anglo-Saxon *middangeard*, etc. In Norse mythology *Miðgarðr* sometimes seems to mean the enclosing rampart rather than the enclosed area, as elsewhere.

[3] The full form of the story is to be found in the *Lebor Gabála*, or 'Book of Conquests', the briefer (older) form in the *Hist. Brittonum*, cap. 13. The latter occurs also in a medieval Irish 'Synchronism' (cf. MacNeill, *Celtic Ireland*, p. 31), which draws from the Annals, and may have been derived from the lost (first) portion of the early Annals.

Gaileoin and Fir Domnann, in which they were successful. The story of the fifth invasion recounts how they were eventually overcome by the sons of Milid, the last invaders. It is universally recognised now that the Tuatha De are really the gods of heathen times; but there is great doubt as to how much of this story is derived from genuine native tradition. The same remark applies to the genealogies. The initial stages are often in accord with the evidence of other stories; but they are carried to a considerable length and eventually traced to Nemed, the leader of the second invasion.

It is to be observed that the third and fourth invasions are those which do not belong to the original scheme. We do not know what was the source which suggested the first two futile invasions—those of Partholon (Bartholomaeus) and of Nemed—or the (fifth) successful invasion of the sons of Milid; but we doubt if it is to be found in native tradition. What is clear is that the native gods, after being eliminated for a time—doubtless by the Church—from the early history of the country, found their way back, under a thin disguise, in the story of the fourth invasion. The cosmological speculations usually associated with such beings are indeed wanting; and in place of these they are provided with a genealogy which connects them with the second invasion[1]—presumably in order to make them fit into the existing scheme. We suspect that traces of such speculations might possibly be brought to light by research in the genealogies; but we have not the detailed knowledge necessary to speak with confidence.

Although we have no direct evidence for the cosmological speculations of the ancient Britons, Greek and Roman writers give us a certain amount of information regarding the cultivation of such subjects among the Gauls. Moreover, Caesar (*Gall.* VI. 13) says that Britain was the chief home of Druidism, with which these studies were essentially bound up, and believed to be its birthplace. He remarks that the training lasted sometimes as long as twenty years and that it involved the learning of an immense body of poetry. Among the subjects taught he specifies the transmigration of souls, astronomy, geography,

[1] Their opponents, the third set of invaders, are provided with similar genealogies. It should be noted that the Gaileoin and Fir Domnann were real peoples, who survived into the historical period; and the same may be true of the Fir Bolg. Why they are brought into conflict with the gods is not clear. A parallel account of the story is to be found in the *First Battle of Moytura*, publ. by Fraser, *Ériu*, VIII. 1 ff. The *Second Battle of Moytura* (publ. by Stokes, *Rev. Celt.* XII. 52 ff.) is the story of a war between the Tuatha De and the Fomori, and is generally believed to contain more genuinely native matter (cf. p. 258).

cosmology and theology.[1] Other writers add further details. In particular we may refer to Strabo, XII. 4. 4, where it is stated as a doctrine of the Druids that both souls (i.e. the individual soul) and the world were indestructible, but that fire and water would some day obtain the mastery. If the last sentence relates to the world[2] it would seem to point either to a doctrine somewhat like that of *Ragnarök* or to an 'alternation' theory such as was propounded by Anaximandros (cf. p. 320). But in any case there is evidence enough that cosmological and theological speculations were cultivated in Gaul, and presumably also in this country—perhaps to an even greater extent than among the other peoples whom we have considered.

We have seen that the material available for this section is limited, owing to the fact that cosmological speculation could not be cultivated by the Christian peoples, the English, Welsh and Irish. Between the Greek evidence and the Norse there are striking analogies. The former shows a more systematised scheme, men, gods and personifications of nature all being brought together in one genealogy. But the underlying principles are the same in both cases—anthropomorphic personification and family relations. In Greece indeed the time came when all this was abandoned, and attempts were made to grapple with cosmological problems on 'rationalistic' principles. The history of thought in the North was cut short; but the passage in the *Gylfaginning* relating to Niflheimr and Múspell indicates that in its last phase it was tending in the same direction. Christianity, however, was introduced before the giant could be got out of the way.

As to the Druids, the records are too meagre to allow us to determine whether their speculations had advanced beyond the mythological stage. On the whole perhaps the evidence suggests a transitional phase in which the old still predominated. Some ancient writers thought that their doctrine of metempsychosis was derived from Pythagoras; for they did not know how widely such beliefs are distributed. But the possibility of external influence upon religious and speculative thought is one which cannot be ignored—either in the mythological or the rationalistic stage. The Gauls had long been subject to the influence of Etruscan and Greek civilisation, the Norse to the influence of Christian

[1] Gall. VI. 14: *Multa praeterea de sideribus atque eorum motu, de mundi ac terrarum magnitudine, de rerum natura, de deorum immortalium ui ac potestate disputant et iuuentuti tradunt.*

[2] The meaning of ποτε is ambiguous. Does the sentence mean one final catastrophe or a series?

Europe, the Greeks to that of Egypt and the East. What we have spoken of as progress or development in thought may often, if not usually, be due to influence from without.

In this chapter we have given little or no attention to that antiquarian learning which prevailed in Southern and Western Europe during the Roman period, and which in the course of centuries gradually spread northwards and overwhelmed the native learning of the various countries, one after another. This Latin learning had of course a history of its own—a genealogy which was partly Classical, partly Hebrew. Thus, when British antiquaries, probably in the seventh or eighth century, began to trace the origin of their nation to Brutus and the early kings of the Latins, they were merely continuing and adapting to their own case work which had been carried on, long before, by Roman antiquaries themselves, when they traced their own origin back to Aeneas and his Trojans. These again were following the example of the Molossoi, the Macedonians and other peoples, whose kings claimed descent from ancient Greek heroes, such as Neoptolemos, son of Achilles, or Temenos, the descendant of Heracles. The prototypes of such genealogies were no doubt to be found in Greece itself, where in some cases they may have been genuine.

The Latin learning introduced by Christianity was of course by no means confined to genealogies and chronicles. Various other branches of learning, represented e.g. in the works of Isidore, were likewise introduced, and eventually supplanted or transformed the native learning in the same subjects. It was only in the British Isles and the North, and more especially in Ireland and Iceland, that the native intellectual life was able to preserve anything of its individual character.

In the native learning itself special features are not wanting in the various lands. We may instance the exceptional activity displayed in Ireland in the etymology of place-names and in the production of genealogies, which must be largely fictitious. But on the whole the resemblances are far more striking than the differences. We may instance in particular the love of catalogues—due largely no doubt to their adaptability to mnemonic purposes—and the extension of the genealogical principle to explanations of the origin of nations and even of objects and phenomena of nature.

The importance of this class of literature lies in the fact that it represents the earliest known attempts to collect and classify knowledge, for its own sake rather than for purposes of entertainment.

Sometimes the information collected may seem futile and trivial enough, e.g. the list of dwarfs in the *Völuspá* or the lists of mermaids and other supernatural beings in the *Theogony*. But on the whole these catalogues must be regarded as serious attempts to bring order into the mass of information supplied by mythology and heroic tradition. It was from such beginnings that the scientific study of history, archaeology and (to some extent) natural philosophy ultimately arose. The length of time during which such studies were continuously pursued is of course difficult to estimate in periods for which no written records are available. But some Norse genealogies come remarkably near the truth in the positions they assign to kings who lived some four centuries before the earliest datable record and at least six centuries before any written records; and we have no reason to doubt that some Irish traditions have quite as long a history. For speculative studies such controlling evidence is hardly to be found. But we think it is possible, in Norse thought, as well as in Greek, to distinguish between different strata—between the childish conceptions of one period or milieu and the attempts at scientific explanation current in another. The changes may be due to external influence; but this could hardly have taken effect without some previous intellectual activity.

CHAPTER XI

POST-HEROIC POETRY AND SAGA

IN Greek, English and Norse the records of times after the Heroic Age differ greatly from those of the Heroic Age itself. The latter, as we have seen, consist almost entirely of poetry, chiefly of Type A, though Type B is also of frequent occurrence in Norse. On the other hand, in 'post-heroic' poetry—by which we mean poetry relating to times after the Heroic Age—Type A (i.e. narrative poetry) is rare, and apparently confined to English. Its place everywhere is taken by saga. Type B is not uncommon in Norse, but these poems are generally believed to be very late. But the prevailing types in post-heroic poetry—excluding, of course, Antiquarian and Gnomic—are D and E, the latter in Greek and Norse, the former in all three languages. It may be observed that English and Norse have now nothing in common and may be treated separately.

In Irish, as we have seen (p. 16), it is difficult to determine when the Heroic Age comes to an end. There is no real break; but stories relating to times later than the beginning of the eighth century are very rare, though poetry of Type D is frequent. In Welsh after the end of the Heroic Age there is a very long period which appears to be almost blank, apart from notices in annals.

The differences between heroic and post-heroic records noted above are by no means limited to form. In Greek and, for the most part, in Norse the differences in tone and in the milieu which they reflect are quite as marked. In English also, where the amount of post-heroic material is small, such contrasts occur not unfrequently, though they are by no means universal. But the Irish post-heroic records, which are mostly fragmentary, are in general such as might have been composed in the Heroic Age itself.

It is to be borne in mind that the definition of the subjects comprised in this chapter is chronological. We are here dealing with records relating to the periods intervening between the end of the Heroic Age and the beginning of the general use of writing for literary purposes. The records with which we are concerned are not the only works dating from these periods; for heroic poetry and saga relating to the past, as well as theological, antiquarian and gnomic poetry, were doubtless cultivated at the same time. But we do not mean to suggest that even the records here treated belong to a uniform category, like heroic records. Even in Norse the poetry of Type D closely resembles heroic poetry of Type D, such as is found in Welsh and Irish, whereas the poems of Type E—often by the same authors—belong to a different world. In Greek also, though heroic affinities are wanting, we shall have to deal with records which have practically nothing in common with one another except the language and perhaps the metre.

It will be convenient to begin with saga, which was perhaps current everywhere, though no examples relating to our period are preserved in Welsh.

In amount, quality and variety Icelandic saga far surpasses anything of the kind which is to be found in the other countries. It provides us with a knowledge of the life, both material and intellectual, of the tenth and eleventh centuries and of the personnel of these times, which can hardly be paralleled in any other barbaric period—indeed perhaps in any period before the sixteenth century. The leading characters in the sagas, such as Egill Skallagrímsson, Njáll, Snorri the Priest and Guðrún, daughter of Ósvifr, differ greatly from the semi-idealised figures which we find in heroic poetry and saga. They would seem to be portraits drawn from life. Otherwise they must be products of a tradition which combined the habit of close personal observation with an unusual development of the imaginative faculty—which is less likely.

In Icelandic saga literature every kind of narrative is represented from the outline story, which may consist of no more than two or three sentences, to long works which contain many changes of scene and personnel and in which the circumstances are often minutely described and conversations given at considerable length. The growth of saga can be traced to a certain extent. Most of the long, detailed sagas relate to the close of the tenth century or the first thirty years of the eleventh. Those which deal with earlier times are few; the earliest, such as *Egils Saga Skallagrímssonar*, relate to the second quarter of the tenth century. For the ninth century, and especially for the reign of Harold the Fair-haired (c. 860–930) and the colonisation of Iceland, which began about 874, we have a large number of short stories which contain speeches and other detailed matter. Many of these are included in the *Saga of Harold the Fair-haired*, while many others are to be found in the opening chapters of various 'Sagas of Icelanders' (*Íslendinga Sögur*), in the *Landnámabók*, or 'Book of the Colonisation of

Iceland', and elsewhere. Some of them, especially those in the first series, appear to be derived from poems, while others are evidently family and local traditions. They are often of an explanatory character—of Type C rather than Type A. Not a few, however, are of the anecdotal kind—short stories of entertainment which culminate in some noteworthy dictum or observation.

For times anterior to the ninth century we have a number of sagas generally known as *Fornaldar Sögur*, or 'Sagas of Ancient Times', some of which run to considerable length and contain numerous speeches and detailed situations. Some of these, as, for example, the greater part of the *Völsunga Saga*, are mere paraphrases of poems. But the rest are generally believed to be imaginative works of the twelfth century—a view for which in one case at least there is definite and early evidence.[1] It is not clear that the authors of these sagas had anything to work upon except family and local traditions in brief outline form, such as we find from time to time in the Sagas of the Kings and elsewhere. Such outline stories perhaps did not differ essentially from the short stories noticed above; for the latter are usually more full in proportion as they deal with more recent times. But the cultivation of saga-telling as an elaborate art, which resulted in the production of such works as the longer of the Sagas of Icelanders, seems hardly to have begun before the second half of the tenth century. In a later chapter we shall see that such evidence as is available is in accord with this view.

In Greece a considerable amount of saga seems to have been current. It is known to us only from Herodotos and later authors, and often only in summary form; but it appears to have entirely displaced the use of narrative poetry, for the cultivation of which, in relation to post-heroic times, we have no evidence before the Alexandrian period. There is indeed nothing to show that Greek saga was ever cultivated up to the pitch which we see in the longer 'Sagas of Icelanders'. But numerous parallels are to be found for the short stories, noticed above, relating to times down to the death of Harold the Fair-haired—i.e. for the earlier phases of Norse saga.

Most of the stories which deal with the earliest (post-heroic) times are of an explanatory or antiquarian character and belong rather to Type C than to Type A. Such are the stories of the 'Return of the Heracleidai', the twin sons of Aristodemos, the expedition of Theras (Herodotos, IV. 147 f.), the abolition of monarchy at Athens, and the

[1] Cf. the *Saga of Thorgils and Hafliði*, cap. 10, and Kershaw, *Stories and Ballads of the Far Past*, p. 58 ff., where this passage is translated.

foundation of the Ionic cities (*ib.* I. 145 ff.)—some of which have been already noticed. It is quite possible that some of these stories are derived from antiquarian poets, such as Cinaithon; but definite evidence is wanting. Saga in some form or other was presumably the source from which the antiquarian poets themselves drew their materials. Saga of Type A relating to this earliest period seems not to be frequently represented. A probable example is the story of Hyrnetho, told by Pausanias, II. 28.

We know practically nothing of the traditions current in most parts of Greece for the period between the first post-heroic generations and the beginning of the seventh century. The stories of which we have any record belong chiefly to Sparta. Of these the best known is the story of Lycurgos, which appears to have been current in various forms. It is bound up with traditions or speculations relating to the history of the Spartan constitution, and would seem therefore to have belonged to Type C rather than to Type A. Other stories, known only from Pausanias, Plutarch and other later authors, appear to have dealt with events of the eighth century—Teleclos and the fall of Amyclai, the death of Teleclos and incidents in the life of Theopompos. It is not clear that these belonged to Type C. As examples of stories relating to other parts of Greece we may cite those of Archias, the founder of Syracuse, and of Philolaos and Diocles, the two Corinthians who settled at Thebes.[1] The stories of the Messenian wars also are presumably derived from saga, though Pausanias' account is taken partly from the late poet Rhianos.

In the seventh and sixth centuries the stories become more numerous and fuller, and are now usually of the anecdotal kind (cf. p. 333). Sparta still possesses the largest number; but they relate also to many other cities in various parts of Greece. They are almost always of a purely personal character—many of them describe the rise and fall, the adventures and intrigues of the tyrants. Indeed it is from these stories, as preserved by Herodotos and later writers, that our knowledge of this period of Greek history is mainly derived.

In Ireland sagas began to be written down about the end of the Heroic Age; but there can be no doubt that in the main they were still preserved by oral tradition. As we have already remarked, there seems to be little difference between heroic and post-heroic sagas; but examples of the latter are quite rare. The *Book of Leinster* contains a list of 187 sagas, and of these apparently only one can be identified with certainty as

[1] Cf. Grote, *History of Greece* (1884), III, p. 360 f.; II, p. 297 f.

relating to post-heroic times in Ireland. This is the story called 'Niall's Love for Gormlaith'. Unfortunately it is lost; but a number of what appear to be extracts from it are preserved in the *Annals of Clonmacnoise*.[1] Gormlaith was married first to Cormac, bishop of Cashel and king of Munster, who was killed in 908, and afterwards to his slayer Cerball, king of Leinster. From the latter she was rescued by Niall Glundub, who subsequently became high-king and was killed by Sigtryggr I, king of Dublin, in 919. Gormlaith is said to have died in poverty in 948. Some poems attributed to her—which may really come from the saga—will be noticed below (p. 340).

Apart from the entry noticed above we know of no direct evidence for post-heroic sagas. We do not doubt, however, that other such sagas once existed—indeed there may be examples still preserved, unknown to us—though we are inclined to doubt if many of them had more than a short life. Mention should be made here of two works of considerable length, which resemble one another rather closely—the *Martial Career of Cellachan of Cashel*[2] and the *War of the Gaedhil with the Gaill*.[3] Both of these contain a large amount of poetry, of Types B and D. The latter, as it stands, is a literary work; cap. 1–40 are derived from Annals, while the rest deals with the life of Brian Boruma, king of Munster and high-king of Ireland, who was killed at the battle of Clontarf, on Good Friday, 1014. This latter part has all the appearance of saga, and the same is true of the story of Cellachan of Cashel (who died c. 954) as a whole,[4] in spite of the very large number of personal names which it contains. Though we are not in a position to speak with confidence, the evidence seems to us to suggest that both these works existed substantially in the form of saga before they were written down—perhaps c. 1100.[5]

In England saga is very poorly represented. In the original language indeed, apart from mere references, we know of only one probable

1 Cf. O'Curry, *MS. Materials*, p. 131 ff.

2 Ed. and transl. by A. Bugge.

3 Ed. and transl. by J. H. Todd.

4 In cap. 65, where a poem is introduced, there is a reference to 'the saga-teller' (*in senchaid*).

5 The question of date depends partly on resemblances in diction to the *Destruction of Troy*; cf. A. Bugge, *Caithreim Cellachain Caisil*, p. xvi ff. We are not qualified to express an opinion. But the fact that Brodar is made to speak English in the *War*, cap. 114, does not prove that this work was written after the English conquest. In cap. 117 he is called 'Brodar mac Oisli, earl of York'. He was perhaps a son of Earl Oslac of York, who was exiled and driven over the sea in 975 (*Sax. Chron.*, *ad ann.*). In any case English would hardly be an unfamiliar language at Dublin in the eleventh century.

example—the story of Cynewulf's death, related in the *Saxon Chronicle*, *ann.* 755. The true date of the event is 786; but the story does not give the impression of being a strictly contemporary record. If it was not written down until the Chronicle began to be kept in English—i.e. probably in the reign of Aethelwulf—it would have had a life of over half a century in oral tradition.

Latin works, chiefly of the twelfth century, contain a number of stories which would seem to be derived from saga. We may refer, for example, to the story of Alfred and the cakes in the *Annals of St Neot* (*ann.* 878). It may be observed that the woman's rebuke to the disguised king is given in verse. Earlier examples are to be found in northern works, especially the *Historia de S. Cuthberto*.[1] We may cite, for example, the story of the appointment of Guthred, the son of Hardacnut, as king (cap. 13). It is true that these stories are of ecclesiastical provenance; but there is no reason for supposing that the Northumbrian church of the Danish period possessed much Latin learning. For earlier times we have the story of Offa II.[2]

In addition to Latin works, mention must be made of Gaimar's *Lestorie des Engles*, which contains a number of such stories. We may cite in particular the story of Beorn Butsecarl and the kings Osbryht and Aella (2589–2836) and that of Edgar and Aelfthryth (3601–3966). The latter is also told more briefly by William of Malmesbury (II. 157), together with other love adventures of the same king. We may also refer to the ghastly story of the death of Prince Alfred (4791 ff.), where the description of the murder somewhat resembles that of the killing of Ásbjörn by the demon Brusi, in *Orms þáttr Stórolfssonar*, cap. 7.

The cultivation of saga in still earlier times may perhaps be inferred from certain passages in Bede's *Ecclesiastical History* relating to the reigns of Aethelfrith and Edwin. If the account of the debate in the Northumbrian council (II. 13) is of this origin, English saga must at that time have attained a high standard. Here again the immediate source is no doubt ecclesiastical, but the reference to the bird points to an English origin, and it is doubtful whether a separate and distinctive ecclesiastical tradition existed in the North until many years after this time. Indeed the beginnings of English saga may go back to a much earlier time—long before the end of the Teutonic Heroic Age. For the story of Hengest and Horsa, especially as told in the *Historia Brittonum*, saga is at all events the most probable source. Such saga may of course have

[1] Publ. in Symeon of Durham (Rolls Series), I, p. 196 ff.

[2] *Vitae Duorum Offarum*, ed. by Wats (1639–40).

been derived from heroic poetry—a process which is likely enough in the case of the story of Offa I; but we have no evidence for (English) heroic poems of which the scene was laid in this country.

There can be no question as to the existence of saga relating to the British Heroic Age. For this we have evidence in the stories of Taliesin and Myrddin, the *Historia Brittonum*, the Romances, and—inferentially—in numerous Triads. Yet, curiously enough, we know of no saga dealing with later times—at least not until the close of the eleventh century, when something of the kind may perhaps be implied in the 'Story of Gruffydd son of Cynan', though the work itself is literary. One can hardly believe that family and local stories ceased to be composed for more than four centuries; but it would certainly seem that attention was chiefly given to the cultivation of stories of the far past.

Except among the Britons it would seem that the cultivation of saga was a general characteristic of post-heroic times. In Greece and England, and in the Norse world before the tenth century, this saga probably embraced no more than family traditions, explanatory stories and anecdotes, all in comparatively brief form, though there are indications—in the passage from Bede cited above, as well as in the *Historia Brittonum*—that English saga had at one time shown a more ambitious development. In Ireland the cultivation of saga as an elaborate instrument of entertainment had without doubt attained an advanced stage of development during the Heroic Age itself; and in the succeeding period new stories dealing with contemporary events and perhaps equally elaborate appear to have been not unknown, though very little of them has been preserved. In Iceland, beginning apparently in the tenth century, saga attained a development far in advance of the Irish, and indeed unparalleled in Europe.

The scarceness of the late Irish sagas and the rise of elaborate saga in Iceland are phenomena which will require notice in a later chapter. Here it need only be noted that Icelandic saga cannot be wholly independent of Irish influence. We may refer,[1] for example, to the *Laxdoela Saga*, cap. 63, where Helgi receives from his shepherd a detailed account of the appearance and dress of each of his approaching opponents and identifies them, one after another, from the descriptions. This is a stock motif in Irish heroic sagas. Such influence is only what might be expected from the fact that much of the population of Iceland and even many of the leading families were partly of Irish blood. But its extent is difficult to determine.

[1] Cf. Thurneysen, *Ir. Heldensage*, p. 61.

Post-heroic narrative poetry (Type A) is found only in English, and even here only one fragmentary piece is preserved—a poem which recounts the defeat and death of Byrhtnoth, earl of Essex, at the battle of Maldon, in 991. This poem,[1] the beginning of which is lost, does not show any striking differences from the early heroic poems, either in substance or form. Courage and personal loyalty are the dominant motifs. Down to 181 ff., where Byrhtnoth is slain, the narrative is such as might have been found in a heroic poem. But the latter part, especially from 205 onwards, consists of a series of short scenes in which a considerable number of Byrhtnoth's knights are introduced, one after another. The connection is very slight, and in spite of the narrative form, one cannot help being reminded of the *Gododdin* (*An.* I). It would seem to be the poet's intention not so much to provide entertainment as to commemorate the fallen—first the earl himself and then his chief followers in succession. If so, the poem, so far as its intention goes, ought perhaps to be connected with Type D.

The *Battle of Maldon* belongs to the latest phase of our period—indeed to a time when writing was already in general use for literary purposes; but we have included it here because we think it was intended for recitation rather than for reading. We know of no other poems of the kind, though it can hardly have been an isolated production. William of Malmesbury and later Latin writers refer to 'songs' (*cantilenae*) dealing with the lives and doings of Aethelstan and other princes; and it is quite possible that these also were poems of Type A. But little definite information is available.[2]

Poetry of Type B is no doubt well represented both in the Icelandic sagas and in the Irish works noticed above; but it is not always easy to distinguish. Most of the 'Sagas of Icelanders' and of the Icelandic 'Sagas of the Kings' contain stanzas which profess to be 'occasional'

[1] Ed. and transl. by Ashdown, *English and Norse Documents relating to the Reign of Ethelred the Unready*, p. 22 ff.

[2] It is possible that some of the stories referred to saga on p. 336 above, may really be derived from narrative poems. Note may also be taken of the fact that the Romances in which the scene is laid in England—*Guy of Warwick*, *Beves of Hampton* and *Havelock the Dane*—are represented as relating to this period, though in the form in which we know them they are works of a later age. The development of Romance may be seen in the story of Gunnhild, daughter of Canute and wife of the Emperor Henry III, as cited by Malmesbury (II. 188) and later writers. The story related, perhaps in the form of a narrative poem, how her honour was vindicated in combat by her English page; cf. Chambers, *Bibliogr. Society's Trans.*, 1925, p. 315 f.

pieces or remarks in verse uttered by the characters at the point indicated in the narrative (i.e. Type E; cf. p. 42), while longer poems, usually panegyrics or elegies (Type D), or fragments of such poems, are not rare. It is commonly held that these poems are in reality what they profess to be, unless they are spoken by children, dead persons or supernatural beings, or there is something in the form or the substance of the poems which militates against the trustworthiness of the record. Thus in *Njáls Saga*, cap. 78, we find a stanza which is said to have been uttered by the dead Gunnarr in his grave-cairn, while in *Egils Saga*, cap. 31, two stanzas are attributed to the hero when he is three years old. Not unfrequently stanzas show linguistic forms which belong to a later period than the times in which the speakers lived. All such cases are of course to be referred to Type B. The rest of the poems may in general be assigned to Types E and D. There can be little doubt that the composition of poetry was a fairly common accomplishment in the Viking Age; and some of the chief characters of sagas, such as Egill, Kormakr, Hallfreðr and Gunnlaugr Ormstunga, were famous poets. Not unfrequently, as, for example, in parts of *Egils Saga*, the narrative seems to have been partly constructed out of the verses. But it is impossible to distinguish with absolute certainty between stanzas actually composed by the characters and those which may have been added by saga-tellers within two or three generations of their time.

The *Fornaldar Sögur* (cf. p. 333) likewise frequently contain a good deal of poetry—not only isolated stanzas but also sometimes poems of considerable length. Some of these latter are much older than the sagas themselves. Thus the *Saga of Hervör and King Heiðrekr*[1] contains the *Battle of the Goths and Huns*, an old heroic poem of Type A, of which we have spoken above (p. 26). This part of the saga (cap. 12–15) is little more than a paraphrase of the poem, including some stanzas which are lost. In the same saga, cap. 4 f., there is a poem of Type B, consisting first of a dialogue between Hervör and a shepherd, who directs her to her father's tomb, and then of a much longer dialogue between Hervör and her father, whom she rouses from the dead in order to get from him his famous sword. Another long poem of Type B, belonging to the same story, is the *Death-Song of Hjalmarr*, which is preserved in *Örvar-Odds Saga*, cap. 14, and (incomplete) in *Hervarar Saga*, cap. 3.[2] These two poems are evidently older than the texts in

[1] Transl. by Kershaw, *Stories and Ballads of the Far Past*, p. 87 ff.

[2] Free verse translation by Kershaw, *op. cit.* p. 148 ff. (following mainly the Hervarar Saga text).

which they are preserved; but they are not believed to be of any great antiquity. Probably they date from the time when these sagas were first composed—perhaps early in the twelfth century. Similar poems of Type B are to be found in *Halfs Saga* and elsewhere. The single-stanza pieces found in such sagas may in general be of the same origin.

It is to be observed that some of the early panegyrics and elegies are in form speech-poems of Type B. Their purpose, however, is so obvious that we shall treat them below, under Type D.

In Irish we may mention first a number of elegies[1] attributed to Gormlaith, the wife of Niall Glundub (cf. p. 335). In nine of these she laments the death of Niall; one (No. 9) is a lament for her son Domnall, while in the remaining one (No. 10) she bewails her own destitution. Not all of these can be genuine. In No. 7 she speaks of herself as married to Cerball after Niall's death, a historical mistake which is found also in the *Annals of Clonmacnoise*. Cerball died ten years before Niall. In No. 11 she speaks of her death-wound, an incident described in the same *Annals*. There is evidently therefore some connection between the poems and the *Annals*. Either the latter are derived from the former, or—what is much more likely—both are taken from the lost saga recorded in the list of sagas in the *Book of Leinster* (cf. p. 334). In that case most, if not all, of the poems may belong to Type B.

The story of *Cellachan of Cashel* (cf. p. 335) contains numerous speech-poems, and there are a good number also in the *War of the Gaedhil with the Gaill*. The speakers are usually kings or princes; and the poems themselves are for the most part of a character which belongs properly rather to Type D than to Type E—elegies, celebrations of victory, exhortations to battle, etc. Sometimes they give information which is not to be found in the prose. Thus Cellachan in cap. 44 speaks of Eric (Blood-Axe), who is not mentioned elsewhere in the story. Yet they can hardly be what they profess to be, although we may believe that Irish princes did cultivate poetry. We may refer, for example, to the poems recited before and during the naval fight at Dundalk, where Cellachan is bound to the mast (cap. 58 ff.), and more especially to the dialogue poems. In the *War*, cap. 54, one of the latter, a dialogue between Brian and Mathgamain—preserved only in one MS.—is said to be composed by 'the poet' (*fili*). It would seem probable that such poems were usually composed by saga-tellers, who, following the model of heroic saga, attributed to their heroes such speeches as they thought appropriate to the occasion. We can believe, however, that the earliest

[1] Ed. and transl. by Bergin in the *Miscellany presented to K. Meyer*, p. 343 ff.

examples of such poems may date from times when the memory of the events was still fresh, and that occasionally they may contain reminiscences of words actually spoken by the princes in question. On the other hand, we are not inclined to doubt the genuineness of the poems attributed to Mac Liac and other poets—although the distinction may seem somewhat arbitrary.

We know of little evidence for (post-heroic) poetry of Type B in England or in Greece, though we do not doubt that it was cultivated to some extent. For the former we may quote the speech of the peasant woman to Alfred, alluded to on p. 336: "Will you not turn the cakes which you see burning? You are glad enough to eat them when they are cooked". For Greek we may refer to the oracle said by Herodotos (I. 65) to have been given to Lycurgos at Delphoi.

Under Type D we have hitherto included only panegyrics and elegies. In addition to these post-heroic poetry furnishes examples of other pieces which may conveniently be treated under this heading, though they are of a somewhat different character—such as hortatory addresses and poems composed in celebration of victories and other public occasions. We are not aware that any parallels to these are to be found in heroic poetry, except incidentally in the course of narratives, as in *Il.* XVI. 269 ff., XXII. 391 ff. Mention may also be made here of prophecies, curses and spells, so far as these relate to political events.

It will be convenient again to begin with the Norse evidence, which is by far the fullest and the most varied. The poems are mostly fragmentary, and their language is unfortunately often very obscure; but with the help of the sagas, which are partly based upon them, they enable us to trace the history of the North fairly well from the time of Harold the Fair-haired. The two earliest poets who require notice here, Thorbjörn Hornklofi and Thjóðolfr of Hvín, both belonged to Harold's court. Considerable fragments of their poems are preserved, especially of the *Glymdrápa*, a poem in which the former seems to have celebrated Harold's battles and exploits seriatim.

Another work of the same poet is the poem now generally known as *Hrafnsmál* or *Haraldskvaeði*[1]—the ancient title has not been preserved. We include it here because it is obviously intended as a panegyric upon King Harold; but in form it belongs properly to Type B. The opening of the poem is as follows: "Hearken, Noblemen, while I celebrate Harold the magnificent and his feats of arms. I will tell of the words

[1] Ed. and transl. by Kershaw, *Anglo-Saxon and Norse Poems*, p. 76 ff.

which I heard spoken by a maiden fair and golden-haired, as she held converse with a raven. The Valkyrie...with white throat and sparkling eyes greeted the skull-picker of Hymir, as he sat on a jutting ledge of rock. 'How is it with you, ye ravens? Whence are ye come with bloody beak at the dawning of day? Torn flesh is hanging from your talons, and a reek of carrion comes from your beaks. I doubt not that ye have passed the night amid a scene of carnage'. The sworn brother of the eagle shook his dusky plumage, wiped his beak, and thought upon his answer: 'We have followed Harold, the son of Halfdan, the youthful scion of Yngvi, ever since we came out of the egg'". Then the raven goes on to describe Harold's ships and the life at his court, the warriors, the poets and the jesters there, in answer to the Valkyrie's questions. The poem is evidently incomplete.

In connection with this piece mention may be made of a fragment relating to the battle of Hafsfjord,[1] which many scholars—erroneously in our opinion[2]—believe to have belonged to the same poem. Most of our ancient authorities attribute it to Thjóðolfr of Hvín, a poet whose other works we have already had occasion to mention (cf. pp. 250, 271). The fragment appears to be not so much a panegyric as a celebration of victory. It approximates rather to Type A than to Type B, but its closest affinities are with the English poem on the *Battle of Brunanburh*. The battle of Hafsfjord was the naval action, fought about 872 in the neighbourhood of Stavanger, in which Harold defeated the allied kings of Hörðaland, Rogaland and the adjacent regions, and which finally established his power as monarch of Norway. We may quote the opening of the poem: "Hearken how the king of noble lineage fought yonder in Hafsfjord against Kjötvi the wealthy (king of Agðir). A fleet came from the east with gaping figure-heads and carved beaks, impelled by desire for battle. They were laden with warriors and white shields, with spears from the West and swords from France. The berserks were howling, the 'wolf-coats' were yelling, and swords were clashing; their warfare was in full swing. They made trial of the resolute monarch of the men of the east, who dwells at Útsteinn—he pointed them the road to flight".

A more personal note of triumph is to be found in a stanza preserved in the *Saga of Harold the Fair-haired*, cap. 32. Rögnvaldr, earl of Moeri, was slain by two of Harold's sons without their father's knowledge. One of them, Halfdan Longlegs, fled oversea to Orkney, which

[1] Ed. and transl. by Kershaw, *op. cit.* p. 88 ff.

[2] Cf. Kershaw, *op. cit.* p. 79 ff.

was under the rule of Einarr (Torf-Einarr), son of Rögnvaldr, and was eventually captured and put to death by him. The following is one of several stanzas attributed to Earl Einarr in connection with this event. They are generally believed to be genuine, since the earl was famous as a poet. "I have done my part in the vengeance for Rögnvaldr's death. Now has the pillar of the host fallen, as the Norns have decreed. Pile up the stones over Longlegs, ye brave boys, for we have won the victory. It is in (such) hard coin I pay him my dues."

Harold the Fair-haired gave up the throne about 930 to his son Eric Blood-Axe. But the latter was expelled from Norway, apparently in 935, by his younger brother Haakon I (the Good) and made his way to Orkney, where the sons of Einarr remained loyal to him. Soon afterwards, according to *Egils Saga*, cap. 59, he was entrusted by Aethelstan with the government of York—a statement which may be correct, though there is no record of the fact in the very meagre English annals of the period. The Icelander Egill Skallagrímsson had incurred Eric's mortal enmity by murdering his son and various other acts of violence in Norway. In 936 (apparently), when he was on his way to seek service—for the second time—under Aethelstan, he was shipwrecked at the mouth of the Humber and fell into Eric's hands. His friend Arinbjörn, who was Eric's chief officer, persuaded him to take the somewhat unheroic course of pretending that he had come of his own free will to make his peace with the king by means of a panegyric which he had composed in his honour. A respite of one night was given him, in which he managed to compose the *Höfuðlausn* or 'Ransom for his head' (i.e. life), which is still preserved complete. The opening stanzas may be quoted, though it is impossible to reproduce the far-fetched kennings or poetic periphrases of the original: "I have made my way to the West[1] across the sea, carrying with me the mead of poetry. Such is the reason of my journey. I launched my (ship of) oak when the ice was breaking up. I loaded the barque of my memory with a cargo[2] of panegyric. The prince has offered me an opportunity; I am commissioned to produce a song of praise. I bring Othin's mead to the land of the English. I have striven to celebrate the prince—assuredly I will glorify him. I beg for a hearing from him, since I have composed a song of praise". In forming an opinion of this poem it is perhaps as well to bear in mind the circumstances in which it was composed and the statement,

[1] A static expression for the British Isles, from whatever direction they may be approached.

[2] The metaphor means properly a cargo of fish.

attributed to Egill in the saga, that he had never before occupied himself with preparing panegyrics upon King Eric.

For Aethelstan himself Egill composed a panegyric, of which only one stanza has been preserved. The poem had a refrain: "The highest mountains now lie beneath (the sway of) the valiant Aethelstan". According to the saga (cap. 55) this poem was composed during Egill's first visit to England, shortly after the beginning of Aethelstan's reign; but the course of events as related in cap. 51–55 cannot be strictly historical. It would seem that memories of the battle of Brunanburh, fought in 937, had been confused by tradition with those of an earlier battle, fought about ten years before—perhaps against Guthfrith—in which Egill's brother Thórolfr was killed. It is not impossible that Egill may have been present at both of these.

After Aethelstan's death York fell for a short time into the hands of the kings of Dublin. Eric Blood-Axe seems to have recovered it more than once. But in 954 he was finally expelled by Eadred; and shortly afterwards he was ambushed,[1] apparently by his Dublin enemies, in Stainmoor Forest and slain with several other princes of his own and the Orkney families. His death forms the subject of the *Eiríksmál*,[2] a fragmentary elegy by an unknown poet, probably composed in Orkney; but the treatment is wholly imaginative. In form the poem follows Type B, like the *Hrafnsmál*; but the scene is laid in Valhalla. Othin dreams that he is welcoming a prince; and on awaking hears the sound of an approaching host. He calls out to his champions: "Sigmundr and Sinfjötli! Arise quickly and go to meet the prince. If it be Eric, invite him in! I have now confident hope that it is he". "Why dost thou hope for Eric rather than for other kings?" asks Sigmundr. "Because he has reddened his sword in many a land", replies Othin, "and carried a bloodstained blade."

Haakon I reigned over Norway c. 934–960, but was eventually slain by the sons of Eric, who succeeded him. His exploits were celebrated by Guthormr Sindri in a poem of which considerable fragments remain. More famous, however, is the elegy[3] on his death composed by Eyvindr Finnsson (cf. p. 271), nicknamed Skaldaspillir or 'Plagiarist'. Eyvindr was present at the battle, but the treatment is purely imaginative.

[1] The Norse account, given in the *Saga of Haakon the Good*, cap. 4, speaks of a battle and differs in other respects from the English authorities (*Saxon Chronicle*, Symeon of Durham and Matthew Paris), which we have followed and which are doubtless correct.

[2] Ed. and transl. by Kershaw, *Anglo-Saxon and Norse Poems*, p. 93 ff.

[3] Ed. and transl. by Kershaw, *op. cit.* p. 101 ff.

(St. 1) "Göndul and Skögul (two Valkyries) were sent by Gautatýr (i.e. Othin) to choose a king of Yngvi's race, who should go to join Othin and dwell in Valhalla". Then follows a description of the king's prowess, in high-flown metaphorical diction, without factual details. Then (st. 11) "the prince heard what the noble Valkyries were saying. Thoughtful was their mien, as they sat on their steeds, with helmets upon their heads, holding their shields before them. 'Why hast thou thus decided the battle, Geir-Skögul?' asked Haakon, 'Surely we have deserved victory of the gods!' 'We have brought it about', replied Skögul, 'that thou hast won the day, and that thy foes have fled'". Then (st. 14) the scene changes to Valhalla, where Othin orders Hermóðr and Bragi to welcome the king. This part is obviously suggested by the *Eiríksmál*. The last stanza (21), if not the whole poem,[1] would seem to have been composed some time after Haakon's death; for it refers to the distress which prevailed during the next reign: "Cattle are dying, kinsfolk are dying,[2] land and realm are laid waste; and many people have been reduced to bondage since Haakon passed away to the heathen gods".

The praises of Harold II (c. 960–975), son of Eric, were sung by Glúmr Geirason, an Icelander, in a poem of which some fragments are preserved. But Eyvindr composed some stanzas in which he contrasted Haakon's generosity with the miserliness of Harold, who was said to have buried his gold. The result was a permanent estrangement between the king and the poet. Eyvindr, however, struck out what appears to have been a new line in poetry by composing a panegyric (the *Íslendingadrápa*) upon all the men of Iceland. The poem is lost; but in the *Saga of Harold Grey-Cloak*, cap. 18, it is said that to reward him a collection was made at the Icelandic General Assembly. A costly treasure was sent to him and came at an opportune moment, owing to the famine then prevailing in Norway.

Eyvindr Finnsson was the last Norwegian poet of whom any considerable remains have been preserved. Our records are almost exclusively Icelandic, and they preserve many fragments of poems by Icelanders who visited the courts of the subsequent rulers of Norway—Earl Haakon the Great (c. 975–995), King Ólafr Tryggvason (995–1000), Earl Eric, son of Haakon (1000–1015), St Olaf (1016–1028),

[1] In st. 18 Haakon is approved for having dealt reverently with the sanctuaries—which his successors are said to have outraged. Both he and they—and doubtless also Eric himself in his later years—were Christians. But the new religion seems to have been confined practically to those who had lived in the British Isles.

[2] This line is perhaps a quotation from the *Hávamál*, st. 76 f.

Magnus the Good (1035–1047), and Harold III (Hardrada, 1046–1066). Indeed it became the custom for the sons of wealthy Icelanders to visit the courts of various foreign rulers and to produce odes in their honour. Thus at the beginning of the eleventh century Gunnlaugr Ormstunga, a grandson of Egill Skallagrímsson, visited in succession the courts of Earl Eric, the ruler of Norway, Aethelred, king of England, Sigtryggr II, king of Dublin, Sigurðr II, earl of Orkney, and Ólafr, king of Sweden. At the first place he lost his temper and was expelled; but the other four princes rewarded him handsomely. The refrains of his odes to Aethelred and Sigtryggr have been preserved: "The whole nation regards the generous ruler of England as a god. The valiant princely stock and men (in general) bow down to Aethelred". The other refrain is very brief: "Sigtryggr feeds the witch's steed (i.e. the wolf) with the bodies of the slain"; but the king was so pleased—perhaps at being credited with such martial prowess—that his treasurer had to restrain him from giving an extravagant reward.

Perhaps the most important of all these poems, from the historical point of view, is the *Vellekla* ('Dearth of Gold'), composed by Einarr Helgason in honour of Earl Haakon. It celebrates the earl's vengeance for his father, his battles in support of the Danes against the Saxons (the emperor Otto II), his return to Norway, where he established himself as supreme ruler after expelling the sons of Eric, and his restoration of the sanctuaries. In *Egils Saga*, cap. 78, it is stated that the earl would not listen to the poem until Einarr threatened to transfer his service to Earl Sigvaldi of Jómsborg, Haakon's chief enemy. Then he gave him a costly shield, which Einarr on his return home presented to Egill Skallagrímsson. Mention should also be made here of the poet Hallfreðr, and especially of his elegy on the death of Ólafr Tryggvason.

Next we may take the *Darraðarljóð*,[1] since it is introduced in *Njáls Saga* as applying to the battle of Clontarf, in 1014. This is a work of the imaginative kind, like the *Hrafnsmál* and the elegies upon Eric and Haakon the Good. It is a poem of Type B in the form of a weaving spell sung by Valkyries at a loom; but its object would seem to be the celebration of a victory. In *Njáls Saga*, cap. 156, it is introduced in the form of a vision seen and heard by a man called Dörruðr in Caithness on Good Friday, 1014. This was the day on which Brian Boruma, high-king of Ireland, fought the battle of Clontarf, near Dublin, against Maelmorda, king of Leinster, Sigurðr II, earl of Orkney, and a crowd of

[1] Ed. and transl. by Kershaw, *Anglo-Saxon and Norse Poems*, p. 111 ff., where the various problems relating to it are discussed.

adventurers, Norse, English and Welsh, whom King Sigtryggr had brought together, though he himself remained neutral. But Dörruðr is an obvious fiction, derived from the refrain *Vindum, vindum vef darraðar*, 'we are weaving, weaving the web of the spear'—a periphrasis for 'battle' which occurs in Egill's *Höfuðlausn*, nearly eighty years before Clontarf. We may also compare the term *mórenglaim*, 'great woof', applied to 'battle' in the (Irish) *Address to Cerball's Sword*, more than twenty years earlier still (see below). There is a passage in st. 7 f. which might refer to the deaths of Sigurðr and Brian, and which doubtless was so interpreted in Iceland: "Even now the earl has been laid low by the spears. The Irish too will suffer a sorrow which will never be forgotten by men. Now the web has been woven and the field dyed crimson. The news of the disaster will travel throughout the world". But the main theme of the poem is the success and fame of a young king. Thus (st. 10) "many spells of victory have we chanted well for the young king. May we have luck in our singing! And may he who hearkens to the Spear-maidens' lay learn it and tell it to men". This cannot be Brian—who was seventy-three—although the sympathy of the saga is wholly on his side. And it can hardly have been Sigtryggr—who must have been at least forty—for according to the Irish account he took no part in the battle. One passage in the poem (st. 7) points to an earlier date: "The people who have hitherto occupied only the outlying headlands shall have dominion over the land". This passage clearly reflects the conditions which prevailed when the Norse power was restored, about a century before the battle of Clontarf. We suspect therefore that the poem was originally composed to celebrate the battle, fought at Dublin in 919, in which Sigtryggr I, the grandfather of his later namesake, defeated and slew the high-king Niall Glundub.[1]

The poems discussed above are in general, so far as tone or feeling is concerned, such as might have been composed in the Heroic Age. It is only rarely that we have noticed any trace of national feeling in opposition to a king. Such is the case in certain of Eyvindr's poems referred to above; and an earlier example occurs in *Egils Saga*, cap. 56, where Egill applies the term *folkmýgir*, 'oppressor of the nation', to Eric, and calls upon the gods to expel him from the country. But we hardly meet with anything which can be described as political criticism before the eleventh century. The most notable case is that of the Icelandic poet Sigvatr, who was in the service of St Olaf. This king's government was so oppressive that in 1028 he had to leave the country; and when he

[1] Cf. Kershaw, *Anglo-Saxon and Norse Poems*, p. 117.

attempted to recover his position, in 1030, he was defeated and killed at Stiklestad. His son Magnus the Good was more fortunate; but having obtained the throne, in 1035, he set his mind on reprisals against those who had led the rising against his father. His councillors were entirely opposed to this policy, and Sigvatr, who was a man of great influence, was chosen to point out to the young king his folly.[1] This he did in a poem known as *Bersöglisvísur*, or 'Stanzas of plain speech'. He begins by recalling the memory of Haakon the Good, whose laws are still kept and whose name will never be forgotten. Then, after referring to Ólafr Tryggvason and the king's father, he goes on to say that Magnus must not be offended with his advisers for speaking plainly. The people are complaining that they are not being governed as he had promised. Who is inciting you to go back upon your words? A king must be true to what he has said. It is never fitting for you to break your promises. Who is inciting you to destroy the property of your subjects? A prince who stirs up warfare within his country shows too martial a spirit. He adds that the men of Sogn are already rising. We will support you with our arms. But how long is the country to be divided? The appeal was successful, and Magnus changed his policy. He is credited with having had the laws committed to writing for the first time—a much disputed statement, to which we shall have to refer in a later chapter.

So far we have noticed only poems relating to rulers or to events of national importance. Numerous elegies, mostly short, on persons in private life are also preserved. Perhaps the longest and most famous is Egill Skallagrímsson's *Sonatorrek* or 'Loss of (my) Sons'.[2] In the saga, cap. 78, it is stated that Egill lost two of his sons within a short time; one of them was drowned at sea. He was so distressed that he shut himself up in his bedroom and refused all food and drink. His daughter Thorgerðr, the wife of Ólafr Pái, was sent for; and she gradually persuaded him to compose an elegy on his sons, which she offered to take down on a rod. His spirits revived with the effort, and he returned to the family circle. The poem contains a number of difficult metaphors, and the diction is frequently far from clear. The following (st. 6 ff.) is one of the more straightforward passages: "The rent which the waves have made in the pale of my father's family has been harrowing to me. Empty and unoccupied I see the place from which

[1] Cf. the *Saga of Magnus the Good* (*Heimskr.*), cap. 16.

[2] Ed. and transl. by Kershaw, *Anglo-Saxon and Norse Poems*, p. 126 ff. (together with translation of the passage in the saga).

the sea has torn my son. Greatly has Rán afflicted me. I have been despoiled of a dear friend. The sea has rent the ties of my kindred and torn a stout thread from me myself. Know that if I could have avenged my cause with my sword, the Ale-brewer would have been no more". The allusion here is to the sea-giant Aegir, who in the *Lokasenna* (cf. p. 248) entertains the gods at a banquet. Rán is his wife, who catches the drowned in her net. Such references to mythology are extremely frequent.

As an example of a brief elegy we may quote that of the same poet on his brother Thórolfr, contained in cap. 55 of the saga: "Thórolfr the bold-hearted, the slayer of the earl, he who feared nothing, strode forth valiantly and fell in Thundr's (i.e. Othin's) great uproar. Near Vina the earth is green over my noble brother. That is a deadly sorrow; but we will suppress our grief". Some scholars doubt the genuineness of this stanza, owing to the resemblance between the name *Vina* and *Weondun*, which is given by Symeon of Durham as an alternative name for Brunanburh. It is clear that Thórolfr was killed some time before the battle of Brunanburh; but the identification of the two names is not convincing.[1]

From the illustrations given above it will be seen that Norse poetry of Type D shows a large amount of variety. And this applies not only to the choice and the treatment of the subject, but also to the metrical form of the poems. The 'imaginative' pieces are in the *Edda* metres, which are no doubt of purely Teutonic origin. The *Darraðarljóð* is in the *Fornyrðislag* metre (cf. p. 29). The *Hrafnsmál* is in the *Málaháttr*, and so also is the ('non-imaginative') poem on the *Battle of Hafsfjord*. The *Eiríksmál* and the *Hákonarmál* are partly in the *Málaháttr* and partly in the *Ljóðaháttr*. The rest of the poems are in what were probably new metres. The *Kviðuháttr* used in Egill's *Sonatorrek*—as also in Thjóðolfr's *Ynglingatal* (cf. p. 271)—is doubtless only a modification of the *Fornyrðislag*, with the first half-line shortened. But the other metres show rhyme or assonance, as well as alliteration, and can hardly be of native origin. The *Rúnhent*, which has end-rhyme, is used in Egill's *Höfuðlausn* and in Gunnlaugr's ode to King Sigtryggr; and analogies are to be found in a few Anglo-Saxon poems. Far more frequent,

[1] We are much inclined to doubt if cap. 51–55 of the saga are derived from early saga tradition. We suspect that they were largely made up at a later date from Egill's poems, augmented by conventional battle-scenes. The stanza which follows the elegy on Thórolfr need not originally have been connected with it. It does not refer to him.

however, is the *Dróttkvaett*, which has internal rhyme or assonance; this is the usual metre in pieces which consist of a single stanza and is employed also in some of the longer poems noticed above. The exigencies of the metre often cause an unnatural order of the words in a sentence—which, taken together with the interweaving of sentences and an extravagant use of periphrases, renders the interpretation of poems in this metre very difficult.

Lastly, it may be remarked that—in contrast with the *Edda* poems—the poetry treated above is almost always of known authorship. Among the poems which we have noticed the only exceptions are the *Eiríksmál* and the *Darraðarljóð*. But it is probably due to a mere accident that the name of the author of the former is not recorded.

In Irish numerous short fragments of panegyrics are preserved in grammatical tracts.[1] The earliest date from the last century of the Heroic Age, but the great majority belong to later times. They are mostly addressed to kings and princes, and in their general character resemble the Norse panegyrics noticed above. A number of abusive poems, directed against enemies of the poets or their patrons, are preserved in the same tracts.

Fragments of elegies, mostly preserved in Annals, are nearly as numerous.[2] The earliest of these also date from the Heroic Age. From later times, however, a few examples have been preserved complete.[3] They have much more in common with Welsh heroic elegies (cf. p. 38) than with the Norse poems treated above. The elegies of Gormlaith for Niall Glundub, noticed on p. 340, whether they are genuine or poems of Type B, are of very similar character. Here also we may mention a number of elegies contained in the story of Cellachan of Cashel. Some of these are presumably to be referred to Type B (BD). Such is the case with the elegy attributed to Cellachan in cap. 42, when he is captured and the heads of his followers are brought to him to identify on the Green of Dublin. Similar cases occur in cap. 75 and 84. On the other hand, the poems in cap. 70 and 78 are not given as speeches in character and may perhaps be derived from contemporary elegies. In any case it is on such elegies that all the poems seem to be based. The *War of the Gaedhil with the Gaill* also contains two elegies, both on the death of Mathgamain, the elder brother of Brian Boruma, in 976. The

[1] A large number are ed. and transl. by K. Meyer, *Bruchstücke der älteren Lyrik Irlands* (Abh. d. pr. Akad., 1919), pp. 5 ff.

[2] Cf. K. Meyer, *op. cit.* p. 37 ff.

[3] Two are transl. by K. Meyer, *Ancient Irish Poetry*, p. 76 ff.

first (cap. 59) is attributed to Brian himself, the second (cap. 62) to Mathgamain's 'blind man' (poet). The latter at least of these may perhaps be derived from a contemporary elegy. But it contains (st. 9) a reference to a prophecy of Brian's high-kingship, which he did not acquire until about twenty-six years later; so that additions would seem to have been made to it.

Next we may mention the *Address to Cerball's Sword*,[1] a poem the object of which is to celebrate the victories won by Cerball, king of Leinster (c. 885–909), and his ancestors. Cerball was the second husband of the Gormlaith whose elegies have been discussed above. The poem seems to have been composed very soon after his death, and is attributed to his chief poet, Dallan mac More. The first stanza is as follows: "Hail, O Sword of Cerball! Often hast thou been in the great woof. Often hast thou been giving battle and taking off the heads of high monarchs". The reference to the 'woof' (of battle) suggests a connection between this poem and the *Darraðarljóð* (cf. p. 346 f.). Possibly the idea of the latter was derived from this passage.

Poems which celebrate specific victories over the Norse are to be found in the story of Cellachan, cap. 19 and 89, and also in the *War*, cap. 54, 67 and 68. The first of the latter is a dialogue (Type B) between Brian and Mathgamain, and the examples from the story of Cellachan are probably to be referred to the same Type. They may, however, be taken as giving some impression of what Type D poems of this kind were like. A fragment of such a poem, also apparently referring to a victory over the Norse, is preserved in a grammatical tract.[2]

For an example of hortatory poetry we may refer to the poem given in the story of Cellachan, cap. 10, in which the warriors of Munster are summoned to attack the Norse city of Limerick. We may quote the first stanza: "Come ye to Limerick of the ships, O children of Eogan, ye of mighty exploits! Around the gentle Cellachan (come) to Limerick of the riveted stones". We know of no parallels to this in Norse; but in its general character the poem is not unlike those of Tyrtaios (cf. p. 355), though it is more personal. Further examples may be found in the same work, cap. 45 and 91, and also in the *War*, cap. 58, where there is an appeal to the Gaill of Limerick and their Munster allies. Note may also

[1] Ed. and transl. by K. Meyer, *Rev. Celt.* XX. 7 ff.; transl. only in *Ancient Irish Poetry*, p. 72 ff.

[2] Ed. and transl. by K. Meyer, *Bruchstücke*, p. 14; transl. only in *Ancient Irish Poetry*, p. 75. The date 994 assigned to the piece in the latter seems to have been given up in the *Bruchstücke*, which were published later.

be made of a poem in the latter work, cap. 73, in which the poet Gilla Comgaill appeals to Aed Ua Neill to take up arms against Brian.

Hortatory poetry of a different kind is represented by a poem known as the *Rights of every Lawful King*,[1] addressed to the high-king Aed Oirdnide, perhaps at his accession, in 798. In it the king is exhorted to assert his rights, to maintain justice and to respect the Church. It may be compared with the *Bersöglisvísur*, though the tendency is different and the matter is much more general. The gnomic element is large; and we shall therefore revert to the poem again in the next chapter. It may, however, be observed here that the author was probably following a custom usual, if not traditional, in his days; for there exist several gnomic 'Instructions' addressed to kings of the Heroic Age, the earliest of which seem to date from about the same time. These also will be noticed in the next chapter.

Welsh poems of Type D dating from the twelfth and following centuries are numerous. They include panegyrics, elegies, and pieces celebrating victories and other public occasions. But these fall outside our period. The earliest poem which can be dated with confidence is a kind of short elegy by Meilyr upon Trahaearn, king of Gwynedd, who was defeated and slain by Gruffydd, son of Cynan, at the battle of Mynydd Carn in 1081. But it is in the form of a prophecy; the poet uses the future both for the battle and for the king's death. Two difficult and obscure poems (*BBC.* III, IV) by a poet called Cuhelyn may be of earlier date. They appear to be panegyrics; but we know nothing either of the poet or of the persons to whom they are addressed. One of them seems to be in honour of a prince called Aeddan. The only Welsh prince of this name known to us is Aeddan son of Blegywryd, who was killed in 1018 by Llywelyn, son of Seisyll.

Mention should perhaps be made here of a number of prophetic (predictive) poems, the purpose of which appears to be partly hortatory and partly to celebrate public events, though the names of contemporary persons are rarely given. On the whole, however, we think it better to treat these poems in Ch. XV, in connection with prophecies of other kinds.

In English the most important example of Type D is the poem on the battle of *Brunanburh*,[2] preserved in the *Saxon Chronicle*, *ann.* 937. This place, now usually identified with Birrenswark, near Ecclefechan, was

[1] Ed. and transl. by O'Donoghue in the *Miscellany presented to K. Meyer*, p. 258 ff.

[2] Ed. and transl. by Kershaw, *Anglo-Saxon and Norse Poems*, p. 59 ff.

the scene of a great victory won by Aethelstan over the allied forces of Constantine II, king of Scots, and Anlaf (Ólafr II), king of Dublin. The poem begins by praising the valour of Aethelstan and his brother Edmund, but it goes on to celebrate the prowess of the English troops, both West Saxon and Mercian: "All day long the West Saxons with troops of horse pressed on in pursuit of the enemies' forces.... Nor did the Mercians refuse hard fighting to any of the warriors who in the ship's bosom had followed Anlaf over the tossing waters to our land to meet their doom in battle". It is a national, not heroic, song of triumph. A large part of it is devoted to exulting over the defeated foes. (37 ff.) "There also the aged Constantine, the grey-haired warrior, set off in flight to his country in the north. No cause had he to exult in that clash of arms. He was bereaved of his kinsmen and friends, who had been cut down in the struggle and lay lifeless on the field of battle.... Then the sorry remnant of the Norsemen, who had escaped the spears, set out upon the sea of Dinge (?) in their nail-studded ships, making for Dublin over the deep waters. Humiliated in spirit they returned to Ireland."

From this point onwards the Chronicle contains various other entries in verse; but most of them do not come within the scope of our work. Some of them are merely metrical annals, obviously composed by the annalists themselves for the places which they occupy in the Chronicle. Such is the case, for example, with the metrical entries in *ann.* 942 (MSS. ABCD), 973 and 975 (ABC). They may be regarded as precursors of the metrical chronicles of later times. Other poems may have been composed independently of the Chronicle, but yet intended for a reading public. It is probable that before the end of the tenth century reading was a fairly widespread accomplishment among the upper classes. Along with these may be mentioned a number of passages in rhetorical prose, e.g. in *ann.* 959, 979 (MS. E), 1011 (CDE), which conform to Type D, though we have no doubt that they were written from the beginning. They are of a homiletic character and were probably written by ecclesiastics, whether for the Chronicle or not. Of poems which may perhaps have been intended for oral production the elegies on the deaths of Edgar and of Prince Alfred may be cited, in *ann.* 975 (DE) and 1036 (C) respectively. They show a partial adoption of rhyme in place of alliteration. Poems celebrating the marriages of prominent persons were also perhaps recited for public entertainment. William of Malmesbury, II. 188, says that a poem on the marriage of Gunnhild, daughter of Canute, with the Emperor Henry III, was still current in this way (*in triuiis cantitata*) even in his own time—more than eighty years after the event.[1]

In Greek no panegyrics of this period have been preserved, so far as we are aware. The Odes of Pindar, composed in honour of athletes and their patrons, belong to a later date; and so also the fragments of panegyrics upon princes, by Simonides of Ceos and others. We see no reason for doubting that such poems were composed in the period with which we are concerned—in honour of the 'Tyrants', who ruled in many cities, or of hereditary princes in more backward parts of the country—but we cannot cite any references to their existence. On the other hand, there is abundant evidence for diatribes in poetry against the leaders of political factions to whom the authors were opposed. Many fragments of such poems by Alcaios have been preserved. Most of them are directed against the dictator Pittacos.

No elegies upon rulers or political leaders appear to have been preserved from our period. Perhaps the nearest approach to such is to be found in an epitaph in hexameters upon a tomb of the sixth century in Corfu:[2] "This is the monument of Menecrates, son of Tlasias, a native of Oianthe; but the citizens (of Corfu) made this for him, for he was a beloved consul of the citizens. But he perished at sea....And this monument was constructed for him, with the cooperation of the citizens, by his brother Praximenes, who had come from his own country". Short memorial pieces of this type are quite common. They belong no doubt essentially to the age of writing, though the opening formula occurs in the *Iliad* (VII. 89). But the type may well have originated, as in Runic epitaphs, at a time when writing was seldom used for literary purposes. Here also we may quote an epitaph on a girl, ascribed to Sappho:[3] "This is the dust of Timas, who died unmarried and passed into the dark chamber of Persephone; and at her death all her companions devoted to the newly whetted steel the lovely hair of their heads".

Longer elegies are not wanting, though they are preserved only in fragments. We may quote from a poem of Archilochos, addressed to a certain Pericles and evidently relating to the death of a relative or

[1] Possibly, however, this was not a poem of Type D, but part of a narrative poem which related Gunnhild's adventures seriatim (cf. p. 338), after the manner of the Romances. The poem on the marriage of Margaret with Malcolm III, quoted in the Chronicle, *ann.* 1067 (D), can hardly have been intended for recitation, except perhaps in religious houses.

[2] Cauer, *Delectus Inscr. Graec.* (1883), p. 54 f.; Solmsen, *Inscr. Graec.* (1910), p. 47 f.

[3] Fragm. 119; cf. Edmonds, *Lyra Graeca*, I, p. 280 f.

friend who has been lost at sea:[1] "Neither the city itself nor any of its inhabitants will take pleasure in feasts, Pericles. They are murmuring at their grievous loss; for such (i.e. so beloved) were they whom the waves of the loud-roaring sea have engulfed. Our hearts are swollen with grief, but the gods, my friend, have devised mighty patience as a balm for incurable ills. Trouble comes first to one, then to another. Now it has fallen upon us, and we groan over a bloody wound; but soon it will pass on to others. Have patience, and put away womanly sorrow as soon as may be". To the same poem probably belongs the following fragment, among others: "Let us hide (perhaps 'bury') the grievous gifts of Lord Poseidon". It is interesting to compare this poem with Egill's *Sonatorrek*, which was composed for a similar occasion. To the modern reader the straightforward style of the Greek poet appeals far more than the affectations of the Icelander.

With Egill's elegy on his brother (cf. p. 349) we may compare a fragment (No. 14) of Mimnermos, which seems to have been part of an elegy on a warrior. The hero's name is not preserved; but the men of the last generation "saw him piercing the serried ranks of Lydian cavalry upon the plain of the Hermos.... He dashed forth in the forefront, in the roar of bloody battle, defying the sharp arrows of his foes".

Hortatory poetry is fairly well represented. The poems in which Tyrtaios rouses the Spartans to battle with the Messenians may be compared with such Irish poems as the one quoted on p. 351, in which the men of Munster are summoned to the attack upon Limerick. But the Greek poems are of a much more general character—tending towards the gnomic—a feature which is even more marked in the only surviving long fragment of Callinos. As an example of this kind of poetry we may take Tyrtaios, fragm. 11: "Now take courage, since ye are the offspring of invincible Heracles. Not yet has Zeus averted his countenance. Have no concern or fear owing to the numbers of your foes; but let every man go straight into the forefront, shield in hand, counting life hateful and the black fate of death as dear as the rays of the sun". Such sentiments recur again and again in these poems.

It should be observed that what Callinos and Tyrtaios appeal to is the spirit of patriotism, not that of personal loyalty to kings, as in heroic poetry. Kings continued to reign in Sparta; but Tyrtaios does not often refer to them. His constant theme is the duty of the individual to

[1] Fragm. 9 ff. Fragm. 12 f. are quoted by Plutarch as referring to the death at sea of the poet's brother-in-law; and some scholars believe these fragments to come from the same poem. For the following passages see note on p. 422.

sacrifice himself to the state. For his attitude to the state we may compare another fragment, from a political poem:[1] "Thus did the lord of the silver bow, Apollo of the golden hair, proclaim from his rich sanctuary, that the kings honoured by the gods, who have under their charge the beautiful city of Sparta—that they and the elders of senior rank should be leaders in counsel, while the men of the commons, who own obedience to straightforward laws, should cultivate honourable speech and justice in all their acts, and devise no evil for the city".

Many fragments of political poetry have been preserved from this period; and everywhere it is in the state or city that the poets' interest is centred. Alcaios seems in more than one poem to have compared his city, Mytilene, which was torn with factions, to a ship foundering among rocks. From Solon we have fragments of a poem[2] in which he roused the Athenians to seize the island of Salamis. This may be compared with the hortatory poems of Tyrtaios, though it would seem to have been of a more specific character. "Then may I change my country and be a citizen of Pholegandros or of Sicinos"—two small islands in the Aegean —"rather than an Athenian; for we should soon have people saying this kind of thing: 'There is a man from Attica, the state which gave up Salamis'." And again: "Let us go to Salamis, to fight for the lovely island and to wipe off our sore disgrace".

Solon, however, was the author of other poems, of a political character, for which no parallels are to be found in the poetry of the northern peoples. We may instance the following (fragm. 5): "To the commons I gave such authority as is fitting—I took away none of their rights, neither was I lavish in presenting them therewith—while for those who had held the power and were respected owing to their wealth, I took care that they should receive no unfair treatment. I took my stand, holding a mighty shield over both parties, and allowed neither of them to gain an unjust victory". In another poem (fragm. 36), in iambic metre—unlike the pieces quoted above, which are in the elegiac—he reviews the results of his legislation. "In the court of Time I shall receive the best of witness from Black Earth, the very great mother of the Olympian deities, from whom I removed the mortgage-stones which everywhere had been implanted in her.[3] Before that she was in slavery,

[1] Preserved by Diodoros, VII. 14.

[2] Fragm. 1 ff. (Bergk).

[3] The allusion is to Solon's measures for the relief of debtors. Much of the land had been mortgaged. According to Greek custom the mortgagee set up stone pillars on land thus acquired.

but now she is free.... These things I did by (my own) authority (as dictator), fitting together force and justice, and I carried them through as I had promised. But I put into writing equal laws for the base and the noble, fitting justice straight to every man." To the last sentence we shall have to refer again in Ch. XVI. It shows of course that we are here approaching the end of our period. Yet note should be taken of the fact that poetry is used as the vehicle of political manifestos. The author expects his words to be preserved by memory rather than in writing.

In the next chapter it will be seen that for some of Solon's other poems rather close analogies are to be found in Anglo-Saxon poetry. The parallelism is such as to suggest that he would not have found the (secular) intellectual atmosphere of Saxon England entirely unintelligible or uncongenial. With such Icelanders as Njáll, the legal expert, he would possibly have been in still closer sympathy. But he would certainly have regarded all the northern peoples as backward politically.

Lastly, it may be observed that prophetical poetry played a by no means unimportant part in the political life of post-heroic times, as may be seen, for example, from the references in Herodotos. It will be more convenient, however, to reserve all poetry of this kind for discussion in Ch. XV.

Type E, i.e. personal or occasional poetry, apart from elegies and from poems dealing with public events, is fairly well represented in Greek and abundantly in Norse. The resemblance between the two literatures here is much greater than in Type D, although the poems belonging to the two Types are frequently by the same authors. It will be convenient in this case to begin with the Greek evidence, though the material is for the most part fragmentary.

The earliest references of a personal character in Greek poetry are to be found in Hesiod's poems and at the conclusion of the Homeric *Hymn to Apollo of Delos* (cf. p. 243 f.). In the latter passage the poet bids farewell to his chorus of maidens and begs them when they are asked who it is whose minstrelsy gives them most pleasure, to say: "It is a blind man, and he dwells in rocky Chios. His minstrelsy will never be surpassed even in the future".

Hesiod in the *Theogony* (22 ff.) refers merely to the 'call' which he received from the Muses, when he was tending the sheep on Mt. Helicon. To this passage we shall have to return in a later chapter. But the *Works and Days* contains much more of a personal character.

The framework is in the form of an admonition to his brother Perses, who has unjustly deprived him of part of his patrimony. He repeatedly exhorts his brother to turn to work of various kinds for a livelihood, instead of devoting his time to lawsuits under corrupt judges. In one interesting passage (631 ff.) he relates how his father had been a trader and spent much of his life at sea. Owing to poverty he had left his home at Cyme in Aiolis and settled at Ascra, near Mt. Helicon, which is described as a bleak and unattractive place. Hesiod himself had only once been on the sea (648 ff.), when he crossed over to Chalcis to compete in a poetic contest at some funeral games. He gained a prize, which he dedicated to the Muses of Helicon.

The earliest poems of a purely personal character of which anything has been preserved are those of Archilochos, who seems to have lived about the middle of the seventh century. He belonged to the island of Paros, but served, probably as a soldier of fortune, in the south of Italy, and settled for a time in Thasos. His poems, which are known only from quotations, are believed to have been quite short; indeed some of them may be preserved complete. Passages from one of his elegies have been given above (p. 355). The fragments are in various metres, including elegiac, iambic and trochaic tetrameter.

In fragm. 1 and 2 he appears to refer to his life as a soldier: "I am a squire of the lord Enyalios (i.e. Ares), versed also in the lovely gift of the Muses". "By the spear I have the kneaded loaf, by the spear the wine of Ismaros, by the spear I can rest and drink". More famous, however, is fragm. 6: "One of the Saioi (Thracians) is exulting in the shield which I left among the bushes against my will. It was an excellent piece of armour. But I myself escaped the fate of death. So bad luck to that shield! I shall get another one which is just as good". This shows his attitude towards heroic ideals, as well as to those of militant patriots like Tyrtaios. The same attitude is perhaps to be seen in fragm. 59: "A thousand strong we are responsible for the slaughter of seven whom we overtook".

Allusions to his adventures at sea seem to occur in the following passages: (fragm. 54) "Look, Glaucos, for the deep sea is already stirred by billows, and a cloud is standing aloft around the peaks of the Gyrai, portending a storm. Danger is falling upon us unexpectedly". (fragm. 4) "Now come, take a flask and run along the benches of the swift ship. Draw the liquor from the hollow casks, and drain the red wine to the dregs; for not even we shall be able to go in for abstinence while we are engaged on this duty".

Some fragments suggest amorous interests or a susceptibility to female charms; but they are perhaps satirical rather than serious. In later times a story was current that the poet had loved the daughter of a certain Lycambes, who at first encouraged and then rejected his suit. Archilochos in revenge lampooned both the father and the daughter so bitterly that they committed suicide. Fragm. 94 would seem to be connected in some way or other with this story: "Father Lycambes, what is this you have been cogitating? Who has been turning askew that wisdom of yours, which in the past was your support? But now you are figuring as an object of great ridicule to the public".

Several fragments deal with the poet's philosophy of life. Thus in 66, which is addressed to his 'soul distraught with cares', he says: "Do not exult in public, when you are successful, and do not collapse and weep in your house, when you are beaten. But in moderation be glad when things go pleasantly, and sad when they go ill. Realise by what sort of 'rhythm' mankind is governed". By 'rhythm' (ῥυσμός) he perhaps means no more than a regular succession of ups and downs—we might say 'see-saw'—for elsewhere his thought does not seem to be abstruse; but he may of course have borrowed the term from more abstruse thinkers. We may also quote the following: (fragm. 15) "Labour and human effort provide all things for men";[1] and (fragm. 25) "I care not for Gyges[2] and his vast wealth, nor has envy of him ever come upon me. I am not indignant at the works of the gods; nor do I long for a great sovereignty, for it is beyond the vision of my eyes". (fragm. 73) "I sinned, and the penalty fell upon somebody else somewhere". Unfortunately the context is lost. The same remark applies to fragm. 63, which may perhaps be contrasted with Tyrtaios' references to the glory of dying in battle.

Sometimes Archilochos seems to be in a playful mood. We may quote fragm. 74, referring to the eclipse, probably on 6 April, 648, by which his floruit is dated: "Nothing in the world can be regarded as unexpected or impossible or marvellous since Zeus, the father of the Olympians, turned midday into night, hiding the light of the sun when it was shining, and grim terror came upon mankind. After that men may believe and expect anything. Let none of you marvel any longer at what he sees—even if wild beasts who have loved the mountains exchange

[1] A different view is taken in fragm. 16: "Fortune and Fate give all things to a man". But this fragment is addressed to Pericles, and may belong to the elegy quoted on p. 355.

[2] King of Lydia in Archilochos' time and famous for his wealth.

with dolphins and take to living in the sea, and find the roaring waves of the deep pleasanter than the land". In other fragments (86 ff.) he makes use of one or more fables, relating to a fox, an eagle and an ape, which we may suspect were made to apply to somebody in no very complimentary way. Here, as elsewhere, the absence of context is much to be regretted. Yet enough of his poetry has been preserved to indicate the wide differences between his individualism and the national collectivism of patriotic poets like Tyrtaios. Both are equally far removed from the Heroic Age.

The other poets who require notice here lived about half a century after Archilochos. A considerable number of the fragments of Alcaios' works seem to come from poems of Type E.[1] But they are much less well preserved than those of Archilochos, and it is often difficult to decide whether a fragment belongs to a political or a personal poem. The latter seem to have borne a general resemblance to Archilochos' poems, so far as one can judge of the subjects and occasions with which they are concerned; but the satirical element is apparently wanting. The metres are usually 'lyric'.

Sappho was a contemporary of Alcaios and belonged to the same city (Mytilene). Many of her poems seem to have been of Type E, and they are better preserved than those of Alcaios—especially the fragments from MSS. recently discovered in Egypt, though most of these require a good deal of restoration. Such treatment must of course be left to specialists; and as good translations are now available, we shall content ourselves here merely with references. Many of the poems appear to have been in the form of letters to Sappho's friends—chiefly women or girls. Some of these must have been fairly long, since they contain speeches. Nos. 35 and 37[2] are addressed to her brother Charaxos, and No. 36 is also concerned with him. The latter contains a most bitter reference to his mistress, Rhodopis. No. 119 is addressed to Alcaios—an indignant rebuke in reply to some remark or message from him. No. 71 makes short work of an uneducated woman, to whom it is said to be addressed. We know of no parallels to Sappho's poems in the early poetry of the north of Europe.

Solon and Mimnermos were contemporary with the last two poets; but little of their poetry comes in for consideration here. The surviving fragments of Mimnermos are chiefly occupied with descriptions of the sorrows of old age; they may be compared with the elegies of Llywarch

[1] Most of the longer fragments in Edmonds, *Lyra Graeca*, I, from No. 121 (p. 396) to the end.

[2] The references are to Edmonds, *Lyra Graeca*, I.

Hen (cf. p. 36). The surviving poems of Solon are mostly either political (cf. p. 356 f.) or philosophical; the latter will require consideration in the next chapter. We may, however, refer here to a story told of the two poets by Diogenes Laertios, I. 2. 13. One of Mimnermos' poems is said to have contained the following couplet (fragm. 6): "May the fate of death overtake me in my sixtieth year, free from diseases and grievous cares". When Solon heard this he expressed his disapproval as follows (fragm. 20): "Now if thou wilt hearken to me even now, remove this, and bear no grudge against me for having hit upon a better thought than thou. But alter thy poem and sing thus: 'May the fate of death overtake me in my eightieth year'". Fragm. 21 belongs to the same context, though it is preserved by a different authority:[1] "When my death comes, may it not be unlamented; rather may I cause my friends to grieve and mourn, when I die". We may also quote fragm. 19, Solon's farewell message to Philocypros, a prince in Cyprus, with whom he had been staying: "Now long mayest thou reign over the Solioi here and occupy this city, thou and the descendants of thy house. And may the violet crowned Cyprian goddess give me a safe voyage in my swift ship from her glorious island. May she grant her favour and glory to this new founded town, and to me a happy return to our native land". All these passages are in elegiac metre.

All these poets belong to the end of our period, and it is probable that many of their poems were written down at once and sent as letters to the persons to whom they were addressed. But oral transmission may still have been the chief channel by which they became more widely known. We may refer to a story[2] which relates how Solon once heard one of Sappho's poems from one of his relations and remarked "Let me learn it and die".

In conclusion something must be said of Alcman, a poet who lived somewhat earlier than the four just mentioned, though later than Archilochos. He belonged to the same city (Sparta) as Tyrtaios, and was apparently not more than a generation later; but the two poets have nothing in common. Most of the fragments of Alcman are very short. So far as one can judge in the absence of context, many of them seem to belong to hymns, which he composed for festivals. We hear also of love-songs and drinking songs by him. A few fragments, e.g. Nos. 46 and 130,[3] apparently come from poems of Type E. But mention

[1] Plutarch, *Comparison of Solon and Poplicola*, cap. I.

[2] Cf. Edmonds, *Lyra Graeca*, I. 140 f.

[3] The references are to Edmonds, *Lyra Graeca*, I.

may perhaps also be made here of the only long piece which survives (fragm. 1). It is a choric hymn, apparently relating to Heracles and the Dioscuroi; but the theme abruptly changes from the legendary heroes to the singers—the ladies of the chorus—who make complimentary remarks on their leader and others of their number. This part of the poem does not fall within our definition of either Type E or Type B. We think it is derived from something akin to the former, viz. the customary interchange of congratulations and criticisms among the members of the chorus when the performance was over. But this conversation—or rather the poet's idea of what it should be—has been incorporated in the ritual poem and become, so to say, part of the performance. He seems indeed to have given as much care to this as to the traditional element—which probably means that it was taken into account by the judges of the competition. It cannot, as it stands, be treated as an example of Type E; for it is not composed by the performers themselves. On the whole it is nearer to Type B. But the speeches are not speeches in character; the performers speak as themselves, though in words composed for them. We know of no parallel to this in the early poetry of the northern peoples. Perhaps the nearest approach is to be found in the epilogues added by minstrels or reciters to heroic poems; but these are less personal than the epilogue to the *Hymn to Apollo of Delos* (cf. p. 357).

In Norway personal poetry can be traced back to the ninth century. Indeed there are examples as early as those of any other kind of poetry from that country in its present form, though some of the poems treated in the previous chapters have doubtless a longer history behind them.

From the tenth and eleventh centuries a large amount of personal poetry has been preserved, chiefly in sagas. It consists for the most part of single stanzas composed on various occasions by the characters of the sagas. The narratives in which they are incorporated give the context and therefore furnish us with more help towards the interpretation of these poems than we are able to obtain in the case of the Greek fragments discussed above. Sometimes, however, in stories dealing with the early part of the tenth century, the narrative seems to be based upon the verses, while in other cases it may be suspected that stanzas have been invented not unfrequently by saga-tellers to fit the narrative. As remarked above (p. 339), it is often difficult and even impossible to distinguish with certainty between Types E and B.

The metrical form of these poems is most commonly the *Dróttkvaett*, of which there are several varieties. The exigencies of this rather complicated metre, as remarked above, tended to produce an obscure and difficult style; and there is no doubt that this was exaggerated intentionally by the poets themselves. Two features in particular repel the modern reader. One is the habit of 'interweaving' two or three distinct sentences in such a way that a literal translation in English would be wholly unintelligible. Even such words as 'and' are frequently displaced. The other is the cultivation to an extravagant degree of kennings or poetic periphrases. From Snorri's *Skaldskaparmál* ('Language of Poetry') the meaning of many of these is known. Yet there remain a good number of stanzas which in whole or part have not been satisfactorily explained. In the following quotations no attempt has been made to preserve either the interweavings or the more extravagant kennings.

The earliest poetry of this kind is attributed to Bragi Boddason, who lived probably before 850. Harold the Fair-haired had several famous poets in his service (cf. p. 341); but the cultivation of poetry of this kind appears to have been pretty general in his day among the upper classes, both men and women. One of the king's sons, named Guðröðr, was brought up by Thjóðolfr of Hvín. He fell into disfavour with his father, and the aged poet used his influence to obtain a reconciliation. They went to the court together in disguise while a feast was in progress. Then said the king:[1] "In great numbers have my heroes of old arrived, even those whose hair is white, exceeding eager for the feast. Why are so very many of you come?" Thjóðolfr replied: "In the service of the wise and generous prince we received wounds in our heads when the swords were clashing. Then there were not too many of us". Then he removed his cloak, and the king recognised him and made him welcome. Each of these speeches occupies half a stanza.

Rögnvaldr, earl of Moeri, one of Harold's right-hand men, had married Hildr, the daughter of a certain Hrólfr Nefja; and one of their sons was called Hrólfr after his grandfather. This son was banished by Harold for piracy. His mother tried without success to induce the king to reverse his sentence. The following stanza is attributed to her:[2] "Ye are driving and hunting out of the country him who is called after Nefja, the wise brother of heroes. Why are ye acting thus, O Prince? It is a bad thing to rage[3] against such a wolf, O deity of the shield! If he

[1] *Saga of Harold the Fair-haired* (*Heimskr.*), cap. 26. [2] *Ib.* cap. 24.

[3] The rare word *ylfask*, used here, means properly 'to rage like a wolf'. There is a certain play upon words, for the second element in the name *Hrólfr* (Anglo-Saxon *Hroðulf*) is the word *ulfr*, 'wolf'.

runs to the forest he will not deal gently with the prince's flocks". Hrólfr (Rollo) made his way first to the Hebrides and afterwards to France, where in 911 he founded the earldom of Normandy.

In *Egils Saga*, cap. 24, the following stanza is attributed to the aged Kveldulfr, whose son Thórolfr had been in Harold's service but had fallen into disfavour and been slain by him: "I have learnt now that Thórolfr has met with his death in a northern island. Too soon has Othin claimed the wielder of the sword. Cruel to me are the Norns. The weight of age (lit. 'Thor's heavy co-wrestler') has rendered it impossible for me to go to battle (lit. 'the Valkyrie's contest'). Not quickly will vengeance be carried out, though my heart impels me thereto". An attempt at reconciliation was made, but failed; and Kveldulfr decided that it would be safer to emigrate to Iceland. He set out with his son Skallagrímr and a large following, but died on the voyage.

Egill, son of Skallagrímr, was the most famous of the poets of Iceland. His life, c. 901–982, forms the subject of the greater part of the saga which bears his name. At his home at Borg in Iceland he was a wealthy and respected landowner; but he travelled much abroad and served as a soldier of fortune under Aethelstan. Both in his character and in his adventures he shows a rather striking resemblance to Archilochos. Several of his longer poems have been referred to above (pp. 343 f., 348 f.). Here we are concerned only with the stanzas relating to his personal experiences and feelings.

These stanzas vary considerably in subject and character. We should have liked to quote one which describes a storm encountered by the poet on one of his voyages (cap. 57); but the metaphors are too obscure. As a rule, however, the subjects are personal. We may first take a stanza (in the same chapter), in which Egill expresses his feelings towards King Eric Blood-Axe and his wife Gunnhildr—in a manner not unworthy of Archilochos. He had claimed certain estates in Norway, which were in the possession of a man high in the royal favour. The court was about to decide the case for Egill, when it was broken up by a band of men instigated by the queen. A scene of uproar followed, in which Egill insulted the king; and on the following day he shot the king's pilot. He was then outlawed. While he was preparing to leave the country he is said to have composed this stanza: "The lawbreaker has slain his brothers[1] and upon me myself has imposed a long journey.

[1] The reference here is to the war in which Eric was engaged against two of his brothers, both of whom were slain. A few months later he was expelled by a third brother, Haakon the Good.

The deity of the land is beguiled by his wife. I have to repay Gunnhildr for this banishment. Fierce is her heart. But I will yet manage to snatch an opportunity of requiting her treachery". He was as good as his word; and before setting sail, he attacked and killed a number of people, including his opponent, the royal favourite, and a young son of the king.

In Egill's poetry we have no exact parallel to Archilochos' poem on the loss of his shield. But his somewhat unheroic behaviour at York, when he saved his head by composing a panegyric upon his enemy, points to a similar cast of mind. And this impression is confirmed by the stanza in which he thanks King Eric for sparing him (cap. 61): "Not unpleasant is it to me, O king, to receive my head, ugly[1] though it be. Where is there to be found anyone who has obtained a more handsome gift from the noble-minded son of a monarch?" This stanza is in the *Kviðuháttr* metre, a modification of the ancient *Fornyrðislag*, and the diction is much simpler than in *Dróttkvaett* stanzas, although the term used for 'head' means lit. 'rock of helmets'.

Another example of Egill's lighter vein may be quoted from cap. 55. After the battle in which he lost his brother (cf. p. 349) he is represented as entering Aethelstan's hall and behaving in a sulky and ill-mannered way until the king presented him with a gold bracelet and other generous rewards. He is then said to have produced two stanzas, of which the simpler is as follows: "The peaks of my eyelids were drooping from sorrow. Now I have found one who has smoothed out these unevennesses of my forehead. With a bracelet the prince has pushed up my lowering eyebrows. That sullen look has gone from my eyes". We have not attempted to translate the periphrases for 'eyelids' and 'eyebrows'.

Egill has not left much in the way of love-poetry. After his first visit to England he went to Norway to stay with the relatives of his brother's widow Ásgerðr, and to acquaint her with her husband's death. While he was there he seemed to be wrapped in gloom and was always burying his head in his cloak; and his friend Arinbjörn supposed that this was due to sorrow for his brother's death. But he replied in a stanza (cap. 56) which may be translated freely as follows: "The young fair-armed goddess does not seek my acquaintance. Formerly I had courage enough to raise my eyes. But when the lady comes into the poet's (i.e. 'my') mind, I have to thrust my nose at once into my cloak".

[1] Egill's appearance, as described in cap. 55, seems to have been by no means prepossessing.

Then Egill confessed that he had set his heart upon Ásgerðr. The marriage took place and proved happy.

Here we may perhaps give an instance of sparring in verse between a youth and a girl—of which examples will be found later in other languages. In cap. 48 Egill, when very young, visits an earl called Arnfiðr in Halland. While the earl's daughter is moving about the hall he takes her seat. She comes back and remarks: "What are you doing, boy, in my seat? You have never given hot blood to the wolf. I wish to sit by myself. You have not seen the raven screaming over blood in the autumn. You have not been where sharp-edged blades were meeting". Egill replies: "I have carried a bloody sword and a screaming spear, and the carrion bird followed me. Fierce was the attack of the pirates. In fury we gave battle. Fire enveloped men's dwellings. I have made bloody corpses to lie in the gates of fortresses".

Egill became blind in his old age. In cap. 85 it is related that one winter day he was lying in front of the fire, and one of the serving women rudely told him to get out of the way. He replied in a stanza, in which he compares his present helplessness with the honours he once received from Aethelstan: "(Now) blind I grope around the hearth and beg the goddess of the fire of her grace to put up with the trouble I suffer from my eyes. (But) once a noble monarch took delight in my words and enriched me with gold".

Stanzas similar in their general character to Egill's have been left by many poets of the next and following generations. Most of these were Icelanders who had travelled much abroad. Some of them, e.g. Kormakr, Hallfreðr and Gunnlaugr, devoted much more attention to love-poetry. Unfortunately in all three cases the object of affection was married to another man. As a specimen of poetry of this kind we may quote a stanza from *Hallfreðar Saga*, cap. 10: "When I catch sight of the goddess of fine cloaks, she seems to me like a ship sailing along the sea between two islands; but when I see the deity of the needle surrounded by other women she looks like a magnificently appointed galley gliding with golden sails". He challenged the lady's husband to combat, but subsequently withdrew, because King Ólafr Tryggvason, to whom he was deeply attached, appeared to him in a vision and forbade it.

Among the later poets perhaps the most interesting career was that of Thormóðr Kolbrúnarskald, which is the subject of the *Fóstbroeðra Saga*. Thormóðr made a covenant of brotherhood with a friend named Thorgeirr; but a coolness arose between them, and they parted. Then

Thormóðr fell in love with a girl called Thorbjörg Kolbrún and composed in her honour some poems which are now lost, but from which he got his nickname 'Kolbrún's poet'. Shortly afterwards, he met a certain Thordís, with whom he had previously been in love. She questioned him about the poems; but he denied that they had been made for Thorbjörg, and re-composed them in her own honour. The following night Thorbjörg appeared to him in a dream and charged him with faithlessness, and added that he would lose both his eyes[1] if he did not make a public declaration of his duplicity. He awoke with severe pains in his eyes; but he announced publicly what he had done and re-composed the verses in honour of Thorbjörg, and then his eyes recovered.

The saga now passes on to Thorgeirr and the events which led to his death. Thormóðr, after spending some time in Norway with St Olaf, went to Greenland to avenge Thorgeirr. Then he returned to Norway and remained with St Olaf to the end, following him into exile in Russia and in his disastrous attempt to regain the throne. On the morning of the battle of Stiklestad (1030) he recited the *Bjarkamál* (cf. p. 19) at St Olaf's command, in order to rouse the army. After the king had fallen he was mortally wounded, but made his way to a barn which was being used as a hospital. He carried firewood for a woman who was attending to the wounded, but she asked him why he was so pale. He replied in a stanza which may be translated freely as follows: "I am not ruddy, but the slender woman (or 'Valkyrie') has got a ruddy husband. The old iron of the spear stands fast in me. I am overcome, good lady, by the pain caused by the deep marks of Danish weapons in Dagr's charge".[2] According to the *Fóstbroeðra Saga*, cap. 24, *ad fin.*, he fell dead to the ground before he was able to complete the stanza, and the last word was added by Harold Hardrada, the king's young brother. But the *Heimskringla* gives a slightly different account.

The amount of poetry of this kind preserved in the sagas is very considerable. After the earliest times—from the middle of the tenth century—it is mostly the work of Icelandic poets; but this may be due largely to the fact that our records, the sagas themselves, are Icelandic.

[1] One may compare the story of Stesichoros' blindness.

[2] Lit. "the deep marks of Dagr's charge and the Danish weapons". Dagr was the commander of the king's bodyguard and led the final charge after his death. The 'Danish weapons' had presumably been supplied to the Norwegians by Canute. The allusion to the 'slender woman' is not clear to us, unless it refers to Hel and the slain. The text of the stanza given in the *Heimskringla* (*St Olaf's Saga*, cap. 247) differs considerably from that of the *Fóstbr. Saga*, quoted above.

'Occasional' poetry was certainly cultivated to some extent in Norway. Some stanzas by St Olaf and Harold Hardrada have been preserved.

We see no reason to doubt that in Ireland also occasional poetry was cultivated during the centuries which followed the close of the Heroic Age. It is not unlikely that such poems are still preserved; but unfortunately we do not know where to find them. Some interesting and attractive monastic poems of this kind have been published and translated;[1] but these do not fall within our scope. Again, the story of Cellachan of Cashel and the 'War of the Gaedhil with the Gaill' contain a considerable amount of poetry; but some of this probably belongs to Type B, while the rest falls under Type D (cf. p. 351) rather than Type E. It is quite possible that some of the poems attributed to Gormlaith (cf. p. 340) may belong to the latter Type—or at least be founded on such poems. But even if they are all to be referred to Type B, they may probably be taken as evidence that secular and royal persons cultivated—or might be expected to cultivate—personal poetry, just as in the heroic sagas. Among the fragments of poems which have been collected and published several appear to belong to Type E, so far as one can judge in the absence of any context.[2]

We have seen (pp. 25 f., 36) that several English and Welsh poems—*Deor*, *Widsith* and the elegies of Llywarch Hen—claim to be, in part or wholly, personal poems of the Heroic Age. For the following period we find nothing of the kind, except a few pieces of religious provenance, such as, for example, the (Christian gnomic) lines recited by Bede on his deathbed.[3] Was personal poetry not cultivated, or was it always of an ephemeral character? Owing to the character of our sources we do not think that either of these conclusions can be regarded as certain. The laity probably did not write very much in either language; and such compositions were not the most likely to find their way into religious houses. Bede in his account of Caedmon (*Hist. Eccl.* IV. 24) represents villagers as coming together in the evening to drink and sing. The harp was passed round, and everyone was expected to take his turn. Unfortunately he says nothing as to the character of the songs, though the context implies that they were in the nature of *friuoli et superuacui poematis*. This expression might apply to personal or occasional poetry,

[1] We may refer especially to *The Monk and his Cat*, ed. and transl. in Stokes and Strachan, *Thesaurus Palaeohibernicus*, II. 293; also transl. by K. Meyer, *Ancient Irish Poetry*, p. 82.

[2] Cf. K. Meyer, *Bruchstücke d. älteren Lyrik Irlands* (cf. p. 350, note 1), especially the last few pieces (p. 69 ff.).

[3] Cf. Plummer, *Baedae Opera Historica*, I. p. clxi.

but Bede would probably have included heroic poetry, as well as folk-songs and other classes of poetry under the same term. All that can be said is that personal poetry may have been cultivated both in English and Welsh; but it did not attain to such fame as to leave permanent record of itself. In Ireland the evidence is better, as we have seen; but for practical purposes we are dependent upon Greek and Norse for the study of post-heroic personal poetry.

The general impression conveyed by the periods discussed in this chapter is, except in Greek and Norse, one of barrenness. It must be borne in mind, however, that the periods were not of the same length in the various countries, and that the conditions which prevailed in them were very different. In Greece we believe that our period—i.e. the interval between the end of the Heroic Age and the time when writing was in general use for literary purposes[1]—covers about four centuries; and most scholars would probably regard this as an understatement. In the Norse world the corresponding period amounts to nearly six centuries. But in England both Latin and English were written within half a century of the close of the Heroic Age. In little more than a century there was a flourishing Latin literature; within two centuries there was probably much written English literature. In Ireland the native language had come to be written perhaps half a century before the end of the Heroic Age, and before long its use for literary purposes seems to have become fairly common. Latin had long been in use. In Wales Latin had been known throughout the Heroic Age and long before. It is uncertain when Welsh began to be written. There is no satisfactory evidence that it was much used for literary purposes before the tenth century—perhaps three centuries after the Heroic Age.

From this it will be seen that the periods with which we are concerned in the British Isles may be described as literary periods, whereas the corresponding Greek and Norse periods were pre-literary. By this we do not mean of course that writing was unknown, but that it was not commonly used for literary purposes—except towards the close of the Greek period. In point of fact the first half both of the Greek period and of the Norse is represented only by antiquarian traditions. The time of great activity in Greece in our period falls within the last century—the period of transition when literature was beginning to be written. In Norse it is otherwise. The 'golden age' of saga ceases c. 1030–1040;

[1] This date will be discussed in Ch. XVI.

and the creative period may have come to an end before the close of the eleventh century—perhaps half a century before the beginning of literary times. Sagas of certain kinds, as well as oral poems, were still composed after this; but the maximum of intellectual output seems to fall between the latter part of the ninth and the latter part of the eleventh centuries. The essential point, however, is this: both in Greece and in the North the best intellects of the age were devoted to the cultivation of oral poetry and saga—including no doubt the elaboration of old themes (heroic, etc.), as well as the creation of new ones, but more especially the latter. On the other hand, the best intellects of the British Isles were now diverted into a different channel, the cultivation of written (primarily ecclesiastical) literature. It was only in comparatively backward circles here that attention was concentrated upon oral poetry and saga.

The absence of Welsh material is perhaps the most striking fact. We have been able to produce very little from Wales in this chapter, nothing from Strathclyde or Cornwall. Yet there is no good evidence for an early written literature in Welsh, as there is in Irish and English, while the output of Latin literature does not appear to have been great. The British Heroic Age is well represented, as we have seen, especially for the northern area. At this time, it is true, the British territories were much more extensive and richer than in later times. But what is more remarkable is that in the twelfth century, when Wales alone remained, a rich new poetic literature begins—a fact which emphasises the barrenness of the intervening period. The *Historia Brittonum* suggests that intellectual activity during this period was largely concentrated upon antiquarian speculations. We have also to take into account the development of imaginative saga, as seen in the *Mabinogion*, and probably a good deal of religious poetry and other (impersonal) kinds of poetry, which will require notice in the following chapters. It would seem at all events that little attention was given to poetry or saga relating to contemporary events.

The records of post-heroic times, like those of the Heroic Age, contain both historical and unhistorical elements. But the proportion between the two varies according to the length of the period in the various countries. In the North, where the period is longest and the record most full, supernatural elements occupy at least as prominent a position in these stories as in those of the Heroic Age. Adventures with monsters are of frequent occurrence; and not seldom deities make their appearance among men. We may refer, for example, to the description of the battle of Hjörrungavágr (c. 990) given in the longer *Saga of Ólafr Tryggvason*, cap. 154 f.,[1] where it is related that Earl Haakon's patron goddesses, Thorgerðr Hölgabrúðr and Irpa, came to assist him, standing on the prow of his ship and pouring showers of arrows upon his enemies. Similar highly imaginative scenes occur even in contemporary poems (cf. p. 344 ff.). It may be remarked too that in the *Íslendinga Sögur* supernatural elements are not least prominent in stories which relate to the end of the saga period—the early part of the eleventh century. We meet here frequently with omens, visions and ghosts, and sometimes even with demons or monsters, as in the story of Grettir, who died in 1031.

Fiction, apart from the supernatural, is of course more difficult to prove, though there can be little doubt that it is used freely in the *Fornaldar Sögur* (cf. p. 333). Unhistorical combinations and chronological errors are likewise frequent in the earlier periods. The most striking case is that of Ragnarr Loðbrók and his sons, who are generally thrown back three or four generations before their true date. Yet it is not to be doubted that from the time of Harold the Fair-haired the narratives of the sagas are to be regarded as historical in their main lines, at least so far as they are concerned with Norway and Iceland.

The Greek evidence is not dissimilar, though the amount of material here is much more limited. It is difficult to determine what is the historical value of the traditions relating to the establishment of the Dorian kingdom in Sparta, though much is doubtless to be attributed to speculations upon personal and place names. The stories relating to Lycurgos also no doubt contain much unhistorical matter; and he is made responsible for institutions some of which were probably of earlier, and some of later, date than his time. Stories relating to the eighth and seventh centuries, however, are generally regarded as historical in the main. Yet supernatural elements occur from time to time, as in the North. We may refer, for example, to an event which is recorded to have taken place not long before the middle of the sixth century—the appearance of Helen at Therapne, when she gave the gift of beauty to the child who afterwards became the wife of Ariston. The story is told by Herodotos, VI. 61. The credulity of the Greeks, even at this time, is pointed out by the same author in another passage (I. 60), in which he describes how Peisistratos recovered his power at Athens—by driving into the city with a woman whom he had dressed up to personate

[1] *Flateyjarbók*, I. p. 192.

the goddess Athena. As illustrating unhistorical situations in saga of this period we may cite the story told by Herodotos (I. 86) of Croisos and his meeting with Solon. Probably, however, such cases are more or less exceptional, as in Norse. At all events it is from these stories that our knowledge of early Greek history is mainly derived.

The English and Irish stories belong, as we have seen, to periods of written literature, and contain but little of the supernatural, other than what is of hagiological character. Such unhistorical elements as they contain would seem to be due in the former to gossip and scandal, in the latter to imaginativeness and the habit of reckless exaggeration.

The parallelism which we have noted in Norse and Greek saga relating to this period is almost entirely wanting in the poetry which we have discussed above (p. 341 ff.) under Type D. The reason for this lies partly in the occasions which gave rise to the poems. The Norse poems are mostly panegyrics or elegies upon princes, whereas the Greek are incitements to battle or political manifestos. Parallels to the former are to be found in Ireland, as we have seen; but the latter have no analogies among the northern peoples in our periods. On the other hand, panegyrics upon princes do not occur in Greek until a later time, though this is probably due to mere accident, while none of the extant elegies are for persons of very exalted position.

There are, however, other and perhaps more important reasons for the differences we have observed. In most of the Greek poems there is to be found a feeling of patriotism for the city or state to which the poet belonged. Alcaios was for a time in exile, while his brother was a soldier of fortune in the army of Babylon; yet he speaks of his native city with the greatest devotion. Similar feelings may be traced in Tyrtaios, Solon and other poets. Parallels up to a certain point may be found also in the English *Battle of Brunanburh* and in some Irish poems. But Norse poems rarely give any hint of such a feeling. The majority of these are, it is true, the work of Icelanders—i.e. aliens to the countries whose rulers they were praising. But even in panegyrics and elegies upon kings of Norway composed by Norwegians the same characteristic is noticeable, except to a slight extent in the poems of Eyvindr Finnsson, the latest of them. In place of patriotism it is everywhere the personality of the ruler himself which is the object of devotion and loyalty, just as in the Heroic Age. Even in the English *Battle of Maldon* the same heroic feature is much in evidence. It is for Earl Byrhtnoth, rather than for their country, that the knights are ready to sacrifice their lives. There is a noticeable difference in this respect between the poems on the battles of Maldon and Brunanburh. The former would seem to be the product of a prince's court, where the old heroic ideals were still maintained, whereas the sense of patriotism and national consciousness in the latter probably points to a different origin.

It would be well, however, not to overestimate the force of the feeling of patriotism in either England or Ireland in these times. The saga of Cellachan represents that prince as a model of patriotism, striving constantly by both actions and words to rouse his countrymen against the invaders. But the *Annals of Clonmacnois* depict him as a mere disturber of the peace and an ally of the invaders. In point of fact, both in England and in Ireland there were usually discontented or ambitious native princes to be found in the armies of the invaders, just as there were usually Norse soldiers of fortune in the native armies. A straight issue between a purely native and a purely foreign army was a rare occurrence. Yet the stress of invasion, and the devastation which inevitably accompanied it, did tend to produce a feeling of patriotism and national solidarity, which we find from time to time reflected in the poems.

The patriotism of the Greek poets is bound up with a more advanced political development; and it is the latter which constitutes the chief difference between Greece and the other countries in the periods under discussion. We have seen that the devotion recognised by Norse poets is personal rather than national, as in the Heroic Age. It is in accordance with this that whenever we hear of internal struggles, they arise not from conflicting political principles, but from family quarrels, as between the sons of Harold the Fair-haired, or from quarrels between two different families, as between the Norwegian royal line and the earls of Lade. The poets are interested in their own immediate friends and in the princes to whom they have attached themselves; but it is very rarely that we hear anything of the rights or wrongs of the people in general. A recognition of public distress appears first in the poems of Eyvindr Finnsson; but it does not go very far, and it is doubtless due in part to the poet's personal dislike of the reigning kings, Harold II and his brothers. More than half a century later popular discontent began to show itself openly against the kings, in risings or threatened risings; but Sigvatr's *Bersöglisvísur* (cf. p. 348) is the first example known to us of political pressure apart from mere violence.

In England and Ireland we know of no parallels to the *Bersöglisvísur*. In England, however, similar political pressure was brought to bear upon Aethelred more than twenty years before the date of this poem.[1] In Ireland nothing of the kind is known to us. The conditions appear to have been more backward.

In Greece political development during our period had reached a far more advanced stage. It is possible that we are inclined to introduce modern ideas too much into the interpretation of the politics of those times, and that the contests between the political factions were more of a personal nature and less due to the recognition of principles than is commonly supposed. But at all events the conception of the state as a common bond, on the welfare of which the security and prosperity of everyone depends, was recognised even in those cities which were governed by individual rulers. The area of the state was as a rule very small; all the citizens lived within easy reach of one another, and could discuss their wishes and grievances at all times. But in the northern countries the areas were too large, the towns too small and few, and the distances between them too great,[2] to allow of such rapid political development. Iceland alone had a 'republican' form of government. But most of those who attended the assembly had to ride from fifty to two hundred miles; and consequently it met only once a year, for a few days.

Taken by themselves the poems of Type D suggest but little analogy between the poetry—and the intellectual development in general—of Greece and that of the North. But a different impression is conveyed by the poems of Type E. The quotations given above (p. 363) will perhaps be sufficient to illustrate the chief resemblances and differences between Greek and Norse poetry of this Type. It will be seen at once that the latter has much more in common with Archilochos than with the melic poets. The reason for this lies no doubt largely in the backwardness of music in the North. There is no satisfactory evidence, so far as we are aware, for choral poetry, except perhaps in spells. It is clear too, that panegyrics and elegies were not usually accompanied by instrumental music. In the Teutonic Heroic Age the harp was regularly employed for the accompaniment of poetry. But the evidence that it was retained in the Viking Age, even for heroic poetry, is slight and somewhat doubtful. These, however, are questions which will require notice in a later chapter.

[1] Cf. *Saxon Chronicle*, *ann.* 1014.

[2] It was in the comparatively populous district of Throndhjem that organised opposition to the kings of Norway first began to show itself.

A comparison between the poetry of Archilochos and that of such poets as Egill Skallagrímsson is much impeded by the conventions of form and diction by which the latter are bound, and which are extremely distasteful to the modern reader. Apart from these perhaps the chief difference lies in the absence, especially in Egill's poems, of the gnomic element and indeed of any kind of generalisation. The themes treated in his stanzas are wholly of personal or particular interest. Observations of general application are hardly admitted even as illustrations. This is the more remarkable because in the *Hávamál*, which can hardly have been unknown to him, gnomic poetry receives a more artistic treatment than in any Greek poem. It is found also in other Norse poems of the period, e.g. in the *Hákonarmál*, Eyvindr Finnsson's elegy on Haakon I (cf. p. 344 f.), which perhaps shows a knowledge of the *Hávamál*. In Anglo-Saxon poetry the gnomic element tends to encroach everywhere.

It is in accordance with this absence of generalisation that we seldom, if ever, find references to the community in Norse poems of this Type. The interests of the poets seem to be wholly individual, and practically never extend beyond their families and personal friends. This is of course only what might be expected from the considerations pointed out above (p. 372 f.).

Far more important, however, than these differences is the element which the Greek and the Norse poets have in common—Sappho and Alcaios, as well as Archilochos, among the former. This may perhaps best be described as the revelation of the author's personality. Hesiod is concerned to a certain extent with his own affairs; but what he tells us about himself amounts to very little, and does not suffice to give us any clear impression as to the kind of man he was. But these poets are primarily occupied with themselves and their own interests. Their experiences and feelings, their pleasures and sorrows, their loves and hatreds are frankly and freely stated. Even in those of their poems which belong to Type D, and which may be intended for a reward of some kind, there is usually some indication of the independence or individuality of the author. We rarely meet with that self-effacement of the author which is characteristic of heroic poetry.

Both in Greece and in the North the poets whom we are now considering were usually persons of independent means, or at least able to make their living in a way which did not involve the sacrifice of their independence. Those of the North might attach themselves to princes in the hope of gaining substantial rewards in one form or another. But such engagements were as a rule only for a short time—after which the poet returned home or resumed activities on his own account. In short, if allowance be made for the unsettled state of society in both periods, the spirit in which the poets composed and the conditions under which they worked were not radically different from those of the modern world.

It is possible that the self-revelation noted above was not entirely a new thing. We know from the case of Gelimer (cf. p. 26) that personal poetry was cultivated in the Heroic Age by princes. Of such poetry, however, nothing has been preserved, except perhaps in Welsh. Elsewhere if any personal poems have come down to us from the Heroic Age, they are the work of professional minstrels. Personal poetry by persons of independent position, whether aristocratic or middle-class, begins for us with the poets treated in this chapter.

In conclusion it may be well to repeat that only poetry and saga relating to post-heroic times fall within the scope of this chapter. The poetry or saga may relate to either the present or the past, though not to the Heroic Age. But it must not be supposed that this was the only kind of poetry or saga cultivated during the periods under discussion. Heroic poetry of Types B and C[1] probably dates largely from these periods. We believe that the history of heroic poems of Type A and of heroic sagas normally goes back to the Heroic Age itself; but as a rule they doubtless underwent elaboration or modification in post-heroic times. These are questions which will require discussion later. Many sagas and poems of all Types (A, B, C, D) relating to the gods seem to date from our periods; and the same is true of much antiquarian poetry, especially in Greece, Ireland and the North. There can be no doubt that most of the poetry discussed in the following chapters belongs to the same periods.

[1] Heroic poetry of Type E must of course, if genuine, date from the Heroic Age itself. The same is no doubt true in general of Heroic Type D, though elegies may occasionally have been composed upon heroes of the past.

CHAPTER XII

GNOMIC POETRY

ACCORDING to Aristotle[1] "a gnome is a statement not relating to particulars, as e.g. the character of Iphicrates, but to universals; yet not to all universals indiscriminately, as e.g. that straight is the opposite of crooked, but to all such as are the objects of (human) action[2] and are to be chosen or avoided in our doings".

Modern writers use the word in a wider sense than this, viz. as defined by Aristotle without his reservation—a statement relating to universals (as opposed to particulars). We know of no satisfactory definition in a dictionary or elsewhere; but the word is commonly applied, for example, to Anglo-Saxon sayings of a kind which are expressly excluded by Aristotle's definition, e.g. 'Good is opposed to evil, youth to age, life to death, light to darkness'.[3]

It will thus be convenient to distinguish two types of gnomes: (I) those which come within Aristotle's definition, and (II) those which are excluded by it. The former are concerned only with human actions, and imply the use of choice or judgment. They are frequently combined with precepts, and may often themselves be converted into precepts. In literature this type appears perhaps most commonly in relation to human action in its moral aspects. But it also includes gnomes in which the governing principle is advisability, as well as those which relate to the practice of industries or to the performance of religious or magical rites.

Type II relates to the properties or characteristics not only of mankind in general and of various classes of mankind, but also of other beings, objects, natural phenomena, etc. The gnomes of this type may in general be regarded as the results of observation, and are not capable of being converted into precepts. Under this type it will be convenient to distinguish gnomes relating to (*a*) human activities or experiences in which no choice or judgment is involved, (*b*) the operations of Fate (death) and the gods, (*c*) all other gnomes belonging to this type—the

1 *Rhetoric*, II. 21.

2 There is no doubt that Aristotle means human actions. But some of the examples which follow seem to indicate that πράξεις includes experiences, as well as actions.

3 *Cotton Gnomic Verses* (cf. p. 380 f.), 50 ff.

characteristics of beings, etc. other than human. Our reason for treating (*b*) as a distinct variety is that gnomes of this kind sometimes occur where other varieties are wholly or almost wholly unknown.

Not unfrequently the same formulae are used in both types of gnomes. We may instance the *sceal* formula in English poetry, e.g. *forst sceal freosan*, 'it is the property of frost to freeze' (Type II *c*); *swa sceal man don*, 'this is how one ought to act' (Type I). The connection between the two types may be seen in such a sentence as *Cotton Gnomes* 14 f., which may be interpreted according to either type:

Geongne æþeling sceolan gode gesiðas
byldan to beaduwe and to beahgife.

This may be translated according to Type I: "Good knights[1] ought to encourage a young prince to warfare and generosity"; but also—and perhaps more probably—according to Type II *a*: "It is characteristic of good knights to encourage", etc. Both types are frequently associated with descriptive poetry of the timeless nameless kind, which will require notice later.

We are not concerned here with the origin of these two types of gnomes, both of which are probably of considerable antiquity, but only with the treatment of them in early poetry. Both types are very important in the history of poetry. Type I may be regarded as the beginning of ethical literature, and Type II as the beginning of scientific literature in general.

It will be convenient to deal first with isolated gnomes, which are introduced incidentally in poems concerned with other themes—especially heroic poems—and secondly with poems, rarely also prose pieces, which consist wholly or largely of collections of gnomes.

In the Homeric poems gnomes are rare. Those which occur mostly belong to Type II *b*, e.g. *Il.* IX. 320: "Death befalls alike him who has done nothing and him whose achievements are many"; and *ib.* XVIII. 309: "Enyalios (the war-god) is impartial and slays him who is about to slay". Similar cases will be found in *ib.* I. 218, XIII. 730 ff. The latter passage shows the influence of the 'gnomic catalogue', which will require notice later. As an instance of Type I we may take *Il.* XII. 243, which is quoted as an example by Aristotle himself:[2] "To fight for one's

[1] Members of the royal comitatus are meant.

[2] *Rhet.* II. 21. 11. Aristotle also quotes the first part of the second of the examples (*Il.* XVIII. 309) given above. But we cannot see how this can be covered by his definition of a gnome (cf. p. 377).

country is better than any omen". This example belongs to the martial, patriotic variety of gnome, which figures prominently in the poems of Callinos and Tyrtaios. Examples of the strictly heroic variety, found in *Beowulf*, seem to be wanting in the Homeric poems.

In the fragmentary poems of the seventh century treated in the last chapter gnomes occur far more frequently than in the Homeric poems. After the patriotic poets Archilochos perhaps supplies the largest number; and these, as might be expected, are of a somewhat specialised character. For instances we may refer to p. 359. Fragm. 8 may also be quoted: "No one who frets over the rebuke of a churl is likely to have too many pleasant experiences". The poems of Simonides and the gnomic poems of Solon will be discussed later.

In *Beowulf* the gnomic element is far greater than in the Homeric poems. Instances of Type II, however, are not frequent, apart from references to God, Fate or death (II *b*). Some of these are of Christian origin, e.g. 700 ff., 930 f. References to Fate and death are more frequent, e.g. 455: "Fate always takes its course"; cf. 1386 f. Type I is of common occurrence. The examples are usually, if not always, of the heroic variety, e.g. 1384 f.: "For everyone it is a nobler course that he should avenge his friend than that he should indulge in mourning". Frequently these gnomes are expressed by the word *sceal*, e.g. 24: "Success is to be attained (*sceal...man geþeon*) in every nation by deeds which evoke praise" (i.e. generosity). Sometimes we find a fuller formula, e.g. 1172: 'This is how one ought to act' (cf. p. 378). In other Anglo-Saxon poems isolated gnomes seem not to be of frequent occurrence.[1] Timeless nameless poems which contain series of gnomes will be noticed below.

In the mythological and heroic poems of the *Edda*, gnomes are of comparatively rare occurrence.[2] Examples of both types occur. As an instance of Type I we may quote *Atlakviða* 19: "Thus ought (*skal*) a brave man to defend himself against his foes"—a 'heroic' gnome similar to those in *Beowulf*. As an example of Type II *b* we may take *Atlamál* 48: "No one can withstand fate". The Trilogy (cf. p. 27 f.) differs greatly from the rest of the heroic poems in this, as in other respects. In the *Sigrdrífumál* indeed the gnomic element outweighs the heroic; and consequently we shall deal with these poems later (p. 385). In the

[1] In religious poetry gnomes are less frequent than one would have expected, though they occur in homiletic pieces, e.g. Grein-Wülcker, *Bibl.* II. pp. 108, 280, and in the verses composed by Bede at his death (cf. p. 368).

[2] The examples are collected by Martin Clarke, *Hávamál*, p. 26 f.

poetry of the Viking Age, discussed in the last chapter, gnomes are of rare occurrence (cf. p. 375), though they are not unfrequent in the sagas themselves.

In Welsh heroic poetry the gnomic element is negligible, except in the elegies of Llywarch Hen, which will require notice below. In early Irish saga and poetry of all kinds incidental gnomes seem to be quite rare. As an example we may quote *Mac Datho's Pig*, cap. 3: "Crimthann Nia Nair said: 'Do not tell your secret to women'. The secret of a woman is not well kept. A treasure is not entrusted to a slave".

Next we have to take poems which are wholly or largely of gnomic character. It will be convenient here to begin with the English evidence, which is unusually full and varied, and supplies many gnomes of a very simple character.

The chief collections are the *Exeter Gnomes*, preserved in the *Exeter Book*, and the *Cotton Gnomes*, which follow the *Menologium* or metrical calendar at the beginning of MS. C of the *Saxon Chronicle*. Gnomic passages occur also in the *Wanderer* and the *Seafarer*.[1] It is to be observed that the gnomes contained in the two latter poems belong to the classes which relate to human activities and experiences (Types I and II *a*), though instances of II *b* occur. On the other hand, in the *Exeter* and *Cotton Gnomes* Type I is comparatively rare, while in Type II the third variety (*c*) is decidedly predominant.

The briefest form of gnomic statements occurs chiefly in catalogues. We may take as an example *Ex.* 130 ff.: "A shield is indispensable (*sceal*) to a brave, a spear to a brigand, a ring to a bride, books to a student, sacrament to a holy man (or 'saint') and sins to a heathen". And again *ib.* 139 ff.: "Counsel is to be spoken, letters (of the Runic alphabet) to be written, songs to be sung, praise to be won, judgment to be declared, and the day to be spent in activity". We may compare the *Wanderer* 65 ff.: "A man of authority must be patient—not too impetuous, or too hasty of speech, or too slack or too reckless in combat, or too timid or jubilant or covetous, or too eager to boast ere he knows full well (the issue)". This last case clearly belongs to Type I, the others to Type II—though one may hesitate whether to assign them to II *a* or to II *c*. Sometimes clear examples of II *a* and II *c* are combined in one catalogue, e.g. *Cott.* 50 ff. (cf. p. 377): "Good is opposed to evil, youth to age, life to death, light to darkness, (one) army to (another)

[1] Also in *Salomon and Saturn*, e.g. 310 f., though this poem does not properly come within the scope of our work.

army, one enemy to another; foe quarrels with foe over (the ownership of) land and charges him with injustice".

The Cotton text contains (16–43) a long list of gnomes which are not very much expanded. Some of them indeed are as brief as possible, without either verb (other than *sceal*) or epithet; others have a verb (infinitive), and others again both verb and epithet. We may take the beginning of the catalogue (16 ff.) as an example: "It is for a knight to show prowess, for a sword to experience fighting in contact with a helmet, for a hawk, wild (as it is) to rest on a gauntlet". Here we have the three stages following one another in succession. Elsewhere we find more than one verb in a sentence, as in *Ex.* 45 f.: "A young man (boy) is to be instructed, disciplined and exhorted until he has full knowledge". And such sentences may be expanded and continued over a passage of considerable length, as in *ib.* 85 ff., which contains several parallel infinitives—the whole giving a picture of the model queen (Type I). The subject begins at 82: "A king buys a queen at a price with (precious) vessels and armlets. In the first place (or 'without delay') both of them must be liberal with gifts. The knight (king) must distinguish himself in warfare and arms, while the wife must succeed in gaining the affections of her subjects. She must be cheerful, and keep secrets. She must be generous with horses and jewels. When mead is served before the company of knights, she is on all occasions first to approach the 'defence of princes' (i.e. the king) and hand the first cup promptly to her lord. And she is to bear in mind the common interest of him and herself, the two owners of the house". It may be observed that relative and conditional sentences are not very common, while causal and final sentences (constituting enthymemes) are quite rare—in the *Cotton Gnomes* they do not occur at all. This is presumably due to the fact that most of the gnomes belong to Type II.

Passages, like the one just quoted, in which a subject is treated at considerable length, occur not unfrequently in the *Exeter Gnomes*. We may quote also 95 ff., the description of the Frisian mariner and his wife: "Welcome to the wife of the Frisian is the arrival of her beloved, when his ship comes to anchor. His vessel has arrived and her husband, who supports her, has come home. She invites him in, washes his sea-stained clothes, and gives him fresh garments. On land there lies at his disposal what his love requires". Here also we may refer to 173 ff., which illustrates the importance of having a brother. Such passages sometimes arise out of a series of gnomes, more or less expanded, on the same or similar subjects; sometimes they are due to the introduction of illustrations. Both processes may be seen in *Ex.* 166 ff.: "Sensible speech is fitting to every man; poetry (is fitting) to the minstrel and discrimination to the man (who listens). There are as many varieties of temperament as there are people upon the earth; everyone has individual characteristics of his own. For example (*þonne*) he who knows numerous lays and can play the harp with his hands can get relief from his sorrows; (for) he has the gift of his minstrelsy, which God has granted to him". Such illustrations differ in no way, except in their brevity, from the descriptive poetry which we shall have to notice later, and which is itself frequently associated with gnomes.

As regards form—both the present indicative (especially *biþ*) and *sceal* with the infinitive are very common in gnomes of Type II. After *sceal* the infinitive is very frequently omitted. In gnomes of Type I *sceal* is almost universal. The imperative occurs in *Ex.* 1 f.: "Question me with words of wisdom; leave not thy mind unrevealed, the deepest secret that thou knowest". But these introductory lines cannot be regarded as precepts. The precept form is indeed wanting in these collections.

On the other hand, the precept—with the verb in the imperative—is the regular form in the piece commonly known as *A Father's Instructions*, which is likewise preserved in the *Exeter Book*. This is a catalogue poem, containing ten counsels given by a father to his son. In its present form it is of a much more definitely Christian character than the poems which we have been considering. It belongs, however, to a rather widespread class, other examples of which will be noticed in the following pages. The present indicative and the *sceal* formula also occur in this piece, though but rarely.

The chief collections of gnomic material in Norse are to be found in the *Hávamál*[1] and in the Trilogy (especially the *Sigrdrífumál*). We will begin with the former.

It is generally agreed that the *Hávamál* is a composite work. Opinions differ much as to its constituent elements; but there can be no doubt that st. 111 to the end are of a different origin from st. 1–110. The god Othin, however, seems to be the speaker throughout, except in st. 111, which serves as an introduction to the second part.

The first part, st. 1–110, consists of a series of gnomic utterances,

[1] Ed. and transl. by D. E. Martin Clarke (Cambridge, 1923). This work contains also the gnomic material found in the other Edda poems, including nearly the whole of the *Sigrdrífumál*.

followed by two short stories of Othin's love adventures, which have already been noticed (p. 249 f.). The second part is addressed to an unknown Loddfáfnir and comprises (i) a series of precepts (st. 112–137), commonly known as *Loddfáfnismál*; (ii) some obscure stanzas (138–145) relating to the myth of the hanging of Othin (cf. p. 250) and to the ritual or magical use of runes; (iii) a list of spells (st. 146–end), each of which is introduced by the formula 'A second I know, if...', etc.

The briefest form of gnomes is to be found in st. 81 ff.: "A day is to be praised when (i.e. not until) evening comes, a wife when she is burnt, a sword when tested, a maiden when given in marriage, ice when crossed, ale when it has been drunk. Wood is to be felled in a wind, the sea to be traversed in a breeze, a girl to be wooed in the dark—(for) many are the eyes of day. A ship is to be handled to make it travel, a shield to obtain protection, a sword to strike a blow, a maiden to get kisses". Most of the gnomes here clearly belong to Type I; but the last two lines (from 'A ship') are rather to be referred to Type II. The same formula (*skal*) is, however, used throughout the passage. Another series of very brief gnomes occurs in the long catalogue of things not to be trusted, given in st. 85 ff.

The first part of the *Hávamál* is as a whole somewhat formless; but in many of the stanzas gnomic poetry receives an artistic treatment which is unsurpassed in any language known to us. The formulae in which the gnomes are stated vary from stanza to stanza. The *skal* (or *skyli*) formula is the most common; but the present indicative also occurs frequently, and the present conjunctive occasionally. Most commonly each gnome occupies a stanza; but sometimes they extend over more than one, while others, as we have seen, are much shorter. Enthymemes are quite frequent. Occasionally they are contained in one line, of which the second half gives the reason for the statement made in the first half. An example has been quoted above from st. 82: "A girl is to be wooed in the dark", etc. More frequently, like other gnomes they occupy a whole stanza, e.g. 84: "No one should trust the words of a girl, nor what a woman says; for their hearts have been shaped on a revolving wheel, and inconstancy is lodged in their breasts". Some gnomes again are introduced by a brief 'descriptive' sentence, somewhat similar to those we have noticed in English gnomic poetry, e.g. st. 21: "Cattle know when they ought to go home, and then they leave their pasture. But a foolish man never knows the measure of his own appetite".

Almost all the gnomes belong either to Type I or to Type II *a*. In the former there is a noteworthy difference between this part of the *Hávamál* and other gnomic poetry of the same Type, whether in Norse or elsewhere. We are not referring to the absence of the heroic element, for that is generally wanting in collections of this kind. We mean rather that the gnomes of Type I which relate to conduct do not as a rule embody ethical principles, as is usually the case with such gnomes. St. 58 may be quoted: "He ought to get up early who means to take his neighbour's life or property". The virtue most frequently inculcated is caution. But more stress is laid upon manners than upon morals. We may refer, for example, to st. 35, which is an enthymeme: "A visitor should depart and not remain always in one place. (For) a friend becomes a nuisance if he stays too long in the house of another". Many of the gnomes of Type II *a* show the same spirit.

It is clear from such passages as st. 66 that this philosophy is not to be taken too seriously: "At many a place I have arrived much too early—at others too late. (Sometimes) the ale had been drunk, at other times it had not been brewed. An unpopular man rarely hits on the right moment". The work is didactic in form, and originally it may well have been didactic also in intention. But if so it has undergone a considerable amount of modification—a process to which such collections as this must have been specially liable in times of oral tradition. As we now have it the object of the work would seem to be entertainment rather than instruction. And this impression is fully borne out by the cynical humour displayed in the stories of Othin's love adventures (noticed on p. 249 f.), which are introduced as illustrations of the gnomes stated in st. 90–95, and which form the conclusions of the work.

The second part of the poem begins as follows (st. 111): "It is time to chant (*þylja*) on the chair of the *þulr*,[1] at the spring of Fate. I saw and kept silence, I saw and pondered, I listened to the speech of men. I heard 'runes' spoken of—nor did they keep silence about the interpretation thereof—at the Hall of the High One. In the Hall of the High One I heard such words as these". This passage will require discussion in a later chapter.

The gnomes, or rather precepts, of the *Loddfáfnismál* are introduced by a formula, which is repeated in each case: "I advise thee, Loddfáfnir, and do thou take my advice; thou wilt benefit if thou take it, thou wilt prosper if thou adopt it". The precepts themselves are expressed

[1] The meaning of this archaic word will be discussed in Ch. XIX. Elsewhere it is used for 'sage' and '(learned) poet'; but the context here suggests 'seer' or 'oracular medium'. The word *þylja* ('chant') is a derivative of *þulr*.

either by the imperative or by *skalt* (2 sing. of *skal*) with the infinitive, usually with a negative. Enthymemes occur fairly often, e.g. (st. 132 f.): "Never hold a stranger or a traveller up to ridicule or mockery. (For) those who are present in a house are frequently without exact information as to the origin (or perhaps 'character') of the visitors. There is no man so good as to be free from imperfection, or so bad as to be entirely worthless".

The subjects here are frequently similar to those treated in the first part—relations with friends, strangers, women, etc. In several cases they deal with the same situations or difficulties, and sometimes there is an obvious relationship between two passages, as e.g. between st. 44 and 119. But the treatment in the *Loddfáfnismál* seems to be uniformly serious. Many of the precepts inculcate caution, like the gnomes of the first part; but the humorous or cynical element is wanting. On the other hand st. 129 and 137 are concerned with magic, which is barely noticed in the first part.

The catalogue of spells, from st. 146 to the end, can hardly be regarded as gnomic; for the character of the spells is never stated. The same remark applies to the list of spells given in the *Grógaldr*. This subject will require notice in Ch. XV.

After the *Hávamál* the chief collection of gnomic material is in the *Sigrdrífumál*. This poem contains two series of precepts given to the hero Sigurðr by the Valkyrie Sigrdrífa. The first (st. 6–13) consists of recommendations for the cutting of Runic letters for (magical) benefit on various occasions. The second (st. 22–37)[1] are very similar to the precepts of the *Loddfáfnismál*. They are introduced by the formula 'First, I advise thee', etc. Many of them are enthymemes, e.g. (st. 23): "Secondly, I advise thee not to take an oath unless thou mean to keep it; (for) dire Fate (lit. 'threads') attends the breaking of an oath. Wretched is he who has violated his plighted word".

The other poems of the Trilogy—the *Reginsmál* and the *Fáfnismál*—also contain a certain amount of gnomic material. Here we need only refer to the list of omens in the *Reginsmál*, st. 20–25. They are perhaps to be connected with gnomes of Type II *b*.

Gnomes occur not unfrequently in prose works. Note may be taken especially of the advice given by the sage and judge Höfundr to his son Heiðrekr in *Hervarar Saga*, cap. 6.[2] The advice consists of eight 'counsels', most of which are gnomic, though one at least is specific.

[1] The rest of the poem is lost.

[2] Transl. by Kershaw, *Stories and Ballads of the Far Past*, p. 103 f.

There is a close relationship between this passage—not only the counsels but also the accompanying narrative—and the Irish story of Flaithri, the son of Fithal, who was a judge under Cormac mac Airt.[1] But parallels are to be found elsewhere, even in distant parts of the world.[2] The form of Höfundr's gnomes may be compared with that of *Sigrdrífumál*, 22–37, though they are in prose. They are, however, briefer and include no enthymemes.

Now if Norse gnomic poetry in general be compared with English, it will be seen at once that there are differences between them of a rather striking character. The former is distinguished by the predominance of Type I, the frequence of precepts, and the absence of gnomes of observation relating to natural history (Type II *c*), which are so numerous in the latter. Such observations do indeed occur not unfrequently, e.g. in *Háv.* 21 (quoted above); but they are not introduced as independent gnomes, but for the purpose of pointing a moral in relation to human life—or at least as connected with human interests in some way or other.[3] The cynical element found in the first part of the *Hávamál* is unknown in the English poems.

On the other hand there are certain rather striking formal resemblances, which must not be overlooked. We may instance especially the very common *skal* (*sceal*) formula, and perhaps also the strings of very short gnomes. Resemblances in substance also are not rare, e.g. the opening of *Háv.* 76 f.: "Cattle (*fé*) die, kinsfolk (*frændr*) die", as compared with the *Wanderer*, 109: "Here wealth (*feoh*) passes away, here friends (*freond*) pass away". We are inclined therefore to think that the beginnings of Norse and English gnomic poetry are to be traced to a common (Teutonic) origin, though the development followed very different lines in the two languages.

Parallels to the English lists of gnomes of Type II *c* are to be found in Norse, though not in gnomic poetry. A very similar catalogue is enumerated in the solemn declaration of peace sanctioned by the law of Iceland and preserved in the Laws and in several sagas.[4] Whoever

[1] Related by Keating, I. cap. 46. Keating's source for this story is apparently unknown; cf. Bergin, *Stories from Keating's History of Ireland*, p. xi.

[2] An interesting example from among the Wayao of Nyasaland, a people of the southern Bantu, is given by Stannus, *Harvard African Studies*, III (1922), 337 f.

[3] This remark applies (e.g.) to such a case as *Háv.* 88: 'Weather determines (the fate of) the crops', which properly belongs to Type II *c*. But the context is to be taken into account.

[4] Cf. *Grágás* (the Icelandic Law-book), ed. Finsen, p. 205 f., cap. 115; *Grettis Saga* (transl. by Morris and Magnússon and by Hight), cap. 72.

violates this peace, it is declared, is to be hunted as an outlaw ('wolf') everywhere—wherever Christians betake themselves to churches or heathens reverence temples, where fire burns or the earth is productive, where the child calls upon its mother, where men light fires, where the ship travels, shields glisten, the sun shines, snow lies, the Lapp shees, the fir grows, the hawk flies throughout the long spring day—with the wind blowing straight beneath both its wings—where heaven extends and the world is inhabited, where wind howls, rivers run to the sea and men sow corn. The resemblance to Anglo-Saxon gnomic poetry here is obvious enough, even in the parenthetic sentence relating to the hawk, while the alliteration which prevails throughout the passage gives some ground for believing that it was itself originally in verse form.

A considerable amount of early Welsh gnomic poetry has been preserved; but, unfortunately, little attention appears to have been paid to it—less even than to the heroic poems. So far as we know, no satisfactory translations or commentaries exist. The translations given below must be regarded as more or less tentative.

Some poems consist wholly of gnomes, while in others the gnomic element is mingled with descriptive poetry applicable to special conditions. The latter will require notice in the next chapter; but it is not always easy to distinguish from gnomes. The descriptive matter in the elegies of Llywarch Hen also contains gnomes.

The great majority of the gnomes—indeed nearly all—belong to Type II, just as in the English gnomic poems. All varieties of this type occur, but observations of nature (*c*) preponderate, as in English. Very often the first part of a stanza consists of such gnomes, while the last line contains an observation relating to human life (*a*); but there is no connection, as in Norse (cf. p. 383) between this and the preceding gnomes. The poems are mostly in stanzas of three lines, an early form of metre which is used also in the poems of Llywarch Hen. The four-line stanzas which are found sometimes in association with these, especially in *RBH*. VI, are believed to be not earlier than the middle of the twelfth century.[1]

The form in which the gnomes are stated is very brief. The verb normally has a form which elsewhere—apart from gnomes—is used as 3 sing. imperative. The commonest word is *bit*, the 3 sing. imperative[2]

[1] Cf. Loth, *Rev. Celt.* XXI. 37.

[2] Strachan, *Introduction to Early Welsh*, p. 98, note 3, speaks of *bit* (in *RBH*. V) as 'consuetudinal'. But the usage is not peculiar to this word. Other imperative forms in *-it*, *-et* are used in the same sense, e.g. *kelet*, *kyrchyt*, *aed* (*RBH*. IV. 24, 28, 36).

of *bot* (*bod*), 'to be', though it is very frequently omitted. This use of the 'imperative' appears to be analogous to that of Anglo-Saxon *sceal* in gnomes of Type II, 'it is characteristic of...' (cf. p. 378 ff.). Frequently we find the word *gnawt* (*gnawd*), 'usual', with or (more often) without *bit*. The present indicative also occurs, but not very often.

We may first take *RBH.* v, which consists wholly of a series of gnomes, mostly in very brief form. The word *bit*, which is here used throughout, may perhaps most conveniently be translated by 'is', though the notion of 'characteristic' is implied. The first two stanzas are as follows: "The cock's comb is red. Vigorous is his cry from his triumphant bed. God commends the rejoicing of man. Joyful are swineherds at the soughing of the wind.[1] The calm is graceful. Misfortune usually falls (*bit gnawt*) upon the wicked". The last but one of these gnomes occurs again in IV. 11, with the substitution of *gnawt* for *bit*: "Usually (or 'it is usual that') the calm is graceful".

In *RBH.* VI the prevailing formula is *gnawt*; but this appears only in the first seven stanzas, of which four belong to the four-line type mentioned above. It is not clear to us that the last four stanzas (8–11) properly belong to the same poem. They are uniformly of the three-line type, and *gnawt* is not used in them; moreover one of them at least (st. 9) is found elsewhere (XI. 14), in a totally different context. We are inclined therefore to regard them as fragments which have come to be connected with the *gnawt*-series.[2] We may quote st. 8 f.: "The stalk is dry,[3] and running water (or 'flood') is in the stream (or 'glen'). The Englishman transacts his business (lit. 'the commerce of the Saxon') with money. Unhappy is the mother of disloyal children. The leaf which the wind carries[4]—unhappy is its fate. It is old, (but) it was born this year".

In certain gnomic poems, as in some other poems, each stanza begins

[1] "Because then the swine would have acorns without his being at any trouble." Pughe (quoted by Skene, *Four Ancient Books*, II. 432).

[2] In the *Myvyrian Archaiology* (p. 102) st. 8 begins a new poem, which includes (after st. 11) *RBH.* VIII and *BBC.* XXX. The connection with the two latter poems can hardly be correct; but the division of *RBH.* VI is perhaps worth noting.

[3] This gnome, if such it be, occurs again in IV. 17, in a different context. But the exact meaning is not clear to us. In *BBC.* XXX. 42 (cf. 9) it occurs in a description of winter conditions. Perhaps this is the case here—as also in the second half of the line.

[4] Translation conjectural. The corresponding passage in XI. 14 (where in general the text is less corrupt) seems to mean "This leaf—the wind shall carry it".

with an expression which is generally unconnected with what follows. Thus in *RBH.* IV every stanza begins with the words *eiry mynyd*, 'mountain snow', often followed by some 'descriptive' phrase relating to the stag, e.g. 'the stag (is) in the wood'; but the rest of the poem consists almost entirely of gnomes, which are unconnected with either snow or stag. There are only a few references to snow, and these occur in the first line of the stanza, in place of the references to the stag. We may quote st. I: "Mountain snow—everywhere is white. The crow is practised in croaking. No good will come from excessive sleeping". And st. 30: "Mountain snow—the stag is on the hill-side. Wind whistles over the top of the ash. To the old his stick is a third foot". In *RBH.* III also thirteen out of the first fourteen stanzas begin with *eiry mynyd*, perhaps in imitation of the last poem. But this is a religious piece, in dialogue form (Type B); the gnomic element is small. On the other hand in *RBH.* IX, which consists mainly of gnomes, each stanza begins with the words *gorwyn blaen*, 'very bright (is) the top' of various trees, hills, etc.

All the poems noticed above are preserved in the *Red Book*.[1] Gnomic poetry is not so well represented in the other early MSS. *BBC.* II is a short piece which consists mainly of gnomes.[2] Unlike the collections noticed above these are concerned only with human activities (Types II *a* and I). The first nine lines of *An.* III also consist of a short series of gnomes, mostly of Type II *a*; but they are followed by what appears to be a specific reference. *Tal.* IV consists wholly of what may be called a gnomic catalogue, but will be treated more conveniently in the next chapter.

A number of gnomes occur also, singly or in small groups, in other poems, especially in the elegies of Llywarch Hen (*BBC.* XXX and *RBH.* XI) and in *RBH.* X, which has much in common with these. These gnomes do not differ in character from those contained in the collections noticed above.

Taking the Welsh gnomes as a whole, it will be seen that in their general character they show a rather striking resemblance to the English gnomes preserved in the *Cotton* and *Exeter* collections. On the

[1] The list is not exhaustive. *RBH.* VIII and XXIV are also mainly or wholly gnomic. The latter contains a considerable, though not predominant, religious element. The former is believed to have been composed in the fourteenth century, in imitation of ancient models; cf. Loth, *Rev. Celt.* XXI. 34.

[2] The connection between the opening lines (cf. Strachan, *Ériu*, II. 60) and what follows is not clear to us.

other hand they have of course marked stylistic features of their own, e.g. in the 'refrains' at the beginning of stanzas and in the form in which the gnomes are expressed. The preference for the three-line stanza is noticeable, though it is not peculiar to gnomic poetry. It may be observed that each of these stanzas most commonly contains three gnomes, though stanzas containing two, four and five gnomes are also of frequent occurrence. The use of this metre for gnomic poetry may possibly therefore be connected with the popularity of the 'Triad.' Gnomic Triads, as well as antiquarian and legal Triads, are preserved in large numbers; but the records are late, and it is quite beyond our power to deal with them.

In early Greek poetry the chief collection of gnomic material is to be found in Hesiod's *Works and Days*. We have already (p. 357 f.) had occasion to mention this poem and the personal references which it contains; but it will be convenient here to give a brief synopsis of the work as a whole. After a short invocation to the Muses and Zeus (1–10) the poet speaks of the difference between good and evil strife, and then (27) begins to address his brother Perses. At 47 ff. he introduces the story of Prometheus and Pandora, and from this passes on (106 ff.) to the description of the Golden Race and the subsequent races of mankind. His account of the depravity of the fifth race—the men of his own time—which is mainly prophetical, leads to the fable of the hawk and the nightingale (200 ff.). From 212 the poem is occupied with gnomic matter, occasionally interrupted by personal references.

The first important gnomic passages are 214–247 and 263–380. These consist of gnomes and precepts somewhat similar to those of the *Hávamál*. The gnomes practically all relate to human experiences, and especially to human acts in their moral aspect; but 'heroic' characteristics are wholly wanting. The poet insists upon work as the condition of success in life. The chief difference from the Norse poem lies in the emphasis laid upon justice, which is constantly associated with the gods, especially Zeus. The tone is truly didactic throughout. There is no suspicion of a desire to entertain rather than to instruct. Nor are the gnomes merely disinterested observations, like those of the English gnomic collections. The 'natural history' variety (Type II *c*) so fully represented in the latter, seems to be entirely absent here. From 248 to 262 the gnomic material is interrupted by an appeal to the princes to beware of vengeance coming upon them from the gods. Descriptive passages are also introduced. The descriptions of the cities of the just and of the unjust (225 ff., 238 ff.) are more on the scale of similar passages in the *Exeter Gnomes* than of those in the *Hávamál*.

After the moral gnomes comes (381–694) a long list of 'industrial' precepts—relating to agriculture and seafaring—subjects to which we have only allusions in the Norse and English poems. This list also contains descriptive passages, especially the long description of the north wind in 505 ff. Next we find (695–723) a short list of precepts and gnomes relating to marriage and friendship. This is followed (724–764) by a list of prohibitions of acts likely to incur the wrath of the gods—based on religious or superstitious rather than practical grounds, like certain precepts in the *Sigrdrífumál* (cf. p. 385). Lastly, from 765 to the end, comes a list of days lucky or unlucky for various occupations. This section may be compared to a certain extent with the omens in the *Reginsmál*, though it contains a good many precepts of the superstitious variety.

In form the *Works and Days* has more in common with the English than with the Norse gnomic poems. Like the former it has the uniform line and—more or less—the continuous running style of heroic narrative poetry, as against the stanza, the unequal lines and the disconnected style of the Norse poems. The descriptive passages also show more resemblance to those contained in the English collections. But the affinities of the gnomes themselves are clearly with the Norse, excluding of course the cynical element so prominent in the first part of the *Hávamál*. The poem is concerned with what should be done rather than with observations of fact, whether in natural history or human activities. Its nearest affinities lie with the *Loddfáfnismál* and the *Sigrdrífumál*.

The expression of the gnomes is somewhat similar to what is found in the Norse poems, though on the whole Hesiod's are rather fuller than the latter. Most of them are enthymemes or contain relative or conditional sentences. They are generally more closely connected with one another than is the case in Norse. The very brief gnomes characteristic of English and Welsh gnomic poetry have no parallels in this poem, though they are not unknown elsewhere in Greek. There are no regular formulae corresponding to *sceal*, *bit*, *gnawt*. Gnomes of Type II are expressed by the present or aorist indicative. In precepts addressed to a particular person (Perses) or group of persons (the princes) the imperative is used. But gnomic precepts, i.e. precepts of general reference, which are much more frequent, are normally expressed by the infinitive. The difference between such precepts and the gnomes of Type I found in the Norse poems and expressed by the conjunctive or by *skal*, is extremely slight, if it can be said to exist at all.[1]

The *Works and Days* is the only extant poem dating from the period before 600 which can be regarded as primarily a collection of gnomes. But there is no reason for doubting that other poems of similar character were current. The *Instructions of Cheiron to Achilles* would seem to have been a somewhat similar collection of gnomic precepts. The framework may have been analogous to that of the *Sigrdrífumál*. The hortatory poems of Callinos and Tyrtaios have much in common with gnomic precepts; but they have specific (local) reference, and we have therefore treated them as political poems. Solon's gnomic poems will be noticed later.

Theognis hardly comes within our period. He is said to have flourished shortly after the middle of the sixth century; but there are references in his poetry (764 ff.) to an impending Median (i.e. Persian) invasion, which cannot date from before the close of the century. In 19 ff. he says that a seal is to be set upon his poems, so that they can be recognised if they are stolen—which is commonly interpreted to mean that they were written. In 237 ff., however, he clearly anticipates that they will be sung at banquets. It is to be noted that the poetry of Theognis is really a collection of poems, apparently numerous and for the most part very short. Many of the pieces are addressed to individual friends of the poet, especially to a certain Cyrnos. The gnomic element is very large; but there is also much personal and political matter, besides appeals to the gods. In 22 f. he speaks of himself as belonging to Megara. In 1209 f., 1213 f. he says that he is in exile and lives at Thebes; but other passages, especially 39 ff., seem to imply that he is in his own city. The state to which he belongs is obviously torn by political factions; and the poet himself is an uncompromising partisan of the aristocracy. Many scholars, however, believe that the poems are a kind of anthology, not entirely the work of one author; and it is obvious enough that such a collection, especially if preserved in the main by oral tradition, is liable to have additions made to it.

There are many parallels between this collection and the first part of the *Hávamál*, which is itself doubtless a collection, though it has

[1] In referring to these infinitival sentences we have used the word 'precept' throughout, in accordance with what seems to be the general custom of Greek scholars. Theognis—and other poets occasionally—seem to use the imperative and infinitive more or less indiscriminately. But Hesiod's infinitival precepts rather suggest gnomes of Type I.

probably had a longer history. The political element is wanting in the latter. But both are largely concerned with social relations and with convivial parties, though the one deals with city life, the other with that of the country. A few examples will have to suffice: (155 ff.) "Never in thy wrath reproach a man for soul-destroying poverty or baneful want of means; for Zeus inclines the scales now one way, now another, so that a man is wealthy at one time but penniless at another". We may compare *Háv*. 75: "One man is wealthy, another poor; but he is not to be blamed for misfortune". And again (363 f.): "Beguile thy enemy with fair words; but when he comes into thy power, take vengeance upon him, without troubling to produce a pretext". With this we may compare *Háv*. 46: "With regard to him in whom thou hast no confidence and of whose motives thou art suspicious, thou shouldst smile upon him and dissemble thy feelings. Gifts ought to be repaid in like coin". But the half-cynical, half-playful element, by which the Norse gnomic collection has been converted into a means of entertainment, is wanting in the Greek poet. Theognis seems always to be serious.

As regards the form of the gnomes, the imperative—or in prohibitions often the conjunctive—is much more frequent than the infinitive in precepts; but there does not appear to be any difference in usage. On the other hand true gnomes of Type I, expressed by χρή, 'it is necessary', with the accusative and infinitive, are not uncommon. The elegiac metre is used throughout.

The Irish material is very extensive, but differs a good deal in character from the rest. We have therefore left it to the end. It may conveniently be divided into three groups: (i) instructions given to a newly appointed king, (ii) instructions given by a father to his son, (iii) anonymous collections of gnomes. Much of the material is in prose.

The instructions to kings represent perhaps the oldest type of gnomic collections in Irish. The earliest example is believed to date from c. 800. But the kings to whom they are addressed are mostly persons of the Heroic Age, while the instructors are either famous heroes—friends of the new kings—or sages. The instructions are therefore to be regarded as speeches in character, somewhat similar to the *Sigrdrífumál* (Type CB, cf. p. 385).

First we may mention the Instructions given by CuChulainn to his friend Lugaid Reoderg, when he became high-king. This incident[1] forms an episode—believed to be a later addition—in the story of

[1] Transl. in E. Hull, *The CuChullin Saga*, p. 231 ff.; cf. Thurneysen, *Ir. Heldensage*, pp. 416, 420 f.

CuChulainn's Sickbed (cf. p. 257). The Instructions, which are quite short, consist of precepts on the duties of kingship and on conduct becoming to a king. It may be observed that there is no reference to achievements in war or to heroic virtues, such as valour and generosity. The duties chiefly emphasised are of an essentially 'non-heroic' type—to see to the proper administration of justice, to avoid arrogance, and to listen to the advice of the wise. The Instructions are given in the form of a series of unconnected precepts, often quite short. They are non-metrical, but contain a good deal of alliteration, somewhat like a *retoric* (cf. p. 57).

Another, still shorter series of Instructions are those given by Conall Cernach to Cuscraid, son of Conchobor, on his appointment to the throne of Ulster. These are preserved in the *Battle of Airtech*,[1] cap. 3. In their form and their insistence upon justice they resemble the last; but heroic elements are not entirely wanting.

The longest and probably the earliest of these Instructions are attributed to Morand,[2] a judge (probably a *fili*) famous in tradition. They are addressed by him to a messenger called Nere for transmission to King Feradach Find Fechtnach. This is the high-king who avenges his father in the *Revolt of the Vassals*, according to one form of that story (cf. p. 171), while Morand is in some accounts son of Cairbre Cenn Cait, who was made king by the revolutionaries. But the Instructions contain no reference to this story. The first part, sect. 2–9, bids Nere to exhort King Feradach to the cultivation of justice. Sect. 10–29 consist of gnomes specifying the blessings which arise from the justice of a ruler—prosperity, peace, wealth, treasures from overseas, good seasons, etc. Sect. 30–43 consist of precepts, specifying the characteristics which should be avoided by a king—lying, arrogance, the killing of relations, etc. Sect. 44–48 discuss various types of princes. The Instructions conclude with warnings against the dangers arising from injustice and falsehood and with a list of the blessings which will follow the observation of the principles enunciated above.

These Instructions are expressed in a form similar to those which we have already noticed. They are unmetrical, but alliteration is frequent. Most of the gnomes and precepts are, however, expressed more fully, and there are numerous enthymemes. A series of gnomes of Type I, expressed by *dligid*, 'deserves', occur in sect. 34, among the precepts. But the most noticeable feature of these Instructions is the almost total

1 Ed. and transl. by Best, *Ériu*, VIII. 170 ff.

2 Ed. and transl. by Thurneysen, *Zeitschr. f. celt. Philologie*, XI. 79 ff.

absence of heroic elements. The ideal which Morand sets forth is that of a reign of peace.

Lastly, mention must be made here of a hortatory poem, the *Rights of every Lawful King*,[1] addressed to Aed Oirdnide, who became high-king in 798, and attributed to a certain Fothad na Canoine, apparently an ecclesiastic. This poem, which is in rhyming couplets, is only partly gnomic; it refers to St Patrick and the church of Armagh, to various dynasties and to heroes of the past. It would seem to have been composed at the beginning of the king's reign,[2] and—like the Instructions noticed above—it frequently insists on the observation of justice. But the tone is far more bellicose; Aed is repeatedly exhorted to maintain his rights with the strong hand. His duties towards the church and the clergy are also much emphasised. The poem is of special importance because it suggests that the Instructions to ancient kings are founded upon a custom which was prevalent in the eighth century, though it may of course have existed earlier.

To the second group belong the *Instructions of Cormac mac Airt to his son Cairbre.*[3] King Cormac lived probably in the latter part of the third century (cf. p. 173) and was regarded by tradition as a sage, or at least as a man of exceptional wisdom; but the Instructions are believed to date from the early part of the ninth century. They consist largely of strings of gnomes or precepts in the briefest form, without metre but with frequent alliteration. Much of the matter, however, is 'descriptive' rather than gnomic. Each subject is introduced by a question from Cairbre.

The first part, cap. 1–6, is of similar character to the Instructions already noticed, and relates to the aims, duties and conduct of kings and minor rulers. In cap. 7–10 Cormac speaks of his own achievements and experiences. Then come in cap. 11, 12 some precepts of a general character, followed in cap. 13–15 by gnomes of Type II *a* and descriptive matter relating to mankind in general. Next, in cap. 16, we find a long and highly uncomplimentary list of the characteristics of women, with a few gnomes on the same subject. Cap. 17 f. deal briefly with weather and housekeeping; cap. 19 contains further general precepts; cap. 20 specifies

[1] Ed. and transl. by O'Donoghue in the *Miscellany presented to K. Meyer*, p. 258 ff.

[2] This is suggested by several passages, e.g. st. 4, 14 f., 25. In st. 68 the king is advised to marry.

[3] Ed. and transl. by K. Meyer, *Todd Lecture Series* (Royal Irish Academy), Vol. XV (1909). Selections also transl. in *Ancient Irish Poetry*, p. 105 ff.

the most lasting things. Cap. 21–28 contain lists of the 'worst' things; the greater part of this (cap. 22–26) relates to public speaking. In cap. 29–34 we have further gnomes and precepts of a general character; in cap. 35–37 the deafest persons, the best seasons, and (again) the worst things.

Most of the gnomes contained in these Instructions belong to Type II *a*. Instead of gnomes of Type I we find precepts, most commonly in the 3 sing. imperative. Gnomes of Type II *c* occur, e.g. in cap. 17 and 36, but they are quite rare. Many of the lists are of great length; but the individual gnomes are expressed as briefly as possible. Enthymemes are rare, while illustrations of any kind are wanting. Most of the subjects seem to be treated seriously and with a didactic object. But the very long section on the characteristics of women (cap. 16) can hardly have been intended otherwise than for entertainment, although humour is wanting, as in the rest of these Instructions. We suspect therefore that the lists are drawn from different sources—perhaps oral—a conclusion which seems to be favoured also by certain variations in the formulae.

A very similar collection is the *Senbriathra Fithail*,[1] attributed to Fithal, who is said to have been a judge in the time of Cormac. Here also the gnomes are expressed in the briefest possible form. Cap. 1–2, 4–5 consist of lists of gnomes of Type II dealing with abstract qualities. In cap. 1, each gnome begins with *tossach*, 'beginning', e.g. 'The beginning of strife is quarrelling'; in cap. 2, with *adcota*, 'begets', e.g. 'Folly begets violence'; in cap. 4, with *ferr*, 'better', e.g. 'A friend is better than ale'; in 5, with *dligid*, 'deserves', e.g. 'Knowledge deserves respect'. Cap. 3 consists of precepts, with the formula: *bat*...*corbat* (*arnabat*)..., 'be...that you may (not) be...', e.g. 'Be humble that you may be exalted'. Cap. 6–9 are variants of the *Instructions of Cormac*, cap. 22, 29–31. There are no references to Cormac or his son; once we find 'said Fithal'. Cap. 10 ff. are in the form of a dialogue between Fithal and his son who is not named. Each of Fithal's sayings is in answer to a question. He tells his son that the 'anvil' (foundation stone) on which his husbandry is to be founded is a good wife. Then in answer to the question how a good wife is to be distinguished, he enumerates various types of women according to their appearance and character, laying special stress on complexion. Then in cap. 11 f. he describes very

[1] Ed. and transl. by R. M. Smith, *Rev. Celt.* XLV. i ff.; cf. Thurneysen, 'Zu ir. Hss.' (*Abh. d. k. Gesellsch. d. Wiss. zu Göttingen*, XIV. 2), p. 3 ff. A variant text of cap. 10 ff. is ed. by K. Meyer, *Zeitschr. f. celt. Philol.* VIII. 112 f.—part of which is transl. in *Ancient Irish Poetry*, p. 110.

briefly the qualities of good and bad wives, and in cap. 13 gives a list of fifteen characteristics of each kind.

From the story referred to on p. 222, it would seem that other wise sayings were attributed to Fithal, though they are not preserved in any early record, so far as we know. In this story—which is probably a form of a widely distributed folk-tale—Fithal's son is called Flaithri.

A third collection of the same kind bears the title *Briathra Flainn Fina maic Ossu.*[1] The Flann to whom they are attributed, whether rightly or wrongly, is the Northumbrian king Aldfrith (r. 685–705), son of Oswio. In this collection cap. 1–3, 5, 6 seem to be derived from the *Senbriathra Fithail*, cap. 2, 3, 5, 1, 4 respectively, though a large number of gnomes have been added. Cap. 4 consists of a similar series of gnomes (Type II), beginning with *descaid*, 'sign', e.g. 'drinking (lit. a drink) is a sign of thirst'. Cap. 7 consists in part of religious gnomes, and is believed to be a later addition.

The third group, consisting of anonymous collections of gnomes, is perhaps best represented by the *Triads of Ireland*,[2] though these contain antiquarian and legal, as well as gnomic elements. The gnomes consist of groups of three (occasionally two, four or more) things or ideas brought under a common heading, e.g. "(There are) three nurses of theft, (viz.) a wood, a cloak, night". They are in prose, but with sporadic alliteration, and stated very briefly. The collection is believed to be not later than the end of the ninth century.

All the collections noticed above[3] are primarily of secular character, though both the *Rights of every Lawful King* and the *Triads of Ireland* frequently refer to ecclesiastical institutions and interests, while similar references occur occasionally in the *Instructions of Cormac*. There is, however, at least one collection of definitely Christian character and doubtless ecclesiastical origin, the *Bid Crinna*,[4] which consists of a very large number of prose precepts, including a few gnomes, based in the main upon Christian ethics. We do not know its date.

In the third group of gnomic collections the Irish material obviously

[1] Ed. and transl. by R. M. Smith, *Rev. Celt.* XLV. 61 ff. In one text this collection is attributed to Fithal.

[2] Ed. and transl. by K. Meyer, *Todd Lecture Series* (Royal Irish Academy), Vol. XIII (1906).

[3] The list is doubtless far from complete. Two four-line gnomic stanzas are ed. and transl. by Marstrander, *Ériu*, v. 142 f. Two short sets of gnomes are ed. by K. Meyer, *Zeitschr. f. celt. Philol.* VI. 260 f. And there are probably many others which we do not know.

[4] Ed. and transl. by Marstrander, *Ériu*, v. 126 f.

has affinities with the Welsh. The *Triads of Ireland* are traceable to a much earlier date than any Welsh collection of prose *Triads*; but we are not prepared to speculate on the nature of the relations between the two until the Welsh material, which is very extensive, has been more thoroughly examined.[1] The other two Irish groups have no Welsh affinities, so far as we are aware. The first group indeed stands very much by itself, though its nearest affinities are with the *Sigrdrífumál*. The second group belongs to a widespread class of 'paternal' instructions, other examples of which will be found in this and the following chapters.

Now if we compare the various gnomic collections discussed in this chapter, it will be seen that—apart from the *Triads*, where there is doubtless a historical connection of some kind—the Welsh and Irish collections have one feature in common, as against the others. This is a tendency to express the individual gnomes as briefly as possible, though in Irish the same idea may be repeated over and over again in successive gnomes. Such brief gnomes are by no means rare in English and Norse, but on the whole they are exceptional and incidental; and there is a general tendency to connect the gnomic sentences—not by mere repetition—and to introduce illustrations.

Far more noteworthy, however, are the features which the English and Welsh collections have in common, as against the Greek, Irish and Norse. These are (i) the predominance of gnomes of Type II *c*, which rarely or never occur in the other collections; (ii) the absence or rareness of gnomes of Type I and of precepts. Again, gnomes of Type II *a* occur everywhere; but it may be observed that there is a noticeable difference in the usage of such gnomes. In Greek, Irish and Norse an element of praise or blame is usually implied, whereas most of the English and Welsh examples seem to be cases of disinterested observation. All this indicates a difference of principle in the collections. The Greek, Irish and Norse are concerned primarily with what should or should not be in human affairs, even when the treatment is cynical and playful, as in the first part of the *Hávamál*; whereas the English and Welsh collections are interested merely in the observation of what is—

[1] It has been inferred from the greater antiquity of the Irish texts that the Welsh *Triads* are derived from them. (Cf. Stern in Hinneberg's *Kultur d. Gegenwart*, I. XI. I. 127.) In view of the character of early Welsh records in general any such inference seems to us hazardous. We ourselves suspect the borrowing to have been in the opposite direction, but perhaps not in the form of written texts.

in the world of nature, as well as among mankind. We are not speaking here of course of short series of gnomes included in other poems, as (e.g.) in the *Wanderer*, nor of collections of Christian gnomes or precepts, like *A Father's Instructions*.

One feature which all the early collections in Greek, English, Welsh and Norse have in common is that they are uniformly in verse. Most of the Irish collections are non-metrical, but it is questionable whether we should be justified in concluding from this that prose was the original form of Irish gnomic collections. The extensive use of alliteration, if not also the cast of the sentences themselves, in the first two groups suggests derivation from the *retoric*—the earliest known form of poetry in Irish. We doubt the antiquity of the third group.

It is doubtful, however, if the history of gnomic poetry followed the same lines in the various languages. In Greece its cultivation would seem to be later than that of heroic poetry. At all events the earliest example, the *Works and Days*, uses the metre (hexameter) and to some extent the diction of Homeric poetry. It should be observed, however, that we have no evidence for the cultivation of any other metres before the seventh century, though they may have been known. Theognis' poetry and the semi-gnomic poems of Solon are in the elegiac metre, which in the seventh century had come into very general use in political and personal poetry and in elegies, though iambic, trochaic and various lyric metres were also widely cultivated. One can hardly say more than that the gnomic poets seem to have made use of the metrical forms generally current in their times.

The Norse gnomic poems do not employ the metres of heroic narrative poetry, the *Fornyrðislag* and *Málaháttr*, except that the latter occurs in a few 'catalogue' stanzas. The metres used are the *Ljóðaháttr*, which consists of alternate long and short lines, like the Greek elegiac, and varieties akin to it, such as the *Galdralag*, which have two or more short lines in juxtaposition. These metres, especially the *Ljóðaháttr*, are regularly used in most of the speech-poems relating to the gods, whether didactic or not, and they also occur in certain elegies, the *Eiríksmál* and the *Hákonarmál* (cf. p. 344 f.); but they are hardly ever found in heroic poems, except in dialogues in the Trilogy and in *Helgakviða Hjörvarðssonar*, and not at all in narrative poems relating to the gods.

In Anglo-Saxon poetry the uniform line like that of the *Fornyrðislag* is almost universal (cf. p. 21). But it is in the *Exeter Gnomes* that most of the exceptions occur—pairs of short lines as in the *Galdralag*, though there are no stanzas. This fact tends to support the view expressed on p. 386 as to the common origin of English and Norse gnomic poetry, and suggests that this early gnomic poetry used a metre different from that of heroic narrative poetry. But the evidence given above shows that the subsequent development proceeded along divergent lines.

Most of the Welsh gnomic poems are in the three-line stanza, which is one of the earliest Welsh metres, though presumably of Latin origin. Apart from gnomic poetry it is used chiefly in antiquarian and religious poems and in elegies.

It may be observed further that Greek,[1] English, Welsh and Norse gnomic poetry shows a contrast with heroic poetry in the matter of social interests. The existence of kings and their courts is not ignored. They may be regarded with hostility, as in the *Works and Days*, or with suspicion, as in the *Hávamál*, or with apparently friendly interest, as in the *Exeter Gnomes*. But royalty is only one of many classes with which these poems are concerned. Attention is paid also to the merchant, the farmer, the destitute man, and even to the thief and other bad characters. The Norse poems are clearly no product of court minstrelsy, any more than the *Works and Days*, while the impartial attitude towards all classes shown in the English and Welsh poems, though less conclusive, at all events affords no ground for supposing that they were of any such origin. It is instructive, by way of contrast, to compare the 'heroic' gnomes, which occur incidentally in Anglo-Saxon and Norse heroic poetry (cf. p. 379).

The Irish evidence is again exceptional, since the first group of gnomic collections noticed above are addressed to kings, while the chief collection of the second group is attributed to a king. But we have seen that the heroic elements in these collections are very slight. The ideal which the authors have in mind is a reign of justice, peace and plenty. It is only in one case, the *Rights of every Lawful King*, that the military side of kingship is markedly emphasised. The other cases represent an attitude towards the kings which is not that of a court. They speak rather as more or less independent advisers, who require justice in a king.

It is probable that collections of precepts and gnomes of Type I figured largely in the unwritten laws of early times. We may compare (e.g.) the Hebrew Ten Commandments. The written Laws which have

[1] We are speaking here only of the *Works and Days*, the only Greek gnomic poem which dates from the times of kingship. Theognis' poems are aristocratic in sympathy.

been preserved vary a good deal in this respect. The Welsh Laws contain a considerable gnomic—or semi-gnomic—element, chiefly in the form of (legal) Triads. In the Anglo-Saxon Laws on the other hand the gnomic element is very slight. These Laws would seem to have been drawn up with a view to meeting cases where doubt might arise; they are rarely comprehensive. Indeed we possess no statement of the principles of Anglo-Saxon law. It may at all events be noted that Morand and Fithal were judges, according to tradition, and the same is said of the legendary Höfundr (cf. p. 385 f.), whose name indeed perhaps means 'judge'. It may also be observed that the Laws of Uppland in Sweden are said in the Preface to them to be based on the 'collections'[1] of 'Wiger the wise (or 'prophetic'), a heathen in heathen times'. There is evidence indeed, which we shall have to consider in Ch. XIX, that in early times both in the North and in Ireland knowledge of law fell within the province of the sage—that it was included in the general knowledge or wisdom which he derived from his gift of second sight.

The Greek and Norse collections, especially the *Works and Days* and the *Hávamál*, have religious associations, whereas the collections from the British Isles date from Christian times and—with a few exceptions, which appear to be of ecclesiastical origin—contain only incidental references to religion. The religious associations of the *Works and Days* and the *Hávamál* are of very different character. The moral gnomes and precepts of the former are permeated by the idea that justice or righteousness (δίκη) is under divine sanction. The righteous man will receive reward and the unrighteous punishment from the gods, especially Zeus. The same idea is prominent in Solon's poetry, though it is foreign to the Homeric poems. There the relations of deities with human beings are governed by purely personal considerations; indeed they are capricious and often unworthy. The deities are helpful to their favourites, cruel and unfair to those whom they dislike (cf. p. 246). It is by personal offences against them, e.g. by the violation of oaths in which they are invoked, that a man incurs their wrath. But in the *Works and Days* and by Solon they are regarded as acting in accordance with moral law.

In the *Hávamál* the connection with the gods is of quite a different character. Nothing is said as to the association of the gods with moral law, any more than in the Homeric poems. The governing principle underlying the gnomes and precepts is utilitarianism, together with the

[1] The word *flokkr*, which is used here, means in Norse either 'body of men' or 'poem'. Possibly therefore poems are meant here.

desire for good fame. But the speaker who gives the advice throughout, in both parts of the poem, is the god Othin. In the first part he is a humourist and a trickster; at the end (st. 110) he declares himself to have been a faithless lover and a perjuror. But the second part is quite serious; and this is introduced (st. 111; cf. p. 384) by words which seem to imply an oracle delivered at a sanctuary. The underlying idea therefore is that this gnomic wisdom is derived from the god. The first part may have originated with the same idea. In the *Sigrdrífumál* the speaker, who gives the advice, is a Valkyrie—either a supernatural being or one with supernatural powers.

The *Works and Days* itself makes no such claim to divine origin; for the invocation of the Muses at the beginning may mean no more than it does in the *Iliad* and the *Odyssey*, or with Solon and many other poets. But there is no valid reason for doubting that the poem is of the same authorship as the *Theogony*, in which (22 ff.) the poet, Hesiod, claims direct revelation and professes to speak as the mouthpiece of the Muses. We are inclined therefore to think that in Greece, as in the North, this kind of learning originally had religious associations—that the poets made claims to inspiration which were more than a mere figure of speech. To this question, however, we shall have to return in a later chapter.

What has been said above applies of course only to the early stages of gnomic poetry. It does not hold good for the first part of the *Hávamál* any more than for Theognis. The latter makes it clear (e.g. 239 ff.) that he expects his poetry to be recited at social gatherings. The milieu suggested in the first part of the *Hávamál* is that of a gathering, apparently small and more or less fortuitous, in a house where hospitality was offered to strangers (travellers) as well as acquaintances—similar to what might be found in an inn. Other gnomic poems may well be of somewhat similar origin—and the same remark applies to some of the descriptive poems discussed in the next chapter. Some of them, it is to be hoped, were intended for male audiences only. But there is no reason for believing that gnomic poetry was a product of court life; it is obviously of a different provenance from heroic poetry. The two may converge occasionally, as in the poems of Llywarch Hen and, to a certain extent, in *Beowulf*—where gnomic elements seem to have invaded the heroic sphere. Sometimes also gnomic collections have adopted the names of famous heroes,[1] whether for the instructor or the

[1] The case of Cormac is peculiar, since he was famed not only as a king but also as a sage. The heroic side is not prominent (cf. p. 100 f.).

person instructed—as in the cases of CuChulainn, Conall Cernach, Sigurðr and Achilles. But the original affinities of gnomic poetry lay doubtless with the non-heroic poetry and saga discussed in Ch. VI.

In Ch. XIX we shall have to consider the class of persons with whom gnomic poetry originated. We may, however, note here that its cultivation was always contemporary, and sometimes connected with that of antiquarian poetry. The products of both often seem arid and futile enough; but both are of incalculable importance in their results. Just as the study of history owes its origin to antiquarian poetry, so gnomic poetry must be regarded as the first systematisation of the study of natural science and of moral philosophy.

CHAPTER XIII

DESCRIPTIVE POETRY

DETAILED descriptions of places—specified and familiar places—seem not to occur in the early stages of any of the literatures which we are discussing. There is a short Anglo-Saxon poem[1] which describes very briefly the situation and antiquities of Durham; but it cannot be earlier than the eleventh century. The far more poetic Irish description of the Isle of Arran[2] is believed to be much later; and this is of such a general character that it might be applied to many other lands. The description of Ireland attributed to St Columba[3] is said to be not earlier than the twelfth century.

The Anglo-Saxon *Ruin*[4] is generally believed to relate to Bath. But the description of the place as the poet sees it is extremely brief: "Wondrous is this masonry, shattered by the Fates. The fortifications have given way, the buildings raised by giants are crumbling. The roofs have collapsed. The towers are in ruins.... There is rime on the mortar. The walls are rent and broken away, and have fallen, undermined by age.... Red of hue and hoary with lichen this wall has outlasted kingdom after kingdom,[5] standing unmoved by storms". The main part of the poem is of an imaginative character, conjuring up pictures of the place as it was in the past, before and during its destruction. The place is peopled, however, not with the health-seekers of a Roman spa, of which naturally the poet knew nothing, but with the military court of an English king, such as he was doubtless familiar with (15 ff.): "Loud was the clamour of the troops; many were the banqueting halls, full of the joys of life—until all was shattered by mighty Fate. The dead lay on all sides". And again (25 ff.): "...where of old many a warrior, joyous hearted and radiant with gold, shone resplendent in the harness of battle, proud and flushed with wine. He gazed upon the treasure... upon this splendid citadel of a broad domain".

[1] Publ. in Grein-Wülcker, *Bibliothek d. ags. Poesie*, I. 389 ff.

[2] Transl. by K. Meyer, *Ancient Irish Poetry*, p. 59.

[3] Transl. by K. Meyer, *op. cit.* p. 85 ff.

[4] Ed. and transl. by Kershaw, *Anglo-Saxon and Norse Poems*, p. 54 ff.

[5] Cf. the short Irish poem called *The Fort of Rathangan*, transl. by K. Meyer, *op. cit.* p. 93.

The descriptions of kings' dwellings which occur in heroic poetry are as a rule quite short and mention nothing particularly distinctive of the place. The palaces of Menelaos and of Hrothgar are represented as being of unusual splendour; but it is not clear that they had any special features of their own otherwise. It is only when the poets are dealing with unknown places or can draw freely on their imagination that longer and more striking descriptions are found—just as in the passage quoted above.[1] We may refer (e.g.) to the account of the city and palace of the Phaeacians in the *Odyssey*, or such pictures as those of the dwelling of Calypso (*ib.* v. 59 ff.) or the den of Grendel, in *Beowulf*, 1362 ff. (cf. 1512 ff.), and above all to the descriptions of Mag Mell in Irish poetry (cf. p. 262 f.).

Descriptions of persons are in poetry generally just as brief and indefinite. Little or nothing is said as to the features, colouring, or even the clothes of the heroes and heroines. Armour, however, is sometimes described in considerable detail. We may instance the arms of Agamemnon described in *Il.* XI. 17 ff. and those borne by Beowulf on his visit to the monsters' den (1441 ff.), and more especially the shield made for Achilles by the god Hephaistos (*Il.* XVIII. 478 ff.). In sagas on the other hand, both Irish and Norse, we meet frequently with descriptions, not only of armour but also of the clothes and the physical appearance of persons. The Irish descriptions are usually of a conventional character. There is a static description of a beautiful woman, which is applied to numerous heroines.[2] Descriptions of heroes, when they differ from the norm, are due apparently sometimes to a desire for differentiation—when they occur in groups or lists—sometimes to the introduction of fantastic features, as in the case of CuChulainn. In Norse sagas of the Viking Age, however, especially the 'Sagas of Icelanders', individualisation is far more advanced. Here also not rarely we find detailed descriptions of the characters, as well as the appearance, of the leading persons.

Descriptions of works of art, though not very common, are sometimes given in great detail. The description of the arms of Achilles in the *Iliad* (XVIII. 478–613) is almost wholly occupied with the designs worked upon the shield. In the *Shield of Heracles* an even longer account

[1] With this passage may be compared the somewhat similar description of a ruin—also obviously Roman—in the *Wanderer* (77 ff.). To this we shall have to return later.

[2] E.g. the description of Etain at the beginning of the *Destruction of Da Derga's Hall* (*Rev. Celt.* XXII. 13 ff.). This is said to be the fullest example.

is given of the shield from which the poem takes its name. The designs upon the former seem to represent only natural objects and scenes typical of various human occupations, i.e. scenes of the timeless, nameless type. The latter, in addition to these, bears also scenes from heroic stories and stories of the gods.[1] With this may be compared the *Ragnarsdrápa* of the very early Norse poet Bragi Boddason, a poem of which only fragments have been preserved, but which evidently gave very full descriptions of the designs painted upon a shield. The shield would seem to have been divided into compartments containing scenes from the stories of Jörmunrekr's death, the adventures of Sigurðr, the tragedy of Heðinn and Högni, and possibly also the creation of Sjælland by the goddess Gefjon. The poem *Haustlöng*, by Thjóðolfr of Hvín (cf. p. 250 f.), likewise appears to have taken its subjects from a shield. Among them were the stories of the goddess Iðunn and Thor's fight with Hrungnir.[2]

In *Beowulf*, 1688 ff., the hilt of the sword found in Grendel's den is said to be engraved with a scene from the story of the Deluge. Again in 994 ff. it is briefly stated that the tapestries in the king's hall presented many wondrous spectacles for those who pay attention to such things. But in *Guðrúnarkviða II*, 15 f. the heroine and her friend Thóra are represented as working in gold thread both scenes from heroic stories and (apparently) timeless nameless scenes. Among the former are Sigmundr's ships and a fight between Sigarr and Siggeirr. Here also we may refer to the *Laxdoela Saga*, cap. 29, where it is stated that the poet Ulfr Uggason composed his poem *Húsdrápa* upon the paintings in the house of the wealthy Icelander Ólafr Pái. Fragments of this poem, dealing with Balder's funeral and the fight between Heimdallr and Loki, have been preserved.

Descriptions of action—not derived from pictorial representations—are of course essential to any narrative poetry which can be called epic.

[1] So far as we are aware, no shields comparable with these have been preserved. But the poets seem to have had in mind schemes of decoration such as are found upon (Phoenician) bronze and silver platters discovered in Italy and Cyprus. The pictures engraved upon these may have been identified by the Greeks with scenes from their own traditions.

[2] According to *Egils Saga*, cap. 78 (83), the Icelandic poet Einarr Helgason (cf. p. 346) was rewarded by Earl Haakon with a magnificent shield of this kind, which on his return home he presented to Egill Skallagrímsson. Egill felt bound to compose a poem upon it. A similar present, likewise followed by a poem, is recorded in the next chapter. No such shields have been preserved, but somewhat similar representations are found on stone sculptures and wood-carvings.

Descriptions of situations of an emotional character are usually treated in speech poems of Type B, dialogues or monologues, in which the speakers themselves are made to express their feelings. Examples will be found in Chapters III, VI and IX. In early poems it is only quite rarely that the poet himself describes such situations in any detail, apart from the speeches. An example may be seen in the opening stanzas of *Guðrúnarkviða I* (cf. p. 27). Some instances of a rather different (timeless, nameless) character will be noticed below.

In the last chapter we had occasion rather frequently to mention 'descriptive' passages which differ somewhat from the descriptive poetry discussed above. These passages are introduced in gnomic poetry by way of explanation or illustration. They are wholly of the timeless, nameless kind, and may be regarded as the counterparts in literature of the designs engraved upon the shield of Achilles.

Such descriptions or illustrations, however, are not confined to gnomic poetry. They occur also incidentally in heroic narrative poems, as well as in antiquarian and other kinds of poetry. Occasionally they form the subjects of poems complete in themselves. Examples may be found in Hesiod's *Theogony*, e.g. the description of the king in 80 ff., and of the distressed man consoled by minstrelsy in 98 ff. The former is of very similar character to the description of the queen in the *Exeter Gnomes*, 81 ff., while the latter is closely parallel to *ib.* 170 ff.—both of which passages have been quoted above (p. 381 f.). It may be observed that the passages in the *Theogony* are introduced as illustrations of a gnome (Type II *b*)—that the eloquence of kings and the skill of minstrels are gifts of the Muses.

Timeless, nameless descriptions are of frequent occurrence in the *Iliad*; but they are introduced not as explanations or illustrations of gnomes, but as similes. Thus when the Myrmidons set out to battle, they are compared (XVI. 259 ff.) to a swarm of wasps, the movements of which are briefly described. These similes illustrate many phases of human and animal life, and of nature in general. We may note that they show a rather striking contrast to the rest of the poem in the fact that they depict the life of the farmer more often than that of the prince. From this it has been inferred[1] with good reason that they belong to the

[1] Cf. Cauer, *Grundfragen d. Homerkritik*, p. 419. The inference is—necessarily of course—rejected by those who hold that the poem is wholly or almost wholly the work of one author. In any case the introduction of similes need not in itself be regarded as a late innovation.

latest elements in the poem and date from a time when heroic poetry had begun to make an appeal to circles wider than the courts. To such they were doubtless attractive additions to the poem, as representing a life with which they themselves were familiar.

Beowulf contains two rather long descriptive passages of this kind.[1] One of these (2444–2462) is introduced as a simile, like the Homeric passages. It describes the grief of an old man who has lost his only son, and is introduced as an illustration of the grief of King Hrethel at the death of his son Herebeald. The second case is the description of a successful and arrogant man (1728–1757). This is introduced by a gnome of Type II *b*, relating to the way in which the gifts of God are distributed. Another—very striking—case occurs in 2233 ff.; but this is of a somewhat different character, and contains a speech of Type B. With other passages of the same kind it will require notice in the next chapter.

Similes of the Homeric kind are rare in *Beowulf* and elsewhere in early Teutonic poetry. But somewhat similar descriptive passages are occasionally introduced in a different way, e.g. 1369 ff.: "Though the heath-ranger, the stag of mighty horns, may make his way to the forest when beset by hounds after a long chase, he will yield up his spirit and his life on the brink before he will be willing to shelter his head therein". This may be compared with such a simile as occurs in *Il.* XV. 271 ff.: "As when hounds and men of the country chase a horned stag or a wild goat, and it is saved by a precipitous rock or dense wood, and they cannot succeed in finding it", etc. The passage in *Beowulf*, however, is not a simile but the description of an imaginary place—the pool in which the monsters have their lair (cf. p. 405).

Descriptive passages similar to those cited above from *Beowulf* (1728 ff., 2444 ff.) occur also in other Anglo-Saxon poems.[2] We may instance the description of old age given in the *Seafarer* (91 ff.): "Old age comes upon him, his face grows pallid; gray-haired he grieves in the knowledge that his friends[3] of old days, the scions of princes, have been

[1] We do not mean to suggest that these passages are necessarily late elements in the poem, though we believe this to be true in one case (1728 ff.). The hunting scene (1369 ff.), quoted below, may be taken from court life—in contrast with *Il.* XV. 271 ff.

[2] Examples occur, though rarely, in religious poems, e.g. *Crist*, 851 ff., *Elene*, 611 ff. Both of these seem to be of Latin or Biblical origin. We may also refer to Grein-Wülcker, *Bibliothek*, II. 221 f. (Prayer IV. 88 ff.).

[3] Perhaps 'lord'. The plurals here may denote one individual, in accordance with a usage very common in Anglo-Saxon and early Norse poetry.

committed to the earth. While his spirit is ebbing his bodily frame cannot relish delicacies, nor suffer pain, nor raise the hand, nor think with the brain". The context here is gnomic. A similar picture occurs more than once in the fragments of Mimnermos, where the sorrows of old age are contrasted with the joys of youth, e.g. (fr. 5): "But hovering immediately over our heads is grievous and unsightly old age, hated alike and dishonoured—which makes a man to be forgotten and injures the eyes and the brain which it overshadows". The same theme recurs in fr. 1, 2 and 3. The subject is treated at much greater length in the Irish *Lament of the Old Woman of Beare*;[1] but this is a monologue poem (Type B) of specific reference, the story apparently being derived from tradition. We may also compare *RBH*. XI, one of the elegies of Llywarch Hen. The first part of this is a lament on the sorrows of old age—a monologue of Type E (or B). But here again the reference is specific; the speaker twice mentions his name. Timeless nameless pictures are not unknown in Welsh religious poetry.[2]

Descriptions of natural phenomena and of the characteristics of the seasons occur incidentally in poetry everywhere. We may refer (e.g.) to the description of the north wind in the *Works and Days* (504 ff.) or to two short similes in *Il*. II. 144 ff., where the movements of the assembled Achaeans in their excitement are compared first to the waves of a stormy sea and then to a field of standing corn battered by a high wind. In Anglo-Saxon poetry references to the storms of winter are especially frequent. We may quote from the *Wanderer*, 102 ff.: "Winter's blast, the driving snowstorm, enwraps the earth, when the shades of night come darkly lowering, and sends from the north a cruel hailstorm in wrath against mankind".

But in Welsh and Irish poetry such descriptions are sometimes treated more fully, and even form the subject of complete poems. Thus *RBH*. VII is concerned mainly with the characteristics of early winter, though it contains also a certain amount of gnomic matter. Each stanza opens with the words *Kalan gaeaf*, 'the beginning of winter' (All Saints' Day), as a kind of refrain. We may quote st. 3 and 5: "The beginning of winter—the stags are lean, the tops of the birches are yellow, the shieling is deserted. Woe to him who incurs shame for the sake of a trifle.... The

[1] Ed. and transl. by K. Meyer, *Otia Merseiana*, I. 119 ff.; transl. also in *Ancient Irish Poetry*, p. 90 ff.

[2] Thus in the religious poem *BBC*. IX (20 ff.) there is a short picture of a miserly, grasping man, followed by a still shorter picture of the sorrows of old age. Such sequences may be compared with *Beow*. 1728 ff.

beginning of winter—the weather is rough, unlike the beginning of summer. Apart from God there is no magician". It will be seen that in the use of the 'refrain' and in the introduction of gnomes of Type II *a*, especially in the last line of the stanza—unconnected with what precedes —this piece resembles some of the gnomic poems discussed on p. 388 f. But the bulk of the matter consists of observations relating in general only to a particular time of the year.

The first part of *BBC*. xxx, one of the elegies of Llywarch Hen, has much in common with the last poem. It employs the same three-line stanza, and most of it is occupied with a description of winter conditions, though the gnomic element is not wanting. One stanza (24) begins with *Kalan gaeaw* (i.e. *gaeaf*). But the latter part of the poem is personal, relating to the speaker's own experiences and the death of his son Mechydd. We may quote st. 4 and 6: "Cold is the bed of the fishes in the shelter of the ice. The stag is lean; the reed-stalks are becoming bearded. The evening is short; the trees are bending... The snow is falling; the hoar-frost is white. Idle is the shield on the shoulder of the aged. The wind is very strong; the young buds are freezing".

An Irish poem describing wintry conditions and dating probably from the tenth century is preserved in *The Hiding of the Hill of Howth*,[1] a short story relating to the flight of Diarmait and Grainne. It is recited to the lovers by an old woman who is acting as a spy for Finn. But the poem may be older than the story; for it contains elements which occur also in a poem preserved in another story of the same cycle.[2] This latter poem is recited to Finn by an attendant called MacLesc, who has been ordered to fetch water but is trying to excuse himself on account of the bad weather. In one text of the story Finn declares that the man is lying, and recites a poem beginning with the words 'Summer has come'. Geographical names occur both in the first poem and in the one on the coming of summer; but the poems can hardly be regarded as local, since the places referred to lie in distant parts of Ireland. We may quote st. 2 of the first poem, which is found also with slight variations in the second: "Deadly cold! The storm has drenched everything. Every furrow in the valley is a river, and every ford a brimming pool". From the poem on the coming of summer[3] we may quote the following

[1] Ed. and transl. by K. Meyer, *Rev. Celt.* XI. 129 ff.; transl. also in K. Meyer, *Ancient Irish Poetry*, p. 57 f.

[2] Cf. K. Meyer, *Rev. Celt.* XI. 126 f.

[3] Ed. and transl. by K. Meyer, *Four Songs of Summer and Winter*, p. 20 ff.; transl. also in *Ancient Irish Poetry*, p. 53.

(final) stanza: "The sun smiles over every land. I feel free from a brood of cares.[1] Dogs bay, stags mate, ravens increase, summer has come".

A somewhat longer and apparently earlier poem on summer,[2] likewise attributed to Finn, is preserved in *The Boyish Exploits of Finn*, cap. 20. This declares briefly the effects of the coming of summer upon various creatures—the blackbird, the cuckoo, the deer, bees, cattle, ants, corncrakes, swallows and mankind—as well as upon the woods and vegetation generally and the sea. The same hero is also made responsible for a very short poem on the coming of winter,[3] preserved in the *Eulogy of St Columba*. Both of these are believed to date from the ninth century.

Lastly, we may mention a series of short poems on the seasons contained in *The Guesting of Athirne*,[4] which is little more than a framework for the poems. Athirne, the *fili* (cf. p. 98), pays a visit to Amargin in the autumn. When he prepares to depart, his host detains him with a poem on the season. The same thing is repeated in the winter and the spring. When summer comes Amargin produces another poem, but allows his guest to go. At his departure a bull is brought in to be killed, and Athirne is asked by the household to give them some poetry. He stops them from killing the bull, and also a calf and a sheep which are brought in, but allows them to kill a pig. He produces poems on all the animals and on the fire, but only the first is intelligible: "The strong-limbed bullock, with thick tail and with horns, vigorous, hairy, broad in the collar, the sportive one of the herd, the father of cattle, the pursuer of every drove is the bull".

There are other Irish poems, attributed to the tenth and eleventh centuries, which are concerned with descriptions of various aspects of nature. Perhaps the most striking is a poem of Type B in which the hermit Marban unfolds to his brother Guaire, king of Connaught, the attractions of his life in the woods. It contains a slight religious element, but most of it is occupied with a description of the woods, the birds and animals which frequent them, and the fruits which grow there. Mention may also be made of a poem on the sea and the storm-winds which sweep over it from various directions.[5]

1 This word is unknown. Meyer suggests 'care, grief'.

2 Ed. and transl. by K. Meyer, *Four Songs*, p. 8 ff. (cf. *Ériu*, I. 186 f.); transl. also in *Ancient Irish Poetry*, p. 54 f.

3 Ed. and transl. by Stokes, *Rev. Celt.* XX. 258 f.; transl. also by K. Meyer, *Ancient Irish Poetry*, p. 56.

4 Ed. and transl. by K. Meyer, *Ériu*, VII. 1 ff.

5 Both these poems are transl. by K. Meyer, *Ancient Irish Poetry*, p. 47 ff. For further references see *ib.* p. 112 f.

Next we may take metrical riddles. This is a widely distributed class of poetry; but it is far more fully represented in English and Norse than in the other early literatures under discussion. It has much in common with the poems treated above. The characteristics of an object or conception are described without its name being mentioned. It is left to the listeners to identify it; sometimes they are invited to do so. Very often the riddles are expressed in intentionally obscure terms; but this is not essential.

A large collection of Norse riddles is contained in *Hervarar Saga*, cap. 11.[1] King Heiðrekr, who is a sage, allows accused men to ask him riddles instead of going to trial. This option is chosen by a certain Gestumblindi, who is really Othin in disguise. But many of the riddles may well be older than the saga. They are all expressed in four-line stanzas, of which the fourth line is a uniform refrain, while the first lines also have refrains running over a number of stanzas. The actual riddles therefore are quite short. We may quote the following examples: "What is that huge one that passes over the earth, swallowing lakes and pools? He fears the wind, but he fears not man, and carries on hostilities against the sun. King Heiðrekr, interpret the riddle". The king replies that it is fog: "One cannot see the sea because of it. Yet, as soon as the wind blows, the fog lifts; but men can do nothing to it. Fog kills the sunshine". These replies are in prose. Again: "What is the marvel which I have seen outside Dellingr's doorway?[2] It has eight feet and four eyes, and carries its knees higher than its body. King Heiðrekr, interpret the riddle". The answer given here is 'spider'.

More than ninety English riddles[3] are preserved in the *Exeter Book*. They vary greatly in length, but nearly all of them are longer than the Norse riddles just mentioned. Many of them are translations or adaptations of Latin riddles, which were very popular with English ecclesiastics of the seventh and eighth centuries. But many others may be of purely native origin, though they were probably collected in religious houses. There is no fixed form, as in the riddles of Gestumblindi. Some riddles are short descriptive poems, not unlike the poems and passages noticed in the earlier part of this chapter or the illustrations of gnomes quoted on p. 381 f.; but a request for interpretation may be

[1] Transl. by Kershaw, *Stories and Ballads of the Far Past*, p. 115 ff.

[2] This is a refrain, which is carried over a number of riddles. The meaning of the expression, which occurs also in *Háv.* 160, is unknown to us. Dellingr is the name of the father of Day (personified); cf. Kershaw, *op. cit.* p. 240.

[3] Ed. by Tupper, *The Riddles of the Exeter Book* (Boston, 1910); Wyatt, *Old English Riddles* (Boston, 1912).

added at the end. We may quote No. 58: "The air here carries little creatures over the hill-sides. They are very black, dusky, dark-coated. Bountiful of song they journey in troops and cry loudly. They tread wooded banks and at times the habitations of men. Name them yourselves". This is variously interpreted as 'gnats' or 'swallows'. Other riddles, however, are, strictly speaking, speeches in character (Type B), in which the object itself declares its characteristics. As an example we may take No. 8: "My robe is silent when I tread the earth or occupy these dwellings[1] or stir the waters. Sometimes my trappings and this lofty air lift me up above the habitations of men; and then the force of the clouds carries me in all directions above mankind. My adornments ring loudly and make music when, as a travelling spirit, I am not in contact with water or earth". The speaker is evidently a swan. It is not always clear that such poems are intended as riddles. This may be seen from the fact that it is still a matter of dispute whether No. 61 is a riddle, meaning 'reed', or the introduction to *The Husband's Message*, a poem which immediately follows it in the MS., and which will require notice in the next chapter.

The *Exeter Book* has no riddles in the Norse form. Two examples, however, occur in the learned dialogue poem *Solomon and Saturn*. We may quote the beginning of the second (281 ff.), which is interpreted by Solomon in his reply (291 ff.) as 'old age': "What is the marvel which passes through this world, taking its course inexorably, beating down barriers, giving rise to tears and forcing its way upon us?" It is possible that the formula may be taken from a Scandinavian source, since the poem is believed to be not earlier than the tenth century. But Scandinavian influence is not evident in other respects; the connections of the poem are Latin. We are inclined therefore to think that this poem has preserved an ancient formula, which originally was common to English and Scandinavian. At the same time it would be hasty to assume that only such formulae were used in ancient riddles, and that the various forms found in the *Exeter Book* are necessarily innovations of later times.

In early Welsh poetry we know of only one riddle. This is the long description of the wind contained in *Tal.* XVII. 1–64.[2] We may quote 1–8 and 25–32: "Guess what (this) is—created before the Deluge, a

[1] Perhaps plural for singular—'my nest'.

[2] The remainder of the piece is of a religious character, beginning with a few gnomes, and has no connection with the riddle. A variant text of the riddle is to be found in the *Hanes Taliesin*, translated in Guest's *Mabinogion* (Everyman), p. 310. The last three lines of this text have nothing corresponding to them in *Tal.* XVII.

strong creature without flesh, without bone, without veins, without blood, without head, without feet. It is no older, no younger than at the beginning...And it is as broad as the face of the land. And it has not been born, and it has not been seen. It is on the sea; it is on the land. It sees not; it is not seen. It is untrustworthy; it does not come when it is desired". Apart from its length it will be seen that this riddle is not unlike the English and Norse examples quoted above, especially perhaps Gestumblindi's 'fog' riddle.

We do not know whether any early Irish riddles have been preserved. The nearest approach to anything of the kind known to us is a passage in the *Eulogy of St Columba*, cap. 63,[1] immediately after the short poem on the coming of winter mentioned on p. 411, and introduced by the words *et alius dixit*: "What life is worse than death?[2] What empty is heavier than full? What lake is wider than any sea?" Parallels to this can be found elsewhere, e.g. among the riddles of Gestumblindi (No. 8): "What lives in high mountains? What falls in deep valleys? What lives without breathing? What is never silent?" Heiðrekr treats all these questions as separate riddles, and gives the answers as 'raven', 'dew', 'fish', and 'waterfall' respectively.

Riddles seem to have been much cultivated in early Greece; but few of them have been preserved in early poetic form. Probably the best preserved is a short riddle on the year—attributed by some authorities to Cleobulos of Lindos in Rhodes, who lived early in the sixth century, and by others to his daughter Cleobuline. It is in hexameters, and may be translated as follows: "There is one father and twelve sons; and each of the latter has two sets of daughters, each thirty in number, which are of quite different aspect. One set are fair in appearance, while the others are dark. They are all immortal, and yet they all pass away".[3]

In riddle poems like those quoted above common features constantly recur. Parallels are to be found in many other languages. But they occur also in certain other forms of poetry, especially in oracles. We may refer (e.g.) to the Delphic oracles quoted by Herodotos, I. 47, 67. Some of the terms used in the *Works and Days*[4] belong to the same type,

1 Ed. and transl. by Stokes, *Rev. Celt.* XX. 258 f.

2 One text has "What death is better than lasting life?" and adds (as answer) "Death of a fat pig". The same text explains the next sentence by "emptiness of the belly".

3 The *Exeter Book* has a very elaborate riddle (No. 23) which may be compared with this; cf. Tupper, *op. cit.* p. 117 f. and the references there given.

4 There seems to be some affinity in the expression of thought between this poem and oracular poetry; compare 231 ff. with the oracle quoted by Herodotos, VI. 86.

e.g. (569) 'house-carrier', applied to the snail. Even the partiality for numeral periphrases, which characterises riddles, occurs sometimes in poems where to us it seems out of place. Thus Bragi Boddason, in a fragment relating to the creation of Sjælland, says that the goddess Gefjon's oxen had four heads and eight eyes (lit. 'brow-stars'). He means no more than that there were four oxen. It is possible that this kind of phraseology is due to the influence of riddles; but the true explanation may be that descriptive, gnomic and antiquarian poetry were largely cultivated by the same class of poets. This is a question to which we shall have to return later.

Next we may take the alphabetic poems which are found in Anglo-Saxon and in Norse.[1] In the Runic alphabet each letter has a name of its own. These names—as also the peculiar order of the letters in the alphabet—date from very early times and were once in all probability common to all the Teutonic peoples, though certain changes took place in the course of time. The names—with the exception of two, which are proper names—denote objects or conceptions of a general character; and consequently the poems take the form of a series of descriptive gnomes of Type II (mostly II *c*). We may quote from the English poem the passages relating to H and I, the names of which were 'hail' and 'ice' respectively: "H is the whitest of grains. It falls from the air of heaven and is tossed by gales of wind. It turns to water afterwards....I is very cold and exceedingly slippery. It glistens as clear as glass, very much like jewels. (It is) a floor fashioned by frost, fair to look upon".

There are two Norse poems on the same subject, one Norwegian, the other Icelandic. Both are very late—probably from the thirteenth and the fifteenth centuries respectively—but there are certain resemblances between them which may be traces or echoes of earlier poems of similar character. The Norwegian poem consists of couplets, of which the second line is usually unconnected with the first. In the majority of cases it is an independent gnome, much like the last line in the stanza of some Welsh gnomic poems (cf. p. 387 ff.). We may quote the following extracts from this poem: "Hail is the coldest of grains. Christ created the world of old....Ice we call a 'broad bridge'. The blind needs to be led". From the Icelandic poem: "Hail is cold grain, and a fall of sleet, and a plague to snakes....Ice is the bark of a river, and the roof of the wave, and a peril to doomed men". The use of the term 'grain' suggests the possibility of a connection in remote times even with the

[1] Ed. and transl. by Dickins, *Runic and Heroic Poems*.

English poem; and it is not unlikely on general grounds that this theme had long engaged the attention of poets.

Lastly, we have to deal with a number of catalogue poems, which have decided affinities with gnomic poetry. Sometimes they contain a considerable gnomic element; sometimes they seem to arise from a gnome of Type II, expressed or implied, such as that 'Men have diverse endowments', or 'Many are the fates to which men are exposed'. We have long hesitated whether to include these poems in this chapter or the last; but on the whole it seems preferable to treat them here as descriptive catalogues of characteristics.

Poetry of this kind developed on very similar lines in Greece and England. But examples are to be found almost everywhere. Some are evidently designed for instruction, others for entertainment; others again seem to be merely the expression of the poet's reflections.

The Greek poems which come in for consideration here are those of Simonides of Amorgos and some of those of Solon. This Simonides is believed to have lived about the middle of the seventh century, and therefore about half a century before Solon. All the remains of his poetry seem to be in the iambic trimeter verse. Mention is first to be made of a piece (fr. 1) addressed to a young man, perhaps his son, on the uncertainty of life. It dwells upon men's ignorance of the future and on the vanity of their hopes, and then proceeds to give a short catalogue of the various ways in which they meet with death: "One is overtaken by wretched old age before he attains his object; others are destroyed by the miserable diseases of mankind; others again are crushed by Ares and sent by Hades down beneath the black earth. Some, tossed by gales upon the deep and by the mighty billows of the dark sea, perish when they could have lived happily, while others through the wretchedness of their lot fit a noose to their necks and quit the light of the sun by their own free will. Thus there is no lack of ills; men are beset by fate in innumerable forms, and by unsuspected troubles and disasters". The fragment concludes with the advice not to seek for evils or to spoil one's life because of troubles.

Another, very much longer, piece deals with different varieties of women, each of which is said to have been formed by the gods from a different kind of animal or other substance. Thus the dirty woman is said to come from the pig and the inquisitive from the fox, while other varieties are derived from the dog, earth, the sea, the donkey, the weasel, the horse, the monkey and the bee. All the descriptions, except the last, are uncomplimentary. This poem is doubtless an example of the application of didactic form to purposes of entertainment, like the first part of the *Hávamál* (cf. p. 383 f.), and, again like it, is evidently designed for male audiences. But it lacks the cynical playfulness of the Norse poem. The lady who is derived from the dog is said (12 ff.) to be just like her mother. "She wants to hear and know everything. She roams and peers about everywhere, and yaps, even if she sees no one. Her husband could not stop her either by threats—not even if in his anger he were to knock out her teeth with a stone—nor yet by gentle words, even if she were sitting in the presence of guests". The woman made of earth (21 ff.) is insensitive and knows nothing either good or bad. "The only thing she understands is eating. If God brings a bad winter and she is shivering, she will not draw her chair nearer the fire".

Solon's political and personal poems were noticed in Ch. XI, and it was pointed out (p. 356 f.) that the political ideas expressed in the former were of a much more advanced type than anything which can be found among the northern peoples in early times. No such remark, however, can be made with regard to the same author's descriptive or gnomic catalogue poems, about which something must be said here. The pieces which concern us are Nos. 13 and 27 of the fragments.

No. 27 is probably complete. It describes briefly the course of a man's life, which it divides into ten stages of seven years each. No. 13 is a much longer piece and embodies Solon's philosophy of life. It begins with a prayer to the Muses to grant him prosperity and good fame, and that he may be revered by his friends and dreaded by his enemies. He desires to attain wealth, but not by unjust means. This leads to a reflection—similar to what we find in the *Works and Days*—that injustice and arrogance will ultimately bring ruin from Zeus. Next, he observes that men live in hopes of the future; the invalid hopes for recovery, the poor man for wealth. Then follows a list of vocations by which men obtain their livelihood, with brief descriptions of the merchant sailor, the agriculturist, the skilled craftsman, the poet, the seer and the physician. "Men's activities lie in different directions. One wanders in ships over the sea teeming with fish, seeking to bring profit to his home. He is driven by grievous winds, but pays no regard to his life. Another clears thickly wooded ground, and serves for the year those whose business lies in curved ploughs. Another has learnt the works of Athena and skilful Hephaistos, and gains his livelihood by his hands. Another we find who has been taught the gifts of the Olympian Muses and understands how to express their beautiful lore". After this list he remarks that Fate brings both good and evil. The gifts of the immortal gods are not to be avoided. There is risk in all one's doings, and no one knows what will be the future of an undertaking, when it is beginning.

It may be mentioned here that several short fragments of the same poet are of a gnomic character, though the context is unknown. Some of them, e.g. No. 9, have a political bearing. The pieces noticed above are in the elegiac metre.

Lastly, we may quote a short catalogue poem included among the Homeric Epigrams (No. 13), which may be compared with the *Addfwynau Taliesin* noticed below: "Children are a garland to a man, as towers to a city and ships to the sea. It is an honour[1] to have horses on the plain. Wealth increases the house. Dignified are kings sitting in the assembly and an honour for others to behold. And when a fire is burning the house is more dignified to look upon, on a winter day when Zeus is sending the snow". The reference to kings in the assembly suggests a rather early date.

Close parallels to some of the above catalogues are to be found in Anglo-Saxon poetry, especially a poem on the *Fates of Men*, preserved in the *Exeter Book*.[2] The poem begins with a gnomic introduction: a man and his wife bring up a young family, but "God alone knows what the years will bring to them when they grow up". Then (10 ff.) follows a lugubrious catalogue of disasters,[3] which may be compared with the first fragment of Simonides quoted on p. 416. "To one it happens that an end, grievous to the wretched people, comes in his childhood. He is devoured[4] by a wolf, the gray ranger of the heath. One is carried off by famine, another cast adrift by storm, another slain by the spear, another destroyed by battle. One passes his life without eyesight, groping with his hands; another, lame in his walk and crippled in his sinews, bewails his injuries and mourns over his destiny, afflicted in heart". Next follows the description of a man who loses his footing at the top of a tree, and after vainly clutching at the branches comes down with a fatal crash to the ground. Then we have the destitute and friendless man, who

1 Can κόσμος mean 'fine sight, fine thing?'—'horses in the plain are a fine thing?' We may compare the use of *atwyn* in *Tal.* IV. We suspect a similar sense in γεραρός. But neither of these usages seems to be recognised by Greek scholars.

2 Ed. by Grein-Wülcker, *Bibl. d. ags. Poesie*, III. 148 ff.; Sedgefield, *Anglo-Saxon Book of Verse and Prose*, p. 45 ff.

3 A very similar list, perhaps suggested by this, occurs in the religious poem *Juliana*, 468 ff., where the Devil is recounting all the evils he has brought about.

4 The gnomic *sceal* (cf. p. 378 ff.) is used in most of the following illustrations.

has to wander in misery through strange lands. Then comes a picture described somewhat more fully—the man who is hanged. The ravens come and peck out his eyes, and then gradually consume his body. Then follows the man who is burnt to death before his mother's eyes; then one who loses his temper and forfeits his life in a drunken brawl; then one who does himself to death by excessive drinking. The list closes, however, with a short description (58–63) of the man who survives the troubles of his youth and lives to a prosperous and happy old age.

This catalogue leads up to another gnome, to the effect that different lots in life are awarded by God. Some obtain happiness, others misery; blessings and endowments are variously distributed. "One is provided with a wondrous gift in the goldsmith's art. Very often he arms and fairly adorns a son of the king of Britain; and the latter as a reward grants him a large estate, which he receives with delight. Another gives entertainment and pleasure to heroes who are gathered together at their beer. Then the banqueters have great joy. Another sits with a harp at his lord's feet. He receives treasure and is ever swiftly plucking the strings", etc. It will be seen that this second catalogue bears a resemblance to one of Solon's poems (No. 13) quoted above.

A very much longer list of endowments is to be found in another poem, known as the *Endowments of Men* and also preserved in the *Exeter Book*. This is of a more religious character than the last poem, and probably originated in a religious house. The introduction (1–29) speaks of the distribution of God's gifts in general terms. Then follows the catalogue (30–96), most of which is given in very brief form. First we hear of the rich, the poor, the strong, the handsome, the eloquent, etc. Then the list becomes more specialised; it describes, rather more fully, the warrior, the councillor, the builder, the minstrel, the sailor, etc. Later, the form again becomes very brief; and there is a good deal of repetition in the subjects. The poem ends with general reflections like those in the introduction. We may add that a somewhat similar, though much shorter, catalogue occurs in the *Crist* (664–681).

In this series we may include one early Welsh poem, which consists wholly of what may be called a gnomic catalogue;[1] its closest affinities lie with the Homeric Epigram noticed above. This poem, *Tal.* IV, bears the title *Aduvyneu* (i.e. *Addfwynau*) *Taliessin*, 'Things pleasant to

[1] Reference may also perhaps be made to *Tal.* XVII. 67 ff., where there is what we may perhaps call a 'negative' catalogue. This latter part of *Tal.* XVII (cf. p. 413) is evidently of religious provenance.

Taliesin'.[1] The items, each of which occupies a line, are arranged in pairs, two or three pairs being included in each (rhyming) stanza. The first line of each pair begins with the word *atwyn* (i.e. *addfwyn*, 'pleasant', in archaic orthography), while the second begins with *arall* ('another') *atwyn*; e.g. (st. 2): "Pleasant is fruit in the time of harvest; another pleasant (thing) is wheat in the stalk".

The nearest Irish parallels we know are the descriptive passages in the *Instructions of Cormac*, especially the long tirade upon women in cap. 16 (cf. p. 395 f.).

Lastly, we have to consider here the Norse poem *Rígsþula*, which is by far the most interesting and ambitious poem of this class. Its purpose is to explain the origin of the various classes of society. A certain Rígr comes to the cabin occupied by a couple called Ái ('Great-grandfather') and Edda ('Great-grandmother'). He is entertained by them for three days, and sleeps between them. Nine months later Edda bears a child, dark, ugly and misshapen, whom they call Þræll ('Slave'). He occupies himself with making loads of bast, and in due time obtains for himself a mate, dirty-footed, sun-burnt and snub-nosed, called Þír.[2] They have a numerous family, who are supplied with names meaning 'coarse, sullen, clumsy, lazy', etc., or derived from such words, and who occupy themselves with making fences, tending pigs and goats, and digging peat. It is added that the 'kindreds of slaves', i.e. the slave population, are descended from these.

Rígr comes to another house (st. 14 ff.) where the conditions of life are much better. The man and woman, who are called Afi ('Grandfather') and Amma ('Grandmother') respectively, are well-dressed. The man is engaged in carpenter's work, the woman is knitting. He is entertained as before. In due course Amma bears a child with ruddy face and twinkling eyes, whom they call Karl ('Man, Freeman'). He busies himself with house-building and agricultural work—ploughs and plough-oxen. For him they get a wife named Snör ('Daughter-in-law'), who is married to him with due ceremony—carriage, veil and ring. These also have a large family, with names like 'Farmer, Smith, Trim-beard'. From them are descended the free population.

Rígr comes to yet another house (st. 26 ff.), where the conditions are still better. The man, who is called Faðir ('Father') is amusing himself with bow and arrows, while the woman, who is called Móðir ('Mother'),

[1] Cf. Rhys, *Rev. Celt.* VI. 55. It may be observed that this poem seems to have been copied from an earlier MS. with orthography somewhat similar to that of *BBC*.

[2] 'Slave-woman' is probably meant. The word occurs elsewhere for 'slave'.

is attending to her dress and ornaments. Rígr is entertained as before, but in better style; we hear of a white linen tablecloth, silver dishes and wine. In due time Móðir bears a child, whom they call Jarl (probably 'Noble'), and wrap in silk. He has fair hair and piercing eyes. When he grows up he learns to use weapons, to amuse himself with horses and dogs, and to swim. Rígr visits him and teaches him (Runic) letters. He adopts him as his son, and gives him his ancestral home. Then Jarl begins to engage in war and to rule territories. He marries Erna (perhaps 'Active'), the daughter of Hersir ('Chief'). Their children have names like 'Son' and 'Heir'. The youngest is called Konr, which also means 'son' or 'offspring'. The others devote themselves to arms; but Konr becomes expert in the magical use of letters and the language of birds. A crow exhorts him to engage in war—but at this point the text breaks off. The rest is lost. In st. 43, 46 f. Konr is called *Konr ungr*, 'young Konr', from which it is generally inferred that the poem represented him as the first *konungr* ('king').

In the prose introduction to the poem Rígr is said to be the god Heimdallr. This may explain why at the beginning of the *Völuspá* (cf. p. 325) the witch addresses her audience as 'major and minor sons of Heimdallr'. The identification, however, is rejected by many modern scholars, who believe the poem to be based on Gaelic sources. They derive the name *Rígr* from Irish *rí* (gen. *ríg*), 'king'; it has been suggested that the Dagda is meant. Others hold that the poem relates to the unification of Norway under Harold the Fair-haired. Neither theory is convincing. The only references to Rígr elsewhere are in connection with legends relating to the origin of the Danish kingdom.

We know of no other descriptive catalogue poems of this kind in Norse; but it is not unlikely that such may once have existed in Denmark. Reference may be made (e.g.) to the description of the four kinds of warriors attributed by Saxo, p. 133 f. (109 f.), to King Wermund the Wise.

In this chapter we have attempted to take note of all the chief varieties of descriptive poetry which occur in our early records. The series may be summarised briefly as follows: i. Imaginative scenes, whether descriptions of imaginary places or of real places under imaginary conditions. ii. Descriptions of works of art. iii. Scenes from human life (timeless nameless) and from nature introduced incidentally, whether as similes or otherwise, in poems concerned with other matters. Descriptions of old age form a special group among these. iv. Complete poems, usually short, occupied with descriptions of nature, especially the seasons and animal life. v. Riddles. vi. Alphabetic poems. vii. Descriptive catalogue poems. We do not think that apart from these the records with which we are concerned contain much descriptive poetry of any importance.

It will be seen that the list is of rather heterogeneous character. No. vii is closely related to gnomic poetry—so closely that we have long hesitated whether to treat it in this chapter or the last. Like gnomic poetry, its connections are in general non-heroic. In the case of the *Rígsþula* some doubt is suggested by the poet's strong aristocratic bias; yet it is the intellectual activities of Konr which are emphasised. No. iii has also gnomic affinities. We believe it to be in the main of the same provenance, though it is perhaps not wholly homogeneous. The description of the arrogant man in *Beowulf* 1728 ff. is definitely non-heroic, influenced by Christian ethics apparently not very well understood, and shows an encroachment of the non-heroic upon the heroic. We believe the same to be true—in quite a different way—of most of the Homeric similes, but not of the other passages from *Beowulf* cited on p. 408. Most of the examples in Nos. v and vi are closely related to No. iv; and this group also has gnomic affinities, i.e. with gnomes of Type II *c*. Nos. i and ii have in general no gnomic affinities.

This cursory analysis must suffice for the moment. The question of provenance and its significance will require notice in Ch. XIX.

Note. For many of the Greek passages quoted in this chapter and in Ch. XI better translations may now be found in Edmonds, *Elegy and Iambus*, which unfortunately was not published before these chapters were in print.

CHAPTER XIV

POETRY AND SAGA RELATING TO UNSPECIFIED INDIVIDUALS

IN the last chapter it was observed that descriptions of human experiences, belonging to the timeless nameless variety and introduced as similes or as illustrations of gnomes, are more developed in English than elsewhere. We have now to consider certain poems and passages which have in general the same character but show a further development. The subject of the picture is no longer a purely hypothetical person or a representative of some class of humanity, but has a definite individuality of his own, though the timeless nameless character remains. These pieces consist wholly or largely of speeches and, in spite of the absence of names, are to be regarded as examples of Type B.

One example occurs in *Beowulf* (2233 ff.), a passage to which reference was made on p. 408. It is the account of the burial of the treasure in the barrow which eventually became the dragon's lair. The man who buries it is represented as the last survivor of his community; and his speech (2247 ff.) is an elegy on the loss of all his friends. The passage is entirely without names and timeless, except that it relates to the far past. We may quote the beginning of the speech: "Do thou, O Earth, keep the treasures of knights, now that heroes have been unable to do so. Was it not from thee that the brave had acquired it? Every man of my company has been carried off by death in battle, by dread mortal ruin....I have no one left to bear the sword or to care for the costly drinking vessel, the flagon of gold plate". Then he describes how the armour will rust and decay; and the elegy concludes as follows (2262 ff.): "There shall be no gladdening harp, no cheering instrument of music. There shall be no good falcon flying through the hall, nor swift steed pawing the castle court. Many families of men have been sped to their doom by murderous slaughter".

The first scene in the *Wanderer*[1] is somewhat similar, though it is introduced by a gnome, and the individuality of the speaker is perhaps not quite so fully developed. The picture is that of a knight who has

[1] This and the following three poems—all of which are preserved in the *Exeter Book*—are ed. and transl. by Kershaw, *Anglo-Saxon and Norse Poems* (Cambridge, 1922).

lost his lord, and is homeless and friendless on a deserted shore in winter. He soliloquises upon his misfortunes (8–29), and then falls asleep and (41 ff.) "dreams that he is greeting and kissing his liege-lord, and laying his hands and head on his knee—just as he used to do when he enjoyed the bounty of the throne in days of old.... His sorrow comes back to him when the memory of his kinsmen passes through his mind. He greets them in glad strains and scans them all eagerly. (But) his warrior comrades again melt away, and as they vanish their spirits bring no familiar greetings to his ear".

The second scene in the same poem (75 ff.) may conveniently be noticed here, though it is not a typical example of the class of poems we are considering. It is concerned with a man who is meditating on ruined cities or castles—evidently of the Roman period—and then (85 ff.) upon one particular ruin, which apparently stands before him; but the man is not individualised in any way. The passage has much in common with the *Ruin*, noticed on p. 404, though there is no indication here that any specific place is in the poet's mind. We may quote from the beginning of the soliloquy (92 ff.): "What has become of the steed? What has become of the squire? What has become of the giver of treasure? What has become of the banqueting houses? Where are the joys of the hall? O shining goblet! O mail-clad warrior! O glory of the prince! How has that time passed away, grown shadowy under the canopy of night, as though it had never been".

The *Seafarer*—or at least the first part of it—is a speech-poem of the type under discussion. The speaker is more clearly individualised than either of those who are introduced in the last poem. He is a mariner, and describes both the hardships and the attractions of his life. More than once there is a somewhat abrupt change of tone, which has led some scholars to the view that the poem is a dialogue between an old mariner and a young man who wishes to go to sea. Different views, however, are held as to the distribution of the speeches; and we are inclined to think that the contrasts are merely rhetorical. We may quote 58 ff.: "Verily my thoughts are now soaring beyond my breast; along the course of the sea my spirit soars, over the home of the whale, and throughout the expanse of earth. Again it comes back to me, eager and hungry, screaming on its solitary flight. Resistlessly it impels my heart to the road of the whale, over the expanse of waters". After this the poem passes into religious and gnomic matter; the original theme seems to be forgotten. It is in this latter part that the description of old age, noticed in the last chapter, occurs.

A much more advanced stage of individualisation is attained in another speech-poem, commonly known as *The Wife's Complaint*. The speaker is a woman who has been forsaken by her husband or lover and ordered to live in a cave beneath an oak, where she passionately bewails her lot. The situation can hardly be regarded as a typical one,[1] and there is no gnomic context—indeed no context of any kind—nor any suggestion of a simile. Consequently it has been thought by some scholars that the poem is a fragment or a scene from some heroic or other story. But it contains no names, and within its limits it is complete. The passage from *Beowulf* (2233 ff.) quoted above shows that such 'nameless' scenes were not unfamiliar to ancient English poets. We may quote 33 ff.: "Lovers there are on earth living in affection and resting in their beds, while all alone before the dawn I pace the round of these caverns beneath the oak. Here I shall have to sit through the long summer day; here I shall have to weep over my misfortunes and my many hardships. Assuredly I shall never be able to get any rest from my distress nor from all the heartache which has come upon me in my life here".

Another somewhat similar case is *The Husband's Message*. The text of this poem is spoiled in parts by serious damage to the MS.; and it is disputed whether certain lines at the beginning really belong to the poem or form a riddle unconnected with it. It is clear, however, that the main part of the piece consists of a message engraved upon a rod in Runic letters—or (less probably) delivered by a messenger who carries the rod—from a husband or lover to his lady. The message is to the effect that the sender has overcome his troubles and become a wealthy prince in a foreign land, and that he desires the lady to take ship and join him as soon as spring comes. The poem probably contains no proper names.[2] It is believed by some scholars to be a sequel to *The Wife's Complaint*—a view which in itself is not unlikely, although the scribe of the *Exeter Book* was evidently unaware of any connection between the two. They do not come together in the MS.

We know of no true analogies to these pieces in Anglo-Saxon religious poetry. The *Dream of the Cross* may be regarded as an anony-

[1] It is worth noting, however, that in the *Helreið Brynhildar* (cf. p. 27), st. 8, the text preserved in *Nornagests Saga* (cap. 9) reads as follows: "In sorrowful wise did the courageous hero make me, the sister of Atli, to dwell beneath an oak". The text of the Cod. Reg. of the *Edda* is quite different here.

[2] One geographical name has been suggested in one of the damaged places, and a personal name has been inferred from an unintelligible group of Runic letters. But these are hazardous conjectures.

mous speech-poem—apart from the speech by the Cross contained in it—but the speaker has no individuality apart from his dream, and this would seem to be claimed as an experience of the poet himself, probably according to poetic convention. The analogy here is with the framework of the *Wanderer*, as distinct from either of the speeches contained in it, though the latter of these also has no individual characterisation, as we have seen.

A closer parallel is perhaps to be found in a piece, mainly but irregularly metrical, which we may call a *Traveller's Prayer*.[1] The speaker invokes Patriarchs, Saints, Angels and Evangelists in turn for protection. He is setting out on a journey, evidently by sea. His destination is not stated; but he has a rod or staff, to which he refers more than once in the first part of the piece. This part, however, uses the formulae and the diction of spells; and the MS. in which the piece is preserved is a collection of recipes and spells. Metrical spells in general may be regarded as speech-poems of the category under discussion—Type DB rather than Type B—but it will be preferable to defer the consideration of all such matter until the next chapter.

There are one or two early Welsh poems of this class. They have something in common with the last piece—they are religious in character, without following the conventions of ecclesiastical poetry; but they are not spells. In *BBC.* XXVII, a monologue poem, the speaker is setting out on a voyage to Rome, apparently as a pilgrim. He hears a sneeze—a sound of ill omen. But he will not believe in omens; where there is a nose there will be sneezing (st. 9). His faith is in God. He gives orders therefore for the saddling of his horse. The first thirteen stanzas are in the old three-line metre. After this point the metre is irregular, and the matter is purely religious. It is not clear that this latter part belongs to the same poem.

A less certain example is to be found in *BBC.* XXVI. The first stanza is as follows: "Black is thy horse, black thy cloak, black thy head, thou art black thyself....Art thou Yscolan?" The rest of the poem is occupied with Yscolan's reply. He says that he is a scholar, that he has been guilty of various sins, including the burning of a church and killing a cow belonging to the school, and that he has undergone severe penance for a whole year. If he had known what he now knows,

[1] Ed. by Grein-Wülcker, *Bibl. d. ags. Poesie*, I. 328 ff., from MS. CCCC. 41, fol. 400. With prayers in general we are not concerned here. The latter part of the prayer publ. by Grein-Wülcker, II. 217 ff., may perhaps be regarded as a religious example of Type E.

he would never have done what he did. The question here is whether *Yscolan* is to be taken as a genuine proper name or a name made up from *yscol*, 'school'. It is not clear[1] that any other proper names occur. Account should perhaps be taken of the possibility that the poem may be connected with the one last noticed, which follows it immediately in the MS. Both are in the same metre, though No. XXVI shows some irregularities, probably through textual corruption.

These two poems show a more advanced technique than the English *Traveller's Prayer*; but they have more in common with this than with the other English poems noticed above. We do not know of any secular Welsh poems of this class. It is possible that *RBH.* x belongs here; but the gnomic element is so large in this poem that the central theme is not clear to us. There are also elements in common with the elegies of Llywarch Hen.

In early Irish and Norse poetry we know of no parallels to the poems treated above. The *Old Woman of Beare* shows a certain general resemblance to some of the English poems. But the speaker is not an 'unspecified' individual; she has definite—indeed partly historical—associations. In general the purpose which the English poems serve is in Irish and Norse served by heroic poems of Type B. We mean that when an Irish or Norse poet wished to produce a study of emotion or of emotional situation, he chose his subject—both the situation and the character—from heroic story, whereas the English poet apparently preferred to invent a situation, with nameless characters.

What has just been said with regard to Irish and Norse poetry appears to be true of early Greek poetry, though only very meagre fragments remain of such heroic poems (cf. p. 24). In Greek, however, there is one piece which, formally at least, may be regarded as an example of the 'unspecified' class—a monologue poem, included among the *Homeric Epigrams* (No. XIV), in which a poet is addressing some potters. No name is given to either party. The poet says that if they will give him his reward he will invoke Athena to protect their kiln. May their work prosper well and find an abundant market. But if they deal unfairly with him, he will summon the foes of their craft, Crasher, Smasher, Shatterer and others, who will spoil their kiln and all their wares. The poem, which is quite short, concludes as follows: "Hither too come thou, Daughter of the Sun, Circe who knowest many spells; cast cruel spells, and injure both them and their wares. Hither too let Cheiron bring a crowd of Centaurs, both those who escaped from the

[1] It is hardly necessary to take the word *bangor* in st. 5 as a proper name.

hands of Heracles and those who perished. May they strike these wares with an evil blow; may the kiln collapse, and the potters lament, as they see their wares ruined.[1] But I will gloat when I see their handicraft smitten with disaster. And may he who is bending over his work have his whole face burnt, so that all may learn to act justly". It is interesting to note that this is another speech-poem derived from spells.

From the instances given above it will be seen that we have to distinguish two varieties of the timeless nameless speech-poem. One variety, represented by the English *Traveller's Prayer*, the Welsh poems and the *Homeric Epigram*, has religious associations, even when, as in the last case, it is not to be taken seriously. It is generally connected with spells or omens. The other variety, to which the remaining English examples belong, has aristocratic associations. These poems possess greater dignity and are evidently the results of more sustained efforts. No true parallels to them are to be found, so far as we are aware, in the other languages now under consideration. Analogies, however, do occur elsewhere, as we shall see in later chapters.

In the preceding pages we have collected all the poems relating to unspecified individuals which are known to us from early records—apart from spells and purely religious pieces. It will be seen that no examples have been given from popular poetry or folksong, the form in which this kind of poetry is most familiar to us in modern times. The reason of course is that no such compositions have been preserved from early times. All our examples relate either to aristocratic or to religious—perhaps we should add professional—life, and there is no reason for doubting that they originated in such circles, or at least in an educated milieu. Poetry relating to humbler spheres of life seems not—or only rarely—to have appealed to those who had the means of recording and preserving it. But we do not doubt that it existed.

In Greek one or two scraps of such poetry have actually been preserved, though we do not know their date. They are songs sung by children, who went round in the spring, begging from house to house. One of these, which comes from Rhodes, may be preserved more or less in its original form:[2] "The swallow has come, has come, bringing fine days and fine weather. She is white in the belly, and black in her back. Roll out the pudding from your rich house, and a beaker of wine and a basket of cheese. Buns too and pulse-cake the swallow will not

[1] Or perhaps 'the sorry deeds'.

[2] Bergk, *Anthol. Lyr.* Carm. Pop. No. 41.

reject. Are we to get it or to go away? If you will give us something (well and good). But if not, we will not put up with it. Let us take the door or the lintel, or the lady who is sitting inside. She is small and we shall easily carry her. But if you will give us something, may you get something big in return! Open, open the door to the swallow. For we are not elders—we are children". The metre is in part iambic; in part it consists of irregular short lines.

The same theme forms the subject of one of the *Homeric Epigrams* (No. XV) known as Eiresione or 'Wreath', from the wreath worn by singing boys at certain festivals. This is doubtless much farther from the original, though the record is probably earlier. The metre is hexameter, except in the last two lines, and the diction more conventional. The children also are better behaved, if somewhat saucy. The last two lines, which are in iambics, are as follows: "If you will give something (well and good). But if not, we will not stop; for we have not come here to make our home with you".

Apart from these passages we know only of brief fragments of popular songs, though references to them—weaving songs, grinding songs, love songs, etc.—are not rare in Greek literature. The earliest reference occurs in the description of the shield of Achilles (*Il.* XVIII. 569 ff.), where a boy is represented as playing a lyre and singing a 'Linos' to the vintagers, who are keeping time with their feet. It is not likely that a timeless nameless song is intended here. In later times at all events Linos is a figure of mythology. He is sometimes said to be a son of one of the Muses; and the fragment of a Linos song which has been preserved speaks of him as slain by Apollo. From other references to folk songs or popular songs it would seem that they were frequently concerned with mythological subjects, while historical or political themes were perhaps not excluded.[1] But timeless nameless themes can hardly have been unknown. Indeed the begging songs just noticed may be regarded as examples of this kind—to be referred to Type D rather than to Type B. Modern analogies would lead us to expect that such themes would be predominant; but we are not sure that this can be assumed with safety.

In the northern languages we confess that we do not know where early examples of popular poetry are to be found, except perhaps in

[1] Yet some pieces which have been taken for folk songs may really be adaptations of folk songs to political propaganda; e.g. Bergk, *Anth. Lyr.* Carm. Pop. No: 43: "The quern is grinding, grinding—even Pittacos is grinding, he who rules over great Mytilene".

spells. The story of Caedmon, told by Bede, *Hist. Eccl.* IV. 24, makes it clear that minstrelsy was much cultivated by villagers in the north of England in the latter part of the seventh century; but unluckily we are told nothing as to the character of the poems they produced. Were the genres cultivated by them the same as those which were cultivated in the courts? Or was the timeless nameless specially in vogue, as in later times? As regards England the two suggestions are not necessarily alternatives. As regards Ireland and the North, the former alternative seems to be the more likely, since we have not been able to find any trace of the timeless nameless. Yet evidence for something similar in the North will have to be considered shortly. In Wales the timeless nameless was known, as we have seen, at least in a religious milieu.

The predominance of the timeless nameless which we find in modern folk songs and popular songs extends also to popular stories, whether told in verse or in prose. When we come to deal with districts like parts of Russia and Yugoslavia, where oral tradition survived in full strength until recently, we shall see that beside heroic stories and other stories relating to historical persons there are current numerous stories dealing with nameless persons or with persons who exist only for a particular story. Similar stories are known in most parts of the world—even in the west of Europe, though here they are used only for the entertainment of children, except in backward districts. We are referring here to 'folk tales'; but it will be convenient—in accordance with general usage—to apply this term only to such stories as have a wide currency, and not to timeless nameless stories in general. When told in verse these stories hardly differ from folk songs of Type A, except that they are generally longer and more detailed. The prose form, however, is much more widespread.

Properly speaking, these stories belong partly to Type A and partly to Type C (CA)—to the former when they are designed purely for entertainment, to the latter when they contain a didactic or explanatory element, as is frequently the case in the true folk tale. In addition to the stories which are strictly nameless there are others, especially perhaps such as belong to Type C, in which some or all of the characters bear descriptive names, invented to suit their characteristics. In other stories again the characters bear non-descriptive names which appear to have been chosen more or less at random. Usually, however, these are names in very common use, like Jack. The presence or absence of such names varies much between one country and another.

Many stories, especially such as belong to Type C, are concerned largely or wholly with animals, which are represented as acting from human motives, and often as speaking. These stories, however, are less common in Europe than in Africa. Others again, though the characters may be nameless, are attached to particular localities. These may be described as local legends, though they frequently belong to Type C.

Folk tales and other timeless nameless stories are not represented as such, any more than folksongs, in the early literatures with which we are concerned. This is perhaps due in part to accident; for the Sicilian Greek poet Stesichoros appears to have cultivated such compositions. One of his poems is said[1] to have told the story of a reaper (apparently unnamed) who was sent to draw water. At the well he found a snake throttling an eagle. He killed the snake and released the eagle, and then went back with the water. The eagle came and knocked the cup out of his hand, before he could get a drink; but all his companions died, because the water had been poisoned by the snake. Stesichoros is also said to have made use of fables,[2] like Hesiod and Archilochos; but these need not be taken into consideration here.

We know of no other early poem which was devoted to the telling of a folk tale or other timeless nameless story as such. Possibly, however, mention should be made here of the Margites, which in form at least may not have been far removed from this description. It was apparently known to Archilochos,[3] and must therefore have been in existence by the middle of the seventh century. Aristotle and other ancient authorities attributed it to Homer. The references to it and the few fragments which remain indicate that it dealt with the adventures of a crazy man, who 'knew many things, but knew them all wrong'; but they seem not to make clear whether it was farce or satire, though the latter is on the whole more probable. The name seems to have been made up from the word μάργος, 'mad';[4] but the scene was apparently laid in Colophon. The poem was in hexameters mixed with iambics.

Next we may take a case of totally different character. There is a

[1] Aelian, *Nat. Hist.* 17. 37 (transl. by Edmonds, *Lyra Graeca*, II. 65, No. 68).

[2] We use the term 'fable' only for a sophisticated variety of animal story (Type C), in which the object is not to explain or illustrate the characteristics of animals, but to draw a moral for human affairs, whether general or specific. The hawk and nightingale scene in the *Works and Days* (200 ff.) seems to belong here. This variety is generally believed to be of Oriental origin.

[3] For the references cf. W. Schmid, *Gesch. d. griech. Lit.* p. 226, note 6; Kinkel, *Epic. Graec. Fragm.* p. 64 ff.

[4] Ancient authorities derived the name from μαργαίνειν, 'to rage' (a derivative of μάργος); cf. Kinkel, *l.c.*

story which was once widely known in the North, and which forms the subject of Swedish and Danish ballads; but the earliest treatment of it is in an early Norse poem (or poems) of Type B. It bears a very close resemblance to a widespread type of folk tale, though it is never entirely without names. The Norse poems, *Grógaldr* and *Fjölsvinnsmál*, are preserved only in very late (paper) MSS., and it is a disputed question whether they date from the heathen period—say the tenth century—or whether they are products of the learned revival in the twelfth and thirteenth centuries. They are sometimes separated in the MSS., but are now generally regarded as parts of one poem. The first part of the *Grógaldr* is a dialogue between Svipdagr and his dead mother Gróa. He desires to win the maiden Menglöð, and has come to his mother's grave to ask her for spells to protect him on his way. The rest of the poem is occupied by the spells—whence the name *Grógaldr* ('spell-singing of Gróa'). In the *Fjölsvinnsmál* Svipdagr appears before Menglöð's home and has an altercation with a certain Fjölsviðr, who appears to be either the porter or the guardian of the maiden. Svipdagr gives himself a fictitious name (Vindkaldr), and puts to Fjölsviðr a long series of questions relating to Menglöð's home and the means by which access to it may be obtained. In the end he learns that Menglöð is in love with a certain Svipdagr, whom she has never seen. He then discloses his real name; Menglöð appears, and they are happily united.

The ballads, which are really only variants of one ballad, treat this theme as a narrative poem (Type A) with a large speech element, though the conversation between Svipdagr (Sveidal, Svendal, etc.) and the 'herdsman' (Fjölsviðr) is quite brief. The early Norse poems are wholly occupied by speeches except one half stanza; but they imply a story. We do not know any folktale exactly corresponding to this story; but the general resemblance is obvious enough. It may be noted also that heroic features are wholly wanting. Svipdagr is a child of luck; all his success is due to external help or to coincidence. As regards the names, Fjölsviðr means 'Very Wise', Menglöð 'Bright with Jewels (necklaces)', or possibly 'Rejoicing in Jewels'. Svipdagr and Gróa are names without obvious meaning, and persons bearing these names figure in other stories. But none of the characters of this story occur elsewhere. Its personnel is peculiar to itself.

Some poems of Stesichoros seem to have been of a somewhat similar character. According to Aelian[1] this poet was the first to compose songs

[1] *Hist. Misc.* x. 18. This passage and the one from Diodoros (iv. 84) cited below are quoted and transl. by Edmonds, *Lyra Graeca*, ii. 36 ff.

about the neatherd Daphnis, of which we have examples in later times from Theocritos. The latter has different accounts of Daphnis; in *Id.* I he perishes through refusal to give way to love, whereas in *Id.* XXVII he is amorous. The story given by Aelian and Diodoros is that he was beloved by a nymph, who threatened him with loss of sight if he should ever have to do with any other woman. He was led to break his vow by a princess, when he was drunk, and thereupon became blind. Aelian's words seem rather to imply that this was the form of the story as told by Stesichoros. In any case its affinities seem to lie with folktales. Diodoros' account in particular suggests that it may have originated in a local legend. Perhaps it was a native Sicilian story, Hellenised by Stesichoros. Mythological associations are not wanting—Daphnis is said to be a son of Hermes—but these may have been added by the Greek poet.

Stesichoros is also said to have composed a song called *Calyce*, which according to Athenaios[1] was sung by women in early times. The subject was as follows: a girl called Calyce prayed to Aphrodite that she might be married to a youth named Euathlos. When he rejected her, she threw herself over a cliff in the neighbourhood of Leucas. Nothing is known elsewhere, so far as we know, either of the story or of the persons who figure in it. It may be observed that the name *Calyce* seems to mean 'bud' (of a flower), while *Euathlos* means 'successful in contests'. Both are quite possible names, and the poem may be founded upon a tragedy of real life. On the other hand it is equally possible that the whole story was invented by Stesichoros.

Another poem by the same author dealt with the fate of a girl called Rhadine. The story is summarised by Strabo,[2] who quotes the first two lines—all that remains—of the poem. Rhadine belonged to a place called Samos, apparently in Elis, but was promised in marriage to a tyrant at Corinth. When she arrived there she was followed by one of her cousins who was in love with her. The tyrant put them both to death and sent off the bodies in a carriage. Then he repented of what he had done and buried them. In this case the evidence, such as it is, favours the theory of fiction. No personal names are recorded except *Rhadine*, which means 'slender' (as applied to a youthful body) and occurs as an epithet of Aphrodite. One fact, however, deserves to be mentioned in connection with the story. Pausanias, VII. v. 6, says that in the island of Samos—off the Asiatic coast—there was a monument

[1] XIV. 619 d (quoted and transl. by Edmonds, *op. cit.* p. 56 f.).

[2] VIII. iii. 20. This passage and the notice in Pausanias, which follows, are quoted and transl. by Edmonds, *op. cit.* p. 56 ff.

(perhaps 'tomb') of Rhadine and Leontichos, at which distressed lovers went to pray. The latter name is presumably that of Rhadine's lover, and may come from the poem, though it is not recorded by Strabo. But Strabo, who evidently knew the poem, was convinced that the poet did not mean the Asiatic Samos. Pausanias' notice therefore can hardly be held to prove that Rhadine and her story were not fictitious. But it is good testimony to the popularity of the story; and it also supplies a rather striking illustration of the readiness with which Greek cities appropriated to themselves celebrities, whatever might be their origin.

It will have been observed that the last four of the poems discussed above were occupied with love themes. Heroic elements seem to have been entirely absent both from these and from the *Margites*. As regards date, Stesichoros belonged to the very end of our period—the early part of the sixth century.[1] The *Margites* was probably a century earlier; the iambics are rather against dating it further back. The date of the Norse poems is disputed, as noted above. We are inclined to think that they belong to the heathen period, but not long before its close. This is suggested in particular by the *Grógaldr*, st. 13: "An eighth (spell) I chant to thee, to the end that a dead Christian woman may have no power to injure thee, if night overtake thee out on a misty road".

Thus far we have dealt only with timeless nameless poems and with poems which as a whole have affinity therewith, whether their themes are invented by the poets or derived from folktales and similar stories. Something must now be said with regard to poems and sagas of essentially different character, especially heroic poems and sagas, which have been influenced by folktales and similar stories, and have apparently incorporated elements of this kind. This subject can only be treated very briefly here. Several instances were noticed in Ch. VIII.

The most striking and obvious examples of this kind are to be found in the long narrative of his adventures which Odysseus gives in the *Odyssey*, Books IX–XII. Some of these have already been referred to (p. 221 ff.). The story of Polyphemos is a widely distributed folktale. The rest are perhaps to be described as travellers' tales rather than folktales;

[1] Some difficulty has arisen from the fact that certain ancient authorities mention two and even three poets of the name Stesichoros, the latest of whom is placed in the early part of the fourth century. Whatever may be the truth about these persons—the second is probably imaginary—there seems to be no adequate reason for doubting that the poems noticed above come from the famous Stesichoros, the first of that name; cf. W. Schmid, *Gesch. d. griech. Lit.* p. 469 ff. (especially p. 469, note 3, and p. 480 ff.).

but we do not profess to be experts in this subject, and consequently find it difficult to draw the line between the two classes. We do not know whether any real parallels to them are to be found in modern folktales; but analogies certainly occur in early stories relating to the north of Europe. Reference may be made especially to the story of the voyage of Gormo and Thorkillus related by Saxo, p. 344 ff. (286 ff.).[1] It may be that the stories belong to an earlier folktale world, in which heathen beliefs and customs were more prominent than in the folktales of modern times. In particular we may notice the violation of the island sanctuary by the slaughter of flocks and herds sacred to the sun or to deities. For such sanctuaries, whether on islands or in coastal districts, there is historical evidence both from the North Sea and the Adriatic. But whether the term 'folktale' be justified or not, it is obvious enough that the stories are such as would circulate most readily in a community which was just coming to be interested in distant lands, as was doubtless the case in the early days of Greek exploration—the eighth rather than the seventh century.

But what we wish to call special attention to is the character of the stories collectively. Heroic elements are virtually non-existent. The hero never uses his sword, except for sacrifice or for cutting a rope. He draws it on two occasions, once against a woman, and once against ghosts. Once he kills a stag with a spear. In the adventure with Polyphemos he saves himself by his own intelligence; but in almost every other case his success or survival is due to some friendly supernatural being, whose advice he obediently follows, like the hero of folktale. His disasters are due either to unfriendly supernatural beings or to the acts of his followers. In this point again we find a contrast with heroic poetry. His relations with his followers are those of captain and crew rather than of lord and comitatus. Sometimes they are friendly, and even affectionate. But he is always ready to throw the blame upon them; and they in turn sometimes show themselves distrustful and rebellious.

It cannot be proved that these stories were timeless nameless before they were introduced into the *Odyssey*: but they show the characteristics which usually belong to such stories. They form a solid block within a heroic poem; but they have not been adapted to their environment, and they contain practically nothing heroic except the names,

[1] Cf. Chadwick, *Heroic Age*, p. 258 ff. It is suggested here that island sanctuaries similar to Heligoland may once have existed in the Mediterranean. When this was written the author had not observed that flocks sacred to the sun are recorded to have been kept near Valona; cf. Herodotos, IX. 93.

which—apart from the (first) Nekyia—are few. They may be contrasted with other cases where heroic poems have incorporated folktales or similar stories, and where the extraneous elements have been adapted to their environment. Such is the case perhaps with the story of the stringing of the bow in the latter part of the *Odyssey* and with the story of Beowulf's adventures with the monsters. Heroic characteristics are obvious enough in both of these.

The story of Beowulf's adventures at Heorot has affinities with the folktale known as the *Bear's Son*,[1] which can hardly be due to accident. But there are differences between the two stories, the importance of which is not always sufficiently recognised. Thus in the folktale[2] the hero has two companions who essay the adventure before him without success; he has an iron mace or club; he rescues three kidnapped princesses in the place to which he descends; the companions haul up the princesses, but treacherously let the rope go when the hero tries to ascend. The hero has provided against the treachery by sending up his mace or a stone in place of himself. Eventually he makes his escape by some other way, convicts his companions of treachery, and marries one of the princesses. These features, with only slight variations, are found in the modern Scandinavian, German, French, Italian, Serbian and Russian versions of the folktale; but they are all wanting in *Beowulf*. Further, in various accounts (Icelandic, French, Italian, etc.)[3] the hero is either the son of a bear or at least brought up in a bear's den. Where this feature is not found it often seems to be implied by the name (Bear's Son, etc.) given to the hero. But Beowulf's origin is of quite a different character. On the other hand Beowulf's adventures have features which are wanting in the folktale. He descends through water, not through a hole in the ground, and the monster he fights with below is different and of a different sex from the one he has encountered in the hall.

A very much closer resemblance to the *Beowulf* story is shown by *Grettis Saga*,[4] cap. 64 ff. This account agrees with *Beowulf* in all the

[1] Cf. Panzer, *Studien zur germ. Sagengeschichte*, I. *Beowulf* (Munich, 1910). A short but good conspectus of the material is given by Chambers, *Beowulf*, p. 369 ff.

[2] The reader must excuse a somewhat summary treatment of the evidence, which is necessary, unless a disproportionate amount of space were to be given to the subject. Details will be found in the works cited.

[3] In Mijatovich's *Serbian Fairy Tales* this feature belongs to the *Bear's Son* (p. 1 ff.), whereas the story given above belongs to *Sir Peppercorn* (p. 55 ff.); but the two stories have common elements.

[4] Transl. by Hight and by Morris and Magnússon (this section also by Chambers, *op. cit.* p. 175 ff.).

features noted above, except that the rôles of the male and female monsters are reversed and that the hero (Grettir) is let down to the water by a rope, which is watched by a priest called Steinn. The priest deserts the rope when he thinks that Grettir is dead. No treachery is implied; but Grettir has to climb the cliff, when he returns. There can be no doubt then that the *Beowulf* and *Grettir* stories form one group (A), as against the folktale (B). It may be that the differences are due to the borrowing by the common original of A of certain features from the folktale. More probably, we think, A represents an earlier northern form of the folktale. If so we may infer that the present wide distribution of B is not very ancient.

A more important fact, however, has yet to be noted. It is agreed by the great majority of scholars—and we cannot admit that there is any reasonable doubt—that Bjarki (the hero of the *Bjarkamál*) is the same person as Beowulf, and that his fight with a monster at the court of Hrólfr Kraki is to be identified with Beowulf's adventure at Heorot. But there is no resemblance in details, beyond the fact that the monster has been committing depredations upon the Danish king's home—the cattle in this case. The monster here is theriomorphic; Saxo, p. 69 (56), referring to the same adventure, calls it a bear. With the folktale and with the story of Grettir Bjarki's adventure has nothing in common. On the other hand two late Norse authorities, the *Hrólfs Saga Kraka* and the *Bjarkarímur* (cf. p. 217), relate that Bjarki was the son of a bear —a prince named Björn ('Bear') who was transformed into a bear— and that he was brought up in a bear's den, like the hero of the folktale. There is no reference to this in the *Bjarkamál* or in Saxo's prose, but the name *Bjarki* is a derivative of 'bear'. The *Hrólfs Saga*, cap. 33, also relates that in Hrólfr's last fight Bjarki remains asleep, and a bear takes his place in the battle. This appearance of the bear is not mentioned elsewhere;[1] but in the *Bjarkamál* the hero refuses to rise from his sleep—a fact which is difficult to explain unless some incident of the kind is implied. The folktale affords no parallel.

There is a general tendency at present to believe that the fight of Beowulf-Bjarki with the monster is derived from the folktale, and indeed that the hero himself is merely the Bear's Son adopted into a heroic story. This view of course implies that the Scandinavian form of the story was in course of time stripped of all the features which belong to the folktale, although the folktale was still familiar—as seen from *Grettis Saga*—and Bjarki himself was credited with associations,

[1] The *Bjarkarímur* deal only with the early part of Bjarki's life.

both old and new, with the bear. It also perhaps involves that the story of Beowulf's origin as given in the poem was an invention of later times. We think that a more satisfactory explanation might be obtained without quite so drastic a treatment of the records. To put the matter as briefly as possible we would suggest something on the following lines. The original story may have been that of an encounter with an animal monster or (more probably) a bear. In England this story has been transformed through the influence of an early variety (A) of the 'Bear's Son' folktale. The incentive to this influence is to be traced to the hero's name *Beowulf*, if this was originally a kenning for 'bear', as seems probable (cf. p. 224). In the North the story of the adventure seems not to have been influenced by the folktale. The name *Bjarki* may have been suggested by the original name *Beowulf*, and may in its turn have given rise both to the birth story and to the story of metamorphosis—the latter perhaps first, if we may draw any inference from the *Bjarkamál*. The former—not the latter—occurs also in the folktale, but need not have been derived from it directly. In the tenth and eleventh centuries, when the name *Björn* was very popular, it was not rare for ancestries to be traced to bears.[1] Notable examples are the genealogies of Earl Siward of Northumberland, who died in 1055, and of Svend Estridsen, king of Denmark 1047–76. Siward's father is described as *Beorn cognomento Beresune, hoc est Filius Ursi*; and it is added that he had the ears of a bear. This is probably the earliest reference to 'Bear's Son'. But the real bear is placed three generations further back.

The story of Beowulf's adventure is of special interest since we know the folktale as a folktale and at the same time can form from the Scandinavian records some idea of the story which it seems to have displaced.[2] Heroic elements are far more prominent than in the *Odyssey* (IX–XII). This may be due in part to the fact that the hero of the folktale is essentially a strong man. But it is quite unnecessary to suppose that the court milieu and pride in weapons were originally

[1] Cf. Chadwick, *Heroic Age*, p. 120, where some of the references are given.

[2] The genealogy of the *Beowulf* story according to our view may be given as follows:

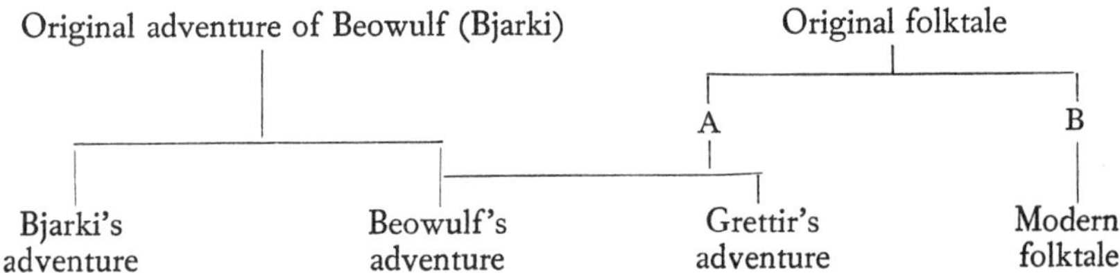

alien to the story of *Beowulf*. They are just as prominent in the story of Bjarki. Beowulf cannot use his sword, owing to the influence of the folktale; but Bjarki is a famous swordsman.

Further examples of stories derived from folktales or something similar have been given in Ch. VIII (p. 222 ff.). By 'something similar' we mean stories which have the general characteristics of folktales, but are not widely enough known to deserve that name. Thus we do not know any close parallel to the interesting story which forms the subject of the first part of the *Lady of the Fountain*. Yet it suggests a heathen sanctuary—which would probably mean that it is of great antiquity. It may be derived either from an obsolete folktale or from a local story. In the *Pursuit of the Gilla Dacker*, which has elements in common with it (cf. p. 224 f.), there is a descent through water, as in the adventures of Beowulf and Grettir. Among other stories which have affinities with the type now under consideration we may note especially those relating to the birth and childhood of heroes (cf. p. 216 ff.). Much material is also doubtless to be found in the stories of Sigmundr and of Heracles, both of which have elements in common with the story of *Beowulf*.

The attachment of floating stories to well-known names is a phenomenon which is common enough even in our own days. In modern society such stories usually lead up to humorous or caustic sayings or to a comic denouement; and the same seems to have been the case in Greece from the sixth century onwards. Such stories often, perhaps usually, have a basis in fact. But unless the original subject of the story is a famous person his name is bound to be forgotten; and the story comes to be attached to somebody who has since attained to note or to 'somebody I knew once', in which case it becomes virtually unattached. In the times with which we are concerned, when little or nothing was committed to writing, such stories must have been far more prevalent, though they were doubtless occupied with deeds—adventures and experiences—far more than with words. That the same process of attachment, first to one person and then to another, prevailed then as now may be seen (e.g.) by the fact that a practically identical story—quite impossible in itself—is told of Beowulf and Grettir.

Unattached stories, whatever may be their origin, seem not to be recorded until comparatively late times. Probably the oldest examples are the poems noticed earlier in this chapter. The surname *Beresune* applied to Earl Siward's father suggests that the *Bear's Son* was known in the eleventh century. Some Norse stories in which the chief character is called Gestr ('guest, stranger') may go back to an earlier date; but they contain also characters who are known from other sources. Yet it would be rash to assume that the unattached or timeless nameless story did not exist before the eleventh century. Beowulf indeed presupposes the existence of a variety of the 'Bear's Son' folktale in the seventh century, and it is not likely that it existed only in attachment to one character or another of (say) heroic story or to persons then living. How then are we to account for the fact that such stories are not recorded?

In order to answer this question it will be well to note the general characteristics of timeless nameless stories. All the evidence is late; but the oldest and best material available is probably to be obtained from widely distributed folktales. Apart from their timeless nameless character the following seem to be the most outstanding features of such stories: (i) the want of individualisation—or perhaps we should say the elementary individualisation of the characters; (ii) the large part played by peasants and other persons of humble rank; (iii) the prominence of the marvellous; (iv) the happy ending of the story, often through the marriage of the hero.

Some of these features are of course not confined to folktales. In heroic poetry the individualisation of the characters is usually not advanced. But even in *Beowulf*, which is much behind the Norse poems in this respect, the characters are far removed from the aimless and irresponsible beings who form the personnel of folktales. The heroes of the latter are sometimes preternaturally strong, sometimes clever; but most commonly their achievements are due solely to external guidance. The 'heroines' are mere puppets; and so also are the other women, unless they are malicious. In heroic poetry it is a very rare thing even among the hero's opponents to meet with a character who is represented in a wholly unsympathetic light. But in folktales there is almost invariably someone of quite inhuman ferocity, and usually others who are guilty of cowardice and treachery beyond all possible consideration.

Again, neither the love of the marvellous nor the happy ending of the story is unknown to heroic poetry. The story of *Waldhere* ends like an orthodox romance. It is the invariability of this kind of ending which is characteristic of the folktale. We are not convinced, however, that this is a feature of great antiquity even in folktales. As regards the love of the marvellous, in heroic poetry this usually appears either in the form of exaggeration or in the introduction of the supernatural (cf. p. 204 ff.). But in the folktale it pervades everything.

It is the second of the features noted above—the prominence of peasant characters—which most sharply distinguishes the folktale from the heroic story. In the latter, as we have seen (p. 64 ff.), such characters are rarely mentioned—which is due doubtless to the fact that these stories were intended primarily for the entertainment of kings' courts. But in folktales the hero himself is usually a peasant—which must mean that such stories were intended primarily for the circles in which they are still current, i.e. for peasant circles. The fact that kings and princesses also figure largely in folktales cannot be admitted as evidence to the contrary, for the interest taken by peasants in the doings of royalty is a different thing from the interest taken by royalty in the doings of peasants. The culminating incident of most folktales—the marriage of the peasant hero with the king's daughter—was likely to please a peasant audience; but we are inclined to doubt whether in court circles it would have roused so much enthusiasm. Moreover the picture of court life which folktales give is not an 'intimate' picture, such as we find in *Beowulf*. It is like a distant view—the view of the court which is obtainable from the cottage door. The life of the courts of petty kings in ancient times was no doubt often aimless and irresponsible enough, but hardly to the degree of inanity which we find in folktales.

The prominence of the marvellous points in the same direction. It is not merely that in the abstract the marvellous appeals more strongly to the uneducated mind. The special character of the marvellous in these stories frequently indicates the workings of the primitive mind, especially perhaps in relation to animals. In heroic poetry practically the only animals mentioned, except collectively, are the horse, the dog and certain hunting animals, especially the stag and the wild boar; and it is only rarely that, as in the case of Achilles' horse, they act unnaturally.

From what has been said it will be seen that the question why there is so little evidence for the existence of folktales in early times is practically answered by the characteristics of the folktales themselves. This internal evidence indicates that they grew up in the milieu in which they are now current. Just as the primary function of heroic poetry was to provide entertainment for the court, so that of the folktale was to do the same for the village audience. Since practically all our records for early times come from the upper and educated classes it is not surprising that we hear so little of the stories which entertained the peasant.

We do not mean of course that every folktale necessarily originated in the village. One must not assume too rigid a line of demarcation. The upper class were probably familiar with folktales from their childhood.

In *Beowulf* we see a folktale making its way into a heroic story and transforming it. It is scarcely possible to doubt that the reverse also took place, and indeed far more frequently. But if so, such stories have been assimilated and accommodated to their environment to such a degree that heroic features are no longer discernible. It is to be remembered that folktales had a very much longer history than our heroic poems before they were committed to writing.

Above all account must be taken of the wide distribution of folktales. Some of the Teutonic heroic stories were known throughout the Teutonic world; but it is only quite rarely that one meets with them in non-Teutonic languages—unless of course they have passed through literary channels. There is evidence for a knowledge of some Irish heroic stories in Wales and some Greek heroic stories in Italy. But such cases are exceptional. On the other hand many folktales are known throughout Europe, and even in Asia and Africa, and are told, with slight variations, in numerous languages. This wide dissemination of folktales opens up a great problem, which cannot be entered upon here, though we incline to the view that the itinerant trader is largely responsible. What we would emphasise is that a Greek folktale need not be of Greek origin, while an English or Norse folktale need not even be of Teutonic origin. It is perhaps only a minority of folktales which are of native origin, even if we use the term 'native' in the widest possible sense. Whatever be the ultimate origin of a story which has passed through two or three languages, even if it be founded on fact, the original names and associations of the characters have obviously little chance of survival.

The timeless nameless story, including the folktale, is without doubt the most widespread of all the forms of literature which we have considered. Yet we have seen that in the periods with which we are concerned it is very difficult to trace. In the north of Europe down to the Middle Ages it seems to have found its way into writing only when it had become attached to a famous character—or at least to a familiar milieu[1]—and treated according to the conventions of the (heroic or other) poetry or saga current at the time. Its timeless name-

[1] We are thinking here more especially of cases like Höfundr in the *Hervarar Saga* (cf. p. 385), who is probably to be regarded as an addition to the heterogeneous personnel of the story. Both his name ('Judge') and what is recorded of him suggest derivation from folktale. It is to be borne in mind that the middle part of this saga is probably a work of fiction, designed to connect the two old stories of the fight at

less character was of course thereby lost. The same seems to be true of early Greece.

The timeless nameless folksong is perhaps almost as widespread,[1] and this is even more difficult to trace in early records. The Anglo-Saxon poems discussed at the beginning of this chapter have analogies with such songs and presumably borrowed the timeless nameless convention from them; but their milieu—except possibly in the *Seafarer*—is heroic, and it is to be remembered that occasional poems (Type E) were by no means unknown to heroic society. In later chapters we shall have to deal with folksongs current among other peoples. It will be seen that they may be divided roughly into two classes—ritual and non-ritual. The former belong to Type D (or DB), the latter to Type A or to Type B. It is clearly the latter (Type B) which have influenced the Anglo-Saxon poems.

Apart from the timeless nameless convention the analogies of these poems are, as we have seen, with heroic poems of Type B. Among other peoples we shall find also theological poems of the same type, as in Norse. For the timeless nameless variety also we shall find analogies elsewhere; but they are rare. The cultivation of poetry of this kind for elaborate studies of situation and emotion is one of the most distinctive features of Anglo-Saxon poetry.

In conclusion it may be observed that the history of the category discussed in this chapter is closely bound up with the development of fiction. Many timeless nameless stories—even folktales—may ultimately have had a basis in fact. But when the persons with whom they were concerned had been forgotten, these were no longer distinguished from other stories, e.g. animal tales, which had been fictitious from the beginning.

In Ch. VIII (p. 233 f.) we saw that fiction appears to be fairly well developed in the *Odyssey*. The stories which the hero invents sometimes introduce well-known characters. But elsewhere, e.g. in his conversation with his father (XXIV. 303 ff.), he uses names with a more or less

Samsey and the battle of the Goths and Huns. The case of Weland-Völundr is less clear and of course much earlier. Apart from the story of Svipdagr it is probably the nearest approach to folktale in early Teutonic poetry. In general the folktale element tends to be more prominent in non-heroic than in heroic stories. We may instance especially the *Mabinogion*. Many examples are also to be found in the *Lives* of Irish saints. The relationship of folktales to stories of the gods is of course a somewhat different question.

[1] We mean as a genre—not the individual themes.

obvious meaning. These are just the kind of names which occur most frequently in folktales.

The Anglo-Saxon timeless nameless poems can hardly be regarded otherwise than as works of fiction, even if the situations which they depict may have been suggested by experiences in real life. The same is probably true of Stesichoros' poems *Calyce* and *Rhadine*; for there is no evidence elsewhere for the former, while the evidence for the latter seems to be of little value (cf. p. 433 f.). On the other hand the story of Daphnis had, at least in later times, a wide currency, like that of Svipdagr. The connections of both are rather with the folktale.

The *Calyce* and the *Rhadine* are of great importance in connection with the romance and novel. And it is essential to note that their author is remarkable also both for the cultivation of folktales and for the freedom with which he treated heroic stories. His activities evidently constitute a landmark in the literary use of fiction.

It is not unlikely that the direction which Stesichoros' activities took was due largely to the fact that he lived in a country which had no local connection with ancient Greek traditions. The Sicilian poet was probably less bound by conventions and comparatively free to give rein to his imagination. Moreover, his own country may have supplied him with new forms of composition, in poetry as well as in music.

England, like Sicily, was a newly settled land; and both of them, unlike Iceland, were lands occupied by a numerous native population. In both cases we have to take into account the effects upon the invaders of comparative isolation from the homes of their kindred, and probably also some influence, however indefinite, from the native population. It may be that the freedom with which heroic story has been treated in *Beowulf* by the incorporation of folktale is due to these causes. At all events we have little doubt that the development of timeless nameless poetry is to be explained in this way. It can hardly be unconnected with the preoccupation shown by the poets with the ruined cities of the Roman period. In both cases alike English poetic activities took a direction for which no true parallel is to be found in the early poetry of the other Teutonic peoples.

CHAPTER XV

MANTIC POETRY

THE material to be discussed in this chapter will appear to be of a somewhat heterogeneous character, at least at first sight. The poems actually preserved in one language have sometimes little or nothing in common with those preserved in another; but we shall see that this is largely due to accident. It will be convenient to give a summary of the material from each country before attempting any classification.

In Greece we may first take the prophecies, many of which have been preserved by Herodotos and other writers. Most of these, however, date from times later than those which fall within our scope, while the genuineness of some of the earlier examples is doubtful. They fall into two classes: (i) answers given at oracular sanctuaries to deputations which had been sent or to individuals who had gone to consult them; (ii) prophecies by seers, whose names are recorded.

The first class is the more numerous. A good number of sanctuaries are represented; but the references to Delphoi are by far the most frequent. Herodotos gives twenty-two answers from this sanctuary, in part at least verbatim. They are all in hexameter verse; but they differ a good deal in character, some using metaphorical diction after the manner of riddles, while others are more or less direct. Examples of the former type may be found in I. 67, III. 57, V. 92 (the second passage), VI. 77. Moral gnomes occur, e.g. in VI. 86, but they are not common.

Herodotos has no certain examples of metrical responses from other sanctuaries.[1] He refers to a number of such responses;[2] but it is not clear that any of them are quoted verbatim. On the other hand he quotes several examples in hexameter verse of the second class mentioned above—prophecies by seers whose names are given. The earliest of these (I. 62)—by Amphilytos the Acarnanian—relates to the year 538 and belongs to the riddle-like type.

[1] A line of uncertain origin relating to Delos is quoted in VI. 98; but the text is doubtful.

[2] A very interesting example from the Oracle of the Dead, on the Acheron, occurs in V. 92; but it is not given verbatim. The responses of the oracle of Apollo at Branchidai quoted in I. 159 are in prose; but the case is obviously exceptional.

Mention may also be made here of the two verses, containing moral gnomes, which are said by Herodotos (v. 56) to have been spoken in a dream to the tyrant Hipparchos before his assassination (in the year 514). Parallels to these are to be found in the North and will be referred to later.

Next we may notice the catalogue of lucky and unlucky days contained in the *Works and Days*, from 765 to the end. It is not clear how far the poet is recording common belief, or to what extent he is giving expression to his own individual wisdom; but in any case the wisdom is of a mantic character. Reference may also be made to the prohibitions which immediately precede this section—from 724 onwards. There is no break in the structure or plan of the poem at this point; but it may be observed that the preceding gnomes (precepts and prohibitions) are moral and industrial, while those which follow are religious and mantic.

The English material consists wholly of spells, and has nothing in common with the Greek. Most of the spells are accompanied by directions in prose, but they themselves are for the most part in verse of a very irregular kind. In their present form they have been Christianised to a certain extent.

One[1] is a spell to counteract the effect of injury done to the crops by witchcraft. It contains four invocations, in two of which the earth is more or less personified. One is addressed to 'Erce, mother of earth', the other to 'Earth, mother of men'. But there is a large Christian element even in these, while according to the directions a portion of the ceremony is to be performed in a church, and the priest takes part in it.

Five spells are preserved in MS. Harl. 585. One[2] of these is directed against a sudden pain—possibly sunstroke. The remedy is "feverfew and a red nettle, which grows in through (the wall of?) a house, and plantain". The spell then proceeds as follows in irregular verse: "Clamorous were they, yea clamorous, when they came riding over the hill (or 'barrow'); fierce (or 'resolute') were they when they came riding over the land. Shield thyself now, if thou wilt have a chance of surviving this attack. If any little dart has found its way into me, out

1 Ed. by Grein-Wülcker, *Bibl. d. ags. Poesie*, I. 312 ff.; Wyatt, *Anglo-Saxon Reader*, p. 128 ff.; Sedgefield, *Anglo-Saxon Book*, p. 354 ff.

2 Ed. by Grein-Wülcker, *op. cit.* I. 317 f.; Sedgefield, *op. cit.* p. 357; Sweet, *Anglo-Saxon Reader*, p. 104 f.

with it! I stood beneath my bright shield of limewood when the mighty dames were arraying their host, when they were shooting the whistling missiles. I will shoot another back, a flying arrow straight in their faces. If any little dart, etc. A smith sat forging a little knife...[1] If any little dart, etc. Six smiths sat making murderous darts. Out with thee, dart! Thou shalt not remain in me, dart! If any piece of iron wrought by witches has found its way into me, it shall melt. If thou hast been shot in the skin or in the flesh or the blood or the limb, thy life shall be in no way harmed. If it has been a shot from the (heathen) gods or from elves or witches, I will now help thee. This shall cure thee from the shot of gods or elves or witches; I will help thee. She shall[2] flee to yon forest. Sound be thou in thy head. The Lord help thee. Then take the knife and dip it in moisture". The last sentence is in prose. It will be seen that the poem regards the pain as due to missiles shot by witches or Valkyries—an idea for which we shall find parallels elsewhere in a later chapter.

The second[3] of these spells is an address to nine herbs seriatim, specifying their properties or what they have done. Much of it is very obscure. We may quote the opening: "Remember, mugwort (Artemisia), what thou didst proclaim, what thou didst determine (?) at the divine assembly.[4] Thou art called Una, chief of herbs. Thou hast power against three and against thirty, against venom and against infection, against hostility which passes through the land". In 30 ff. a reminiscence of heathen days seems to be preserved: "A snake came creeping: it bit a man. Then Woden took nine glorious shoots (or 'twigs of glory'); then he smote the adder so that it flew into nine pieces". The poem concludes with a list of the various venoms, etc., against which the nine herbs are potent.

The third spell[5] is for recovering lost or stolen cattle. This spell is entirely Christian. The fourth[6] is a very obscure spell, apparently against some malady caused by a dwarf. Part of it is in narrative form. The fifth[7] consists of a series of spells for childbirth, with directions for their use. The first of them is to be said by the woman herself at the grave of a dead man.

[1] Text apparently corrupt.
[2] Text corrupt. Perhaps to be emended to a pl. form.
[3] Ed. by Grein-Wülcker, *op. cit.* p. 320 ff.; by Sedgefield, *op. cit.* p. 359 ff.
[4] Uncertain. Taken by some to be a proper name.
[5] Ed. by Grein-Wülcker, *op. cit.* p. 323 f.
[6] Ed. by Grein-Wülcker, *op. cit.* p. 326; by Sedgefield, *op. cit.* p. 358.
[7] Ed. by Grein-Wülcker, *op. cit.* p. 326 f.

Another small collection of spells[1] is preserved in MS. CCCC. 41. Two of these are spells for the recovery of lost or stolen cattle. The second is addressed to an unknown Garmund, 'thegn of God'. A third spell is to be used at the swarming of bees, to prevent them from being injured by witchcraft or from flying away to the woods.

Somewhat similar spells are found in a few early German MSS.[2] One of these, for the swarming of bees, bears a certain resemblance to the case last mentioned, though it has assonance instead of alliteration. Two spells of a rather different character are preserved in a Merseburg MS. of the tenth century. The first is as follows: "Once there were women seating themselves here and seating themselves there. Some were fastening the chains, others were hindering the host, others again were plucking at the shackles. Spring from thy bonds and make thy escape from the warriors". This may be compared with the English spell against sudden pain quoted in full above. Here also the women appear to be Valkyries. The second of these spells, which is likewise in narrative form, describes how Wodan and four goddesses healed a lame horse by their incantations.[3] Both these spells use the alliterative metre.

Spells similar to the English and German examples just quoted are by no means unknown in the North. But no early examples seem to have been preserved, though spells are frequently referred to in sagas. The Norse material to be discussed here consists mainly of speech poems (Type B), which contain mantic elements. Some poems are indeed wholly cast in the form of a spell or prophecy. A number of such cases have already been noticed, so far as their subject-matter is concerned, in previous chapters. Here we are concerned only with their form. The speakers are usually supernatural beings or persons endowed with supernatural powers.

First we may refer again to the *Darraðarljóð*, discussed on p. 346 f. This is in the form of a weaving spell, sung by Valkyries who have set up a loom, and its object is to secure safety and victory for the 'young king'. In st. 7 it contains a prophecy of the future dominance of the Norse power in Ireland.

1 Ed. by Grein-Wülcker, *op. cit.* pp. 324 f., 319 f.; the second also by Wyatt, *op. cit.* p. 130 f.; the third by Sweet, *op. cit.* p. 104, Sedgefield, *op. cit.* p. 359.

2 All are to be found in Braune, *Althochd. Lesebuch*, pp. 81 and 158.

3 Later (Christianised) forms of this are given by Grimm, *Teut. Myth.* (4th edn.), p. 1232 f., from Norway and Scotland.

Next we may take the *Grottasöngr*, which is preserved in certain MSS. of the *Prose Edda*. This poem contains a few narrative stanzas; but most of it is in the form of a grinding spell. Fróði, the mythical peace-king of the Danes, has bought two girls who are seeresses, sprung from the *jötnar* (cf. p. 253), and set them to grind wealth for him at the quern called Grotti. We may quote st. 5: "We are grinding for Fróði, grinding riches unstinted, grinding[1] wealth in abundance at the quern of joy. May he abide in riches, may he sleep on feather cushions, may he wake to his pleasure! Then has the grinding been well done". Fróði allows them not a moment's rest. In wrath they sing of their origin and the deeds of their youth; then they prophesy the coming of a raid and the end of Fróði's kingdom. Finally the quern falls in pieces. Snorri, in the *Skaldskaparmál*, cap. 43—where this poem has been inserted—seems to have had in mind a somewhat different version of it. He says that the bond-maidens 'ground a raid' against Fróði, bringing against him a sea-king called Mýsingr, who is not mentioned in our text of the poem. Mýsingr slew Fróði and carried off the quern and the maidens. He made them grind salt, persisting until the ship went down. It will be seen that no clear line appears to be drawn in the poem between spell and prophecy. The bond-maidens' prophecy seems to bring about its own fulfilment.

An account of the *Skírnismál* was given on p. 248. This poem is not in the form of a spell, like the two last; but when Gerðr refuses to give in to Skírnir's entreaties and threats, he pronounces (st. 25 ff.) a long spell or curse against her. She is to live a life of continuous misery and horror. We may quote st. 32 f.: "I went to the wood, to a succulent tree, to get a potent (i.e. magic) wand. I have got a potent wand. Wroth with thee is Othin, wroth with thee is the chief of the Aesir; Frey shall hate thee, thou most wicked girl—and thou hast incurred the potent wrath of the gods". He ends his speech (st. 36) by saying that he is inscribing (the letter) *þurs* ('giant') and what appear to be three magic signs.

The *Sigrdrífumál* is in the form of a monologue addressed by the Valkyrie Sigrdrífa to the hero Sigurðr. It has already been referred to in connection both with heroic poetry, Type C (cf. p. 27f.), and with

[1] The repetition of the predicate is a frequent characteristic of poetry of this kind; cf. *Darraðarljóð*, st. 4 ff., and some of the English and German spells noticed above. We may also compare the Lesbian fragment quoted on p. 429, note, which is evidently based on a quern song or spell. Lancashire weavers used to sing "Ticketum tacketum gee bow-wow".

gnomic poetry (cf. p. 385). The first part of it, however, must be noticed here somewhat more fully. The address begins with an invocation to Day, Night, the deities and the earth (st. 2 f.). Then, in st. 4, the Valkyrie mentions the magic ingredients in the beer which she offers to Sigurðr. In st. 6–13[1] she specifies the kinds of (runic) letters which should be used for various purposes and the objects on which they should be inscribed. We may quote st. 11: "Thou shalt know *Limrúnar*, if thou wilt be a doctor and know how to look after wounds. They are to be inscribed upon the bark and the boughs of a tree whose branches bend to the east". St. 14 ff. contain a brief account of information—given apparently to Othin by Mímir's head—with regard to the objects upon which runes had been inscribed and the dissemination of these runes. After this the speaker passes on to the moral gnomes. It may be observed that the word *rún* means both 'letter' (of the alphabet) and 'mystery'. Both ideas are involved here. Only one recognisable letter (T in st. 6) is mentioned. Some of the terms used are unintelligible to us.

Here we ought perhaps to refer also to the *Reginsmál*, which is closely connected with the *Sigrdrífumál* (cf. p. 27). St. 20 ff.[2] contain a short list of omens, which are declared to Sigurðr by Hnikarr—the disguised Othin. They are all of general application and belong to the same class of mantic composition as the list of lucky and unlucky days in the *Works and Days*, though the resemblance is of course not very close.

It has already been mentioned (p. 383) that the last part of the *Hávamál*, from st. 146 to the end, consists of a list of spells. The nature of these is never described, though the objects for which they are available are stated in each case. We may take st. 149 as an example: "A fourth I know: if men place gyves upon my arms and legs, I chant such spells as will enable me to go free. The fetter flies from my feet and the shackle from my hands". This list is preceded by a passage relating to the magical use of runes, which may be compared with the passage from the *Sigrdrífumál* noticed above. It is to be remembered that Othin is the speaker throughout the poem.

Another list of spells, nine in number, is contained in the *Grógaldr*, st. 6 ff.[3] (cf. p. 432). They are sung by the dead Gróa to her son

[1] From st. 6 to the end this poem is ed. and transl. by Clarke, *The Hávamál*, p. 88 ff.

[2] Ed. and transl. by Clarke, *op. cit.* p. 98 f.

[3] Ed. and transl. by Clarke, *op. cit.* p. 100 ff.

Svipdagr, who has roused her from the grave, and their object is to protect him from various dangers which may beset him on his quest for Menglöð; but they are all of general application. As in the *Hávamál*, it is not the nature of the spells which is described, but the circumstances for which they are available.

Another case of necromancy forms the subject of the *Vegtamskviða*—sometimes called *Balder's Dreams*. Othin wakes up a dead seeress or witch (*völva*), in order to ascertain from her the meaning of the dreams by which Balder was troubled. She foretells to him the death of his son. This case has a certain affinity with Greek prophecies in the fact that the consultation and response are concerned with a specific event, though the story belongs to mythology.

The *Völuspá* is another 'prophecy of a seeress' (*völ(v)u spá*). The contents of this poem were discussed on p. 320f. They embrace both the origin and the future fate of the world and the gods—in fact the whole of mythological cosmology. In such cases the word *spá* properly means 'vision' of things unseen, whether future, present or past, rather than 'prophecy' in the modern sense.

In the *Hyndluljóð* (cf. p. 278f.) Freyja goes to consult the giantess Hyndla as to the ancestry of her devotee Óttarr the son of Innsteinn. This is another specific case, and interesting from the fact that all the questions and answers relate to the past.

All the examples given above are referred to supernatural beings and, with the exception of the *Darraðarljóð*, all relate to mythological events. But in heroic poetry also prophecies and prognostications of various kinds are by no means rare. The poem *Grípisspá* ('Prophecy of Grípir') consists of a dialogue between Sigurðr and his mother's brother Grípir, who is said to have knowledge of the future. In alternate stanzas Sigurðr asks questions and Grípir gives answers, in which the whole course of the hero's life is revealed. A somewhat earlier example of the same kind, though in monologue form, occurs in *Sigurðarkviða hin Skamma*, st. 51 ff., where the dying Brynhildr prophesies at length the course of events which will follow her death.

Moreover there is no reason for doubting that both prophecies and spells played an important part in real life. In point of fact spells are frequently mentioned in sagas; but the actual words are rarely given. The following passage may be quoted from *Egils Saga*, cap. 57—relating to Egill's departure from Norway, after he had been outlawed by King Eric Blood-Axe: "When they were ready to sail, Egill landed on the island. He took a hazel pole in his hand, and went to a promontory of the cliffs, which looked towards the mainland. Then he took a horse's head and fixed it on the pole. Then he pronounced a curse, saying: 'I set up a "pole of cursing", and direct this curse against King Eric and Queen Gunnhildr'. He turned the horse's head towards the coast. 'I direct this curse upon the spirits of the land, who inhabit this country, that they shall all lose their way, and none of them shall find or reach its dwelling, until they drive King Eric and Gunnhildr out of the country.' Then he thrust the pole into a rift in the rocks, and left it standing there. He turned the head also towards the mainland, and he inscribed on the pole runes which expressed all this curse". The whole passage is in prose. Egill appears to have been following a recognised practice.

Prophecies also are by no means rare; but they are seldom given in verse.[1] We may, however, cite the story of a dream prophecy, which presents a rather striking parallel to the story of Hipparchos, mentioned on p. 446. It is preserved in a short piece known as the *Dream of Thorsteinn son of Hallr á Síðu*. Three women appear to Thorsteinn on three successive nights and warn him in verse against his Irish slave. He is unable to find the slave, and on the fourth night is murdered by him. The poems are extremely obscure. This Thorsteinn had fought under Earl Sigurðr at Clontarf in 1014; but his death did not take place until thirty or forty years later. His father was one of the leading men in Iceland at the beginning of the eleventh century.

Reference may also be made to the dream of Earl Gilli of the Hebrides, mentioned in *Njáls Saga*, cap. 157.[2] A man appeared to him in a dream and declared in verse that he had come from Ireland, and that Earl Sigurðr and King Brian had fallen. This, it is added, was a week before news of the battle was brought by the survivors. The case may be regarded as an instance of prophecy relating to the present, though to things not ascertainable in the ordinary course.

In the Norse evidence, taken as a whole, three features deserve to be emphasised: (i) the very frequent association of spells with (runic) writing; (ii) the absence of a clear line of division between spell and prophecy; (iii) the fact that 'prophecy' applies to the past and the present, as well as the future.

[1] Examples occur in 'Sagas of Ancient Times' (cf. p. 333), e.g. the prophecy of the witch Heiðr in *Örvar-Odds Saga*, cap. 3. But these are generally believed to be late compositions.

[2] The passage, including the prophecy, is transl. by Kershaw, *Anglo-Saxon and Norse Poems*, p. 118.

As regards (i), the association of spells with runes[1] is not found in any extant English or German spells; but this is a mere accident. Bede (*Hist. Eccl.* IV. 22) speaks of *litteras solutorias*, which were credited with the power of liberating a prisoner from his bonds, like the spell quoted above from *Háv.* 149. There can be little doubt that the association goes back to early Teutonic times. The unintelligibility of many of the earliest inscriptions suggests that they may have been cut for magical purposes.

(ii) The connection between spells (including curses) and prophecies may be illustrated from various stories relating to the Norns or Fates. Sometimes these are represented as prophetesses; sometimes their operations are regarded as weaving or spinning spells. To this question we shall have to return later. The antiquity of the connection is made probable by the story of the Roman prince Drusus, who died on his return from the Elbe in 9 B.C. It is stated[2] that he had been deterred from advancing beyond the river by a woman of superhuman size, who called out to him: "The Fates forbid thee to advance. Away! The end of thy deeds and of thy life is at hand".

(iii) For the application of 'prophecy' (*spá*) to the past and present, as well as to the future, it will be sufficient here to compare what is said in the *Iliad* (e.g. I. 70) of Calchas, the seer of the Achaeans—that he knew the present, the future and the past. Practically the same description is given of the Muses in Hesiod, *Theog.* 38. Instead of 'prophecy' it would of course be more correct to speak of 'vision (or sometimes 'declaration') of things not ascertainable by ordinary means'.

Early Welsh poetry also contains a considerable amount of material, though unfortunately much of it is very obscure.

We may first take a rather large group of prophetic poems. Of these three are preserved in the *Black Book*, seven in the *Red Book*, and six in the *Book of Taliesin*. The majority of these are concerned with the future deliverance of the Cymry from the oppression of the Saxons or the Normans; and many of them show a well-developed national sentiment.

As between the specific and the general there is considerable variation in the prophecies. Some poems mention a number of geographical names; but the personal names are few. Some poems speak of Henri

[1] We may compare Hrabanus Maurus, *De Inuentione Linguarum* (in Goldast, *Script. Rer. Alem.* II. i. p. 67): *Litteras quippe quas utuntur Marcomanni, quos nos Nordmannos uocamus, infra scripta habemus...cum quibus carmina sua incantationesque ac diuinationes significare procurant*, etc. This is followed by a Runic alphabet (partly German, partly English).

[2] Dion Cassios, LV. I.

(i.e. Henry I) or the 'son of Henri' (i.e. Earl Robert of Gloucester) as the enemy.[1] Almost the only national leaders mentioned[2] are Cadwaladr and Cynan, who are to reappear in order to deliver the country. The former was the son of Cadwallon, and died in the plague of 682, according to the earliest text of the *Annales Cambriae*.[3] We do not know who Cynan was. Cadwaladr is mentioned in eight poems (*BBC.* XVI–XVIII, *RBH.* I, *Tal.* VI, XII, LII, LIII), and in five of these (*BBC.* XVII, XVIII, *Tal.* VI, XII, LII) Cynan is associated with him.[4] In one poem (*RBH.* XXII) there is reference to a deliverer who is not named.

There can be no doubt that the majority of these poems date from times subsequent to the Norman conquest, at least in the form in which we have them. References to Henry or his son, which cannot be earlier than the twelfth century, occur in six of them (*RBH.* I, II, XIX, XX, XXI, *BBC.* XVIII), while two others (*BBC.* XVI, *RBH.* XVIII) speak of the 'Franks', i.e. Normans. But caution is necessary in dealing with such poems as these. It is not safe to apply to them the principle that a work cannot be earlier than the date of the latest event recorded in it.

We may first take *BBC.* XVII, commonly known as *Afallenau*, or 'Appletrees' (cf. p. 106). This is a poem of Type B, constructed on a rather ingenious scheme and consisting of what we may perhaps describe as scenes in two different planes. The speaker is Myrddin; and the matter in part, including several whole stanzas, relates to his own experiences and to Rhydderch Hael and other persons of his own time. But intermingled with this are a number of prophecies relating to much later times; and it is with these that we are now concerned. Now the poem is known not only from the *Black Book* but also from later texts.[5] In these latter the poem contains twenty-two or twenty-three stanzas, whereas the *Black Book* has only ten. The order of the stanzas in the various texts is quite different.

Now certain stanzas in the later texts relate clearly to the time of

1 The fact that no other Norman kings are mentioned by name suggests that these names came to be used generically.

2 Except of course in *RBH.* I, where the names are numerous. In *RBH.* XX. 20 there is apparently a reference to Owein the Red; cf. p. 457, note.

3 The two later texts say that he retired to Brittany. These date from the late thirteenth century, and their evidence cannot stand against the first (Harl. 3859), which dates from c. 960 (cf. p. 146). The date 682 is perhaps a mistake for 664; cf. Lloyd, *History of Wales*, p. 230, note 9.

4 Cynan is mentioned also in *Tal.* X. 16 f., a poem to which we shall have to refer later.

5 One of these is publ. and transl. by Stephens, *Literature of the Kymry*, p. 223 ff. Another text is publ. in the *Myvyrian Archaiology*, p. 115 ff.

Henry II and the closing years of Owein Gwynedd (c. 1165–70). But these stanzas do not occur in the *Black Book*. The only precise predictions found in the latter are those of a victory (st. 1) over the English on the Machawy—near Glasbury, on the borders of Radnor and Brecknock—and of another victory (st. 3) over the men of Dublin. The latter event, which is evidently much exaggerated, cannot be identified with confidence; but the former is generally believed to be one of the victories of Gruffydd ap Llywelyn, c. 1055.[1] The general opinion now seems to be that the *Black Book* preserves the original text of the poem and that the stanzas found only in the other texts are later additions; and we think that this view is correct in the main, though it requires some modification. One stanza which is found only in the later texts[2] predicts the coming of a youth who will be known as Gruffydd of the line of Iago. This must surely be the Gruffydd who was brought up in exile and after two unsuccessful attempts—in 1075 and 1081—finally secured the throne of Gwynedd in 1094. He is described in the Annals as *nepos Iacob*, presumably because his father (Cynan) never returned from exile. It would seem then that stanzas which occur only in the later texts may be old; for probably no one would want to compose such a stanza as this nearly a century after Gruffydd's return.

Our view therefore is that the history of the poem goes back at least to the latter part of the eleventh century, but that stanzas were added to it from time to time, chiefly—not wholly—for purposes of political propaganda. The framework, relating to the prophet's own experiences, was preserved. The earlier predictions were sometimes preserved, sometimes discarded.

RBH. I is another poem of Type B (or CB), in the form of a dialogue between Myrddin and his sister Gwendydd. We have already referred to this poem (p. 106 f.); but we may repeat here that the opening stanzas deal with the power of Rhydderch Hael, and that these are followed by the enumeration of a very long list of kings. The form of the dialogue is somewhat like that of the *Grípisspá*. One stanza is devoted to each king, the alternate stanzas being occupied by questions from Gwendydd as to the successor in each case. Next after Rhydderch come Morcant and Urien, and then Maelgwn and his descendants down to Howel the

[1] Cf. Loth, *Rev. Celt.* XXI. 53, where it is identified with the defeat of Earl Raulf. It may, however, be the defeat of Bishop Leofgar, in 1056; cf. Lloyd, *History of Wales*, p. 368.

[2] No. 15 in Stephens' text; No. 10 in the *Myv. Arch.*

Good, who died c. 950. After this follow a long series of kings, who are recorded not by their true names but by descriptions, which are difficult or impossible now to recognise. There are, however, a few exceptions—Gruffydd, Owein, the 'son of Henry', and the revenants Cadwaladr and Cynan. The first of these is doubtless Gruffydd son of Cynan, who died in 1137, and the second probably his son Owein,[1] who reigned from 1137 to 1170—although he is separated from his father by many stanzas. The text in the latter part of the poem seems to be in a state of much confusion;[2] and we think that additions have been made to it from time to time.

RBH. II is another speech poem of Type B, addressed by the dead Myrddin from his grave to his sister Gwendydd. The predictions here relate in st. 6 to the reign of William Rufus, in st. 7 to that of Henry II, in st. 8 to that of Henry I, in st. 9 apparently to Thomas à Becket. Surely these were not all composed at one time and by one author. All of them have reference to specific events. St. 7 is the prophecy quoted by Giraldus Cambrensis, *It. Kambr.* I. 6,[3] and which he says the Welsh interpreted as referring to the crossing of the Usk by Henry II, during his campaign in 1163. They were much discouraged by it and abandoned their resistance. We may suspect therefore that it was inspired or manipulated by partisans of the king. As a rule, however, the prophecies are strongly national in feeling. We suspect that a careful examination of them would be of considerable historical value; but we have not the knowledge necessary for more than a cursory survey.

For this poem also there is a later text[4] which contains thirteen extra stanzas at the end. These are occupied with a prophecy of the destruction of Llandudoch (St Dogmael's) by 'black Brithwyr from Man'. Whatever may be the meaning of the name *Brithwyr*, the reference is apparently to a Viking raid—which is actually recorded in the chronicles

[1] This Owein seems to be intended also by the name *Gwyn Gwarther* in st. 57 f., which immediately follows his father Gruffydd; cf. Loth, *Rev. Celt.* XXI. 34.

[2] The poem is preserved also in later MSS., from one of which the text printed in the *Myv. Arch.* (p. 108 ff.) is taken. From this it appears that a number of stanzas, chiefly questions of Gwendydd, are omitted in the *Red Book.* St. 66–80 (Skene) are wanting in one MS. A critical edition of *RBH.* I and II is greatly needed.

[3] The first two lines of the stanza—"When a strong freckled one shall come as far as the ford of Pencarn"—hardly permit any doubt as to its identity with the prophecy known to Giraldus. But there is no verbal resemblance in the last two lines. Has the text been changed?

[4] *Myv. Arch.* p. 104 ff. For the various texts of this poem see Phillimore, *Y Cymmrodor*, VII. 112 ff.; for the contents *ib.* 116 ff. The MS. origin of the last 13 stanzas in the *Myv. Arch.* seems not to be known.

for the year 988. Unfortunately the whole passage is obscure to us; but if this is the event referred to—as has been suggested[1]—and the prophecy dates from the same period, it must be nearly two centuries older than some of the stanzas in the poem to which it has been added, and more than half a century older than the earliest datable element in the *Afallenau*.

Thus far we have spoken only of poems of Type B, in which Myrddin is the speaker or one of the speakers. To these is to be added *BBC.* XVIII, which is a late imitation of *BBC.* XVII. But this series, consisting of four poems in all—or five if we include the Llandudoch prophecy—forms only a small minority of the predictive poems. The rest can hardly be regarded as speeches in character. In *Tal.* VI. 17 a prophecy is introduced by the words 'Myrddin foretells', as a variation of 'the Muse (*Awen*) foretells' which is found elsewhere in this poem. It is possible therefore that some of these poems were regarded as prophecies of Myrddin; but they contain no personal elements.

As already mentioned, most of the poems are concerned with the national struggle between the Welsh and the English and Normans. In addition to the speech poems noticed above, this forms the subject of *BBC.* XVI, *Tal.* VI, XII, LIII, *RBH.* XVIII–XXI. Several of these poems, as we have seen, mention 'Henri' or the 'Franks'; and the others, so far as our observations go, do not seem to show any features which suggest an earlier period. We are therefore inclined to believe that they all date from the period after 1050. One or two seem to be as late as the thirteenth century. But it ought to be possible, from the historical allusions[2] and perhaps the style, to date several of them more precisely. To the list given above we should in all probability add *RBH.* XVII, which appears to belong to the same series, though the beginning and the end of it have been taken from panegyrics upon Urien (cf. p. 40). In view of the incongruity of the subjects this is a remarkable phenomenon, even in early Welsh poetry.

The remaining predictive poems are all very obscure; but they do not seem to be occupied primarily with the struggle against the English. *RBH.* XXII is concerned with movements of the Brithwyr and the

[1] Cf. Stephens, *Literature of the Kymry*, p. 222; but the reference might of course be to some later (unrecorded) raid.

[2] The Owein mentioned in *RBH.* XX. 20 seems to be Owein the Red, brother of Llywelyn, the last prince of Gwynedd. Loth, *Rev. Celt.* XXI. 56, dates the poem between 1253 and 1277, and assigns the following poem (*RBH.* XXI) to the same period.

disasters arising from them—which seems to indicate raids of the Vikings. Such raids appear to have been at their worst c. 1000; but the chronicles record occurrences of the kind until late in the eleventh century at least. *Tal.* XLVII, XLIX and LII are unintelligible to us. Both the two former contain antiquarian references to Beli. The first four lines of *Tal.* XLVII are taken from *Tal.* VI. *Tal.* XLIX appears to date from the time of Henry II. *Tal.* LII seems to refer to Viking raids.

From what has been said it will be seen that the material as a whole is very unsatisfactory and obscure. It is clear enough that most of the poems date from the Norman period and that they arose out of the national propaganda, set on foot to resist the invaders. The first impetus may have been given by Harold's invasion. But there is some evidence for the cultivation of prophetic poetry before this time—partly in connection with Viking raids and partly as a framework for antiquarian compositions. The significance of both will be seen by a comparison with the Irish evidence. As regards the latter, we believe that *RBH.* I contains elements which are earlier than the eleventh century. This earlier prophetic poetry would seem to have been either 'elegiac' or learned, rather than stimulating, in character; the prophetic form was apparently more of a literary convention than in the later nationalistic poetry. It is to be remembered, however, that prophecy in national interests is found in the *Historia Brittonum* (cap. 42) and can be traced back even to the time of Gildas.

What was the origin of the national deliverers Cadwaladr and Cynan? It is tempting to suppose that the latter was at first[1] identical with the exiled prince Cynan, the father of Gruffydd, and that the original prophecies were issued during his lifetime by a party who favoured his return. At all events the fact that both names are found among Gruffydd's immediate descendants would seem to indicate that this family were interested in the prophecies. Cadwaladr the revenant must of course have been known before the rise of Cadwaladr the son of Gruffydd, of whom nothing is recorded before 1136. Yet it is curious that a person of the far past so obscure as Cadwaladr the son of Cadwallon should be chosen as the national deliverer. Is it possible that prophecies were current in his own time to the effect that he would live to avenge his father's fall, and that some remembrance of these was preserved down to the eleventh century, when his true history had long been forgotten?

[1] The association with Cadwaladr suggests that later he was thought of as a revenant from the far past—perhaps the Cynan of the *Dream of Maxen Wledig*.

There is another rather large group of poems which in general have little or nothing in common with these and are even more obscure. This group is almost confined to the *Book of Taliesin*. The only example found in any other early text, so far as we know, is *RBH*. XXIII, the conclusion of which is also preserved at the beginning of the *Book of Taliesin* (*Tal.* I).

One poem (*Tal.* X) which may be regarded as belonging to this group is of a prophetic character and mentions Cynan as a future ruler. Apart from this the prophetic (predictive) element is limited to one or two short passages (especially in *RBH*. XXIII). In most of the poems it is entirely wanting. Indeed these poems bear no very close resemblance to any of the material discussed in this chapter. The language which they employ has much in common with that of spells; but they can hardly have been intended as spells themselves. They may perhaps best be described as declarations of bardic wisdom, of a more or less esoteric character. In some of them indeed this is stated explicitly; but the object for which they were composed is not made clear. It will be seen later that certain analogies are to be found in Irish records, both spells and other pieces.[1]

Short passages of a religious character occur in most of these poems. Such is the case in *Tal.* III, VII, VIII, XIII–XVI, XXV, XXX, XLVIII. One or two others, especially *RBH*. XXIII (*Tal.* I), show a mixture of Latin and native learning. Most of them, however, are primarily concerned with wisdom which seems to be of native origin.[2]

Certain rhetorical features are of rather common occurrence in poems of this class. In VII. 221–48, VIII. 3–23, 205–8, XXV. 58–68 we find catalogues with the word *bum*, 'I have been', e.g. "I have been a journey (?), I have been an eagle, I have been a sea coracle...I have been a sword in the hand, I have been a shield in battle, I have been a string in a harp". In *RBH*. XXIII. 87–93, *Tal.* III. 9–13, 25 f., XLVIII. 31 f. (cf. 1–22) we find other catalogues with the word *wyf*, 'I am'. These catalogues, especially the former series, include the names of various animals, birds, reptiles, etc., which may point to some belief in either transmigration or transformation; but they also contain the names of inanimate and even incorporeal things, as in the passage quoted above. Another catalogue, with *gogwn*, 'I know', occurs in VII. 173 ff. Again,

[1] There is also a resemblance—of a rather indefinite kind—to the second part of the *Hávamál* (cf. p. 383), though the Welsh poems do not contain catalogues of precepts or spells.

[2] Poems of Latin origin, like *Tal.* LV, are of course not included here.

in *RBH.* XXIII. 2–42, *Tal.* VII. 95–212, and throughout *Tal.* IX we find long lists of questions relating in the main to natural law and natural history, and beginning with *pwy*, *py*, etc. ('who, why', etc.), but especially with *pan* in the sense of 'whence, from what cause?' As examples we may quote *RBH.* XXIII. 12 ff.: "Whence come night and day? Whence (is it that) the eagle becomes gray? Whence (is it that) night is dark? Whence (is it that) the linnet is green?" And *Tal.* VII. 128 ff.: "Whence (is it that) milk is white? Whence (that) holly is green?... Whence (that) brine is salt? Whence (that) ale is intoxicating? Whence (that) the alder is red?... Why does the string of a harp complain? Why does the cuckoo complain? Why does it sing?" Other catalogues occur in *Tal.* XIII and XV.

Heroic names are of rare occurrence in these poems, except in *Tal.* XIV, which records the poet's visits to various princes (cf. pp. 104, 582). On the other hand mythological or legendary names are frequently found. Many of these are known from the *Mabinogion.* Thus Pwyll and Pryderi are mentioned in *Tal.* XXX, the latter also and Bran and Manawyd in XIV, Math in VIII and XLV, Mathonwy in X, Gwydion in VII, VIII, XIV, XVI, XLV and *RBH.* XXIII, Don and Arianrod in XVI, Lleu in XIII, XIV, XVI and *RBH.* XXIII. Of the characters mentioned in the *Hanes Taliesin* (cf. p. 103 f.) Ceridwen appears in *Tal.* IX and XIV, and she is obviously the speaker in XVI, though her name is not mentioned here; Afagddu is referred to in XVI and XLVIII, and Gwion perhaps in VII, XIII, and *RBH.* XXIII, though these passages are obscure. What is said of Gwydion in *Tal.* XVI is easily recognisable as a brief summary of some of the adventures attributed to him in the *Mabinogi* of *Math.* But otherwise the poems give little definite information about these persons. They contain also many other names which seem to belong to the same class.

Taliesin is said to be the speaker in *Tal.* VII. The same authorship is obviously claimed for *Tal.* XIV, though the poet's name is not actually mentioned; and the same may be said of *Tal.* XV, at least if we may judge from the last two lines.[1] We think that *Tal.* XIV is in part comparable with *Widsith* (cf. p. 25 f.) and presents similar problems, though it contains more heterogeneous elements. But there can be no doubt that *Tal.* VII is a speech poem in character (Type B). It contains (234 ff.) the legend of Taliesin's origin, which is preserved in a

[1] *Tal.* LV (*ad fin.*) also claims Taliesin's authorship. The last four lines are a variation of the last four lines of *Tal.* VII, and are doubtless taken—with the two preceding lines—from some poem ascribed to this poet.

late form in the *Hanes Taliesin*. We have already (p. 103 f.) given a summary of this story and also noticed (p. 263) other references to Ceridwen, who appears to have been regarded as a goddess of poetry. Again, there seems to be a reference to the same story in *Tal.* XV. 35 f., which speaks of three *awen* of *Gogyrwen* coming from a cauldron. These can hardly be other than the three drops of inspiration mentioned in the story; for, although the meaning of the name *Gogyrwen* is far from clear, it is associated with Ceridwen in *Tal.* XIV. 11 f. and in *BBC.* III. 3 and IV. 1. In the two latter passages indeed it would seem to be an epithet of this person. In *Tal.* VII. 75 it occurs again in connection with *awen*, though the meaning is obscure.

The word *awen* is of rather frequent occurrence in this group of poems. In addition to the passages cited above we may refer to *Tal.* VII. 170 f., XIII. 7, XIV. 8, XV. 2. In IX. 2 it is again used in connection with Ceridwen; but the sense is not clear. Usually, if not always, the meaning is 'inspiration', as in various other early poems. References to cauldrons are also fairly frequent. Apart from *Tal.* XV. 35 f., which has been cited above, we may note VII. 17, 198, 201, XIII. 65, XXX. 2 and especially XIV. 11 (the 'cauldron of Ceridwen') and XVI. 24, where Ceridwen speaks of her cauldron. Several of these passages are obscure; but at least in XIV. 11 and XXX. 2, if not in all, the reference is to cauldrons of inspiration.

The poems with which we have been dealing present many difficulties. But it is clear that—whatever the purpose for which they were composed—they are intimately connected with magic. Apart from the passages noticed above, we may refer to *Tal.* VIII. 150 ff., where the speaker says that he was formed out of various elements, including fruits and flowers. With this may be compared XVI. 14 f., where it is stated that Gwydion ap Don formed by magic (*hudwys*) a woman out of flowers. Again, the phrase 'I was enchanted by Math' (*am swynwys i Vath*) in VIII. 162 is doubtless to be taken in connection with the magic wand (*hudwyd*) of Math mentioned in XLV. 10—and perhaps also with that of Mathonwy (Math's father), referred to in X. 12. Both the magic wand and the creation of a woman from flowers will be found in the *Mabinogi* of *Math*.

We hope that a certain amount of help towards the interpretation of these poems may be obtained from a consideration of the Irish material.

Analogies to most of the forms of poetry discussed above are to be found in Irish records. To the Welsh poems in particular the resemblances are sometimes so close that it is difficult to doubt the existence of an historical connection.

We know of no true analogies in Irish to the Welsh patriotic prophecies discussed on p. 453 ff. above. Such may exist; but we have not been able to find them. Irish parallels, however, are certainly to be found for the 'elegiac' prophecies relating to the devastations of the Viking Age, as represented perhaps by the Llandudoch stanzas (cf. p. 456) and by *RBH.* XXII. Examples occur in the *War of the Gaedhil with the Gaill*, cap. 9 f. They are concerned with the depredations upon the Irish churches committed by Vikings and by the Norse of Dublin. They are attributed to early saints and prophets, Columba, Berchan and Bec Mac De; but in reality they are not earlier than the tenth century, if so early. We do not know what is the nature of the relationship between the Irish and the Welsh poems, or whether the question has ever been raised.

Historical prophecies which give a long succession of kings, like *RBH.* I, are well represented in Irish. Poems of this kind, also attributed to St Berchan and giving the succession of the kings of Ireland and of Scotland,[1] appear to have been composed about the close of the eleventh century. The last king of Scotland mentioned seems to be Edmund, who died in 1097, while the last Irish king is Muircertach Ua Briain, who was reigning at the same time. A much closer parallel, however, to *RBH.* I is to be found in the story called *Baile in Scáil* ('Ecstasy of the Champion'), to which we have referred briefly in an earlier chapter (p. 206). When Conn is brought into the palace of (the god) Lug, he sees there a maiden wearing a golden diadem and having beside her a vat of ale. She is said to be the sovereignty of Ireland. Lug says that he will reveal to Conn the length of his reign and name every king who shall rule in Tara after him. The maiden asks who the ale is to be given to, and Lug replies that she shall give it to[2] Conn. Then he pronounces a short prophecy in verse with regard to Conn's reign. The maiden then again asks who the ale is to be given to; and he replies that it is to be given to Art, son of Conn. Of him too Lug prophesies; and the process is repeated for each succeeding high-king, most of the prophecies being at least partly in verse. One of the two MSS. (Harl.

[1] The prophecy relating to Scotland is ed. and transl. by Skene, *Chron. of the Picts and Scots*, p. 79 ff. For the Irish prophecy see O'Curry, *MS. Materials*, p. 412 ff. There is a new critical edition (without transl.) by Anderson, *Zeitschr. f. celt. Philol.* XVIII. 1 ff.

[2] The context suggests that *for* here means 'on behalf of', rather than 'to'.

5280)[1] ends with Fergal, who was killed in 722 (cf. p. 54); the other (Rawl. B. 512)[2] continues down to (apparently) the twelfth century, ending with a purely imaginary king. But this latter text has been extended; the *Baile* is known to have been in existence c. 1050, for it is cited by Flann Mainistrech, who died in 1056.

The parallelism between *RBH.* I and the *Baile* can hardly be due to accident. In both cases a prophet or prophetic god foretells the succession of a long line of kings, in response to the interrogation of a woman, which is repeated on each occasion. The kings are named by their ordinary names in the *Baile* down to Niall Glundub, who was slain in 919, and in *RBH.* I down to Howel the Good, who was Niall's contemporary. After Niall the majority of the Irish kings have descriptive names applied to them after the fashion of riddles. After Howel this is the case with almost all the Welsh kings. A careful examination of the two texts would probably bring other common features to light. Thus in *RBH.* I. 63 one king is described as 'Youth of (the) Two Halves' (*Mackwy Deu Hanner*), while in the *Baile* Domnall (son of Muircertach), who died in 979, is called 'Son of (the) Two Halves' (*Mac Dá Leithi*). The text of *RBH.* I is obviously in a state of great confusion; but we know of no Welsh king whom this description would suit better than Owein, son of Howel, who inherited the kingdom of Dyfed from his mother and claims to North Wales from his father, and evidently prided himself on his two lines of ancestry (cf. p. 149). He was contemporary with Domnall.

The nature of the relationship is a question which we would prefer to leave to experts. It is always tempting in such cases to derive the Welsh from the Irish. Early Irish records are numerous, and it is often possible to trace with confidence the history of a text back to a remote date; but early Welsh poetry consists largely of sparse and neglected fragments of wreckage. In this case the question is complicated by the existence of a much earlier Irish prophecy called *Baile Chuinn* or 'Ecstasy of Conn',[3] a treatment in prose of the same theme, in which Conn himself is the speaker. We think that the beginning of *RBH.* I contains ancient elements and that there is a relationship between this poem and the *Baile in Scáil*, dating possibly from about the close of the tenth century; but the whole question requires investigation.

[1] Ed. by K. Meyer, *Zeitschr. f. celt. Philol.* III. 457 ff.

[2] The latter part is ed. by K. Meyer, *Zeitschr. f. celt. Philol.* XII. 232 ff.

[3] Ed. by Thurneysen, *Zu ir. Handschr.* I. 48; cf. O'Curry, *MS. Materials*, p. 385 ff.

There is no doubt as to the antiquity of prophecy in Ireland. It plays a great part in ecclesiastical records, e.g. in Adamnan's *Life of St Columba*, and it occurs by no means rarely in heroic and other stories relating to heathen times. In the latter prophecies are usually given in the form of rhetorics (cf. p. 57) or poems of Type B. Sometimes they are attributed to supernatural beings, as in the case noticed above, sometimes to Druids or other persons endowed with second sight. Sometimes they are solicited, especially in the case of Druids, at other times they are offered spontaneously. Sometimes they are of particular, sometimes of general application.

Among the earliest examples we may mention the *Verba Scathaige*.[1] CuChulainn visits Scathach in order to be instructed in feats of arms, and she prophesies to him the course of his adventures in the impending great raid (the *Táin Bó Cuailnge*). The prophecy is in the form of a rhetoric and very obscure. Scathach seems to have much in common with the Valkyries of the North. Her home is sometimes, as here, said to be in the Alps, sometimes in Britain.

Next we may take the prophecy of Fedelm in the *Táin Bó Cuailnge*.[2] Fedelm is a prophetess (*banfáith*), who appears to Medb when the host of Connaught has assembled for the raid, but before they have actually set out. In the oldest text she says she is a woman of Connaught and has learnt 'poetry'[3] in Britain; but in the *Book of Leinster* she declares that she is from the shee-mound of Cruachan—i.e. she is a supernatural being. In reply to Medb's enquiries she says she sees a vision of blood; and when the queen expresses incredulity she describes in poetry CuChulainn and his feats and the havoc he will make of the host.

Druids are frequently consulted in the sagas. Two instances occur in the *Táin*[4] not long after the incident just mentioned. Fergus appeals to them to interpret the significance of objects left by CuChulainn in the way of the army. On both occasions the Druids' answers are given in verse. Among other cases of this kind we may refer to the story of Derdriu's birth, at the beginning of the *Exile of the Sons of Uisliu* (*Uisnech*). Before the child is born the Druid prophesies in verse of her beauty and the disasters it will bring upon the men of Ulster.

1 Ed. by K. Meyer, *Anecdota from Irish MSS.* v. 28, and Thurneysen, *Zeitschr. f. celt. Philol.* IX. 487; cf. Thurneysen, *Ir. Heldensage*, p. 376 f.

2 *YBL.* 37 ff. (publ. in *Ériu*, I, Suppl. p. 4); Windisch, 215 ff.; Dunn's transl. p. 14 f.

3 *Filidecht*, properly the 'art of the *fili*'. The context shows that what is meant here primarily is knowledge of spells.

4 Windisch, 596 f. (cf. *YBL.* 257 ff.), 727 ff.; Dunn's transl. pp. 31 f., 39.

It may be observed that the prophecies are seldom, if ever, attributed to inspiration by a deity or other supernatural being. They seem to be due, as in Norse, to a faculty possessed by the prophet himself. The same faculty appears frequently in dreams and visions. We may refer (e.g.) to the dream and vision of Derdriu in the *Fate of the Children of Uisnech*, cap. 12 f. Here also the prophecies are given in the form of poems of Type B.[1]

An interesting example of 'prophecy' relating to the past is to be found in the story of Mongan and the *fili* Forgoll, a short summary of which was given on p. 98. It is true there is no prophecy in set form, whether verse or prose; but the whole story turns upon the possession of a faculty of this kind, which in this case is bound up with metempsychosis. In another story belonging to the same—very early—series[2] Mongan is said to sing to his wife a *Baile*, or 'Ecstasy', relating to his adventures; but this poem is not recorded.

As a specimen of prophecy of purely general reference we may cite the long speech of Ferchertne in the 'Colloquy of the Two Sages',[3] noticed on p. 97. Nede has given a description of the good things actually existing. Ferchertne replies with a prophecy of evils to come—famine, destitution, devastation and demoralisation—referring apparently, in quite general terms, to conditions which are said to have prevailed at certain times during the Viking Age. Nede recognises his opponent's superiority and acknowledges him to be a great *fili* and prophet (*fáith*).

Next we may take the *ges* or 'tabu', which figures so largely in stories of the Heroic Age. These tabus are perhaps most nearly related to the 'magical' prohibitions in the *Works and Days*, but they have also something in common with the omens in the *Reginsmál*. In contrast, however, with both of these they are of special (individual) application. References to such tabus are frequent enough, but examples of the actual declaration of them seem to be rare. An instance occurs in the story of

1 In the poem given in cap. 13 Derdriu speaks of a cup presented ('to me', in one text) by Manannan. Can this mean a gift of inspiration?

2 Ed. and transl. by K. Meyer in *The Voyage of Bran*, I. 42 ff. This incident occurs in No. IV (p. 56 ff.). All the first four stories come from the book of *Druim Snechta*, which was written apparently early in the eighth century (cf. Thurneysen, *Ir. Heldensage*, p. 15 ff.).

3 *Rev. Celt.* XXVI. 36 ff. Analogies are to be found elsewhere, e.g. in a prophecy of Badb in the *Second Battle of Moytura* (*Rev. Celt.* XII. 110 f.) and in a prophecy ascribed to Bec Mac De in the *Death of King Dermot* (O'Grady, *Silva Gadelica*, II. 85).

the *Destruction of Da Derga's Hall* (cf. p. 98 f.), where they are imposed upon Conaire Mor by Nemglan the bird-king. The story relates how all these tabus eventually come to be violated, and Conaire realises that he is doomed.

References to the pronouncement of curses by Druids and *filid* occur occasionally, as (e.g.) in the *Fate of the Children of Uisnech*, cap. 34, where the Druid Cathbad curses Emain Macha for the murder of Naoise (Noisiu) and his brothers. But the actual words are rarely given. An example is to be found in Cormac's Glossary, s.v. *gaire.*[1] It is said to have been pronounced by the *fili* Nede mac Adnai against Caier, king of Connaught, with whose wife he was involved in an intrigue. The words of the curse seem to mean that Caier is soon to meet with a violent death and to be laid in his grave. But the story told in the Glossary (cf. p. 97) is that it produced boils on his face, which made him give up his kingdom to Nede and eventually to die from shame. It is rather curious that the same curse appears in the *Book of Ballymote*[2] as part of the ritual employed in former times by a *fili* who had been defrauded of his due fee by a prince.

The learning of spells (incantations) formed part of the regular training of a *fili*. Examples of such spells are given in the *Book of Ballymote*;[3] but they are obscure. One appears to be for the recovery of stolen cattle, like the Anglo-Saxon spells referred to on p. 447 f. It is to be sung on the track of the lost beast or—if the track cannot be found—through the singer's right fist. The thief will then be shown to him in a dream.

The most interesting of these spells is one for long life,[4] called *Cétnad n-Áise* or 'Song of Long Life'. It invokes first 'the seven daughters of the sea', and then 'Senach of the seven periods of time', and contains a short catalogue with *am* ('I am'), similar to the Welsh catalogues with *wyf*, noticed on p. 459. The speaker says, repeating the word *am* in each case, that he is an indestructible fortress (*dún*), an unshaken rock, a precious stone, and the luck of the week. The spell is in the form of a rhetoric.

[1] Ed. and transl. by Stokes, *Three Irish Glossaries*, p. xxxvi ff.; cf. Thurneysen, *Ir. Heldensage*, p. 523 f.

[2] Ed. in Windisch, *Ir. Texte*, III. 97 (*Verslehren*, Text III, Sect. 155). It dates from cent. XI, according to Thurneysen, *loc. cit.*

[3] Windisch, *op. cit.* III. 51 ff., 117 ff. (Text II. 95 ff.). Collections of spells are also to be found elsewhere. An early example, from a St Gall MS., will be found in Stokes and Strachan, *Thesaurus Palaeohibernicus*, II. 248.

[4] Windisch, *op. cit.* III. 53 f. Also text and transl. by K. Meyer, *Learning in Ireland in the Fifth Century*, p. 16 ff.

A spell for promoting the increase of fish is preserved in the *Leabhar Gabhála* or 'Book of Conquests',[1] cap. 186. It is said to have been composed by the mythical *fili* Aimirgin (Amorgin) Glunmar, son of Mil, who came to Ireland with his brothers Eremon and Eber (cf. p. 312); but it contains nothing which would not be appropriate in a fishing spell of general application.

In the same work, cap. 185, Aimirgin is credited with another rhetoric, which he is said to have uttered when he first set foot on Irish soil. This is not a spell but a composition very similar to some of the Welsh poems noticed on p. 459 ff. The first part of it is a fairly long catalogue with *am*; the speaker says that he is wind on the sea, a wave of the ocean...a powerful ox...a salmon in pools...the strength of art (poetry?), etc. Then follows a short series of questions: "Who clears the stone-place of the mountain? What the place in which the setting of the sun lies?"[2] and others. The last few lines are obscure.

In conclusion we would again revert to the 'Colloquy of the Two Sages', in order to call attention to the character of the work, taken as a whole. The framework of the piece was described briefly on p. 97. The young *fili* Nede has seated himself in the chair of the *ollam* (chief *fili*), previously occupied by his father. The old *fili* Ferchertne disputes his right to it and asks him a series of questions. The same questions are also put to Ferchertne by Nede. They are as follows: (i) Whence hast thou come? (ii) What is thy name? (iii) What art dost thou practise? (iv) What is it thou undertakest? (v) What is the path thou hast come? (vi) Whose son art thou? (vii) Hast thou tidings? The answers are given in metaphorical and frequently obscure language. Ferchertne's last answer is in the form of a prophecy, and has been noticed briefly above. The point of the contest would seem to lie not so much in the matter as in the diction of the speeches. But the milieu is obviously mantic.

This Colloquy, we think, gives a clue to the obscure series of Welsh poems noticed on p. 459 ff. It is not clear that any of these poems are dialogues. But several of them speak in disparaging terms of opponents who are also bards. We would suggest that these were either composed for production at bardic contests or taken from stories of such contests. In some cases, especially *Tal.* xxx, more importance seems to have been

[1] Ed. and transl. by R. A. Stewart Macalister and J. MacNeill.

[2] This is the transl. given by Macalister and MacNeill. The text ed. by them seems to have omitted one question, and there appear to be other variants. The transl. given by Nutt, *Voyage of Bran*, II. 92 (without text) is as follows: "Who spreads light in the gathering on the mountain? Who foretells the ages of the moon? Who teaches the spot where the sun rests?"

attached to form and diction than to the treatment of the subject—indeed one might say that the latter has been entirely sacrificed to the former. On the other hand *Tal.* VII and perhaps one or two other poems may well come from an early form of the story of Taliesin's encounter with Maelgwn's bards. Note was taken on p. 105 of the curious analogy between this story and the account given in the *Historia Brittonum*, cap. 42, of the dialogue between the boy Ambrosius and Gwrtheyrn's magi. In both stories the mantic element is prominent. In the former it takes the form of spells, in the latter of prophecy.

As regards the obscure subject-matter of the Welsh poems, in particular the 'transformation' catalogues and the questions on natural law, there can be no doubt as to the existence of a relationship with the Irish rhetoric noted above from the *Leabhar Gabhála* and the spell for Long Life. It may be observed that in both the Irish passages, as in the Welsh, the catalogues include inanimate and even incorporeal things. But we have yet to take note of a third Irish parallel, which throws light, if not on the origin of such compositions, at least on the time when they were current. This occurs in the second poem contained in the *Voyage of Bran*,[1] a poem of Type B, in which the god Manannan mac Lir is the speaker. The poem may be divided into three parts. The first of these (st. 33–44[2]) is occupied with a description of Mag Mell (cf. p. 262 f.). The second (st. 45–8) is a statement of Christian doctrine, added apparently as a corrective of the preceding, but quite out of harmony both with it and with what follows. The third (st. 49–59) is a prophecy of the birth, life and death of Mongan, who is Manannan's son (cf. p. 206). It is in this third part that the catalogue occurs. Here the future (*biaid*, *bíd*, 'he will be') is used: "He will be in the shape of every beast...a wolf ...a stag...a spotted salmon in a full pool[3]...a seal...a swan", etc. This catalogue seems to contain only the names of animals, birds and fishes.

It cannot be said that this catalogue explains the others, but it certainly throws light on the milieu in which poetry of this kind was produced. The *Voyage of Bran* comes from the *Book of Druim Snechta* (cf. p. 47), which also contained the *Four Stories of Mongan* and various other—chiefly non-heroic—stories in which visions and

[1] Ed. and transl. by K. Meyer, *Voyage of Bran*, I. 16 ff.

[2] These are the figures given in Meyer's edition, where the stanzas are numbered from the beginning of the saga. The true figures for the poem itself are 1–12.

[3] A similar description occurs in the *Leabhar Gabhála*, cap. 185; cf. also *Tal.* VII. 221 f., VIII. 206.

prophecies were prominent. The *Book* was written in the early part of the eighth century and is believed to have been compiled by a *fili*. The *Voyage of Bran* was presumably already in existence; it has been dated to the beginning of the eighth or the end of the seventh century.[1] Since Mongan died in 624, according to the Annals, the legends relating to him must have been current within a century of his time.

Whatever may be the date of the other poems, both Irish and Welsh, we see no reason for doubting that poetry of this kind goes back in both countries to the seventh century—which is not long after the time of Taliesin (cf. p. 155 ff.). Both the catalogues and the questions on natural law must surely be of heathen origin, and the same is true of the personnel mentioned in the Welsh poems and the frequent references to magic (cf. p. 460 f.)—which are characteristic also of the stories of Mongan. One passage (*Tal.* XIV. 45 ff.) shows a rather close parallel to the description of Mag Mell.[2] The poet says that his chair is prepared in Caer Sidi. Disease and old age afflict no one who is there.... Around its peaks are the streams of the ocean. Above it is the fountain which contains liquid sweeter than white wine. In the poem which we are discussing—the second poem in the *Voyage of Bran*—Mag Mell lies not beyond but beneath the sea. This is of course combined with an idea of illusion—what appears to Bran to be sea is to the speaker (Manannan) a flowery plain with woods and inhabitants, the salmon which Bran sees playing are really calves and lambs. But at the same time his boat is said (st. 42) to be passing over the top of a wood and across ridges. Here, as elsewhere, Mag Mell is blessed with delicious drink and with freedom from old age and frailty.

It is remarkable that so many heathen ideas should be represented in poems which make no claim to date from times anterior to the introduction of Christianity. Mongan lived two centuries after St Patrick. Some of the Welsh poems, including *Tal.* VII and XIV, claim to be the work of Taliesin, who lived at a time when Britain had long been a Christian country. The open—or barely disguised—heathenism of the poems therefore requires explanation. The question is one which cannot be discussed adequately here; but we would suggest that a reasonable answer might be found on the following lines. There can be no doubt that in early times the functions of the *filid* were primarily mantic;[3] and

[1] Cf. K. Meyer, *Ancient Irish Poetry*, p. 111.

[2] Cf. Morris-Jones, *Y Cymmrodor*, XXVIII. 236 ff.

[3] The word *fili* is related to W. *gweled*, 'to see', and seems originally to have meant 'seer'.

consequently the change of faith must have been unwelcome to many of them. A prince who was wholeheartedly in sympathy with heathen ideas, as Mongan apparently was,[1] would be eagerly adopted by them as their leader and their hope. As for Mag Mell, it has been pointed out (p. 262 f.) that this doctrine seems to have grown in popularity at a comparatively late period. We would suggest that it was developed—not necessarily originated—by the *filid* in order to counteract the attractions of the Christian doctrine of a future life, and that it was perhaps not entirely uninfluenced by this doctrine.[2] In short we would suggest that the stories and poems relating to Mongan reflect a temporary heathen reaction under the influence of the *filid*. But this reaction had evidently only a short life, and the *filid* had to give way to the new religion. To this later phase we would attribute the introduction of the Christian elements in the poems in the *Voyage of Bran* (st. 26–9, 45–8) and also the poems in which—in contrast with the other records—Mongan is represented as a friend and admirer of St Columba. It was natural enough for the *filid* to choose this saint, who had saved them when their order was threatened with extinction.

In the Welsh poems heathen elements are quite as prominent as in the Irish. They are frequently punctuated by passages which profess faith in Christian doctrine, e.g. in *Tal.* XIV *ad fin.*, immediately after the reference to Caer Sidi cited above; but such passages may quite well be explained in the same way as the Christian elements in the poems relating to Mongan and Mag Mell. The heathen elements themselves must be due to a continuance of heathen tradition—or to a reaction in favour of it—in the poetry of the bards, who evidently had much in common with the *filid*. Unfortunately, however, our knowledge of Welsh (British) society in the sixth and following centuries is sadly defective. The *Lives* of saints, including Jocelin's *Life of St Kentigern*, frequently suggest a society which, so far as the upper classes are concerned, was virtually heathen, though it showed respect and obedience from time to time to scattered bodies of monks. But conditions may have varied greatly from one district to another. The references in the poems to Maelgwn and to Math and Gwydion and their family seem to point to Gwynedd, and in particular to Carnarvonshire, as a centre of

[1] Cf. *Voyage of Bran*, st. 52: "He will delight the company of every fairy-knoll (*síd*), he will be the darling of every goodly land" (Meyer). Does the last expression (*dagthír*) mean the same as *síd*?

[2] We may compare the reference to Gimlé, the future and everlasting abode of the righteous, in the *Völuspá*, st. 64.

bardic activities; and what we know of Maelgwn—e.g. that he had been a monk and renounced his vows—is not incompatible with the supposition that he may have patronised heathen poetry. But similar conditions may have prevailed in the north,[1] where all local records were subsequently obliterated.

Taking the evidence as a whole, it will be seen that there is a close relationship between the mantic poetry of Ireland and Wales. This relationship is the more remarkable because it is not paralleled—in anything like the same degree—in heroic poetry and saga, or indeed in any of the categories discussed in previous chapters, except possibly in descriptive poetry. It is found both in the prophetic poetry, which seems to have flourished chiefly in the eleventh and following centuries, and still more in the 'mystical' poetry, which evidently belongs to an earlier period, and in Ireland at least can be traced with certainty back to the seventh century. There is no doubt that the British and Irish Churches were in close touch in the sixth century. The evidence noticed above shows that a similar community of ideas and activities was shared by intellectual circles in the two countries, which were virtually, if not professedly, heathen.

It was remarked at the beginning of this chapter that the material would seem to be of a somewhat heterogeneous character. The Greek and the English poems, which we took first, have nothing in common. The former are prophecies, together with a list of omens and 'mantic' prohibitions; the latter consist only of spells. The Norse and Irish material, however, supplies both prophecies and spells—whether in their original form or in the form of speech poems of Type B—and also yields evidence which serves to connect these two genres. Lists of omens are found in Norse, as well as in Greek poetry. In Irish and Welsh we also find declarations of mantic lore, which, at least in the former, belong to contests represented in the form of Type B.

There can be little doubt that the apparent differences between the various languages are largely due to accident, and that most of the genres under discussion were cultivated everywhere. Spell poetry was certainly cultivated in Greece from very early times. A reference occurs in the *Odyssey*, XIX. 457 f., where it is related that Odysseus, when a boy, was injured by a wild boar, and that his companions bound up the

[1] This is suggested by various passages in the *Lives of St Kentigern*, if their evidence on such a point is to be trusted. The theory that the battle of Arderydd was connected with religious divisions seems to be without foundation.

wound and stopped the black blood with an incantation. In later literature spells are to be found in poems of Type B. An elaborate instance forms the subject of Theocritos' second *Idyll.*

On the other hand prophecies, dreams and visions are of very frequent occurrence in records of the Anglo-Saxon period. They are preserved, it is true, almost entirely in Latin works and come doubtless from 'ecclesiastical saga' (cf. p. 336); but it can hardly be supposed that they are invariably products of foreign influence. The story of the dream of Breguswith, the mother of St Hild, recorded by Bede, *Hist. Eccl.* IV. 23, relates to a time anterior to the conversion of the Northumbrians. But perhaps the most interesting case is the story in which the same writer in his *Life of St Cuthbert*, cap. 24, describes the meeting of the saint with the abbess Aelffled, sister of King Ecgfrith. During the conversation the abbess falls on her knees and beseeches the saint to tell her how long Ecgfrith would continue to live and reign. After some hesitation he replies that the king has only one year left. Then she begs him to say who will succeed to the throne. He intimates that the successor will be a brother to her. Then, pointing to the sea—the meeting is in Coquet Island—he adds that from one of its numerous islands God can provide a man to rule over England. The reference is to Ecgfrith's illegitimate brother Aldfrith, who was studying in Ireland or Iona. This picturesque story cannot have had a life of more than half a century before it was written down. Its affinities do not seem to us to be Latin. They lie rather with the dialogue of Myrddin and Gwendydd and with the Mongan poetry in its Christianised form.[1] The story was presumably put into shape by someone who had been brought up in the traditions of the Celtic Church, and who may have been familiar with the conventions of Irish or British poetry.

One rather striking difference between Greek prophecies and those of the northern peoples lies in the fact that the former are usually represented as due to inspiration from a deity, whereas the latter appear to proceed from some faculty within the speaker himself. The *awen* of the Welsh poems, which we have rendered by 'inspiration' or 'Muse', forms no real exception; for this is clearly regarded as a property of the poet. Yet this distinction between Greek and northern prophecy must not be pressed. It may very well be that inspiration predominated in the

[1] The reference to the islands may be compared with st. 25 of the *Voyage of Bran.* A variant form of this stanza occurs in Mongan's poem on St Columba (ed. and transl. by K. Meyer, *op. cit.* p. 88 f.), a poem of Type B—for which it may originally have been composed.

former and 'vision' (or second sight) in the latter. But the difference is not essential or invariable. In the *Eyrbyggja Saga*, cap. 3 f., a wealthy landowner and priest, called Thórolfr, in one of the Norwegian islands, receives a summons from the king (Harold the Fair-haired) to submit to him or else to quit the country. He offers a great sacrifice to Thor, and then consults him as to whether he shall surrender or emigrate to Iceland. Such cases differ little, if at all, from the usage followed at various Greek sanctuaries—not Delphoi—where oracular responses were given. We may also cite a passage in Rimbertus' *Life of St Ansgar*, cap. 26. When St Ansgar arrived in Sweden on a missionary expedition, his efforts were frustrated for the moment by a man who stated that he had been present in a dream at an assembly of the gods, and that they had commissioned him to tell the Swedes that they were opposed to the introduction of the new religion. On the other hand we hear sometimes in Greece of seers, who prophesied from a faculty of 'vision', apparently without the intervention of a deity. Such is the case with Theoclymenos in the *Odyssey*, XX. 351 ff. The faculty was sometimes, as in this case, hereditary in families.

It was pointed out above (p. 451 ff.) and must be repeated here that prophecy may relate to the present and the past, as well as to the future. This applies to prophecy from inspiration or revelation, as well as to prophecy from vision. We may refer (e.g.) to the response of the Delphic oracle, quoted by Herodotos, I. 67, as to where Orestes was buried. This case may be compared with the dispute between Mongan and Forgoll, noticed on p. 465, in which case of course there is no hint of revelation from an external source. Indeed examples of prophecy relating to the present or past will probably be found almost everywhere. We have not noticed any instances in the Welsh prophetic poems; but they may be found in the story of the boy Ambrosius and the *magi* in the *Historia Brittonum*, cap. 42.

The relationship of prophecies to spells noted on p. 452 f. must also be emphasised here. Curses and blessings may be regarded either as spells or as prophecies which carry with them their own fulfilment. The same ambiguous character sometimes appears in references to the operations of the Norns, as we shall see in a later chapter.

It will be seen that the category with which we have been dealing in this chapter is rather intimately connected with what we have called non-heroic poetry and saga. The personnel with which we were concerned in Ch. VI was largely the same as that which has figured in this chapter, viz. the prophets and sages of the Heroic Age, though here we have also had to take account of deities and other supernatural beings. Now one of the most widespread themes of story relating to such persons—and also to mantic gods—is that of the mantic contest, or perhaps we should say the contest in wisdom. The best Norse example of this is the *Vafþrúðnismál*, in which the god Othin contends with the learned giant (*jötunn*) Vafþrúðnir. The contest here is in antiquarian (cosmogonic and mythological) lore; but from what has been pointed out above this comes at least partly within the scope of prophecy. Perhaps the same may be said of the contest between Mongan and Forgoll, though the contest in this case turns upon one special fact. But Greek legend furnishes much closer parallels to the contest of Ferchertne and Nede. In particular we may refer to the story of the contest between the rival seers Calchas and Mopsos, which was treated in the *Melampodia*. From a fragment of the poem which survives it appears that Mopsos was made to win by what may be described as a prophecy relating to the present. He gave a correct answer to the question how many figs there were on a certain tree. Apart from the languages we are considering, one of the most interesting cases of this kind is the contest between Väinämöinen and Joukahainen, described in Rune III of the *Kalevala*. Here Väinämöinen wins by means of spells, which reduce his opponent to helplessness and almost submerge him in a bog.

Lastly, with regard to spells we have to admit that there is one side of the subject which we are not able to treat, though we fully recognise its importance. This is the connection between spells and music. In *Thorfinns Saga Karlsefnis*, cap. 3, the Greenland witch Thorbjörg cannot get any attention from her spirits until she has obtained a good singer to sing the spells; and it would not be difficult to collect a good deal of interesting information on the subject, at least in the North. Linguistic evidence makes it probable that spells played a very important part in the early history of both music and poetry.

CHAPTER XVI

LITERATURE AND WRITING

TO all the peoples whose records we are now studying the art of writing was known from early times. In later chapters we shall see that these records were largely preserved by oral tradition. But there can be no doubt that in all cases the art of writing was known at least before they assumed their final form.

The beginnings of writing are generally obscure. On the whole, however, more information is available for the early history of the art in the north of Europe than in Greece, where its antiquity is doubtless much greater. We will therefore begin with the former.

In the north of Europe, at least among the Teutonic peoples and in Ireland, two forms of writing were in use in early times, the native and the Roman. In each case the former was of unknown antiquity. It was employed chiefly for writing upon objects of wood, bone, metal and stone. Parchment was doubtless unknown before the introduction of Roman writing; and even after this it appears to have been very rarely used for the native form of writing. The purposes for which the latter was employed were chiefly (i) denoting the owner or worker of the object inscribed, (ii) correspondence, (iii) memorial notices, (iv) magical formulae. There is no evidence that it was extensively used anywhere for literary purposes. The materials employed were unsuitable for records of any considerable length; they involved too great an expenditure of labour.

Roman writing appears to have come into use everywhere with the introduction of Christianity. In Britain of course, which had been a Roman province, its use was very much earlier. At first it was employed only for writing Latin. But sooner or later it became adapted everywhere to writing the native languages; and it is in this that almost all our records are preserved. Parchment was doubtless introduced along with this form of writing; and it may perhaps be assumed that the missionaries usually carried writing materials, as well as books, with them. Hence it is customary to take the date of their arrival as the beginning of the historical period—or more properly the period for which contemporary records are available. More important for us is to bear in mind that to the Roman, and to the ecclesiastics who inherited his tradition, the connection between literature and writing was essential.

The Runic alphabet was known to probably all the Teutonic peoples in the fourth century, and there is no cogent reason for believing that it was then of recent origin. A number of inscriptions dating from about the fourth and fifth centuries have been found in Angel and the adjacent districts, and there can be no reasonable doubt that this form of writing was brought over to Britain by the English invaders, although there are hardly any inscriptions in this country which can be dated before the seventh century. From then to the ninth century they are not uncommon. The inscribed objects consist for the most part of coins and monumental stones, though other articles of metal (weapons and ornaments) and bone (especially combs) are not unknown. Inscribed wooden rods were also in use, for correspondence; but none of these have been preserved. The latest coins belong to the Northumbrian kings of the ninth century (before 867); and it would seem that after this time Runic writing was merely a matter of antiquarian knowledge. Runic letters occur sometimes in MSS., especially in the Riddles in the *Exeter Book*; but they seem often to be incorrectly used.

Evidence for the literary use of this form of writing is very slight. Some passages from the *Dream of the Cross* are inscribed on the Ruthwell Cross, while the Franks Casket, a small whalebone box now in the British Museum, bears several lines which were perhaps specially composed for it. Otherwise the inscriptions rarely, if ever, contain more than one line of verse.

The Roman alphabet was in use from the time of St Augustine's arrival in 597. At the beginning of the eighth century there was a flourishing Latin literature in this country, which reached its zenith in the course of the next generation, under Bede. Yet it had not a very long life; within a century of Bede's death (735) it seems to have come to an end.

The script used in this period, whether in Latin or English writing, was of an archaic type, similar to what was in use in Ireland and Wales rather than to the contemporary Continental script. It is commonly held that this form of writing was derived from Irish monks and missionaries settled in this country, especially from those who were introduced by King Oswald (634–42) from Iona. We think that the possibility of British influence, even before this, ought not to be disregarded. But there is no reason for supposing that Roman writing was in common use among the English before the seventh century.

The earliest English document of which we have any record is the Laws of Aethelberht, which were written between 597 and 616. These Laws, together with those of other kings of Kent, viz. Hlothhere and

Eadric (c. 685) and Wihtred (c. 694), are preserved only in a MS. of the twelfth century—in a modernised form of language, but probably without substantial change. The Laws of Ine, king of Wessex, approximately contemporaneous with those of Wihtred, are preserved in several MSS., one of which dates from the early part of the tenth century. Apart from these Laws we have nothing except glosses and glossaries which can with confidence be said to have been written before the eighth century. It is clear, however, both from the glosses and other sources, that a recognised system of orthography for English words and names was already in existence by this time, though it varied somewhat from one kingdom to another.

The earliest evidence for a MS. collection of English poetry is to be found in Asser's *Life of King Alfred*, cap. 23, in a story relating to the king's childhood, not long after 850. Some forty years later we have a statement from Alfred himself, in the introduction to his translation of the *Cura Pastoralis*, that the ability to read English was now fairly widespread; and the various translations which he himself undertook show that there was something of a reading public for English. It may be added that the beginnings of the Saxon Chronicle, as an English work, seem to date from shortly before the middle of the ninth century, and that there is a translation of the Psalms dating from the same time or a little earlier. From the first half of the ninth century, especially from c. 825 onwards, we have also a number of legal documents (conveyances, agreements and wills) in English—which suggest that it was no rare accomplishment to be able to read in the vernacular.

It is more difficult to determine what was the case in the eighth century. Bede was engaged on a translation of St John's Gospel at the time of his death; but he had only got as far as cap. VI, and his work is believed to have perished. At the same time he also composed a short poem, which was taken down and is preserved in a letter from one of his companions named Cuthbert to a friend called Cuthwine. The copy of Caedmon's Creation Hymn written on a fly-leaf of the earliest (Moore) MS. of the Ecclesiastical History is also believed to date from the eighth century. But these pieces, together with two lines in a letter to St Boniface, are the only examples of written English poetry which can be dated with certainty to that period. Caedmon himself, the founder of English religious poetry, was composing before 680; but it is not clear from Bede's account, our only source of information, that his poems were committed to writing. And the same is true of Anglo-Saxon poetry in general. Much of what has come down to us was doubtless composed in the eighth century or even earlier; but, with insignificant exceptions, it is preserved only in MSS. which were written c. 1000.

The great MSS. of Anglo-Saxon poetry—the *Beowulf* MS. in the British Museum, the *Exeter Book*, the *Vercelli Book*, and the *Junius MS.* at Oxford—are obviously copied from earlier MSS. Their language normally is what is generally known as 'late West-Saxon'—a type of language which originated in Wessex but was taught in schools throughout the greater part of the country in the latter part of the tenth century. But they contain many forms belonging to earlier periods; and many obsolete or poetic words appear in forms which are not West-Saxon at all, but would seem to have been copied from MSS. written in parts of the country where West-Saxon had not yet been introduced. It is not clear, however, that any of this evidence[1] points to times earlier than the ninth century. We practically never meet with (e.g.) traces of the orthographic features which distinguish English texts of the earlier period.[2] Such negative evidence is not conclusive, but, so far as it goes, it is rather against the view that a large body of written English literature existed in the eighth century.

Four religious poems, the *Crist*, the *Elene*, the *Juliana* and the *Fates of the Apostles*, contain the name of the author, *Cynewulf*, in (Runic) acrostics. This may probably be taken to mean that the author himself committed his poems to writing. But we know nothing of him except what he tells us in the poems; and this gives no clue to his date. His syntax suggests that he lived not earlier than the ninth century. This was a time when the practice of introducing acrostics was popular on the Continent. A good example may be found in the introduction to Otfried's versified translation of the *Gospel Harmony*.

For the existence of English prose texts, apart from laws, there is hardly any evidence before the ninth century. Indeed we know of no certain case except Bede's translation of St John, mentioned above. The few legal documents which are preserved in English appear to be late translations from Latin originals.[3] In documents before 800 it would

[1] *Beow.* 1382 has been cited as an example; cf. Chambers' note *ad loc.* But, like most of the editors, we find it difficult to believe that successive scribes have preserved an archaism which must long have been unintelligible—especially in a familiar phrase.

[2] E.g. *th* or *d* for þ, ð; *u* (*uu*) for *w*; *ch* (final) for *h*; *ct* for *ht*.

[3] Birch, *Cart. Sax.* No. 171 claims to be a grant from the Mercian king Aethelbald, who died in 757; but in its present form it must be more than a century later than that date. All the other examples known to us are much later than this.

seem that the use of English was limited to statements of the boundaries of estates. Taking the evidence as a whole therefore we are inclined to doubt whether a reading public for English existed before this date. What we mean is that we doubt whether there were persons at this time who could read English but yet were without knowledge of Latin. A certain amount of English poetry, especially religious poetry, may already have been written down. But we suspect that the rise of English as a written language was connected and contemporaneous with the decline of Latin in England—about the close of the eighth century.

With regard to the question of a reading public it would be of importance to know whether any provision was made for the education of the laity. We hear of schools instituted even in the seventh century, e.g. by the East Anglian king Sigberht and by Adrian at Canterbury. But were they attended by those who were intended for a secular life? King Alfred gives instructions in his introduction to the *Cura Pastoralis* that the sons of the nobility are to be taught to read English in their childhood. He himself according to Asser, cap. 22, had remained *illiteratus* until he was twelve years old or more; but it is added that this was due to neglect on the part of his parents. One may perhaps infer from this that in the ninth century some education was customary, at least for the sons of princes. But can this be inferred also for the eighth century, when (written) English was apparently much less used? We are not aware of any evidence. In a number of charters of the eighth century a distinction is drawn between the signatures of ecclesiastics and those of the laity. The former employ some such formula as *Ego... subscripsi*, while the latter have *Signum manus*...(the name being often in a genitive form). More frequently we find either the one formula or the other used throughout; but the distinction must have some traditional basis. It is not often that anyone definitely states that he is illiterate. Wihtred, king of Kent (689–725), says on several occasions that he has made his mark *pro ignorantia litterarum*; but other examples are rare. Yet the distinction seems to us to imply a tradition that only the clergy were expected to be able to sign their names.

With the evidence at our disposal it is at all events a precarious hypothesis that the writing of English poetry—or prose—was cultivated by the laity in the times we are discussing; and a still more precarious hypothesis that it was cultivated, either by laymen or ecclesiastics, for the benefit of a lay reading public. The writing of English began presumably in places where writing was customary and easy, i.e. in religious houses—where also English religious poetry had its origin. And one would naturally expect that the first poems to be written down would be religious poems. The writing of secular poems, designed for the entertainment of a lay public, belongs surely to a later phase.

In the Norse world and in all parts of the North the Runic alphabet continued in use until much later than in England—a fact due doubtless to the late introduction of the Roman alphabet. Inscriptions are not so common in Norway and in Norse colonies as in Sweden, where they are preserved in very great numbers; but even in the former they extend over a period of more than a thousand years. The inscribed objects are similar to those found in England, except that coins with Runic legends appear to be wanting, at least in Norse lands, whereas memorial stones are infinitely more numerous. The Norse inscriptions yield little or nothing which can be regarded as literature; but poetry is not uncommon on Swedish and Danish memorial stones. The stone of Rök in southern Sweden, dating from the tenth century, contains a good deal.

References to Runic writing are of very frequent occurrence in poems and sagas. Most often it is mentioned in connection with magical formulae and spells, as in the *Sigrdrífumál* (cf. p. 449 f.); but we also hear of its being employed for sending messages. Sometimes also it is said to be used for recording poems. Thus in *Egils Saga*, cap. 78, when Egill is composing his poem, the *Sonatorrek*, his daughter Thorgerðr inscribes—or offers to inscribe—it on a rod (cf. p. 348). In *Grettis Saga* also, cap. 66, Grettir records his adventures at Sandhaugar in two stanzas, which he inscribes on a rod and leaves in the church porch; and though the story is fictitious, it testifies to the prevalence of the custom. There seems to be no evidence, however, which would lead us to suppose that any of the surviving texts owe their preservation to such records.

The Roman alphabet was introduced into Norway and its colonies in the course of the eleventh century, chiefly from England. Occasional instances of its use are found earlier, e.g. on the coins of Earl Haakon the Great (975–95); but these may be the work of foreigners. In the first half of the eleventh century the relations between Norway and England appear to have been very close, especially during the regency of Alfifa (Aelfgifu), an Englishwoman who held the government for her son Sveinn (1030–5). Before the end of the century a certain amount of Latin literature was produced in the Norse world. We may mention especially the Icelandic scholar Sæmundr.

The first documents of any appreciable length in the native language seem to have been the Laws of the various provinces—*Gulaþingslög*, *Frostaþingslög*, etc. These are believed to have been committed to writing c. 1100,[1] or very shortly after, though they are now preserved only in later recensions. The same is true of the Laws of Iceland, which are said to have been first written down in 1118.

The development of literature can best be traced in Iceland. The earliest known scholar who wrote in the vernacular was the priest Ari, who produced his history of Iceland (*Íslendingabók*) within a few years of the appearance of the Laws, c. 1130, though the text which now survives is believed to be an abridgment subsequently made by the author. During the next half century a considerable number of religious works appear to have been written both in Iceland and in Norway, while in the former country many sagas also were committed to writing apparently before 1200. MSS. of poetry are rare. Our knowledge of early Norse poetry is derived in the main from quotations in sagas and other prose works; and consequently the great majority of the poems are incomplete. It is generally believed, however, that the original MS. of the *Edda* poems, from which the surviving copies are derived, was written before 1200. The next following period was the great age of Icelandic literature, especially under Snorri Sturluson, who died in 1241. It was also a time of considerable literary activity in Norway; but this country was now almost entirely under foreign influence, in secular as well as religious literature.

On the Continent, apart from Jutland, Runic inscriptions are rare, though they are scattered over a wide tract of country, from France to the Ukraine. The inscribed objects are almost entirely of metal, and consist of weapons and ornaments, especially brooches. They contain little or nothing which can be regarded as literature, though one brooch from Nordendorf in Bavaria preserves the names of the gods Wodan and Thonar, perhaps in a magic formula. After the eighth century the Runic alphabet appears to have been known only to a few antiquarian scholars, and these had at best only an imperfect acquaintance with it.

[1] Snorri states in the *Heimskringla* (*Magnus Saga Góða*, cap. 17) that there was in his time in the Throndhjem district a law-book written by order of Magnus the Good, who reigned 1035–47. Snorri is a most trustworthy authority; but this statement is not generally credited by modern writers.

Among the Goths about the middle of the fourth century a new alphabet was introduced, derived mainly from the Greek. In this a certain amount of religious literature was produced. What remains consists of a translation of the greater part of the New Testament, some fragments of the Old Testament and of a homily, and a few insignificant fragments.

Many of the Teutonic peoples became acquainted with Roman writing before the close of the fifth century. The earliest documents are the Laws of the various kingdoms; but these, like everything else, are written in Latin. In the vernaculars, apart from Gothic, there is little or nothing before the eighth century, and even then the remains consist almost entirely of glosses and fragments of translations of religious works. In the ninth century we meet with religious poems on a large scale, such as Otfried's *Gospel Harmony* from the south of Germany and the *Heliand* (on the same subject) from the north. But of poetry—or prose—on native lines there is nothing except the fragment of the *Hildebrandeslied*, written about the close of the eighth century, and a few spells, chiefly from the ninth. The great mass of German heroic poetry is preserved only in texts dating from the thirteenth century and in a form (metre, etc.) which cannot be much older than that time. From earlier times we have two historical poems, of which one (the *Ludwigslied*) celebrates the victory of Louis III over the Northmen at Saucourt in 881, while the other (*De Heinrico*) is concerned with the meeting of Otto the Great and his brother Heinrich in 952. But the former is entirely under foreign influence both in style and metre, while the latter consists of alternate half lines in Latin and German.

Taking the Teutonic evidence as a whole, it is of interest to note how the output of written vernacular literature was governed by the amount of attention devoted to Latin studies. On the Continent, where Teutonic and Latin populations were included under the same rule, the output of Latin literature never ceased. The early writers were usually native Romans; but from the eighth century onwards there was an unceasing stream of Latin literature—chronicles, histories, biographies, poems, etc., in addition to religious and legal works—produced by scholars of German nationality. In England, where no Latin-speaking population existed, this phase began earlier but had not a very long life. In the ninth century English was being commonly written, and in all probability for literature on native as well as Roman lines, whereas Latin was then moribund, though it revived in the tenth century. In

Iceland the Latin phase was shorter and much less productive, and the native language was widely written, for secular as well as religious literature, within considerably less than two centuries after the introduction of Christianity. In Norway the case was much the same, except that French literature took the place of the native literature of entertainment.

Three phases therefore are to be distinguished in the early history of (Roman) writing among the Teutonic peoples. In the first phase Latin only is written. In the second the native language is employed for writing religious and other works derived from Roman sources or based on Roman models. In the third purely native works are written. But this third phase did not arise on the Continent before the twelfth century, and then only in a much modified form, while even the second phase was largely local and hardly recognised in the highest circles. In the main writing continued to be bound up with a foreign language. But in England Latin learning could not be maintained permanently. In the ninth century very few even of the clergy understood their services. In Iceland doubtless the difficulty was still greater. Hence the impetus to the adaptation of writing to the native languages was more pressing—with the rather curious result that education, at least the ability to read and write, was apparently more widely diffused in proportion as each country was more remote from the centres of civilisation. It is less surprising that the third phase is better represented in Iceland than in England; for England had been affected to a much greater extent by the foreign influence.

There is evidence that a reaction in favour of native Teutonic poetry was not wholly unknown on the Continent. Charlemagne himself according to his biographer Einhard (*Vita Karoli Magni*, cap. 29) had ancient German heroic poems written down, and learned them by heart. But nothing has been preserved, unless indeed the fragment of *Hildebrand* comes from this source, and we hear no more of them. Presumably there was no reading public for such things at that time. Einhard (cap. 26) assures us that Charlemagne himself could read quite well, but he adds that he would never read aloud, nor would he sing except in a low voice and together with the rest of those who were present. He was never able to write (*ib.* cap. 25), though he was always trying to do so; he had begun too late in life. Yet Charlemagne was without doubt a man not only of outstanding ability but also of quite exceptional intellectual activity. His attainments may be taken as an index of what a prince or nobleman might at best achieve during the

'Latin phase'.[1] They would be quite useful for the purpose of reference to the written Laws; but such persons would not be likely to read very much for pleasure. It was not, we think, before the ninth century in England and the latter part of the twelfth century in Iceland that conditions were changed in this respect. Even then the term 'reading public' is perhaps somewhat misleading. What we mean is that it would then not be difficult to find laymen who were in the habit of entertaining their friends and neighbours either by reading aloud or by reciting to them after perusal of a MS. In earlier times we believe there were plenty of persons who could recite without reference to a MS., but very few to whom the MS. would have been any use.

It is a curious fact that the ancient rule, derived from Greek, of writing each verse in a separate line was not applied to the poetry of the northern languages. Poetry was treated as prose. Presumably the convention was originally set by persons who were not familiar with MSS. of Latin poetry.

In Britain Roman writing was of course known in much earlier times—long before the Heroic Age. Both in Wales and elsewhere inscriptions occur from the early part of the Roman period. The vast majority are in Latin, though Greek is not rare, and even Oriental languages are found; but there are no inscriptions in the vernacular. The proper names naturally belong to many lands; British examples are quite frequent. Such names sometimes show British pronunciation, e.g. *Catuallauna* in an inscription, half Latin, half Aramaic, at Carlisle, and even a British case ending, e.g. *Brigomaglos* at Chesters (Chollerford); but such cases are rare. Even when they occur the rest of the sentence is in Latin.

In addition to the Latin (Greek, etc.) inscriptions there are a number of stones inscribed with Ogam writing, of which the earliest, e.g. at Silchester, may date from the fourth century. Some of these contain Gaelic forms; and the prevailing view at present is that all of them are of Irish origin. If that is correct we have hardly any British inscriptions until comparatively late times. Probably the earliest example is a difficult inscription in half-uncials at Towyn in Merioneth. The reading here is complicated, because more than one inscription seems to have been cut upon the stone; but the earliest is believed to date from the

[1] Exceptional cases doubtless occurred, such as the Northumbrian king Aldfrith and, in earlier times, the Frankish king Helpric (Chilperic); but they were probably very rare.

seventh century.[1] To the sixth and seventh centuries also doubtless belong many inscriptions in Wales, Cornwall, Devon, Dorset and the south of Scotland, which are either in Latin or contain only proper names. Some are in capitals, some in half-uncials; but the lettering is always very rude in comparison with inscriptions of the Roman period. Perhaps the most important monument is that of Voteporix (Vortiporius), the king of Dyfed attacked by Gildas, which must date from about the middle of the sixth century. The stone, which was found near Llanfallteg (Carmarthenshire), bears inscriptions both in Roman and Ogam letters.[2] In the former the king's name is given in British, in the latter in Gaelic form. We may also mention a monument to two sons of Nodus Liberalis, i.e. Nudd Hael, a cousin of Rhydderch Hael, found in Yarrow, Selkirkshire (cf. p. 143), and another to Catamanus, i.e. Cadfan, father of Cadwallon, preserved in the church of Llangadwaladr, Anglesey. Of these the former dates probably from the second half of the sixth century, the latter from the early part of the seventh. From later times the most important example is the inscription on the column near Valle Crucis set up by Cyngen, king of Powys, who retired in 850. It is now unfortunately illegible, but a partial copy was made by Llwyd at the beginning of the seventeenth century.[3]

Latin literature seems never to have wholly perished. It is true that there is little or nothing which can be dated with absolute certainty between the middle of the sixth century and the early part of the ninth. But we have seen (p. 154 ff.) that in all probability a good deal of antiquarian tradition and speculation found its way into writing during this period. We may refer especially to the 'Book of St German' and to traces of chronicles, especially perhaps in the north; and Nennius (*Hist. Brit.*[4]) refers to previous writers on the same lines as himself. Religious literature also can hardly have been at a complete standstill, although the *Lives* of saints which we have belong to a later period. Some knowledge of Latin poetry is shown by the hexameter verses—not very correct, it is true—which occur sometimes in monumental inscriptions.[5] Grants of land and privileges, some of which may be derived from originals of the eighth century or earlier, are recorded

[1] Cf. Morris-Jones, *Y Cymmrodor*, XXVIII. 266.

[2] *Ib.* p. 200.

[3] Given by Hübner, *Inscr. Brit. Christ.* No. 160 (p. 57 f.).

[4] ...*de ciuitatibus et mirabilibus Britanniae insulae, ut alii scriptores ante me scripsere, scripsi*—in texts of the Cambridge group after cap. 56.

[5] E.g. Hübner, *Inscr. Brit. Christ.* Nos. 82 (Pant y Polion, Carmarthenshire), 149 (Llangadwaladr, Anglesey), and perhaps 209 (Yarrow, Selkirkshire); cf. p. 143.

in the *Book of St Chad*, the *Book of Llandaff* and the *Life of St Cadoc*.

Probably the earliest extant example of written Welsh is a memorandum of a reconciliation entered on the title page of the (Gospel) *Book of St Chad*, which was transferred from Llandaff to Lichfield some time in the latter part of the tenth century. There is some reason for believing that the memorandum was copied, perhaps in the seventh century, from an original which may have been written in the sixth.[1] The same MS. also contains some early notices of donations in Welsh. From the ninth century there are a number of glosses; and two short poems in the Cambridge MS. of Juvencus are believed to date from the same period. From the tenth century we have a fragment of a 'Computus',[2] somewhat similar to one of Bede's tracts. All these, like many of the inscriptions, are written in the insular variety of half-uncial, which is used also in Anglo-Saxon and Irish.

The early Laws claim to have been drawn up by Howel the Good. The original text was probably written during the later years of his reign, c. 942–50; but the texts which have come down to us represent 'recensions' (doubtless much modified and expanded) not earlier than the twelfth century. The earliest Welsh MS. dates from c. 1200. One or two Latin MSS. are a little earlier.

Of the MSS. which contain collections of poetry the earliest is the *Black Book of Carmarthen*, part of which was written probably not long after 1150. By this time the insular script had given way to ordinary medieval writing. In orthography the MSS. differ a good deal.[3] But all of them preserve forms which show earlier features; and probably a number of poems have been copied from texts not later than the tenth century. Such forms are especially frequent in the *Book of Aneirin* (*ad fin.*).

The oldest texts differ from the later both in language and in orthography, but more especially perhaps in the latter. They rarely use *y*,[4] which may perhaps have been taken over from Anglo-Saxon some time

[1] Cf. Morris-Jones, *Y Cymmrodor*, XXVIII. 268 ff.

[2] Ed. and transl. (with facsimile) by Quiggin, *Zeitschr. f. celt. Phil.* VIII. 407 ff.

[3] Thus for the sound *đ* (Mod. W. *dd*) *BBC.* uses *t*, whereas the other MSS. have *d*. For *v* the other MSS. often use *f*, as in Anglo-Saxon. For *w Tal.* and *RBH.* commonly use a symbol which may have been suggested by A.S. *w*, though it does not resemble it. If these features are really due to English influence, they must have been taken over before 1150. But they seem not to occur (except occasional *f*) in the earliest part of *BBC.*

[4] In the 'Computus' only after *o*; in Harl. 3859 chiefly after *o*, *a*, *e*.

between the tenth and the twelfth centuries. But the most striking feature is that they use several letters with double phonetic values. Thus *c*, *m*, *p*, *t* at the beginning of words normally have their ordinary values. But in other positions—with certain exceptions—they must have represented the sounds *g*, *v*, *b*, *d* respectively. This is shown by the later language. Medieval texts commonly keep *c*, *p*, *t* (not *m*) for these sounds only at the end of words. In such cases their retention must be due to traditional orthography; and the same remark applies also to the regular use of (non-initial) *c*, *m*, *p*, *t* in the early texts. In the great majority of cases the sounds denoted by *c*, *m*, *p*, *t* had actually been the sounds *c*, *m*, *p*, *t*. The sounds changed in the course of time; but the traditional orthography was retained. It is important, however, to observe that these sound changes took place as far back as the seventh century, as may be proved by the representation of Welsh names in English records of that time. Thus we find *Ceadwalla* for *Catguollaun* (later *Cadwallon*) and *Maban* for *Mapon* (later *Mabon*). Indeed the change from *t* to *d* can be traced with certainty back to the sixth century in a number of names, e.g. *Cerdic* for *Ceretic* (later *Ceredig*). The change from *m* to *v* is not quite so old, as may be seen in *Caedmon* for *Catman* (later *Cadvan*, *Cadfan*) and in (Dat. pl.) *Deomedum* for *Dimet* (later *Dyfed*). But it must have taken place before 700, as may be seen from *Melfoben*: *Musa* (i.e. *Melpomene*) in the *Epinal Glossary*—a gloss which evidently comes from a British-Latin source. The salient features of early Welsh orthography must therefore date from the seventh century—indeed in all probability from the sixth.[1]

The double phonetic use of *c*, *m*, *t* is found also in Irish; but here it cannot (except in the case of *m*) be explained by native sound laws. It appears to have been taken over from Welsh orthography and, as we shall see below, confirms the conclusion stated above as to the time when this became fixed. Another conclusion which is indicated both by the conservatism of the orthography and by the Irish evidence is that Welsh must have been written in these early times to a greater extent than one would infer from the extreme paucity of the records which have been preserved. And here it is necessary to bear in mind that British civilisation was on the decline from the fifth century

[1] Early W. *c* (Mod. *g*) is usually represented by Engl. *c* (*ck*) in place-names; but the sound was *g* by c. 700 at latest, as may be seen by the personal name *Baeglog* (W. *baglog*) in the Durham *Liber Vitae*. It is worth noting that original *g* is sometimes preserved in the earliest Welsh records, though the English evidence (e.g. *Luel*, *Cumbra*) shows that it had ceased to be pronounced in the seventh century.

onwards. The Church itself was out of touch with the rest of the world, except the other Celtic peoples. It is likely enough therefore that, as in Ireland and in England in the ninth century, Welsh may have begun to displace Latin as a written language.

The absence of records is not necessarily fatal to such a supposition. We have practically no literary records from the Roman period, when they must have existed in abundance. In the latter part of the sixth century a good half of England was still British territory; but within the next century it was nearly all gone. Our records come only from Wales; and here there seems to have been no revival before the tenth century.

The question would be of great importance for us if it could be shown that secular native literature was ever written in these times—or that any of the poems with which we are concerned could be traced to early written texts. In the following chapters it will be seen that many of our poems must have been preserved by oral tradition, probably for a considerable time. Yet in some cases the possibility of derivation from an early written text is not wholly to be ignored.

In Ireland the earliest examples of writing are the monumental Ogam inscriptions,[1] which are very numerous. They are always in Gaelic, but never contain more than a few words. They are believed to date chiefly from the fourth, fifth and sixth centuries, though the evidence is almost wholly of a philological character and inferential. Occasionally they are accompanied, as in Wales, by brief Latin inscriptions of the early Christian type in Roman letters.

References to the use of Ogam writing occur frequently in sagas. Often it is stated that a hero's name is inscribed in Ogams at his funeral. In other cases they are used for spells, the inscribed objects being sometimes weapons, sometimes wooden rods, apparently of birch. These latter seem to have been used also for the purpose of conveying messages. A knowledge of Ogams was required in the education of the *fili* (cf. p. 603). It is stated that he is to learn fifty in each of the early years of his training, though what is meant by this is not quite clear. In one story,[2] relating to the time of Art, the father of Cormac, we hear of 'Rods of *Filid*' upon which were inscribed many stories of visions and courtships. And a very early, though unhistorical, reference to the use of Ogam writing for poetry occurs in the *Voyage of Bran* (*ad fin.*),

[1] Cf. Macalister, *Studies in Irish Epigraphy*.

[2] The story of Baile mac Buain. Text and transl. in O'Curry, *MS. Materials*, p. 472 ff.; cf. p. 464 ff.

where Bran is said to have written the poems in Ogam. But it is hardly credible that so cumbrous an alphabet can have been used to any appreciable extent for literary purposes. The sagas, however, imply that the knowledge of Ogam writing was not confined to *filid*. In the *Táin Bó Cuailnge* CuChulainn on several occasions cuts and inscribes rods, which he leaves behind him for Medb's warriors to read; and these are interpreted by Fergus.

Tombstones inscribed in Roman writing, usually half-uncial, are preserved in great numbers in the cemeteries of ancient monasteries, especially Clonmacnois.[1] The earliest which have been identified as yet belong to the eighth century; but many of them may be still earlier. The inscriptions are very frequently in Irish.

Latin literature began with St Patrick, or possibly even earlier.[2] It is not unlikely that a considerable amount has been preserved from the next two or three centuries; but for the most part it is embedded in later works. It is mainly of ecclesiastical character.

The earliest vernacular texts are likewise almost wholly ecclesiastical. They come from various monasteries on the Continent and consist chiefly of glosses. Many of them date from the eighth century. The oldest, together with fragments of a homily, preserved at Cambrai, are believed to have been written c. 700. Of matter other than religious there are some scraps of poetry written in the margins of the MSS., but these also appear to be chiefly of monastic origin.

The Irish Laws present very difficult and complicated problems, owing to the amount of additions and commentaries which have been incorporated with the original text. These problems are now being thoroughly investigated for the first time. All that can be said here is that the original text seems to date from very early times—probably as early as the seventh century.

The MSS. which contain sagas, heroic and non-heroic, are not earlier than the twelfth century. In the oldest of them, the *Lebor na-hUidre*, the original hands date from c. 1100, while the *Book of Leinster*, which contains the largest collection of all, was written about sixty years later. Many of the stories are preserved only in much later MSS. But there is no doubt that a large number of them were committed to writing in much earlier times. Some MSS., e.g. the *Yellow Book of Lecan*, a MS. of the fourteenth century, preserve to a great extent the forms and orthography of the eighth or ninth century. Not unfrequently references

[1] Cf. Macalister, *Memorial Slabs of Clonmacnois*.

[2] Cf. K. Meyer, *Learning in Ireland in the Fifth Century*, p. 4 ff.

occur to earlier MSS., from which the surviving ones are derived. Of these lost MSS. the earliest and most important seems to have been the *Book of Druim Snechta*, which is known to have contained many stories, especially non-heroic (cf. p. 468 f.). From a comparison of the forms which occur in the MSS. derived from it with those which are found in the earliest glosses it is clear that this MS. must have been written in the first half of the eighth century.[1]

The history of Irish writing is in its early stages closely connected with the history of British writing. The script is practically identical in both cases, and there can be little doubt that Ireland obtained it from Britain.[2] Moreover early Irish writing, like early Welsh, uses the letters *c*, *p*, *t* with double phonetic values, i.e. for the sounds *g*, *b*, *d*, as well as for the sounds *c*, *p*, *t*; and it can scarcely be questioned that this usage also was derived from Britain, where its origin was due, as we have seen (p. 487), to phonetic causes. Lenition of consonants took place in Irish, as well as in Welsh; but it took a different form. And it is important to observe that in Irish the lenited sounds derived from *c*, *p*, *t* are expressed differently from the sounds from which they are derived—they are written *ch*, *ph*, *th*.[3] This seems clearly to indicate that early Irish orthography became fixed at a somewhat later stage in the history of the language than was the case in Welsh, viz. after the lenition was completed, or at least far developed. Such evidence as we have suggests that lenition took place about the same time in both languages. Consequently it would seem that Irish orthography became fixed later than Welsh—which is quite in accordance with the observations noted above.

The early Ogam inscriptions and the proper names which occur in St Patrick's writings belong to a totally different stage in the history of the language from what we find in the earliest vernacular texts. On the whole they are closely parallel to the British forms which are found in inscriptions of the Roman period. Without doubt the period from the fifth to the seventh century was a time of rapid linguistic change in both countries. On the other hand the forms of the names in Adamnan's *Life of St Columba*, which was written shortly before 700, are in

[1] Cf. Thurneysen, *Ir. Heldensage*, p. 16.

[2] Together with a large number of words denoting practices and ideas connected with the Church—which were derived from Latin through the medium of Welsh; cf. Thurneysen, *Handbuch des Alt-Irischen*, I. 517 f.

[3] The lenited sounds derived from the other consonants (including *m*) are expressed by the same letters as the unlenited sounds. The lenition of *m* seems not to have been quite the same as in Welsh.

general far more in accord with the forms of the earliest vernacular texts than with those of the Ogams. There are, however, even here a certain number of exceptional forms, which represent an earlier stage of language.[1] In particular we may note the (not very rare) use of *u* for *f*, e.g. in *Uinnianus*, *Uirgnous* for *Finnian*, *Fergna*—a relic of the time previous to the change of *w* to *f*, which had taken place before Irish orthography became fixed. It is probable, however, that such names were taken over from earlier records, for the persons who bear these names belonged to the past—Fergna died in 623, Finnian long before. The evidence then, taken as a whole, tends to indicate that it was in the course of the seventh century—perhaps about the middle of it—that early Irish orthography became fixed.

It would seem then that Roman writing must have been known in Ireland for at least two centuries before it was adapted to use for the vernacular. There is some reason for believing that during that period a not inconsiderable amount of Latin literature was produced. At all events Irish learning was already famous in the seventh century, and had by this time doubtless outstripped that of Britain. But the chief contrast in the history of literature between the two countries is to be found in the period which followed the beginning of writing in the vernacular. It is clear that in the eighth and ninth centuries great activity was developed in the writing of Irish literature, secular as well as religious, whereas there is no satisfactory evidence for any considerable body of Welsh written literature at this time.

The writing of Irish secular literature may have been very largely due to the *filid*.[2] It has been pointed out[3] that the contents of the *Book of Druim Snechta* suggest that it was the work of a *fili* rather than of an ecclesiastic. They are of a most pronouncedly heathen character. The heroic elements are slight; but deities figure very prominently in the stories. There is also much about visions, tabus, reincarnation, and other subjects which might be expected to interest a *fili*. Now the *filid* were originally seers; and they must have felt their influence to be seriously threatened by the growth of the Church. But unlike the Druids, who disappeared, they came to terms with the Church and continued to maintain their position as a kind of what we may call literati. According to a widely spread story an attempt was made at the Convention of Druim Ceta in the year 573 to suppress them, on

[1] Archaic forms in names derived from Irish sources occur also occasionally in Bede's *Eccl. History*, e.g. *Meilochon* (III. 4).

[2] See Addenda.

[3] Cf. Thurneysen, *Ir. Heldensage*, pp. 18, 72.

account of their arrogance and extortionate demands; but St Columba intervened on their behalf and saved them. The *Eulogy of St Columba* is said to have been composed by the *fili* Dallan mac Forgaill in commemoration of this.

It may be that not all the *filid* made peace with the Church at this time. This is at least what is suggested by the stories and poems relating to Mongan (cf. p. 469 f.), whose court would seem to have been one of the last strongholds of the old faith. Yet it may be observed that the poems contained in the *Voyage of Bran* are in a metre of Roman derivation, which would seem to indicate that even this milieu was not long free from Roman influence.

Between the *filid* in general and the Church a sort of compromise seems to have been brought about, though we do not know that it was ever stated in formal terms. The *filid* were allowed to retain their traditions of the gods and to commit them to writing; but the gods were no longer represented as objects of worship, and the use of the word 'god' was avoided. The result of this compromise was that Ireland has preserved a richer store of traditions relating to the heathen age than any other European country except Greece; for the *filid* were doubtless the best informed and most intellectual class of people in the country. In theory their training seems to have remained purely oral, apart from the Ogams; but in point of fact in the tenth century they were often authorities on Roman as well as native learning and must have got much of their information from books. We shall have to speak of them more fully in Ch. XIX.

What we would emphasise here is the part played by this class in the literary history of Ireland. In Wales we find a class, the bards (*beirdd*), who in the sixth century may have resembled the *filid* very closely. It is quite possible that literary activities may have begun among the British bards earlier than among the *filid*. But if so they were cut short by the political conditions—by the fact that all the best of the British territories were lost soon afterwards. There is no satisfactory evidence that in Wales itself the bards cultivated writing until a much later period.

There is no evidence in the records of early Greece for any foreign influence equal in magnitude to the influence which was exercised by Rome upon the literary history of northern Europe. Yet both the forms and the names of the letters show that the alphabet was derived from a North Semitic source, presumably Phoenician. In the Bronze Age a different kind of writing, which has not yet been deciphered, was current, at least in Crete; but the general opinion now seems to be that this died out without influencing the writing of historical times—indeed probably before the latter came into existence. The alphabet of historical times varied considerably in different parts of the Greek world; but it was clearly of uniform origin. Only in Cyprus, down to the fourth century, there existed a totally different—syllabic—form of writing. We do not know whether this was connected in any way with the prehistoric writing of Crete.

The earliest datable Greek inscription is one of a number which are inscribed on the leg of a statue of Rameses II at Abu Simbel. It states that it is the work of soldiers in the army of King Psammetichos—presumably Psammetichos II, who reigned c. 593–589 B.C. But a number of inscriptions which are undated may well go back to the seventh century. A still earlier date for the use of the alphabet may be inferred from the fact that the various Greek colonies in Italy, Sicily and elsewhere usually employ the same forms of alphabet as the cities by which they were founded. Several of these colonies were founded before the close of the eighth century, and it would seem that by this time a good number of well-marked local varieties already existed. Some scholars hold that the names of the winners at the Olympian Games, which are preserved from 776, are derived from contemporary written records. However that may be, if the materials used in early times were of a perishable character, the alphabet may have been known long before that time. The Semitic evidence seems to point to the period between the tenth and the eighth century. Datable inscriptions in the North Semitic alphabet are said to be rare. But the stone which commemorates the victories of Mesha, king of Moab, and which dates from c. 850, bears a rather close resemblance to the earliest Greek writing, in spite of certain differences in details.

The purposes for which writing was employed in early times seem on the whole to have been much the same as in the North,[1] though from the sixth century onwards we meet with very long inscriptions containing treaties and other public notices, for which no Northern

[1] An interesting analogy to the inscriptions of Abu Simbel may be found in the Runic inscriptions cut on the walls of the great pre-historic tomb of Maeshowe in Orkney. At least fourteen persons seem to have inscribed their names there. Two inscriptions say they are the work of Crusaders who have broken into the tomb. These were doubtless the followers of Earl Ronald of Orkney, who went to the Holy Land in 1151. The Norwegian part of his force spent the previous winter in Orkney, and apparently occupied their time in this way. Cf. Dickins, *Runic Inscriptions of Maeshowe* (Kirkwall, 1930).

parallels are to be found. The materials also were apparently similar, though the Greek articles were doubtless often of more advanced types. We hear of letters written on folded wooden boards even in the *Iliad* (VI. 168 f.). In later times at least these boards were covered with wax. Another form of letter—apparently referred to by Archilochos (fragm. 89)—was the *scytale*. It was used especially for secret despatches. The letter was written on strips of leather and had to be wound round a rod of a certain thickness in order to be read. Inscriptions are also frequently found on painted pottery.

The question which primarily concerns us is the application of writing to literary purposes. It is commonly held now that the works of the early Greek poets, including even Homer and Hesiod, were written from the beginning. This means of course that writing on a large scale was practised as far back as the eighth century or earlier. The records give no evidence to justify such a belief. Writing may well have been known from the ninth century. But down to the sixth century its scope seems to have been little more extended than that of Runic writing in the North.

Written literature usually begins with the writing of the Laws. Such was the case in England, in the North—apparently in Sweden and Denmark, as well as in Norway and Iceland—and probably also in Ireland. In Greece the first written Laws are said to have been drawn up by Zaleucos for Locroi Epizephyrioi, in the south of Italy, c. 660. At Athens the first written Laws appear to have been those of Dracon, enacted in 621. Many other cities are believed to have had their laws committed to writing about the same time. But of prose works apart from Laws there is no record before those of the philosophers Pherecydes and Anaximandros, who flourished not long before 550.

The ability to read and write was doubtless widespread in the seventh century; and poems may frequently have been written down, as in the case of Egill's *Sonatorrek* (cf. p. 348). But we cannot believe that writing was the medium by which poetry was commonly disseminated at this time. Writing is probably necessary for the circulation of a prose literature, if—as distinct from saga—an author's actual words are to be preserved. At least we know of no exceptions other than ritual works which are preserved by a priestly organisation. But poetry is obviously easier to preserve; and before the existence of a reading public it is by this means alone that an author can hope to obtain a wide circulation for his actual words. The political poems of Solon, Tyrtaios and others indicate that such were the conditions in Greece in their times.

For the existence of a reading public the knowledge of reading and writing is not alone sufficient. There must also be abundant and convenient writing materials. But it is much to be doubted if such was the case in Greece before the close of the sixth century. Laws were inscribed upon wooden boards or rods[1] or on blocks of stone. For less permanent requirements, as we have seen, leather or some kind of skin was used besides the wooden tablets, which were apparently more common; but there is no reason for supposing that this was anything like the vellum or parchment which played so great a part in the history of literature from the Roman period to the Middle Ages. The latter was an invention of the third century (B.C.), inspired by the necessity of finding a substitute for papyrus, which had become too dear owing to the excessive demand. From the fifth century, and indeed probably from the sixth, onwards papyrus had been the material regularly used for literary purposes.

The importance of papyrus for the history of literature was perhaps greater even than that of parchment was in later times—at least if the various vegetable substances used as writing materials in the East were originally suggested by it. At all events it is clear that not long before the middle of the first millennium (B.C.) some great impetus to written literature was experienced throughout the East, as well as in Greece, and that the types of writing adopted in India were derived from Semitic sources. Papyrus was probably known to the Semitic peoples—both the Arameans in Assyria and the Hebrews and Phoenicians in Palestine —from the eighth century, indeed sporadically even earlier;[2] but there is no evidence which would lead one to infer that it was used in Greece so early. The first record of a Greek merchant in Egypt relates to the year 688;[3] but the real development of Greek trade with this country seems not to have taken place before the latter part of the century. Before that time papyrus may of course have found its way sporadically into the Greek world, whether through Greek or Phoenician channels. But it did not lead to the discovery of any native vegetable substitutes, as in the East; the Ionians, who had the Egyptian trade mainly in their hands and who doubtless first began to use papyrus, called it 'skins' (διφθέραι). Herodotos (v. 58), in explanation of this, says that

[1] Solon's Laws are said to have been inscribed on ἄξονες, apparently wooden boards, which seem to have been set up in the Prytaneion ('City Hall') and fitted with some contrivance for turning; cf. Plutarch, *Solon*, cap. 25.

[2] Cf. Cook, *Cambridge Ancient History*, III. 424.

[3] Cf. Ure, *Origin of Tyranny*, pp. 103, 118.

formerly owing to the scarcity of papyrus they had used the skins of sheep and goats.

From what has been said it seems to us unlikely that papyrus came into general use in Greece much before the close of the seventh century. In the absence of precise evidence we have to depend unfortunately upon general considerations. In the early part of that century the civilisation of the Greek world was evidently very similar to that of the Norse world in the tenth century (A.D.), and we see no reason for believing that the art of writing was more developed. But from this time the progress in Greece was more rapid. First came the demand for written Laws, and within a century from this we find the beginnings of a prose literature. The sequence would be natural if suitable writing materials became generally available during the intervening period.

The linguistic evidence seems to us to point quite definitely to the same conclusion. The remains of the early poets, Hesiod, Callinos, Archilochos, Simonides, Tyrtaios, Mimnermos, Solon and others are all preserved in a more or less uniform type of language. This is also in general the language of the Homeric poems, though here we find also a considerable number of quite alien (Aeolic) forms and also numerous archaic forms, which occur likewise in Hesiod's poems and to some extent elsewhere. The only important exceptions down to the beginning of the sixth century are the poems of Alcman, Sappho and Alcaios. Now the language to which we are referring is not exactly Attic, though it is not far removed from it. Such a language may have served quite well as a common literary medium for Athens and the neighbouring cities of the Cyclades. But it is incredible to us that Tyrtaios can have employed such a form of language in his poems, which are addressed to the Spartans,[1] and very unlikely that Hesiod can have employed it, at least in the *Works and Days*, which is surely intended in the first place for Boeotians. 'Translation' then in some form or other is involved. But, if so, why are the poems of Alcman, Sappho and Alcaios not translated? The explanation cannot wholly lie in the fact that these latter were lyric poets, although in the case of lyric poems 'translation' may have been more difficult. From Sappho we have also elegiac poems, which are preserved in their original (Aeolic) language, like the lyrics.

[1] There was a widespread story, known to Plato, that Tyrtaios was of Athenian birth. It is doubted by Strabo, VIII. 4. 10. Whatever may be the truth, Tyrtaios in his poems clearly identifies himself with the Spartans. He is a very model of patriotic nationalism.

Moreover we have lyric poems from Archilochos, Solon and others in the same form of language as the rest of their poems.

The true explanation seems to us to be as follows. In the fourth century, before the rise of Alexandria, when Athens was the intellectual centre of the Greek world and its language had been adopted everywhere as the language of literature, it is more than probable that the texts of authors of the past which were current there came to be generally accepted as the standard texts everywhere. There is no reason for doubting that, with the exception of the Homeric poems and perhaps Hesiod, these texts had been current at Athens from the times of the authors themselves or shortly afterwards. Now if we leave out of account the Ionic authors—for whom little 'translation' was required—it will be seen that it is the earlier authors who are 'translated', while the later authors are untranslated. The difference in time between Tyrtaios and Alcman was probably not great; but almost all Doric and Aeolic authors after the latter are preserved in their original language.[1] There can be little doubt that Pindar's poems circulated in written form; and we need not hesitate to believe the same in the case of Alcman and the poets who followed him, Sappho, Stesichoros, etc., for even by Alcman's time—towards the close of the seventh century—facilities for writing may have been generally accessible.[2] The difference in the treatment of the earlier poets points, we believe, to oral transmission of their poems. We mean that they did not come to Athens in writing.

It may be observed that in passages quoted by an author from poems in a different form of language 'translation' appears to have been the usual practice. Numerous examples may be found in Herodotos. In a score of Delphic oracles quoted by him we have noticed forms which are definitely Doric only in one case—an oracle given to the Cyreneans (IV. 159)—and even in this the Doric forms are mixed with Ionic. Yet Doric was the language of the Delphic sanctuary, as is clear from numerous inscriptions found there. The inscriptions quoted by the same author are also reproduced in Ionic, whatever their source. We may refer in particular to the famous epitaphs, quoted in VII. 228, upon the Spartans and their Peloponnesian allies, who fell at Thermopylai in

[1] Theognis' poetry is an exception. The explanation may be that this is in reality an anthology (cf. p. 392), perhaps made for educational purposes.

[2] It is worth noting that Mytilene had trade connections with Egypt about this time. Sappho's brother Charaxos was engaged in trade at Naucratis in Egypt; cf. the passage from Athenaios quoted and transl. by Edmonds, *Lyra Graeca*, I. 148 ff. Alcaios also is said to have visited Egypt (*ib.* p. 410 f.). Alcman according to some authorities was a Lydian slave (*ib.* p. 44 f.).

480. These monuments are not preserved, but there can be no reasonable doubt that the inscriptions were in Doric. We may compare the inscription upon the serpentine column of the tripod dedicated at Delphoi from the spoils won at Plataiai in 479, which is referred to in IX. 81 and is still preserved at Constantinople. The inscription is in Doric and the form of writing is that of Sparta, although the armies of Athens and of most of the other Greek states took part in the battle.

It is difficult for us to believe that Herodotos had not written copies of the oracles and inscriptions which he quotes. But we suspect that even with the leading literary men of the fifth century speech and memory were of much greater importance—in comparison with writing—than they are with us. Even if his information did come from written copies—whether in the original languages or not—it may well have been less trouble to him to remember the verses than to write them down. We may note that he regularly gives Doric and Aeolic names in Ionic form. Good examples may be found in the long genealogies of the Spartan kings, recorded in VII. 204 and VIII. 131. Other writers are less consistent. Thucydides apparently more often preserves the native forms. But the 'translated' forms are common enough everywhere, and doubtless reflect the usage of ordinary speech. For the preservation of the Doric and Aeolic texts we are probably indebted to professional scribes from the beginning.

The language of the Homeric poems is a subject which has been debated so frequently and fully that it is impossible to do more than state an opinion here.[1] The poems were familiar throughout the Greek world; and their archaic language and diction is frequently reproduced in poetic inscriptions.[2] We are unable to believe that they were commonly either recited or learnt in an alien form of language. The fact that the language of the inscriptions which contain the Homeric forms and formulae is always the native language—whether it be the Doric of Corfu or the Ionic of Naxos—is definite evidence to the contrary. Evidence to the same effect is furnished by the forms of heroic names, especially on painted vases, where they are written over the figures depicted. Such forms as *Wekaba* and *Daiphobos* cannot possibly be derived from our text—or any Ionic text—of the poems. The (presumably Chalcidian) form *Ainees* is equally incompatible with our text.

Our text itself represents the form in which the poems were known at

[1] The writer's views have been expressed more fully in *The Heroic Age*, p. 207 ff.

[2] For references cf. *The Heroic Age*, p. 217, notes. The inscription upon the bronze discus from Cephallenia (there quoted) is especially interesting.

Athens. Its origin can be accounted for satisfactorily enough by the story which credits Peisistratos with having ordered the poems to be written down. The only serious objection to the story is that there is no evidence for it before the time of Cicero. In any case it seems to us highly improbable that writing on this scale was undertaken much before the middle of the sixth century. We are far more ready to believe that the complete written text dates from a still later time. It was presumably due to the magnitude of the task that, so far as we know, no other texts were ever committed to writing, though in Italy they apparently survived in oral use long enough to influence Latin poetry.

As for the original language of the poems we believe this can be traced only in the alien element embedded in our text—which belongs to the Aeolic of Asia. If we could recover the versions of the poems current in (say) Sparta or Corfu, we should doubtless find the same element embedded in a Doric text. We see no satisfactory evidence for the presence of true Ionic elements in our text. But in regard to the early history of the poems certain questions will require notice in the following chapters.

From the evidence discussed in this chapter it will be clear that in the early history of writing two phases are to be distinguished everywhere, except perhaps among the Britons. In the first phase writing is employed for messages, for inscriptions denoting ownership, for memorial inscriptions, perhaps for spells, and for other purposes for which a small amount of writing will suffice—but not to any considerable extent for literary purposes. In this phase writing is a difficult and slow business owing to the nature of the materials available. In the second phase writing is easy, owing to improved materials, and regularly used for literary purposes. The first phase lasted everywhere for a considerable time—two or three centuries both in Ireland and in Greece, much longer among the English, four or five times as long in the North—but the two phases overlap to some extent, especially among the northern peoples.

In no case was the transition from the first to the second phase due to purely native development. In the north of Europe it is accompanied by the introduction of a new kind of writing and a new language. Here we have to distinguish three periods or sub-phases in the new phase. In the first only the new language is written in the new writing and with the new materials. In the second the new writing is adapted to the native language, but only for laws and for subjects connected with the new influence. In the third it is applied to purely native literature. These three divisions of the phase are found everywhere; but they differ much in length in the different countries, and there is of course much overlapping. In England the first two sub-phases may be said to be in part contemporary;[1] for the earliest Laws date practically from the beginning of the phase. Otherwise the second sub-phase is not much in evidence for the next century and a half, while the third begins perhaps half a century after that. In Ireland the first sub-phase lasts some two centuries before we see any trace of the second, while the third begins between half a century and a century after the second.

For Greece there is no need to adopt any such divisions of the second phase. No new form of writing was introduced; the writing of the second phase was a continuation of that of the first. Nor was any new language introduced. What brought about the new phase in Greece was the acquisition of new writing materials from Egypt. But at the same time it is to be noted that this was only one of many new things which Greece learnt from Egypt and the East in the course of the seventh century. It was in this century and through knowledge thus gained that Greece passed very rapidly from barbarism to civilisation. There is no trace of any organisation like the Church, by which the northern peoples were brought under Roman influence. But it is significant that several of the intellectual leaders of the early sixth century, such as Thales and Solon, are said to have visited Egypt and the East in quest of knowledge.

It would appear that written vernacular literature usually begins with Laws. In England the earliest Laws were written long before any other writings in the vernacular of which we have record. In one Greek city at least, the Italian Locroi,[2] the Laws are said to have been written at a date which seems to fall within our first period. And for this we have an analogy in early Roman history, if we are to believe the story of the Ten (or Twelve) Tables; for the date assigned by tradition to these Laws is more than two centuries earlier than any Latin literature of which we have record. This, however, is not incredible, in view of the proximity

[1] The explanation of this peculiarity is, we think, that the ability to read English was at first probably limited to a very small number of persons—perhaps only to certain royal officials.

[2] It seems strange at first sight that a place which plays so small a part in Greek history should be the first to have its laws written, however large and wealthy it may have been. But mercantile interests may have been responsible, as elsewhere. There was great wealth in Italy about this time, as may be seen from the Etruscan and Praenestine tombs.

of flourishing Greek cities, e.g. at Naples, whose merchants must have been well known to the Romans. When Latin literature began it was as much indebted to Greek models as Anglo-Saxon ecclesiastical literature was to Latin models.

Unfortunately we have no information as to what forms of literature were first written down, apart from laws, legal documents and works of ecclesiastical interest. It seems to us most improbable that long epic poems or sagas should be among the first to receive this treatment. But positive evidence is wanting.

The case of Britain is obviously different from all the rest, owing to the exceptional history of the country; but unfortunately our information is defective at many points. We do not know whether the Britons ever had a native writing of their own, whether Ogam or other; but Roman writing would seem to have been current to some extent even before the Roman conquest. Throughout the Roman period good writing materials, including papyrus or parchment, were doubtless obtainable in many parts of the country. This implies the prevalence of conditions which we have described above as the second phase—presumably the first division of it. It is not likely that the use of parchment ever died out, even when the territories of the Britons had become restricted to the poorer and more backward parts of the country. But we are very much in the dark as to the beginnings of the second and third divisions of the second phase, i.e. as to when Welsh began to be written (*a*) for ecclesiastical and (*b*) for secular literature. We have no record of any written Laws before those of Howel the Good (c. 942–50); and there is no doubt that about this time a good deal of Welsh secular poetry was written, in addition to ecclesiastical works. There is good reason also, as we have seen, for believing that Welsh was written at a much earlier period—three or four centuries earlier—but we do not know whether this applies to secular literature; nor do we know to what extent or in what localities it was written at this time. Welsh tradition and history, intellectual as well as political, tends to centre in Gwynedd. But the intellectual activities of which we are speaking may have belonged to some other part of the country, which was subsequently lost.

CHAPTER XVII

THE TEXTS

IN the last chapter we saw that there is abundant evidence for the writing of English in the ninth century. It is certain that the language was written to some extent in earlier times—in Laws from the beginning of the seventh century. But we do not know how far it was written for literary purposes before the ninth century. With the exception of the few short texts mentioned on p. 477, no MSS. of earlier date have been preserved. Indeed nearly all Anglo-Saxon poetry is contained, as we have seen, only in MSS. dating from the end of the tenth or the beginning of the eleventh century. It is clear enough that most of the poems were written before this time; but the date when they were first written is generally difficult to ascertain.

The poems in general show a mixture of forms belonging to different periods and different parts of the country. In this respect they show a certain resemblance to the Homeric poems. The prevailing type of language is what is commonly known as late West Saxon, since it originated in Wessex; but by the end of the tenth century it had come to be the school language of the greater part of England. Embedded in this, however, we find earlier forms, sometimes belonging to Wessex, more often to other parts of the country. But it does not appear that, as in the case of the Homeric poems, the preservation of these forms is usually due to metrical considerations. There is a good deal of variation between one poem and another; but the tendency seems rather to be for non-West Saxon forms to occur in archaic and poetic words, while words which belong to the language of everyday life usually appear in the normal late West Saxon form. Thus in *Beowulf* the West Saxon form is invariable in *eald*, 'old', whereas in the poetic word for 'life' the West Saxon *ealdor* and the non-West Saxon *aldor* are about equally frequent.

The existing MS. of *Beowulf* is written in two hands, the second of which begins at 1939. There are considerable differences in orthography between the two portions; and it is clear that one of the two scribes, probably the first, introduced extensive changes. Behind the present text, however, we can detect at least two MS. strata, one of which was West Saxon, apparently of a somewhat earlier type, but probably not very early, while the other, which was still earlier, was evidently not West Saxon. It is of interest to notice that this earlier stratum appears to have used the digraph *oe*,[1] which is alien to the orthography even of early West Saxon; the sound had been lost in Wessex before 850. On the whole the evidence for this early stratum seems to point to a text written in the Mercian orthography, which was current in Kent and various other parts of the country during the first half of the ninth century, as a result of the Mercian political supremacy. We doubt, however, whether there is sufficient material for determining the kingdom or province to which the writer belonged. The traces of Kentish or other dialect which have been suggested are not convincing. Our impression is rather that the different strata represent in general the different standard school languages which successively obtained currency.

We think that the mixture of forms which is to be found in most other Anglo-Saxon poems is usually to be explained in the same way, in spite of differences in detail. It is quite possible, however, that some poems are derived ultimately from the Northumbrian kingdom, where a different orthography prevailed. Such may be the case with some at least of the Riddles, which seem to show traces of the loss of final *-n*,[2] an exclusively Northumbrian characteristic. One Riddle (No. XXXVI) is preserved (in a Continental MS.) in Northumbrian form. Caedmon's *Hymn* is of course of Northumbrian origin, and so also any other poems by the same author which may have been preserved; but we do not know whether the scribal tradition is Northumbrian. The same remark applies to the *Dream of the Cross*. The inscription upon the Ruthwell Cross shows at least that this poem was known in the north at an early date.

The most important evidence bearing upon the date of Anglo-Saxon poems is that of syntax.[3] In particular there is considerable variation in the use of the definite article. In the *Battle of Maldon* it is nearly three times as frequent as in *Beowulf*, while all the religious poems fall between

[1] The text several times has *æ* for *e*—a mistake due apparently to misunderstanding *oe*, which was unfamiliar to the scribes. For examples see Klaeber, *Beowulf*, p. lxxix. We believe that the forms *Hrædles*, *Hrædlan*, beside the more frequent *Hreþel*, etc., are to be explained in the same way, in spite of the Norse forms. A very convenient summary of the linguistic characteristics of *Beowulf* will be found in Klaeber, *op. cit.*, Introduction, cap. VII (p. lxii ff.).

[2] E.g. in Rid. XV. 1, where we think *wæpen wiga* (for *wigan*) should be read.

[3] The conclusions which certain scholars have drawn from the metrical evidence seem to us unconvincing; cf. Chadwick, *The Heroic Age*, p. 464 f.

these two extremes. In those which are generally believed to be the earliest, *Genesis* and *Exodus*, the occurrences are only about 20–30 per cent. more frequent than in *Beowulf*, but in others they are more than twice as frequent. The significance of this is that in *Beowulf*, as in the Homeric poems, the word is still a demonstrative (or relative) pronoun, and has not yet become an article. With rare exceptions it is only in combination with the adjective that it is used as an article—a phenomenon which is regular also in early Norse poetry, though the word used here is of a different origin. It may be remarked that the archaic character of *Beowulf* in this respect is shared also by the Gnomic poems. In these the use of the article is even more rare; but the peculiar nature of the subject-matter may be partly responsible for this.

The most striking evidence for date is to be found in the presence or absence of the article with the (weak) adjective in combination with a noun. In Cynewulf's poems the article occurs in such combinations eight times for every time that it is wanting, whereas in *Beowulf*, omitting certain doubtful cases, it is wanting five times for every time that it is found—i.e. it is forty times more common than in Cynewulf's poems. Here again the earlier religious poems occupy an intermediate position. The nearest approach to the usage of *Beowulf* is that of the *Exodus*, which has ten examples with the article to fourteen without.

All this evidence tends to show that *Beowulf* belongs to an earlier phase of language than any of the religious poems. It does not necessarily follow, however, that the poem was written down at a very early date. To this question we shall have to return in the next chapter. It may be mentioned that the other heroic poems show no marked divergences from the usage of *Beowulf*. But they are too short for any safe conclusions to be based on statistics of their syntax; and the same remark applies in general to the poems discussed in Ch. XIV.

Very few Anglo-Saxon poems are preserved in more than one MS., and consequently the material available for study by a comparison of texts is very limited. First we may take the five poems or metrical pieces which are preserved in more than one MS. of the *Saxon Chronicle*. Throughout these five pieces there is only one variant[1] which is not due either to mere corruption, through carelessness, or illegibility of the original, or to modernisation of orthography.

In all other cases the text seems to be treated with somewhat greater freedom. Riddle XXXI, of which two texts occur in the *Exeter Book*,

[1] In the poem on the *Battle of Brunanburh* (*ann.* 937), where MS. B (18) has *forgrunden* for the archaic word *ageted*.

presents several variations which cannot be accounted for by either of the processes mentioned above. One case affects a whole line. In Riddle xxxvi, which is preserved in an early Northumbrian form (see above), as well as in the *Exeter Book*, apart from minor variations the last two lines are wholly different in the two texts. In Caedmon's *Creation Hymn* the only variant to be noticed here[1] is that the early Northumbrian text (cf. p. 477) has *alda* against the *eorþan* of the other texts. But the passages from the *Dream of the Cross* inscribed upon the Ruthwell Cross contain several important variants from the text of the poem preserved in the *Vercelli Book*.

All the pieces noticed in the last paragraph are very short. There are only two poems of any length preserved in more than one MS. One of these is the *Address of the Soul to the Body* contained in the *Exeter* and the *Vercelli Books*. Here, apart from cases of corruption, omission, and modernisation of orthography, there are a considerable number of variants. In one case (12 ff.) two *Exeter* lines correspond to three *Vercelli* lines, owing to a fuller text in the latter; and something similar is to be found in 84 f., though the *Vercelli* reading here is hardly metrical. In sixteen cases the *Vercelli* text has pronouns, pronominal and other adverbs, prepositions or the word 'all', which are wanting in the *Exeter* text, while the latter has three such cases which are wanting in the *Vercelli* text. In between fifteen and twenty cases the two texts use different words (e.g. *bewitige—geþence*), where the variation cannot be attributed to misreading. In one case (123 f.) we find transposition of a whole line, in three cases transposition of individual words. The common part of the text[2] amounts to 120 lines in the *Exeter Book* and to 126 lines in the *Vercelli Book*; but the omissions in either case may be due, at least partly, to accident. Yet in view of what has been pointed out it is clear that the textual tradition is of a different kind from what is found in the *Saxon Chronicle*.

In the other case the textual tradition shows even greater freedom of treatment. There can be no doubt that the first part (1–75) of the poem generally called *Azarias* in the *Exeter Book* is of identical origin with a portion (280–365) of the poem *Daniel* in the *Junius MS.*, though a good number of lines found in the latter are wanting in the former. The variations are much the same as in the previous case; but out of the seventy-five lines common to the two poems only twenty-three are

1 The later texts have *wera* against the North. *uerc*—which gives a different sense. But this change may be due to misreading or misunderstanding of the original.

2 The rest of the poem is preserved only in the Vercelli MS.

identical.[1] Usually the variation affects only one word in the line—perhaps a preposition or an added pronoun—but occasionally it affects a whole line. The correspondence between the two poems ends with the fourth verse of the hymn *Benedicite, Omnia Opera*. The rest of the hymn is contained in both poems, but they have only an occasional line or half-line in common. After the conclusion of the hymn also they are independent, except in one passage (*Daniel*, 412–16; *Azarias*, 170–5). In this case no single line is identical, but there are agreements which cannot be due to accident.

The two cases just noticed are of course not quite parallel. *Daniel* and *Azarias* are not the same poem, though they contain a large common element, which must have been taken either by one of them from the other or by both from a common source.[2] But the divergences noted above give rise to the question whether the relationship is due to copying. In the later passages (*Az*. 94 f., 105 ff., 170 ff.) it seems to us much more probable that the resemblances are due to memory. In the first part (1–75) the case is not quite so clear. We think there is a third possibility, intermediate between copying and the unaided use of memory. There may have been persons to whom it was easier or more natural to make use of their memory than to copy even when they had a written text at hand. This of course means treating the material as spoken poetry rather than as script; and it is much easier thereby to account for the frequent alterations of the text—whether deliberate or not. It is to be observed that, with rare exceptions, both readings are metrically correct and give good sense.[3] We are inclined to think that this is the true explanation of the variants in the *Address*—possibly also of the divergences between *Azarias* (1–75) and *Daniel*, though in regard to this we are doubtful.[4]

Whatever the explanation may be, we have in *Daniel* and *Azarias* the case of two poems beginning with a common opening and subsequently diverging. For this we shall find parallels later in oral poetry. Now we may take the case of a portion of one poem incorporated in another

[1] We have not counted differences in inflectional endings in either poem.

[2] It is commonly held that ll. 280–409 are an addition to *Daniel*. But the relationship between the two poems is not clear to us and hardly essential to the present discussion.

[3] As against readings produced in the scriptorium. Thus in the *Battle of Brunanburh*, 13, the oldest MS. (A) has *secgas hwate* for *secga swate*. The words are correct in themselves, but give no sense.

[4] The question might perhaps be settled by a careful examination of the orthography, especially the use of equivalent letters, such as þ and ð.

poem. The *Genesis* is the longest and perhaps the earliest of the religious poems; quite possibly it may be the work of Caedmon himself. But after l. 234 one or more leaves are lost in the only MS., and then, from 235 to 851, comes a long passage translated from a German (Old Saxon) poem on the same subject. The rest, from 852 to the end (2935), belongs to the original English poem. There is no break in the narrative at 852; so it may be presumed that a portion of the original poem was omitted, when the foreign passage was incorporated. But owing to the damage to the MS. it is impossible to determine exactly how the latter was introduced.

The German poem was presumably either acquired by an Englishman on the Continent or brought over here by a German. In the latter case it is natural to think of John the Old Saxon, who was made abbot of Athelney by Alfred the Great. The German poem appears to have been composed not long before his time. Only fragments of it now remain, and of these only one, consisting of twenty-five lines, belongs to the portion preserved in the English *Genesis*.[1] Here the treatment is very similar to what we have observed above. Only four lines are identical in the two texts; but in nine others the difference affects only a single word or expression. The majority of the other changes are also slight; but in two cases the English version has expanded one line of the original into two. Some changes, it may be observed, are doubtless due to the occurrence of words which were not current in English. These cases, however, are comparatively few; and in point of fact the translation retains a fair number of words which were either unknown in English or known only in a different sense. Many of the variants are clearly analogous to those which we have noticed in the *Address* and in *Azarias*; and we are no more certain than in the latter case as to whether a MS. was used. It is not impossible that our text is the work of an Englishman listening to the dictation or recitation of a German.

In all the cases noticed above, whatever explanation be adopted, the treatment of the text involves a relationship between authorship and copying—or writing from memory—which is foreign to modern ideas. The nearest analogy is probably to be found in pirated hymns and popular songs. In the next section we shall see that similar phenomena occur in poems which are without doubt derived from oral tradition. Here we shall find examples not only of verbal variation between two texts of the same poem, but also of passages more or less identical which

[1] The two passages are printed side by side in Cook and Tinker, *Translations from Old English Poetry*, p. 184 f.

are contained in two different poems. The evidence seems to us to show that the Anglo-Saxon faculty of improvisation or 're-composition' and the habit of transferring passages from one poem to another are inherited from times when poetry was preserved only by oral tradition.

There can be no question as to the importance of oral tradition in the history of early Norse poetry. It is universally agreed that a considerable body of poetry survives from the tenth century and an appreciable amount—though fragmentary—from the ninth. Yet nothing was committed to writing[1] until a much later period—apparently the latter part of the twelfth century. This means a period of nearly three centuries from the time of Harold the Fair-haired; but from the evidence at our disposal there seems to be no reason for doubting the authenticity of the poems dating from that reign. Snorri, in the prologue to the *Heimskringla*, states that these poems were still known to many people in his time; and many fragments of them are preserved in quotations in his own works and elsewhere. It is generally believed that some of the anonymous (*Edda*) poetry is quite as old.

None of the MSS. in which the poems are preserved are older than the thirteenth century; but they are all copies of earlier MSS. Consequently the language shows a mixture of thirteenth- and twelfth-century forms, though the former predominate. The syntax, however, is that of a much earlier period, as in some Anglo-Saxon poems. In particular we may note the complete absence of the article with nouns. The suffixing of the article to the noun is believed to date from c. 1100; but this of course must have been preceded by a transition period when the article was more or less commonly associated with the noun.

Norse poetry, apart from the *Edda* poems, is mostly preserved in sagas and other prose works. The texts show much the same variants in the poetry as in the prose. In general they are not unlike what we find in the *Saxon Chronicle*—especially substitutions of more modern for earlier forms, and misreadings. The variants shown by texts of poems or fragments of poems which are preserved in two or more different works are generally of a similar character. Poems preserved both in a Norwegian work like the *Fagrskinna* and an Icelandic work like the *Heimskringla* show Norwegian forms in the one and Icelandic forms in the other. Such is the case (e.g.) with the poem on the *Battle of Hafs-*

[1] We are referring of course to Roman writing. Poems were sometimes written down in Runic writing in much earlier times (cf. p. 480); but there is no evidence that the texts of any existing poems have been affected by such writing.

fjord and with the *Hákonarmál.* There are cases, however, of variants which are not so easily explained. Thus in st. 1 of the *Eiríksmál*, as quoted by Snorri (*Skaldskaparmál*, cap. 2), there are two variants from the text of the poem contained in the *Fagrskinna*, which give a different meaning to the opening lines. And sometimes still greater variations are found.[1]

The text of the *Edda* poems shows analogous phenomena. There are two early MSS. which contain (or rather have contained) many of the poems—the *Codex Regius* (*R*), of the late thirteenth century, and the *Arnamagnean* (*A*), of the early fourteenth—while a few of the poems also occur singly in other MSS. Large portions of *A* are unfortunately lost; but so far as it is preserved, the variants between it and *R* are of the usual scribal character. On the other hand the text of the *Völuspá* found in the *Hauksbók*, another MS. of the early fourteenth century, differs in many respects from that of *R*. In *A* this poem is wanting. Some stanzas are peculiar to the *Hauksbók*, others to *R*. The order of the stanzas differs greatly, and there are many differences of wording in the stanzas which both texts have in common. Again, the *þáttr af Nornagesti* contains a text of the *Helreið Brynhildar* which differs frequently from that of *R*. The differences are not of such a striking character as in the last case, but they give a different meaning to several passages. We may further note that Snorri's quotations from the *Edda* poems often show a different text from that of *R* and *A*. In all these cases we have to deal with alternative readings, both of which as a rule conform to the rules of metre and convey at least an intelligible meaning.

The question has sometimes been debated whether Snorri's quotations were drawn from MSS. or from memory. To us it seems incredible that a man of Snorri's knowledge can have been wholly dependent upon written sources. Half a century before his time the poems were preserved by memory alone, and it is hardly conceivable that he did not know many of them by heart. Doubtless MSS. were accessible to him, and he may well have consulted them from time to time; but we do not see why he should take the trouble to copy MSS. of poems which he could write out from memory. The disuse of the memorising faculty, which is a result of the printing press, must not be assumed for Snorri's time.

[1] For an example we may refer to a stanza relating to the marriage of Harold the Fair-haired with Ragnhildr, which some scholars believe to have belonged to the *Hrafnsmál*. Text and transl. in Kershaw, *Anglo-Saxon and Norse Poems*, p. 79.

It is impossible of course in a work like this to enter upon a discussion of the elaborate theories which have been proposed in regard to the structure of some of these poems and the relationship of the texts. These theories too frequently rest upon the assumption that a writer who had MSS. before him must have been wholly dependent upon them—an assumption which seems to us inadmissible when applied to Snorri and other well-informed men of his time. It is perhaps in regard to questions of 'interpolation' that this assumption is most prevalent.

Of all these poems the *Völuspá* is probably the one which presents the most complex textual problems. In st. 9 both MSS. speak of the creation of dwarfs, and then (st. 10 ff.) give a long list of them. Snorri also in the *Gylfaginning*, cap. 14, quotes almost the whole passage, and it is clear from the context that he knew it as occurring at the same point in the poem as we find it in the MSS. Most of the names are the same in all three texts—*R*, *Hauksbók* and Snorri's—but the differences, especially in the order, are sufficiently great to make it difficult to believe that any one of them is derived from either of the others. This, however, is one of the passages usually regarded as interpolations. To the modern mind the list may seem a futile enough effort and—what is more serious—it appears out of place in a poem in which dwarfs otherwise play practically no part. But this objection applies with at least equal force if it be an interpolation. We have to account not only for the introduction of such an inappropriate passage but also for the fact that it was accepted by all subsequent writers, including the chief literary man of the age. Snorri would surely have been less inclined to incorporate the passage in his work if he had known that it was an interpolation made during his own lifetime than if he had believed it to belong to the traditional text of the poem.

We do not see why the list of dwarfs should not have come down from the days of oral tradition, whether it formed an original part of the poem or not. A good parallel to it is to be found in the list of mermaids (Nereids) which occurs both in Hesiod's *Theogony* (243 ff.) and, with considerable variations, in the *Iliad* (XVIII. 39 ff.). To the latter poem learned catalogue matter of this kind is essentially foreign. But the *Theogony* is a poem of the same type as the *Völuspá* and comprises both the chief elements of the latter—cosmogony and the conflict between gods and demons, though there are differences in arrangement and in proportion. It is true that the list of mermaids is one of a series of long catalogues in the *Theogony*, whereas the other catalogues in the *Völuspá* are few and brief, and themselves regarded as interpolations by many scholars. Yet such catalogues are not necessarily out of place in a cosmological poem; and the truth may be that the poem has suffered more from omissions than from additions—though we do not mean to suggest that what survives is entirely the work of one man or of one period.

The sequence of ideas is certainly very far from clear. Various attempts at reconstruction have been proposed, involving changes of the most drastic character. We have not the courage to attempt anything of the kind—which indeed we regard as quite hopeless. We are prepared, however, to venture the following remarks:

1. The two MSS. (*R* and *Hauksbók*) are not wholly independent; for they have at least one scribal error in common.[1] But we certainly do not believe that either MS. is wholly derived from the other. There is no satisfactory evidence for a relationship between Snorri's quotations and either of the MSS. He may of course have had a written copy of the poem, but there is nothing to prove it.

2. The order of the stanzas in *R* is more intelligible than in *Hauksbók*; and editors are doubtless right in taking the former as the basis of the text. But we cannot understand how any scribe who had a text arranged like this could have come to rearrange it in the order (or disorder) found in the *Hauksbók*. We are therefore inclined to the view that the copy in the *Hauksbók*, though it is a later MS., represents the original written text of the poem; that the scribe of *R*, or rather one of his predecessors, had this text before him, but that he knew the poem from memory in what he rightly believed to be a better form; and consequently that he substituted his own version in many places for the one he was copying—especially in the central part of the poem.

3. We see no reason for supposing that the text of *R*, though doubtless the better of the two, preserves even approximately the original form of the poem. The impression it conveys to us is that many stanzas have been forgotten, while others may have been added. From the variety in the formulae with which stanzas are introduced—sometimes 'I saw, I know', etc., sometimes 'she saw, she sees' (relating to the seeress)—we are inclined to infer that it was derived from more than

[1] *þriar* for *þrir* in st. 16 (*R*; st. 17, *H*). The mistake can be accounted for in *H* more easily than in *R*. In the former it is followed by *þussa brudir*—which does not connect with what follows. It would seem that the openings of two different stanzas had been confused (cf. st. 8). The evidence for other common scribal errors seems to us inconclusive.

one version, probably in a ruinous state. As to the origin and date of the poem we are not prepared to speculate. One stanza (*R.* 61) suggests the period of transition between heathenism and Christianity, like the Mongan poems. But this stanza stands in no relation to the rest and may be one of the additions.

We may next take the case of poems of which only one text is preserved, but which contain elements—stanzas or lines—which occur also in other poems. Very frequently there is some variation. For an example we may refer to the passage from the *Grímnismál* (st. 41 f.) quoted on p. 321. The first of these stanzas recurs in the *Vafþrúðnismál*, with slight variations as follows: "The earth was formed from Ymir's flesh, and the cliffs from his bones; the sky from the skull of the ice-cold giant, and the sea from his blood". The context of the two passages is quite different.

It is perhaps in poems which deal with the story of Sigurðr and Guðrún that these identical or similar passages occur most frequently. We may refer to a few cases from *Guðrúnarkviða I*, *Guðrúnarkviða II* and *Sigurðarkviða hin skamma*. Thus *G. I* begins as follows: "It was long ago that Guðrún was like to die as she sat by (the dead body of) Sigurðr. She did not weep or wring her hands or make lamentation over (her trouble), as other women do". The scene here is laid in the palace. But in *G. II*, which is a retrospective poem of Type B, the murder is said to have taken place out in the forest. In st. 11 Guðrún says she went to the forest to find the body, and then continues: "I did not weep or wring my hands or make lamentation over (my trouble), as other women do, when I sat consumed (with grief) for Sigurðr". Again, in *G. I.* 18 Guðrún says: "In comparison with the sons of Gjúki my Sigurðr was like a garlic standing out above the grass, or a bright stone, a precious stone, set in a collar worn by a prince". So in *G. II.* 2 she says: "Beside the sons of Gjúki Sigurðr was like a green leek standing out above the grass, or a high-stepping stag beside nimble deer, or fiery red gold beside gray silver". The following passages may also be compared. In *G. I.* 16 it is said that when her sister removed the covering from Sigurðr's body, Guðrún gave way to such violent weeping that "the geese in the courtyard screamed at the sound, the splendid birds which the girl owned". The first part of this sentence occurs also in *Sigurðarkviða*, 29; but here it is introduced as a result of Guðrún's screams immediately after the murder, and it is also said that the crockery rattled. In *G. I.* 25 Brynhildr says: "Atli is solely responsible for all the trouble". In *S.* 27 the mortally wounded Sigurðr says: "Brynhildr is responsible for all the trouble". The reference is in both cases to the same event.

The significance of such parallels as these—which are numerous—seems to us to have been somewhat incorrectly estimated. They have been used as criteria for determining the relative antiquity of the poems. It is assumed that a poem which borrows an expression from another poem must of necessity be the later of the two. If we were dealing with written poetry this would doubtless be true. But it is clear from modern oral poetry—and the same may be said of ballad poetry—in which some freedom of treatment is allowed, that no inference can safely be drawn from such parallels, except that the two poems must once have been current in the same community. *Guðrúnarkviða I* may be a later poem than *Guðrúnarkviða II*, since the latter is called 'the ancient *Guðrúnarkviða*';[1] and both may be later than *Helgakviða Hundingsbana II*, where Sigrún says (st. 39) that her dead husband Helgi excelled (other) heroes as a splendidly shaped ash excels thorns. But the question of priority must be determined by other considerations, if it can be determined at all. The comparison found in the *Helgakviða* and the two *Guðrúnarkviður* may well be a convention of the poetry of the period. Very little Norse heroic poetry survives except the poems relating to Sigurðr and Guðrún and to Helgi; but this is a mere accident. If we may judge from references in other early poems these stories were surpassed in popularity by several other heroic stories—relating (e.g.) to Hamðir and Sörli, to Hagbarðr and Signý, to Heðinn and Högni—which are now known only from one poem, or only from prose paraphrases or from Saxo. It is only when an expression is applied to the same person, as in the two *Guðrúnarkviður*, that one can feel any confidence as to the existence of a connection. Even then it is usually difficult to determine which of the two poems the expression originally belonged to; and this poem is not necessarily the older of the two.

An interesting passage may here be quoted from the poem just referred to—*Helgakviða Hundingsbana II*. In the prose which follows st. 18 it is related that Helgi went with a fleet to attack a king called Granmarr, and that Guðmundr, a son of the latter, espied them from the cliffs. "Then said Guðmundr, as is written above in the *Helgakviða*:

[1] But this expression does not necessarily mean more than that *G. II* was known before *G. I* in the circle where the name was first used. *G. I* was apparently not a widely known poem; it is not used either by Snorri or by the *Völsunga Saga*. But we fail to see how the silence of the *Völs. Saga* can justify a date c. 1150 for the origin of the poem, as has been suggested. There is one good piece of evidence which suggests a date about three centuries earlier (cf. p. 232).

'Who is the leader who commands the fleet and is bringing a terrible host to shore?' Sinfjötli, son of Sigmundr, answered, and this also has been written. Guðmundr rode home with news of the raid", etc. The reference here is to *Helgakviða Hundingsbana I.* 32, where the same event is related; but *H. H. I*, unlike *H. H. II*, is a narrative poem, and contains no prose. "The noble Guðmundr made enquiry: 'Who is the prince who commands the host and is bringing a terrible host to shore'". It will be observed that there are two variants[1] here from the quotation given in *H. H. II.* Then follows Sinfjötli's answer, which leads to a long and abusive altercation between the two (st. 34–44). Finally Helgi intervenes (st. 45 f.) and stops Sinfjötli from replying further. In *H. H. II* the passage translated above is followed immediately by a short account of the battle, also in prose, and this by some speeches in verse by Sigrún and Helgi (st. 19–23). Then (st. 24 ff.) comes a short altercation between Guðmundr and Sinfjötli, which is evidently out of place here, since all Granmarr's sons are said to have perished in the battle. The altercation itself seems to be an abbreviated variant of *H. H. I.* 32–46. Guðmundr begins: "Who is the Skjöldungr (probably used here for 'prince') who commands the ships and flies a golden standard at his prow?" The beginning of Sinfjötli's speech in st. 25 is also a variant of part of the same hero's speech in *H. H. I.* 35. The next two stanzas (26 f.) have little or nothing corresponding to them in *H. H. I*; but in Helgi's speech (*H. H. I.* 45 f., *H. H. II.* 28 f.), which concludes the altercation, the variants, although definite enough, are few in number. *H. H. II.* 29 contains an extra line.

The text of *H. H. II* is obviously much confused. It refers to a passage in *H. H. I*, but the only (very short) piece which it quotes contains variants—although the whole of the MS. (*R*) is said to be in the same hand. Then, later, it introduces the same dialogue again, in a wrong place—after the death of one of the speakers—and with more serious variants. The whole passage may very well have been taken mechanically from an earlier MS. But whoever was responsible, it would seem (1) that the passage referred to has not been copied from the other poem, and (2) that a third variant form has been introduced later—its identity with the others apparently not being recognised. We can only conclude that variant versions of the poems were current at the time when they were committed to writing.

We may next take the poems *Guðrúnarhvöt* and *Hamðismál.* In this

[1] *H. H. I* has *landreki* ('prince') and *liði* ('host') against *fylkir* ('leader') and *flota* ('fleet') in *H. H. II.*

case it will be convenient to give a translation[1] of the opening stanzas of each poem, omitting st. 1 of the *Hamðismál*, which is extremely obscure. The *Guðrúnarhvöt* begins as follows:

(1) "That was the bitterest altercation I have heard of—words difficult of utterance, spoken in great distress—when Guðrún the fierce-hearted incited her sons to violence with cruel words.

(2) 'Why do ye sit? Why do ye sleep away your lives? Why are ye not distressed to talk gaily, when Jörmunrekr has had your young sister trodden down on the highroad by white and black steeds, by the gray horses, the trained coursers of the Goths? (3) Ye have not grown up like Gunnarr and his brother, nor have ye any of the courage which Högni had. Ye would have sought to avenge her, if ye had had the spirit of my brothers or the fierce heart of the kings of the Huns'.

(4) Then spake Hamðir the great-hearted: 'Little wast thou minded to praise the doings of Högni, when they woke Sigurðr from his sleep. Thy black and white coverlets were dyed and drenched in the blood of thy slain husband. (5) A cruel and grievous revenge didst thou take for thy[2] brothers, when thou didst murder thy sons. (Had they survived) united in one purpose we should all have been able to exact vengeance from Jörmunrekr. (6) (But) bring out the treasures of the kings of the Huns. Thou hast incited us to battle'".

In the *Hamðismál* the best we can do is as follows:

(2) "It was not just now nor yesterday, it came to an end much longer ago—there is nothing more ancient, this was twice as far back—that Guðrún, daughter of Gjúki, incited her young sons to avenge Svanhildr.

(3) 'Your sister was called Svanhildr, and Jörmunrekr has had her trodden down on the highroad by white and black steeds, by the gray horses, the trained coursers of the Goths. (4) Ye have fallen below the standard (?) of the great kings; (but) ye are the only surviving strands of my line. (5) I am left in solitude like an aspen in a wood,[3] bereaved of kinsfolk like a fir of its branches, robbed of pleasure like a tree of its foliage, when 'the branch-destroying'[4] comes on a warm day'.

(6) Then spake Hamðir the great-hearted: 'Little wouldst thou have

[1] The translation must in some places be regarded as tentative. Both poems present great difficulties, especially the *Hamðismál*.

[2] The word 'bold' is probably omitted.

[3] Or perhaps 'on a heath'.

[4] We know of no satisfactory explanation. The word is fem.; 'wind' (the usual interpretation) is masc. More probably the reference is to a summer forest fire. *Eldr* is masc.; can *brenna* be intended?

been minded (thus) to praise the doings of Högni, when they woke Sigurðr from his sleep—when thou wast sitting on the bed while his slayers laughed. (7) Thy black and white coverlets, woven by skilled workers, were dyed with his life's blood. Then did Sigurðr die, and thou didst sit beside his dead body with no thoughts of joy. Thus did Gunnarr will it for thee. (8) Thou thoughtest to injure Atli by slaying Eitill and taking the life of Erpr. Still worse for thyself was that. One who uses the murderous sword for a death-struggle with another should not injure himself'".

The common elements in these narratives are obvious enough; but they cease at the points at which we have broken off. In *G.* Guðrún brings the armour from her store-room, and her sons mount their horses. Hamðir prophesies his own and his brother's death. The rest of the poem is a soliloquy by Guðrún, who reviews the sorrows of her life. In *H.* Sörli stops the altercation and prophesies his own and Hamðir's death; but the prophecy is different in detail from the other. Then the brothers set off, and the rest of the poem is occupied with the narrative of their adventures.

The portions of the poems which we have translated amount to twenty-six lines in *G.* and twenty-seven in *H.* Three of these are identical and several others nearly so, while in other passages also there is a close resemblance. *H.* is believed to be the earlier poem, and *G.* is supposed to have borrowed from it. But the latter poem has in places without doubt the better text. Thus in *G.* 4 the speech of Hamðir is clearly an answer to the speech of Guðrún in st. 3. But in *H.* 6 f., which correspond to *G.* 4, his speech is left without explanation. It is held by some scholars that one or more stanzas here have been lost in *H.*, while others regard st. 6 f. as an interpolation (from *G.*). But in reality Guðrún's speech is not lost, though 'great kings' has taken the place of Högni and Gunnarr, and the point is consequently obscured. In the same way the names of the murdered sons are omitted in *G.* (st. 5).

We think that a much simpler explanation of the relationship between the two poems is to be found. It may be observed that they not merely deal with the same incident, but that they are structurally almost identical, so far as the portions translated above are concerned. We find (i) an introductory statement as to the incitement by Guðrún of her sons (*G.* 1, *H.* 2); (ii) the death of Svanhildr by the order of Jörmunrekr (*G.* 2, *H.* 3); (iii) an unfavourable comparison of Guðrún's sons with her brothers (*G.* 3, *H.* 4); (iv) Hamðir's reply referring to the death of Sigurðr (*G.* 4, *H.* 6 f.); (v) the continuation of Hamðir's speech, relating to the killing by Guðrún of her own sons (*G.* 5, *H.* 8). On the other hand there is only one passage of importance which is peculiar to either poem, viz. in *H.* 5, where Guðrún refers to the trees by way of comparison with her solitary and bereaved state.

The analysis seems to us to show clearly that the two passages under discussion (*G.* 1–5, *H.* 2–8) must be regarded as variants, i.e. that the two poems originally had a common introduction. Whatever the explanation may be, the case is parallel to that of the Anglo-Saxon religious poems *Daniel* and *Azarias*. In later chapters we shall find analogies in modern oral poetry.[1]

The *Hamðismál* presents other features of interest for the study of textual history, but these can only be referred to very briefly here. In st. 2 the clumsy and long drawn out passage which indicates the remoteness of Guðrún's time can perhaps best be accounted for if the second and third lines were originally variants, both of which have been recorded, probably by the man who first committed the poem to writing. More interesting is the fact that the *Völsunga Saga*, cap. 42, gives a different account of the fight in Jörmunrekr's hall. The weapons of the defenders prove useless against Hamðir and Sörli; and then an old man, who is obviously Othin, enters the hall and advises Jörmunrekr to attack them with stones. Saxo, p. 338 (281), has the same account and mentions the god by name. But in our text of the poem there is no reference to Othin. The person who gives the order to stone the assailants (st. 24) appears to be Jörmunrekr himself; and this is how Snorri (*Skaldsk.* 42) understood the passage. In this case the variant may have a longer history.[2] It may be added that the poem shows a good deal of metrical irregularity—variation between *Málaháttr* and *Fornyrðislag*. One stanza (27) is in *Ljóðaháttr*—a very rare occurrence in poetry of this kind and usually regarded as an interpolation.

The examples given above will be sufficient to show that numerous variants were current in the *Edda* poems about the time when they were

[1] We may refer especially to the Serbo-Croatian poems relating to Mušić Stefan (Bušić Stjepan) at the battle of Kossovo.

[2] The saga passage is partly derived from the poem and quotes half of st. 26, with insignificant variants. But it also contains some matter—apart from the introduction of Othin—which is not found in the poem. This matter is of a rather childish character and suggests derivation from a popular prose narrative. The question is whether the passage had two independent sources or whether this matter had been incorporated in a text of the poem, like the prose passages in the *Völundarkviða*, etc. Apart from the reference to Othin, the saga passage has nothing in common with Saxo, whose account is quite different.

committed to writing. There is no reason for supposing that they are due in any considerable measure to scribes. When a poem is preserved in both *R* and *A*, the agreement between them is as a rule very close and suggests that scribal tradition in Iceland was not peculiarly free; and the texts of the sagas and of the poems contained in them point to the same conclusion. There can be no doubt that in general the variants are due to oral tradition; and the same may be said of cases where a passage occurs in more than one poem—whether it consists of a line or two, as in the examples noticed on p. 512 or of a long series of stanzas, as in the *Guðrúnarhvöt* and the *Hamðismál.* We may presume that the common elements belonged originally to one of the two poems and were borrowed by the other; but it is quite incredible, at least in the latter case, that they were taken from a written text. The same remarks apply to the elements common to the two *Helgakviður Hundingsbana*, which were noticed on p. 513 f. In this case we have presumably a rather large borrowed element in the interior of a poem—in short what is commonly called an 'interpolation', though we would prefer not to apply the term to such cases.

Another case of such 'interpolation', on a larger scale, is believed by the great majority of editors to have taken place in the *Hyndluljóð*. This poem, which was noticed briefly on p. 278 f., is not preserved in either of the Edda MSS. (*R* and *A*), but only in a much later MS., the *Flateyjarbók*, written c. 1386. It is largely occupied with genealogies and lists of heroes from whom a certain Óttarr is descended. But st. 29–44 deal with a different set of subjects—the origin and relationships of certain gods and other supernatural beings, and various incidents relating to them. St. 29 repeats a refrain which occurs in the first part of the poem—"All this is thy ancestry, Óttarr"—but otherwise it is not easy to trace any connection. The last few stanzas, 45–50, return to the original subject. Snorri (*Gylf.* 5) quotes st. 33 as belonging to 'the short *Völuspá*', which is commonly interpreted as meaning not the *Hyndluljóð* as a whole, but the shorter theological poem incorporated in it. If the prevailing view is mistaken and the theological element belonged to the poem from the beginning, we can only conclude that it has suffered very badly in the course of oral tradition; but this, unfortunately, is in itself by no means improbable.

It was pointed out above that the borrowing of elements by one poem from another need not have taken place when the former was first composed, and consequently that such borrowings cannot prove the relative antiquity of poems, even if we are satisfied as to which of two poems was the borrower. If the opening series of stanzas in *Guðrúnarhvöt* are derived from *Hamðismál*, it is not unlikely on general considerations that they were borrowed when the former poem was composed. But if they were taken by *Hamðismál* from *Guðrúnarhvöt*, we think it less probable that the former only came into existence when they were borrowed; for we think there is reason for believing the main part of this poem to be more ancient than the *Guðrúnarhvöt*. The question of antiquity, however, can in our opinion be determined only by general considerations—by the general character of a poem, not by particular passages.

In this connection it deserves to be noticed that the *Edda* poems, like the great bulk of Anglo-Saxon poetry, are anonymous. In the latter case it is true that our ignorance as to the authors may sometimes be due to the paucity of our information regarding the history of vernacular literature. But in the case of Norse poetry it is possible to speak with more confidence. The fact that we do not know the author of the *Eiríksmál* (cf. p. 344) is doubtless due to mere accident. The prose authorities, when they quote, sometimes give the name of the poem, sometimes that of the author; and in this case both Snorri and the *Fagrskinna* give the former only. But it cannot possibly be due to accident that in all his numerous quotations from the *Edda* poems Snorri never once mentions an author's name; and the same is true of the quotations from these poems in other authorities. It may be regarded as certain that, in spite of all the literary activity of the twelfth and thirteenth centuries, the authors of the *Edda* poems were not known.

How is this anonymity to be explained? The poets of the reign of Harold the Fair-haired were well known; and Bragi Boddason lived apparently even before the time of that king. None of the *Edda* poems are usually believed to be earlier than this. Anonymity can hardly have been necessitated by the nature of the theme; for stories of the gods are treated in Thjóðolfr's *Haustlöng* and in Eilífr Guðrúnarson's *Þórsdrápa*. Yet it is true that heroic poems of Types A and B which date from times of oral tradition are as a rule anonymous. This applies not only to Anglo-Saxon and other ancient poems, which some scholars believe to have been written, but also to Yugoslav, Russian and Turkish poems, where writing is out of the question. We believe that the same is commonly true also of similar poems relating to the gods. But account is also to be taken of the variants noticed above, which show that these poems were treated with very great freedom. And it is to be borne in mind that the metre and diction are much simpler and more archaic than what we find in most of the poetry of the ninth and following centuries.

The conclusion to which all these considerations seem to point is that the *Edda* poems were regarded as ancient—in a sense which modern scholars will not allow. It is customary now to assign some poems to the ninth century, others to the tenth, others again to the eleventh and even the twelfth centuries. This may in general be more or less true of the form in which we now have them, though we must confess to some scepticism in regard to the precise dates usually assigned. It is at all events significant that in a good number of cases opinion varies very greatly. It is also significant that one of our leading authorities assigns six of the heroic poems to Greenland and almost all the rest to Norway, while another holds that the majority of them come from Iceland. The evidence is in fact ambiguous. One passage in a poem may suggest a certain date and place of origin, while another passage in the same poem may point in quite a different direction. But in spite of differences in detail it is generally agreed that the evidence, such as it is, applies to the composition of the poem—which is regarded as a new work, though concerned with an old theme. We doubt if this represents the contemporary view. We suspect that what was produced at a certain place at some date—say in the eleventh century—was regarded at the time not as a new poem, but as a 'rendering' of an old poem, however drastic the changes which were introduced.

To the modern reader this idea seems strange. To take an extreme case, we cannot regard the *Atlakviða* and the *Atlamál* otherwise than as two distinct poems. Both are concerned with the same series of events—the treacherous invitation sent by Atli to his brothers-in-law, Gunnarr and Högni; the attack made upon them on their arrival; their deaths; and the vengeance taken upon Atli by his wife Guðrún, who is their sister. Both poems are described by their titles in the MS. as belonging to Greenland. It is commonly held that this is correct only for the *Atlamál*; but one cannot deny the possibility that the man who first collected or wrote down the poems may have obtained them both from Greenland. The *Atlamál* refers (st. 18) to white bears, which suggests Greenland, and contains (st. 88) a definitely Christian expression, which is unparalleled elsewhere among the heroic poems and can hardly be earlier than the eleventh century. On the other hand it also refers (st. 105) to ship burial, which points to a somewhat earlier date. More important, however, than these details is the general treatment of the story, which seems to reflect the colonial life of the northern seas. There are no great palaces or armies; even Atli has only thirty warriors. The brothers set out on their journey by sea, not on horseback, as in the *Atlakviða*.

There is but little verbal agreement between the two poems, and each of them has various features peculiar to itself. We may instance the dreams of Gunnarr's and Högni's wives, which occupy eighteen stanzas in the *Atlamál*. Yet in spite of all differences it is impossible to deny a connection between the poems. Not only is the general course of events the same in both; but what is more important is that both have in common a number of incidents which can hardly be due to anything but poetic invention. One of these is the ring sent by Guðrún to warn her brothers; it may be observed that the details are quite different. Still more interesting is the introduction of a person who appears to be a fictitious character,[1] the cowardly Hjalli. In the *Atlamál* he is a cook; but in the *Atlakviða* his position is not stated. The incident in which he figures is different in the two poems—he is killed in one, but apparently not in the other—and so also is the motif of the scene; but in both cases his introduction is bound up with the fate of Högni.

If the two poems are of a common origin the differences between them must be due to difference of treatment. In the *Atlamál* the treatment has evidently been what we may call revolutionary. The milieu has been adapted to that of settlers in a maritime land, such as Iceland or Greenland. It may be noted that even the burial ship is to be bought. This freedom of treatment is what might be expected from the metre, in regard to which the poem stands by itself in the *Edda* collection. It is regarded as the standard example of *Málaháttr*, which is generally believed to be a rather late development from the mixed type found in the *Atlakviða* and the *Hamðismál*. On the other hand the *Atlakviða* appears to be very conservative. Gunnarr and Högni are represented as wealthy princes. The scene is laid among the great forests and grasslands of the Continent; and the horse is all-important. We may note too that it is only in this poem (st. 18) that the historical name 'Burgundian' is preserved. Moreover, in spite of the great difference in motif between the Norse and the German versions of the story, there is a remarkable resemblance between one incident in the poem (st. 26 f.) and a passage in the *Nibelungenlied* (st. 2370 f.), which cannot be accidental. In the former passage Gunnarr, when he sees the heart of Högni brought to him, says to Atli that he alone now knows where the

[1] We cannot see any ground for identifying him with Rumolt in the *Nibelungenlied*.

treasure of the Niflungar is hidden and that he will never disclose the secret. In the latter Kriemhilt brings the head of Gunther to Hagen, who says that he and God alone now know the secret of the treasure and that he will never reveal it to her. Here the rôles of Gunnarr and Högni are reversed, and Atli's part is taken by his wife, as throughout; but an ancient poetic motif is clearly preserved.

The story of Hamðir and Sörli is preserved only in one poem, though we have seen (p. 517) that there are traces of variants. But the main features of the story were known in the ninth century, as may be seen from the fragments of Bragi's *Ragnarsdrápa*, which describes the heroes as descendants of Gjúki (i.e. sons of Guðrún) and mentions Erpr, the third brother, and the cutting off of Jörmunrekr's hands and feet. A somewhat different form of the story is given by Saxo, p. 338 (280 f.). He records the last feature and also the quarrel on the way, though he does not mention Erpr's name, nor even those of his brothers. He also knows of the barbarous death of Svanhildr, and that they had set out for the purpose of avenging her. Before the attack he makes them consult a witch called Guðrún (Guthruna), who blinds their opponents. But this person is not their mother—to whom there is no reference. The unhistorical feature, found in all the Norse sources, that Jörmunrekr's assailants were the sons of a sister of Gunnarr, who died nearly seventy years after Jörmunrekr, is unknown to Saxo. Indeed he does not refer to the stories of Sigurðr, Guðrún and Atli. Jörmunrekr's men are helpless until Othin removes their blindness and instructs them to stone their enemies.

Apart from the connection with the story of Guðrún, the main features of Saxo's account, which is wholly in prose, agree with the poem. The common original of the two must go back beyond the ninth century. References to the story are found also in German and Gothic sources. The former mention the cutting off of the king's hands and feet. Jordanes, cap. 24, representing the Gothic account, says merely that he was wounded, and that he died later, partly in consequence of the wound, partly through old age and distress at the Hunnish invasion. It is generally agreed that Jordanes is here trying to reconcile two different accounts, one of which he knew from poetic, the other from historical sources. We know from a contemporary authority, Ammianus Marcellinus, XXXI. 3. 2, that Jörmunrekr committed suicide through fear of the Huns. We do not know what foundation in fact there was for the poetic account. But the chief features of the story—the death of Svanhildr and the vengeance attempted by her brothers, whom Jordanes calls Sarus and Ammius—were familiar by the middle of the sixth century. There is no need to suppose that the story was then new.

We see no reason for doubting that the poem written down in Iceland about the close of the twelfth century is the direct descendant of a poem current in the Ukraine or the Balkan peninsula seven or eight centuries previously. Russian poems relating to the time of Vladimir the Great, who reigned in the Ukraine during the latter part of the tenth century, were collected and written down less than a hundred years ago; and the collectors found the poems best preserved in the Governments of Olonetz and Archangel. Now they are said to be best preserved in remote parts of Siberia. From Iceland or Greenland we have also poems which give an account of Attila's death. The account is unhistorical, but in all probability it was connected, as we have seen (p. 185 f.), with a story which was current in the Roman Empire within a century of the event. We do not doubt that the history of the Atli poems goes back to the fifth century.

It may perhaps be objected that we are here confusing 'poem' and 'theme'. But the theme cannot have existed without being incorporated in some form of poetry or saga; and there is no evidence for any intensive cultivation of saga among the Teutonic peoples in early times. It is not unlikely that Saxo derived his material from saga, since his narratives are always in prose; his verse passages are all speech poems of Type B. But Saxo's material, whether Danish or Norse, was such as was current in the twelfth century. It does not follow that heroic narrative poetry was unknown in Denmark several centuries earlier, when the stories made their way to the North. The facts are as follows: (i) Heroic poetry of Type A was current in England and Germany in the eighth century, and it was certainly cultivated by the Frisians until the end of the seventh century at least. (ii) Similar poetry is found in the Norse world. It is much abbreviated in form, but it bears all the marks of antiquity; and there is no narrative poetry relating to later times. The natural conclusion would seem to be that such poetry was once known also in Denmark—the intermediate region—but that it died out there some time before the twelfth century, as it did apparently among the North Germans and the Frisians. In this connection we may note that though the Danes figure more prominently than any other people in stories of the Heroic Age, both Norse and English, we have no traditional records relating to Denmark between the sixth and the ninth centuries. Our knowledge of that period is a blank. It would seem then that the cultivation of saga in Denmark, as in the North, was a development of the Viking Age. Its traditions reached back no further than the beginning of the ninth century. What remained of heroic narrative poetry after this may have been transformed into saga—a process for which, in its initial stages, analogies are to be found in the North, e.g. in the *Battle of the Goths and Huns* and probably in the *Völundarkviða.*

We have spoken only of poems of Type A. Poems of Type B may originate in more than one way, as will be seen in a later chapter. We are inclined to think that all the Norse heroic poems of this type are of secondary origin—that they are scenes taken from heroic stories, or rather from heroic poems of Type A, for intensive study of situation or emotion. A transitional phase is to be seen in such a poem as *Guðrúnarkviða I*, which contains a number of narrative stanzas. We do not think that poems of this type relating to the gods, such as the *Skírnismál*, are to be explained in the same way; but we prefer to postpone discussion of such poems until parallels from other languages have been considered. It is quite possible of course that the existence of these has contributed to the development of the heroic Type B, though the fact that most of them are in the *Ljóðaháttr* metre is rather against the suggestion. More likely the influence came from 'post-heroic' poems like the *Hrafnsmál*, which sometimes contain a small narrative element.

It should be mentioned that a view directly opposed to ours has been expressed by various scholars, viz. that the speech poem (Type B) is the earlier type and that the narrative was originally given in prose, as in *Helgakviða Hundingsbana II* and *Helgakviða Hjörvarðssonar*. This view has frequently been associated with a theory that all early Teutonic poetry was originally strophic (stanzaic) and that even *Beowulf* was composed in stanzas—a theory which we are unable to accept (cf. p. 21) and which we believe is now not so widely held as it was formerly. Apart from the strophic theory and from general considerations, which cannot be discussed here, it is an argument for this view that of the two *Helgakviður Hundingsbana* No. I, which is of Type A, is generally believed to be a later—we should prefer to say less conservative—work than No. II, which is of Type B, with the narrative in prose. But a poem may belong to an earlier type and yet be less conservative than another poem; and we believe that nearly all scholars would agree that some poems of Type A, e.g. the *Hamðismál* and the *Atlakviða*, are at least as old as any heroic poems of Type B.

At all events the evidence noticed above seems to us to leave no doubt that poetry of Type A was the common property of the Teutonic peoples about the close of the Heroic Age. It is possible that this poetry had developed out of poetry of Type B, with the narrative in prose, as in Irish sagas; but we must defer consideration of this question until we have discussed the heroic poetry of other peoples. We would only say that, should this prove to be true, it is possible that poetry of the earlier phase may have survived in the North. But we think it more probable that this poetry was a product of the Viking Age, perhaps not uninfluenced from Ireland, and that it represents a phase midway between the old Teutonic heroic poems of Type A and the narratives interspersed with poems of Type B which are found in some of the *Fornaldar Sögur*, especially *Hálfs Saga* and *Hervarar Saga*. Type A was a dying type, which seems to have found its last home in Greenland; but the poems of this type had had a very long history.

The Welsh evidence is on the whole very similar to the Norse. We have seen (p. 33 f.) that almost all the early poems are contained in one or other of four MSS., the oldest of which—the first part of the *Black Book of Carmarthen*—is hardly earlier than the middle of the twelfth century. Archaic orthography, however, which is much more frequent than in Norse, shows that many poems are derived from texts written in the tenth century, or possibly even in the ninth. This is the earliest point to which the history of the texts can be traced, though a good number of the poems are addressed to persons of the sixth century, while others claim to be the work of poets who lived in the same period.

Very few poems are found in more than one of these MSS., and consequently the material available for the study of variants is limited. An example occurs in *Tal.* I, which corresponds to *RBH.* XXIII. 84–123 (the end). The first part of the poem is wanting in *Tal.* I, owing to the loss of a leaf. In what remains the differences from *RBH.* XXIII are of a purely scribal character.

Another case occurs in *BBC.* XIV, which corresponds to *Tal.* XXI. 58–67 (the last stanza). The differences here are somewhat greater, and cannot in all cases be due to carelessness on the part of scribes. They are perhaps to be compared with the variants found in certain Anglo-Saxon religious poems, noticed on p. 505 f.

In other cases there can be no doubt that the variants are due to oral tradition. Thus the last three lines of *RBH.* XVII—a poem to which we shall have to refer again shortly—are clearly a variant of the four lines which appear at the end of the panegyrics upon Urien in the *Book of Taliesin* (XXXI–XXXVI, XXXIX). But the differences are not of a scribal character.

The same remark applies to the whole of the poem which celebrates Gereint, preserved in *BBC.* XXII and *RBH.* XIV. This poem contains in the former text eighteen (three-line) stanzas, in the latter twenty-four, of which two are incomplete. Two stanzas are peculiar to the *Black Book*, and eight to the *Red Book*; and, apart from these, one stanza in each poem has only one line in common. In regard to the order of the stanzas the two texts have hardly anything in common. Thus, if we take the first nine stanzas of the *Black Book*, we find that in the *Red Book*, so far as they occur, they come in the following order: 4, 3, –, 6, 10, 8, –, 15, 14. The last stanza in the *Black Book* corresponds to the first stanza in the *Red Book*. Moreover, there are many variants in the stanzas which correspond. Thus in the *Black Book*, st. 8, we find "In Llongborth I saw Arthur"; but the corresponding passage in the *Red Book* (st. 15) has "In Llongborth Arthur was slain". Such textual variation as this points clearly to a long period of independent oral tradition.[1]

These appear to be the only cases in which a whole poem or a considerable part of a poem is preserved in more than one of the four ancient MSS. The *Book of Aneirin* itself, however, frequently contains more than one text of a stanza, sometimes with remarkable variants. The last six stanzas of *An.* I, which are in a different hand from the rest of the poem, are all variants of stanzas which have occurred previously. In two cases, st. 89 and 92, which correspond to st. 78 and 86 respectively, the resemblance is very close, amounting to substantial identity. In the remaining cases, st. 90, 91, 93, 94, which correspond to st. 52, 48, 40, 41, the variations are considerable and materially affect the meaning. It will be observed that there is little agreement in the order of the stanzas.

Still more striking evidence is to be found in a series of stanzas, thirty-seven in number, which are preserved at the end of the MS., after *An.* V, apparently as a kind of supplement. It is recognised that at least fourteen of these are connected with stanzas in *An.* I. The nature of the connection varies greatly from case to case. No. 35 is substantially identical with I. 63, while in other cases the connection is obvious only in a few lines. The great majority of the cases lie intermediate between these two extremes. Here again there is a total want of agreement in the

[1] From the somewhat fatuous character of the latter part of the poem, in which the hero's horse is compared to eagles of various colours, one is tempted to suspect that the poem had suffered pretty badly even before the two (traditional) texts had come to diverge. But it is unsafe to apply modern aesthetic criteria to poetry of this kind. An analogy may be found in *BBC.* XXXII.

order of the stanzas. The stanzas in the 'Supplement' which show a connection with *An.* I are Nos. 1, 6, 7, 8, 10, 13, 19, 20, 24, 27, 28, 34, 35, 37, while the stanzas in *An.* I to which they correspond respectively are 51, 23, 20, 22, 62, 26, 48, 42, 68, 70, 69, 65, 63, 66.

It is clear from this comparison that at least one of the texts must be in an advanced state of disintegration; and the fact that the poem is still very much of an unsolved problem renders it more than probable that this is true of both of them. Hence we do not regard it as legitimate to draw conclusions as to the date of the original composition of the poem from isolated words or expressions which occur in it; and the same remark applies to most of the early Welsh poems. It has sometimes been inferred from certain words[1] that the *Gododdin* poems cannot be earlier than the ninth century. To such inferences the same objection holds as in the case of the *Edda* poems; but here it is stronger in proportion as the texts are worse preserved.

We have seen (p. 160) that this collection of poems, or at least a nucleus of them, is concerned with a body of heroes who went to battle inflamed with drink under a prince, otherwise unknown, called Mynyddawg. The scene of the disaster was a place called Catraeth, which is probably to be identified with Catterick. The names given to the enemy are Deivyr and Brenneich, i.e. Deiri and Bernicii. The date cannot have been later than the close of the sixth century. Yet in I. 89 (78) we hear of the death of the Scottish king Domnall Brecc, which took place in 642. Moreover the poems contain a suspicious number of references to Gwynedd and Anglesey. It is of course by no means impossible that heroes from North Wales took part in such a distant expedition—Cadwallon invaded Yorkshire and Northumberland in 633–4. But the number of such references rather suggests that considerable additions have been made to the original matter.

For such additions we find a good parallel in the *Appletrees* (*BBC.* XVII). It was noted above (p. 454 f.) that this poem is known from two later texts, of which one contains twenty-three and the other twenty-two stanzas against the *Black Book*, which has only ten. The latter seem to refer to no events later than the eleventh century—from which

[1] E.g. from the word *Gynt*, 'heathen' (usually 'Vikings') in I. 94; cf. *Rev. Celt.* XX. 204, XXXII. 209. This stanza is a variant of st. 41, and is obviously to be taken in connection with the preceding stanza (93; cf. 40). The same inference has been drawn from the word *taryaneu*, 'shields', in *An.* II. 10. Such words prove only that the poems were treated freely in the Viking Age—which is in full accord with what has been pointed out above.

we may infer when the poem was originally composed. But some—not all—of the stanzas which occur only in the later texts are concerned apparently with the politics of the twelfth century. It may be observed that here again there is little agreement in the order of the stanzas, as between the *Black Book* and the later texts. The stanzas in Stephens' text corresponding to the stanzas (1–10) contained in the *Black Book* come in the following order: 23, 17, 13, 10, 5, 6, 18, 19, 20, 8. Between the other texts there is more agreement; but the discrepancies are considerable. Thus corresponding to Stephens' st. 1–6 we find in the *Myvyrian* st. 1, 6, 7, –, 13, 14. On the other hand, the variations within the stanzas themselves are comparatively slight between all three texts and limited to one or two words in each stanza, with occasional omission of lines. Most of them indeed appear to be scribal.

This poem is of great importance as an illustration of the statement quoted on p. 130 from Giraldus Cambrensis, *De Vaticiniis*, that the bards were in the habit of adding new prophecies to the old. We may remark that in the light of the *Gododdin* poems it would seem that the application of his statement might be extended to other forms of poetry, as well as prophecies—at least as regards the bards of earlier times. The poem is also of interest as showing that sometimes—apparently in the twelfth century—the words of stanzas were preserved more or less exactly, while complete freedom or negligence prevailed in regard to the order of the stanzas. It is to be remembered of course that the poem as we have it, even in the *Black Book*, is comparatively late; not more than a century need have elapsed between the composition of the oldest and that of the latest political prophecies contained in it. Yet there is no valid reason for doubting that the framework (cf. p. 454), as distinct from the prophecies, preserves elements—whether one prefers to say 'reminiscences' or 'nucleus'—dating from times as early as the *Gododdin* poems. We suspect that these elements have had a history comparable to some extent with that of *Guðrúnarkviða I* or *Guðrúnarkviða II*. But the problems of textual variation, with which we are here primarily concerned, relate only to the twelfth century.

RBH. I and II present many interesting textual problems; but in the absence of a critical edition we do not think that any useful purpose would be served by discussing them. A later text of the second poem seems to have had a much earlier poem attached to it (cf. p. 456 f.). But we do not know at what stage this took place.

Next we may take the case of poems which have one or more stanzas in common. A striking example occurs in *BBC*. XXXIX, which is concerned with the sons of Llywarch Hen. Here four stanzas (Nos. 7, 8, 10, 11) correspond to stanzas in *BBC.* XXX (Nos. 33, 35, 8 and 20 respectively), and two other stanzas (Nos. 6 and 12) to stanzas in *RBH.* XI (Nos. 58 and 66). The variants are merely graphic, except as between st. 6 and *RBH.* XI. 58, where different words are used in two cases, though there is little difference in meaning. As *BBC.* XXXIX contains only twelve stanzas, half of it is shared with the other two poems. All three claim to be the work of the princely poet Llywarch Hen.

BBC. XXX. 8 has two lines in common with st. 17 of *RBH.* X,[1] a poem which makes no claim to be Llywarch's work, while *RBH.* XI has one stanza (No. 14) corresponding, with slight variations, to a stanza (No. 9) in the gnomic poem *RBH.* VI (cf. p. 388). Those who are more familiar with these poems than we are will probably know of other parallels. Our examination is doubtless far from being exhaustive.

Of all the textual problems presented by early Welsh poetry perhaps the most remarkable is to be found in *RBH.* XVII. The greater part of this poem belongs to the predictive series (cf. p. 457), relating to affairs of the twelfth century or slightly earlier. But the first eight lines are a panegyric upon Urien; and after the predictive portion (9–37) the same subject is reverted to in 38 ff. The last three lines, as we have seen (p. 525), are a variant of the formula with which several of the panegyrics on Urien conclude. Immediately before this (42 f.) the poem claims to be the work of Taliesin and also speaks of Aneirin. Whatever may be the explanation of this last passage, it would seem that a political prophecy of the twelfth (or eleventh) century has been inserted in the middle of a panegyric upon a king of the sixth century. The former relates to Wales (Gwynedd and Powys), the latter to the north; and in other respects also the two have nothing in common.

Yet even this case is not wholly without analogy. We have already (p. 460) had occasion to refer to *Tal.* XIV, a speech poem of Type B, in which the speaker is obviously Taliesin. The poem relates how he sang before Brochfael of Powys and Urien—a passage much like *Widsith*—and how he rescued Elphin at the court of Maelgwn. It refers also to some purely legendary experiences of Taliesin, partly connected with the story of Branwen. Finally the speaker says that his chair is prepared in 'Caer Sidi', of which a description is given similar to that of Mag Mell in the poems contained in the *Voyage of Bran.* All this may well be of quite early date, in spite of the mixture of historical and unhistorical elements. But the poem contains also two passages, each

[1] This poem (*ad fin.*) has an unusual reference to reading.

probably of eight lines, which are wholly out of harmony with the rest. They are concerned with the national troubles of the Cymry and appear to be taken from late predictive poetry. Two lines (39 f.) are practically identical with two lines in *BBC.* XVIII, st. 22. These insertions—for they can hardly be described otherwise—may perhaps be connected with the adaptation of the story of Myrddin to the political propaganda of the eleventh and twelfth centuries. At this time political prediction was evidently the most popular form of poetry and would seem to have been able to force its way into any early poetry preserved by oral tradition—Taliesin poems among the rest.

From what has been said it will be clear that early Welsh poetry has been subject to a very large amount of change and disintegration—more even than the *Edda* poems—in the course of oral tradition. We can never be sure that we have the original words of the authors before us. Some poems, however, even very early poems, may have suffered less than those which we have discussed. The best preserved are perhaps to be found among the panegyrics in the *Book of Taliesin* and the elegies in the *Red Book*—not including the poem upon Gereint. Irish analogies (cf. p. 466 ff.) suggest that some of the 'mystical' poems in the former book also contain elements which are ancient in form, as well as substance. All these groups of poems present difficulties enough; but that is only what might be expected if they are as old as they claim to be. It is quite possible that some of these may have been committed to writing in early times. But the Norse evidence shows that even in times of purely oral tradition some poems are more faithfully preserved than others. In particular the panegyrics and elegies composed for kings of the tenth century appear to have been treated far more conservatively than most of the *Edda* poems.

We regret that we are unable to deal with the question of variants in early Irish poetry and 'rhetorics'. As regards the relations of the two, it is believed that in various passages in sagas poems have been substituted for rhetorics. But we do not know whether in any case both the poem and the rhetoric have actually been preserved—whether in the same or different texts.

Stanzas certainly occur sometimes in more than one poem—usually in somewhat variant form. An example may be found in the first poem in the *Voyage of Bran*, st. 25; this occurs also, with variants, in a poem which Mongan is said to have composed in honour of St Columba.[1]

[1] Text and transl. in Meyer and Nutt, *Voyage of Bran*, I. 88 f.

The former poem bears also a general resemblance to other poetic descriptions of Mag Mell, e.g. in the *Sickbed of CuChulainn* and, more briefly, in the *Adventure of Connla the Fair* (partly rhetorics) and the stanzas[1] in the third *Courtship of Etain* (cf. p. 52), in which Midir invites Etain to return to him. In the last case the description of Mag Mell—here called *Mag Mor* or the 'Great Plain'—seems to be somewhat out of place.

References to Christian ideas occur in most of these poems, as also in other poetry relating to heathen times. Thus Adam's sin is referred to in the poems both in the *Sickbed* and in the *Courtship of Etain.* If we are right in believing (cf. p. 262 f.) that the doctrine of Mag Mell flourished especially during the period of transition from heathenism to Christianity, it is possible, though not very likely, that this poetry contained such references from the beginning. But both the long poems in the *Voyage of Bran* contain series of stanzas (26–8 and 45–8) which can hardly be explained in this way. In both cases they are quite out of harmony with the rest of the poem; and they appear to have been inserted as correctives to the heathenism by which the poems are permeated. Analogies are to be found in the Welsh mystical poems, e.g. at the close of *Tal.* XIV, immediately after the passage relating to 'Caer Sidi' (cf. p. 469).

Early Greek literature offers comparatively little scope for the study of textual problems like those which have been discussed above. The reason for this lies partly in the fact that, apart from the Homeric and Hesiodic poems, the remains consist almost entirely of fragments—passages quoted in the works of later authors. On the other hand the text of the Homeric and Hesiodic poems themselves appears to have been more or less fixed in early times.[2]

Variants similar to the Norse and Welsh examples noticed above are, however, by no means unknown in the Homeric Hymns. Thucydides (III. 104) quotes two passages from the *Hymn to Apollo of Delos* (cf. p. 357), which he ascribes to Homer. In the first passage, corresponding to ll. 146–50 of the Hymn, four lines out of the five show appreciable variations from our text, though only one gives a marked difference of meaning. In the second passage, corresponding to 165–72, there is

[1] Transl. by Stern, *Zeitschr. f. celt. Philol.* v. 532 f.

[2] Some remarks on the text of the Homeric poems will be found in Excursus II, following this chapter.

only one variant worth noting. But taken as a whole the variants are clearly not such as could be due to scribal error. They certainly come from oral tradition in some form, whether Thucydides himself was quoting from a written text or from memory.

Again, it was noted on p. 244 that the opening lines of Hymn III are a variant of Hymn XVIII. In point of fact only three of the nine lines are exactly identical; but the variations in the others are comparatively slight and quite parallel to those which we have just spoken of in Hymn I. 146–50. The last two lines of Hymn III (579 f.) similarly correspond to the last two lines of Hymn XVIII (10 f.), one of the two being identical. But between the exordium and these concluding lines Hymn III narrates a long story of Hermes' adventures, whereas Hymn XVIII passes straight from the exordium to the conclusion. There can be little doubt that the elements common to the two Hymns are variants of the conventional exordium and conclusion appropriate to hymns to Hermes.

Parallels extending over a few lines are to be found in other Hymns, e.g. between Hymn XVII and Hymn XXXIII. In Hymn XXV four of the seven lines are practically identical with Hesiod, *Theog.* 94–7; but they may of course be taken from it direct.

The parallelism between Hymns III and XVIII suggests that the resemblances between the lists of mermaids (Nereids) found in Hesiod, *Theog.* 243–62, and in *Il.* XVIII. 39–48 may be due to some similar cause. The names, which are for the most part obviously poetic inventions, number fifty-one or fifty-two in the former list and thirty-three in the latter. Of these only eighteen are common to both lists. But one line (*Theog.* 248, *Il.* 43) is identical in both, and another (*Theog.* 250, *Il.* 45) differs only in one word, while there are resemblances also in two other lines (*Theog.* 245 f., *Il.* 40, 42). Moreover it may be observed that the last eight names in the *Iliad* do not occur in the *Theogony*, while only one of the last twenty-one names in the *Theogony* occurs in the *Iliad.* The common elements therefore are practically confined to the first parts of the lists; and here the distribution of the names points to a common origin. In the *Theogony* this is merely one of a number of imaginative lists, whereas the *Iliad* contains no parallel. But there is no reason for supposing that the former poem was the first essay in catalogue poetry of this kind. One of the verse catalogues, current in oral tradition, from which it drew, may well have been the source—differently expanded—of the list incorporated in the *Iliad.* We may compare the list of dwarfs in the *Völuspá* (cf. p. 510).

Another example of such catalogue poetry is to be found in the list of the distinguished women seen by Odysseus in the home of Hades (*Od.* XI. 235–327). We do not know of any passage which bears a relationship to this comparable to the relationship between the passages from the *Iliad* and the *Theogony* noticed above. But its affinities clearly lie with the Hesiodic Catalogue (*Eoiai*, etc.) and with the last part of the *Theogony*. Indeed it hardly differs from these except in the recurrent formula ('I saw—'). On the other hand it has no bearing upon the context in which it stands in the *Odyssey*.

This passage, however, is merely an incident in the long narrative which the hero gives of his adventures to Alcinoos, and which occupies the whole of Books IX–XII. It has been observed above (p. 435) that this narrative as a whole shows a striking contrast to all that we know of heroic poetry elsewhere. In the fact that it consists of a series of adventures similar to folktales it has an analogy in *Beowulf*. But it has not been assimilated, like *Beowulf*, to heroic story; heroic characteristics are practically wanting. The milieu is that of the age of exploration rather than that of the Heroic Age.

In Greek unfortunately there is little evidence available from independent poetic traditions, such as we find in English, Norse and German, by which the history of a heroic story—or rather of a heroic poem—can be traced back to the far past. For the story of Agamemnon and his family an independent tradition does appear to have been preserved (cf. p. 183 ff.), probably in the form of saga; but for the subject of the *Odyssey* we have nothing. Consequently any attempt to trace the history of the poem must depend upon internal evidence, which is unsatisfactory at the best. Yet few of those who admit the principle of growth in any form will doubt that the history of the poem began with the return and vengeance of the hero, and that all the three narratives which occupy the first half of the poem are of secondary origin. The characteristics of these three narratives, which differ greatly, as was noted on p. 234, seem to us to point to a chronological sequence in their (original) composition. All of them are works of fiction; but one (the *Telemachy*) is concerned with a heroic milieu, the second with a milieu which is imaginary but shows reminiscences of the Heroic Age, the third with a milieu which is remote from the heroic. It is difficult to believe that any of them can have come into existence except as subsidiary, or rather preliminary to the heroic story which forms the subject of the second half of the poem. But they may well have originated as poems of a series, rather than as parts of one poem. The object of the second and the third was presumably to satisfy curiosity as to the adventures of the hero during his absence.

One is naturally reluctant to add to the number of hypotheses which have been put forward with regard to the history of the Homeric poems. But the evidence admits of nothing better—apart from analogies in the heroic narrative poetry of other peoples, which will require consideration later. Provisionally the case may be stated as follows. We have a very long narrative poem (over 12,000 lines), the latter part of which is concerned with what appears to be a heroic story (A). The first half consists of three fictitious narratives (B, C, D), which lead up to this story, and the characteristics of which seem to reflect different ages. In the poem as we have it C is introduced within B, shortly before the end, and D within C, also towards the end.[1] Our suggestion is that these narratives were originally separate poems, and that the *Odyssey* has attained its present proportions partly by incorporating them. But the original story itself has also doubtless been greatly expanded and transformed. We should hesitate to allow that either the incident of the bow or the prominent part played by the swineherd Eumaios belonged to this. The other elements also may of course contain different strata.

Analogies in the form of fictitious stories or scenes connected with a heroic story are not wanting in early Norse heroic poetry. As an instance we may cite the *Helreið Brynhildar* (cf. p. 221), perhaps also the *Oddrúnargrátr* (cf. p. 234). The second part of *Beowulf* may have had the same origin. All these, however, are sequels, not preliminaries, to the original story. We know of no Teutonic examples of the latter, apart from stories, like those of the Trilogy (cf. p. 27 f.), relating to a hero's birth and childhood. Instances, however, are to be found in Irish heroic sagas, especially in some of the 'Stories preliminary (*Remscéla*) to the *Táin Bó Cuailnge*'. Such is the case with the *Táin Bó Regamna*, where the Bodb encounters CuChulainn and prophesies to him the evils which she will bring upon him during the raid. A somewhat looser connection is to be found in the *Táin Bó Dartada* and the *Táin Bó Regamain*.[2] Further analogies occur in the heroic poetry of other peoples, as we shall see later.

It may be observed that, though the fictitious accretions to the story

[1] D occupies Bks. IX–XII, except for the interlude XI. 330–84. C occupies Bks. V–VIII and resumes at the beginning of Bk. XIII. B occupies Bks. I–IV and resumes at the beginning of Bk. XV. Bk. XIV is occupied with Odysseus and Eumaios—a scene which resumes at XV. 495. We are not prepared to speculate as to whether this belonged originally to C. It is doubtless fiction and probably late.

[2] Cf. Thurneysen, *Ir. Heldensage*, p. 303 ff.

of Odysseus included in the *Odyssey* cease with the hero's return,[1] there is clear evidence for the existence of imaginative poems dealing with his subsequent career and fate. This formed the subject of the *Telegony*, a poem attributed to a certain Eugammon of Cyrene, who is said to have lived early in the sixth century, while a different form of the story is implied in Hesiod, *Theog.* 1011 ff. Indeed at least one passage in the *Odyssey* itself (XI. 118 ff.) betrays acquaintance with speculations on the subject—from which we may probably infer that it was treated in poetry at the same time as the hero's earlier adventures, or soon afterwards.

We believe that the growth of the *Iliad*—as of other similar long epics—is to be explained on the same principles, partly by expansion, and partly by the incorporation of supplementary (mainly fictitious) stories and scenes. As an example of the latter process we may probably take the Doloneia (cf. p. 233). But the history of the *Iliad* is more complex than that of the *Odyssey*.

With regard to the lost poem *Cypria* two interesting items of information have been preserved. In the Epitome[2] contained in Proclos' *Chrestomathy* the poem is said to have concluded with a catalogue of the allies of the Trojans. If this was the same list which we find in the *Iliad* (II. 816 ff.)—and there is no reason for thinking otherwise—we must infer that some doubt prevailed as to which of the two poems it belonged to. Again, Herodotos (II. 117) states that according to the *Cypria*, when Alexandros (Paris) abducted Helen, he had the advantage of a favourable breeze and a smooth sea and consequently arrived at Troy within three days of leaving Sparta. He also notes (II. 116) that in the *Iliad* (VI. 289 ff.) Alexandros is said to have gone out of his way on this voyage and visited Sidon. From this discrepancy he concludes that the *Cypria* was not the work of Homer. But according to the Epitome of the *Cypria* Alexandros was overtaken by a storm on the voyage and driven to Sidon, which he captured. This suggests the existence of rather serious variants in the text of the *Cypria*—unless of course it was emended after Herodotos' time, so as to bring it into conformity with the *Iliad*.

When one is reading the Epitome, it is difficult to resist the suspicion that the *Cypria*, or at least a good part of it, was originally composed as an introduction to the *Iliad*, and that some of the incidents treated in it were suggested by passages in the latter poem. But inferences relating

[1] The closing scene of the poem—at Laertes' home—may be a further example.
[2] Printed in Kinkel, *Epicorum Graec. Fragmenta*, p. 16 ff.

to the characteristics of lost poems are unsafe. Possibly the *Iliad* itself may in some cases be drawing from the *Cypria* or its sources.

In a book like this it is obviously impossible to attempt anything like a comprehensive treatment of saga texts. The material both in Irish and in Norse is far too great. In general it must suffice to observe that the variants between different texts of a saga are on the whole comparable with those between different texts of a poem, though MSS. of sagas are often much more numerous. Sometimes the variants are slight and of the ordinary scribal character; sometimes they are great and due to deliberate alteration. A text may be abbreviated or expanded; and in the latter case the expansion may be due to the incorporation of matter from known or unknown sources. If the source is unknown the question often arises whether it has been invented by a scribe or 'editor' or derived by him from a lost document or from oral tradition. Lastly, we meet not unfrequently with a story or series of events treated by two sagas which appear to be more or less independent, though they may have common elements or features. We propose to confine our attention to this last case, taking one Norse and two Irish stories.

An interesting example of this kind is to be found in the story of Guðríðr daughter of Thorbjörn, the family of Eric the Red, and the discovery of America. This story is told in two quite different forms—one in *Þorfinns Saga Karlsefnis* (*Þ. K.*), sometimes called the *Saga of Eric the Red*, the other in the *Flateyjarbók*.[1] We will first give a synopsis of *Þ. K.*

Cap. I coincides, to a large extent verbally, with the *Landnámabók*, II. 15, and is believed to be derived from it. It describes how Auðr, widow of Ólafr the White, king of Dublin, went first to Scotland and then to Iceland. The conclusion of the chapter corresponds, though not quite so closely, with a passage in *Landn.* II. 17, which is concerned with one of the queen's freedmen named Vífill and relates how she gave him land.

Cap. 2 agrees, again to a large extent verbally, with *Landn.* II. 14. It relates how Eric the Red left Norway and settled in Iceland. There he

[1] Both works are transl. by G. M. Gathorne-Hardy, *The Norse Discoverers of America*. An account of the MSS. will be found *ib.* p. 100 ff. It should be observed that *Þ. K.* is here called the 'Saga of Eric the Red', whereas in the Reykjavík edition this name is applied to the first part of the story as told in the *Flateyjarbók*. Both usages can be justified; but in order to obviate ambiguity we have avoided using the name. The greater part of both works is also transl. by J. I. Young, *Narratives of the Discovery of America*. Here also the 'Saga of Eric the Red' is what we call *Þ. K.*

becomes involved in a feud, in which he is supported by Thorbjörn, son of Vífill,[1] among others. In consequence of this feud he has to leave Iceland. He goes to Greenland, which he colonises.

In cap. 3 the saga becomes independent. First (*a*) we have an account of Thorbjörn Vífilsson and his daughter Guðríðr. (*b*) A certain Einarr proposes marriage with Guðríðr; but Thorbjörn, who is a very proud man, takes offence at the proposal, and decides to go to Greenland to join his friend Eric. (*c*) The ship loses half its company through plague; but the survivors eventually arrive at the settlement of a certain Thorkell, where they stay for the winter. (*d*) Greenland is suffering from famine; and Thorkell invites a witch to prophesy what will happen. She requires someone to sing a certain spell in order to attract the spirits. Guðríðr is the only person present who knows the spell, and sings it, somewhat reluctantly—for she is a Christian—but with great success. The witch foretells the end of the famine and then prophesies Guðríðr's own future—a prophecy which turned out to be quite correct. (*e*) Thorbjörn and Guðríðr continue their voyage till they reach Eric's settlement.

In cap. 4 (*a*) Leifr, son of Eric, sets out for Norway, but is delayed in the Hebrides. (*b*) Thence he comes to Norway and joins the court of King Ólafr Tryggvason, who commissions him to preach Christianity in Greenland. (*c*) The next summer he sets out for home, but sails far out of his course, and lights upon an unknown land, where he finds self-sown wheat and vines. (*d*) Eventually he reaches Greenland, and on the way he rescues people (unnamed) on a wreck, and brings them home with him. (*e*) He converts many of the people of Greenland, though not his father, to Christianity. (*f*) Curiosity is aroused by Leifr's account of the unknown lands he had seen; and his brother Thorsteinn persuades Eric to join him in an attempt to find them. (*g*) As they are starting, Eric falls from his horse; but nevertheless they both set out on Thorbjörn's ship. But the voyage proves unsuccessful.

In cap. 5 (*a*) Thorsteinn, son of Eric, marries Guðríðr. (*b*) They go to live at a place called Lýsufjörðr, where they join another Thorsteinn, whose wife is called Sigríðr. (*c*) Plague breaks out; Thorsteinn, son of Eric, and Sigríðr die—a detailed and gruesome scene. (*d*) Guðríðr goes to live with Eric, her father-in-law. Thorbjörn, her father, dies.

In cap. 6 (*a*) Karlsefni and Snorri set out to Greenland. (*b*) The same

[1] It is generally believed that one or two intermediate generations have been forgotten. Nearly a century must have elapsed between the arrival of Queen Auðr in Iceland, and Eric's settlement of Greenland.

summer another Icelander, named Bjarni Grímolfsson, also sets out. (*c*) They all arrive at Eric's home, and are hospitably entertained by him for the winter. (*d*) Karlsefni marries Guðríðr.

In cap. 7 (*a*) curiosity again rises about the land of vines (Vínland); and in the summer three ships set out to look for it. The first is that of Karlsefni and Snorri, the second that of Bjarni. The third is the ship which had belonged to Thorbjörn; it is manned by Greenlanders, under Thorvarðr, husband of Eric's illegitimate daughter Freydís, Thorvaldr, son of Eric, and Thórhallr, surnamed the hunter. (*b*) They follow Leifr's directions, and come in succession to the various lands described by him—to which they give names, Helluland, Markland, etc. On one headland they find the keel of a ship, and this they call Kjalarnes ('Headland of the Keel'). (*c*) A Scotch man and woman, called Haki and Hekja, who had been given to Leifr by Ólafr Tryggvason, and who are exceedingly swift on their feet, are sent out to explore, and come back with grapes and self-sown wheat. (*d*) The expedition camps at a place called Straumfjörðr. (*e*) Provisions run short. Thórhallr the hunter is lost. When they find him he is engaged in an incantation to Thor, as a result of which they find a whale, but are all sick after eating it.

In cap. 8 a division of opinion occurs as to the direction to be taken. Thórhallr with a small party sets off on one ship, but lose their way. Eventually they are cast up on the coast of Ireland, where they perish.

In cap. 9 f. the rest of the expedition proceed to a place called *í Hópi*, where they form a settlement. Here they are visited by natives called Skrælingjar, who come in boats by sea and trade with them. In cap. 11 however they are attacked by the same natives, and take to flight. They are saved only by the courage of Freydís. In cap. 12, thinking the place unsafe, they return to Straumfjörðr, which they had left a year before. But it is stated that according to another form of the story, Karlsefni and Snorri with the greater part of the company had only been away two months, while Bjarni and Guðríðr had remained at Straumfjörðr.

In cap. 13, Karlsefni sets out to look for Thórhallr; but Thorvaldr is shot by a native, a 'one-leg'. In the following winter there is much disorder, the unmarried men attacking those who had wives. When summer comes, they start on their homeward journey. It is remarked that Karlsefni had a son born the first year, called Snorri, and that the child was three years old when they returned.

Cap. 14 is concerned with the fate of Bjarni Grímolfsson, whose ship, after leaving Greenland, proved to be unseaworthy. In cap. 15 it is related that Karlsefni and Guðríðr returned next summer to Iceland; and the saga closes with an account of their descendants.

Now we may take the story as told in the *Flateyjarbók*. The first three chapters of this are given in Vol. I, pp. 429–32, under the title *þáttr Eireks Rauða*, or the 'Episode of Eric the Red'; the remainder in Vol. I, pp. 538–49, under the title *Groenlendinga þáttr*, or 'Episode of the Men of Greenland'.

Cap. 1 corresponds, in part verbally, to *þ. K.* 2, and is doubtless derived from the same source.

In cap. 2 Leifr, son of Eric, is said to have gone to Norway sixteen years after his father had settled in Greenland. He attaches himself to King Ólafr Tryggvason, and is baptised. Cap. 3 is concerned with one of Eric's friends named Herjulfr and his son Bjarni. The latter is an active merchant sailor, constantly voyaging between Iceland and Norway. Once on his return home he finds that his father has gone to Greenland; so he sets off after him, but loses his way. He comes first to one unknown land, then to another, then to a third; but holds on his way till he comes to Greenland. There he settles with his father and gives up voyaging.

In cap. 4, when the story begins again (p. 538), we find (*a*), in contradiction to what has just been said, Bjarni is again in Norway, at the court of Earl Eric (r. 1000–1014). (*b*) When he returns to Greenland, there is much curiosity about the lands which he had seen. Leifr buys his ship, and persuades his father Eric to join him in an expedition to look for them. (*c*) As they are starting, Eric falls from his horse, as in *þ. K.* 4 (*g*); but he turns back, and Leifr proceeds alone. (*d*) Leifr comes in succession to the various lands described by Bjarni. He gives the name Helluland to the first, and Markland to the second. This passage corresponds to *þ. K.* 7 (*b*). (*e*) In the third land he builds houses, and prepares to explore. In cap. 5 (*a*) a German called Tyrker is lost; and Leifr sets out with a party to find him. (*b*) Tyrker soon appears with grapes—with which they fill their boat. Leifr calls the country Vínland. (*c*) On his return voyage, Leifr finds a ship-wrecked party on the rocks. Among them is a Norwegian called Thórir with his wife Guðríðr. (*d*) Leifr rescues the party, and takes Thórir and his wife home with him; and Thórir dies shortly afterwards of plague. (*e*) Eric the Red dies. (*f*) Thorvaldr desires to explore Vínland and borrows Leifr's ship.

Cap. 6 deals with Thorvaldr's expedition to Vínland, where he stays two winters in Leifr's houses. We may note (*a*) that he gives the name Kjalarnes to a certain headland, but the circumstances are different from the account given in *þ. K.* 7 (*b*). Here the name is due to an accident to Thorvaldr's ship which is repaired at the place. (*b*) Eventually a battle takes place with the Skrælingjar. Here again the circumstances are quite different from those of Thorvaldr's death in *þ. K.* 13. Thorvaldr is buried in Vínland, and his followers return home.

In cap. 7 (*a*) Thorsteinn, son of Eric, marries Guðríðr, daughter of Thorbjörn, and widow of Thórir. (*b*) Thorsteinn and Guðríðr start for Vínland to recover Thorvaldr's body. (*c*) They lose their way and come to Lýsufjörðr in Greenland. (*d*) They are invited to stay with Thorsteinn the Black and his wife Grímhildr. (*e*) Grímhildr and Thorsteinn, son of Eric, die of plague. This scene closely corresponds to *þ. K.* 5 (*c*). (*f*) Thorsteinn the Black brings Guðríðr to Leifr.

In cap. 8 (*a*) Thorfinnr Karlsefni arrives from Norway. (*b*) Guðríðr marries Karlsefni by the advice of Leifr. (*c*) Karlsefni and Guðríðr go to Vínland and stay at Leifr's houses. (*d*) Skrælingjar come from the forest and trade with Karlsefni. (*e*) Guðríðr's son Snorri is born. While she is tending him in his cradle, the Skrælingjar come again to trade; and one of their women visits Guðríðr and says that she also is called Guðríðr. (*f*) The trading leads to a fight, and the Skrælingjar flee to the forest. (*g*) Karlsefni and his party return to Greenland.

In cap. 9 two Icelanders arrive from Norway. Freydís, daughter of Eric, gets them to join in an expedition to Vínland with her. When they arrive at Leifr's houses, she breaks the agreement with them, and eventually persuades her husband Thorvarðr and his men to massacre the whole party.

In cap. 10 (*a*) Freydís, on her return, tries to suppress all news of what had happened; but Leifr eventually finds it out, and is deeply indignant. (*b*) At this time Karlsefni sails for Norway, where he disposes of his wares, and then returns to Iceland. (*c*) Karlsefni dies, and Guðríðr keeps house for her son Snorri. Afterwards she becomes a nun. (*d*) The story ends with a list of her descendants. It is added that Karlsefni gave a clearer account than anyone else of all the events related.

Now, if we compare the two stories, it will be seen at once that they have much in common, though each of them has a good deal peculiar to itself.

We need not attach any importance to the resemblances between *þ. K.* 2 and *Flat.* 1, for these chapters appear to have been taken from the *Landnámabók*, probably when the stories were committed to writing. But attention should be paid to the similarity between *þ. K.* 5 (especially (*c*)) and *Flat.* 7 (especially (*e*)), which clearly have a common origin, although different names are given to the wife of the second Thorsteinn. The same is also clearly true of *þ. K.* 10–11 and *Flat.* 8 (*d*) and (*f*). We may note here especially that in both stories reference is made in the first passage to the bellowing of a bull, and in the second to an axe which was picked up by one of the Skrælingjar, though the details in the latter case are quite different. A common origin is also probably to be sought for the incident of the wreck described in *þ. K.* 4 (*d*) and in *Flat.* 5 (*c*); and for that of the accident to Eric in *þ. K.* 4 (*g*) and in *Flat.* 4 (*c*)—although it is to be observed that in *þ. K.* Eric proceeds on the expedition in spite of the accident, whereas in *Flat.* he turns back.

Next we may notice the differences between the two accounts. (1) Each story contains a number of incidents peculiar to itself. The more important of these have been noted in the analysis given above. (2) Important discrepancies are not infrequent. Thus in *þ. K.* 4 (*c*) Leifr discovers Vínland by accident, but in *Flat.* 4 (*d*) he sets out on a voyage of exploration to look for it and builds houses there. Again, Thorvaldr, son of Eric, meets with his death in Vínland according to both stories (*þ. K.* 13; *Flat.* 6). But the date and circumstances are quite different in the two accounts. Again, Guðríðr comes to Greenland unmarried, with her father, in *þ. K.* 3 (*e*), while in *Flat.* 5 (*d*) she is married, and comes with her husband, named Thórir.[1] In the latter case the story of her arrival is connected with the incident of the wreck. (3) The same incident is sometimes related of different persons. Thus, the accidental discovery of the new land is ascribed to Leifr in *þ. K.* 4 (*c*), to Bjarni Herjulfsson in *Flat.* 3 (*b*). Again, the voyage of Karlsefni in *þ. K.* 7 (*b*) seems to correspond to that of Leifr in *Flat.* 4 (*d*). We may also note that after Thorsteinn's death, Guðríðr seems to be under Eric's care in *þ. K.* 5 (*d*) and 6 (*d*), whereas in *Flat.* 7 (*f*) and 8 (*b*) (cf. 5 (*e*)) she is under Leifr's care; Eric is dead. (4) Differences may also be noticed in such cases as the explanation of the name *Kjalarnes* (*þ. K.* 7 (*b*); *Flat.* 6 (*a*)). The story told of Tyrker in *Flat.* 5 seems to be connected in some way with the incidents related of Haki and Hekja and of Thórhallr in *þ. K.* 7 (*c*) and (*e*).

The agreements and the differences noted above can hardly be explained otherwise than by oral tradition. Indeed the existence of a divergent tradition in regard to one part of the story is noted in *þ. K.* 12

[1] It may be suspected that this Thórir (who died of plague) is due to some confusion between her father Thorbjörn and her first husband Thorsteinn. If so, of course, the passage must have a different origin from cap. 7. But this is merely conjecture.

(cf. p. 538). It has been suggested[1] that the story preserved in the *Flateyjarbók* comes ultimately from Greenland. But this story, like the other, ends with Karlsefni's return to Iceland. It contains no reference to events in Greenland after his departure, except a sentence in cap. 3, which may well be due to the writer of the saga. The saga itself contains a passage (*ad fin.*) which suggests that the story is believed to be derived from Karlsefni—though actually he is less prominent in it than in *þ. K.*

But *þ. K.* is concerned far more with Guðríðr than with Karlsefni. The latter does not appear before cap. 6, whereas the saga follows the life of Guðríðr from her girlhood in cap. 3 to her return to Iceland at the end. If convention had allowed sagas to bear the names of women, this saga would surely have been called 'Guðríðar Saga'. We may note in particular a number of personal details affecting Guðríðr's history, which are not otherwise of importance, e.g. in the account of the witch (cap. 3 (*d*)), in the story of her husband Thorsteinn's death (cap. 5 (*c*)), and in the reference to the birth of her child Snorri (cap. 13). Such passages point definitely to Guðríðr as the source of the story.[2] But it may be observed further that the two incidents last mentioned are treated also in the *Flateyjarbók* (cap. 7 (*e*), 8 (*e*)). And here the birth of the child is followed by an adventure of Guðríðr's which is not mentioned in *þ. K.* Indeed from the beginning of cap. 7 the *Flateyjarbók* points to Guðríðr as its source just as much as does *þ. K.* The two stories appear to be variants, derived ultimately from Guðríðr's account of her experiences. This explains the large amount of attention paid to women in both stories. It also perhaps accounts for the fact that both of them are of much greater interest in regard to human relations than as records of exploration. On the latter side they are indeed far from satisfactory.

Extraneous elements are of course not wanting in either case. The first part of the story in the *Flateyjarbók* (cap. 1–6) bears no relation to Guðríðr. The only passage in which she is mentioned (cap. 5 (*d*)) seems to have come from someone who did not know her history. In *þ. K.* the greater part of cap. 13 and cap. 14 probably come from different sources. Some of these notices may ultimately be derived perhaps from members of Karlsefni's crew. The point, however, to which we would

[1] Cf. Gathorne-Hardy, *The Norse Discoverers of America*, p. 139 ff.

[2] The variants in the plague scene are especially interesting. Both stories introduce the supernatural—the activities of the victims after their deaths—at the same points; but the supernatural here may be due to the interpretation put upon the events, rather than to the events themselves.

call attention is that the evidence, in our opinion, points to Guðríðr as the ultimate source of the story; but that in course of time variant forms of it arose, each of which independently received accretions from different sources.

In Ireland, saga has had a much longer history than in Iceland. It began in much earlier times, and even today it is not wholly dead. The problems, however, presented by variants in early and in late texts are not quite the same. It will therefore be necessary to take examples from both; and consequently we shall treat the material more briefly.

First we will take the *Conception of CuChulainn*, a story which is preserved in two early forms, I and II.[1] The chief features which both of these have in common are as follows: (1) The fields round Emain (Macha) are continually stripped by a large flock of birds. In I they are 180 in number; in II, 250. (2) Conchobor and the Ulster chiefs set out in nine chariots to hunt them. (3) Their route lies to the south, over Sliab Fuait. (4) They are overtaken by night. (5) Someone (in I, Bricriu and Conall; in II, Fergus) finds a little house occupied by a married couple, who invite them in. (6) The house proves able to hold them all comfortably, and to provide for them. (7) A child is born in the house during the night.

These agreements clearly prove a common origin for the two forms of the story; but the differences between them are numerous and important. The following especially may be noted. (1) In I Deichtine, Conchobor's daughter, takes part in the hunt as her father's charioteer; in II Dechtire, Conchobor's sister, has been lost for three years with fifty companions. (2) In I nothing is said as to the origin of the birds; in II the birds are Dechtire and her companions. (3) In I nothing more is said of the birds after night comes on; in II Bricriu finds a fine large house, in which are Dechtire and her companions. They have enticed the Ulstermen in the form of birds, but are now in their human form. (4) In I the child is born by the wife of the owner of the little house, who is tended by Deichtine; in II the child is born by Dechtire, when she has been brought from the big house to the little house. (5) In I the

[1] A detailed synopsis of both forms of the story is given by Thurneysen, *Ir. Heldensage*, p. 268 ff., with references to the various MSS. etc. in which they are found. I is transl. by Thurneysen, *Zu ir. Hss.* I. 41 ff.; II by Thurneysen, *Sagen aus dem alten Irland*, p. 59 ff.; by Duvau, *Rev. Celt.* IX. 4–9; by Hull, *The Cuchullin Saga*, p. 15 ff. (from Duvau). The text transl. by Duvau, *Rev. Celt.* IX. 9–13, belongs to I, but does not preserve this version in its original form.

house and its owners vanish during the night. The child is taken to Emain, but soon dies; but after the funeral Deichtine swallows a small creature in a drink of water, through which she becomes pregnant, and bears CuChulainn. In II the child born in the little house is CuChulainn. (6) In I, when Deichtine is pregnant, a man appears to her in a dream and says that he is Lug mac Ethnenn, that he was the owner of the little house and the father of the child, which has now entered into her womb. In II no name is given to either the owner of the little house or to the owner of the big house. Dechtire is the wife of the latter and pregnant (apparently by him) when she comes to the little house. Apart from these differences, each form of the story has a number of features peculiar to itself.

It is hardly possible that either version of the story can have been derived from the other in written form. Both of them can be traced back to early times. I comes from the *Book of Druim Snechta*, which appears to have been written early in the eighth century (cf. p. 490); II is believed to be derived from a text written in the eighth or ninth century. If both of them are derived by oral tradition from a common origin, as we see no reason for doubting, the original story must have been in existence by the seventh century, if not earlier. Incidentally we may observe that this story itself clearly belongs to the class of 'secondary' stories, and could never have come into existence before CuChulainn had become a famous hero. It affords good evidence therefore for the antiquity of the primary story or stories relating to him.

In later times some stories are preserved in a number of widely different versions. As an example we may take the story of the *Sons of Uisliu*, or *Uisnech* (cf. p. 50). The oldest form of the story, known as the *Exile of the Sons of Uisliu*, and preserved in the *Book of Leinster* and two other early MSS., dates perhaps from the ninth century. A much longer version, known as the *Fate of the Children of Uisnech*, is preserved in a number of MSS., the earliest of which dates from c. 1500. This version comprises only the latter part of the story, beginning with Conchobor's decision to invite the sons of Uisnech back to Ulster. It is believed to date from the fifteenth century, or slightly earlier. In addition, several versions of the story, both prose and verse, were taken down from recitation in Ireland and the Scottish islands in the course of the nineteenth century. It is believed that other versions are still current, or were so until recently. There is no doubt that some of the versions had long been preserved by oral tradition. Hence, if all the material were easily accessible—which unfortunately is not the case—

the story would afford good opportunities for studying the growth of variants. Here, however, we can only notice cursorily a few of the questions involved.

First we will take the story obtained by Carmichael from John Macneill in Barra (Hebrides) in 1867.[1] The latter part of this story, rather less than half of the whole, bears a general resemblance to the fifteenth-century version. Sometimes there are even verbal resemblances; but it is much simplified. The only persons mentioned by name are Conchobor, Fergus and his sons, the Sons of Uisnech, Derdriu (Deirdire), and also the following characters who are not mentioned elsewhere: Gealbhan Greadhnach, son of the king of Lochlann, and a druid called Duanan Gacha Draogh. Of these two latter the first is the man—called Treundorn in the fifteenth-century version—who peeps through the keyhole and gets his eye knocked out, while the druid makes the magic sea, and in this respect corresponds to Cathbad in the fifteenth-century version. The 'foster-mother' is sent by Conchobor to look at Deirdire, but her name, Leborcham (Leabarcham), is not mentioned. Cuilionn, who in the fifteenth-century version is Fergus's shield-bearer, appears here as one of his sons. None of the other characters who figure in the fifteenth-century version occur. No place-names are mentioned, except one or two in Scotland. The story is simplified in many respects. Naoise and his brothers perish from exhaustion through struggling with the magic sea. Short poems are introduced from time to time, somewhat similar to those contained in the fifteenth-century version and in similar places; but verbal resemblances are rare.

The first—and rather longer—part of the story deals with Deirdire's life from the prophecy of her birth to her departure from Scotland, and has nothing corresponding to it in the fifteenth-century version, though the subject is treated in the early 'Exile'. This part of the story is less well preserved. The place of Fedlimid, Conchobor's story-teller, is taken by Colum Cruitire ('the harper'), who has nothing to do with Conchobor. The prophecy of Deirdire's birth, and the troubles which were to arise therefrom, is attributed, not to Cathbad, who is not mentioned, but to a nameless and apparently itinerant fortune-teller. No other persons are mentioned by name in this part of the story except Conchobor (Conachar), Fergus, and Naoise and his brothers. Deirdire is brought up in a secret place by the midwife, and discovered there by a hunter, both of whom are unnamed. It is Deirdire's father who sends her to be brought up in the secret place; Conchobor hears of

[1] *Deirdire*, text and transl. by A. Carmichael, 2nd edn. Paisley, 1914.

her first from the hunter. Otherwise the story corresponds in general to the narrative in the *Exile*; and it is remembered that Conchobor is king of Ulster. This part of the story contains no poetry.

The *Lay of the Children of Uisne* was taken down by Carmichael from a smith called Donald Macphie, also in Barra, and in the same year.[1] It is partly narrative, but has more in common with Type B than with Type A. There is no reference here to the early part of the story. The poem deals only with the voyage of Dearduil (Deirdriu) and the Sons of Uisne from Scotland, and their arrival at Conachar's town, which is represented as on the coast. The fight takes place at once; Naois and his brothers are killed in their boat. Dearduil asks permission to go and kiss them, and then borrows from a ship-wright a knife with which she stabs herself to death, after reciting an elegy over the brothers. No other persons are mentioned, and no names of places except one or two in Scotland. From all this it will be seen that the poem differs widely from all the versions mentioned above. But the concluding elegy bears a close and sometimes verbal resemblance to part of the elegy which is preserved at the end of the fifteenth-century version.

Next we may take a story recited to the late Prof. Dottin in 1891 by Thomas Ford in Galway.[2] This story again covers the whole life of Deirdre; but it differs greatly from any of the versions mentioned above. The part played elsewhere by Conchobor is here assigned to a king Manannan, who is not king of Ulster. He is Deirdre's father. At her birth a wizard prophesies that she will be the cause of much bloodshed, and the other kings want to have her put to death; but her father has her shut up in a tower. When she grows up she dreams of a man, and her mother tells her that the description corresponds to Aille (Andle), son of Uisneach. Her mother gets Aille to walk in front of the tower with his brother Ardan and his companions; and when Manannan goes to visit the king of Ulster, she arranges for Deirdre to escape with Aille to Scotland. The king of Scotland (unnamed) recommends them to go to the earl of Dun-an-treoin. There they are followed by Manannan with an army. A battle takes place in which Manannan is defeated, and has to return to Ireland. His adviser now suggests that he should offer a free pardon to the fugitives, and attack them treacherously when he has enticed them back to Ireland. They come; but Naois—who has barely been mentioned up to this point—suspects treachery, and warns his brothers. They beat off the attacking party, but in the

[1] Text and transl. by Carmichael, *Deirdire*, p. 114 ff.

[2] Text and transl. by Dottin, *Rev. Celt.* XLV. 426 ff.

confusion and excitement of the fight they fall upon and slay one another. Deirdre calls upon the grave-diggers to dig the grave big enough for all the three brothers and herself, and celebrates their prowess in a poem, which is not given. The last passage recalls Deirdre's dirge in the fifteenth-century version, especially st. 11. Otherwise this account has no special resemblance to that version, except possibly in the suspicions of treachery, which, however, are here attributed to Naois. The story contains no verse; and it mentions no place-names and no personal names except those which we have noted. It will be seen that Aille has taken the place of Naoise.

Lastly, we may notice a version contained in a MS. dating from about 1800 preserved in the Belfast Museum. Its origin is unknown. It appears to be of considerable length; but only the first part of it has been published[1]—down to the departure of Deirdre with Naoise and his brothers to Scotland. This version is much closer than either Carmichael's or Dottin's to the *Exile*. It preserves the names of Deirdre's father (Feidhlim), the druid (Cathfaidh), and the nurse (Leabharcam), as well as of Conall Cernach and Fergus, and several place-names. But the actual wording has little or nothing in common with the *Exile*. It is expanded a good deal and contains modern ideas. The name *Cailcin* is given to Deirdre's 'tutor'. The published part of the story contains no verse, but there are said to be six stanzas in the later part of it. The later part appears to have more in common with the fifteenth-century version than with the *Exile*. But at the close of the story, before the druid delivers his curse, he and Conall see the king returning with Deirdre, after the sons of Uisneach are dead.

It will be seen that, apart from the last version—the history of which is not clear—the first part of the story in the modern (prose) records differs a good deal from the *Exile*. Yet certain elements are common to all accounts. Thus all contain a prophecy delivered by a druid or fortune-teller in connection with Derdriu's birth, relating to the disasters of which she would be the cause. All accounts also contain a passage in which Noisiu—or the man beloved by Derdriu—is said to have the three colours of the raven, of newly shed blood, and of snow, or a swan. In the latter part of the story all the modern accounts resemble the fifteenth-century version rather than the *Exile*.

At the present time it appears to be the prevalent view[2] that late versions of sagas are usually derived from earlier texts, and that the

[1] Ed. and transl. by D. Hyde, *Zeitschr. f. celt. Philol.* II. 138 ff.

[2] Cf. Thurneysen, *Ir. Heldensage*, pp. 72 ff., 327 ff.

versions now current orally are likewise ultimately derived from written sources. Thus in this case it is held that the fifteenth-century version is derived, as a literary work, from the *Exile*, and that the various versions current orally, whether in Ireland or Scotland, are derived from the former. For the derivation of oral stories from written works plenty of analogies are to be found in ballads. We may refer e.g. to the ballads current in the Faeroes, many of which are avowedly derived from Icelandic books.[1] The simplification and disintegration of the story observable in some of the cases noted above is no greater than what may be found in some of these ballads.

Yet we are inclined to think that in the case of native stories, such as those with which we are concerned, the current view needs reconsideration. It can hardly be doubted that the practice of story-telling has always prevailed in Ireland; and although the possibility of influence from written works is always to be taken into account, we hesitate to believe that the latter would very easily displace the traditional narrative, especially among the numerous reciters who were illiterate. In the case with which we are concerned, it is a serious objection to the current view that apparently all the current prose versions of the story begin with Derdriu's birth, whereas the fifteenth-century version from which they are supposed to be derived begins only with Conchobor's treacherous design of bringing the fugitives back from Scotland. Whence then did the modern versions obtain the first part of the story?

It is true that at least one MS. of the fifteenth-century version, viz. Edinburgh LVI, which was written c. 1700, has prefixed to the text an account of the first part of the story copied from Keating's *History of Ireland*. The same text has likewise taken from Keating the close of the story—after the elegies. One or both of these additions may occur in other MSS.[2] The first, however, is wanting not only in the earliest MS., Edinburgh LIII,[3] which was written c. 1500, but also in O'Flanagan's eighteenth-century text.[4] The conclusion of Edinburgh LIII is unfortunately lost;

[1] Cf. Kershaw, *Stories and Ballads of the Far Past*, p. 166 f.

[2] The first addition (not the second) is prefixed to the edition of the story published by the Society for the Preservation of the Irish Language (2nd edn. 1914). It is not clear to us whether it is derived from the MS. (c. 1740), or added by the editor.

[3] Ed. and transl., with variants from Edinburgh LVI, by W. Stokes in Windisch's *Irische Texte*, II. ii. 109 ff.

[4] Text and transl. by O'Flanagan, in the *Transactions of the Gaelic Society of Dublin* (1808), p. 16 ff.

but the second addition is not found either in O'Flanagan's text, or in the text published by the Society for the Preservation of the Irish Language. The two latter have a quite different and much shorter conclusion, which according to all probability was the original conclusion of the fifteenth-century version—whereas the passage taken from Keating in Edinburgh LVI is inconsistent with what has been stated just before in that MS.; it makes Deirdriu live for a year with Conchobor (as in the *Exile*) after she has gone into the tomb.

It appears to us most improbable that the first part of the story, as told in the modern versions,[1] can be derived from Keating, through the medium of such a text as Edinburgh LVI. Keating, it is true, follows the *Exile* so closely that it is very difficult to trace any differences between the two in texts so remote from both as the modern versions. Yet in two points at least, Carmichael's *Deirdire* agrees with the *Exile* as against Keating and Edinburgh LVI. In the two former Deirdire makes up to Naoise herself, whereas in the two latter Naoise goes secretly to see Deirdre. Again in *Deirdire*, Naoise's brothers try to dissuade him from the adventure—a trait which is not found in Keating or Edinburgh LVI. And apart from this, it is scarcely credible, in view of the great number of place-names in Scotland derived from the story,[2] that it was not known there before c. 1640—a conclusion which would virtually be involved by the hypothesis that it was obtained from a source derived partly from Keating.

We ourselves see no reason why the modern versions should be derived from a literary source at all, though in the latter part of the story they certainly have more in common with the fifteenth-century version (the *Fate*) than with the *Exile*. But we have yet to consider the relationship between the two latter. The theory that the *Fate* was in origin a literary work derived from the *Exile* seems to us unproved, and indeed to be open to serious objections. In the first place, why is the poetry entirely changed? The poems contained in the first part of the story are naturally wanting in the *Fate*. But the place of the elegies at the end has been taken by other (quite different) elegies. In these latter it will be seen that there are important variations between the different texts. In the second elegy (Deirdre's last poem), the variants consist in differences

1 Except possibly Hyde's version, the history of which is obscure.

2 Cf. Carmichael, *Deirdire*, p. 135 f., especially p. 140 f., where it is implied that some of these names, in the neighbourhood of Loch Etive, were in existence before the Reformation. This question might be worth investigating.

in detail, and in the order of the stanzas. But the first (short) elegy, which precedes this in Edinburgh LVI, is a different poem from the elegy which occupies the same position in O'Flanagan's and the Irish Language Society's texts. The latter is mainly occupied with a love-adventure between Naoise and the daughter of the earl of Dun Treoin—a story to which we have no reference elsewhere. Other poems—monologues by Deirdre, and dialogues between her and Naoise—have been introduced at various places in the narrative. At least one of these, the poem beginning 'Beloved land, the land in the east, Britain', etc. must surely be of Scottish origin; for it is full of references to localities on the west coast of Scotland—a parallel to which is hardly to be found elsewhere in Irish saga literature. Probably the poem relating to the daughter of the earl of Dun Treoin is of similar origin, since it refers to a gathering of the host of Alba at Inverness. The evidence of the poetry therefore points to a widespread cultivation of the story.

In the narrative itself it is difficult to see why so many changes were introduced if it was really taken from the *Exile*. We may note especially that the names of nearly all the minor characters have been changed. If the story was preserved by oral tradition, it is easily enough intelligible that confusion should take place (e.g.) between the various persons called Fiacha (or similar names) and Maine. But if the *Fate* was based merely on the written text of the *Exile* these changes must have been deliberate; and it is difficult to see why they should have been made. Moreover there is evidence for the existence of variants long before the fifteenth century—indeed even in the text of the *Exile* itself. Thus in the second prophecy attributed to Cathbad, it is stated that certain heroes will lose their lives through Derdriu. Those mentioned by name are Fiachna, son of Conchobor; Gerrce, son of Illadan; and Eogan, son of Durthacht. But in the narrative itself, towards the end of the saga (cap. 16), it is related that Dubthach and Fergus, in revenge for the sons of Uisliu, slew Mane, son of Conchobor, Fiachna, son of Fedelm, and others, though not the persons mentioned in the prophecy; Eogan is spoken of as alive at the end of the story. Fiacha or Fiachra, son of Conchobor, it is to be observed, is one of the heroes slain in the *Fate*. It is held that this prophetic poem is a later addition to the story; but it is found even in the earliest MS. the *Book of Leinster*. The same list of casualties occurs also elsewhere in this MS., in a poem[1] attributed, probably wrongly, to Kenneth O'Hartigan (d. 975). There can be no doubt there-

[1] Cf. *Rev. Celt.* XXIII. 308 f. (st. 17 f.). In view of the gloss given on p. (*ib.*) 326 (cf. p. 337) it would seem that the translation 'by Eogan' in st. 18 is erroneous.

fore as to the existence of important variants, at least by the middle of the twelfth century.

From what has been said it will be seen that the theory of a literary tradition is beset with difficulties. We see no reason for doubting that the story has had a continuous history in oral tradition. It was written down in the ninth century according to the form—or rather according to a form—then current. It is likely enough that variants already existed. By the twelfth century their existence can be demonstrated. The latter part of the story was again written down, independently as we think, in the fifteenth century, according to a form then current. This incorporated a different and presumably later set of poems than those included in the *Exile*. Some of them came from Scotland,[1] and one points to a ramification of the story which is otherwise unknown. Lastly, the story has been written down in various forms, still from oral tradition, in recent times. These modern versions in general show a greater resemblance to the fifteenth-century version than either to the *Exile* or to one another. We believe the explanation of this to be as follows: in the Middle Ages saga was so prevalent, and the saga-tellers so constantly in touch with one another, in Scotland as well as in Ireland, that a popular saga was bound to develop everywhere on similar lines—whereas from the seventeenth century onwards such conditions no longer existed.

The wordy and florid style which characterises the fifteenth-century version is similar to that of various works dating from the Middle Ages —we may refer especially to the *War of the Gaedhil with the Gaill*— but we doubt if it is properly of literary origin. The love of alliteration suggests that it is derived from the art of the story-teller. It may not be the style which was cultivated by the *filid*; but sagas were told by many other persons besides *filid*, as we shall see in a later chapter. The style of the *Exile* is so concise that one is tempted to suspect that what the writer has given us is for the most part a summary, rather than the actual words in which the story was narrated in his time. This is a

[1] The fact that the two earliest MSS. belong to Scotland may perhaps suggest that the story itself was written down there. Ireland—especially in connection with heroic stories—was doubtless far better known to the Gaels of western Scotland than Scotland was to the Irish; but we are not inclined to attach much importance to the argument. Nothing can be made of the date 1238—with the name *Gleann-masain*—written on one of the leaves of the oldest MS. (cf. Thurneysen, *Ir. Heldensage*, p. 327 f.)—although Glen Masan is one of the places referred to in the poem mentioned above, p. 550. The date is presumably a mistake for MDCXXXVIII, or MDCCXXXVIII.

question, however, which affects many other short sagas, and we prefer to leave it to those who are better qualified than ourselves to express an opinion.[1]

EXCURSUS II

THE WRITTEN EPIC

The last quarter of a century has seen a noteworthy change of opinion with regard to the composition of the Homeric poems and of *Beowulf*. In place of the elaborate and often conflicting theories which had long prevailed among the majority of scholars, the view has been gaining ground that each of the epics is the work of a single author, who wrote his poem much as a modern poet would do. On the question whether both the *Iliad* and the *Odyssey* are the work of the same poet there is less tendency to agreement; but this is, comparatively, a minor question.

This view is attractive from its simplicity. It puts an end to a large amount of speculation which has led to no definite conclusions. In the case of the Homeric poems it has the sanction of ancient opinion. In the case of *Beowulf* no opinion earlier than last century is recorded. Possibly an Englishman of the eleventh century, if questioned, would have expressed a similar belief; but this is quite uncertain.

We regret that we are unable to subscribe to this view. It appears to us to involve the assumption of modern conditions in times for which we have no warrant for believing that they existed. From the fifth century onwards the Greeks thought and worked much as we do. But reasons have been given above (p. 494 ff.) for doubting whether such conditions can have prevailed in (say) the middle of the seventh century—i.e. probably before the date of the earliest extant Greek inscription. We doubt also the existence of a written *Beowulf* in the first half of the eighth century (A.D.). Yet few scholars will propose later dates than these for the composition of the poems.

Apart from these considerations the chief fact to be taken into account is the knowledge of past times shown by the poems. *Beowulf* preserves record of an event which is known to have taken place about two centuries before the time assigned to the composition of the poem, and of many princes, living about the same date, whose historical existence cannot reasonably be questioned (cf. p. 135 ff.). For the persons

[1] Cf. Hyde, *Zeitschr. f. celt. Philol.* II. 141.

and events recorded in the Homeric poems contemporary evidence is wanting; but we have seen (p. 181 ff.) that there is good reason for believing that they also contain a large historical element. How then were these records preserved? The answer is given clearly by the poems themselves, in which we hear not unfrequently of heroic poems sung by minstrels. As we shall see in the next chapter, these heroic poems are sometimes said to be concerned with very recent events. But they had a long history, for they were still current in Hesiod's time; and he speaks of them (*Theog*. 95–101) as dealing with men of old.

Some scholars do not deny that the existing poems are in part at least derived from such poems as these. But they draw a distinction between the two classes of poems, describing the former as literary works, the latter as 'lays'. It is this distinction which requires justification; it appears to us purely arbitrary. Minstrelsy in connection with heroic poetry seems to have died out in Greece before the beginning of the historical period. But it was still current in Hesiod's time; and Hesiod is generally thought to have lived much later than Homer, though some ancient authorities believed them to have been contemporary. In England we have contemporary evidence (cf. p. 556) for heroic minstrelsy, i.e. 'lays', towards the close of the eighth century—at least half a century after the time when *Beowulf* is held to have been written. There can be no question therefore as to the survival of the lay at—and indeed after—the time when the 'literary' poets are supposed to have been at work. It is this literary work itself for which evidence is wanting. The burden of proof therefore rests upon those who assume its existence—those who draw a distinction between the two classes of poems.

No argument can be drawn from the length of *Beowulf*. In other countries, where heroic minstrel poetry is still living—or was until lately—'lays' of over three thousand lines, even such as deal with contemporary events,[1] are not rare, while lays of over two thousand are common. With the Homeric poems the case is different. We do not know of any 'lays'—or indeed of oral poems of any kind—dealing with contemporary events, which run to such a length. Our view is that they were greatly expanded in the course of time—a process for which a certain analogy is to be found in the *Mahabharata*. This expansion was due largely, we think, to the desire to provide consecutive entertainment

[1] We may refer (e.g.) to one of the poems dealing with Omer Pasha's attack upon Montenegro in 1852, which contains 3042 lines; publ. in Vuk St. Karadžić, *Srpske Narodne Pjesme*, v (Vienna, 1865), p. 70 ff.

for festivals which extended over a number of days. We see no reason for believing that a written text was involved. The effort of memorisation involved would doubtless be beyond our powers. But we shall meet with equally remarkable feats of this kind in later chapters.

Expansion may take place either from within, by fuller treatment, or from without by adding new matter or joining one poem to another. There is a widespread impression that the 'lay' was essentially a short poem, in which the action moved rapidly; and the fragmentary poem *Finn* is often cited as the solitary survivor in Anglo-Saxon of this class of poetry. *Finn* may have been a short poem of this character, though it is a little hazardous to judge from a fragment of under fifty lines. But there is certainly no ground for believing that such a description is true of all 'lays', if this means heroic minstrel poems. For the addition of new matter Norse and Welsh examples have been cited above. A probable example may also be found in the latter part of *Beowulf*, from 2200 to the end, which may well have been composed as a sequel to what goes before, though perhaps originally intended for a separate recitation.[1] We think too that similar additions on a much larger scale may be traced in the *Odyssey*, though here they are prefixed to, or included within, the previously existing matter. It may be observed that—apart from the Telemachy—the additions are in the main of an imaginative character, though they contain references to heroic stories. Their object, we would suggest, was to satisfy curiosity as to previous or later adventures of the hero. A parallel to the latter part of *Beowulf* in this respect was supplied by the lost *Telegony*.

The chief cause which prevents *Beowulf* from being generally recognised as minstrel poetry is probably to be found in the fact that the poem is, superficially at least, Christian and contains a large number of Christian expressions, though traces of heathen times, both in practices and in thought, are by no means wanting. A Christian minstrel poem is of course nothing impossible; but the existence of poetry coming down from heathen times is involved in the preservation of historical information, as noted above. The question at issue is whether *Beowulf* is an early minstrel poem, originally heathen but adapted to a new

[1] In this case the connection is very slight and affects only a few lines (2200–2208). Changes similar in principle, though still slighter, were apparently introduced at the beginning and end of Greek heroic poems, when they were treated as parts of a continuous cycle. We may refer to the opening of the *Aithiopis*, as implied in a scholion to the last line of the *Iliad* (cf. Kinkel, *Epic. Gr. Fragm.* p. 34). This last line was apparently adapted so as to serve as the first line of the following poem.

environment, or a new Christian literary work, which has drawn its materials from heathen lays.

A somewhat similar question arises from the linguistic phenomena in the Homeric poems. Superficially, the language is Ionic or something close akin thereto (cf. p. 496); but forms of an earlier, Aeolic, type of language are very numerous. According to the current theory the poems are works of an Ionic writer (Homer), deriving his materials from Aeolic lays, just as *Beowulf* is the work of a Christian writer, deriving his materials from heathen lays.

The evidence for this theory is of course primarily of a negative character: the Homeric poems, being Ionic, cannot themselves be of Aeolic origin; *Beowulf*, being Christian, cannot itself be of heathen origin. And if we were concerned with the possibility only of written poems, such inferences would no doubt be sound enough—apart from exceptional circumstances.[1] But when it is applied to oral (minstrel) poetry, the theory rests on the assumption that this likewise is necessarily rigid—an assumption which is proved to be false by the evidence of the oral poetry current among various unlettered peoples of the present day. In narrative poetry a good deal of freedom is usually allowed to the singer or reciter; he may expand or contract the poems included in his repertoire, and modify the treatment in various other respects. The amount of freedom varies from one country to another and probably from one period to another. Instances will be given in later chapters. For the moment perhaps it will be sufficient to refer to the Norse variants noticed on p. 513 ff., though the treatment here is more conservative than what is usually found in modern oral poetry.

It cannot be admitted for a moment that any great difficulty would be experienced by a minstrel in adapting a heathen heroic poem to Christian conditions, at least if he had any acquaintance with the phraseology of current Christian poetry. As for the translation of the Homeric poems from Aeolic to Ionic, the difficulties to be faced here would be much less than those which were surmounted in translating German poetry into English. It is a question, however, whether this translation of the Homeric poems was not a more superficial thing than is generally supposed. To this we shall have to return shortly.

[1] One must bear in mind the possibility that the translation of the Old Saxon *Genesis* (cf. p. 507) was made from a written text, though we think the alternative explanation is more likely.

With regard to *Beowulf*[1] several scholars have recently expressed the opinion that the author was not only a Christian but a man of learning—even an ecclesiastic 'informed with a spirit of broad-minded Christianity'. We fear that this is crediting the eighth century with the feelings of modern times. The attitude of the Church of that day towards heroic poetry is clear enough from a letter[2] written by Alcuin in 797 to Hygebald, bishop of Lindisfarne. He denounces the clergy for inviting harpists to entertain them when they dine together, and then proceeds as follows: "What has Ingeld to do with Christ? Strait is the house it will not be able to hold them both. The king of heaven will have no part with so-called kings who are heathen and damned; for the one king reigns eternally in heaven, the other, the heathen, is damned and groans in hell". Alcuin, the leading scholar of his age, will have nothing to do with the heroes, because he knows they were heathens.

It has been suggested that in Bede's time, some three-quarters of a century earlier, when the poem is supposed to have been written, a more liberal view may have prevailed among the learned. But there is no evidence for this. It is a remarkable fact that Bede himself never refers to heroic poems or stories, unless indeed, as is possible, these are the *fabulae* and *fabulationes*, which he censures certain monasteries and ecclesiastics for listening to.[3] In either case he cannot have considered them worthy of cultivation. Further, it is clear enough from many passages in his works[4] that he held the same view as Alcuin with regard to the destiny of the heathen. Indeed this was not an individual opinion but the doctrine of the Church[5]; and consequently the hostility of ecclesiastical scholars to stories of heathen times was perfectly logical.

[1] The questions of Christian and of literary influence in *Beowulf* have been discussed more fully in *The Heroic Age*, pp. 47 ff., 73 ff. What is said below is intended to be merely supplementary to this discussion—occasioned by some important works which have been published subsequently. We may refer in particular to Klaeber's edition of *Beowulf*, especially pp. xlviii ff., 437 ff., Chambers, *Beowulf* (*Introduction*), especially pp. 121 ff., 329 ff., Heusler, *Altgerm. Dichtung*, p. 184 ff. In a book like the present it is of course impossible to discuss such questions as these in detail.

[2] Mon. Germ., *Epist. Carol.* II. 124.

[3] E.g. *Hist. Eccl.* IV. 25; *Ep. ad Ecgbertum Episc.* cap. 4. See Addenda.

[4] E.g. *Hist. Eccl.* IV. 13, where Wilfrid is said to have saved the people of Sussex *ab erumna perpetuae damnationis*.

[5] We may cite the story of the Frisian king Redbad, who is said to have withdrawn from the font (in the year 718), when he learned that his heathen ancestors were *in Tartarea damnatione*. He said that he could not do without the company of his predecessors and take his seat with a small party in the kingdom of Heaven. Cf. Plummer, *Baedae Op. Hist.* II. 289, and the references there cited.

Obviously the passage from Alcuin's letter noticed above shows that in his time there were ecclesiastics who took pleasure in the stories. We think it is probably to the influence of such persons that the poems owe their Christian phraseology and also the fact that they were ultimately committed to writing. But we doubt if the time for the latter had come in Bede's day. It is more likely to have been inspired by the action of Charlemagne (cf. p. 483), in whom the national element was strong enough to defy ecclesiastical scruples. By the ninth century too both ecclesiastical learning and ecclesiastical discipline had declined in England. But what we cannot assent to is the description of the persons who patronised the poems as 'learned', in the ecclesiastical, Latin, sense. The learned 'liberal churchman' of the eighth century seems to us as much of an anachronism as the literary epic. The learned clergy would have nothing to do with heroic poetry, because they knew that the heroes were heathens. There is not the slightest suggestion that the ecclesiastics censured were persons of liberal views; they seem rather to be regarded as slack and pleasure-loving. The associations in which they are depicted are not those of the study or the library, but of the banquet; in the references to *fabulae* indeed there are implications of drunken revelry (*potationes*, *ebrietates*). It is to be suspected that as a rule they were persons of defective education, to whom reading and writing were irksome.

Now we may turn to the internal evidence, furnished by the poem itself.[1] It has been contended that the author was a student of the

[1] We cannot take seriously the suggestion, which has frequently been made, that the syntax and diction of the poem show Latin influence—apart from certain theological terms and descriptions of God, which may quite well be derived through the medium of (Anglo-Saxon) religious poetry. Since the same suggestion is made for all other Anglo-Saxon poems—and early German poetry obviously yields nothing free from suspicion—we have to depend upon early Norse poetry for undoubted examples of Teutonic usage. It is unfortunate therefore that the Norse evidence appears to have been disregarded; for nearly all the supposed Latinisms are in common use in the *Edda* poems. Thus *ylda bearn* cannot be separated from *alda börn*, while impersonal constructions like *Beow*. 1787 f. are more characteristic of Norse poetry than Latin. Constructions like 642 f., 1629 f. are very frequent in Norse (e.g. *Atlakv*. 16); so also constructions like 1368 ff., 2350 (cf. *ib*. 21, *Brot* 15, *Guðrkv*. *II*. 5). With 183 ff. we may compare *Háv*. 77, with 1392 ff. *Háv*. 84 ff. [The references are to Bugge's edition.] There is no exact equivalent of *hwilum*... *hwilum*...; but similar usages like *sumir*...*sumir*... are common enough. Hunting for 'influences' in *Beowulf* without reference to early Norse poetry—or any poetry other than Latin—can only lead to mare's nests. The same remark applies to attempts to trace the influence of Virgil without reference to the Homeric poems—or any other heroic poetry. On this question we may refer to *The Heroic Age*, p. 75 f.

Bible. If so, we fear that he did not persevere very far with his studies. There are references to the Creation, the story of Cain and Abel, and the Deluge, but not to any later event, except the Great Judgment. The first of these references (90 ff.) is to a poem in which the Creation was described. The last (1688 ff.) is to a work of art—the hilt of a sword—which depicted the 'beginning of the ancient struggle' between God and the 'race of giants', when the latter were destroyed by the Flood. Neither of these passages proves direct acquaintance with the Bible. Caedmon's *Hymn on the Creation* (cf. p. 477) was famous.

To Cain there are two references. In the first (107 ff.) it is stated that when he had slain Abel, God banished him far from the human race. "From him"—or possibly "from this" (crime or exile)—"sprang all evil broods (*untydras*), *eotenas* (demons) and elves and *orcneas*,[1] also the giants who for a long time struggled against God." The second passage (1261 ff.) is similar, though somewhat shorter. Here it is stated that after the murder Cain made his way to the wilderness. "From him (or 'this') sprang many spirits of fate (?), one of whom was Grendel." The closing words of the former passage are probably to be taken in connection with the passage relating to the Flood. But the Bible says nothing about demons and elves. We suspect that this idea also was suggested by vernacular poetry—possibly by a passage in the poem *Genesis* (987 ff.), which, after relating how Cain slew Abel and the earth drank up his blood, describes the growth of troubles and strife arising therefrom under the simile of the growth (*tuddor*) of a tree.[2] If so, the idea has taken a much more concrete form in *Beowulf* than was intended in the original. But in any case we cannot believe that the demons and elves were introduced by a theologian. They betray a 'barbaric' mentality more appropriate to the professional minstrel.

The longest religious passage in the poem is a kind of sermon (1722 ff.), contained in a speech by Hrothgar, in which he warns the hero against certain sins and bids him remember that death in some form or other will one day overtake him. In a speech of congratulation and thanks—for *Beowulf* has just rendered the king a great service by slaying the monsters—the whole passage strikes us as strangely out of place. The 'sermon' is believed to show the influence not of the Bible itself, but of the religious poems *Daniel* and *Crist*, especially the second part of the latter, which contains the name of Cynewulf. There is

[1] Meaning unknown. The word is supposed to denote monsters of some kind.

[2] A similar idea but expressed in purely abstract terms occurs in the *Exeter Gnomes*, 196 ff.

certainly a remarkable resemblance between *Beowulf* 1743 ff. and *Crist* 761 ff.; and though the other parallels are less convincing, we are not inclined to doubt that the whole sermon is largely derived from poetry of this kind. To those who believe in a 'literary' *Beowulf* the influence of *Cynewulf* presents of course a certain difficulty; for it is admitted that *Beowulf* must have come into existence before Cynewulf's time. The difficulty has been met by the unconvincing suggestion that Cynewulf himself interpolated the poem.

It has not been sufficiently recognised that the resemblances between the passages in *Beowulf* and *Crist* apply to the phraseology and figures of speech rather than to the essentials. Hrothgar specifies three sins—arrogance, avarice, meanness—none of which figure in the latter passage, though the first is prominent in *Daniel*. The same sins—or at least the first and the last of them—are referred to elsewhere in *Beowulf*, e.g. in the account of Heremod, which immediately precedes the 'sermon'. They were sins quite as repugnant to the court as to the Church, the latter (meanness) perhaps more especially to the court minstrel. Indeed one passage (1749 f.) indicates clearly, we think, who was responsible for the 'interpolation'—if such a word is justifiable: "He (the sinner) does not proudly (*on gylp*) present the golden rings (armlets)". The word *gylp* ('boasting, pride') occurs frequently in religious poems in a bad sense, but rarely, if ever, as a thing to be commended. It is a minstrel, not a theologian, who is speaking. He has picked up a denunciatory passage from a religious poem and adapted it to sins which came within his own knowledge. If his source really was Cynewulf's *Crist*, it is of interest to note that additions to the poems could be made as late as the ninth century. There is no need to suppose that all the religious passages date from the same time.[1]

In addition to the long passages noticed above the poem contains numerous expressions and short passages which are likewise of Christian character. This feature is by no means peculiar to *Beowulf*. It is found in all Anglo-Saxon secular poems which run to more than fifty lines, whether they are heroic, gnomic, historical or 'timeless nameless'. It is only in very short poems or fragments, such as *Finn*, the *Ruin* and the *Wife's Complaint*, that such expressions are wanting.[2] Similar

[1] We are inclined to think that most of them are early; but this can hardly be the case (e.g.) with the 'otiose' line *on þæm dæge þysses lifes*, 'in the time of this life' (with accentuation of the article, etc.), which occurs three times in the poem.

[2] It is to be remembered that in some parts of *Beowulf* they occur in less than 1 per cent. of the lines. See Addenda.

expressions occur in the very scanty remains of German secular poetry which survive from the same period. It would seem therefore that they were required by the public opinion of the times, whatever the position of the poet or reciter.

There can be no doubt that the poetry of heathen times also, like Norse poetry, frequently referred to religious ideas and practices; and it is very probable that many of the Christian expressions found in the poems were originally introduced as substitutes for heathen expressions. In this connection we may cite a passage in *Nornagests Saga*,[1] cap. 9, where Gestr is represented as reciting the *Helreið Brynhildar* at Ólafr Tryggvason's court. The members of the court are delighted with the poem and ask him to continue. But the king says: "You need not tell us any more of things of that kind"—and turns abruptly to another subject. The saga is late; but the tenor of the story is quite in accord with what is said of the same king elsewhere. Thus in *Hallfreðar Saga*, cap. 6, he repeatedly reproves the Icelandic poet Hallfreðr for introducing the gods into his poems.

In England too, as elsewhere, when the courts had been converted, minstrels had to adapt their poems to the new conditions, if they were not to scrap their entire repertoire. Here also it was evidently regarded as improper for Christians to listen to purely heathen poems;[2] but heroic poetry still retained its attractions, even for the slacker and less learned ecclesiastics. The minstrel then had two alternatives before him: he had either to represent the heroes as Christians or to denounce them as heathens. Naturally he chose the former course, and accordingly introduced Christian expressions in their speeches, as well as in the narratives. This expedient apparently succeeded in preserving the poems, though the more learned ecclesiastics knew what the heroes really were and repudiated them. But it is to be remembered that in one passage in *Beowulf* the alternative course has been followed, viz. in 175 ff., where the Danes are definitely represented as heathens, praying at heathen shrines, and denounced accordingly in a rather long homiletic adjunct. No satisfactory explanation of this passage is to be obtained from the hypothesis that the poem is the work of a learned Christian writer; one can only conclude that he must have been a very stupid

[1] Transl. in Kershaw, *Stories and Ballads of the Far Past*, p. 33 f.

[2] It is only in spells (both English and German) that heathenism of a pronounced character, unaccompanied by censure or disparagement, is preserved. These presumably come from a humbler class of society; and in any case they were not intended for public entertainment.

fellow.[1] But if it has come down from heathen times and acquired its Christian character gradually and piecemeal from a succession of minstrels, such inconsistencies are natural, perhaps inevitable. Heathenism of a less flagrant kind peeps out often enough both in ideas and in practices.

In later chapters we shall see that transformations of this kind are by no means unknown elsewhere. Here it must suffice to refer to the Irish poems relating to Mongan noticed on p. 468 ff., the heathen nature of which is counteracted by insertions of a Christian character. In Irish saga the treatment of heathen elements was less drastic than in English poetry. Even the gods are allowed to remain, though their true character is obscured—they are made to appear more like ghosts—and the use of the word 'god' (*dia*) is scrupulously avoided. Heathen customs are frequently mentioned, but references to actual worship or sacrifice are suppressed. Sanctuaries and festivals are referred to only in their social aspect. The fact that the heroes were heathen was often realised, and various attempts were made to overcome the difficulty; thus (e.g.) stories were invented to the effect that Conchobor and Cormac mac Airt were converted. And disapproval of the stories is occasionally expressed in MSS. by the scribes themselves.[2]

The text of the Homeric poems received in ancient times, especially in the Alexandrian period, a far greater amount of attention than was ever paid, until recently, to the poetry of the northern peoples. By means of numerous scholia and commentaries it is possible to trace the existing text back to the third century (B.C.).[3] Variants are said to be comparatively few and unimportant; but certain lines and groups of lines are known to have been marked as spurious by some of the scholars of that age. Very early fragments of papyri, however, contain a considerable number of lines which are not found in our texts, though they do not yield much evidence of textual variation in other respects. In regard to these lines much difference of opinion still prevails; some believe that in general they belonged to the original text and that they were eliminated

1 The Danes are Christians in 90 ff. and again in 316 ff., and regularly after this.

2 E.g. in a note appended to a MS. of the *Táin Bó Cuailnge* (p. 369 in Dunn's translation).

3 The only evidence available from earlier times apparently is from quotations in works of the fifth and fourth centuries; and unfortunately we have not sufficient knowledge of Greek literature to deal with this subject. Variants are not unknown. Thus (e.g.) in a quotation from *Il.* XV. 494 ff. Lycurgos (*Leocrates*, cap. 103) has three examples in six lines. None of these affect the sense; but they are not of a scribal character. But we do not know how far this case is typical.

arbitrarily by scholars of the Alexandrian age, while others hold that most of them were additions made at various times.

Alexandrian records speak of texts belonging to individuals and also of texts belonging to certain cities, even as far away as Marseilles; but there seems to be no evidence available, so far as we are aware, which would enable one to determine how long these texts had been independent. The absence of evidence for linguistic variation suggests that their independent existence had not been very long. In the fourth century, before the rise of Alexandria, Athens was the intellectual centre, and doubtless also the bookshop, of the Greek world; and it is most probable that all the texts were ultimately derived from this source, though they may of course have been affected by previous local knowledge of the poems.

The language of the poems points to Athens as the original home of the texts as we know them. It is not true Attic, but—apart from the Aeolic element—it is virtually identical with the language of Solon's poems; and it may well have been the form of language employed in his Laws. The origin of this form of language is not to be considered merely in relation to the Homeric poems; for it is found, as we have seen (p. 496), in the remains of most of the early poets, whatever parts of Greece they belonged to. It appears to have been the form regularly used in Athens for literary purposes down to the close of the sixth century; and we may probably infer that by this time the Homeric poems had begun to be written, though it does not necessarily follow that a complete text was already in existence.

The mixture of forms belonging to different 'dialects'—Aeolic and what we may call Attic-Ionic[1]—which characterises the Homeric poems, may be compared with the somewhat similar mixture which we find in Anglo-Saxon poetic texts. In both cases some process of 'translation' is involved. But the Homeric mixture has this peculiarity, that the Aeolic forms are preserved only where they are required by the metre,

[1] We use this term to distinguish this form of language—'dialect' is of course not strictly correct—from the Ionic of the Asiatic coast. We see no satisfactory evidence for the presence of the latter in our Homeric texts. The preservation of *h* (involving aspiration in various cases) is definite evidence against the prevalent view that our texts originated in that region. In Ionic the loss of *h* must go back at least to the beginning of the seventh century; for the use of *H* for *ē*, which presupposes this loss, had spread to Dorian communities by the beginning of the sixth century, as may be seen from the inscription at Abu Simbel. On the other hand there is no evidence for early Ionic forms—e.g. there is no gen. sg. in *-ēo*. The very early forms are always Aeolic.

i.e. where the corresponding Attic-Ionic forms would be unmetrical. Within these limits, however, the Aeolic forms are more frequent than the non-West-Saxon forms in Anglo-Saxon poetic texts. Thus the word λαός, with all its compounds, including the name of the very prominent hero Menelaos, invariably appears in Aeolic form. The Ionic forms λεώς and Μενέλεως are unknown to our Homeric texts. In other cases we find variation, though the Aeolic forms are usually in an overwhelming majority. Thus in the gen. sing. ending of masculine ā-stems we find both -αο (dissyllabic) and -εω (monosyllabic), the former being more than three times as frequent as the latter. But the proportion in reality appears to be much greater than this; for the great majority of the latter forms—about four out of five—occur before initial vowels, with hiatus, whereas -α' (with elision) before initial vowels is not recognised in our texts. In such cases (e.g. *Il.* I. 1) -εω has clearly been substituted for -α'. The remainder—i.e. the cases (e.g. *Il.* V. 16) where the monosyllabic ending is required by the metre—amount to less than nine per cent. of the total number.[1]

In view of such evidence the often-repeated statement that Aeolic elements are preserved only in stereotyped phrases and formulae cannot for a moment be admitted. Moreover these elements are distributed without noteworthy variation throughout the poems; Homeric poetry as a whole is essentially Aeolic.[2] It is overlaid throughout with an alien (Attic-Ionic) element; but this element is late, as may be seen from the following consideration. In the history of the gen. sing. ending discussed above three phonetic stages are involved in all varieties of Ionic, viz. (i) -*āo*, (ii) -*ēo* (dissyllabic), (iii) -*eō* (monosyllabic). But the second (early Ionic) stage is unrepresented. The Ionic (Attic-Ionic) forms belong to the third (late Ionic) stage.

On the other hand there is no evidence that the poems were ever written in Aeolic.[3] Neither is there any ground for supposing that they

[1] According to Reichelt, *Zeitschr. f. vergl. Sprachforschung*, XLIII. 68, -αο occurs altogether 247 times, -εω before vowels 49 times, before consonants 27 times. For reference to this paper we are indebted to the kindness of Dr P. Giles.

[2] An argument for the Ionic origin of the poems has been drawn from the fact that the name *Homeros* (with Ionic ē for ā) can be traced in non-Ionic records. But nothing is known of 'Homer'; we do not know when the name first became connected with the poems (cf. Chadwick, *Heroic Age*, p. 217, note), though the form suggests that it was at Athens. The whole question is discussed more fully, *ib.* p. 215 ff.

[3] We mean of course complete texts. A line of the *Little Iliad* is preserved in some non-Ionic form of language (Kinkel, *Epic. Gr. Fragm.* p. 43, No. 11); but the ultimate source of the fragment seems not to be known. It may of course have been quoted by some Doric or Aeolic writer.

were ever recited in Aeolic, except presumably in Aeolic communities. Such evidence as is available (cf. p. 498) suggests that they were everywhere 'translated' into the local dialect. When speculation arose as to Homer's birthplace, various Dorian and Ionic cities, including Athens, claimed the honour—a claim which could hardly have been made if the language of the poems had shown obviously and unambiguously the stamp of its origin. In Athens the poems may have been adapted to the native language long before they were committed to writing.

The evidence discussed above tends to show that the text was not modified to any great extent either in the course of translation or later. We have seen that in the case of the gen. sing. of masculine *ā*-stems there is an appreciable, though small, percentage of cases where the Aeolic ending *-āo* is metrically impossible and where the text would seem to have required the Ionic -εω from the beginning. But even this evidence is not unambiguous, for the latter may be a substitution for the (metrically equivalent) later Aeolic *-ā*, contracted from *-āo*. In general we are inclined to think that this is the true explanation; for in the gen. sing. of *o*-stems the contracted form -ου (from *-oo*) is so frequent[1] that it would be very strange if contraction was never found in the case of the ending *-āo*. But on general grounds we are not inclined to doubt that the text did undergo a limited amount of change through (and after) the change of language.[2] At all events, apart from difference of dialect, the forms noticed above belong to different—earlier and later—strata of language.

The Homeric poems contain a very large amount of repetition. As in *Beowulf* and, to a less extent, in Norse narrative poetry, speeches are

[1] The gen. sing. of *o*-stems has two different forms, -οιο and -ου. Where the latter stands unshortened (i.e. with hiatus) before initial vowel, it has probably been substituted for the former, which is never written before vowels in our texts. Apart from this case the two forms are about equally frequent in the *Odyssey*; but the former is much more frequent in the *Iliad*. The ending -ου is contracted from *-oo* (dissyllabic); but this uncontracted form is only rarely required by the metre (e.g. in *Il.* XXI. 104). The contracted form seems to be required in nearly half of the cases in the *Odyssey* (rather less in the *Iliad*); cf. Reichelt, *op. cit.* p. 72 ff. No question of dialect is involved here; for the contracted *-ō* (-ου or -ω), from *-oo*, appears in most of the Greek dialects, including Aeolic, as well as Ionic and Doric. But an element of uncertainty is introduced by the extreme frequency of this ending, especially perhaps the contracted form, in pronouns. The other ending (-οιο) is comparatively rare in pronouns. We do not know whether these facts have been explained; but they may perhaps have some bearing on the frequency of contraction in this case.

[2] Some (metrically non-equivalent) doublets may be explained in this way, e.g. ξείνιος—ξένιος. But the majority of these cases hardly admit of such an explanation. They seem rather to point to a time when the metre was less rigid.

usually introduced by a line which consists of one of a limited number of recurrent formulae, followed by the name of the speaker with a standing and frequently recurring epithet. It will be seen later that this is a regular feature of oral narrative poetry among many peoples—perhaps everywhere.

Longer repetitions are by no means unfrequent; sometimes they extend over a large number of lines. As a general rule they are not incompatible with either of the contexts in which they occur; and they might have been designed by the original poet. But there are cases where this is very improbable. Thus in *Il.* IV. 163 ff., Agamemnon consoles his brother, who has been wounded treacherously, with a reflection that the Trojans will ultimately suffer vengeance for such deeds: "For well I know in my heart and soul that a day will come when holy Ilios will perish, and Priam and the army of Priam with his good ashen spear". The same passage occurs again in VI. 447 ff. in a speech by Hector, when he is confessing to his wife that he has no hope of the future. The latter part of it is to be found also in IV. 46 f., where Zeus is addressing Hera.

Again, in *Il.* III. 355 ff. it is stated that Menelaos "cast his spear of long shadow and struck the round shield of Priam's son (Paris). Through the bright shield went the massive spear, and forced its way through the very skilfully wrought breastplate; and right against his side the spear tore his tunic. But he swerved, and escaped black fate". The same passage, amounting to five and a half lines, occurs again in VII. 249 ff.; but here it refers to Aias, while 'Priam's son' is here not Paris, but Hector. Part of it is to be found also in XI. 434 ff., again in relation to other heroes.

Interesting examples of such repetitions occur in the fictitious accounts which Odysseus gives of his adventures on his return home. In the long story he relates to Eumaios (*Od.* XIV. 299 ff.) he makes himself out to be a Cretan. In 301 ff. he describes a shipwreck which he says that he had experienced near Crete. This passage has much in common with the 'true' story of the shipwreck he experienced before his arrival at Calypso's island, as related to Alcinoos in VII. 249 ff. and XII. 403 ff. Thus 302–4 are identical with XII. 404–6, 305 f. with XII. 415 f., 308 f. with XII. 418 f., and 314 with VII. 253, while close resemblances occur in 301 to XII. 403, in 307 to XII. 417, in 313 to XII. 425, and in 314 f. to 448 f.[1] Then he proceeds to relate how he had just come from the land of the Thesprotoi and had there heard news of

[1] XII. 448 is identical with VII. 254. The next following lines may also be compared.

Odysseus. This is practically the same (fictitious) story which he tells later, while still in disguise, to his wife Penelope; and here again there are close verbal resemblances. Thus XIV. 323 is identical with XIX. 293, XIV. 325 with XIX. 294, XIV. 327 f. with XIX. 296 f., XIV. 330 with XIX. 299, XIV. 332–5 with XIX. 289–92, while the differences between XIV. 326, 329, 331 and XIX. 295, 298, 288 respectively are very slight. It will be observed that there is a difference in the arrangement of the narrative and that the story as told to Eumaios contains one line (XIV. 294) which does not occur in the other account.

The variants between the stories told to Eumaios and to Alcinoos are obviously intentional. But it is by no means clear that this is the case with the variants between the former and the parallel account given to Penelope. The latter are in general similar to the Anglo-Saxon variants noticed on p. 505 f. Variants of this kind seem not to be of frequent occurrence in the Homeric poems. The description (e.g.) of the wound inflicted on Menelaos in *Il.* IV. 135 ff. is not a variant of the passages quoted on p. 565, though it is not altogether independent of them. On the other hand true variants are doubtless to be found in the descriptions of the river Axios (Vardar) given in *Il.* II. 850 and XXI. 158. It is of interest to note that the latter of these passages was marked as spurious by Aristarchos—a fact which suggests that similar variants may have been removed or corrected by ancient scholars.

The most famous variant in the *Iliad* is of quite a different kind. We refer to II. 557 f., a passage in the 'Catalogue of Ships'. Our text reads here: "Aias led twelve ships from Salamis; he led them and stationed them where the forces of the Athenians stood". It was recognised by ancient critics that the statement made in the second line appears to be untrue; when the disposition of the Achaean army is referred to, Aias is not found with the Athenians. Indeed it was widely believed that this line had been added by Solon—or possibly by Peisistratos, who is said to have supported him—in order to justify the Athenian claim to Salamis. Strabo, IX. I. 10, states that in Megara, which had been deprived of the island by Solon, a different text was current: "Aias led ships from Salamis and from Polichne and Aigirussa and Nisaia and Tripodes" —which, he says, were places in the territory of Megara. It is curious that both versions devote only two lines to Aias and his contingent, although no other contingent in this Catalogue has less than four lines allotted to it, and Aias is one of the most important heroes.

There appears to be no adequate reason for doubting the story that in the struggle for Salamis, in the early years of the sixth century, both sides appealed to the witness of Homer. It is of interest therefore to note both that Homer was already accepted as a historical authority and that the text was still capable of manipulation. But the poverty of invention shown by both variants suggests that the time of free treatment was practically at an end. And the same is true of the other references to Athens which may have been introduced into the poems for the purpose of gratifying Athenian audiences. This inference is quite in accord with the linguistic evidence discussed above (p. 563 f.). The creative period and even the period of really free composition would seem to have been past when the poems became naturalised in Athens.

CHAPTER XVIII

RECITATION AND COMPOSITION

IT will be convenient to treat this subject by 'Types', where possible, rather than by the 'categories' (heroic, etc.) in which we have hitherto arranged the material—i.e. according to the character of the works themselves rather than that of the subject-matter. The general categories, such as antiquarian and gnomic, in which such distinctions of Type do not occur, will be treated last.

In Greek for Type A practically only the Homeric poems come in for consideration. In early historical times—the sixth and fifth centuries—these were declaimed by professional reciters (rhapsodists), especially at public festivals. The earliest reference (Herodotos, v. 67) relates to the time of Cleisthenes, tyrant of Sicyon in the first half of the sixth century. The rhapsodists appear to have gathered large audiences; and they recited in a loud voice, and apparently with an emotional delivery.[1] The reciter carried a staff, but there appears to have been no musical accompaniment. At festivals the recitations, sometimes at least, seem to have been in the nature of a competition, with prizes awarded for the best performances.

Ancient writers, when they cite the *Iliad*, sometimes refer to what appear to be the names of sections of the poem; and it is generally believed that these sections were divisions adopted by the rhapsodists. At Athens it is said to have been ordained by Solon[2] that rhapsodists were to follow the order of the poems; the second was to begin where the first stopped—thus avoiding omissions and repetitions—a regulation which suggests that if the choice was left to them they tended to choose certain sections. The sections may, however, have served other purposes also; they may (e.g.) have been utilised for educational purposes—for committing portions of the poem to memory.

The internal evidence of the poems points to quite a different kind of recitation. It is always accompanied by the lyre. The recitations are

[1] Cf. Plato, *Ion*, 535 B–D.

[2] Diogenes Laertios, cap. 58 (*Solon*). The regulation was perhaps intended for the Panathenaia, a festival at which recitations of the Homeric poems are known to have taken place.

usually given in kings' palaces for the purpose of entertaining the court and visitors. One example, however, takes place at a public gathering (*Od.* VIII. 261 ff.), though the king and his court are present. In this case—but only in this—the recitation is accompanied also by dancing; the theme is a story of the gods. The minstrels are usually professionals. They seem to be attached in some way to the kings' courts; and sometimes, as we shall see in the next chapter, they are held in high honour. Princes themselves also sometimes practise minstrelsy (*Il.* IX. 186 ff.), for the entertainment of themselves and their friends.

There is a yet more important difference, however, between the recitations of the historical period and those mentioned in the poems. From quotations in writers of the fifth century, it is clear that the text of the poems was then established and more or less familiar to the educated world, and that the recitations must have conformed to this text, whether the reciters had written copies of it or not. But the minstrels mentioned in the Homeric poems appear to be creative poets. Phemios, the minstrel in Ithaca, says to Odysseus (*Od.* XXII. 347 f.): "I am self-taught; it was a deity that implanted poems of all kinds in my heart". Practically the same is implied in the case of the Phaeacian minstrel Demodocos, to whom Odysseus says (*ib.* VIII. 487 ff.): "I praise thee far above all mortals. Verily thou hast been taught either by a Muse, a child of Zeus, or even by Apollo; for thy poems give a most accurate account of the fate of the Achaeans, of all they did and suffered, and of all their toil, as though thou hadst been present thyself or hadst heard it from someone (who had been present)". In full conformity with this is what Telemachos says (*ib.* I. 351 f.): "Men attach most value to the latest poem which has come to their hearing". This remark is in answer to Penelope's complaint that Phemios is always harping on the sad subject of the Achaeans' return from Troy.

In Hesiod's *Theogony*, 94 ff., there is a passage which suggests a form intermediate between the two types of recitation described above: "It is through the Muses and far-shooting Apollo that men upon the earth are minstrels and harpers...and blessed is he whom the Muses love.... For even if one is suffering from a recent sorrow to his soul, and pining in anguish of heart, yet if a minstrel, the squire of the Muses, shall celebrate the glories of men of old and the blessed gods who occupy Olympos, he will at once forget his distress", etc. This passage indicates that the reciter was still a minstrel, accompanying his poetry with a lyre; but his themes have become fixed; he is no longer concerned with the most recent events, but with the glories of men of old.

For Type B there is little evidence. Stesichoros's heroic poems, if we are right in regarding them as belonging to this Type, would seem to have borrowed their form from Type D.

For Type C the only evidence we know comes from the Homeric *Hymn to Apollo of Delos*; and this is perhaps better regarded as an example of DC (cf. p. 244). This Hymn, which is generally believed to be of early date, was evidently composed for recitation at a religious festival (at Delos), like the other Hymns. The poet, who is evidently also the reciter, describes himself as a blind man from Chios. Thucydides, III. 104, calls him 'Homer'. Is he a rhapsodist? He has a 'choros' of girls—just as Demodocos has a 'choros' of boys—but unfortunately we are not told whether he uses a lyre or not. And it is not clear whether the choros has to sing, as well as dance. Perhaps true choral singing was not yet cultivated. In *Il.* I. 604 and *Od.* XXIV. 60 the Muses are said to sing in turns.

Type D is all-important in the history of Greek poetry. In the eighth and seventh centuries great changes appear to have been made in music; and we now find choral music in the modern sense. Every state maintained 'choroi', which sang as well as danced at festivals; sometimes also they were sent to perform at festivals elsewhere. The poems sung were primarily hymns to the gods; but Stesichoros is said to have applied the same treatment to heroic themes, while later we find choral songs celebrating the successes of athletes and the inauguration of magistrates. The songs were often composed by the trainers of the 'choroi'—who may be regarded as professional musicians—but often also by private persons who might live far away, and who made their living by such compositions.

From the seventh century also there survive many fragments of war songs, political songs, and songs for various social functions—marriages, convivial parties, etc.—by well-known poets. Some of these appear to be intended for collective singing. All of them were probably designed for singing rather than for recitation.

On the other hand the patriotic and political poems of a hortatory character, chiefly in the elegiac metre, which are found among the fragments of Callinos, Tyrtaios, and Solon, were evidently intended for recitation. Probably they were declaimed in the first case by the authors themselves, though subsequently they may have been communicated to their supporters and partisans. It would seem that during this period poetry was much used on occasions which called for formal speech or impassioned oratory—occasions for which, in later times, rhetorical prose was cultivated. The same remark applies to letters of a formal character, though these were committed to writing.

Of Type E little need be said here. We can only conjecture that of the personal poems of Archilochos, Alcaios, and Sappho some were written down and sent to friends or patrons, while others were circulated orally among the poets' companions, or published at small social gatherings.

In the history of Greek poetry, especially perhaps of antiquarian poetry, great importance is to be attached to the custom of holding poetic contests, both at public festivals, and even at celebrations of a more or less private character. For an example we may refer to Hesiod, *W. D.* 652 ff., where the poet states that he had won a prize by his poetry at the funeral games of Amphidamas at Chalcis. Reference may also be made to the 'Contest of Homer and Hesiod', which was perhaps founded on this passage. On some of these occasions poems of Type D (hymns and elegies) were doubtless produced, and possibly also poems of Type E, but antiquarian and general (social) themes were perhaps the most usual. For antiquarian poetry good openings also were no doubt available in the service of states and of aristocratic families. Pseudo-gnomic poetry, such as Simonides's poem on women, probably owed its origin to social gatherings.

Thus far we have spoken only of the ways in which poetry of the seventh century was first made known. We have yet to consider how it was preserved. There can be no doubt that the intellectual people of this period were in general fairly well informed as to what was going on in this way, even in cities far distant from their own. It is clear enough from the poems that there was a great deal of social life—what we may perhaps call 'club life'. Trade and communication between different parts of the Greek world, and indeed throughout the Mediterranean, were very active. Towards the end of the century written copies of poems were probably circulating to some extent; but for the most part it is scarcely to be doubted that a man's memory served as his library—just as was the case in Iceland down to the twelfth century (cf. p. 581 f.).

In illustration of what has been said above we may refer to the story cited on p. 361, where Solon is represented as criticising and emending one of the poems of Mimnermos, with which he did not agree. The story shows that he was familiar with the work of a contemporary poet who lived on the other side of the Aegean. So also the story (*ib.*) which relates how one of his companions recited to him one of Sappho's odes. Solon was so charmed with it that he begged him to teach it to him. In this case it is implied that the poem was carried by memory, not by writing—although as we have seen (cf. p. 496 f.) Sappho's poems in general seem to have been written down very early, if not by the poetess herself.

Some of the early poets, however, may owe the preservation of their works to the fact that they were used for educational purposes. It is known that boys at school were expected to learn a large amount of poetry by heart. Among the authors whose works were learnt in this way were Homer, Hesiod, Tyrtaios, Phocylides, Mimnermos, Solon and Theognis.

We are not aware of any evidence as to the way in which saga was carried on in ancient Greece. The stories told by Herodotos, Plutarch, and others rather suggest that they were originally told in small social gatherings of educated men. There is no evidence that they were treated as a regular form of entertainment for large gatherings, as we find in Iceland. In some states, such as Sparta, saga may have been more assiduously cultivated—possibly as part of the educational curriculum.

Anglo-Saxon records show nothing like the variety in which ancient Greek poetry was recited and preserved. References to the recitation of poetry are not rare; but, except in the case of ecclesiastical poetry, it is probably always of the Homeric type, i.e. minstrelsy, or recitation to the accompaniment of the harp. There appears to be no evidence for collective or choral singing or for dancing, any more than for recitation without accompaniment. We will first take references to recitation in which the character of the poetry recited is not specified.

The story told by Bede, *Hist. Eccl.* IV. 24, of the poet Caedmon suggests that the cultivation of minstrelsy was pretty general in the early Saxon period. In this story we are told that when villagers met together in the evening to drink and amuse themselves, it was the custom that everyone should take his turn in singing to the harp. Caedmon, who had never been able to learn a song, used to leave the festivities and make his way home as soon as he saw the harp coming in his direction. Unfortunately the passage gives us no information about the character of these poems. Neither does it say whether they were improvised for the occasion or prepared beforehand, or acquired from others and sung from memory. The words 'He had never been able to learn a song'[1] might mean any of these things. Caedmon's own poems, after he had acquired the gift of poetry, were clearly prepared beforehand. He acquired his subject-matter from the monks, and then converted it into

[1] *Nil carminum aliquando didicerat.*

poetry by going over in his mind all that he could learn from hearing them, like a cow chewing the cud.[1] Caedmon lived during the abbacy of Hild, who died in 680.

A story relating to the same period is told of Aldhelm,[2] who later was bishop of Sherborne, and died in 709. It is said that he used to take up his position on a bridge, like a professional minstrel, and sing to the people in order to call them back to church. Again, unfortunately, we are not informed as to the character of the poems recited.

Here also we may repeat a passage from the *Exeter Gnomic Verses* (170 ff.), quoted on p. 382 above: "He who knows numerous lays and can play the harp with his hands can get relief from his sorrows; (for) he has the gift of his minstrelsy, which God has granted to him". It will be seen that this passage presents a rather interesting parallel to the one quoted from Hesiod's *Theogony* (94 ff.) on p. 569.

In this connection we may perhaps refer also to *Be Manna Cræftum*, 49 f. and to *Be Manna Wyrdum*, 80 ff., though in both these cases only instrumental music is actually mentioned—unless the latter passage is to be taken in connection with the preceding lines (77 ff.).

An interesting reference to minstrelsy in connection with heroic poetry is to be found in the letter of Alcuin to Hygebald quoted on p. 556: "When priests dine together let the words of God be read. It is fitting on such occasions to listen to a reader, not to a harpist, to the discourses of the Fathers, not to the poems of the heathen. What has Ingeld to do with Christ?...In your houses the voices of those who read should be heard, not a rabble of those who make merry in the streets".

The heroic poems themselves refer not unfrequently to minstrelsy. Thus in *Beowulf*, 1063 ff., at the feast which follows the killing of Grendel, we hear that "There was recitation and music combined.... The harp was brought into play and much poetry declaimed, when Hrothgar's minstrel was called upon to recite and entertain the banqueters in the hall". Then follows the subject of his recitation, namely the story of Finn and Hengest—an example of Type A—which is told at considerable length.

The reciter here is in some sense a professional—the court minstrel, or one of the court minstrels. Perhaps he is the same person who recites the religious poem in 90 ff., again to the accompaniment of the

[1] *Cuncta quae audiendo discere poterat rememorando secum, et quasi mundum animal ruminando, in carmen dulcissimum conuertebat.*

[2] William of Malmesbury, *Gesta Pontif.* v. cap. 190 (from King Alfred's *Handboc*).

harp. But minstrelsy is cultivated by other members of the court, even by the king himself, as in the *Iliad* (cf. p. 569). We may quote 2105 ff., where again the reference obviously is to poetry of Type A: "Then there was poetry and music. The aged Scylding (Hrothgar) related stories of old time out of his great store of information. Now the martial hero would lay his hands on the joyous harp, the instrument that makes good cheer; now he would recite a poem, true but sad; now a story of marvel would be related correctly by the noble-hearted king. Now again, bowed with age as he was, the old warrior would begin to lament that he had lost the martial vigour of youth. His heart surged within him, as he called to mind the manifold experiences of a long life". The last two sentences suggest Type E, as well as Type A.

More interesting still is a passage (867 ff.) in the description of the rejoicings which take place during the morning after the killing of Grendel: "Now one of the king's squires, a man full of grandiloquent phrases and intent upon poetry, who remembered a very great number of stories of the past—(wherein) one expression led to another in due sequence[1]—(this) man in his turn began to describe Beowulf's adventure in skilful style, declaiming with success a well-constructed narrative, with varied phraseology. He related everything that he had heard told of Sigemund and his deeds of prowess", etc. He then goes on to speak of Sigemund's exploits. It is not clear whether the reciter is the same person as the court minstrel mentioned above. But the passage is of special interest for the light which it throws on the genesis of a heroic poem. The poet evidently thought it natural that a poem celebrating the adventure should be composed within a few hours after the adventure itself. Perhaps he has in mind a poem of Type D, rather than of Type A; but it is evidently a poem which contains a good deal of narrative. The other important point to notice is that after describing Beowulf's adventure this poem, apparently, passes on to an account of the adventures of Sigemund. We know of no relationship of any kind between Beowulf and Sigemund—so it would seem that the introduction of the latter hero must be due to a simile or comparison of some kind. Possibly such comparisons may to some extent account for the transference of stories of marvel from one hero to another.

Further references to court minstrelsy occur in *Widsith*. We may quote 103 ff., where a duet seems to be described: "Then Scilling and I began to sing with clear voices before our victorious lord. Loudly rang out our music as we played the harp. Then it was frankly acknowledged

[1] Cf. *Hávamál*, st. 141, and Klaeber's note *ad loc.* (*Beowulf*, 870 ff.).

by many brave-hearted men, who were good judges, that they had never heard a better song". Most of the references in this poem are to poetry of Type D, as in the lines (99 ff.) immediately preceding this passage, where the poet says of Ealhhild, daughter of Eadwine: "Her praise has resounded through many lands, when I have had occasion to declare in poetry where I knew of a queen, adorned with gold, who showed the noblest generosity (of any) under heaven". Further examples occur in 54 ff., 66 f.

The Continental evidence available from early times relates almost wholly to heroic poetry. Much of it dates from the Heroic Age itself, though it comes from foreign sources. The references point to minstrelsy of the same kind as in England.

First we may take a passage in the Life of Saint Liudger,[1] relating to a Frisian minstrel named Bernlef, who became a disciple of the saint, some time before the year 785. He had been blind for three years, but it is stated that "he was greatly loved by his neighbours because of his geniality and his skill in reciting to the accompaniment of the harp stories of the deeds of the ancients and the wars of kings". Clearly this is a case of Type A, similar probably to the contemporary English minstrelsy mentioned in Alcuin's letter to Hygebald (cf. p. 556).

A much earlier reference to heroic poetry of Type A is probably to be found in Jordanes, cap. 5, where it is stated that the Goths "used to sing to the strains of the harp ancient poetry dealing with the deeds of their ancestors, Eterparmara, Hanala, Fridigernus, Vidigoia and others who are very famous in this nation".

Usually it is court minstrelsy which is referred to. Thus in a poem addressed to Lupus, Duke of Aquitaine, about the year 580, Venantius Fortunatus (*Carm.* VII. VIII. 61 ff.) says: "Let the Roman sound your praise with his lyre and the barbarian with his harp....Let us frame verses for you, while barbarian poets compose their lays". The reference obviously is to poems of Type D.

The historian Priscus was a member of an embassy which visited Attila, king of the Huns, in the year 448. After describing the banquet given by the king to his guests, he proceeds as follows[2]: "When evening came on torches were lighted and two barbarians stepped forth in front of Attila and recited poems which they had composed, recounting his victories and his valiant deeds in war. The banqueters

[1] *Vita S. Liudgeri*, II. 1 (Mon. Germ., *Script.* II. 412).
[2] K. Müller, *Fragmenta Historicorum Graecorum*, IV. 92.

fixed their eyes upon them, some being charmed with the poems, while others were roused in spirit, as the recollection of their wars came back to them. Others again burst into tears, because their bodies were enfeebled by age and their martial ardour had perforce to remain unsatisfied". If we are right in taking these poems to be Gothic rather than Hunnish—it is stated that both languages were used during the evening—the passage may be compared with the duet mentioned in *Widsith*, 103 ff., referred to above, though instrumental music is not actually mentioned. The poems would seem to be of Type D or Type A (perhaps DA), specially prepared for the occasion.

A curious case of royal minstrelsy (of Type E) is recorded by Procopios (*Vand.* II. 6) in his account of the siege of Mount Papua (A.D. 534). Gelimer, king of the Vandals, wrote a letter to Faras, the Herulian chief who commanded the besieging army, begging him to send him a harp, a loaf and a sponge. The explanation given by the messenger was that the king had composed a song upon his misfortunes, and as he was a good minstrel he was anxious to accompany it with a mournful tune on the harp as he bewailed his fate.

The last two references may be compared with the passage from *Beowulf* (2105 ff.) quoted on p. 574. Further, from a comparison of the English evidence in general with the Continental evidence,[1] it is clear that the cultivation of heroic poetry and minstrelsy among the early Teutonic peoples was very similar to what we find recorded of early Greece in the Homeric poems and in Hesiod.

In early Norse literature, references to the recitation of heroic poetry are rare. A famous case, to which we have already referred (p. 367), occurs in the account of the battle of Stiklestad, in *St Olaf's Saga* (*Heimskr.*), cap. 220, where the Icelander, Thormóðr Kolbrúnarskald at St Olaf's request recites the *Bjarkamál* on the morning of the battle. There is no suggestion that he used any musical instrument; but it is said that he recited the poem so loud that he aroused the whole army.

In the *Nornagests Saga* (cf. p. 560) Gestr is represented as reciting several heroic poems to King Ólafr Tryggvason and his court. One of these is the *Helreið Brynhildar*, which is given practically complete; another was perhaps *Guðrúnarkviða II*, while a third may have been the *Oddrúnargrátr* or one of the Atli poems—though some scholars think that the reference is to purely imaginary poems. Gestr has a

[1] For other early references to recitation and minstrelsy on the Continent see Chadwick, *Heroic Age*, pp. 80, 85 f. Cf. also p. 588, note, below.

harp and is said (cap. 2) to 'play'[1] (*slá*) the two latter. The saga is late, but there is no clear indication of foreign influence.[2] We see no reason why the author of the saga should have invented this feature; and therefore we are inclined to think that the recitation of heroic poetry to the harp may not have been unknown—in Norway perhaps rather than in Iceland. We know, however, of no other case where the recitation of poetry of any kind is accompanied by instrumental music; and there can be no doubt that the recitations of which we are about to speak were usually, if not always, unaccompanied.

Among the poems of the Viking Age relating to contemporary persons and events we may take first those of Type D, beginning with panegyrics in honour of princes. Harold the Fair-haired had several famous poets permanently attached to him; and the same is probably true of some later kings. But the poets of whom we hear most were Icelanders. It was customary, as we have seen (p. 346), for young Icelanders, when travelling abroad, to try to get themselves attached temporarily to the courts of princes; and those who claimed to be poets usually had panegyrics ready. For examples we may refer to *Gunnlaugs Saga Ormstungu*, cap. 7–9, where the young poet visits in succession the courts of England, Dublin, Orkney and Sweden. On entering the king's presence he says: "It has been my wish to visit you, my lord, because I have composed a poem in your honour and would like you to give it a hearing"—or some similar formula. It is evident that such poems were composed beforehand for the occasion and committed to memory.

An exceptional case of this kind is to be found in *Egils Saga Skallagrímssonar*, cap. 59 f. (cf. p. 343). Egill had fallen into the power of his enemy, King Eric Blood-Axe, at York; and his friend Arinbjörn advised him to compose a panegyric (*drápa*) of twenty stanzas in the king's honour, in order to save his life. Egill replies: "I will try this plan, if you wish; but I have never occupied myself with composing encomia on King Eric". Arinbjörn tells him to sit up all night and have the poem ready when he has to be brought before the king in the morning. After a while he comes to see him, and asks how he is getting on. Egill replies that he has made no progress, owing to the twittering of a swallow at the window. Arinbjörn then sits outside the window; and

[1] Mogk (Paul's *Grundriss d. germ. Philologie*, 2 edn., p. 822) translates "singt zu der Harfe".

[2] We do not believe that the story of the Norns (cap. 11) is derived from Classical sources.

by the morning Egill has got the whole poem composed and committed to memory. Arinbjörn insists on the king's hearing it, and Egill recites it in a loud voice before him—with the result that his life is spared. The opening of the poem (*Höfuðlausn*) has been quoted on p. 343.

References occur also to the composition of elegies in memory of private friends and relatives. The most interesting examples again come from *Egils Saga*. One of these—Egill's elegy on the deaths of his sons (*Sonatorrek*), in cap. 78—has already been discussed (p. 348 f.). His daughter Thorgerðr persuades him to compose an elegy before starving himself to death: "I hardly think that your son Thorsteinn could compose a poem on Böðvarr, and it is not right that he should not be celebrated"....Egill said that he was not likely to be able to compose anything, even if he attempted it: "However I will try", said he....Egill began to recover his spirits as he proceeded with the poem. And when it was finished he took it to Ásgerðr (his wife) and Thorgerðr and his household.[1] Thorgerðr had offered to inscribe the poem on a Runic rod.

Poems of Type E are usually quite short, consisting of one—or less frequently two—four-line stanzas. Sometimes it is stated or hinted in the saga that the poet had been preparing what he was going to say; but more often these poems are represented as improvisations. Such is the case, of course, with stanzas which are said to have been produced on the spot in unexpected situations, and especially with repartee stanzas. Examples will be found in Ch. XI (cf. p. 363 ff.). We may refer in particular to the dialogue stanzas in *Egils Saga*, cap. 48, quoted on p. 366. It is true, of course, that a large proportion of these occasional stanzas belong probably in reality to Type B rather than to Type E. Sometimes we find them attributed to infants, and even to dead persons.[2] In other cases they may have been recast by the authors themselves long after the events with which they are brought into connection. But there can be no doubt that the art of improvisation was widely and intensively cultivated in the Viking Age—a phenomenon for which we shall find parallels in other lands.

There is little or no evidence relating to the composition and recitation of poems belonging to the impersonal category. It cannot be doubted, however, that antiquarian poems like the *Ynglingatal* (cf. p. 271) were the result of long preparation. They have something in common with the panegyrics on princes, since they were composed for the glorification of the ancestry of the poets' patrons.

[1] The passage is transl. in Kershaw, *Anglo-Saxon and Norse Poems*, p. 132.

[2] Cf. *Landnámabók* (*Hauksbók*), 314; *Njáls Saga*, cap. 77.

A brief notice of the recitation of a (heathen) hymn or prayer occurs in *Thorfinns Saga Karlsefnis*, cap. 7. Karlsefni's expedition (cf. p. 538) on one occasion ran short of food, and their prayers met with no response. Thórhallr the Hunter, who was a heathen, disappeared for three days, and eventually they found him lying on the top of a crag, and staring up into the sky with open mouth and distended nostrils, and chanting something. He came back to the camp with them, but refused to answer any questions. Then a whale came, and Thórhallr said: "The Red-beard has now proved mightier than your Christ. I have got this as a reward for the poetry which I composed for Thor, in whom I put all my faith; never has he failed me". The word *þylja*, 'chant', is found elsewhere in a religious connection, e.g. in the *Hávamál*, st. 111, the introductory stanza of the second part of that poem (cf. p. 384). But it is also used for the reciting of panegyrics, e.g. in Egill's *Höfuðlausn*, though *kveða* ('say') is more usual.

It is not easy to make out from the records how far singing, as distinct from recitation, was cultivated. But it would seem that the words *gala*, and *syngva*, both of which are used for the chanting of spells, mean something different from ordinary recitation, though *kveða* is often used in this case also. The account of the spells pronounced by Kotkell and his family in the *Laxdoela Saga*, cap. 35, 37,[1] certainly suggests singing rather than recitation. The latter passage says that they were beautiful to hear. The same impression is conveyed by other passages, e.g. when Guðríðr chants the spell for the witch in *Thorfinns Saga Karlsefnis*, cap. 3. But we do not know of any references to singing, except in spells, before the introduction of church music. The word *gala* appears not to be used for any other kind of recitation, while *syngva*, though commonly applied to church music, occurs elsewhere only in the *Darraðarljóð* and in the *Grottasöngr*, both of which are in the form of spells.

References to choral singing likewise occur only in connection with spells, though even here they are never, so far as we know, free from ambiguity. Thus Kotkell and his family may have sung their spells in turn, though it is perhaps more natural to take the singing as collective. The *Darraðarljóð* once has the verb in the first person singular but for the most part it uses the plural. In the legendary *Örvar-Odds Saga*, cap. 2, we hear of a witch called Heiðr who is accompanied on her visits by a troop of fifteen boys and fifteen girls. They play no part in

[1] These passages may perhaps be compared with the Irish *filid's* curses referred to on p. 587 below.

the scene where she utters her prophecies; but in one text they are described as *raddlið*, which probably means 'singing company'. Musical instruments seem never to be mentioned in such cases; but to these questions we shall have to return at the end of the chapter.

Sagas sometimes refer to the telling of stories, which in Iceland was cultivated as a fine art. On p. 540 it was mentioned that at the end of the *Groenlendinga þáttr* Karlsefni himself is said to have told the story of the adventures related in the work. But the most interesting reference of this kind is a passage in *Njáls Saga*, cap. 153; which describes the Christmas party given by Earl Sigurðr II of Orkney in 1013. Among the guests were King Sigtryggr II of Dublin and Earl Gilli of the Hebrides. The Icelander Flosi was also present with a number of his followers, who had been banished from Iceland for the murderous attack upon Njáll. King Sigtryggr wanted to hear an account of the tragedy. Gunnarr Lambason, one of Flosi's companions, was chosen to tell the story, and took his seat on a chair in front of the king and the earls. He gave a biassed and unfair account of the occurrence; and when the king asked how Skarpheðinn had behaved in the burning house, he replied that he held out for a good while, but eventually broke down and wept. At this moment it happened that Njáll's son-in-law, Kari, who was prosecuting the vendetta, and who had just arrived unexpectedly in Orkney, was standing outside the door and listening. He rushed in with drawn sword and cut off Gunnarr's head. Sigurðr gave orders for him to be seized; but Kari was a well-known and popular man in Orkney, and no one took any notice of the order; so he went away unmolested to Caithness. The dead man was then carried out, and the blood cleaned away; and the story was resumed by Flosi, who told it fairly and in a way which met with general approval.

We may also cite a passage from the *Fóstbroeðra Saga*, cap. 23. The Icelandic poet, Thormóðr Kolbrúnarskald, made his way to Greenland about the year 1025, in order to obtain vengeance for the death of his friend Thorgeirr. There he hired a servant called Egill, who was dull-witted. When the time came for the assembly, he went to it with his friends. One day he falls asleep; and on waking he is surprised to find nobody about. Then Egill comes in and says that he has missed a great entertainment. In answer to Thormóðr's enquiries Egill explains that nearly the whole assembly is gathered in front of the tent of a certain Thorgrímr, a great man in the district. Thorgrímr himself is sitting on a chair in the centre of the crowd, and telling a story which they are all listening to. He cannot give a clear account of the story; but he says that a great hero called Thorgeirr figured in it, and that Thorgrímr himself had also played a great part. Thormóðr realises that this is the man he is looking for, and joins the crowd. A storm suddenly comes on, and people run for shelter. Thormóðr finds Thorgrímr alone and kills him.

In these two cases we see saga in its first stage. The story-teller himself is one of the chief characters in the story; he tells of what he has seen and done himself. We may now take an example of saga in its second stage, where the story has been derived from someone else and is told at second hand.

In *Haralds Saga Harðráða* (*Fornmanna Sögur*), cap. 99, we hear of a young Icelander, whose name is not given, but who came to visit Harold III, king of Norway (1047–66). The king asks him if he has any stories to tell—for Icelandic story-telling was already becoming famous. The young man says that he has; and the king agrees to take him into his service on condition that he shall tell stories to any member of the court who shall want them. This goes on throughout the autumn; he tells stories both night and day, and becomes very popular in the court. But towards Christmas he becomes very depressed; and the king suspects that his repertoire is coming to an end. In answer to the king's questions he admits that he has only one story left; and this he dare not tell because it is concerned with the king's own exploits abroad. The king says there is no story he would more like to hear. He releases the Icelander from further story-telling till Christmas; and tells him he must make his story-telling last over the twelve days of the festival. Each day the king stops him after a certain time, so as to make the story last out. The Icelander is naturally very uneasy about the result; but when the story is finished the king tells him he has liked it very well, and asks him where he got it from. He says that it has been his custom in Iceland to go every year to the general assembly, and there each summer he has got something from the stories told by Halldórr Snorrason. Halldórr is known to have accompanied Harold when he was fighting in the Mediterranean, in the service of the Greek emperor.

As regards the preservation of both poems and sagas in later times—before they were committed to writing—most valuable information is given by Snorri Sturluson in the Prologue to the *Heimskringla*. He says: "There were poets with Harold the Fair-haired: and people still (i.e. in the early part of the thirteenth century) know their poems, and poems relating to all the kings who have since reigned in Norway". He then goes on to speak of Ari, the priest and historian, with whom written Icelandic literature begins. We possess Ari's history of Iceland (*Íslendingabók*) only in an abbreviated form, written about 1135; but this and Snorri's Prologue together supply good information as to the cultivation of the history of the past by intellectual Icelanders in the last days of oral tradition. Ari was born about 1067, and his chief source of information was his foster-father Hallr, an old man and famous for his wisdom, who in early life had been acquainted with St Olaf. Among his other informants are mentioned Teitr, another foster-son of Hallr, and grandson of Gizurr the White; Oddr, a grandson of Hallr á Síðu; and Thuríðr, a daughter of Snorri Goði. Gizurr, Hallr á Síðu, and Snorri Goði are among the most prominent characters who figure in sagas relating to the beginning of the eleventh century. Ari himself belonged to the most distinguished family in Iceland. He was a descendant of Queen Auðr of Dublin, and a great-grandson of Guðrún, the heroine of the *Laxdoela Saga*.

In early Welsh poetry references to the recitation of poems are very common. They occur most frequently in poems of Type D. Two of the panegyrics upon Urien (*Tal.* XXXIII, XXXIX) are largely occupied with the subject; and the same is true of one panegyric upon Gwallawg (*Tal.* XXXVIII). References occur also in the *Gododdin* poem (*An.* I), e.g. st. 5, 21, 24 f., 33, 66—passages which declare the duty of celebrating the valour of heroes who fell at Catraeth and extol their generosity to poets.

Here also we may cite *Tal.* XIV, a poem of Type B—perhaps derived in part from Type E (cf. p. 460)—in which the speaker, who is obviously Taliesin, relates how he had sung for various princes: "I sang before a famous prince in the meadows of the Severn, before Brochfael of Powys who loved my Muse. I sang before Urien in the morning on a pleasant terrace" (7 ff.). But he had also sung before the sons of Llyr in Aber Henvelen (4)—a passage connected in some way (like 31 ff.) with the legendary story of Bran. Again in 42 he says he had sung before princes (unnamed) over the mead vessels.

References are to be found also in gnomic poetry, e.g. *RBH.* v. 3: "Whoever loves a bard will be a handsome giver". We may refer also to *Tal.* IV. 27, 30.

In *Tal.* XXX, a very obscure poem,[1] each stanza begins apparently with a reference to the recitation of poetry. The passages suggest that this

[1] Transl. by Rhys in the Preface to Malory's *Morte d'Arthur* (Everyman), p. xx ff.

piece is in the nature of a graduation essay. The 'mystical' poems discussed on p. 459 ff. frequently refer to recitation and to bards.

None of the passages cited above allude to musical accompaniment. References to instrumental music in any form are rare in the poems. The mystical poems, however, occasionally mention the harp (*telyn*), e.g. in *Tal.* VII. 148; VIII. 19 (cf. 60). In *Tal.* XLVIII. 31 ff. the speaker says that he is a bard, a harper, a piper, a fiddler (*crythawr*), etc.

From the twelfth century onwards, when fuller historical evidence becomes available, bardism was an important element in Welsh life. The Laws contain regulations for the recitation or singing of poems in the king's household. The texts vary greatly, but the general drift is as follows:[1] When the king wishes to hear poetry the *Pencerdd*[2] (lit. 'head of poetry') is to recite or sing two poems (or one poem) of a religious character and another about princes. One text defines that the latter poem shall be about the king to whom the palace belongs if possible—i.e. presumably a panegyric. When the queen wishes to hear a poem in her bower, the bard of the household is to sing three poems in a low voice, so as not to disturb the hall. A variant here specifies 'three odes about Camlan'. In another passage it is stated that a bard of the household recites the *Monarchy of Britain* before the household in the day of battle and fighting. A variant says that this is recited when they divide the spoil. We do not know the *Monarchy of Britain*; but the former passage may perhaps be compared with the recitation of the *Bjarkamál* before the battle of Stiklestad (cf. p. 367).

The Laws seem to imply that poems were accompanied on the harp, though we do not know whether this is ever precisely stated. It is clear at all events that the harp is an indispensable property of the bard. In one passage[3] it is stated that a bard of the household receives a harp from the king, which he is never to part with. Elsewhere[4] we find that every *Pencerdd* has a right to receive a harp from the king, and that every pupil of a *Pencerdd*, when he leaves him, has a right to receive a harp from him.

The institution of the Eisteddfod can be traced back to the twelfth century. The first satisfactorily authenticated gathering was held by the

[1] Cf. Wade-Evans, *Welsh Medieval Law*, p. 33 f. (transl. p. 180), 22 (transl. p. 167), 304. Variants will be found in the Venedotian Code (ed. Aneurin Owen), I. xiv, xli.

[2] A *Pencerdd* is defined as 'a bard, when he shall gain a chair'. In the Vened. Code the term *bard cadeiriawg* ('chaired bard') is sometimes used for *Pencerdd*.

[3] Cf. Wade-Evans, *op. cit.* p. 22 f. (transl. p. 167).

[4] Cf. Wade-Evans, *op. cit.* p. 304 f.

Lord Rhys at Aberteifi (Cardigan) in 1176.[1] Two competitions were arranged, one for bards and poets, and the other for harpers, fiddlers, pipers, and various kinds of music; and a chair was awarded as a prize to the winner of each competition. It is not clear that minstrelsy was included. Giraldus Cambrensis (*Descr. Walliae*, I. 10, 12), who wrote shortly after this time, says that both poetry and music were much cultivated. Harps were to be found in every house; but he also does not speak of minstrelsy. In view of the evidence of the Laws the absence of references to minstrelsy is perhaps due to accident. Nearly a century earlier we hear of a certain Gellan, a harper and *Pencerdd*, who was killed at Aberlleiniog[2] in 1094. But the *crwth*, whether it was originally a fiddle or a harp, had been cultivated for long ages before this time; for the *chrotta Britanna* is mentioned by Venantius Fortunatus (VII. 64), about the year 580.

From Giraldus Cambrensis (*ib.* I. 13) it is clear that choral singing was much practised in his day. In particular he speaks of the proficiency of the Welsh in part singing. We do not know whether any of the early poems were intended for part singing.

With regard to the preservation of poems, some information is perhaps to be obtained from the introduction to the Gwarchan of Maelderw (*An.* V). Unfortunately the passage is far from clear to us, but it seems that a certain value was attached to a knowledge or recitation of each stanza of the *Gododdin* and of each of the *Gwarchaneu*.[3] The expression used here (*atal*, i.e. *a dal*, 'is worth') is prefixed also to certain poems in the *Book of Taliesin*—to No. XII with the numeral *XXIV* and to No. XVII with the numeral *CCC*—while other poems have numerals alone: *XXIV* in Nos. XIII, XIX, XX, *CCC* in Nos. XV, XVI, and *XC* in No. XXII. Whatever may be the exact meaning it would seem that a bard was entitled to a fixed payment for the recitation of certain poems. If we may judge from the variants in the *Gododdin* (cf. p. 526 f.) considerable freedom must have been allowed in the treatment, unless the memorisation was very poor.

For the recitation of saga also there is some evidence from Wales. We may refer especially to a passage in the *Mabinogi* of *Math*, where Gwydion and his brother Gilfaethwy with ten others visit Pryderi, king

[1] Cf. Lloyd, *History of Wales*, p. 548 f.

[2] *Hanes Gruffydd Ab Cynan*, cap. 8.

[3] The passage is transl. as follows by Morris-Jones, *Y Cymmrodor*, XXVIII. 5; "Each stanza of the *Gododdin* is worth a song of one measure (i.e. of one unit) according to privilege in song-contest. Each of the *gorchaneu* is worth 363 songs (i.e. units)", etc.

of Dyfed, in the guise of bards. In the course of the evening Pryderi asks Gwydion if one of the young men will tell a story. Gwydion replies that with them it is the custom for the *Pencerdd* to tell stories on the first night; and then it is stated that Gwydion, who was the best of story-tellers, entertained the court for the rest of the evening. The story is interesting as showing that saga, as well as poetry, was cultivated by the bards. Evidence to the same effect is given by the last sentence in the *Dream of Rhonabwy*.

From the records at our disposal it would seem that both poetry and saga were largely, if not exclusively, in the hands of the bards, who evidently formed something in the nature of a learned profession, not entirely without organisation. With this question we shall be concerned in the following chapters. Here it is sufficient to call attention to the numerous references to recitation, which, taken together with the absence of satisfactory evidence for early written literature, as pointed out in Ch. XVI, and the large amount of textual variation noted in the last chapter, indicate without doubt that Welsh poetry was mainly preserved by oral tradition down to a comparatively late date. There can hardly be any question that the same is true of saga.

In Ireland, as we have seen, a large amount of poetry of Type D has been preserved, though down to the eleventh century the greater part of it is fragmentary. We do not know of any early description of the recitation of such poetry, except in heroic sagas—in scenes where women are represented as lamenting the deaths of their husbands. An example may be found in the lamentation or elegy uttered by Deirdre over Naoise and his brothers at the end of the *Fate of the Children of Uisnech*. A much earlier instance is the rhetoric in which Emer laments the death of CuChulainn.[1] These descriptions may be compared with those of the lamentations uttered by Andromache, Hecabe and Helen over the death of Hector at the close of the *Iliad*. There is no reference to the presence of minstrelsy in either of these Irish cases—as in the *Iliad* (XXIV. 720 ff.)—though some kind of formal lamentation is mentioned in connection with the funerals of other Irish heroes. Modern analogies will be noted in later chapters. There can be little doubt that most of the panegyrics and elegies composed for princes of the early historical period were intended for recitation.[2]

[1] *Book of Leinster*, fol. 123 a. This passage does not appear to have been translated.

[2] Sometimes they are said to have been composed by the prince's widow, as appears from the phrase *ut coniunx dixit* in *Ann. Tig.* (*Rev. Celt.* XVII. 162, 174).

Irish poetry of Type B is usually contained in sagas. References to the recitation of these are not rare. Thus according to the *Battle of Allen*,[1] cap. 3, Fergal, the northern king, takes with him on his campaign a youth called DonnBo, who is to entertain his warriors both with 'stories of the kings' and with poetry. From cap. 7 it appears that he also played the pipes. But on the night before the battle he cannot provide them with any entertainment; and at his suggestion they call upon a certain Ua Maglainni, who "began reciting the battles and valiant deeds of Conn's Half and of Leinster from the Destruction of...Dinn Rig...down to that time". We may compare the story of Thormóðr at the battle of Stiklestad. In cap. 18 it is stated that all Fergal's poets are killed in the battle; but after their death they all make music for him, 'poets and horn-players, and pipers and harpers'. In cap. 22 f. DonnBo's head sings in the presence of the Leinster warriors.

In one story of Mongan (cf. p. 98), which comes from the very ancient *Book of Druim Snechta*, the king has a *fili*, named Forgoll, who is said to recite to him a different story every night from November 1 to May 1. We may compare the story of Harold Hardrada and the Icelander noticed on p. 581.

Here also reference may be made to the story[2] of Urard mac Coise, chief *fili* of Ireland, who died in 990. Having had his house destroyed by a raid, he makes his way to the high-king Domnall mac Muirchertaig (d. 980). The king asks him to recite a saga; and he thereupon offers him a choice of all the sagas known, ending with a story which he has composed on the injury done to him, but with the names disguised. The king asks for this because, he says, he has not heard it before.

From these passages it will be seen that the *filid* cultivated the recitation of sagas. Later we shall see that they were required to learn a very large number of them in the course of their training. But the training also included the learning and composition of poetry. In fact the combined cultivation of poetry and saga which we find implied in stories of the Welsh bards is definitely attributed to the *filid* in Irish sources, especially the *Book of Ballymote*. Doubtless we owe to them, not only much poetry of Type C and other antiquarian pieces, but also many of the poems of Type B included in the sagas.

This combination of poetry and saga was probably not confined to the *filid*. There is no evidence, so far as we know, that DonnBo was a

[1] Ed. and transl. by Stokes, *Rev. Celt.* XXIV. 41 ff.; cf. p. 54 above.

[2] Ed. by K. Meyer, *Anecdota from Irish MSS.* II. 42 ff.; cf. Thurneysen, *Ir. Heldensage*, p. 21 f.

fili; and he, as we have seen, was a musician, as well as a story-teller and poet. In the text of the *Exile of the Sons of Uisliu* preserved in the *Book of Leinster*, Fedlimid, the father of Derdriu, is described as 'Story-teller (*scélaige*) and harper (*cruittire*)' to Conchobor. The latter word is not found in the other texts, and consequently may have been added; but the addition shows at all events that the combination was regarded as natural. In the *Fate of the Children of Uisnech*, cap. 1, we find harping combined with antiquarian poetry, recited by druids and *filid*; but this is of course a late work as we have it. We do not know of any definite evidence from early texts as to the way in which recitation and music were combined, whether by *filid* or other reciters—e.g. whether the poems included in the stories were accompanied on the harp, or whether the recitation was interrupted from time to time by purely instrumental music.

There is no doubt as to the general cultivation of the harp or its antiquity in Ireland. Giraldus Cambrensis[1] states that the Irish surpassed all other peoples in this art. In the *Destruction of Dinn Rig*, which relates to earlier times than any other heroic story, an important part is played by the harper Craftine—though it is not stated that he was a poet or story-teller. Even the Dagda, the chief of the gods, has a harp, which is described in the *Second Battle of Moytura* (cf. p. 258).

It is generally believed that many of the sagas which we have, especially those which were written down in early times, come from *filid*. We have little doubt, at all events, that the preservation of poetry, in particular antiquarian poetry, was largely due to this class and their educational system. In this system the learning of spells also formed an important element. Instances were noticed in Ch. XV (cf. p. 466 f.). We may refer also here to the elaborate account, given in the *Book of Ballymote*,[2] of the proceedings which attended the pronouncement of a curse upon a prince with all his belongings. The account seems to imply collective singing by *filid* of different grades; and it is the only reference to collective singing which we have noted in early Irish records.

From the evidence discussed above it is clear that in all the periods with which we are concerned recitation of poetry or saga (or both) was

1 *Topographia Hibernica* (Rolls Series, Vol. V, p. 153 f.).

2 This portion is ed. by Thurneysen in Windisch's *Irische Texte*, Series III, p. 96 f. (cf. p. 124 f.). Cf. also O'Curry, *Manners and Customs*, II. p. 216 f.; Atkinson, *Book of Ballymote*, p. 13 a.

extensively cultivated. Three forms of production may probably be distinguished: I. Recitation without musical accompaniment. II. Recitation to the accompaniment of the harp (or other stringed instrument). III. Choral singing (whether accompanied or not). We ought, perhaps, to distinguish a fourth variety, viz. singing, as distinct from recitation, by an individual. Something of this kind seems to be implied by the Greek non-choric lyric poetry of the seventh century, as found e.g. in the poems of Sappho and Alcaios; and it may have existed in earlier times—we may refer e.g. to the Linos song mentioned in *Il.* XVIII. 569 ff. Possibly the spell song sung by Guðríðr in *Thorfinns Saga Karlsefnis*, cap. 3, may belong here; but this would be difficult to prove. Indeed we know of no clear evidence, except in Greece.

It must be admitted that even for III the evidence in general is far from satisfactory. Choral hymns to the gods were clearly cultivated in Greece in the seventh century, if not earlier. In the sixth century we find other choral songs, especially those which celebrate victories in athletic contests. A choral hymn to Apollo seems to be meant in *Il.* I. 472 ff., and perhaps a choral song of triumph over the fall of Hector in XXII. 391 f. A choral dirge over the same hero appears to be implied in XXIV. 720 ff. But the reference to the dirge sung by the Muses over Achilles in *Od.* XXIV. 60 f. suggests alternate rather than choral singing. In Norse the only examples we have been able to find are spells, with which we may compare the Irish spell in the *Book of Ballymote*. But in all these cases the possibility of alternate singing is to be taken into account. The same remark applies to the elegy pronounced over Beowulf (3169 ff.) by the twelve princes who ride round his tomb, and perhaps to the elegy over Attila described by Jordanes, cap. 49. It would seem, at all events, that choral singing began in these types of poetry—spells, hymns to the gods, dirges and songs of triumph.[1]

It is clear that heroic narrative poetry (Type A) was in early times recited according to Form II, both in Greece and among the Teutonic peoples. In England and on the Continent this form of recitation was still preserved in the time of our historical records; but in Greece and in the North—in the latter perhaps not universally—Form II had been displaced by Form I, i.e. the instrumental accompaniment had been discarded. In the *Edda* poems we find references to the harp, e.g. in the *Völuspá*, st. 42, and in the story of Gunnarr's harping in the snake-pit; but in sagas and poetry relating to the Viking Age such references are

[1] A number of probable references in Latin works to (Teutonic) choral singing are given by Heusler in Hoops, *Reallexikon d. germ. Altertumskunde*, I. 447 ff.

curiously rare—so rare as to suggest that the use of the harp generally had gone out of fashion. Yet both in Greece and in the North the chief reason for the change is probably to be sought in the influence of other kinds of poetry. This is a subject to which we shall have to return later.

For the recitation of poetry of Type B, found in Norse, Irish and Welsh, the evidence is not satisfactory. It may be suspected that in Norse the history of this Type is similar to that of Type A. In *Nornagests Saga* we find what are apparently poems of this Type accompanied by the harp. As regards the Irish and Welsh poems, the fact that the saga-tellers were also harpers suggests that the harp may have been used for accompanying the poems (Type B) included in the sagas. It is possible, however, that the harp was used merely for musical interludes. Presumably this was the case with the pipes, which are mentioned sometimes with the harp. As regards Type D it is clear from *Widsith* and Venantius Fortunatus (cf. p. 574 f.) that in the Teutonic Heroic Age panegyrics were, sometimes at least, accompanied by the harp. On the other hand there can be no doubt that the panegyrics and elegies of the Viking Age were as a rule unaccompanied. The Welsh and Irish evidence is again uncertain. We know also of no explicit evidence in the Homeric poems. In later Greece this Type, as we have seen (p. 570), had many ramifications, some of which, e.g. choral hymns, doubtless had musical accompaniment; while in other cases, e.g. political hortatory poems, we may presume that such accompaniment was wanting.

In the case of Type E very little evidence is available. Gelimer wanted a harp for the poem which he had composed on his misfortunes. But we do not know of any other certain examples.

There is another question affecting poetry of Types B and D, apart from that of musical accompaniment. Such poems are not unfrequently in the form of dialogues. Was it customary for more than one person to take part in the recitation? The only case for which we know any definite évidence is the recital of the *Helreið Brynhildar* in *Nornagests Saga*; and here the whole poem is evidently recited by Gestr himself. But in the poetry of Type D described in *Widsith*, 103 ff., two minstrels take part in the recitation; and in the panegyric described by Priscus at Attila's court (cf. p. 575 f.), two reciters come forward simultaneously. Are we to think of such cases as duets, or as dialogues? We may refer e.g. to the elegy on Niall Noigiallach, which is in the form of a dialogue between Torna and his son (cf. p. 55), or to the *Hrafnsmál*, a panegyric on Harold the Fair-haired in the form of a dialogue between a raven and a Valkyrie (cf. p. 341 f.). We may also refer to *BBC.* 1, a poem which consists of a dialogue between Myrddin and Taliesin. Such cases may well have been suggested by panegyrics or elegies which consisted of a real dialogue between two poets. We are, therefore, inclined to think that this is the more probable explanation.

For the recitation of didactic (antiquarian or gnomic) poetry or prose hardly any direct evidence is available. It may be observed, however, that many of the pieces have the form of Type B, i.e. they are dialogues or monologues in character. Perhaps the most widespread form is that of a contest in wisdom between two sages. The subject may be antiquarian or mythological or mantic lore, or it may take the form of a series of riddles. The disputants are usually famous sages or prophets of the past, or supernatural beings. In later chapters we shall see that in various parts of the world there is evidence for the existence of such contests. Among the peoples with whom we are now concerned we cannot produce such evidence; but we would suggest that a tradition of this kind may have been perpetuated as a form of intellectual entertainment, in which the speakers took assumed names. In view of Russian analogies the dialogue of the *Fjölsvinnsmál* may indicate the survival of a similar custom in somewhat more popular circles down to a comparatively late date.

The monologues in character are usually either addresses by a sage to his son or disciples, or revelations of wisdom by a supernatural being. In Ireland we find a third variety in the form of hortatory addresses by sages or heroes to newly appointed kings. Some of the poems in which the speaker is a supernatural being may be based upon religious usage—in connection with sanctuaries or festivals. Other monologue poems were perhaps designed for educational purposes and owe their preservation to such use. What we would suggest is that this form of literature originated in a time when it was customary for sages to give instructions to those who resorted to them, but that it was preserved later as a stereotyped form. It is difficult to avoid the suspicion that the very peculiar framework of Snorri's *Gylfaginning* is derived from a tradition of this kind.

Many of the poems which are not speeches in character had probably a similar origin. Among these we may mention especially the English and Welsh gnomic poems. The opening lines of the *Exeter Gnomes* are in the form of an address—probably by a teacher to a disciple, though a debate between two sages is not impossible. We suspect also that the form of Hesiod's *Works and Days* is derived from compositions of this kind. It is only in Greek that the personality of the poet himself is introduced, unless we are to admit that certain 'mystical' poems which claim to be by Taliesin are really genuine works of that poet.

We do not know of any evidence for the use of an instrumental accompaniment to didactic poetry. Instances may occur; but it is to be doubted whether accompaniment was usual. In Greece, as we have seen, the reciters of Homeric poetry in later times carried a staff or wand instead of a lyre; and we suspect that this change was due in part to the influence of didactic poetry. At all events Hesiod (*Theog.* 30 f.) receives a staff from the Muses as the badge of his calling; and this was at a time when heroic poetry was apparently still accompanied by the lyre. To this question, however, we shall have to return later.

CHAPTER XIX

THE AUTHOR

IN the last chapter we saw that Greek heroic poetry was recited in early times by minstrels, in later times by rhapsodists, and that the former phase was still existing in the time of Hesiod (*Theog.* 94 ff.). Consequently this phase must have existed also when the Homeric poems were composed, unless it be maintained that they date from a later time than Hesiod's *Theogony*. By this we do not, of course, mean that they had assumed by this time exactly the form in which we have them. It is significant, however, that they refer fairly often to minstrelsy, but never to rhapsodists.

Two professional minstrels are mentioned by name in the *Odyssey*. Phemios regularly performs in Odysseus' house. It is possible that he may perform elsewhere also; but this is not stated. He has derived his poems from a deity (cf. p. 569). Much the same is said of the Phaeacian minstrel Demodocos. He is blind; but he occupies an honourable position at Alcinoos' court and is described as *hērōs* (*Od.* VIII. 483).

In the 'Catalogue of ships' (*Il.* II. 595 ff.) we hear of a Thracian minstrel called Thamyris, who is said to have come to Nestor's land from the court of Eurytos at Oichalia and to have been disabled by the Muses and deprived of his poetry and harping on account of his boasting.

Again, in *Od.* III. 267 f. Nestor says that when Agamemnon set off to Troy he entrusted his wife to the care of a minstrel, whose name is not given. It is not stated that he was a professional minstrel; but in any case he was presumably a person of important rank.

Whatever may be the case with the two persons last mentioned, it is clear that minstrelsy was cultivated by princes as well as by professional minstrels. In *Il.* IX. 186 ff. Achilles is reciting heroic poetry to the accompaniment of the lyre. In *Il.* III. 54 Paris is said to play the lyre, though poetry is not mentioned. In the description of the shield of Achilles (*Il.* XVIII. 569 ff.) we hear of popular minstrelsy, where a boy is singing and playing to vintagers (cf. p. 429).

Of the authors of the Homeric poems themselves nothing definite is known; and it is evident, e.g. from the number of places which claim the honour of being Homer's birth-place, that even in the earliest historical times no certain information was available. Strabo, XIV. i.

35, says that the people of Chios supported their claim to Homer by pointing to a family in their island called Homeridai, who were descended from him. But elsewhere the name *Homeridai* is applied to reciters, and even students of Homer; and in the former sense this use goes back to the time of Pindar (*Nem.* II, *ad init.*). Not much value perhaps should be attached to the scholion on this passage which states that the name was originally applied to members of Homer's family who acquired the poems from him, and then later to other rhapsodists. We see no reason for dissenting from the view held by many scholars that Homer was probably a reciter, to whom the authorship of his repertoire came to be attributed. He must already have been famous in the early part of the seventh century, for Callinos[1] is said to have attributed to him the authorship of the *Thebais*. It would seem therefore that he belonged to the period of (more or less creative) minstrelsy, rather than to that of rhapsody. In any case we do not doubt that the poems themselves in general originated in the former period.

The lost poems of the Epic Cycle were attributed by ancient scholars to various poets, of whom practically nothing is known. Thus, for example, the *Cypria* was attributed sometimes to Homer, sometimes to a certain Stasinos, who is said to have been Homer's son-in-law. But no trustworthy evidence is available, though this poem at least was probably as early as the eighth century.[2] No more evidence is available for the authors of the Homeric Hymns. For the 'blind man of Chios', who speaks at the conclusion of Hymn I, we may refer to what was said on p. 570.

Hesiod seems, from the *Works and Days*, to have been a farmer or small landowner. His father was a merchant (cf. p. 358). There is no evidence that he was a professional poet. He competes in a poetic contest (*ib.* 652 ff.), but dedicates his prize to the Muses. In the *Theogony* (22 ff.) he claims direct inspiration from them. He says that they taught him beautiful poetry as he was keeping sheep on the slopes of holy Helicon. They gave him as a staff the branch of a well-grown laurel, and "inspired me with a voice divine to celebrate both the future and the past". Hesiod never describes himself as a prophet or mantis; but the words just quoted practically imply this character as we shall see later. Various elements in the *Works and Days*, especially the

[1] Fragm. 6, from Pausanias, IX. 9.

[2] Cf. Wilamowitz-Möllendorff, *Hermes*, LXV. 267 ff., who points out a quotation from the *Cypria* upon an ivory comb found in the sanctuary of Orthia at Sparta, in a stratum dating from c. 700–635 B.C.

lists of prohibitions and omens, point to the same conclusion. His poetry is essentially didactic. The *Works and Days* is largely concerned with agriculture, but in spite of this it is a learned rather than a 'bucolic' poem.

In the eighth and seventh centuries there appear to have been a number of such learned poets. We may mention Eumelos, who is said to have belonged to the Bacchiadai, the ruling family at Corinth, and who composed a processional hymn for the Messenians at the festival at Delos, as well as antiquarian (genealogical) poetry. Some of these learned poets were of a definitely mantic character. Such was the case with Epimenides, who is said to have been summoned to Athens in the year 596 to purify the city from a plague. We may also refer here to the legendary poet Musaios, though the date and authorship of the fragments attributed to him is quite uncertain. It is not clear how far the learned poets were professionals. They may have been rewarded for their poems. Epimenides is said to have refused the reward offered him for his services at Athens.

From the seventh century onwards, or even earlier, there were poets who were trainers of state *choroi*, and who may be regarded as professional musicians. To this class apparently belonged Alcman and Stesichoros, and, in earlier times, perhaps Terpandros. Other poets were maintained by tyrants at their courts. Among these may be mentioned Ibycos and Anacreon, though they hardly fall within our period.

But the majority of the poets of the seventh century seem to have been men of rank or of independent means. Among them were statesmen who employed poetry for patriotic or political purposes, such as Solon and Alcaios. With them we may class Callinos and Tyrtaios, though there are divergent stories as to the origin of the latter. Alcaios was a nobleman and a revolutionary leader. He composed poems for recitation at social gatherings, as well as political poems. It was for social gatherings also that the poems of Archilochos and Simonides were composed. Archilochos was a dissatisfied nobleman, who had become a soldier of fortune, whereas Simonides appears to have been a successful man, and led a colony from his native island (Samos) to Amorgos. Theognis was an exiled nobleman. Sappho appears to have been a teacher, belonging to a well-to-do and perhaps noble commercial family.

From what has been said it will be seen that both professional and non-professional poets were known in all periods. Among the professional poets we have to include especially (1) minstrels and (later) rhapsodists who were occupied with heroic poetry and stories of the gods; and (2) persons who were connected with religion in some way or other. To the latter belong (*a*) trainers of state *choroi*; (*b*) probably some persons of prophetic or mantic character, though such were not always professionals; (*c*) the priests of oracular sanctuaries, e.g. the *Hosioi* at Delphoi and the *Tomuroi* at Dodona—educated citizens who converted the oracles into poetry. Among those poets who were not primarily professional there were probably many who competed for prizes and from time to time received rewards for composing elegies, wedding songs, triumphal odes, etc.

In the early history of Greek poetry, taken as a whole, we may conveniently distinguish three chief phases. The first (I) which we may call 'Homeric' consists of the poetry of entertainment, intended primarily for kings' courts. The subjects are stories of the Heroic Age and of deities. The second (II), which we may call 'Hesiodic', consists of learned didactic poetry. The subjects are antiquarian, religious and gnomic. The third (III) which we may call after Archilochos—though he is typical only of a section of it—consists of poetry which was composed for various purposes, but is not primarily didactic. The subjects were mainly of present-day interest. Its affinities are in general with modern literature. The milieu is urban. The society in which the authors lived, and for which they composed, was that of the city state.

This classification is primarily chronological. We shall probably not go very far astray if we take the flourishing creative period of I before 750, of II between 750 and 650, of III after the latter date. But it is not to be assumed that no learned poetry was composed before 750, and no 'modern' poetry before 650. The dates indicated are approximately those at which poetry of the various phases came to be cultivated as a fine art.

To Phase II we may assign oracular poetry, which seems to have followed old tradition, and also most of the Homeric Hymns, though many of them may have been composed in later times. Sagas (of Type C; cf. p. 333 f.) relating to early times belong to the same phase; but sagas of Type A relating to the seventh and sixth centuries belong to Phase III.

It is to be observed that Phase I and Phase II have a common uniform metre—the hexameter. Phase III, on the other hand, shows great variety of metrical form.

The transition between Phase I and Phase II may be seen rarely in the *Iliad* or *Odyssey*—the most important evidence is in the first Nekyia (*Od.* XI)—but appears to have been more frequently exemplified in the lost Cyclic poems, if one may judge, for example, from the references to 'purification' and the numerous explanatory elements contained in the summaries. Instances are also to be found in a few of the Homeric Hymns (cf. p. 243 f.).

The transition between Phase II and Phase III may be seen (*a*) in form—in the fragments of Asios, which are partly in hexameters, partly in elegiacs, and in the *Margites*, in which the hexameters are interrupted from time to time by iambics. We may also refer to what we may perhaps call experimental adaptations of the hexameter found in early poets.[1] (*b*) In subject—the transition from didactic (gnomic) to political or patriotic (hortatory) poetry may be seen in Callinos and Tyrtaios, and also (in a different direction) in Solon. The transition from the didactic to the satirical may be seen in Simonides, while Asios apparently produced both antiquarian and satirical poems. For the latter we may also refer to the *Margites*.

Among the early Teutonic peoples the development seems on the whole to have followed much the same lines as in Greece.

Phase I is represented both in English and in Norse. The earlier (minstrel) form was long preserved both in England and on the Continent. In the North it was given up, at least for the most part (cf. p. 588). We have very little information relating to the poets who cultivated heroic poetry (Types A and B) in the North. For the passages relating to Thormóðr Kolbrúnarskald and Nornagestr we may refer to p. 576 f. It may be observed that in Norse, as in Greek, stories relating to gods are treated in the same metre as heroic stories, and that the differences in style between the two sets of poems correspond in general to the differences between the two sets of poems in Greek. It is not unlikely, therefore, that here also heroic stories and stories of the gods were treated by the same poets. From England and the Continent we have only heroic poetry, owing to the early adoption of Christianity in these regions.

The minstrels of whom we hear in the English poems are court minstrels. In *Beowulf* King Hrothgar has a minstrel (*scop*)—perhaps more than one—who entertains the court from time to time (cf. p. 573). Deor at the close of his elegy (35 ff.) gives the following account of himself: "With regard to myself I will say that formerly I was the minstrel of the Heodeningas and dear to my lord....For many years I had a good office and a gracious master. But now Heorrenda, a skilful

[1] E.g. Terpandros, fragm. 4; cf. Edmonds, *Lyra Graeca*, I. 32.

poet, has received the domain which the king had given to me." Widsith again is a traveller who prides himself on the large number of nations he has visited. He states also that he has been handsomely rewarded by various princes for his poetry. In 94 ff. he says that on his return home he presented to his lord, Eadgils, prince of the Myrgingas, a valuable 'ring' which had been given him by Eormenric. This present was a reward to Eadgils for his kindness in granting the poet the land which had previously been held by his father. It would seem then that he is a man of good position. In the prologue it is stated that he accompanied a princess named Ealhhild, apparently a sister of Eadgils, to the court of Eormenric.

Such minstrels are known also in the medieval German poems. Horant (Heorrenda) is one of the leading characters in *Kudrun*. In the *Nibelungenlied* the invitation sent by Etzel (Attila) to the Burgundian king is conveyed by two of his minstrels.

But minstrelsy is by no means confined to professionals. We have seen (p. 575 f.) that in *Beowulf* King Hrothgar himself recites to the harp, and perhaps other members of his court do the same. Gelimer, the last king of the Vandals, was a poet and harper (*ib.*). In the *Atlakviða* (st. 31) and elsewhere Gunnarr is represented as a harper. We may refer also to Folker in the *Nibelungenlied*, who is said to be a nobleman and a minstrel.

In works relating to later times we hear of minstrels who entertained the general public with heroic poetry accompanied by the harp. Such are the minstrels mentioned in Alcuin's letter to Hygebald quoted on p. 573. Bernlef, the blind Frisian minstrel (cf. p. 575), belongs to this class. It may be added that in Frisian law[1] a special compensation was fixed for injury to the hand of a harper.

Phase II is also represented both in England and in the North. From Bishop Daniel's letter, referred to on p. 325 f., we may infer also that it was known in Germany, though nothing of this kind has survived. Unfortunately we have no information relating to poets of this phase in England. Neither do we know anything of the poets responsible for the *Edda* poems belonging to this phase. The only passage which gives us any indication as to the source of these poems (*Háv.* 111) will be discussed later.

Of the authors of Norse antiquarian (not gnomic) poetry, however, some are known to us. Bragi Boddason evidently occupied a high position; he was a friend of kings, such as Hjörr and Ragnarr. Thjóðolfr

[1] Mon. Germ., *Leg.* III. 699 f.

of Hvín was a distinguished member of Harold the Fair-haired's court, and the fosterer of one of his sons. Eyvindr Finnsson was a member of the court of Haakon I, and a descendant of Harold the Fair-haired.

Phase III is widely represented in the North, though little is known of it elsewhere. Most of the examples are either panegyrics and elegies (Type D), often in honour of kings, or short occasional poems (Type E), like those of Archilochos. For details we may refer to Ch. XI. The affinities of the former frequently lie with Phase I rather than with Phase III, as represented in Greek; but practically all the authors also have poems of Type E attributed to them. In some cases also they are authors of antiquarian poems (Phase II). The few English poems which may be assigned to this phase have little in common with those of the North (cf. pp. 338, 352 f.). Nothing is known as to the authors.

It may be observed that in England all phases generally use the same (uniform line) metre. The same metre was used also in Germany for Phase I; from Phase II nothing has been preserved. From the same metre again comes doubtless the Norse *Fornyrðislag*, in spite of its (often irregular) stanzaic character. This is the metre employed in most of the Norse heroic poems, and also in some of the *Edda* poems relating to the gods—including a few antiquarian, as well as narrative, poems. The *Málaháttr*, which is used in the remaining heroic poems, was probably of identical origin with the *Fornyrðislag* (cf. p. 29 f.).

The other Norse theological poems and the gnomic poems contained in the *Edda* use quite a different metre, the *Ljóðaháttr*, or metres akin to this, such as the *Galdralag*. These metres, in some form or other, are probably ancient; for English gnomic poetry contains a few passages which show a metrical form related to them. There cannot of course be any question as to the antiquity of the uniform line metre.

Thjóðolfr and Eyvindr, in their antiquarian poems, employ the *Kviðuháttr*, apparently a new modification of the *Fornyrðislag*; and this is occasionally used in poetry of Phase III (Type D), as are also the *Málaháttr* and the *Ljóðaháttr*. But the great majority of the poetry belonging to Phase III (both Type D and Type E) uses new metres involving the principle of rhyme or assonance. This goes back even to Bragi Boddason; but it is never found in the *Edda* or in any anonymous traditional poetry. In England rhyme occurs only in religious poetry, and probably not before the ninth century.

The transition between Phase I and Phase II may perhaps be seen in *Widsith*, which consists for the most part of catalogues, though the milieu is heroic. A similar transition may be traced in the *Edda* Trilogy, which preserves slight elements of heroic Type B, though in the main it has become a didactic work.

The transition from Phase II to Phase III may be illustrated from the poems of Bragi, Thjóðolfr and Eyvindr, all of whom are credited with occasional poems of Phase III, as well as with antiquarian poems. A similar transition may be seen in the *Hávamál*, st. 1–110, where a didactic (gnomic) collection has largely been converted into a satirical poem of entertainment. The transition between these phases, however, is less marked than in Greek.

Phase III is not represented with so much variety in Norse as in Greek. There is probably no choral poetry. The milieu is somewhat similar to that of Greek poetry of the seventh century, though it is not properly urban, but rather that of a travelling and trading society in which persons from distant lands were frequently meeting. For the most part it may be described as a middle-class milieu.

As regards professionalism in Phases II and III there is no evidence available except for the North. Many poets are attached to the courts of kings for varying lengths of time; but we do not know of any evidence for any other form of professionalism.

Sagas for the most part belong to Phase III. This applies to the 'Sagas of Icelanders' in general and to most of the stories contained in the 'Sagas of the Kings'. There are, however, a number of stories, mostly short, contained in both classes and more especially in the *Landnámabók*, which are of essentially antiquarian character and may be referred to Phase II. Sagas are practically always anonymous; but we think it is sometimes possible to trace with more or less probability the source from which they ultimately come. In Iceland saga was developed to a far greater extent than in Greece.

Women poets are often referred to and quoted; but the poems consist almost always of single occasional stanzas, generally improvised. A few fragments are preserved, however, of what appears to have been a longer poem by a certain Jórunn 'the Poetess', of whom nothing is known. The poem was apparently of Type D and celebrated the doings of Harold the Fair-haired. The question is perhaps worth raising whether heroic poetry was cultivated by women. We know of no external evidence to this effect; but it is remarkable that in the heroic poems of the *Edda* feminine interest greatly predominates and a large preponderance of the speeches are by women. This remark applies only to the poems composed in *Fornyrðislag*. Is it possible that this metre was cultivated by women after it had been given up by men? The *Grotta-*

söngr and the *Darraðarljóð* suggest the same question. We are inclined also to the view that a few sagas come ultimately from women. It has been suggested above (p. 542) that the greater part of *Thorfinns Saga Karlsefnis* and a portion of the *Groenlendinga þáttr* come ultimately from Guðríðr, daughter of Thorbjörn. We suspect that in the same way a large part of the *Laxdoela Saga* may be traced to Guðrún, daughter of Ósvífr. Mention has already been made (p. 582) of the fact that Snorri Sturluson speaks of Thuríðr, daughter of Snorri the Goði, as one of Ari's authorities—he says that Ari obtained much information (*froeði*) from her. It is perhaps worth observing that Snorri the Goði was an intimate friend of Guðrún and that Ari himself was her great-grandson.

As regards the chronology of the phases we have seen that in Greek Phase II seems to follow Phase I, making its first appearance in the eighth century, while it in its turn is followed by Phase III, which appears first in the seventh century. In the North such chronological sequence of the phases is not obvious. So far as we know, Bragi Boddason is the earliest poet of whose work anything has been preserved. Thjóðolfr is also one of the earliest. Yet both these poets belong in part to Phase III. But it is to be observed that both these poets, like all the poets of Phase III, use metres which can hardly be of early Teutonic origin, whereas no such question can arise with regard to the origin of the metres employed in the (anonymous) heroic poetry of Phase I. Phase II employs either the same metres as Phase I, or modifications thereof, or else a metre which also is probably ancient in some form or other (cf. p. 598). It would seem, therefore, that although all three phases can be traced back to the ninth century, Phase III was then probably more or less recent, whereas Phases I and II were already old.

As regards the sequence of Phases I and II, it is to be borne in mind that the features common to English and Norse in the latter are by no means so numerous, either in form or subject, as in Phase I. It would seem then that in the form in which we know it Phase II was of later development than Phase I. Yet both, without doubt, are very ancient. Both can be traced back to the first century. Tacitus, *Ann.* II. 88, speaks of poems (evidently heroic) in which Arminius was celebrated, while in *Germ.* 2 he refers to 'ancient poems', which treated of the mythical ancestry of the various Teutonic peoples, and which must have been of an antiquarian character, somewhat similar to the Hesiodic *Catalogue*.

In early Welsh there is little or no poetry which corresponds exactly to the Greek-Teutonic Phase I; but we have a good number of panegyric and elegiac poems which relate to the Heroic Age. Phase II is represented by many antiquarian and gnomic poems. The chronological relationship of these to the former can hardly be determined with certainty. The majority of them probably belong to a later period; but it is clear from the *Historia Brittonum* that Welsh antiquarian speculation had a long history. Evidence for the existence of Phase III is slight and doubtful,[1] apart from the late predictive poems discussed on p. 453 ff. Saga is first known with certainty from the twelfth century; but references in the *Historia Brittonum* and the *Mirabilia Britanniae* suggest that it had been cultivated for a long period. It has nothing in common with the saga of Phase III found in Greek and Norse. Its affinities and connections are rather to be sought in the first two phases.

As we have seen, there appears to be no evidence for different classes of poets who occupied themselves with different kinds of themes. The only bard whose name occurs at all frequently is Taliesin; and what we know of him is preserved in a very late and legendary form. The poems which claim to be his work vary greatly in character. Some are heroic panegyrics, while others are 'mystical' poems which have nothing in common with heroic poetry. Myrddin may also have been a professional bard, in view of *RBH.* I. II. But the records relating to him are likewise legendary; and the poems which bear his name are in their present form prophecies composed in much later times. There may have been bards who devoted themselves wholly to religious subjects; but even this cannot be proved. In the Laws (cf. p. 583) it is stated that when the king wishes to hear a poem the *Pencerdd* is to sing two religious poems, and a third upon the king himself or other princes. The recitation of sagas seems also to have been a function of the bards (cf. p. 584 f.).

There were however differences of status among bards, according to their attainments. Several early poems contain rather obscure references to a 'poetic chair'; and these are probably to be explained by a passage in the Laws (cf. p. 583), where it is stated that a bard becomes a *Pencerdd* when he wins a chair. A *Pencerdd* had certain very definite privileges at the king's court.

[1] The difficult stanzas preserved in the Cambridge MS. of Juvencus, and dating from the ninth century, seem to belong here. From the twelfth century onwards there is a large amount of poetry, chiefly of Type D (panegyrics, elegies, etc.), which is somewhat similar to the Norse poetry of this type.

There may have been poets who were not professional bards. At all events we hear of a poet of princely rank—Llywarch Hen, from whom the later kings of Gwynedd traced their descent, and who, according to the genealogies, was first cousin to Urien. The elegies which claim to be his work represent him as a vassal or subject of Urien and Owein; but he is evidently a warrior and the father of warriors. Among these elegies we may include *RBH.* XII, the author of which, though his name is not given, speaks (st. 20) of Urien as his lord and cousin.

From Ireland corresponding to the Greek-Teutonic Phase I we have a very large amount of heroic saga, much of which is preserved in early form, and also a good deal of heroic poetry of Type B contained in the sagas. Phase II is also largely represented in both poetry and prose. For Phase III there are numerous poems of Type D (panegyrics and elegies), mostly fragmentary, which, like the Norse examples of this Type, seem to have more in common with Phase I than with the Greek Phase III. On the other hand, there appears to be very little poetry corresponding to Greek and Norse occasional poetry; and this is mostly of ecclesiastical origin.

The Irish evidence relating to poets and saga-tellers is far fuller than that which is available for any other country included in the present survey; but unfortunately much of it is late and of doubtful value. Discrepancies indeed are frequent. It is clear, however, that poetry and saga were regularly cultivated by the same class or classes of persons.

In Ireland, as in Wales, we find the term *bard.* From the thirteenth century onwards, if not somewhat earlier, the bards were the chief intellectual force in the country; but in earlier times the term is comparatively seldom mentioned. Their training is said to have included the knowledge of certain metres.[1] It would seem from a passage in the *Book of Rights*[2] that they were regarded with contempt by the *filid.* The evidence, such as it is, suggests that they were an order of poets inferior to the *filid.*

The *filid* themselves would appear to have been primarily antiquarian poets but all kinds of poetry were apparently cultivated by them; and consequently the word *fili* is commonly translated by 'poet'. Again, the stories of Mongan (cf. p. 586) and Urard mac Coise

[1] *Metrical Tract. I* from the *Book of Ballymote*, of which tracts the text and summaries are published by Thurneysen, *Irische Verslehren* (Windisch, *Irische Texte*, III. 5 ff.; 109 f.).

[2] Ed. O'Donovan, p. 183.

represent them as providing entertainment to kings by the recitation of sagas; and according to the second tract on poetry contained in the *Book of Ballymote*[1] and dating from the eighth or ninth century,[2] and also other authorities, they were required by their training to know a very large number of these. The story of Mongan, however, suggests that they paid special attention to the antiquarian elements in the sagas.

The gnomic compositions which have survived are, it is true, attributed mostly to either princes or judges of the prehistoric period. There was, however, a tradition that the *fili* and the judge had once been identical. According to one (late) story[3] the *filid* were deprived of legal functions—which had hitherto belonged to them alone—on account of the obscurity of the language used by Ferchertne and Nede in their dispute. According to another story,[4] likewise late, the first laws were drawn up by a body of nine persons—three kings, including Loegaire, three bishops, including St Patrick, and three *filid* (*ollam*)—who evidently are regarded as the more or less professional element. Of the two chief gnomic collections attributed to judges, it is believed[5] that one, which bears the name of the legendary judge Morann, is actually the work of a *fili* who was also a judge. The other collection is attributed to the legendary judge Fithal (cf. p. 396), who elsewhere[6] is described as a *fili*.

The *filid* are said to have a long course of training. According to the second tract on poetry contained in the *Book of Ballymote* and dating, as we have seen, from the eighth or ninth century, this training occupied many years—the number is stated or implied variously as seven, ten and twelve years.[7] It consisted in learning a large number of sagas each year, in the study and cultivation of metres, in antiquarian lore of various kinds—especially in connection with *Dinnšenchas* or topographical poems—and, during the last years, in the study of spells and magic. The training was apparently oral in the main, though it included a knowledge of ogams. According to one tract the early part of the training was common to the *fili* and the bard; but the latter stopped at

1 Thurneysen, *Metr. Tract.* pp. 50, 117.
2 Thurneysen, *Ir. Heldensage*, p. 67.
3 Contained in the commentary on the *Senchas Mór* (*Ancient Laws*, I. 18).
4 Contained in the Introduction to the *Senchas Mór* (cf. MacNeill, *Studies*, XI. 23).
5 Cf. Thurneysen, *Zeitschr. f. celt. Phil.* XI. 78.
6 In *Cormac's Adventure in the Land of Promise* (*Irische Texte*, III. 257).
7 Cf. Thurneysen, *Metr. Tract.* in Windisch's *Irische Texte*, III. 29 ff.; 110 ff.

the seventh year. Among the *filid* themselves there were various grades, the highest of which was the *ollam*.

The powers and privileges claimed by the *filid* are said to have been very great in early times. They were entitled to rewards for their poems, graduated, it is said,[1] according to the metres employed—a statement which perhaps explains some mysterious notices in the Welsh poetic MSS. It was dangerous to refuse any request made by them; for they were credited with the power of causing disease, especially eruptions on the face, and even death (cf. p. 97). As an instance of the extravagant demands attributed to them by legend, we may cite the story, referred to on p. 98, of the *fili* Athirne, who visited Luain, a one-eyed king in Connaught, and demanded his eye—a request which the king was obliged to accede to.[2] In general their influence both with kings and with the community seems to have been very great.

Filid seem also to have been instructors of the young—at least of those who desired to become *filid* themselves,[3] if not of other young people also. It is commonly held that Gemman, the teacher under whom St Columba studied as a deacon,[4] was a *fili*. The laymen who are sometimes found teaching in monastic schools in later times, e.g. Flann Mainistrech at Monasterboice, also presumably belonged to the same class.

Filid were sometimes attached to the service of princes. Such was the case with Ferchertne who was in the service of CuRoi mac Dairi, while Amorgein was attached to the service of Conchobor. Elsewhere, however, we find *filid* who appear to be more or less independent and pay visits to various kings. As an example we may take Athirne, who belongs to Ulster, but acts in a very independent manner towards Conchobor and outrageously towards other kings. Indeed they are sometimes said to have had a kind of organisation extending throughout the country with an *Árd-fili* or *Árd-ollam hErenn* ('Chief Ollam of Ireland') at their head.

The *ollam*, who was a *fili* of the highest class, wore a dress composed wholly or in part of feathers,[5] had a retinue of his own, sometimes of

1 Cf. Thurneysen, *Metr. Tract.* (Windisch, *Irische Texte*, III. 109).

2 In the *Battle of Howth*, ed. and transl. by Stokes, *Rev. Celt.* VIII. 47 ff.

3 Thus Athirne is said to have been the instructor of Amargin; cf. Thurneysen, *Metr. Tract.* (Windisch, *loc. cit.* pp. 29, 31; cf. p. 114). Cf. also p. 411, above.

4 Adamnan, *Vita Columbae*, II. 25.

5 Cf. Cormac's *Glossary*, s.v. *tugen*; and the *Colloquy of the Two Sages*, cap. 8 (*Rev. Celt.* XXVI. 12 f.).

considerable size,[1] and was treated with great respect. Sometimes also we hear of what seems to be an official 'chair of the *ollam*' (*cathair ollaman*).[2] It is clear, therefore, that he corresponded closely to the Welsh *Pencerdd*.

Owing to their great numbers and the arrogance of their pretensions the *filid* are said to have come to be regarded with jealousy by the kings. This is stated[3] to have been one of the causes which led to the Convention of Druim Ceta, in the year 574, when an attempt to expel them was made by the high-king Aed mac Anmerech. On this occasion they were saved by the intervention of St Columba, though their numbers were reduced. The *Eulogy of Columba* is said to have been composed as a thankoffering by Dallan mac Forgaill, the chief *fili*. There was also a story that they had been expelled in much earlier times, but that they had then been protected by Conchobor.[4]

There seems to have been a tendency for the profession of *fili* and perhaps even for the rank of *ollam* to become hereditary. Thus in the *Colloquy of the Two Sages* (cf. p. 97) Nede, on hearing of the death of his father Adna, comes to claim the 'chair of the ollam' which the latter had held. The same remark is apparently true of bards also. In the first tract of the *Book of Ballymote*[5] we hear of a *bard áne* who is not a practising bard, but who has inherited the bardic rank from his ancestors. So in later times the office of scribe to certain noble families was hereditary.

The terms *fili* and *ollam* are, however, applied to certain princes of the legendary period. Such is the case with the legendary Leinster prince Finn Fili, from whom the kings of Leinster claimed descent. To him certain early poems[6] are attributed, though they must be several centuries later than the date assigned to him in the genealogies. Still farther back in the genealogies we find a (presumably mythical) king of the Ulster line named Ollam Fodla, who is famed as a lawgiver.

In sagas princes are credited not merely with poems (of Type B) but also with a knowledge of obscure poetic circumlocutions and with antiquarian lore. For an example of the former we may refer to the

1 Cf. the *Eulogy of Columba* (*Rev. Celt.* XX. 38 f.).

2 Cf. the *Colloquy of the Two Sages*, cap. 8 (*Rev. Celt.* XXVI. 12 f.).

3 Cf. the *Eulogy of St Columba* (*loc. cit.*).

4 *Loc. cit.*

5 Cf. Thurneysen, *Metr. Tract. I* (Windisch, *Irische Texte*, III. 5; cf. p. 108).

6 Cf. K. Meyer, *Abh. d. k. pr. Akad. d. Wissenschaften*, 1913, Phil.-Hist. Cl., Nr. 6, p. 38 ff.; Nr. 10, p. 9 ff.

Courtship of Emer,[1] where the dialogue between CuChulainn and Emer is said to be unintelligible to the rest of the party present. Speeches in the form of 'rhetorics' in this kind of language are of frequent occurrence. For the latter we may refer to the story noticed on p. 98, which describes how Mongan became involved in a dangerous antiquarian discussion with a *fili*.

It has been noted above (p. 586 f.), in connection with the recitation of stories, that the rank or position of the reciter is not always stated. There is no indication that DonnBo (in the *Battle of Allen*) is a *fili*, though he is said to be the best story-teller in Ireland. In the same passage we pointed out that the same ambiguity occurs with regard to Fedlimid, who is described as Conchobor's 'saga-teller' (*scélaige*). There is no hint that these persons were thought of as bards. Their position is quite uncertain. They appear to have been entertainers who were primarily concerned with heroic stories, and therefore correspond presumably to the Greek-Teutonic Phase I.

The *filid* were, however, undoubtedly reciters of heroic stories, but it will be clear from what has been said above, especially with regard to their training, that this was only one side of their activity. The list of sagas contained in the *Book of Leinster* concludes with a note as follows:[2] "He is no *fili* who does not synchronise and harmonise all the stories". Antiquarian study was presumably their chief preoccupation; and it may well be due to their activities that we find so much explanatory matter, e.g. speculations upon place-names, in the texts of the sagas. But it is also to be remembered that their training involved the learning of spells; and there are passages (cf. p. 466 f.) which illustrate how these were performed. There was therefore a mantic side to their character. This had naturally to fall into the background when Ireland became Christian; but the word *fili* itself indicates that manticism was their primary characteristic. For it is generally agreed that the word originally meant 'seer', and is closely connected with Welsh *gweled*, 'to see'. An earlier feminine form of the word is to be found in *Veleda*, the name of the prophetess of the Bructeri, mentioned by Tacitus, *Hist.* IV. 61 etc. The Romans would seem to have taken the Gaulish word for 'prophetess' as a proper name. It is clear then that the *fili* originally belonged to Phase II. In assuming the functions of a narrator of heroic sagas he seems to have encroached on the domain of Phase I.

[1] Ed. and transl. by K. Meyer, *Archaeological Review*, I. (1888); the transl. is also published by Hull, *Cuchullin Saga*, p. 57 ff. See especially, p. 63 ff.

[2] Cf. O'Curry, *MS. Materials*, p. 583; cf. also MacNeill, *Celtic Ireland*, p. 37 f.

From a comparison of the Welsh with the Irish evidence it will be seen that the two have much in common. Both in Wales and in Ireland we find a class of persons who cultivate both poetry and saga; and this class appears to be more highly organised, and probably more influential than any similar class to be found in Greece or in Teutonic lands. The *Pencerdd* obviously corresponds to the *ollam*; but it should be observed that the Welsh bard seems to correspond rather to the Irish *fili* than to the Irish bard, of whom little is known in early times. No word corresponding to *fili* is known in Welsh.

We must now turn for a moment to consider the evidence available for the ancient Gauls. No Gaulish literature has been preserved. But ancient writers, Greek and Latin, supply us with a good deal of information about the intellectual classes in the population; and the evidence which they yield throws some light on the early history of the Welsh and Irish classes which we have been considering. The most important references are as follows:

Strabo (IV. iv. 4) says that "there are three classes of persons who are especially honoured by the Gauls, viz. Bards, *Vates*, and Druids. The Bards are singers (or 'panegyrists'—ὑμνηταί) and poets, while the *Vates* are sacrificers and interpreters of nature (φυσιολόγοι). But the Druids practise both the interpretation of nature and moral philosophy. They are considered to be most just; and for this reason they are entrusted with the decision of all cases, both private and public. Formerly they even settled wars, and parted those who were on the point of fighting. Above all they were entrusted with the settlement of suits for manslaughter".

According to Diodoros (V. 31) the Gauls "have also composers of songs,[1] whom they call Bards. These accompany their songs with instruments resembling lyres, and in their songs they praise some persons and revile others. And there are certain philosophers and theologians who are called Druids and who are honoured exceedingly. They make use also of Seers (μάντεις) and reward them handsomely. These foretell the future by augury and the sacrifice of victims, and have the whole population under their influence....It is their custom never to offer sacrifice except in the presence of a philosopher. For they say that offerings acceptable to the gods must be made through those who are acquainted with the nature of the deity, since they only know their language; and they think that it is only through them that

[1] Ποιηταὶ μελῶν. We understand μελῶν to mean poetry accompanied by instrumental music.

benefits can be asked for. Moreover it is not only in regard to the ordinary requirements of peace time that these persons and the poets are obeyed, but even in war time too—and that not only by their friends, but also by their enemies. Often when armies have met one another in battle array, when swords have been drawn and lances hurled, these men have stepped in between the combatants and stopped the fight, like people who charm wild beasts".

Ammianus Marcellinus (xv. ix. 8), speaking of Gaul, says that "When people in these parts had gradually become civilised, praiseworthy intellectual pursuits, initiated by Bards and *Vates* and Druids,[1] began to flourish. The Bards sang to the sweet strains of the lyre the brave deeds of illustrious men, composed in epic poetry. The *Vates* began to examine and explain the system and the glories of nature. Among them the Druids, who were of loftier intellect, and bound by the rules of brotherhood as decreed by Pythagoras' authority, were exalted by investigations in deep and secret study, and despising human affairs, declared souls to be immortal".

It is clear that these three passages are not wholly independent, though there is little or no verbal agreement among them, and we cannot point to a common source with any certainty.[2] The discrepancies are noteworthy and somewhat tantalising. Diodoros clearly represents the bards as cultivating poetry of Type D; but Ammianus just as clearly means heroic narrative poetry of Type A, while Strabo is ambiguous. We are, therefore, left in doubt as to what the original writer said. He may of course have stated that the bards cultivated both types of poetry. Or again there may be more than one original authority. It is clear from other sources[3] that the Gaulish bards did cultivate panegyric poetry (Type D). A similar ambiguity prevails with regard to the functions of the *vates* and the druids. There appears to be some confusion between these two orders.

We may next quote Lucan, *Pharsalia*, I. 447 ff. The poet is describing how the Gauls are left in peace now that Caesar's armies have set out for Italy: "Ye Vates also, who by your praises celebrate for all eternity brave souls who have been cut off by war, to very many poems, ye Bards, have ye given utterance in security. Ye too, Druids, have

[1] The MSS. have various corrupt forms of these names, e.g. *euhages* and *drasidae*, obviously derived from a Greek text.

[2] Ammianus refers to Timagenes shortly before this passage; but Poseidonios is perhaps more likely to be the source.

[3] Cf. Appian, *Celtice*, cap. 12; Athenaios, IV. 37; VI. 39.

returned to your barbaric rites and your forbidding mode of worship, now that warfare is laid aside". Here again the same three names are mentioned; but it would seem that the *vates* are identified with the bards. The poems in this case might belong either to Type A or to Type D.

Lastly we may give a brief summary of Caesar's account (*Gall.* VI. 13 f.) of the druids, though he does not refer to the other two classes. He says that the druids had the entire control of religion and the direction of both public and private sacrifices. All suits of whatever character, whether private or public, were brought before them, and the decision was left entirely in their hands. They could enforce their sentences under penalty of excommunication, which was equivalent to outlawry. They were presided over by an arch-druid, who was elected for life; and they met annually in a consecrated place within the territories of the Carnutes, a district which was regarded as the centre of Gaul. But the institution was believed to have originated in Britain; and many still went there in order to acquire a more perfect knowledge of the system. The druids were excused from all tribute and military service, and devoted themselves to the study and exposition of natural philosophy (cosmology) and theology. Large numbers of young men resorted to them for instruction, which was given entirely in oral form—no writing was allowed—and involved learning by heart a large amount of poetry. Sometimes the training lasted twenty years.

It may be added that the druids do not appear to have been a distinct caste. They were, sometimes at least, drawn from the nobility. In Caesar's time the chief men among the Aedui were two brothers named Deiuiciacus and Dumnorix, the latter of whom was endeavouring to obtain the kingship. The former, according to Cicero (*De Diuin.* I. 41), was a druid and claimed to have the power of foretelling the future.

It will be seen from the passages noticed above that there are said to have been three different classes or orders among the Gauls, viz. the Bard, the *Vates* and the Druid. The two former are apparently confused by Lucan; but in view of the clear distinction drawn by the other authorities, this would seem to be due to misunderstanding on his part. On the other hand the distinction drawn between the *vates* and the druid by the first three authorities quoted is not altogether clear. Caesar makes no mention of the first two orders, but gives a detailed account of the druids. What he says of them has much in common with what we know of the Irish *filid*. We may refer in particular to the educational activities and the long training attributed to both these classes, and also to the fact that both are credited with having possessed judicial functions. There can be little doubt that the studies of the druids, like those of the *filid*, were largely of an antiquarian character.[1] It is to be borne in mind, however, that Ireland also possessed druids in heathen times.

The difficulty of distinguishing between the *vates* and the druid lies chiefly in the fact that Strabo and Diodoros represent both of them as taking part in sacrifices. In the passage quoted above indeed Strabo does not connect the druid with sacrifices; but in the next chapter he says that the Gauls never sacrifice without druids. Caesar and Lucan on the other hand attribute the sacrifices solely to the druids. It is true that the former does not mention the *vates*; but his words are quite explicit,[2] and seem to us to leave no doubt that he regarded the druids as responsible for the sacrifices. As the word *vates* and its cognates in Celtic, Latin and other languages—as we shall see later—are always connected with the ideas of prophecy, inspiration, poetry, etc., and never with that of sacrifice, the natural inference is that the *vates* attended the sacrifices as diviners, while the druids were the priests.

To this explanation it has been objected[3] that we hear sometimes of priests (*sacerdotes*) who are not described as druids. Thus Caesar (VII. 33) says that a certain man was appointed chief magistrate of the Aedui by the priests—i.e. probably with due formality—while Lucan (III. 424 f.) mentions the priest of a sacred wood near Marseilles, which he describes at length. It is held that the true Gaulish name for the priest of a sanctuary was *Gutuater*, which occurs in several inscriptions of the Roman period[4] and which has been interpreted as 'father of invocation'. But there is nothing to show that the *Gutuater* was not a druid, though after the Roman conquest the latter term was probably avoided in official records. Again, Lucan's description of the sacred wood with its *barbara sacra*, i.e. human sacrifices (III. 403 ff.), distinctly recalls the passage quoted from the same poem on p. 608 f., which goes on to say

[1] Caesar speaks only of cosmology and theology; but Ammianus (XV. ix. 4) refers to the druids as authorities upon the history of the nation.

[2] VI. 13: (Druides) *sacrificia publica ac priuata procurant*; cf. VI. 16: *administrisque ad ea sacrificia Druidibus utuntur.*

[3] Cf. Dottin, *Antiquité Celtique*, p. 364 f.

[4] It seems to occur also (much corrupted in the MSS.) in Caesar, VII. 3, VIII. 38, as the name of a man of the Carnutes, who was responsible for the great revolt of the Gauls in 52 B.C. Is it a title here? He must have been a person of very great importance.

(I. 453 f.): "Ye (druids) inhabit deep glades in secluded groves". It is difficult to believe that the poet was thinking of a different class of persons. The association of druids with sacred groves and human sacrifices offered in them occurs again in Tacitus' account (*Ann.* XIV. 29) of Suetonius Paulinus' attack upon Anglesey. We may refer also to Maximos Tyrios' statement (VIII. 8) that "the Celtic image of Zeus is a lofty oak", and to a passage in Pliny's *Natural History* (XVI. 95), where he says that the druids "select groves of oaks and perform no religious rites without leaves from them". After the latter passage Pliny goes on to describe the ceremonial cutting of the mistletoe from an oak; but before doing so he suggests that the name *Druidae* is derived from the word for 'oak'. We see no reason for doubting that this etymology is correct.[1]

For this association of the druids with the sacrificial grove analogies are to be found in the priesthoods of various European peoples. Teutonic and Greek parallels will be noticed later. But the most interesting examples come from Lithuania and neighbouring regions—especially the national sanctuary of the heathen Prussians at Romove, where the priests lived and performed their rites beneath the sacred oak. The evidence seems to us to leave little room for doubt that druidism was of similar origin. As regards the intellectual activities of the druids analogies are to be found, not only in India, but also, and more especially, among the Thracian Getae,[2] where the priests are credited with very similar learning, in natural philosophy as well as theology.

We have not spoken of Irish druids in this chapter, because their

[1] Cf. Chadwick, *Journ. R. Anthr. Inst.* 1900, p. 34, note. The origin of the name must of course be sought in a Celtic word corresponding exactly to the Gk. δρῦς (not in the Greek word itself, as Pliny seems to suggest). This Celtic word must originally have had two slightly different forms **drū-s* and **dr̥u-s*, from the latter of which come Ir. *daur*, W. *dar*, 'oak'. To the former we may trace not only the name *Druidae*, but also Δρυνέμετον, the name of the meeting place of the Galatian council (cf. Strabo, XII. v. 1)—which would seem originally to have meant 'oak-sanctuary'. These etymologies, which were current long before our time, have been disputed for many years by the majority of philologists. But we are glad to see that the leading Celtic scholar of the day has recently come back to them; cf. Thurneysen, *Zeitschr. f. celt. Philol.* XVI. 276 f. For a partial analogy we may compare the name of the Lithuanian thunder-god, *Perkunas*, which would seem originally to have meant 'the (god) of (or 'in') the oak' (cf. Chadwick, *loc. cit.*).

[2] Cf. Dottin, *Antiquité Celtique*, p. 389 f. Unfortunately we are almost wholly dependent upon Jordanes, *Get.* 5 ff., especially the ludicrous rhetorical account in cap. 11. See Addenda.

connection with the history of literature is not obvious. But in view of the Gaulish evidence we must now notice briefly what is said of them.[1] Sagas refer to them chiefly in connection with their mantic faculties. Thus in the *Táin Bó Cuailnge*[2] Medb consults her druid as to the success of her expedition before she sets out. It is the druid Cathbad who prophesies the disasters that would arise from Derdriu's birth, at the opening of the *Exile of the Sons of Uisliu*; and it is a prophecy of the same druid which in the *Táin Bó Cuailnge*[3] induces CuChulainn in his boyhood to ask Conchobor for arms on a certain day. They are also frequently represented as working spells, as in the *Destruction of Da Derga's Hall*, cap. 144, where they bring a thirst upon Conaire, and in the *Fate of the Children of Uisnech* (531 ff.), where Cathbad produces a sea in front of the heroes. But they are also teachers. In the passage of the *Táin* last noticed Cathbad has eight pupils—a hundred in the earlier text—to whom he teaches druidic learning. The numbers of the druids, however, seem to be quite small. In each kingdom there is apparently one who has close relations with the king, e.g. Cathbad with Conchobor, and—in the *Battle of Cnucha*[4]—Nuadu with Cathair Mor. The latter story shows that the office was sometimes inherited. The position of the druids was very high, and they were intermarried with the royal families. Indeed, according to one story, Cathbad is Conchobor's father.

The druids soon came into conflict with the Church. They are frequently mentioned in Lives of the saints, and almost always as working in opposition to the saints. They do not seem to have become wholly extinct before the seventh century. It may be observed that the *magi* of the Picts, frequently mentioned in Adamnan's *Life of St Columba*, appear to have been persons of the same class. One of them, Broichan by name, is the foster-father of King Brudeus. The same term (*magi*) occurs also in the *Historia Brittonum*, in the story of the boy Ambrosius (cap. 40 ff.), where it is presumably a translation of W. *derwydd*, 'wizard', 'druid'. The latter word is not strictly identical[5] with Gaulish-Latin *druida*, Ir. *drui*, 'druid'; and there is no satisfactory

[1] A valuable list of references to Irish druids (and *filid*) will be found in Plummer, *Vitae Sanctorum Hiberniae*, I. clviii ff.

[2] Windisch, 194 ff.; p. 13 in Dunn's translation.

[3] Windisch, 1073 ff.; p. 60 in Dunn's translation.

[4] Ed. and transl. by Hennessy, *Rev. Celt.* II. 86 ff.

[5] It appears to have been influenced by the word for 'oak' (W. *dar*, for earlier *daru-s*); cf. Thurneysen, *Zeitschr. f. celt. Philol.* XVI. 277. This influence is noteworthy as showing the continued connection between druid and oak.

evidence for the survival of druids as a class in the historical period in Wales. But we do not think it is justifiable on these grounds to deny a connection between the two words or to deny that the history of the Welsh word may go back to the days of druidism.

It will be seen that the difference between the druid and the *fili* in Ireland is hardly more clear than the difference between the druid and the *vates* in Gaul, as represented by ancient writers. For the *fili*, like the druid, had a mantic side to his character; and, to judge from the name (cf. p. 606), this must originally have been his primary function. The only thing which is clear is that the position of the druid was incompatible with Christianity, while that of the *fili* was not. The cause of this is presumably to be found in the druid's relations with the heathen gods, especially perhaps in sacrifices.[1] He may also have been connected with sanctuaries; but these are seldom referred to in Irish records.

It is difficult to doubt that there was some connection between the *fili* and the Gaulish *vates*. The two words are unconnected; the word *vates* recurs in Irish in the form *fáith*, 'prophet', which is only seldom applied to a *fili*—e.g. in the *Colloquy of the Two Sages* (272). More frequently it is used for Biblical prophets; but in sagas it seems to occur chiefly in the compound *ban-fáith* (*banfáid*), 'prophetess', a term which is applied e.g. to Fedelm, the seeress who prophesies to Medb in the *Táin Bó Cuailnge*.[2] In the later text (*Book of Leinster*) she comes from the shee-mound of Cruachan; but in the earlier text (*Yellow Book of Lecan*), where she is also called *ban-fili*,[3] she seems to be a mortal. Yet the mantic functions of the *fili* must not be forgotten, though they doubtless tended to fall into the background in Christian times. Here again too the Welsh evidence should not be overlooked. We know nothing of a Welsh class corresponding to the *filid*, except the bards (cf. p. 607); and there is probably no trace[4] of a word exactly identical with Gaul. *vates*, Ir. *fáith*. But there are closely related words, *gwawd*, 'poetry', 'panegyric', or 'abusive poem', 'mockery'; and *gwawdydd*, 'panegyrist', 'lampooner', which point to the former existence of

[1] References to sacrifices are rare, but there can be little doubt that even human sacrifice was practised; cf. *Rev. Celt.* XVI. 35 f. (from the Rennes *Dinnšenchas*); and K. Meyer, *Ériu*, II. 86.

[2] Windisch, 221; p. 15 in Dunn's translation. Cf. *YBL.* 43 (in Medb's speech).

[3] *YBL.* 38 (where the later text has *banfáid*).

[4] The *Hist. Brit.* cap. 62, mentions a certain poet called Cian, surnamed *Gueinthguaut*, which is commonly taken to stand for *Gwenith-gwawd*, 'Wheat-poem'. Could it not mean 'Wheat-poet'? But similar names occur elsewhere.

Welsh *vates* with the functions of the Irish *filid*. We think, therefore, that *vates* and *fili* were originally synonymous terms.

We may now summarise the Celtic evidence. There appear to have been three intellectual classes both in Gaul and Ireland. The evidence suggests that these classes were originally common to the various Celtic peoples.[1] The bard was originally occupied with heroic minstrelsy of Type D—also presumably with Types A and B, if these existed. Between the other two classes, the *vates-fili* and the druid, it is not easy to distinguish clearly, either in Gaul or in Ireland. Both seem to have claimed the power of prophecy or of second sight. The druid was apparently a priest, connected with the worship of the gods—hence his disappearance in Ireland as a result of the conversion. In Gaul law was in the hands of the druids; in Ireland it is said to have been in the hands of the *filid*. It is possible of course that the *filid* only obtained this power when the druids disappeared or lost their influence, though we know of no evidence to this effect in sagas or elsewhere. But no sagas or other records make clear what was the relationship between the *filid* and the druids in heathen times. One is tempted to suspect that the druids may have been promoted from the *filid*—and in Gaul from the *vates*. In that case the *ollam* was perhaps a substitute for the druid in Christian times. Yet we are inclined to regard any such suggestion as hazardous, though we think it probable that the *filid* encroached upon the functions of the druids, as they did apparently also upon those of the bards (cf. p. 606).

In Wales we find only one class, the bards; but their position and functions seem to correspond in the main with those of the *filid*, and their poetry is often described as *gwawd* which recalls the *vates*. The word *derwydd*—and also the plural word *drywon*[2]—survives as a reminiscence of the druids; but the class which properly bore this title doubtless disappeared at an early date. It would appear, therefore, that the three classes had been reduced to one—which, like the Irish *filid*, occupied itself with poetry of various kinds and saga-telling. The stories suggest that magic also, perhaps in the form of spells, was likewise cultivated by them. The *Pencerdd* corresponded to the *ollam*.

In addition to these professional classes there were probably in both

[1] This question has been frequently discussed. We may refer especially to Zimmer's article in Hinneberg's *Kultur d. Gegenwart*, I. II. i, p. 46; but we fear that the conclusions there drawn go a good deal beyond what the evidence warrants.

[2] We do not know the history of this word; but it seems to occur in early poetry (e.g. *Tal.* LIII. 37).

countries persons, especially of princely rank, who cultivated poetry. In Ireland we also hear of saga-tellers who are not described as *filid*. We are inclined to attribute to them the heroic 'saga of entertainment' (Type A), and to the *filid* the non-heroic saga, as well as all sagas with a moral, and the explanatory and synthetic elements in other sagas. Thus we would suggest that the *Destruction of Da Derga's Hall* had its origin among the *filid*, but that the *Táin Bó Cuailnge* has been merely worked over by *filid*. The *Courtship of Etain* may have elements from both sides, according as the sympathy lies with the king or with the god. But it would hardly be justifiable to assume that court entertainers like Fedlimid mac Daill were non-professional. They may have been bards, corresponding to the Welsh 'household bard' (*bardd teulu*). In such questions one can hardly get beyond conjecture. But the Welsh bards were saga-tellers.

There is no evidence for a new class of poet belonging to Phase III. Apart from ecclesiastics the poets would seem to have been persons of the same classes as those of earlier times. For women poets and saga-tellers the evidence is uncertain.

Between the Celtic evidence as a whole and the Teutonic evidence the differences are perhaps at first sight more noticeable than the resemblances. But this impression is due partly to the nature of the records. The evidence for the Teutonic peoples relates in the main to individuals, except in Phase I. The evidence for Gaul relates wholly to classes of persons, and the same is largely true of the Irish and Welsh evidence. For Ireland especially much of our information comes from antiquarian tracts and traditional regulations for which Teutonic records offer few analogies. If allowance be made for this difference in the records, we think that Teutonic parallels are to be found for all the classes or orders discussed above, though the organisation was probably not so highly developed.

The heroic minstrel of the Teutonic peoples must have had much in common with the bard. Our information with regard to the latter is meagre; but he was certainly a minstrel, and probably supplied entertainment, whether in poetry (Type A or B) or saga, as well as poetry of Type D.

Again, analogies to the druids are to be found in the Teutonic priests of heathen times. We have not referred to these before, because their connection with poetry or saga is nowhere expressly recorded; but the influence of such a class upon intellectual history cannot safely be ignored, any more than that of the druids. The priests mentioned in the earliest times[1] were state-priests. They had charge of the state sanctuaries (groves) and of the sacred objects preserved there, which they carried into battle. They presided over the assembly, which was also a court of justice; and both there and on the battle-field they were the only persons who were entitled to coerce and punish offenders. The excommunication of cowards, mentioned by Tacitus, *Germ.* 6, was doubtless pronounced by them. It was their function to interpret omens on behalf of the state, and presumably also to conduct the sacrifices, though this is not explicitly mentioned. It is probable that the state-priests were sometimes, if not always, of noble or princely rank; for a priest of the Chatti is included by Strabo (VII. i. 4) in a group of princely personages mentioned in connection with the triumph of Germanicus. The priests of the English, at least in Deira, were not allowed to bear arms, according to Bede (*Hist. Eccl.* II. 13), and the high-priest was a member of the king's council. The priests of later times in the North—frequently mentioned in sagas—were usually local chiefs who had temples of their own. They also had courts of justice over which they presided. Even after the conversion of Iceland they preserved the title *goði*, 'priest', though they were now purely secular magistrates without religious functions.

An important difference between the ancient Teutonic priests and the druids lies in the fact that we have no evidence in the former case for any priestly organisation extending over the whole country, nor for courts composed solely of priests. Yet in later times the *Lögrétta* or legislative council of Iceland approximated, in principle at least, to the druidical system; for it was composed of the various priests (*goðar*) together with two assessors nominated by each of them. Again we have no information to the effect that either the ancient Teutonic priests or the Norse priests of the Viking Age possessed an extensive and organised educational system. But it can hardly be doubted that the priest, both of early and late times, was expected to preserve the law and the traditions of the community—whether state or district—to which he belonged. It is only in a somewhat elementary form that analogies to druidism are to be sought among the Teutonic peoples. But the 'ancient poems' referred to by Tacitus, *Germ.* 2 (cf. p. 305 f.) testify to a long cultivation of antiquarian studies; and that these were connected with

[1] E.g. Tacitus, *Germ.* 7, 10 f., 40, 43. For further details and for Caesar's statement that the Germani had no druids, see Chadwick, *Folk-Lore*, XI. 268 ff.

sanctuaries—and consequently with the priesthood—is rendered probable by such passages as *ib.* 39 (see below), where we hear of a festival attended by deputies from all peoples of the same stock.

For the cultivation of such antiquarian studies analogies are to be found in the religious organisations of many peoples, as we shall see later. It will be sufficient here to refer to the Lithuanians, who retained much of their ancient religion down to the seventeenth century, and for whom consequently more information is available than for peoples converted in much earlier times. For an example we may quote from Matthaeus Praetorius[1] who wrote about 1670–80. He describes a sacrifice seen by one of his informants which took place close to an oak—presumably one of the holy oaks which figured so much in Lithuanian and Prussian religion. When the sacrifice was at an end the worshippers seated themselves round the oak. The priest (*Weydulut*) sat upon a large stone beside it and "delivered a sermon about their origin and ancient customs, beliefs, etc., mentioning Zemyna [the earth goddess], Perkuns [the thunder god], and others".

In connection with this passage we may perhaps refer to Tacitus' account (*Germ.* 39) of the great sacrifice in the sacred wood of the Semnones, where he says that "the whole of their religion is centred on this spot, their idea being that it was from there that the nation was sprung, and that there is the god who rules over all". For 'educational' addresses, like the one reported by Praetorius, we have no direct evidence among the Teutonic peoples—except possibly in *Háv.* 111 ff. (see below)—but in view of the nature of our information it cannot safely be assumed that they were unknown.

More important for our purpose is the question whether antiquarian learning and the other forms of learning and poetry comprised under Phase II were cultivated specially by any other class of persons among the Teutonic peoples—whether these peoples ever possessed an intellectual class or order corresponding to the Irish *filid*. In Icelandic sagas experts in antiquarian learning and in (traditional) law are most commonly described as *spakir menn*, which may be translated 'wise men'; but there is usually an implication of second sight, or at least of (mantic) skill in the interpretation of dreams. For an example we may refer to Ari's *Íslendingabók* (cf. p. 581 f.), cap. 4, where the term is applied to Thorsteinn Surtr and Ósvífr. Thorsteinn has a dream which is interpreted by Ósvífr as relating to the reform of the calendar, which was proposed by the former and accepted by the assembly of Iceland (c. 960).

[1] *Deliciae Prussicae* (Extracts, ed. by W. Pierson, Berlin, 1871), p. 24.

A derivative of the word *spakr* is the substantive *spekingr*, which may be translated 'sage'. It is occasionally qualified by *framsýnn*, 'foreseeing', or used with reference to the interpretation of dreams; but we find it also applied to members of kings' councils. Another derivative is *speki*, 'wisdom', occasionally qualified as 'wisdom relating to things which have not yet happened'. The word *spámaðr*, 'seer', is sometimes used in connection with these words, though it is not related to them, except perhaps in a very remote degree.

But there is an older word, *þulr*, which occurs only in the *Edda* poems, and occasionally in the learned and archaistic poetry of later times. In the latter it seems to mean 'poet', in which sense perhaps it is used by the learned Earl Rögnvaldr of Orkney (c. 1150) in reference to himself. In the *Edda* poems we find it in the *Vafþrúðnismál*, st. 9, where the learned giant Vafþrúðnir calls himself 'the old *þulr*', when Othin comes to compete with him in antiquarian learning. In the *Fáfnismál*, st. 34, Reginn is called 'the hoary *þulr*'. The same expression occurs again in *Háv.* 134, where Loddfáfnir is exhorted not to laugh at 'a hoary *þulr*'. In all these cases the word may be translated 'sage'. It may be observed that in the prose introduction to the *Reginsmál* Reginn is described as 'wise, cruel, and learned in witchcraft' (*fjölkunnigr*). A somewhat different use of the word, however, is to be found in *Háv.* 111, the introductory stanza of the second half of the poem (cf. p. 384). It will be convenient to quote this stanza again: "It is time to chant (*þylja*) on the chair of the *þulr*, at the spring of Fate. I saw and kept silence, I saw and pondered, I listened to the speech of men. I heard 'runes' spoken of—nor did they keep silence about the interpretation thereof—at the Hall of the High One. In the Hall of the High One I heard such words as these". Then begin the precepts of the *Loddfáfnismál*, followed by the mystical matter and the list of spells. The milieu is here that of a sanctuary, and so the meaning required for *þulr* appears to be 'prophet'. In what follows the god Othin (the 'High One') is the speaker, and we take the poem from this stanza to the end to be the utterance of a revelation by him.

The verb *þylja*, 'chant', which occurs in the last passage, and is closely related to the word *þulr*, is used elsewhere for the chanting—perhaps in a low voice—of hymns to heathen gods. An example from *Thorfinns Saga Karlsefnis* has been noticed on p. 579. The word also means 'to mutter', or 'talk to oneself'. More than once it is used in sagas of men of second sight, denoting a habit attributed to them. Another related word is *þula*, 'poem'—a term applied especially to catalogue poems, e.g. the *Rígsþula* (cf. p. 420 f.), and also the *þorgrímsþula*, the fragments of which consist of lists of legendary horses and oxen.

At Snoldelev in Denmark there is a memorial stone bearing an inscription which states that it belongs to Gunnwaldr, son of Hroaldr, *þulr* at Salhaugar. The inscription is believed to date from about the beginning of the ninth century. The word *þulr* would here seem to be a descriptive title.

The English form of the same word (*þyle*) occurs in Anglo-Saxon glosses and elsewhere as a translation of *orator*. In *Beowulf* we find a person called Hunferth (Unferth) who sits at the Danish king's feet, and is obviously an important member of his court. The word here is commonly translated 'spokesman'; but the part which he plays rather suggests that he is a 'man of information'—the person whose business it was to know all about visitors and their origin.

Taking all the evidence together the word *þulr-þyle* would seem to have the following meanings: (1) a poet, perhaps a specially learned poet; (2) an (old) sage, especially one who is versed in antiquarian lore; (3) a prophet; (4) a spokesman, or 'man of information'. It will be seen that these characteristics, taken as a whole, approximate closely to those of the *fili*. We may add that, like the latter, the *þulr-þyle* is sometimes connected with the king's court, as may be seen from *Beowulf*.

On the other hand, in contradistinction to the *filid*, there is nothing to show that the *þylir* formed an organised class, or that they possessed any educational system, whether for their own disciples or for the community in general. The peculiar framework of Snorri's *Gylfaginning* does indeed suggest a tradition of oral instruction in antiquarian lore by way of dialogue, as we might expect; but even here we find only one inquirer. If there had been any organised system in the North, such as existed among the *filid* of Ireland and among the druids of Gaul, we should almost certainly have heard of it.

At all events there can be no doubt that, just as the *filid* were responsible for Phase II in Ireland, so the *þylir* and *spakir menn* whom we have been discussing were the people mainly responsible for the same phase in the North. In the *Vafþrúðnismál* a *þulr* is an expert in antiquarian lore. In the *Loddfáfnismál*, a collection of gnomic precepts, mystical lore, and spells is recited from the chair of the *þulr*. In English sources *þyle* is an 'orator' and probably a man of general information. Moreover *þula* is the technical term for a catalogue poem, while the verb *þylja* is used for the chanting of the *Loddfáfnismál* and of hymns to the gods, as well as for the (audible) musings of second-sighted men. Lastly, the *spakir menn* of later times are experts in antiquarian lore and traditional law; frequently also they are interpreters of dreams or possess second sight. These are precisely the activities comprised in Phase II. It may be observed that some of the antiquarian poets, such as Thjóðolfr and Eyvindr, like the *þyle* Hunferth in *Beowulf*, are attached to courts; but on the whole such cases seem to be rather the exception than the rule.

Did women share in these activities? We know of no direct evidence to this effect. Yet prophecy and witchcraft are usually associated with women from Roman times down to the end of the saga period. In the *Völuspá* (cf. p. 320 f.) the speaker is a seeress or witch (*völva*). In the *Sigrdrífumál*, which consists of mystical lore and moral precepts, the speaker is a Valkyrie. For other examples we may refer to Ch. XV (p. 448 ff.).

Traces of a terminology common to the Celtic and the Teutonic languages are not wholly wanting. No word corresponding to *fili* exists in the latter; but the words *spámaðr*, *spákona*, 'seer', 'seeress' (from *spá*, 'vision', 'prophecy'), spring from the same idea. Again, though there is no word exactly corresponding to Gaul. *vates*, forms identical with the very closely related Welsh *gwawd* are to be found in Anglo-Saxon *wōþ*, Norse *óðr*, 'poetry', 'eloquence'. We may compare the word *Óðrerir*, the name of the mythical vessel in which the poetic mead was kept (cf. p. 249), but originally, doubtless, the name of the mead itself. The word would seem to have meant 'that which stirs poetry (or eloquence)'. The name of the god *Wōden-Óðinn* is in all probability related; the original meaning may have been 'inspired'. The words *gwawd*, *wōþ*, and *óðr* without doubt come from a common original denoting the activities or gifts from which the *vates* derived his name.[1] Among other mantic terms which are common to the Celtic and Teutonic languages we may mention Welsh *coel*, Anglo-Saxon *hǣl*, Norse *heill*, 'omen', and Welsh *hud*, Norse *seiðr*, 'witchcraft'.

[1] In the *Vafþrúðnismál*, *oeði*, a derivative of *óðr*, is repeatedly used for the intellectual endowments of the giant, who is a *þulr*. So too in Anglo-Saxon the words *þylcræft* and *wōþcræft* seem to be synonymous. In view of the phonetic changes which have taken place in the various languages it may be convenient here to give what are believed to be the original forms of the words which we have been discussing: Ir. *fáith* is believed to come from **wātis*; N. *óðr*, and probably W. *gwawd*, from **wātus*; A.-S. *wōþ*, from **wātā* (perhaps deflected from **wātus*); W. *gwawdydd*, from **wātios*; N. *oeði*, from **wātiom*; A.-S. *Wōden*, N. *Óðinn* from **Wātenos*. A.-S. *wōd*, N. *óðr*, 'frenzied', 'mad', is probably also related to these words.

From what has been said it will be seen that classes of persons corresponding within certain limits to the three intellectual classes of Gaul and Ireland are to be found among the Teutonic peoples of heathen times. We have no evidence, however, for an organisation extending over a whole country, or for an elaborate educational system, such as we find among the druids of Gaul and the *filid* of Ireland. Some sort of organisation must have existed in connection with state sanctuaries and sacrifices, and also for the sanctuaries and sacrifices to which whole districts in Norway[1] resorted, and which were presided over by bodies of leading men, presumably priests. But it is uncertain to what extent these persons resembled the druids; there is no ground for believing, for example, that they abstained from warfare. In the case of the *þylir* or *spakir menn* there is no evidence for any organisation; we ought perhaps to describe them as a type of persons with certain qualifications, rather than as a class. But it is not clear that the Gaulish *vates* were organised, unless they were included in the druidical system.

How far can these same classes be traced in Greece?

It has been seen above that the Homeric minstrels closely resembled the heroic minstrels of the Teutonic peoples. The resemblance of both to the Celtic bards depends on the extent to which the latter were entertainers, whether by poetry of Types A or B or by saga, as well as panegyrists. Minstrel poetry of Type D seems not to be mentioned in the Homeric poems, except perhaps in *Il.* XXIV. 720 ff.

Priests are mentioned fairly often in the *Iliad*; but most of the references are merely incidental—they are referred to as fathers of Trojan warriors. They are said to be greatly honoured, and sometimes at least they are among the leading nobles. Each of them is said to be the priest of a special god, e.g. Hephaistos, Zeus of Ida, the river-god Scamandros. Probably they had charge of the temples of these gods, though this is actually stated only in the case of Theano, the priestess of Athena. On the occasion of a ceremony (*Il.* VI. 297 ff.) she opens the door for the procession and offers prayer to the goddess. She is the wife of Antenor, who appears to be the most important man in Troy after the royal

[1] We may refer to the sanctuary at Mæren in the upper part of the Throndhjem Fjord, the sacrifices at which are described in *St Olaf's Saga* (*Heimskr.*), cap. 115. Earlier references to the same sanctuary may be found in *Hákonar Saga Góða*, cap. 19, and *Ólafs Saga Tryggv.* cap. 74 f. The sacrifices were governed by a body of leading men of the district (twelve in St. Olaf's time), whose connection with the sanctuary seems to have been hereditary. In *Yngl. Saga*, cap. 2, the gods themselves are said to have a body of twelve priests, who are also judges.

family. There are no references to priests in the Achaean army; but the allusion (*ib.* IX. 575) to the Aetolian priests who are sent to placate Meleagros shows that Trojan custom was not regarded as alien from that of Greece in this respect.

In addition to the priests mentioned above, who seem to be connected with temples in cities, we hear in the *Iliad* (I. 11 ff.) of a priest of Apollo at a place called Chryse on the coast, apparently far from any city. He invokes his god to send a plague upon the Achaeans and, later, offers sacrifice to him to stop it (*ib.* 462 f.). He carries a golden staff, like a king; but no indication is given as to whether he was a local chief, like the Norse *goði* (cf. p. 616), or a person of purely religious functions. In the *Odyssey* (IX. 197 ff.) there is mention of another priest of Apollo, named Maron, at a city called Ismaros in Thrace—perhaps the later Maroneia. He dwells in a grove of trees belonging to Apollo; but it is not stated whether this is inside the 'city'—which is apparently quite small—or outside, like the grove of Athena outside the city of the Phaeacians (*ib.* VI. 291 ff.). The priest is evidently a wealthy man, and gives Odysseus wine and other presents, because he spared his household when he sacked the city.

Another type of priesthood—quite different at least from the Trojan—seems to be implied in Achilles' prayer to Zeus of Dodona (*Il.* XVI. 233 ff.), where he says that "thy interpreters (if this is the meaning of ὑποφῆται) dwell around thee with unwashed feet, making their beds upon the ground". This also was a tree-sanctuary; Zeus' oracles were delivered from a lofty oak (cf. *Od.* XIV. 327 ff.), as in later times. In Herodotos' day the interpreters of the oracles were three women, whom he calls (II. 55) both prophetesses (προμάντιες) and priestesses; but there appear to have been men also, called Tomuroi, according to Strabo, VII. vii. 11. In general the sanctuary seems to have borne a close resemblance to the oak-sanctuary at Romove (cf. p. 611).[1]

In later times also priests are regularly associated with temples of various deities. The office was frequently hereditary, at least in the sense that the priest had to be chosen from a special (noble) family, such as the Eumolpidai and the Eteobutadai at Athens. In some cases he had to wear distinctive robes and to follow a course of life different from other men. But there appears to have been great diversity of usage.

This diversity of usage, both in Homeric and in later times, is a characteristic which the Greek priesthood shares with the Teutonic.

[1] Cf. Chadwick, *Journ. R. Anthr. Inst.* (1900), pp. 32, 36; Welsford in Hastings' *Encyclopaedia of Religion and Ethics*, art. *Old Prussians.*

Indeed the differences in general between the two systems are hardly more than would necessarily arise between a people concentrated in cities from early times and a people who knew no cities except in conquered lands. As against the druidical system neither of the two had an organisation extending throughout the country nor an elaborate course of education connected with it, so far as we know. Yet the Greeks had confederations ('Amphictyonies'), somewhat similar to those in Norway mentioned on p. 621, but on a larger scale, for the observation of certain festivals, which were governed by representatives of the various states or groups of states participating. Indeed the festivals at Olympia and elsewhere, as well as the oracle at Delphoi, were resorted to by all Greece. It is true that these festivals were not controlled by a Pan-Hellenic priestly organisation. Yet the analogies are important; and in general the difficulty of reconciling the grove-sanctuary with the Pan-Gallic intellectual activities of the druids is materially reduced by a consideration of the Greek evidence. There is no need to assume uniformity of the sacerdotal class in Gaul, any more than in Homeric Greece.

More important for our purpose is the Greek evidence for the cultivation of antiquarian learning at sanctuaries. The Teutonic evidence, as we have seen, is merely indirect and inferential. But Herodotos (II. 55) states explicitly that he derived his information regarding the origin of the sanctuary at Dodona from the priestesses themselves. Again, the 'men of Delos', from whom he says he received much information of this kind, can hardly have been persons unconnected with the temple. And many other passages both in his *History* and in later works point clearly to a similar origin. Indeed there can be little doubt that we are largely indebted to the sanctuaries for the mass of (often discrepant) tradition and speculation which has come down to us.

Apart from minstrels and priests the Homeric poems refer not unfrequently to the *mantis* or seer. In the *Iliad* we hear chiefly of Calchas, who accompanies the Achaean army evidently as a professional seer, though it is not clear that he is in the personal service of Agamemnon or any other prince. The Hesiodic *Melampodia*, as we have seen (p. 474), contained an account of a contest between him and a rival seer named Mopsos, which ended in the death of Calchas. In the surviving fragment the test—which is decisive—lies in reckoning the number of figs upon a certain tree.

Seers of princely rank are also mentioned in the Homeric poems. Among these is a son of Priam named Helenos, who is described as 'best of augurs',[1] and who comprehends a conversation between Athena and Apollo (*Il.* VII. 44 f.). A more striking case occurs in the *Odyssey*, XX. 351 ff., where Theoclymenos, a descendant of Melampus, has a vision of the impending slaughter of the suitors. The genealogy of this man, given *ib.* XV. 225 ff., shows clearly that mantic faculties were already believed to be hereditary.

Of other seers belonging to the Heroic Age the most famous are Melampus himself—who appears both as seer and as healer of mental diseases, and subsequently also as king of Argos—and Teiresias the Theban, grandfather of Mopsos. Here also we ought perhaps to mention Cheiron, 'the most just of the Centaurs', who appears sometimes as a prophet, sometimes as a teacher or educator. In the *Iliad* he is said to have taught surgery to Asclepios and Achilles and to have presented Peleus, the father of Achilles, with a spear. There was a Hesiodic poem called *Instructions of Cheiron*, which would seem to have been of a gnomic character, if we may judge from one or two short fragments which have survived (cf. p. 392). It is to be observed that all these persons appear to have figured much more largely in non-heroic stories (cf. p. 116 f.) than in heroic poetry. The notices which we have of them are derived probably for the most part from Hesiodic poetry.

In later times we hear not rarely of 'state-seers'. In decrees of the Boeotian confederation the name of the official mantis is recorded as late as the fourth—or perhaps the third—century. At Sparta a similar office was held by persons who claimed descent from Calchas. We may also refer to the Iamidai, a famous family of seers, traditionally connected with Olympia. Greek armies of the fifth century frequently had seers attached to them.

In this class of persons we must also include the *Promantis*, who spoke as the mouthpiece of a deity at oracular sanctuaries. The most famous of these were the prophetesses of Apollo at Delphoi. Many of the oracles have been preserved; in early times they were always in hexameter verse (cf. p. 445). Sometimes, as at Dodona (cf. p. 622), the mouthpieces of deities are described as priests or priestesses.

Hesiod does not apply the term *mantis* or *promantis* to himself; but in the account of his 'call' (*Theog.* 22 ff.) he says that the Muses "inspired me with a voice divine to celebrate both the future and the past" (cf. p. 593). This is almost the same expression as that by which he describes (*ib.* 38) the activities of the Muses themselves: they tell of "the

[1] *Il.* VI. 76: οἰωνοπόλων, lit. those who study birds or omens. In XIII. 70 Calchas is called θεοπρόπος οἰωνιστής.

present, the future and the past". In the *Iliad* (I. 70) the same description is given of Calchas: "he knew the present, the future and the past". It is probably a static description of a seer. In the *Works and Days* also mantic elements are well represented in the lists of prohibitions and omens. Consequently, whether Hesiod called himself a *mantis* or not, there can be little doubt that his poetry is derived largely from this class of persons. The same remark applies to some lost poems which were often attributed to him. The *Melampodia* was apparently concerned with the stories of a number of famous seers; and some authorities credited him with a poem called *Ornithomanteia* ('Divination from Birds'). We may also refer to the *Instructions of Cheiron*.

Among later poets who occupied themselves with similar subjects mention may be made in particular of Epimenides, who seems to have been a seer, though he is also described occasionally as a priest. The list of works attributed to him includes the following titles:[1] (1) *Argonautica*, (2) *Purifications*, (3) *Origin of the Curetes and Corybantes, and Theogony*, (4) *Of Minos and Rhadamanthys*, (5) *Story of the Telchines*, (6) *Oracular Responses*. Of these Nos. 1 and 3–5 were presumably of antiquarian character, though the three latter had probably also interests in connection with religion, like Hesiod's *Theogony*. It is always to be borne in mind that in Greece, as in the North (cf. p. 451 f.)—and probably everywhere—prophecy and mantic vision applied to the unknown past, just as much as to the future.[2] Antiquarian studies or speculations therefore fell properly within the sphere of the *mantis*.

From what has been said above it will be seen that analogies to the three intellectual classes of Gaul and Ireland are to be found in Greece. Indeed they are more clearly distinguished here than elsewhere, though there is some overlapping between the priest and the seer—e.g. in oracular sanctuaries like Dodona[3] and perhaps in the case of certain individuals like Epimenides—which may help to the solution of certain difficulties in the Celtic evidence. With the Teutonic evidence the Greek has still more in common—thus, for example, Hesiod would have been recognised at once as a *þulr* in the North. It is true that neither Greek nor Teutonic parallels are to be found for the widespread organisation of Gaulish druidism or for the elaborate educational system of

[1] For the authorities see Kinkel, *Epic. Graec. Fragmenta*, p. 232.

[2] Cf. Aristotle, *Rhet.* III. 17 (with reference to Epimenides).

[3] At Delphoi this does not appear to have been the case. The prophetesses are said to have been uneducated, while the educated *Hosioi*, who presided over the temple, are presumably to be regarded as priests. But we are not sufficiently acquainted with the records to express an opinion with any confidence. The sanctuary had a long history.

the Irish *filid*. But the Greek Amphictyonies seem to have approximated to the former, within certain limits.

We may now return to the consideration of the 'phases'. Phase I is represented everywhere by composers and reciters of either narrative or panegyric poetry or both. In early times such recitations were in the form of minstrelsy, i.e. accompanied by stringed instruments, in Gaul as well as among the Teutonic peoples and the Greeks. Where narrative poetry was not cultivated its place was taken, at least in Ireland, by heroic saga of Type A. The minstrels were frequently professionals, attached to the service of princes;[1] but minstrelsy was cultivated by other persons also, including princes themselves. In Ireland heroic saga was cultivated both by *filid* (see below) and by other persons, who sometimes—as in the case of Fedlimid (cf. p. 587)—were attached to the service of princes. We do not know whether these saga-tellers were usually or ever identical with the bards who cultivated panegyric poetry. We suspect that such was frequently the case; but the Irish evidence relating to bards is meagre and unsatisfactory, while Wales had only one class corresponding to both *filid* and bards. The frequent occurrence of poetry of Type B in Irish sagas points at least to the cultivation of poetry by saga-tellers.

Phase II is at least as widely distributed as Phase I and covers a larger number of categories. Among these we may include not only antiquarian, gnomic and mantic poetry, but also probably 'descriptive' poetry, which is commonly associated with gnomic, and theological poetry, except such as was intended merely for entertainment. Non-heroic stories are also connected with this phase. In Gaul the representatives of this phase are to be sought among the druids and *vates*, in Ireland among the druids and *filid*. The druids disappeared soon after the conversion of the Irish; and it may be in part due to this fact that the *filid* have various functions which in Gaul are attributed to the druids. The Gaulish evidence rather suggests that there may be some confusion between the two classes in the traditions which represent the *filid* as judges. But we are not inclined to speak with much confidence as to the characteristics which differentiated the two classes.

In the North the representatives of Phase II are to be sought chiefly among the *spakir menn* and *þylir*; but the influence of the priesthood—from ancient Teutonic times onwards—is not to be disregarded, whether in theology, law or antiquarian learning. The Greek evidence differs

1 Gaulish examples are to be found in Appian, *Celtice*, cap. 12; Athenaios, VI. 49.

little from that of the North. In both cases we find at the beginning of the historical period a class—quite unorganised—of learned poets or sages, distinct from professional seers or priests. In both cases the history of intellectual life—or, perhaps we should say, of synthetic thought—seems to be bound up with this class. Yet the history of this class, like that of the *filid*, who represent the intellectual life of early Ireland, must be traced back apparently to the learning of the seer; neither Hesiod nor the *spakir menn*, any more than the *filid*, have parted with their mantic associations.

Both in Gaul and in Ireland Phase II is flourishing in the times of our earliest records. This is strictly true also in the case of the Teutonic peoples, whether we take the Norse evidence alone—which goes back only to the ninth century—or include the evidence relating to the peoples of the Continent in very much earlier times. In Greece on the other hand Phase II seems to be definitely subsequent to Phase I. It is not to be assumed that Phase II did not exist before the eighth century, the time of our earliest known authors. But the evidence tends to show that its cultivation as a fine art was later than that of heroic narrative poetry, and that it was greatly influenced by the latter both in matter and form. Such evidence as is available for the Teutonic peoples points to a similar development among them—perhaps to a less extent in the North than elsewhere, though even here we find the old heroic metre used sometimes for poems of a didactic (antiquarian) character.

It is important to observe that there appears to be a tendency everywhere for Phase II to encroach upon Phase I. Traces of this may be seen even in the Homeric poems, e.g. in the catalogue of Nereids in the *Iliad* (XVIII. 39 ff.) and, more especially, in the account of Odysseus' visit to the home of Hades (*Od.* XI. e.g. 235 ff.). In the lost Cyclic poems elements of this kind seem to have been much more prominent—we may refer, for example, to the purifications, the attention given to seers, and what appear to have been attempts at synthesis or explanation of the stories. A large amount of poetry belonging to Phase I was doubtless forgotten in early times; and the heroic stories with which it was concerned were known in the historical period only from antiquarian poets. With such poets the story of the voyage of the Argo seems to have been especially popular.

With the encroachment of Phase II is also probably to be connected the change in the method of recitation noted in the last chapter (p. 568 f.). In historical times the reciter had to seek his audience not in kings' courts but at social and public gatherings, especially when festivals took place at sanctuaries. There is no reason to doubt that hymns to the gods were recited by the same persons. Instead of a lyre the reciter now carried a staff or wand—which is probably to be connected with the staff of laurel given by the Muses to Hesiod as a symbol of his commission. It would seem then that the minstrels of the Heroic Age had been succeeded by a class of persons who originally were associated with religion—or derived their style of recitation from persons associated with religion. The sanctuary may have been the governing factor in the change. To the period when this change took place may perhaps be assigned many of the descriptive similes, which are calculated to appeal to a public gathering rather than to a king's court.

Among the Teutonic peoples the encroachment of Phase II takes different forms in different lands. In England heroic minstrelsy long maintained itself; but the influence of Phase II is shown by the large amount of gnomic matter—and descriptive matter connected therewith—incorporated in the poems, if we may judge from *Beowulf*. In the North, on the other hand, minstrelsy seems in general to have been given up, as in Greece; but we do not know when or through what circumstances this change took place. In the Trilogy we have a heroic story used as a framework for antiquarian, gnomic and other compositions belonging to Phase II. But gnomic elements are not introduced to any appreciable extent in the other poems. The influence of Phase II is also perhaps to be seen in the 'synthesis' of different stories, e.g. the stories of Guðrún and Jörmunrekr.

In Ireland we know that heroic sagas were largely cultivated and recited by *filid*, while in Wales the class called 'bards' have taken over the functions of the *filid* or *vates*. The influence of Phase II (i.e. the *filid*) is doubtless to be seen in the extensive use of synthesis and explanatory matter in the Irish sagas—most of all perhaps in the explanations of place-names.

We have yet to consider the characteristics of Phase III. The materials for this study are in general to be found only in Greek and Norse. In the other languages—apart from religious works—'post-heroic' poetry and saga offers little which is distinctive except the evidence for a growth of national feeling, which finds expression most clearly in the *Battle of Brunanburh* and a group of (late) Welsh predictive poems (cf. p. 453 ff.). Similar evidence is to be found in the works of certain Greek poets, especially Tyrtaios (cf. p. 355 f.). Such poetry is as a rule the product of times of stress; but its appearance is of great importance as marking the change from the principle of personal allegiance—which governs the society of the Heroic Age—to that of patriotism.

Apart from this the chief characteristic of Phase III, both in Greek and Norse, seems at first sight to be the prevalence of Type E, i.e. personal or occasional poetry, dealing with the poet's feelings, experiences and surroundings. Further enquiry, however, shows this impression to be misleading. Poems of Type E were composed in the Heroic Age itself. We may refer to the story of Gelimer, noticed on p. 576. Indeed traces of such poetry seem to be preserved in *Widsith* and *Deor* (cf. p. 25 f.). Moreover poetry of Type E flourishes among many peoples who are now—or were until very recently—living in the Heroic Age. Examples from the Tartars, Abyssinians, Gallas and Tuaregs will be noticed in the next volume.

The fact that so little heroic poetry of this type has come down to us from ancient times is due in part to the essentially ephemeral character of such compositions. Poetry of Type E seems to be preserved only under the following conditions: (i) if it is written down soon after composition; (ii) if it is attached to the name of a person of high position or distinction; (iii) if it is regarded as of conspicuous merit by later generations. The two latter conditions in general account for the preservation of Greek poems of this type dating from the seventh and sixth centuries[1] and of Norse poems dating from the Viking Age. As regards time—most of the Greek poems were probably committed to writing either by the authors themselves or at least within a century after their composition. In the case of the Norse poems this was doubtless quite exceptional (cf. p. 480). Most of them owe their preservation to being included in sagas. This means that many of them must have been preserved by memory for two centuries; but any poems surviving from the Heroic Age would have had to be remembered for at least six centuries.

Apart from the lapse of time account is to be taken of the fact that under 'post-heroic' conditions the second of the considerations noted above is to some extent dependent upon the third. It is true the preservation of panegyrics upon princes is doubtless often due to the fame of the princes themselves, and also that the sagas have preserved a good deal of poetry by practically unknown persons, much of which may be genuine, though it is of no conspicuous merit. But on the whole the preservation of the

[1] We refer of course to their preservation in Classical times. Now unfortunately we have only fragments; and many of these owe their preservation to mere accident—like many fragments of Norse and Irish poetry—through being quoted as illustrations of peculiarities of metre, diction or grammar.

poetry in, for example, *Egils Saga* is no doubt due in the main to Egill's fame as a poet. He was not a man of very high rank, though he had an adventurous career. It was owing to the social and political conditions of his time that he was able to achieve fame. And the same remark probably holds good for the Greek poets of the corresponding period.

The characteristics which seem really to be distinctive of Phase III may be summarised briefly as follows:

1. Innovations in form, especially metre. The new Norse metres are partly, but not wholly, due to foreign influence. They are used occasionally in antiquarian poems, but only by authors who also composed poems of Type E in new metres. We do not know the origin of the new Greek metres.

2. A tendency to humour, satire and cynicism, as in Simonides' poem on women and various poems of Archilochos. These features are very rare, though not absolutely unknown in Phase I. They appear to be quite foreign to Phase II.

3. A disregard or contempt for traditional standards, as in Archilochos' poem upon the loss of his shield (cf. p. 358). This feature is foreign to both the earlier phases.

These two characteristics are by no means so well represented in Norse as in Greek. Norse panegyrics upon princes (Type D) follow traditional lines and are generally such as might have been composed in the Heroic Age. Norse poetry of Type E has much more in common with Greek, but is more conventional. Yet a good example of No. 2 is to be found in one of Egill's stanzas, quoted on p. 365. And cynicism is nowhere better expressed than in the first part of the *Hávamál*, which appears to be a collection of gnomes—originally of Phase II—adapted to purposes of entertainment. For Norse examples of No. 3 we shall have to turn to sagas. Egill's behaviour at York, as described in the saga (cap. 59), is quite in the spirit of Archilochos' poem.

4. An absence of the (more or less conventional) idealism with which the characters of heroic poetry are depicted. This can be appreciated much more from sagas than from the short poems and fragments of poetry belonging to Phase III, which have come down to us. It does not apply of course to the Norse panegyrics. But good examples are supplied by many of Herodotos' anecdotes, while numerous lifelike pictures are to be found in Norse sagas. For an instance we may refer to the description of Egill's last conversation with his father (cap. 58), where the close and grasping propensities of the pair are well brought out, though not in an unfriendly manner. Less vivid, but quite sym-

pathetic, is the account given in *Thorfinns Saga Karlsefnis*, cap. 11, of the unheroic way in which Karlsefni and his men took to their heels, when they were attacked by the Skrælingjar.

The difference in the treatment of character between Phase I and Phase III may be explained briefly as follows. The authors of Phase I, in both Greek and Teutonic, were for the most part court minstrels—dependents of princes—whose business it was to idealise both the heroes individually and the princely class in general. Such treatment was quite in keeping with the boastfulness and love of display shown by the heroes themselves, not only in poetry but doubtless also in real life. The authors of Phase III, saga-tellers as well as poets, were doubtless persons of more or less independent position, while the characters with whom they were concerned belonged usually to the same class—at least in Iceland. Their business was to give an interesting and, in general, sympathetic account of these persons. Sometimes we meet with characters who are represented in a very unfavourable light; but flattery or idealisation is rare. 'Heroic' characters, it is true, figure not unfrequently in sagas. Usually they get into trouble, like Grettir; but they are often treated very sympathetically and sometimes credited with impossible feats. The treatment, however, as well as the milieu, is different from what one finds in heroic poetry.

It is easier to contrast Phase III with Phase I than with Phase II, for the latter is in general of a less personal character. The *spakir menn*, who properly represent this phase, are frequently mentioned in sagas, as we have seen. But they seldom play a leading part in them—indeed only when, like Njáll, they are the victims of circumstances. They are usually stay-at-home people, like Hesiod, whereas the men who are prominent in the sagas are nearly always persons who have travelled a good deal. The latter statement seems to be true also of most of the poets belonging to Phase III, whether Norse or Greek. We cannot say whether it is true of the authors of sagas, because these are generally unknown to us. But what can be said with confidence is that the sagas are the product of a society which was familiar with travel and with distant lands. It is to this extended horizon, we think, that the resemblances between Greek and Norse are mainly due.

In our opinion the three phases of literature discussed above represent phases in the history of intellectual life; but it is to be remembered that Phase II is to a large extent contemporary with Phase I and—probably to a much less extent—with Phase III.

Phase I represents the intellectual life—primarily the entertainment—

of court circles in the days of military kingship. It is the product of a society whose governing principles are prowess in arms, loyalty, generosity—in short, action, not thought.

Phase II represents the activities of the learned in barbaric times and is intended for instruction. It arises in a milieu where the governing principle is thought, accompanied by inspiration or second sight, or at least by the cultivation of mantic lore.

Phase III is the product of more advanced and complex conditions, which cannot well be brought under one head. It represents the activities of a much larger proportion of the population than either of the earlier phases. In the North and in Greece it shows characteristics which are due to a widely extended horizon. In Greece also and elsewhere we find evidence of the growth of national feeling. But it is to be remembered that in Christian countries intellectual life was now mainly concentrated in the Church.

The three phases discussed above do not of course include all the forms of literature current in ancient times. In the description of the shield of Achilles (*Il.* XVIII. 569 ff.) and in Bede's account of Caedmon (*Hist. Eccl.* IV. 24) we hear of what appear to be peasants' songs. Examples of such poetry will require notice in the next volume; but hardly anything of the kind seems to have been preserved from ancient times, at least in the languages treated above. The Greek children's song noticed on p. 428 f. may belong here; and there are a number of other short Greek pieces, mostly fragments, which are supposed to be of the same origin, though some of them are doubtful. Probably also some of the Anglo-Saxon spells referred to on p. 446 ff. are of the same milieu.

The Anglo-Saxon spells here referred to are doubtless derived ultimately from mantic poetry of Phase II; and the same may be true of the Linos-song mentioned in *Il.* XVIII. 569 ff. We shall see later that a good deal of peasant poetry seems to be of similar origin, while much also is probably derived from poetry of Phase I. On the other hand it is likely that the *Grottasöngr* is based on a peasants' grinding spell; and the same may be the case with the fragment of a Lesbian political song noticed on p. 429, note. The timeless nameless poetry and saga discussed in Ch. XIV may likewise have originated in a peasant milieu. Discussion of these questions, however, must be deferred until more material has been considered.

There is one question which the reader may feel to have been somewhat neglected in this chapter—the question of recognised authorship and anonymity. The first impression one obtains from a consideration of the evidence is that the personality of the author tends to be forgotten in the course of time. Authors of Phase I are commonly unknown, while those of Phase III have usually had their names and something of their history preserved. And there is a good deal of truth in this impression. But it will not explain everything. The authors of the 'Sagas of Icelanders' are unknown; it is only in rare cases that one can even hazard a guess as to their origin. Yet we have poems, mostly fragmentary, by known authors, who lived long before these sagas can have originated—before the persons who figure in them were born. So also in Ireland some (anonymous) sagas, such as the *Battle of Allen*, relate to times later than those of a number of known poets whose remains have not entirely perished.

A better answer is to be found, we think, in the Types. Poems of Type E are recognisable as such only when the author is known. If he is forgotten they cannot be distinguished from those of Type B. In Type D the author is usually known, except in hymns and songs designed for ritual purposes. But the authors of narrative poetry and saga (Type A), which comes from oral tradition, seem never to be known. In poetry the most one can find is a name like 'Homer'. Heroic and theological poetry of Type B is likewise usually anonymous.

It would seem then that in Types A and B, as also in ritual hymns, the authors were soon forgotten. This must mean that no sense of ownership or 'copyright' was recognised in such works. The poems or sagas were suitable and available for use by anyone who cared to acquire them for his repertoire; and there was nothing to prevent him from treating them according to his own inclination. In poems of Types E and D (apart from ritual poems)[1] such freedom apparently was not generally permissible.[2] These poems were composed for specific purposes and occasions, and not for general use. If they were remembered later, this was due to the fame either of the poet himself or

[1] We are thinking here primarily of the Homeric *Hymns*. But in point of fact there is much difference of usage in regard to such compositions. In some countries, as we shall see later, the text of hymns is most carefully preserved; and very frequently the author's name is preserved in it.

[2] The most striking examples of textual variation in Type D are to be found in certain Welsh poems (cf. p. 526 f.). The period of oral tradition here was probably very long.

of the person celebrated. Those which have been preserved usually bear the names of men who seem to have been the most distinguished poets of their times. Elegies, however, are often said to be composed by the widow or a near relative of the deceased. This is a widely distributed custom, evidenced by historical records, as well as in heroic poems and sagas.[1]

Antiquarian, gnomic, descriptive and mantic poetry, together with heroic and theological poetry of Type C, is usually anonymous. The personal element in Hesiod's poems is exceptional even in Greece, while the Norse genealogical poems of known authorship have a panegyric purpose in view, apart from their antiquarian interest. Most commonly poems—and even prose compositions—belonging to these categories have a form similar to that of Type B; the speaker or speakers are generally either famous seers or sages of the past or supernatural beings. Such compositions could be preserved and utilised, like poetry and saga of Type A, when the author had been forgotten, although they were not intended for purposes of entertainment.

From what has been said it would seem that in regard to authorship a broad line of distinction may in general be drawn between Types A and B on the one hand and Types D and E on the other, and that the didactic and impersonal categories approximate more to the former. In the former case authorship appears to be less clearly defined, and the use of some such expression as 'original author', for the person who first gave form to a theme, would perhaps be more appropriate. It remains to be seen, however, how far these observations will be found to apply to the literatures of other peoples.

[1] References to elegies by widows will be found in *Ann. Tig.* (*Rev. Celt.* XVII. 162, 174) and in Irish heroic sagas (cf. p. 585); also in *Il.* XXIV. 723 ff., in *Guðrúnarkviða I.* 17 ff., and probably in *Beow.* 3150 ff. For elegies by mothers see *Ann. Tig.* (*ib.* 177), *Il.* XXIV. 747 ff., *Ragnars Saga Loðbrókar*, cap. 9; cf. *Beow.* 1117 f. Examples of elegies by fathers and brothers will be found in *Egils Saga*, cap. 24, 55, 78 (cf. p. 348 f.).

CHAPTER XX

INSPIRATION

THE *Iliad* opens with the words "Sing, O Goddess, of the wrath of Achilles". The *Odyssey* begins with a similar invocation: "Tell me, O Muse, of the man", etc. In several other passages in the *Iliad* the Muses (in the plural) are appealed to for information. The formula regularly used is: "Tell me now, ye Muses who occupy Olympian homes". In the *Odyssey* certain minstrels are said to have received inspiration from a Muse (or 'deity'), in passages which have already been noted (cf. p. 569).

These are doubtless traditional formulae, the force of which, as evidence for a belief in inspiration, is not to be pressed. And the same may be said of similar formulae which occur in Hesiod's poems, e.g. *W. and D.* 1 f., *Theog.* 114 f., 965 f. But we do not think that the story of Hesiod's call, told in *Theog.* 22 ff. (cf. p. 593), can fairly be explained in this way. It is obviously to be compared with the story of Caedmon's dream (cf. p. 572); and the natural interpretation is that the poet believed he had received a commission from the Muses in person—whether we take it as dream, vision or hallucination. And it is not likely that he was the first poet who held such a belief. The traditional formulae of the *Iliad* imply the existence at some time of a genuine belief in inspiration from the Muses.

The gifts which are said to be inspired by the Muses are as follows:[1] (i) prophecy, relating both to the past and the future (*Theog.* 31 f.; cf. p. 624); (ii) eloquence or persuasiveness of speech, which will enable a king to settle all disputes (*ib.* 81 ff.); (iii) poetry (*ib.* 98 ff.; cf. *Od.* VIII. 64, 480 f., XXII. 347 f.). Perhaps we should include (iv) memory. It is not necessary to interpret in this way the frequent appeals to the Muses for information found in the *Iliad*, except possibly II. 488 ff.: "I could not tell or name the multitude, even if I had ten tongues...if the Muses of Olympos...did not bring to my mind all those who came to Ilios". In general such passages can also be taken—perhaps more correctly—as prophecies relating to the past. But it is to be noted that the mother of the Muses is always called

[1] Cf. Hesiod, fragm. 205, which may perhaps be translated: "...the Muses who make a man very wise, inspired and eloquent". But we are far from certain of the exact meaning both of the words themselves and of Clement's commentary upon them.

Mnemosyne or Mnama (Mneme), i.e. 'Memory'. Lastly, we may refer to the curious words with which the Muses address Hesiod in *Theog.* 26 ff.: "Ye shepherds of the fields, evil things of shame, no more than bellies! We know how to say many false things which resemble reality; but when we wish we know how to relate things which are true". The 'false things' are usually taken as referring to Homeric poetry;[1] but it is possible that some power of illusion is meant.

Solon in his address to the Muses (cf. p. 242) speaks of other gifts—happiness, good fame, success, etc.—which do not appear to be attributed directly to them in earlier poetry. On the other hand the Homeric poems occasionally speak of their destructive activities, as in the case of Thamyris (noticed on p. 592), who has offended them by his boasting. So in *Od.* VIII. 63 f. Demodocos is said to have been blinded by a Muse, though she loved him and granted him the gift of poetry.

Little evidence for inspiration of this kind is to be found among the northern peoples. A good parallel to Hesiod's call is certainly offered by the story of Caedmon's dream; but here the milieu is Christian. The best instance we can think of from a heathen milieu is the introductory stanza of the *Loddfáfnismál* (*Háv.* 111), quoted on p. 618: for revelation in the form of messages from the gods we may refer to the story in the *Life of St Ansgar* noticed on p. 473. To the Muses themselves a parallel is to be found in the Valkyrie Sigrdrífa in the *Sigrdrífumál* (cf. p. 449 f.); but in this case there is no reference to inspiration.

Better parallels are perhaps offered by the Welsh *awen*, though this word does not properly denote a person. Giraldus Cambrensis (*Descr. Kambriae*, I. 16) says there are persons in Wales called *Awenithion* (i.e. *Awenyddion*), who prophesy in a state of ecstasy or frenzy, as if possessed by a spirit. They have to be brought back to their senses by violence; and if consulted again they express themselves quite differently. The gift of prophecy is usually conferred upon them in dreams. They use religious (Christian) expressions in their prophecies; but it is clear from Giraldus' account that these prophets were not of ecclesiastical origin—though Wales had been Christian for seven or eight centuries.

In predictive poetry the word *awen* seems to be used in the sense of 'prophetic spirit', as might be expected from Giraldus' description of the Awenyddion. Thus in *Tal.* VI the expressions *dysgogan awen*, 'the *awen* predicts', and *dysgogan Myrdin*, 'Myrddin predicts', appear

[1] Is there any ground for believing that the heroic stories were regarded as 'false' in Hesiod's time?

to be used indiscriminately. But elsewhere, especially in the 'mystical' poems, which in general belong no doubt to an earlier period (cf. p. 469 f.), the word can hardly have this meaning. Owing to the obscurity of this class of poetry it is not easy to determine the exact meaning; but the sense generally required seems to be 'poetry' or 'poetic inspiration'. Such is the case apparently in *Tal.* VII. And in *Tal.* XIV. 7 f. Taliesin says: "I sang before a famous prince in the meadows of the Severn, before Brochfael of Powys, who loved my *awen*". So also in *ib.* LV. 56 f., where the meaning seems to be "My *awen* has made me to praise Urien".[1] In the *Historia Brittonum*, cap. 62, we hear of a poet Talhaern, surnamed *Tat aguen* (i.e. *Tad awen*), 'Father of poetry'; and the same expression occurs also in *BBC.* XIX. 10 (st. 4). In *Tal.* XV. 35 f. the three *awen* which "came from the cauldron of Gogyrwen" are clearly to be identified with the three drops which flew from Ceridwen's 'cauldron of inspiration', as related in the *Hanes Taliesin* (cf. p. 103).

The word *awen* is often translated 'Muse'; and we have sometimes followed this usage ourselves. But it does not mean an external personality; so far as we are aware, it is never used for anything external, except the drops (of inspiration) which came from Ceridwen's cauldron. In general it is used to denote the poetic or prophetic spirit within a man. It corresponds to the gifts of the Muses rather than to the Muses themselves. What we wish to call attention to is that no rigid distinction is drawn between poetry and prophecy—the same word is used for both—just as in Greek both are said to be gifts of the Muses. Moreover, it is not merely the form of poetry or prophecy for which the *awen* or the Muses are responsible, though eloquence or power of speech may well be implied in the former. The *awen* which predicts doubtless supplies the substance as well as the form of the predictions, just as in the *Iliad* and the *Theogony*, as we have seen, the Muses are besought to supply the poet with information.

For the combination of prophecy, poetry and information we may refer back to the history of the Irish *fili* (cf. p. 606) and to the discussion on p. 620 of the words W. *gwawd*, N. *óðr*, A.-S. *wōþ*, etc., in relation to *vates*; so also the various meanings of the word *þulr-þyle* (p. 619). It is clear that throughout the ancient languages of northern Europe the

[1] Reading *Uryen* for *vyren*. These lines are attached to a learned poem of Latin connections; but we think they must originally have belonged to a panegyric. *Awen* in the sense of 'poetry' is by no means confined to the mystical poems. It appears to have the same meaning, for example, in one of Llywarch Hen's elegies (*RBH.* XI. 23).

ideas of poetry, eloquence, information (especially antiquarian learning) and prophecy are intimately connected. Further, we may perhaps repeat here (cf. p. 619 f.) that gnomic lore and mantic and mystical lore of various kinds belong to the same circle of activities. Thus the *Loddfáfnismál*, which opens with a statement of inspiration or revelation, contains gnomic precepts, mystical lore and spells. The *Sigrdrífumál* contains mantic lore and gnomic precepts, while the preceding poems in the same Trilogy include omens and antiquarian lore. A reference to Hesiod's poems will show how these covered a very similar series of interests. We may also refer to the list of poems ascribed to Epimenides, noted on p. 625.[1] Lastly, we may add, there can be no doubt that mantic and mystical lore were included in the sphere of the *awen*—as may be seen, for example, from *Tal.* VII.

We have now seen (1) that the activities of the learned followed very similar lines in Greece and among the northern peoples; (2) that in Greece these activities were regarded as due to inspiration from supernatural beings; (3) that among the northern peoples, though they included a large mantic element, they were regarded as due, not to inspiration from without, but to something inherent in the poets or seers themselves. Exceptions occur on both sides, though among the northern peoples they seem not to be common. The Greek evidence is not quite so clear.

In the first place it is to be observed that the Muses are not the only supernatural beings from whom poets and seers were believed to derive inspiration. The god Apollo is also to be taken into account. In the historical period he was regarded as far more important than the Muses in the domain of prophecy; the activities of the latter were now restricted to poetry. But in early poetry this distinction is not clear. Thus in *Theog.* 94 f. Apollo and the Muses are associated as the source of minstrelsy; and the same association is found again in *Il.* I. 603 f., where Apollo seems to accompany the singing of the Muses with his lyre. Again in the Homeric poems some seers are said to have received their mantic powers from Apollo. Such is the case, for example, with Calchas in *Il.* I. 72 and with Polypheides in *Od.* XV. 252 f., while Amphiaraos is said to have been beloved by Apollo (*ib.* 245). The two latter, however, belong to a mantic family, descended from the great seer Melampus, of whom nothing of the kind is said. There are many

[1] It is instructive also to compare a list of the works attributed to the legendary poet Musaios; cf. Kinkel, *Epic. Graec. Fragmenta*, p. 220 f.

other seers also, e.g. Teiresias and Helenos, son of Priam, who are never associated with Apollo. In later works several of these persons are brought into contact with him; and the absence of such associations in early poetry may be due to accident. But the evidence on the whole rather suggests that the tendency to connect seers with Apollo was a growing one—that in early times they might be inspired either by him or by the Muses;[1] but that the possession of mantic powers might be independent of any deity, as among the northern peoples.

In the North also we find mantic supernatural beings; but they operate differently from those of Greece. They impart their information usually, not through a medium, but directly. It is not clear whether Sigrdrífa is an essentially supernatural being or a human being[2] endowed with supernatural properties. But sometimes we meet with seeresses in poems where the scene is laid among the gods themselves, e.g. the seeress who is the speaker of the *Völuspá*, the dead seeress who prophesies Balder's death to Othin in the *Vegtamskviða* ('Balder's Dreams'), the witch Hyndla, who declares Óttarr's ancestry to Freyja in the *Hyndluljóð*. These characters are evidently counterparts of the human witches or seeresses whom we meet with in sagas, e.g. *Thorfinns Saga Karlsefnis*, cap. 3, and *Örvar-Odds Saga*, cap. 3. In *Helgakviða Hundingsbana I* (*ad init.*) Norns come to the hero at his birth and prophesy, or rather determine, his future fame. These appear to be supernatural beings. But it is not clear whether the prophetesses—also called Norns—who visit Nornagestr and determine his fate, are supernatural or human. Saxo, p. 223 (181), relates how a certain king named Fridleuus went, in accordance with ancient custom, to consult the oracles of the Fates (*Parcarum oracula*) about the destiny of his child. In the house of the gods (*deorum edes*) he saw three maidens (*nymphis*) seated, who in answer to his request determined the character of his son. Here again it seems probable, though hardly certain, that the supernatural Norns are meant.

The chief mantic deity of the North is Othin; but he has little in common with Apollo. In the *Loddfáfnismál* he appears to speak through a medium—by inspiration, or rather perhaps by revelation. More usually he appears in person, generally disguised, as when he declares

[1] If the legendary oracular poet Musaios is a fictitious character, as is generally believed, the association of prophetic inspiration with the Muses must still have been prevalent when his name was invented.

[2] In other poems she is generally identified with Brynhildr; but there is no trace of this in the *Sigrdrífumál* itself.

the omens in the *Reginsmál* or discourses on cosmology in the *Grímnismál*. But elsewhere, especially when the milieu is entirely supernatural, he shows a character which seems to be quite alien to the Greek pantheon. He is constantly trying to acquire, rather than to impart, information. He wakes up a dead seeress in order to ascertain Balder's fate; and in the *Völuspá* we find him consulting another seeress. At other times he gets information from his ravens or from Mímir's head. Again, we frequently hear of him striving to effect his purposes by witchcraft or cunning. It is by skill of speech that he gains possession of the poetic mead in *Háv.* 104 ff. (cf. p. 249 f.); but in *ib.* 140 it seems to be implied that he used spells for this purpose. Spells and poetry in general are his invention.[1] He has spells at his command for everything he wishes to effect; a list of eighteen is given *ib.* 146 ff. It will be seen that the picture presented is that not of a deity who possesses inherent power and knowledge, but of a wizard who is exerting himself to obtain power and knowledge. The picture is the more remarkable because Othin is the god of the princely (warrior) class. Yet he is never represented as fighting in person, though he is the giver of victory.

The character of Othin cannot be derived from the *spakir menn* of the Viking Age, who would doubtless have regarded some of the proceedings attributed to him as discreditable. The Anglo-Saxon *Nine Herbs Spell* (cf. p. 447) shows that Woden—the same god—was known to the ancient English as a wizard, although nearly all the English royal houses claimed descent from him. In Germany he was regarded as an expert in spells, as is clear from one of the *Merseburg Spells* (cf. p. 448). The main lines of his character therefore were fixed in very early times. From the name *Mercurius* applied to him by Latin writers, from the time of Tacitus onwards, it appears that even in the first century he was thought of at least as an intellectual rather than a fighting deity.

Yet, in spite of the antiquity of the wizard god, and consequently also of the human wizards from whom the conception must have been derived, it is to be observed that Roman writers attribute mantic powers to women much more frequently than to men among the Teutonic peoples. They seem to have regarded prophecy as primarily, if not essentially, a property of the women. We have already (p. 606) had occasion to mention Veleda, the famous prophetess of the Bructeri in the time of Vespasian, and also another seeress (p. 452) who is said to have prophesied the death of Drusus, nearly a century earlier. Tacitus,

[1] Cf. such kennings as *galdrs faðir*, 'father of the spell', i.e. Othin; *Óðins mjöðr*, 'Othin's mead', i.e. poetry.

Germ. 8, refers to other prophetesses, and states that the Germani attribute to women or girls in general "an element of sanctity and a faculty of foresight; they do not disdain to consult them, neither do they neglect their answers". In *Hist.* IV. 61 he says that they regard some women as prophetesses and even as goddesses, though he rejects the latter statement in *Germ.* 8. In *Germ.* 10 he speaks of divination practised by men both in family and state affairs: but according to Caesar, *Gall.* I. 50—a century and a half before Tacitus' time—Ariouistus' army depended upon the *matres familiarum* for divination. Half a century earlier still we hear of women practising both sacrifice and divination in the army of the Cimbri, according to Strabo, VII. ii. 3.

The evidence as a whole rather suggests that manticism in general was originally cultivated only by women and only later taken over gradually by men. But the information available before Tacitus' time is extremely meagre. What we may conclude with confidence is that in his time prophecy was regarded as belonging at least predominantly to women, while divination was cultivated by men, though not necessarily by men only. Such a distribution of functions is of course not inconsistent with the evidence of the *Völuspá* and the *Vegtamskviða*, where we find the wizard god seeking knowledge of the future from witches. The history of the latter clearly goes back to ancient times. But at the same time we cannot doubt the antiquity of the wizard god, expert in spells and poetry, who was the chief deity and the deity *par excellence* of the princely (warrior) class. We do not see how such a doctrine can have obtained acceptance except at a time when the wizard was of outstanding importance in society.

The evidence from the Christian countries relating to (heathen) inspiration and manticism is, naturally enough, much less full and satisfactory. The story of Caedmon comes from a Christian milieu. Irish sagas refer not unfrequently to prophecies by druids, but without specifying whence their knowledge of the future is derived. But we hear also of prophetesses and seeresses, both human and supernatural. As an example we may cite the case of Fedelm, the seeress in the *Táin Bó Cuailnge* (cf. p. 464). In the earlier text she seems to be human, but in the later she comes from a shee-mound to prophesy to Medb. Another human seeress is Deirdre, who prophesies in the *Fate of the Children of Uisnech*, though not in the earlier *Exile*. An earlier example is to be found in Scathach, who foretells to CuChulainn the course of the great raid. She bears some resemblance to the Valkyries; but she appears to be human. The deities, however, have a seeress, Badb, who prophesies in the *Second Battle of Moytura* (*ad fin.*).[1] Her name suggests affinity with the Valkyries.

The Irish stories of the gods are mostly preserved in a late and unsatisfactory form. But they are clearly neither omnipotent nor omniscient; nor are they, for the most part, of a military character. In Manannan mac Lir mantic elements predominate, as may be seen, for example, from the second poem in the *Voyage of Bran* (cf. p. 468) and from *Cormac's Adventure in the Land of Promise*. Possibly this may once have been the case with other deities also, including the Dagda himself. It is difficult to believe that the chief of the gods was invariably portrayed as the helpless figure which we find in our stories. Brigit, daughter of the Dagda, is described in Cormac's *Glossary* (s.v.)[2] as 'poetess' and 'goddess of poets'.

In the *Mabinogi* of *Math* Gwynedd is governed by a family of wizards. Some scholars regard these persons as deities—a proposition which seems to us unconvincing. It is of some interest, however, to note that the same district is the scene of the mantic contest in *Hist. Brit.* 42 and also of a somewhat similar contest in the story of *Taliesin*. The scattered notices which we have relating to Ceridwen point to a deity of poetry like Brigit; but she is evidently a witch. Apart from her we seem to have no record of prophetesses or poetesses, whether human or divine.

Early records relating to Gaul present a contrast to those relating to the Teutonic peoples in the fact that the former speak of a class of seers, who are doubtless men. In view of the paucity of these records it would no doubt be rash to assume that mantic activities were limited to one sex in either country, especially with the Irish evidence before us; but the existence of a contrast in this respect is not to be overlooked. The names of a number of Gaulish goddesses are preserved; but nothing is known of their attributes. From the fact that the most prominent god among the Gauls is called 'Mercurius', just as among the Teutonic peoples, one is naturally tempted to connect the two deities. At least we may infer that they were both of intellectual rather than military character. Unfortunately we do not know the native name of the

[1] *Rev. Celt.* XII. 110 f.

[2] Transl. by Stokes, *Three Irish Glossaries*, p. xxxiii f. The first part of the entry might also be transl. as follows: "Brigit, a female *fili* (*banfile*), daughter of the Dagda. Brigit is a learned woman (*baneceas*) or a woman of learning (*be neicsi*). Brigit a goddess (*bandee*) whom *filid* worshipped". The word *éceas* means both 'poet' and 'learned man'; *écse* both 'poetry' and 'learning'. These words doubtless had special application to antiquarian poetry (like *fili*).

Gaulish god.[1] If he is really to be identified, as some scholars hold, with Ogmios, whom Lucian[2] speaks of as represented under the name and attributes of Heracles, he may well be connected with Othin; for Ogmios is clearly a god of eloquence.[3] He was depicted as leading a crowd of persons by thin and fragile chains, one end of which was fixed in their ears, the other in the god's tongue.

There is one piece of evidence, from a different quarter, which renders it probable that there was some connection between the Gaulish and the Teutonic Mercurius. Herodotos, v. 7, states that the Thracians in general worshipped Ares, Artemis and Dionysos, but that their kings worshipped Hermes and said that they were descended from him. Now the Thracian peoples bordered upon Celtic peoples (Boii, Scordisci, etc.) to the west and upon Teutonic peoples to the north. What Herodotos says here reminds us of the aristocratic connections of the cult of Othin-Woden (cf. p. 640). Further, the northern Thracians, the Getai or Daci, are said to have had an elaborate educational system, which seems to have something in common with that of the druids, while all the Thracians, like the Gauls and the Teutonic peoples, appear to have given great attention to speculations upon a future life. It is true that the Graeco-Roman god Hermes-Mercurius has various characteristics and that different characteristics may have led to his identification with the gods of different peoples. But the evidence just pointed out renders such an accident unlikely in this case. It is obviously more probable that the gods of the three neighbouring groups of peoples—who between them occupied about one third of Europe—had in reality some striking characteristics in common.

It has been seen that in the character and distribution of mantic properties among human beings and in the conception of mantic deities both resemblances and differences are to be found among the peoples with whom we are concerned. Where resemblances occur it is

[1] Eighteen different Gaulish surnames are applied to Mercurius in inscriptions of the Roman period; cf. Dottin, *Antiquité Celtique*, p. 304.

[2] *Heracles*, cap. 1 ff. Lucian makes the Gaul, who is his authority, explain why Ogmios is identified with Heracles rather than with Hermes—viz. because the former is stronger. This suggests at least that the identification of him with Hermes was current.

[3] In Ireland his name (*Ogma*) survives only as that of a minor figure among the gods—apparently a warrior; but it must be connected originally with *ogam*, the native form of writing. Indeed the Irish version of the *Hist. Brittonum* (p. 155 in Mommsen's edn.) says that he invented the letters of the Irish.

sometimes a question whether they are due to contact in ancient or recent times or to independent causes. In general it will be preferable not to attempt to answer such questions until the evidence of other peoples has been taken into account. On certain points, however, a provisional—not final—opinion may perhaps be formed from the evidence already considered.

If we are right in believing that the Gaulish Mercurius and the Thracian Hermes were probably deities of similar character to Othin-Woden, it would seem likely, in view of the geographical position of the peoples, that the three gods were not wholly of independent origin. We know of no deity really resembling Othin in the south of Europe, in spite of the identification with Mercurius. But even if we allow that the gods were not independent, a further question arises—whether they were borrowed by one people from another ready-made, or whether the resemblance is due to the existence of similar human prototypes. The earliest Teutonic evidence, noticed on p. 640 f., might seem to favour the former alternative; but the human character of Othin (*ib.*) gives little support to the suggestion that he was not of native growth.

The Thracians bordered not only upon the Celtic and Teutonic peoples but also upon the Greeks; and here in the south of Europe contact is easier to trace than in the north, although it dates perhaps from much earlier times. The Greeks believed that some of their deities were derived from Thrace—we may refer in particular to Dionysos. More important perhaps is the fact that some legendary poets, especially Orpheus and Philammon, to whom certain mantic and antiquarian poems were attributed, were believed to be Thracians. The story of Orpheus is sometimes located in Pieria,[1] sometimes in the district of the Hebros (Maritza). With these poets again were connected the 'Mysteries', which likewise were believed to be mainly of Thracian origin. The chief Mysteries were those of the island of Samothrace, not far from the mouth of the Hebros, and those of Eleusis in Attica. The latter were believed to have been founded by a Thracian named Eumolpos, from the Hebros district; his name—presumably fictitious—suggests that he was regarded as a poet. It may be observed that both the Mysteries and the Orphic poems seem to have been largely concerned with speculations upon the future life—with which the Thracians, like the Gauls, are known to have been much occupied. We may refer to Herodotos'

[1] This is hardly consistent with the fact that he is described as belonging to the Cicones—who lived near the Hebros.

account (IV. 94 ff.) of Salmoxis, who was said to have been a wizard of the Getai and a disciple of Pythagoras, though Herodotos himself suspected that he was a supernatural being.

Orphism appears to have flourished chiefly in the sixth century. The stories—perhaps poems—and the mystic rites connected with it may have become known to the first Greeks who settled on the coast of Thrace, early in the seventh century.[1] Thracian influence in the cult of Dionysos would seem to be of earlier date—Semele is apparently a Thracian name—and the same may be true of the festival at Eleusis. But in the Homeric and Hesiodic poems evidence for Thracian connections—at least for connections which are demonstrably Thracian—is comparatively slight.[2]

Some ancient authorities[3] apparently thought that the Muses were of Thracian origin; but this seems to have been due to the belief that Pieria—the district between Mt Olympos and the sea—had once been occupied by Thracians. At all events the formulae in which their name occurs in the Homeric poems show that they had long been Hellenised. Hesiod's references to the Muses suggest that there were originally various groups of Muses belonging to different localities. The Muses to whom he dedicates his prize (*W. D.* 656) are called 'Muses of Helicon'; and it is the same Muses whom he invokes in *Theog.* 1 ff., though he identifies them shortly afterwards with the Muses of Olympos—called 'Muses of Pieria' in *W. D.* 1 ff. Only the Muses of Olympos occur in the Homeric poems; they are incorporated in the divine community of Olympos. These were perhaps the first Muses to be associated with Apollo. But Eumelos in one fragment (17) is said to have stated that there were three Muses, daughters of Apollo; the names given to them (Cephisus, Apollonis, Borysthenis) are wholly different from those used by Hesiod. Another fragment (16), however, speaks of nine Muses and gives them the usual parentage, from Zeus and Mnemosyne. The Muses

1 It is to be observed that the names are Greek—or at least completely Hellenised. The name *Philammon* points either to Aiolis or Thessaly, or possibly to Ainos, an Aeolic colony (cf. Strabo, VII. fragm. 52). It should also perhaps be mentioned here that many modern scholars believe the Mysteries to have been largely due to Egyptian influence. That may be so; but ancient belief must have had some ground for connecting them with Thrace.

2 Ares is connected with Thrace more than once in the Homeric poems, though in *Theog.* 921 ff. he is said to be son of Hera, as well as of Zeus. The case of Apollo is too complicated for discussion here. His associations in the Homeric poems seem to lie with the north-east corner of the Aegean.

3 Cf. Strabo, IX. ii. 25; Pausanias, IX. 29.

of Helicon are also said to have been three in number originally.[1] They do not seem to be associated with Apollo;[2] at all events Hesiod does not mention Apollo when he refers to them. There is no reason for supposing that the Muses of Olympos and those of Helicon were the only Muses. It is doubtless due to the accident of Hesiod's fame that we know of the latter. Elsewhere we meet with somewhat similar beings under a different name. Thus the Muses have much in common with the Charites of Orchomenos, at whose festival contests in poetry and music were held. One of them (Thaleia) has the same name as one of Hesiod's Muses. Less close is the resemblance to the Moirai; for these were doubtless regarded as older. But it may be observed that in both cases we find the encroachment of a male deity; *Moiragetes* ('Leader of the Fates'), as applied to Zeus or Apollo, is parallel to *Musagetes*, also applied to Apollo. More usually, however, the Moirai remain independent.

The Muses, Charites and Moirai can hardly be of a different origin from the groups of female supernatural beings, usually three or nine in number, which are found in the North and elsewhere. The Norns correspond very closely to the Moirai; they are always three in number and independent of any male deity. Skuld, the youngest of the Norns, is also a Valkyrie. The Valkyries have not the specialised functions of the Muses; but there can be little doubt that they were originally associated with witchcraft—an association which was preserved at least in England. In the North they are usually, though not always, subordinated to Othin; elsewhere there is no evidence for this. Their names and numbers vary, but most commonly they appear in bands of nine. Such is the case, for example, in the prose narrative of *Helgakviða Hjörvarðssonar*, in that of *Helgakviða Hundingsbana II* and in the *Helreið Brynhildar*, st. 6. We may compare the story[3] of Thiðrandi, son of Hallr á Síðu, who was slain by nine blackrobed women on horseback. Nine whiterobed women on white horses arrived at the same time, but failed to save him. The event was interpreted by a sage as foreshadowing the change of faith; the blackrobed women were the ancestral spirits of the

[1] Cf. Pausanias, IX. 29. The names given here are *Melete* ('Practice'), *Mneme* ('Memory') and *Aoide* ('Song').

[2] Apollo does not seem to have been specially honoured at the sanctuary of the Muses (cf. Pausanias, IX. 29 ff.). There was a statue of him struggling with Hermes for the lyre; but this was only one of numerous statues representing legendary persons (Linos, Orpheus, Thamyris, etc.) connected with poetry and music.

[3] Related in the *Flateyjarbók*, I. 418 ff., and elsewhere. The text is publ. in Garmonsway, *Early Norse Reader*, p. 75 ff.

family, the whiterobed were the spirits of the new faith. The story deserves notice here because the conception involved is in all probability based upon that of Valkyries.

The last case—however it be explained[1]—illustrates how conceptions of a more or less abstract character can come to be personified on the model of existing types. But the types themselves cannot have arisen out of such personifications. Valkyries and Norns are sometimes supernatural beings; but there are other Valkyries and Norns who are represented as human beings, endowed with supernatural powers. In historical times these latter survived only as witches and fortune-tellers. Archbishop Wulfstan in his sermons classes Valkyries (*wælcyrian*) with wizards, murderers, robbers, perjurers and other undesirable characters. But there can be no doubt that in earlier times they were honoured—and so also the Norns, whether they were itinerant or established at sanctuaries, the prototypes of those noticed on p. 639. In any case the origin of both classes is to be traced back to the mantic women of Tacitus' time. We have no doubt that the Greek groups of supernatural female beings were of similar origin. Their human prototypes survived in the historical period, as prophetesses at certain oracular sanctuaries, such as Delphoi and Dodona, though they had come to be regarded as the mouthpieces of gods.

Celtic parallels are naturally not frequent, since among these peoples manticism seems to have been cultivated more by men than by women. It may be noted, however, that in Cormac's *Glossary*[2] the goddess Brigit is said to have had two sisters of the same name as herself. Other references of an obscure kind to groups of female supernatural beings occur occasionally in Irish and Welsh poetry. The Irish *Song of Long Life* (cf. p. 466) contains an invocation to 'the seven daughters of the sea'. In *Tal.* XXX. 13 ff. we hear of nine maidens whose breath warms the cauldron of 'the Head of Annwfn'. Annwfn would seem to be a conception similar to Mag Mell (cf. p. 264). We may also refer here to the nine witches of Gloucester, who figure in the story of *Peredur*. Lastly, mention may be made of the *Matres* or *Matronae*, to whom numerous altars dating from Roman times are dedicated, and who appear to be partly Celtic and partly Teutonic. The title *Fatae Deruones*[3]

[1] Hallr was a very prominent man in Iceland, and largely responsible for the official recognition of Christianity there in the year 1000.

[2] S.v. *Brigit*; see Stokes, *Three Irish Glossaries*, p. 8 (transl. p. xxxiii f.).

[3] Cf. Dottin, *Antiquité Celtique*, pp. 112, 316, where the name is connected with Welsh *derw*, 'oaks'.

(beside *Matronae Deruonnae*) suggests a conception similar to the Norns and the Moirai.

It would seem that groups of beings of this kind were once known also in ancient Italy. The Parcae were probably a group of three, similar to the Moirai, whose attributes they eventually took over. The Camenae were identified with the Muses and eventually displaced by them. Together with the goddess or nymph Egeria, who perhaps belonged to them, they were said to have instructed the legendary king Numa Pompilius in drawing up the religious and social institutions of Rome. He dedicated to them the grove—said to be near the Porta Capena—where he used to meet them, and devoted the spring to the use of the Vestal Virgins. It should be observed that this is a case, not of inspiration, but of revelation through direct personal interviews—somewhat similar perhaps to the scene in the *Sigrdrífumál*, but taking place on repeated occasions.

Next, we may consider briefly the nature of the localities, where inspiration, revelation or 'vision' is said to be acquired. Hesiod receives his call when he is tending sheep at the foot of Helicon (*Theog.* 23). The exact spot is not specified, though the Muses are said to dance on the top of the mountain and round an altar of Zeus and to bathe in certain springs. The sanctuary of the Muses was—at least in later times[1]—a grove near a spring called Aganippe, which according to some authorities was credited with the power of inspiring anyone who drank from it.

Elsewhere both mountains and springs are places of inspiration. Examples of the former seem to be rare in the countries which we have been considering, though they occur in modern folklore. An instance from early times is to be found in the *Sigrdrífumál.* Springs are more frequent in early, as well as modern, times. It is at the 'Spring of Fate' that the *Loddfáfnismál* is pronounced (*Háv.* 111). A Spring of Fate lies also beneath Yggdrasill's Ash, the sanctuary of the gods, where the Norns dwell. The Norns are said[2] to pour loam from the spring upon the tree. Under the Ash there is also what is said to be another spring, belonging to Mímir, which contains information[3] and wisdom. It is

[1] Described by Pausanias, IX. 29 ff. Cf. also Frazer's notes (V. 150 ff.).

[2] *Gylf.* 16. This is perhaps Snorri's interpretation of *Völuspá*, st. 19 f., from which the rest of the description comes. It is to be observed that the eldest of the Norns is called Urðr ('Fate')—the same word as A.-S. *wyrd*, 'Fate'.

[3] *Spekt*; cf. *spakr*, etc. (p. 617 f.). This is stated in *Gylf.* 15; cf. *Völuspá*, st. 28.

said that when Othin wished to get a drink from this he had to pay for it with one of his eyes.

Early Irish references to springs of inspiration or knowledge are very obscure. In the Rennes *Dinnšenchas* (cf. p. 283 f.), cap. 59,[1] we hear of "a well at which are the hazels and inspirations of wisdom, that is the hazels of the science of poetry". The fruit and blossom falls into the well, and seven streams of wisdom spring forth. "Sinend went to seek the inspiration, for she wanted nothing save only wisdom." This well is said to be below the sea. Yet *Sinend* is the name of the Shannon, and the reference seems to be to a personification of that river.[2] We may also compare the *Colloquy of the Two Sages* (cf. p. 467), sect. 24,[3] where in one text Nede says he has come from the nine hazels of the Segais (the mound from which the Boyne rises), while in the others he says he has come from the hazels of poetic art. It would seem therefore that inspiration or wisdom was to be obtained from springs which were the sources of rivers, or rather perhaps from the hazels which grew over these springs.

We do not know of any similar references in early English or Welsh records, though mention should perhaps be made of the spring in 'Caer Sidi', spoken of in *Tal.* XIV. 50 f.—where the context is mantic and the description analogous to that of Mag Mell. Indeed early references to holy springs of any kind in this country seem to be rare. But they were certainly known in Roman times. We may cite in particular the temple-spring beside the fortress of Procolitia, on the Wall, in which a large number of antiquities were found. Among these were ten altars to a Dea Couentina and a sculptured slab depicting three female figures, each of whom is in one hand holding up a cup and with the other pouring out liquid from another cup.[4] The figures and the deity herself doubtless represent the spirits of the spring. The locality still preserves the Gaelic name Teppermoor ('great spring').

It will be observed that in most of the cases noticed above the spring of inspiration is situated in a holy grove or beside a holy tree. In the Irish case, where the sanctity of the place is not stated, the inspiration seems

1 Cf. Stokes, *Rev. Celt.* XV. 456 f. A somewhat similar story will be found in cap. 19 (*ib.* 315 f.).

2 There is perhaps some confusion between the spring at the source of the Shannon and the spring in Mag Mell. For the personification of the river we may compare the story told of Boand (the Boyne personified) in cap. 19, and other stories relating to the same person (cf. p. 256).

3 Cf. Stokes, *Rev. Celt.* XXVI. 18 f.

4 Cf. Bruce, *Handbook to the Roman Wall* (7th edn.), pp. 119 f., 129.

properly to come from the tree. The conception of Yggdrasill's Ash is clearly derived from an earthly sanctuary such as that at Upsala, where there was a sacrificial spring in the neighbourhood of the holy tree; but holy trees or groves with springs were apparently not rare either in the north of Europe or in Greece. We may refer also to the grove and spring where Numa was accustomed to meet the Camenae. There were other holy trees and groves where we hear little or nothing of a spring, and some of them, as at Dodona and Romove, were oracular; but these cases seem to have been less frequent.

From some of the cases noticed above it is clear that inspiration was obtained by drinking from the water of the spring. The spirit of knowledge (prophecy, eloquence, etc.) was evidently believed to be inherent in the water. We may compare the fact that the prophetesses at Delphoi had to drink water from one of the holy springs before giving their oracular responses. But this was perhaps not the only way springs were used for mantic purposes. According to the *Colloquy of the Two Sages*, sect. 2, the *filid* believed that the brink of water was always a place for the revelation of knowledge; and consequently Nede, who is walking by the sea, casts a spell upon the wave in order to learn the meaning of a certain sound. We do not know any parallel to this, as applied to the sea; but in the case of springs such a belief would seem not unnatural.[1]

In a few of the cases noted above, e.g. the incident of Hesiod's call and the story of Numa, 'inspiration' takes the form of revelation from supernatural beings. The scene is similar to that of the *Sigrdrífumál*. With these may be compared certain Norse poems, the *Grógaldr* and the *Vegtamskviða*, in which the chief speaker is a dead seeress. In these cases the scene is laid at the speaker's tomb. We do not know any exact parallels in the other languages; but the utterances from Greek 'oracles of the dead', such as we hear of in Herodotos, v. 92, were doubtless similar in principle. A similar ancestry is to be sought for a late Welsh predictive poem, *RBH.* II, which claims to be an utterance of Myrddin from his grave. At the conclusion of this poem the speaker says that he has received information from certain 'mountain spirits' (*wylyon mynyd*); but these are perhaps local spirits rather than ghosts.[2]

[1] Possibly we may refer to *Il.* II. 305 ff. In the *Laxd. Saga*, cap. 33, it is at a spring that Gestr interprets Guðrún's dreams; but no significance is attached to this fact in the story.

[2] On this passage see Phillimore, *Y Cymmrodor*, VII. 115, where variants are given; cf. also *BBC.* I. 11; XVII. 7.

Next we may consider cases where inspiration proceeds not wholly from supernatural beings nor from a—more or less—sacred place, but is produced or aided by stimulants of various kinds. The influence of the spring, when it is used for drinking (or bathing), may of course be brought under this head.

First we may take the use of music. We have seen (p. 579) that such evidence as there is in the North for choral singing, or for singing of any kind, as opposed to recitation, relates to spells. In *Thorfinns Saga Karlsefnis*, cap. 3, Guðríðr by the excellence of her singing succeeds in getting the attention of the spirits which the witch has been trying in vain to attract. In the *Laxdoela Saga*, cap. 37, when Kotkell and his family work the fatal *seiðr* against Hrútr's child, the beauty of their singing is specially noted. We may repeat here that the name *Galdralag*, 'metre of spells', is applied to the most elaborate of the old native metres. The stanza normally contains two long and three short lines and gives more scope for musical variation than any other variety of metre. No early metrical spells have been preserved, so far as we know, except in poems of Type B; but the name must mean that the metre in question was largely used, if not invented, for them.

We know of no direct evidence elsewhere. But there is good reason for suspecting that Greek melic poetry was in part at least derived from spells. The fragment of a Lesbian political song (cf. p. 429, note), containing the words 'the quern is grinding, grinding', was doubtless based on a grinding song or, more properly, a grinding spell, like the *Grottasöngr* (cf. p. 449). Moreover, the earliest choric poet whose name has been preserved, Thaletas the Cretan, is said to have composed *Katharmoi*, lit. 'purifications', by means of which he stopped a plague at Sparta, about the year 665. *Katharmoi* are attributed also to the first known melic poet, Terpandros the Lesbian, who lived very early in the seventh century and is said to have revolutionised Greek music—as well as to Epimenides and other early poets. No remains of these *Katharmoi* seem to have been preserved; but it can hardly be doubted that they were either spells or invocations to deities. The legends relating to Orpheus—to whom likewise *Katharmoi* were attributed—suggest that his fame too was originally derived from spells. Lastly, we may refer to the large part played by music of various kinds in the Mysteries and in the cult of Dionysos.

Next we may take the stories of inspiring drink. We have seen that there is an unmistakable resemblance between the story of Ceridwen's cauldron and that of Othin's theft of the mead. Allusions to the cauldron of inspiration are not rare in early Welsh poetry; but it is only in the very late *Hanes Taliesin* that we learn anything of the contents. Ceridwen had spent a whole year in gathering herbs for it. Óðrerir has a long and complicated history. Originally the mead was made out of the blood of a wise person called Kvásir, who had been formed out of the spittle of the Aesir and the Vanir.[1] This was mixed with honey, and eventually came into the possession of the giant Suttungr, who gave it into the charge of his daughter Gunnlöð. Othin stole it from her, as related in the *Hávamál* (cf. p. 249) and elsewhere. Poets constantly refer to this mead as the origin of poetry.

In the *Sigrdrífumál*, when Sigurðr has awakened the Valkyrie, she takes a horn full of mead and gives him a 'cup of memory' (*minnisveig*). A little later (st. 5) she says: "I am bringing thee beer, mixed with 'virtue' and the 'glory of virtue' (or 'mighty glory'). It is full of verses and healing letters, of good spells and runes of joy". Then she goes on to explain the magic use of runic letters. The terminology employed here seems to be that of witchcraft. The word *megin* ('virtue') denotes the magic potency of anything—here perhaps the potency of the ingredients, rather than that of the beer itself. We may compare *Guðrúnarkviða II*, 21 ff., where Guðrún is given a cup of beer to make her forget Sigurðr's death. It is strengthened with the 'virtue of earth' —whatever that may be—and with runes, as well as with herbs, acorns, soot, entrails, pig's liver, and various other delicacies. We may also refer here to *Hyndluljóð*, st. 45, where Freyja requests the witch Hyndla to give 'ale of memory' to Óttarr, when she has enumerated his ancestry (cf. p. 278 f.).

Ale-drinking seems to have formed an important element in the religious ceremonies of heathen times,[2] as in social life generally; and it is possible that the myth of Óðrerir ('that which stirs poetry or eloquence'; cf. p. 620) is to be traced back to an attempt to account for the origin of ale. But in the light of the passages just noted we are inclined to doubt if it means more than a belief in the potency of a witch's brew—as in the story of Ceridwen. Brewing was women's work, and

[1] There would seem to be some confusion in this story, which is found only in the *Skaldskaparmál*, cap. 1 (*Bragaroeður*). According to *Yngl. Saga*, cap. 4, Kvásir was the wisest of the Vanir and was given to the Aesir as a hostage. Possibly in the original story Óðrerir contained both spittle and Kvásir's blood. For the use of spittle in brewing we may compare *Hálfs Saga*, cap. 1.

[2] So in the Lithuanian ceremony described by Praetorius and noticed above (p. 617) a well-dressed old lady brings a jug to the Weydulut, which he drinks off, after offering prayer. This takes place before he addresses the worshippers.

witches may well have been credited with the power of imparting special properties to their brews. The evidence points perhaps rather to mead than to ale, though the two terms are used more or less indiscriminately in early Norse poetry.

Óðrerir has obviously something in common with the Greek cult of Dionysos. In both cases the governing idea is that of inspiration arising from an intoxicating drink. How deep the resemblance goes we do not know—the history of the Greek cult seems to be obscure in many respects. Dionysos himself appears to have little or nothing in common with Othin. Moreover the Greek cult was apparently bound up with popular feasts and revelry. If that was ever the case with Óðrerir the association was forgotten—Óðrerir seems to be a possession of the chosen few.[1] But we are not prepared to speak with any confidence upon this subject.

Lastly, mention may be made of certain objects which are found in association with inspiration or manticism. In some cases doubt may be felt as to their significance; but in view of their rather wide distribution it will be well to make a note of their occurrence, for the sake of future reference.

When the Muses reveal themselves to Hesiod, they present him with a staff (σκῆπτρον) of laurel. It has been suggested above (p. 628) that this staff is to be connected with the wand (ῥάβδος) carried by rhapsodists when they recited. But is this wand really of different origin from the wand (ῥάβδος) used by Athena, when she changes the appearance of Odysseus (*Od.* XVI. 172 ff.), or the wand used by Circe, when she turns Odysseus' followers into pigs (*ib.* X. 237 f.)? It is to be remembered that Circe has prophetic powers, as well as the power of causing metamorphosis. Again, is there any connection between the laurel staff presented to Hesiod and the branches or sprays of laurel carried by those who came to consult the oracle at Delphoi? Laurel belongs to the Muses, as well as to Apollo, and was perhaps taken over by him from them together with the sanctuary. We may refer to the story of Daphnis, the 'laurel man' (from δάφνη, 'laurel'), beloved by the Muses and celebrated by Stesichoros (cf. p. 433) and later poets. He seems to have no more to do with Apollo than Hesiod has.

[1] It should perhaps be mentioned that in the *Grímnismál*, st. 19, Othin is said never to take any food or drink except wine. This may raise a suspicion that Óðrerir was originally wine. But wine is never mentioned in this connection; and in view of the evidence noted above we think it is more probably to be explained as a witch's brew. Parallels from other countries will be considered later.

In northern Europe also we find a staff or wand used in witchcraft, the antiquity of which is shown by the identity of the terminology (W. *hud*, N. *seiðr*, Lith. *saitas*, etc.; cf. p. 620). It is with a magic wand (*hudlath*) that Math son of Mathonwy, in the *Mabinogi* which bears his name, ascertains whether Arianrod is a virgin and turns Gwydion and his brother into various kinds of animals. Gwydion himself uses a magic wand to transform Llew back into his true form. It may be recalled that Gwydion is an expert saga-teller and represents himself to be a *Pencerdd* (cf. p. 585). References to the cultivation of witchcraft by this family occur also in poetry. In *Tal.* x. 12 we hear of the magic wand of Mathonwy. We may also refer to *Tal.* XLV. 10, though the passage is obscure.

In *Thorfinns Saga Karlsefnis*, cap. 3, the dress and appurtenances of the witch Thorbjörg are minutely described. She carries a knobbed staff, decorated with brass and studded with stones beneath the knob. In the *Laxdoela Saga*, cap. 76, the bones discovered by Guðrún beneath the church floor are declared to be those of a witch because, among other reasons, a large magic staff (*seiðstafr*) was found with them. Indeed it would seem that witches regularly carried a staff, for the word *völva* ('witch') is believed to be derived from *völr*, 'staff'. We may also refer to the *Skírnismál*, st. 26, where Skírnir is cursing Gerðr: "I strike thee with a 'wand of subjection' and will subject thee to my wishes". Hypnotic subjection seems to be meant. Again (st. 32): "I went to a wood and to a young sapling, to get a 'potent' shoot. I got a potent shoot". The reference is to magic potency.[1]

An English example[2] occurs, strangely enough, in a religious poem—a 'Traveller's Prayer' (cf. p. 426): "I chant a spell of victory, I carry a rod of victory". What is actually meant is perhaps a cross. But the language used in the opening lines of the poem is that of witchcraft; and we may infer from it that the magic wand or staff was known in England.

In Ireland we hear of a 'wand of the *fili*' (*flesc filed*) which was regarded as possessing a divining power.[3] A magic branch also figures in

[1] The exact meaning of the word *gambanteinn* ('potent shoot') is not known; but it is probably to be compared with the A.-S. *wuldortanas* ('shoots of glory') in the *Nine Herbs Spell*. These shoots are used in witchcraft by Woden against a snake or dragon, which he strikes with them.

[2] Text in Grein-Wülcker, *Bibl. d. ags. Poesie*, I. 328 ff.

[3] Cormac's *Glossary*, s.v. *Coire Breccain*; cf. Stokes, *Three Irish Glossaries*, p. lvii. We have not noticed any references in sagas.

some stories. Mention has already been made (p. 100) of the branch with three golden apples given by Manannan mac Lir to Cormac mac Airt—which had the power of turning all sorrow into joy, and for which Cormac was willing to barter his wife and children. In the *Voyage of Bran* it is related that Bran heard music of extraordinary sweetness, which lulled him to sleep. When he awakes he finds beside him a silver branch with white blossoms, which he takes with him to the palace. When the court assembles an unknown lady appears and chants the first of the poems contained in the story. In it (st. 1) she says that this is a branch of the appletree of Emain—a distant island—and she invites Bran to follow her thither.[1] At the conclusion of the poem she vanishes and takes the branch with her. The appletree mentioned here seems to be identical with the silver tree described in a poem in the *Sickbed of CuChulainn*, when Laeg returns from Mag Mell (cf. p. 257). It stands beside the castle of Fand—who is the wife of Manannan.

In the *Colloquy of the Two Sages*, sect. VI, Nede carries a branch of silver. It is explained that this was what it was proper for an *anruth* to carry—an *anruth* was a *fili* of the highest grade next to an *ollam* (cf. p. 604)—whereas an *ollam* carried a branch of gold and any *fili* of lower grade a branch of copper. If any value is to be attached to this statement —the metals may be disregarded—it would seem to suggest an analogy to the use of laurel in Greece. Was the 'Appletree of Emain' derived from a tree sacred to the *filid*?

The evidence for the association of manticism or inspiration with a special seat is less clear; but, such as it is, it requires to be noted. In early Welsh poetry references to the bard's chair (*cadeir*) are not rare. They occur also in the Laws (cf. p. 601), where it is stated that a bard becomes a *Pencerdd* when he obtains a chair. In general the term may mean no more than a seat of honour, denoting a certain rank. Yet it may be observed that in *Tal.* XVI. 24, Ceridwen is made to speak of her chair, together with her cauldron and her laws (or rights), while in *Tal.* XIV. 45, Taliesin says that his chair is prepared in Caer Sidi.

In the *Colloquy of the Two Sages* Nede, at the instigation of Bricriu, takes the chair (*cathair*) of the *ollam*, which has been occupied by his father. His right is disputed by Ferchertne. As in Wales the chair evidently indicates a position of honour; but here the position coveted is that of '*Ollam* of Ireland'. The robe of the *ollam* is also in dispute.

[1] One may perhaps compare the story told by Saxo, p. 37 f. (31), about the journey of Hadingus. The milieu is similar; but hemlocks take the place of the silver branch.

In *Háv.* 111 (cf. p. 618) the *Loddfáfnismál* is said to be declaimed 'on the chair of the *þulr*, at the Spring of Fate'. The chair (*stóll*) of the *þulr* may be similar to that of the bard; but the following words indicate mantic associations. Elsewhere the chair of the *þulr* is not mentioned; but the word *þulr* is rare. In *Beow.* 1165 f. the *þyle* sits at the king's feet.

When witchcraft (*seiðr*) was in progress the witch occupied a *seiðhjallr*, which appears to have been a raised platform of some kind. This platform is frequently mentioned and would seem to have been necessary for the operation. Apparently it could be occupied by several persons at a time—at least this is what seems to be implied in the *Laxdoela Saga*, cap. 35. If there is any connection between this platform and the chair of the *þulr*, it must be remote. Possibly we may refer to Saxo's description of the Norns (*Parcae*), cited on p. 639. More important perhaps is the fact that Othin has a throne or seat of honour (*hásæti*) called Hliðskjölf, from which he can see everything in the world. This throne is said[1] to be in a hall (called Valaskjölf); so it has evidently a mantic property. On one occasion Othin and Frigg are seated in it together.

Very little evidence seems to be available from Greek. The word θρόνος, 'chair'—used especially for a ruler's throne—is applied occasionally to Apollo's sanctuary at Delphoi.[2] The seat actually used by the prophetess, when giving oracles, appears to have been a high tripod, carrying a bowl. We are not aware that it had anything in common with the *seiðhjallr*, except the idea of height.

In conclusion it may be mentioned that in Greek legend manticism is often connected with snakes. Such is the case, for example, in stories relating to Melampus and Teiresias. Some of these seers are said to have acquired the power of understanding the speech of birds through the fact that their ears have been licked by snakes. The snakes sometimes live in trees.

The other countries under discussion supply but little evidence of this kind. In the *Fáfnismál* Fáfnir has become a snake; and when

[1] *Gylf.* 17. Some scholars hold that Hliðskjölf was originally a name for the hall itself; but Snorri clearly did not understand it in that sense. The seat of honour given to the witch in *Thorfinns Saga Karlsefnis*, cap. 3, is called *hásæti*; but it is not clear that this was the *hjallr* mentioned shortly afterwards.

[2] E.g. Aischylos, *Eumen.* 616; Euripides, *Iph. Taur.* 1282. The expression μαντικοῖσιν ἐν θρόνοις in the former passage is possibly worth noting, in view of *Háv.* 111.

Sigurðr has killed him and tasted the blood of his heart he understands what the birds in the trees above him are saying. According to the *Grímnismál*, st. 34, there are numerous snakes beneath the Ash of Yggdrasill; but they are not said to be connected with manticism. They are presumably a relic of the time when snakes were kept in tree sanctuaries—as was the case with the Lithuanians and kindred peoples down to the end of the heathen period.

It will have been observed that a large proportion of this chapter has been taken up with mythology and legends of the far past. In point of fact the amount of evidence available for historical and even semi-historical times is not great. But the myths and legends may be taken as evidence of what the learned men of early historical times, or their predecessors, thought of the inspiration or manticism of the past. With regard to the inspiration or manticism of their own times—the times of our earliest records—a few remarks may be added.

Ecstasy of the frenzied type does not seem to have been widely prevalent.[1] We have seen that this occurred in the case of the Welsh Awenyddion in the twelfth century; and the prophetesses at Delphoi are said to have been affected in the same way. More widespread perhaps are premonitions in the form of visions. Instances are of frequent occurrence in the 'Sagas of Icelanders'. We may cite, for example, *Njáls Saga*, cap. 126, where Njáll, before the fatal attack, sees the walls falling and the table and food covered with blood. This case is parallel to examples in heroic poetry, e.g. Theoclymenos' vision of the death of the suitors (*Od.* XX. 351 ff.), and Deirdre's vision of the red cloud, in the *Fate of the Children of Uisnech*, cap. 13 (280 ff.).

Within the limits of our enquiry it is only from Iceland that we have detailed and living descriptions of 'mantic' persons; and here we have to distinguish between two classes—those who practised *seiðr* and those who did not. The form of *seiðr* most commonly referred to in the 'Sagas of Icelanders' consisted apparently of spells, used for the purpose of raising storms and causing death either by this or other means. It was practised occasionally by landowners, but more often by persons of humbler position, who were employed, sometimes even by people of high rank, to bring death or disaster upon their enemies. This was of course a dangerous practice; sooner or later it generally came about that

[1] The fury of the *berserkir* may be related pathologically; but the *berserkir* were essentially fighting men. The *berserkr* described in *Njáls Saga*, cap. 99, seems to be merely a dangerous lunatic.

the practitioners were set upon and lynched, and their employers seldom ventured to bring the case before the courts. There was, however, another form of *seiðr*, directed towards obtaining knowledge of the future, as in *Thorfinns Saga Karlsefnis*. Here the witch, who appears to be a professional, is received publicly with great honour. In the ninth century we hear of a Norse queen practising what would seem to be *seiðr* of this kind upon the altar of Clonmacnois.[1] Gunnhildr, the wife of King Eric Blood-Axe, is credited with a more mischievous form of *seiðr*; but she was a very unpopular character.

But the sagas also speak of many more persons who are credited with mantic powers, including a knowledge of the future, but who never practise *seiðr*. They are not professionals in any way, though they may be willing to interpret dreams and predict the future for their friends. Usually they are landowners of good position, and sometimes among the leading people in the country. The degree to which mantic power is shown seems to vary greatly from case to case. Gestr Oddleifsson, a most influential man and much in demand as an arbitrator, knows exactly what will happen to his friends and their families. Others have merely a presentiment of impending evil. But the sagas rather tend to convey the impression that some element of foreknowledge was implied in a reputation for wisdom.

Little or nothing that can be called distinctive is recorded as to the behaviour of mantic sages. When Njáll first hears of Christianity it is said (cap. 96) that he frequently retires into solitude and talks to himself. We may compare the behaviour of Thórhallr the Hunter in *Thorfinns Saga Karlsefnis* (cf. p. 579), when he is composing a hymn to Thor; the same word (*þylja*) is used in both cases (cf. p. 618). Again, in Ari's *Íslendingabók*, cap. 7 (cf. *Njáls Saga*, cap. 101), when the general assembly breaks up into two camps on the question of Christianity, and Thorgeirr, the Speaker of the Law, is invited to give an official pronouncement, it is stated that, before doing so, he lay all day and the night following, with a cloak spread over him, and without speaking a word. In such cases the solitude or silence was doubtless utilised by the sage not only for reflection, but also for composition, or at least for giving coherent expression to his thoughts. The differences from modern custom, such as they are, may be explained partly by the fact that the Icelanders had no private studies, partly by the absence of written literature and serviceable writing materials.

[1] *War of the Gaedhil with the Gaill*, cap. 11; cf. Kershaw in Hastings' *Encyclopaedia of Religion and Ethics*, art. *Teutonic Religion*.

In *Egils Saga*, cap. 1, it is stated that Kveldulfr, Egill's grandfather, was a wise man and a good adviser; but in the evening he was drowsy and difficult to speak to, and it was commonly believed that he was *hamrammr*. This means that his soul was wandering in some other (probably animal) form, while his body lay motionless at home. The drowsiness might be satisfactorily accounted for by the fact, stated just before, that he was an early riser and spent his days out in the fields. But it is quite possible that many mantic sages did cultivate the habit of bringing themselves into a kind of trance, in which they were oblivious of their surroundings, while their minds were concentrated upon some thought or some object not present. At all events they paid great attention to dreams—and not merely to the interpretation of other people's dreams. It is said of Gísli Súrsson (in his Saga, cap. 12) that he was a 'clear dreamer' (*berdreymr*), which seems to mean that the future was made clearly known to him in dreams. A number of his poems, which are generally believed to be genuine, speak of two 'dream women' who appear to him, and advise him or warn him as to his fate.

In different countries various expedients were in use for inducing a mantic sleep. In some Greek sanctuaries, especially those which belonged to seers of the far past, the person who consulted the oracle had to sacrifice a sheep or ram, and then sleep upon its hide.

We may refer also to the Irish rite called *imbas forosnai*, which, according to Cormac's *Glossary* (*s.v.*), "makes known whatever thing a *fili* wishes and whatever it is expedient for him to reveal. It is performed as follows. The *fili* chews a piece of the raw flesh of a pig or dog or cat, and then places it on a stone behind the door, and chants a spell over it, and offers it to the 'idol gods' and summons them to him, and does not leave them on the following day. Next he chants over his two palms, and again summons the 'idol gods' to him, to ensure that his sleep may not be disturbed. Then he covers his two cheeks with his palms and sleeps; and people watch over him, so that he may not turn over, and so that no one may disturb him—whereupon there is revealed to him whatever lies before him during the following week (?) or two or three, according to the length of time that he shall have provided for at the offering."

It would seem that this rite was originally an attempt to obtain revelation from deities. The *Glossary* adds that it was banned by St Patrick, 'as a denial of baptism' (i.e. Christianity). In heroic sagas references to it are not rare. It is practised by the seeress Fedelm, who warns Medb of the coming disaster to her army (cf. p. 464), and by the seeress Scathach (*ib.*), who prophesies of the same events to CuChulainn.

The Norwegian sage and lawgiver Thorleifr the Wise (*spaki*) is credited with a simpler recipe. King Halfdan the Black, father of Harold the Fair-haired, is said in his Saga (cap. 7) to have been much concerned because he could never dream. He consulted Thorleifr, who told him that when he desired to get knowledge of anything, it was his custom to go and sleep in a pigsty. Then dreams never failed to come.

That the future could be ascertained, whether from dreams or otherwise, was a belief inherited doubtless from ancient times and not generally questioned even by the more intellectual. And there can be no question that similar beliefs prevailed in all the periods included in our survey. A parallel to Gestr Oddleifsson is to be found in the Gaulish statesman and druid Deiuiciacus (cf. p. 609). Herodotos' *History* supplies numerous examples of the importance which the Greeks attached to dreams and visions, and more especially to oracles, even in the sixth century. All these facts have to be borne in mind if one will form a true estimate of the influence of manticism. To a certain extent thought is bound to proceed along traditional lines—more especially when there is no written literature to expedite the interchange of ideas. Further discussion of the subject, however, must be deferred until we have considered the evidence available from other lands.

ADDENDA

P. 53, line 11 ff. Reference should have been given to K. Meyer, *Fianaigecht* (R.I.A., Todd Lecture Series XVI, 1910), which contains an account of various stories relating to Finn and his cycle, especially those preserved in early texts.

P. 72. The custom of presenting an infant prince with horses foaled at the time of his birth was perhaps both Teutonic and Celtic; cf. the passage in the *Conception of CuChulainn* referred to on p. 74. A somewhat similar incident occurs in the story of Pwyll.

Pp. 96, 102. There can be little doubt that the stories contained in the Lives of British and Irish saints are largely derived from monastic saga. In the later Lives the hand of the author or compiler has often been heavy; but it is sometimes not difficult to see that the sagas themselves must have reflected a different type of mentality. The records of St Kentigern suggest that some of the stories current in the church of Glasgow were utilised as much for entertainment as for edification. These stories may have been Gaelic in their last phase. At all events the vernacular expressions found in the Lives are Gaelic; and in Bishop Herbert's time Kentigern was already regarded as a Scottish saint (cf. the poem published in the Rolls Series edition of Symeon of Durham, II. 386 ff.). On the other hand the strange story of the saint's residence in Wales may date from a time when his British nationality was still recognised.

P. 116, line 31. The true form of this name is probably *Melampodia*, though there seems to be good authority for both forms.

P. 119. It would seem that mantic properties were attributed to smiths in Ireland; cf. Stokes, *Tripartite Life*, p. 50 f.

P. 162, line 2 ff. It is quite possible that the name was derived ultimately from a certain L. Artorius Castus (or Iustus), of the Sixth Legion, who lived some time in the third or fourth century; cf. Chambers, *Arthur of Britain*, p. 170.

P. 171. A story found in various records of St Patrick has sometimes been brought forward as evidence that the different saga-cycles were originally not so clearly distinguished as we find them—and consequently as an argument against the antiquity of Irish saga-tradition. In Tirechan's *Collections* (Stokes, *Tripartite Life*, p. 324 f.), our earliest authority, the story is given as follows. St Patrick raises from the dead a man who states that he was killed a hundred years previously by the soldiers of MacCon's son (*fian maicc Maicc Con*) in the reign of Cairbre Nia Fer. This Cairbre belongs to the time of CuChulainn and Conchobor (cf. p. 172); but MacCon is a contemporary of Cormac mac Airt. The discrepancy, however, may be explained easily enough by a mistake on the part of an ecclesiastic who was not well acquainted with heroic tradition and confused Cairbre Nia Fer with Cairbre Lifechar. The latter is a contemporary of MacCon's sons (Fothad Airgtech and his brother) and is succeeded by them in the high-kingship. The interval between Cairbre Lifechar's time and that of St Patrick was doubtless more than a century; but one must not expect to find exact reckonings in a record of this kind. Our experience has been that the more alleged discrepancies of this kind we have examined the greater has become our respect both for Irish saga-tradition and for the work of the synthetic historians.

P. 210, note, and elsewhere. Reference should have been given to a fragment of Cormac's Glossary from Laud 610, ed. and transl. by Stokes, *Trans. Philol. Soc.* (London), 1891–4, p. 149 ff.

P. 332. A very interesting account of the 'Sagas of Icelanders' in general will be found in Phillpotts, *Edda and Saga*, chs. VII–IX.

P. 415. Reference should have been made to the frequent use of kennings in early Irish poetry. In this respect, as in others, Irish poetic diction has much in common with Norse; cf. K. Meyer, *Rev. Celt.* XIII. 220, note.

Pp. 433, 444. Stesichoros' authorship of the *Rhadine* and the *Calyce* is disputed by Rose, *Class. Quarterly*, XXVI. 88 ff. Some of the questions raised are of a kind which can be decided only by Greek scholars; but we would remark that other works attributed to the same poet (cf. p. 431 ff.) suggest that he was capable of such innovations.

P. 436 ff. Reminiscences of the folktale in its earlier form seem to be preserved in the late *Saga of Samson the Fair*; cf. Lawrence, *Beowulf and Epic Tradition*, p. 188 ff.

Pp. 454, 527. For yet another text of the *Appletrees* see I. Williams, *Bulletin of the Board for Celtic Studies*, IV. 121 ff., from MS. Peniarth 3. This text is nearest to the one given in the *Myvyrian Archaiology*; but it contains only sixteen stanzas. The same article (p. 112 ff.) gives also a variant text of part of *RBH.* I from the same source.

P. 463. It should have been mentioned that the *Baile Chuinn* appears to have been contained in the *Book of Druim Snechta* (cf. Thurneysen,

Ir. Heldensage, p. 17). This form of prophecy therefore was very old in Ireland.

P. 491, note 2. Reference should be made to two interesting papers by MacNeill, *Studies*, XI. 13 ff., 435 ff., on Cenn Faelad, known as *Sapiens*, a prince who was wounded at the battle of Mag Rath (cf. p. 53), and died c. 679. He is claimed as the author of some historical poems and of Irish tracts on law and grammar, which are still preserved in a fragmentary condition. He is said to have attended both a Latin school and also schools of Irish law and learning, and to have written down from memory what he learned. The date suggests, as Prof. MacNeill points out, that we are brought here practically to the fountain head of written Irish learning. The *filid* at this time may still have been opposed to the use of (Roman) writing in their teaching; and a student of princely rank, who combined their learning with that of a Latin school, was peculiarly qualified to introduce an innovation of this kind. An interesting parallel from New Zealand will be noticed in a later chapter.

P. 493, line 1 ff. A fragmentary inscription on the remains of a bowl found recently at Asine and dating from the end of the Mycenean period has been interpreted as Greek (cf. Lindquist, *Kungl. Hum. Vetensk i Lund, Årsb.* 1930–1, p. 111 ff.). The form of writing is thought to be akin to the Cypriot syllabary of later times. If this is correct, the art of writing was known to the Greeks long before the introduction of the North Semitic alphabet. But was it preserved, apart from Cyprus, during the three intervening centuries? The reference in *Il.* VI. 168 f. (cf. p. 494) may be due to a reminiscence of ancient writing.

P. 520. When this was printed we had not seen Neckel's *Altnordische Literatur*, which (p. 79 ff.) gives a view of the Edda poems much more in accordance with our own.

P. 541, last line. Similar references to divergent traditions occur also in texts of Irish sagas. We may instance *Mac Datho's Pig*, cap. 18, where after the reference to Fergus one text adds: "Others say that it was CuRoi mac Dairi who took the oak to them"—with further details.

P. 556. On consideration, however, we are inclined to the view that *fabulae*, etc. relate to saga-telling—perhaps chiefly anecdotal—which was evidently much cultivated in monasteries.

P. 556, note 1. Reference should be added to Chambers, *Beowulf* (*Introduction*, new edn, 1932), pp. 389 ff., 486 ff.

P. 559. For the introduction of religious expressions, etc., in secular poems parallels may be found in Russia; cf. Chadwick, *Russian Heroic Poetry*, p. 12: "Gilferding...adds that the *kalêka*, or wandering psalm singer, Ivan Feponov, generally known as 'blind Ivan', when reciting *byliny*, always gave a religious colouring to his narratives, representing the heroes as constantly praying to God." This, however, is stated as characteristic of an individual—or of the *kalêki* as a class—not of the reciters of heroic poetry in general, as in England.

P. 611, note 2. We are by no means inclined to dispute the existence of pre-Celtic—and possibly also southern—elements in Druidism; but the important affinities it had with the religions of central Europe should not be overlooked.

P. 624, line 4 ff. Among the northern peoples also there seems to be a tendency for both professional manticism and the possession of mantic faculties to run in families, though definite evidence is rare. *Filid* are sometimes sons of *filid*; Nede's father was an *ollam*. Gwydion is nephew to Math. Kotkell's sons join him in his incantations and have the same injurious powers. Thorbjörg, the Greenland witch, is said to have had nine sisters, all of whom were seeresses. We may compare the nine witches of Gloucester in the story of *Peredur*. The seer Thorleifr who figures in *Hallfreðar Saga*, cap. 6, belongs to a younger generation of the same family as his more famous namesake, the sage and lawgiver; and the Icelandic lawgiver Ulfljótr comes from the same stock.

P. 637, line 12. The surname *Tad awen* is applied also to Tydain (presumably the same person as in *BBC*. XIX. 10) in *Triad* III. 92 (*Myv. Arch.* p. 409). In explanation it is added "qui, le premier, fit du chant un art et régla l'inspiration" (Loth).

P. 649, line 3 ff. Reference should have been given to a *Dinnšenchas* poem *The Fate of Sinann*, ed. and transl. by Joynt in the *Miscellany presented to Kuno Meyer*, p. 193 ff.

Reference should also have been given to the 'Fountain of Knowledge' in *Cormac's Adventure*, mentioned on p. 100. In (*ib.*) cap. 35 this spring is said to be overshadowed by nine hazels, while according to cap. 53 "no one will have knowledge who drinketh not a draught out of the fountain itself and out of the streams. The folk of many arts are those who drink of them both" (Stokes).

Holy springs seem to have been reverenced in Ireland as much as elsewhere. We may refer to the spring called Slan, which is described as *aquarum rex* in Tirechan's *Collections* (Stokes, *Tripartite Life*, p. 323), and was revered as a deity by the druids. But it is not definitely stated that the spring was regarded as a source of inspiration, though this may possibly be implied by the belief that a prophet (*profeta*) had been buried in it.

INDEX